CHASING
SAM MAGUIRE

DERMOT REILLY has had a lifelong affiliation with the GAA as a player, supporter and administrator. In a true labour of love, he has dedicated years of painstaking research to the history of the All-Ireland Football Championship since 1928, the season Dermot's beloved Kildare became the first team to win the Sam Maguire Cup. Now retired, Dermot was formerly a Partner with PwC.

A sports journalist his entire career, Meath-born COLM KEYS has accumulated a formidable knowledge of the players, personalities and politics that have shaped the modern GAA. He started at the *Meath Chronicle* and was the *Irish Mirror*'s GAA correspondent and chief sportswriter before joining the *Irish Independent* where he has been the GAA correspondent since 2003.

CHASING SAM MAGUIRE

THE ALL-IRELAND FOOTBALL CHAMPIONSHIP
1928–1977

DERMOT REILLY & COLM KEYS

THE O'BRIEN PRESS
DUBLIN

First published 2023 by
The O'Brien Press Ltd,
12 Terenure Road East, Rathgar,
Dublin 6, D06 HD27, Ireland.
Tel: +353 1 4923333; Fax: +353 1 4922777
E-mail: books@obrien.ie
Website: obrien.ie
Reprinted 2023.
The O'Brien Press is a member of Publishing Ireland.

ISBN: 978-1-78849-380-2

Text © Dermot Reilly & Colm Keys 2023
The moral rights of the authors have been asserted.
Editing, design and layout © The O'Brien Press 2023
Cover and text design by Emma Byrne

8 7 6 5 4 3 2
27 26 25 24 23

Printed and bound in Poland by Bialostockie Zaklady Graficzne S.A.
The paper in this book is produced using pulp from managed forests.

Cover photographs
Front: Kerry's Mick O'Connell (centre) and Down's Sean O'Neill (left), vie for possession
in the 1968 Final. *Image courtesy of the GAA Museum at Croke Park*
Back: Winning captains and their representatives at an event to mark the seventy-fifth
anniversary of the first presentation of the Sam Maguire Cup, in 2003. *Reilly Collection*

Published in

CONTENTS

FOREWORD	7	1953 (FINAL: KERRY V ARMAGH)	207
ALL-IRELAND FINAL RESULTS 1928-1977	9	1954 (FINAL: MEATH V KERRY)	216
INTRODUCTION	11	1955 (FINAL: KERRY V DUBLIN)	225
1928 (FINAL: KILDARE V CAVAN)	14	1956 (FINAL: GALWAY V CORK)	233
1929 (FINAL: KERRY V KILDARE)	22	1957 (FINAL: LOUTH V CORK)	242
1930 (FINAL: KERRY V MONAGHAN)	29	1958 (FINAL: DUBLIN V DERRY)	251
1931 (FINAL: KERRY V KILDARE)	36	1959 (FINAL: KERRY V GALWAY)	260
1932 (FINAL: KERRY V MAYO)	42	1960 (FINAL: DOWN V KERRY)	269
1933 (FINAL: CAVAN V GALWAY)	48	1961 (FINAL: DOWN V OFFALY)	277
1934 (FINAL: GALWAY V DUBLIN)	55	1962 (FINAL: KERRY V ROSCOMMON)	285
1935 (FINAL: CAVAN V KILDARE)	64	1963 (FINAL: DUBLIN V GALWAY)	293
1936 (FINAL: MAYO V LAOIS)	71	1964 (FINAL: GALWAY V KERRY)	302
1937 (FINAL: KERRY V CAVAN)	80	1965 (FINAL: GALWAY V KERRY)	310
1938 (FINAL: GALWAY V KERRY)	89	1966 (FINAL: GALWAY V MEATH)	318
1939 (FINAL: KERRY V MEATH)	98	1967 (FINAL: MEATH V CORK)	327
1940 (FINAL: KERRY V GALWAY)	106	1968 (FINAL: DOWN V KERRY)	336
1941 (FINAL: KERRY V GALWAY)	112	1969 (FINAL: KERRY V OFFALY)	346
1942 (FINAL: DUBLIN V GALWAY)	119	1970 (FINAL: KERRY V MEATH)	354
1943 (FINAL: ROSCOMMON V CAVAN)	125	1971 (FINAL: OFFALY V GALWAY)	364
1944 (FINAL: ROSCOMMON V KERRY)	134	1972 (FINAL: OFFALY V KERRY)	372
1945 (FINAL: CORK V CAVAN)	142	1973 (FINAL: CORK V GALWAY)	384
1946 (FINAL: KERRY V ROSCOMMON)	150	1974 (FINAL: DUBLIN V GALWAY)	396
1947 (FINAL: CAVAN V KERRY)	157	1975 (FINAL: KERRY V DUBLIN)	405
1948 (FINAL: CAVAN V MAYO)	165	1976 (FINAL: DUBLIN V KERRY)	414
1949 (FINAL: MEATH V CAVAN)	173	1977 (FINAL: DUBLIN V ARMAGH)	423
1950 (FINAL: MAYO V LOUTH)	182	CONCLUSION	433
1951 (FINAL: MAYO V MEATH)	190	ACKNOWLEDGEMENTS	434
1952 (FINAL: CAVAN V MEATH)	198	INDEX	436

FOREWORD

Tá an-áthas orm gur iarradh orm an réamhrá a scríobh don leabhar tábhachtach seo a cheiliúrann Corn Mhig Uidhir.

I am delighted to welcome the publication of *Chasing Sam Maguire*, the latest addition to the ever-growing library of GAA publications that chart the popularity and importance of Gaelic games to this country.

In September 2022, I had the privilege of representing the Association at the unveiling in Kildare of a life-size statue to Bill 'Squires' Gannon, captain of the All-Ireland winning Kildare team of 1928 and first-ever recipients of the Sam Maguire.

It remains Kildare's last All-Ireland senior football triumph and the level of pride and the depth of feeling at the unveiling that day left no one in any doubt about the significance which that team of players and that victory still has in the county and among the people.

Such is the power of the Sam Maguire Cup and the allure that surrounds it and envelops those fortunate to claim it and be a part of its rich history.

Modelled on the famous Ardagh chalice, it has few equals in world sport in terms of size and beauty, and it forever celebrates the GAA contribution of Sam Maguire. Born in Cork, he joined the civil service after school and upon his arrival in London he became immersed in the GAA and in the republican movement, where he was prolific and instrumental on both fronts. He recruited people like Michael Collins into the IRB in London and was later a Major General and Chief Intelligence Officer of the IRA in London.

A superb organiser, he was a major asset to various GAA committees in London. He was London secretary and chair and later a GAA Trustee. He was also a gifted athlete and a great footballer and was a key figure and captain on the London Hibernians who contested the 1901, 1902 and 1903 All-Ireland football finals.

He is also unique in that the eponymous cup also features a stencilled portrait of him on the front of the chalice. The original cost £300. The replica in use since 1988 took 500 hours to complete.

The Sam Maguire Cup is the most iconic and prestigious trophy in Irish sport and its size befits the enormous significance that the annual pursuit of the silverware commands in the nation's psyche.

The scale of the task undertaken by the authors is monumental. This book chronicles the first fifty years. Within that, there is a history of Gaelic football and the GAA and Irish cultural life and of the nation itself told through the record of the heroes who fought it out for the honour of bringing

CHASING SAM MAGUIRE

'Sam' home to their county, their clubs and communities for the winter.

Not everyone is fortunate to see the Sam Maguire Cup in their home place during their lifetime – but even so, the chase and pursuit of the Sam is something that enthrals all football supporters and for many of us it is a chase that defines the Irish summer year after year, decade after decade.

I want to thank Dermot Reilly and Colm Keys for the work undertaken and for preserving this important chronicle of our history and heritage, and trust that you will find it as informative and entertaining as I did.

Thar ceann Chumann Lúthchleas Gael, Comhghairdeas agus míle buíochas,

Is mise le meas,

Uachtarán

1928 Kildare 2-6 Cavan 2-5

1929 Kerry 1-8 Kildare 1-5

1930 Kerry 3-11 Monaghan 0-2

1931 Kerry 1-11 Kildare 0-8

1932 Kerry 2-7 Mayo 2-4

1933 Cavan 2-5 Galway 1-4

1934 Galway 3-5 Dublin 1-9

1935 Cavan 3-6 Kildare 2-5

1936 Mayo 4-11 Laois 0-5

1937 Kerry 4-4 Cavan 1-7 (Replay)

1938 Galway 2-4 Kerry 0-7 (Replay)

1939 Kerry 2-5 Meath 2-3

1940 Kerry 0-7 Galway 1-3

1941 Kerry 1-8 Galway 0-7

1942 Dublin 1-10 Galway 1-8

1943 Roscommon 2-7 Cavan 2-2 (Replay)

1944 Roscommon 1-9 Kerry 2-4

1945 Cork 2-5 Cavan 0-7

1946 Kerry 2-8 Roscommon 0-10 (Replay)

1947 Cavan 2-11 Kerry 2-7

1948 Cavan 4-5 Mayo 4-4

1949 Meath 1-10 Cavan 1-6

1950 Mayo 2-5 Louth 1-6

1951 Mayo 2-8 Meath 0-9

1952 Cavan 0-9 Meath 0-5 (Replay)

1953 Kerry 0-13 Armagh 1-6

1954 Meath 1-13 Kerry 1-7

1955 Kerry 0-12 Dublin 1-6

1956 Galway 2-13 Cork 3-7

1957 Louth 1-9 Cork 1-7

1958 Dublin 2-12 Derry 1-9

1959 Kerry 3-7 Galway 1-4

1960 Down 2-10 Kerry 0-8

1961 Down 3-6 Offaly 2-8

1962 Kerry 1-12 Roscommon 1-6

1963 Dublin 1-9 Galway 0-10

1964 Galway 0-15 Kerry 0-10

1965 Galway 0-12 Kerry 0-9

1966 Galway 1-10 Meath 0-7

1967 Meath 1-9 Cork 0-9

1968 Down 2-12 Kerry 1-13

1969 Kerry 0-10 Offaly 0-7

1970 Kerry 2-19 Meath 0-18

1971 Offaly 1-14 Galway 2-8

1972 Offaly 1-19 Kerry 0-13 (Replay)

1973 Cork 3-17 Galway 2-13

1974 Dublin 0-14 Galway 1-6

1975 Kerry 2-12 Dublin 0-11

1976 Dublin 3-8 Kerry 0-10

1977 Dublin 5-12 Armagh 3-6

INTRODUCTION

As All-Ireland football final stories go, there is scarcely a more compelling one than that of the Maguire brothers, rivals in the 1952 decider between Cavan and Meath.

The family originally lived in Cornafean in Cavan but sometime in the years before 1952 they moved across the Meath border to just outside Oldcastle.

Older siblings Des and Liam switched clubs, but not counties. The younger brother, Brendan, by then a student in Gormanston College on the other side of Meath, and still eligible for minor, opted to declare for his county of residence, however, putting the trio on a most unlikely collision course.

So they went their separate ways that weekend, drawing the family in different directions and provoking different emotions.

Apply it in a modern context and you could equate it to Marc Ó Sé leaving the family home in Ard a' Bhóthair on Kerry's Dingle peninsula and heading across to Cork to join his colleagues on the train journey to Dublin, while Darragh and Tomás made the shorter trip to Killarney for their connection with the Kerry squad to the capital ahead of the 2009 Final between the Munster neighbours.

Different as those directions and emotions clearly were for the Maguires on that 28 September morning, their goal was the same: the most treasured piece of silverware in Irish sport. A prize so resonant that it has the endearment of being known by its first name by those who pursue it, cherish it and follow the pathway to it, from armchair to terrace, through each Irish summer.

'Sam' has been a North Star for so many for close to a century, a mission for talented and ambitious young Irish sportsmen that has become a way of life. Men like the Maguires who share the surname with the man whose memory is perpetuated in the silverware that marks the conclusion of the All-Ireland football championship each year.

When Kildare defeated Cavan in the 1928 All-Ireland Football Final, it was the first time the Sam Maguire Cup, named after a Dunmanway-born Irish republican who spent much of his life in London and who had died the year before, was presented.

Since then it has been to sixteen counties (at the time of writing) and has brought joy to many. But it has also brought despair and exhaustive effort with no return. Most pursuits of 'Sam' haven't ended in success. Thus, not everyone gets to see it at close quarters. Our project seeks to reflect that, to explore the routes taken by those who set off on that pursuit but who did not ultimately gain the prize.

Their part in the story of 'Sam' is just as important as those who eventually got their hands on the 'canister'.

The detail from the first fifty years is deep-rooted, from the names of the two brothers who played on opposite sides in the 1928 Ulster Final between Cavan and Armagh to the reason why

Roscommon captain Jimmy Murray left the field with just minutes remaining in the drawn 1946 Final, and how a future government minister had to be escorted from the field half an hour after a game's conclusion in 1957 are some of the moments crystallised in the pages that follow.

And of course there's 1947, when an All-Ireland Final was exported to New York where Cavan defeated Kerry, maybe the most memorable occasion of all. Try applying modern context to that!

Our journey began with what we felt was a simple concept, to attach the names of clubs to All-Ireland Final players from 1928 onwards, to give some order and context to those who contributed to one of Irish sport's blue riband days. As great as all the literature relating to the GAA's storied past is, those club details were not something that, we felt, had been captured comprehensively before. It was something we wanted to collate. But as we began sourcing the information through newspaper archives, club histories, obituaries, old programmes and expert word of mouth in the counties, we realised how complex and layered the club archive of so many famous players was. And how hard it was to establish.

The great Kerry player during their four-in-a-row from 1929 to 1932, Paul Russell, a garda by occupation, is estimated to have played with as many as eight clubs, from his native county to Dublin, Waterford, Meath, Kildare, Cavan and Galway from the 1920s to the 1940s!

Even the definitive list of All-Ireland Final panels is not a matter of official record. Twenty All-Ireland medals were routinely presented to winners but 'training' panel numbers were greater than that and we sought to reflect that as much as we could.

Seamus Mac Gearailt, for instance, was brought on to the Kerry Senior All-Ireland Final day panel as a substitute goalkeeper in 1962 as they beat Roscommon, having already played on the county's minor team that had beaten Mayo in the All-Ireland Minor Final beforehand. But he was one who didn't get an All-Ireland senior medal.

What we present is not definitive lists of All-Ireland medal winners but comprehensive lists of those who were involved in All-Ireland Finals in pursuit of the Sam Maguire Cup from 1928 onwards.

It was a laborious task. Quite often, the attachment a player had was to his home club, not the club he was part of in a particular year. The magnet of Dublin for young men in pursuit of work and a different life was, and is to this day, very strong, but particularly in those early years when inter-club movement to the capital was so seamless that multiple clubs could register in the space of a few short years. University education and army service also brought players to 'declare' for different counties.

It left us with a dilemma – to omit home clubs or to build a short profile through the known club attachments of each player. We opted for the latter, choosing to list the player's club of that particular year, where possible. The association with the other clubs listed came either before or after, in many cases charting their personal journeys.

The help from certain people with such extensive knowledge and records of their own in various counties was invaluable. They really are treasure troves of information who, in the absence of a central database, perform an incredible service and they are warmly referenced in our acknowledgements.

Ultimately, we made the final determination ourselves, based on all information gathered.

As our research deepened, the idea took shape to expand our interest in charting the course of 'Sam Maguire' championships to much more than just matching clubs with players. The journeys those players took to reach the summit, and those who rarely got out of the foothills, were fascinating.

Our research began with Kildare's 1928 win when Bill 'Squires' Gannon was the first to receive the Cup. To this day it remains their last championship success. Kerry achieved their first four-in-a-row from 1929 to 1932, while Cavan's prominence as a football stronghold grew in the two decades that followed, interspersed by first wins for Mayo, Roscommon and Meath. Inevitably, Kerry were never too far from the top while Galway consistently brought teams to All-Ireland Finals in each of the decades we covered.

By the 1950s Armagh had become the first 'Six Counties' team to reach an All-Ireland Final since Antrim over forty years previously. They were followed by Derry and Down within a few short years, with the Mourne men going all the way in 1960. In between, Louth's 1957 success stands the test of time. The 1970s saw Offaly's breakthrough with back-to-back All-Ireland titles and then the Dublin–Kerry duopoly which packaged Gaelic football in such a different way.

The volume of stories and information grew so much that a decision was taken to focus on chronicling the first fifty years of 'Sam' in this book. In that time, there were twelve winners while four more counties, Monaghan (1930), Laois (1936), Armagh (1953) and Derry (1958) contested finals.

'Sam' is an aspiration for many but an attainment for so few; 'chasing' it is the journey we wanted to shine a greater light on.

1928

The 1928 Championship was the first for which the Sam Maguire Cup was presented to the winning team. While there had been forty-one championships previously, there were, in fact, only thirty-eight finals. In 1888, an exodus of leading players to raise funds by competing in a series of athletic contests in the United States led to the abandonment of the championship. In 1910, finalists Kerry had a dispute with the Great Southern Railway Company in relation to travel arrangements for their supporters. The upshot was that they refused to travel and Louth were awarded the title, their first. A whole series of objections and counter-objections ultimately led to Galway being crowned 1925 champions without any final being played.

Back in the 1920s, coverage of Gaelic games in the national media was very patchy. Despite this, it is clear that hurling and football had by then become central to heated debates in every parish in the country. It is certain that the early predictions of the likely winners of the 1928 football championship would have focused on the two dominant forces at the time – Kerry and Kildare. These

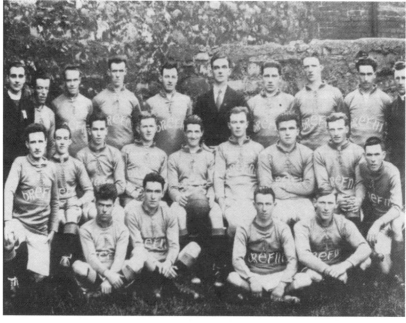

The Cavan team of 1928, pipped by Kildare in their bid to become the first holders of the Sam Maguire Cup.

counties had captured the imagination of the GAA world with a series of nail-biting contests. The 1926 Final needed a replay before Kerry emerged as champions on a score of 1-4 to 0-4. In 1927, it was the turn of the Lilywhites to take the title as they edged out the Kingdom, 0-5 to 0-3, at Croke Park on 25 September.

The reigning champions were far from impressive when they launched their 1928 campaign against Laois at Athy on 20 May. Facing a determined Laois side that was handicapped by the absence of Paddy Whelan and Bill Irwin, it took a late point by Tom Keogh to give Kildare victory. Reporting on this lacklustre display, the *Leinster Leader* concluded that their prospects of retaining the All-Ireland crown were 'none too rosy'.

Three second-half goals gave Longford a sensational win over hot favourites Meath at Mullingar on 22 April. This qualified them for a semi-final tilt with Kildare and, noting the absence of 'the dreaded Doyle' from Kildare's line-up, the *Longford Leader* expressed confidence in the county's prospects. When they met at Croke Park on 10 June, however, it was one-way traffic all the way as the Jack Higgins-inspired Lilywhites romped to a thirteen-point victory.

The opposite side of the draw saw Dublin struggle to a two-point win over Louth at Athy on 20 May, before qualifying for the final with an easy 3-3 to 0-4 win over Wexford on 8 July. A common feature of Dublin's run to the provincial final was the repeated brilliance of their goalkeeper, Johnny McDonnell.

The crowd of over 15,000 that turned up to see Dublin challenge Kildare for their Leinster crown was treated to a robust spectacle. After holding a commanding six-point lead at the break, Kildare began to lose their grip on the game. With brothers John and Joe Synnott to the fore, Dublin began to close the gap and when Morgan Durnin found the net for the Metropolitans, the fat was well and truly in the fire. The departure of Jack Higgins through injury seemed to signal curtains for the Lilywhites, but the pendulum swung again when Dublin's captain, Paddy McDonnell, was sent off after an altercation with Bill 'Squires' Gannon. A long-range point by ace marksman Paul Doyle finally settled the matter, 0-10 to 1-6 in Kildare's favour.

In the immediate aftermath of this game, a number of Dublin supporters, angered at the sending off of team captain McDonnell, sought out referee Jim Byrne, himself a former All-Ireland winning captain with Wexford. Showing true sportsmanship, the first man into the breach to protect the referee from the baying mob was … Paddy McDonnell.

The first round of the Munster Championship saw Kerry ease past Clare, 3-4 to 0-5, at the Cricket Field in Kilrush on 10 June. Their next 'routine' assignment was against Tipperary on 8 July. In what must rank as one of the greatest ever championship upsets, the men from the Premier County toppled the mighty Kingdom on a score of 1-7 to 2-3. Reporting on Kerry's shock defeat, the *Irish Independent* noted that the result 'will be a disappointment to those who had been looking to their having another meeting with Kildare'.

Tipperary were not able to maintain their momentum, however, as they suffered an eleven-point defeat to Cork in the provincial final at Dungarvan on 5 August. The headline of the match report in the *Irish Independent* highlighted the contribution of two UCC doctors, Joe Kearney and Eugene 'Nudge' Callanan, to this victory which saw Cork become Munster champions for the first time since 1916.

Compared to the modern game, scoring was generally much lower in the 1920s. Kildare's ten points in the Leinster Final was the only occasion in the entire 1928 Championship when a team brought its points tally to double figures. Even by the standards of the day, however, Galway and Leitrim took matters to another level when they met at Roscommon on 10 June. They failed to raise a single white flag between them as they fought out a 'fast and exciting contest' which ended in a draw, one goal each. Leitrim introduced Peter Masterson for the replay two weeks later and he was the central figure as they took the laurels, 0-7 to 0-3.

As reigning Connacht champions, Leitrim were favoured to advance to another final when they met Sligo at Boyle on 15 July. However, from the moment Tom 'Click' Brennan scored a point in the opening salvo, it was Sligo who dominated. Their star in this six-point victory was Paddy Colleran, who, despite being knocked out on two occasions, played brilliantly all through. For Leitrim, their shining light was John 'Nipper' Shanley, whose ability to take the ball from end to end was a feature of the game.

The two games between Leitrim and Galway were refereed by Roscommon's Tom Shevlin. On

An artist's impression of the Kildare team which retained the All-Ireland title in 1928, thus becoming the first recipients of the Sam Maguire Cup. *Courtesy Gaelic Art.*

the Sunday before the replay, he busied himself by lining out, and starring, in Roscommon's semi-final encounter with Mayo. His efforts were in vain, however, as Mayo progressed to the final on a score of 1-5 to 0-2. The wonderful play of Dick Creagh and Gerald Courell, as well as Tom and John Forde, gave Mayo great optimism that the Connacht title was within their grasp.

The Connacht Final at Tuam on 5 August was a close affair between two evenly matched teams. Aided by the breeze in the first half, Sligo built up a three-point lead. While they failed to score in the second half, brilliant defending by Jim 'Red' Flynn, Paddy Colleran and goalkeeper George Higgins kept Mayo at bay as Sligo held on for a one-point victory, and their first ever provincial title.

For many years, Cavan had been the dominant force in Ulster football. They had been slighted in 1927, however, when neighbours Monaghan stole in to take the provincial crown. The men of Breffni set out on the 1928 Championship trail when they met Antrim at Belturbet on 17 June. With Jim Smith and Jimmy Murphy in top form, they had a comfortable six-point win. While giving due credit to Cavan's stars, *The Anglo Celt* described the performance of Antrim midfielder Art Thornbury thus: 'brilliant as usual'.

Cavan's semi-final opposition was presented by Tyrone, who had earlier trounced Derry, 7-3 to 2-3. With Packy Devlin in sparkling form, the Breffni men had a comfortable 4-3 to 0-4 victory.

While the general expectation was that Cavan and Monaghan would contest the Ulster Final, the men of Armagh had different ideas. Amid scenes of wild jubilation among their supporters, they overcame Monaghan, 0-4 to 0-1, at Carrickmacross on 1 July. Monaghan's cause was not helped by the fact that four of their players, including team captain Paddy Kilroy, had taken part in a Garda v Army match at Croke Park earlier in the day.

The most remarkable feature of the 1928 Ulster Final, played at Breffni Park on 29 July, was that the two goalkeepers were brothers. Keady's Charlie Morgan lined out with Armagh while his brother, John, a garda based in Cavan, was his opposite number.

Cavan's status as favourites to regain the crown suffered a serious blow in the days before the game. Two of its stalwarts, Jim Smith and Harry Mulvany, had to withdraw through illness. When the game got underway, Armagh grabbed an early goal through Gerry Arthurs and continued to pile on the pressure in the opening half. When they extended their lead to four points midway through the second half, a championship shock was on the cards. Cavan rallied, however, and late goals from Andy Conlon and Jimmy Murphy saw them take the title on a scoreline of 2-6 to 1-4.

Sligo were unfortunate in having to travel to Breffni Park to take on Cavan in the first of the All-Ireland semi-finals. Despite showing well initially, Sligo eventually ran out of steam and Cavan were comfortable 2-5 to 0-4 winners. The returning Jim Smith was Cavan's outstanding player, while Andy Conlon and Packy Devlin were their goal scorers. Paddy Colleran, 'Click' Brennan and Kieran Kenny were especially prominent for Sligo.

With home advantage, Cork were tipped by many to topple All-Ireland champions Kildare in their 2 September semi-final clash. Within minutes of the throw-in, however, it was clear that the

Lilywhites were in a different class. As Paul Doyle, Joe Curtis and Bill Mangan proceeded to cut through the Cork defence, Kildare led 1-5 to 0-0 at the break. Cork's gallant efforts in the second half came to nought against a defence where Gus Fitzpatrick, Frank Malone and Jack Higgins were outstanding, while goalkeeper Martin Walshe was unbeatable. Kildare's winning margin was fourteen points. Now only Cavan stood between them and a second successive All-Ireland crown.

THE FINAL – 30 SEPTEMBER

Underdogs Cavan were to belie that label in a tense, closely fought encounter. It was only by the narrowest of margins, and in somewhat controversial circumstances, that red-hot favourites Kildare retained their crown.

In a game that newspapers at the time described as being of the highest standard, the Cavan men raced into an early three-point lead. Driven on by their inspirational captain, Jim Smith, they matched the Lilywhites in every facet of the game. Their early advantage would have been greater but for the outstanding play of Kildare's central defenders Matt Goff and the inimitable Jack Higgins. As the game approached half-time, Kildare veteran Paul Doyle slammed home a well-taken goal to leave his team two points ahead at the break – Kildare 1-2, Cavan 0-3.

In the second half, there was no let-up in the frantic exchanges and the advantage shifted between the two teams. A goal from Packy Devlin looked to have turned the tide in Cavan's favour but another from Kildare's Paddy O'Loughlin put the Lilywhites back in the driving seat. Many allege that this score was thrown into the net and 'Pato' (P.D. Mehigan), reporting in *The Irish Times*, was emphatic on this: 'Let it be written quickly, P. O'Loughlin threw the ball into the Cavan net.'

Cavan battled back to draw level with the help of a Willie Young goal. Bill Mangan then kicked what proved to be Kildare's winning point. With Young and Devlin to the fore, Cavan's all-out siege on the Kildare goal looked certain to yield an equaliser but corner-back Gus Fitzpatrick saved the day for the Lilywhites with a magnificent interception and clearance in the dying seconds. With exactly the same line-out as in the previous year's final, Kildare retained the title on a scoreline of 2-6 to 2-5, thus becoming the first holders of the Sam Maguire Cup.

Over the years, unbounded exuberance has grown to become part and parcel of the All-Ireland Final presentation experience. Celebrations were more subdued in 1928, as this extract from the *Leinster Leader* shows: 'A pleasant little ceremony followed the match when Willie Gannon, the Kildare captain, was called to the Grand Stand and there presented by Dr McCartan, a close friend of Sam Maguire, with the beautiful silver cup which commemorates the memory of that great Gael and true Irishman.'

FINAL STATISTICS

	Kildare	Cavan
Full-time:	2-6	2-5
Half-time:	1-2	0-3
Scorers:	P. Doyle 0-5 (0-3 frees)	P. Devlin 1-2
	B. Mangan 1-0	W. Young 1-0
	P. O'Loughlin 1-0	J. Murphy 0-1
	T. Keogh 0-1	J. Smith 0-1
		S. Farrelly 0-1
Attendance:	24,700	
Gate Receipts:	£2,007 (€2,548)	
Referee:	Tom Burke (Louth)	

FINAL MISCELLANY

- For the 1928 Final, reserved seating in the Hogan Stand was priced at five shillings (€0.32).
- At the end of the 1928 Championship, the leading counties in the All-Ireland roll of honour were:

  Dublin: 14

  Kerry: 7

  Wexford: 5

  Tipperary: 4

  Kildare: 4

- While Kildare lined out with the same fifteen as in the 1927 Final, this was only brought about through a last-minute intervention by Cavan officials. Suffering from broken ribs after a cycling accident, Joe Curtis was due to be replaced by Rathangan's Peter Pringle. The arrival of a Breffni contingent into the Kildare dressing-room, armed with photographic evidence showing that Pringle had played illegally in a Laois club game, prompted his demotion. Curtis was duly strapped up for action, given a swig of whiskey to numb the pain, and proceeded to make a major contribution as the Lilywhites retained their title.
- The Cavan centre half-back, Patsy Lynch, was sixteen years old when he lined out in the 1928 Final.
- Star Kildare forward Paul Doyle, who also won All-Ireland medals with Kildare in 1919 and 1927, had lined out for Cavan in the 1923 All-Ireland semi-final.
- At the GAA Annual Congress of 1928, a motion was passed whereby the expense allowance for teams participating in inter-county matches was increased from £5-10-0 (€6.98) to £7-10-0 (€9.52).

1928 — THE YEAR THAT WAS

- Irish coinage was circulated for the first time in 1928.
- According to the *Leinster Express* of 29 September 1928, one Thomas Kirwan of Thurles was fined ten shillings (€0.63) at Abbeyleix District Court. He had been 'speeding' at 25 miles per hour.
- Clery's Department Store on Dublin's O'Connell Street was promoting a special deal on made-to-measure overcoats for men. They were priced at four and a half guineas (€6).
- In Amsterdam, the Irish tricolour was raised for the first time at the Olympics when Pat O'Callaghan took gold in the hammer throw.
- Mickey Mouse, one of the most recognisable and enduring characters in the world of entertainment, made his debut in 1928.
- Alexander Fleming's accidental discovery and isolation of penicillin, on the weekend of the 1928 All-Ireland Final, marked the beginning of modern antibiotics.

1928 TEAM LINE-OUTS

KILDARE (WINNERS)

1. Martin Walshe
(Kildare Round Towers)

2. Mick Buckley
(Caragh)

3. Matt Goff
(McKee Barracks, also Leixlip)

4. Gus Fitzpatrick
(Naas)

5. Frank Malone
(Caragh)

6. Jack Higgins
(McKee Barracks, also Naas)

7. Jack Hayes
(Kildare Round Towers)

8. Bill 'Squires' Gannon
(Kildare Round Towers) Capt.

9. Joe O'Loughlin
(Rathangan)

10. Joe Curtis
(Naas)

11. Paddy Martin
(Ellistown)

12. Paul Doyle
(McKee Barracks, also Maddenstown and Suncroft)

13. Bill Mangan
(Kildare Round Towers)

14. Paddy O'Loughlin
(Rathangan)

15. Tom Keogh
(Crumlin Independents, Dublin, also Kildare Round Towers and Portlaoise, Laois)

Subs: Dan Ryan (Naas), Played; Joe Reilly (Rathangan); Tom 'Towe' Wheeler (Naas); Paddy Ryan (Carbury); Frank O'Toole (Griffith Barracks); Peter Pringle (Rathangan); Jack Connell (Milltown); Pat 'Darkie' Ryan (Milltown); Mick Connor (Caragh)

CAVAN (RUNNERS-UP)

1. John Morgan
(Drumbo)

2. George Malcolmson
(Bailieboro)

3. Tom Campbell
(Crosserlough)

4. Herbie Clegg
(Cootehill)

5. Harry Mulvany
(Maghera)

6. Patsy Lynch
(Bailieboro)

7. Jack Clarke
(Cavan Slashers)

8. Jim Smith
(Garda, also Erin's Own, Kells, Meath,
Bailieboro and Virginia) Capt.

9. Hughie O'Reilly
(Tullyvin, also Cootehill)

10. William A. Higgins
(Drumbo, also Ballyhaise)

11. Packy Devlin
(Killeshandra, also Cornafean)

12. Jimmy Murphy
(Cornafean)

13. Andy Conlon
(Cavan Slashers)

14. Willie Young
(Cornafean)

15. Seán Farrelly
(Drumbo, also Cavan Slashers)

Subs: Tom Crowe (Cavan Slashers); Frank Fitzpatrick (Cavan Slashers, also Cornafean); Tom Mulvany (Maghera); Benny O'Reilly (Cornafean); Benny Fay (Cornafean); John O'Reilly (Templeport)

Other Panel Members: John Carolan (Cross); Paudge Masterson (Cornafean); Packy Joe O'Reilly (Cornafean); John Young (Cornafean); Hugh B. Carolan (Cross)

Pat Leddy (Cornafean) and Pat Fox (Cross) had played throughout the campaign but returned to college before the final and were unavailable for selection.

Also unavailable for selection was John P. Murphy (Cornafean). He spent several weeks in hospital after suffering a serious shoulder injury in the semi-final against Sligo.

1929

Kerry's dramatic exit from the 1928 title race at the hands of Tipperary was one of the greatest ever championship shocks. Few doubted that the men from the Kingdom would return with a vengeance, most likely to renew their rivalry with reigning champions Kildare.

With Paul Russell in commanding form, Kerry's campaign started in routine fashion with a comfortable four-point win over Cork at the UCC Grounds on 26 May. On the same day, Tipperary met Clare at Kilrush in the second semi-final. Having been treated to a civic reception by the local urban council on the Saturday evening, the Tipperary men got an altogether different reception the following day. The captain of their All-Ireland winning minor team of 1929, George Comerford, led the way as Clare stunned their visitors and ran out comfortable 3-3 to 1-4 winners.

Clare's hopes of a first ever win over Kerry were well and truly dashed in the Munster Final at Killarney on 14 July. Leading 0-10 to 0-0 at the break, the Kerry men regained their provincial crown with a facile 1-14 to 1-2 victory. The manner of Kerry's win did not, however, inspire confidence and *The Kerryman* went so far as to suggest that their great run had come to its natural end. This was one prediction that proved to be somewhat wide of the mark.

In Connacht, champions Sligo got off to a winning start when they had one point to spare over Leitrim at Boyle on 16 June. Luke Colleran and Tom 'Click' Brennan were the key men as Sligo progressed to the semi-final. When they lined out against Galway at Roscommon on 7 July, however, they fell victim to a brilliant display by Galway's Mick Donnellan. At the wrong end of a 1-7 to 0-0 scoreline, Sligo's defeat would have been much greater but for the heroic display of goalkeeper George Higgins.

Gerald Courell ran amok as Mayo trounced Roscommon 6-6 to 0-4 in the second semi-final on 9 June. Despite this big win, it was Galway who took the favourites tag into the Connacht Final at Roscommon on 21 July. Once again, it was Courell who came up trumps, scoring all of Mayo's points in their 1-6 to 0-4 victory.

In Leinster, the Lilywhites started their campaign in Drogheda on 12 May when they were fortunate to secure a draw against a Meath side that had one 'M. Fahy' in scintillating form. Otherwise known as Fr Michael McManus, this Westmeath native would go on to become Chairman of the Meath County Board many years later.

In the dying minutes of the game, and with Meath on the offensive, Kildare resorted to kicking the ball out of play repeatedly. The *Meath Chronicle* lamented the shameful use of these 'Tullyallen' tactics to avoid defeat. The replay on 9 June attracted a crowd of over ten thousand to Drogheda, where, after another epic battle, Kildare progressed, 3-5 to 0-9, with Albert O'Neill accounting for two of their goals.

Fresh from their surprise win over Louth, Kilkenny provided Kildare's opposition in the provincial semi-final at Portlaoise on 7 July. The Lilywhites proved far too strong, however, and ran out comfortable fourteen-point winners.

Dublin were favoured to emerge from the opposite side of the Leinster draw and, with Mick 'Ginger' O'Brien and Paddy McDonnell starring, they duly opened their account with a seven-point win over Longford on 26 May. The Metropolitans were then expected to prevail in the semi-final against Laois at Athy on 30 June. With Danny Douglas in commanding form, Laois embarked on a five-goal scoring spree and held a nine-point lead late in the game. After a dramatic rally, spearheaded by Paddy McDonnell, Dublin looked to have saved the day. However, Joe O'Shea had different ideas, striking the winning point for Laois several minutes into time added on.

Aiming for their fifth title in a row, Kildare were firm favourites against their inexperienced Leinster Final opponents. When they met at Croke Park on 21 July, it was Laois who took the

The Kerry team of 1929, which started the county's run of four-in-a-row titles, thus equalling the achievement of the great Wexford team of 1915–1918. Back (l–r): Paul Russell, Con Brosnan, Sammy Locke, J. O'Connor, John Joe 'Purty' Landers; middle (l–r): Jackie Ryan, Ned 'Pedlar' Sweeney, Tim O'Donnell, Micheál Ó Ruairc, Jack Walsh, John Joe Sheehy, Paud O'Sullivan; front (l–r): Miko Doyle, Bob Stack, Jimmy Baily, Joe Barrett (captain), Dee O'Connor, Johnny Riordan, Joe O'Sullivan. *Image courtesy of the GAA Museum at Croke Park.*

initiative and they proceeded to dominate in the possession stakes. But their preoccupation with going for goals proved to be their downfall, with Kildare goalkeeper Joe Reilly in unbeatable form. The *Irish Independent* recorded that his performance 'under hot pressure was equal to anything ever witnessed on a Gaelic field'.

While Kildare retained their provincial crown on a score of 2-3 to 0-6, it was widely acknowledged that Laois had put the champions to the pin of their proverbial collar.

In Ulster, reigning champions Cavan travelled to Belfast on 26 May and had little difficulty easing past Antrim. Their next engagement was against an Armagh side which had been showing very impressive form. Fresh from their McKenna Cup Final win over Monaghan, and an easy first-round victory over Down, the Armagh men were expected to trouble the champions. When they met at Belturbet on 30 June, the game turned out to be a totally one-sided affair, with Cavan romping to an easy 4-10 to 0-2 victory. But the result faded into insignificance when Armagh's James Kernan, injured during the game, sadly passed away two days later.

As expected, Monaghan progressed from the other side of the draw to contest the Ulster Final. They followed up their 2-8 to 0-1 victory over Donegal with an equally impressive 3-7 to 1-2 win over Tyrone in the semi-final.

A crowd of over ten thousand had to endure a continuous downpour as they watched Cavan and Monaghan serve up a thrilling encounter at Breffni Park on 28 July. With Jim Smith and former Sligo star Paddy Colleran lording it at midfield, Cavan stormed into an early five-point lead. Monaghan fought back, however, and a goal from Rev. Fr T. McDonald brought the sides level at half-time. It was helter-skelter all the way to the end as these great rivals fought out a battle of endurance which ended all square, 1-4 each.

The replay took place two weeks later at Carrickmacross, but this was far from being a close affair. Before a crowd of over eight thousand, Monaghan took command early on and with 'the elusive 'Blayney postman', Christy Fisher, in top scoring form, they ran out comfortable 1-10 to 0-7 winners.

The stage was now set for the All-Ireland semi-finals and the consensus was that Kerry would overcome Mayo while Kildare would beat Monaghan and so renew one of the great All-Ireland Final rivalries.

Kerry were complete masters over Mayo when they met at Roscommon on 18 August. Without ever moving into top gear, they cruised to a 3-8 to 1-1 victory. Not satisfied with victory, *The Kerryman* bemoaned the absence of any real challenge on the way to the All-Ireland Final and worried that this would leave them vulnerable in the September showdown.

The second semi-final was equally one-sided, with Kildare emerging 0-9 to 0-1 winners over Monaghan at Croke Park on 25 August. Monaghan's principal weakness was in attack where they repeatedly failed to convert the chances that came their way. Kildare's staunch defence, particularly Joe Reilly, Gus Fitzpatrick, Jack Higgins and Bill Hynan, proved too strong for the less robust

Farney men. In the words of *The Anglo Celt*, 'the tall Kildare backs seemed to be a mass of arms and legs, which was a considerable handicap to the low-sized Monaghan forwards'.

THE FINAL – 22 SEPTEMBER

A then record crowd of 43,839 flocked to Croke Park on 22 September to witness a renewal of the Kerry–Kildare rivalry. Under what the *Irish Independent* described as 'a burning sun', Kerry relieved Kildare of their crown in one of the greatest struggles in championship history.

The Lilywhites started the game in whirlwind fashion and star forward Paul Doyle had notched two points before Kerry got off the mark. The Kerry men soon got into their stride, however, and scored 1-5 without reply to hold a six-point (1-5 to 0-2) half-time lead. Ned 'Pedlar' Sweeney scored Kerry's goal, while the outstanding John Joe Sheehy struck points from all angles.

In the second half, Kildare staged an impressive comeback and Paddy Martin's thirty-five-yard piledriver to the back of the Kerry net closed the gap to three points. Further scores from Paul Doyle left the score at 1-6 to 1-5 and paved the way for a grandstand finish. Late points from Sheehy and John Joe 'Purty' Landers saw Kerry emerge victorious on a 1-8 to 1-5 scoreline.

Newspaper reports on the game were effusive in their praise of the Kerry fifteen, with *The Cork Examiner* noting that '[O']Sullivan, Russell, Sheehy and Sweeney were mainly responsible for the downfall of the champions'.

For Kildare, goalkeeper Joe Reilly had a brilliant game and could not be faulted for conceding what was the only goal scored against him in the championship. Scorer-in-chief Paul Doyle produced another fine display while Frank Malone was unbeatable in defence. *The Kerryman* report on the game described Kildare midfielder Joe O'Loughlin as a 'master craftsman'.

As the dust settled on the 1929 Championship there was general agreement that the country's two best teams had contested the final. Such was the quality of Kerry's play that many predicted an era of sustained success for the Kingdom. Time would confirm just how well these predictions were founded.

FINAL STATISTICS

	Kerry	Kildare
Full-time:	1-8	1-5
Half-time:	1-5	0-2
Scorers:	J.J. Sheehy 0-6 (0-2 frees)	P. Doyle 0-5 (0-2 frees)
	N. Sweeney 1-1	P. Martin 1-0
	J.J. Landers 0-1	
Attendance:	43,839	
Gate Receipts:	£3,994 (€4,010)	
Referee:	Peter O'Farrell (Roscommon)	

FINAL MISCELLANY

- From the *Irish Independent*, Monday 23 September: 'Feminine screams rose above the tumult, and strong men had difficulty in rescuing women in danger of being trampled on. Some men protested that it is not fair that they should have been allowed in at all when the grounds were so crowded.'

- Writing in the *The Nationalist and Leinster Times* of 28 September, Jack Winter reported:

  'It was the first time I had been to Croke Park, if I leave out those early days, long ago, when the field was but an ordinary centre with practically no accommodation beyond the ordinary country centre, and Gaelic football was a game, not of science, but of strength. My old eyes were gladdened therefore, when on Sunday last, I saw the great improvements that have been achieved in this venue, and still more to see the thousands of people that flocked from all over Ireland to view the final contest for the nation's prize.'

- On 29 May 1929, Kilkenny beat Louth in the Leinster quarter-final on a scoreline of 0-10 to 0-4. This remains their most recent championship win.

- The inaugural Minor Championship took place in 1929, with Clare beating Longford, 5-3 to 3-5, in the final.

- When the *Meath Chronicle* criticised Kildare's use of 'Tullyallen' tactics, it was referring to an ingenious strategy employed by the men from that Louth parish in the early days of the Association. Prior to 1892, each team comprised twenty-one players, while the goals were just fifteen feet wide. Further, a goal counted for more than any number of points. An early goal for the Tullyallen team meant just one thing: twenty-one sturdy young men would crowd the goalmouth, rendering the likelihood of a goal for the opposition a virtual impossibility.

- It was common at the time not to report the names of clerics in newspaper reports, but to substitute a false name instead. An exception here is *The Anglo Celt*'s account of the 1929 Ulster Final between Monaghan and Cavan when two priests were in direct opposition: 'McAleer … sent on towards Father McDonald, but Father Leddy got there first and pulled down the ball, driving to touch.'

- Pádraig Ó Caoimh was appointed General Secretary of the GAA and Manager of Croke Park in 1929. His salary was £300, rising in annual increments of £10 to a maximum of £400. He was also provided with a free house and 'electric light'.

- According to *The Nationalist and Leinster Times* of 26 November 1929, the Chairman of the Carlow County Board was critical of the practice of giving young players a half-time shot of intoxicating liquor. 'It was,' he said, 'deplorable to see young fellows taking whiskey which only tended to injure their nervous systems and make them irritable for the rest of the game.'

1929 – THE YEAR THAT WAS

- Staunch republican and former government minister Austin Stack, who had captained Kerry to win the 1904 title, passed away on 27 April. He was forty-nine years old.
- The Ardnacrusha power plant in County Clare, at that time the world's largest hydroelectric station, opened on 22 July.
- The Wall Street Crash began on 24 October, with financial markets collapsing on 29 October (Black Tuesday), thus heralding the onset of the Great Depression. Also in New York on 29 October, future Dublin star Jim Crowley arrived into the world.
- Originally completed in 1818 at a cost of £50,000, and largely destroyed during the 1916 Easter Rising, Dublin's GPO was reopened to the public in 1929.
- Lasting just fifteen minutes, the first ever Academy Awards ceremony took place in Hollywood on 16 May.

1929 TEAM LINE-OUTS

KERRY (WINNERS)

1. Johnny Riordan (John Mitchels)

2. Dee O'Connor (Kilcummin, also Dr Crokes)

3. Joe Barrett (Austin Stacks) Capt.

4. Jack Walsh (Asdee)

5. Paul Russell (Dr Crokes, also Garda, Dungarvan, Waterford and Oldcastle, Meath)

6. Joe O'Sullivan (Dingle)

7. Tim O'Donnell (Camp, also Dr Crokes)

8. Con Brosnan (Moyvane)

9. Bob Stack (Ballybunion)

10. Jackie Ryan (John Mitchels, also Austin Stacks)

11. Miko Doyle (Austin Stacks)

12. John Joe 'Purty' Landers (Austin Stacks)

13. Ned 'Pedlar' Sweeney (Austin Stacks)

14. Jimmy Baily (Ballymacelligott, also Austin Stacks)

15. John Joe Sheehy (John Mitchels)

Subs: Micheál Ó Ruairc (John Mitchels); Paud O'Sullivan (Moyvane); Sammy Locke (Kerins O'Rahillys); Richard Clifford (Dr Crokes); Denis 'Rory' O'Connell (Austin Stacks); Sean Stack (Dingle, also Geraldines, Dublin); Mick Healy (Austin Stacks); Dan Joe Conway (Kerins O'Rahillys); Dan Ryan (Austin Stacks)

KILDARE (RUNNERS-UP)

1. Joe Reilly
(Rathangan, also Garda)

2. Jack Hayes
(Kildare Round Towers)

3. Matt Goff
(McKee Barracks, also Leixlip)

4. Gus Fitzpatrick
(Naas)

5. Mick Fenneral
(Milltown, also Army)

6. Jack Higgins
(McKee Barracks, also Naas) Capt.

7. Frank Malone
(Caragh)

8. Paddy O'Loughlin
(Rathangan)

9. Joe O'Loughlin
(Rathangan)

10. Paddy Martin
(Ellistown)

11. Bill Hynan
(Carbury)

12. Paul Doyle
(McKee Barracks, also Maddenstown
and Suncroft)

13. Tom Wheeler
(Naas)

14. Peter Pringle
(Rathangan)

15. Bill 'Squires' Gannon
(Kildare Round Towers)

Subs: Mick Buckley (Caragh); Christy Graham (Kildare Round Towers); Mick Connor (Caragh); Joe Curtis (Naas); Mick Behan (Rathangan); Albert O'Neill (Kildare Round Towers); John McEvoy (Athy)

1930

As the 1930 Championship got underway, it was generally considered that Kerry would once again be the team to beat. Receiving a bye into the Munster Final, they looked on as Cork, Clare and Tipperary battled it out for the right to face the champions in the provincial showdown. Cork advanced to the semi-final by virtue of a 3-8 to 3-4 victory over Clare at the Athletic Grounds on 1 June. When they met Tipperary at Clonmel on 20 July, the early stages of play were marred by a torrential downpour. While conditions improved dramatically in the second half and the game was played out in blazing sunshine, there was little comfort for anyone involved. According to the *The Nationalist* (Tipperary), 'The players were soaked and so were the many spectators who ventured out without topcoats and umbrellas.' Team captain Dick Mockler, Paddy Arrigan and agile goalkeeper John Weston were the key men as Tipperary advanced to the final on a score of 2-6 to 1-3.

When they met Kerry in the provincial showdown on 10 August, there was a quiet confidence among Tipperary supporters that they could repeat their sensational win of two years earlier. Few doubted that they had highly talented players in such as Tom Lee, Mick Barry, Bill Barrett, Tom Power and especially John Weston. The problem, however, was that they simply couldn't match the experienced Kerry men when it came to team combination. Intricate play produced goals from John Joe Sheehy, Con Brosnan and Jackie Ryan as Kerry took their twenty-first Munster title on a score of 3-4 to 1-2.

The Connacht Championship got underway at Sligo on 18 May where Mayo had a comfortable 3-4 to 1-1 semi-final victory over Leitrim. Describing an otherwise drab affair, *The Connaught Telegraph* reported the highlight of the day's proceedings: 'There was a good deal of amusement among Mayo spectators when a Leitrim player showed inclination to strike Hearns, the international amateur boxer. The referee also had a sense of humour – so has Hearns.'

The other side of the draw saw Sligo play Galway at the Mental Hospital Grounds, Castlebar, on 1 June. The crowd of 8,000, a record attendance for Connacht, was treated to a great game, at the end of which Sligo emerged 2-4 to 1-5 winners. The loss of goalkeeper George Higgins, who was badly injured in a goalmouth melee, was a major handicap for Sligo. However, the Trojan efforts of midfielder Paddy Colleran and the opportunism of Mickey Noone finally got them over the line.

Sligo's prize for this victory was a semi-final joust with Roscommon at Boyle on 29 June. Lavishing praise on this encounter, *The Sligo Champion* reporter said he had never seen a better game, further enhancing the match's status by noting that it 'started only 15 minutes after the scheduled time'. Perhaps the reporter's view was swayed by the fact that Sligo took the laurels on a scoreline of 2-7 to 0-5.

After their comprehensive win over Leitrim, Mayo were strongly favoured to overcome the Sligo men when they met at Tuam on 10 August. Within minutes of the throw-in, Sligo's Paddy Colleran struck a goal from fully forty yards out to put his team into the driving seat. While the teams were level at the break, Sligo had wind advantage to come, and an upset seemed on the cards. On the resumption, however, Mickey Moran took a serious hand in proceedings. He registered a goal and a point in quick succession to put Mayo into the ascendancy. Sligo's best efforts to retrieve the situation came to nought, and Mayo took the title on a score of 1-7 to 1-2.

In Leinster, Kildare were expected to prevail and they duly started their campaign with a facile 6-7 to 3-3 win over Offaly at Tullamore on 11 May. With a 4-2 to 2-1 victory over Kilkenny, Wexford advanced to meet the Lilywhites in the quarter-final at Croke Park on 6 July. After opening impressively, it was downhill all the way for the Slaneysiders, as they slumped to a ten-point defeat. Laois qualified to meet Kildare in the semi-final when Jack and Har Browne hit the headlines in a 2-7 to 0-3 victory over Louth.

No fewer than nine members of the army were on duty when Kildare and Laois lined out on 20 July at Kilkenny. The Laois men got off to a lightning start and were 1-2 to the good before Kildare registered their first score. But the Lilywhites eventually settled into their rhythm, and with Bill Hynan and Paddy O'Loughlin controlling midfield, the scores began to come. Harry Burke took full advantage of Kildare's midfield dominance, finding the net three times in an emphatic 4-4 to 1-4 victory.

At Mullingar on 8 June, Dublin and Meath emerged victorious from their respective quarter-final encounters with Westmeath and Longford. Their much-anticipated semi-final clash attracted a crowd of 17,000 to Drogheda on 29 June where a blistering start by Meath set them on the road to a famous victory. If names such as Russell, Rogers, McGuinness, Nulty and Meade formed the backbone of this new footballing force, one 'P. Donoghue' was the team's outstanding performer. Hopes were now high that the men from the Royal County could bring an end to Kildare's years of dominance.

It was only on the day of the Leinster Final that news of 'Donoghue's' omission from the team became public knowledge. Despite this setback, Meath gave as good as they got, and ended on level terms with their exalted opponents. It was a different story the following week when the craft of Jack Higgins and Paul Doyle paved the way for a comfortable six-point win for the Lilywhites.

When the dust settled on the Leinster campaign of 1930, there was widespread consensus that Meath would have taken the title if they had been able to line out as selected for the drawn game. Supporters were left frustrated that Fr Michael McManus, otherwise known as 'Donoghue', had been omitted from the team when the Bishop of Mullingar refused the request of the Meath selectors that he be allowed to play. Their annoyance was all the more acute against the backdrop of his not needing permission to start in the earlier rounds, nor indeed throughout the 1929 campaign when Fr McManus gloried under the *nom de plume* 'M. Fahy'.

While the other provincial championships were progressing relatively smoothly, matters became seriously complicated in Ulster.

For a start, Cavan had the distinction of playing, and winning, provincial semi-finals against two different counties in the same year. In the quarter-final game at Enniskillen on 1 June, Antrim beat Fermanagh on a scoreline of 3-3 to 1-5. Fermanagh objected on the grounds that Patrick Canning's name had not been included on Antrim's official list of twenty players. They were duly awarded the game by the Ulster Council on 14 June and they proceeded to play Cavan in the semi-final at Belturbet on 22 June. Cavan won 2-3 to 1-0.

Antrim were unhappy about the Ulster Council ruling and appealed the matter to the GAA Central Council. The outcome of this appeal was to reverse the original Ulster Council decision and so Antrim were awarded the laurels from their earlier clash with Fermanagh. Cavan were now obliged to play a second semi-final and they duly beat Antrim 1-5 to 1-2 at Belfast on 6 July.

Even though they struck 7-8 in a cakewalk victory over Down on 8 June, not many predicted an extended run for Monaghan in the 1930 Championship. With Cavan having overcome both Fermanagh and Antrim in successive 'semi-finals', the Farneymen were now pitted against neighbours Armagh in the 'third' semi-final. They emerged three-point winners and, despite a subsequent objection by Armagh, they seemed set for a straightforward shoot-out with their arch-rivals. But there was nothing straightforward about what happened next.

The Ulster Council fixed the game for Carrickmacross on 27 July. Cavan objected on the basis that the playing pitch there was totally unsuitable and the expected crowd could not be accommodated. In the weeks leading up to the game there were several 'emergency' meetings involving various combinations of the Cavan County Committee, the Monaghan County Committee, the Ulster Council and the Central Council. Cavan offered to play the game at any other Monaghan venue and passed a motion, on the casting vote of chairman Seamus Gilheany, not to fulfil the fixture unless it was moved from Carrickmacross. For their part,

The 1930 football final programme cover.

Image courtesy of the GAA Museum at Croke Park.

Monaghan were adamant that a change of venue would not be conceded and their County Secretary, Paddy Hoey, set out their position in a letter to Cavan's local newspaper, *The Anglo Celt*: 'Our team will take the field on the date fixed by the Ulster Council, viz: 27th July, and at the venue fixed by the Ulster Council, viz: Carrickmacross.'

All of this came nearly ninety years before Kildare's Cian O'Neill coined the immortal phrase 'Newbridge or Nowhere!'

Further confusion ensued when, at the urging of the Ulster Council, a number of Cavan officials fielded a weakened team for the Carrickmacross showdown. Monaghan duly won this encounter easily, 4-3 to 1-5. Cavan were deemed to have suspended themselves from the GAA while, in turn, the officials responsible for fulfilling the fixture were suspended by the Cavan County Committee.

At Roscommon on 24 August, Kerry had their expected win over Mayo, winning on a scoreline of 1-9 to 0-4. John Joe Sheehy was the outstanding performer on the day, scoring the game's only goal.

Also on 24 August, the second semi-final, which was played at Croke Park, was expected to pave the way for the by now routine Kerry versus Kildare showdown. The men from Monaghan had other ideas, however, and in one of the biggest shocks in championship history, they overpowered the Lilywhites, 1-6 to 1-4, in a Croke Park downpour. While Kildare could point to the absence of Larry Stanley and Paddy O'Loughlin, Monaghan fully deserved this famous victory. The Lilywhites simply couldn't penetrate the Farneymen's rock-like defence, in which goalkeeper Tommy Bradley was inspirational.

THE FINAL — 28 SEPTEMBER

The sense of excitement in the build-up to the final was abruptly shattered on the Friday before the game. Dick Fitzgerald, the legendary Kerry player and coach, died after a fall from a roof in Killarney. Described by Dr William O'Sullivan, county coroner, as 'probably the greatest exponent of Gaelic football that ever lived', Fitzgerald's death cast a long shadow over the final. It was only after long deliberation that it was decided to proceed with the match and, at the request of the Kerry County Board, the funeral was delayed until the day after the game.

On the day of the final, all six teams lining out in Croke Park wore black armbands as a mark of respect, while The Artane Boys Band played Chopin's 'Funeral March' before the throw-in.

The final itself was most disappointing. In ideal conditions, Monaghan were first out of the traps, with Peter McConnon launching the opening score in the first minute. Thereafter, it was downhill all the way for the Ulster champions as the speed and movement of the Kerry forwards created havoc. Kerry led 1-6 to 0-2 at half-time and piled on even more pressure in the second half. Holding Monaghan scoreless in the last half hour, the Kingdom had a runaway 3-11 to 0-2 victory. The final minutes of the game were marred by a number of unsavoury incidents, including a pitch invasion which took several minutes to quell.

A feature of the game was how, as described in *The Anglo Celt*: 'A number of players came to grief, the more serious accidents being to O'Carroll, whose leg was fractured, and Mason, who was carried off in the last five minutes by members of the Saint John Ambulance Brigade.'

It was generally acknowledged that Kerry had reached a new level in this final. In a team of stars, special praise was heaped on Sheehy, Landers, the 'dazzling' Ryan, and the 'lightning fast' Sweeney.

Despite conceding three goals, Monaghan goalkeeper Tommy Bradley gave a brilliant display. Jimmy Duffy was generally accepted as being their best performer, and while Mickey McAleer was said to have done very well, 'he, like the rest of the team, met with plenty of hard knocks.'

Kerry's status as the best team in the land was now unquestioned. The county's sense of confidence was captured by 'Liam' De Scriobh in *The Kerry Champion*: '… as we left the scene of our latest victory we felt we could look forward to struggles for the title in coming years with rare confidence and faith'.

FINAL STATISTICS

	Kerry	Monaghan
Full-time:	3-11	0-2
Half-time:	1-6	0-2
Scorers:	J.J. Landers 1-4	P. McConnon 0-1
	J.J. Sheehy 1-3 (0-1 free)	H. Brannigan 0-1
	J. Ryan 0-3	
	M. Doyle 0-1	
	N. Sweeney 1-0	
Attendance:	33,280	
Gate Receipts:	£3,038 (€3,857)	
Referee:	Jim Byrne (Wexford)	

FINAL MISCELLANY

- The referee for the 1930 Final was Jim Byrne. A native of Carlow, he had captained Wexford to All-Ireland success in 1918.
- In a very one-sided game, and at a time when kick-outs were usually taken by one of the full-back line, Kerry goalkeeper Johnny Riordan did not touch the ball during the 1930 Final.
- Monaghan captain Paddy Kilroy won senior provincial medals in three provinces: with his native Galway in 1922, with Wexford in 1925, and with Monaghan in 1927, 1929 and 1930.
- Monaghan's goalkeeper, Tommy Bradley, who was a native of Belfast, had been a member of the Royal Irish Fusiliers and had seen action at the Somme during World War I.

1930 – THE YEAR THAT WAS

- The 'planet' Pluto was discovered in 1930. It retained this status until 2006 when it was redesignated a 'dwarf planet'.

- The sliced pan went on sale in Britain for the first time.
- Uruguay won the inaugural soccer World Cup Final by beating Argentina 4-2 in the deciding game.
- A special meeting of Mayo County Council was convened on 27 December to discuss the Local Appointments Commissioners' decision to appoint Miss L.E. Dunbar of Dublin to the position of county librarian. After almost three hours of lively debate, the Council voted, twenty-one votes to six, to reject the proposed appointment. While the official decision for this rejection was the candidate's alleged inadequate knowledge of Irish, some of the contributions to the debate suggested that broader issues were at play. A member of the Protestant faith, Ms Dunbar was a graduate of Trinity College and so, in the words of one councillor, 'was bound to be West British'. One supporter of the appointment suggested that the combination of the library committee's responsibility for the selection of books, and the state censorship laws, should ensure that the requisite moral standards were preserved.

1930 TEAM LINE-OUTS

KERRY (WINNERS)

1. Johnny Riordan
(John Mitchels)

2. Dee O'Connor
(Kilcummin, also Dr Crokes)

3. Joe Barrett
(Austin Stacks)

4. Jack Walsh
(Asdee)

5. Paul Russell
(Dr Crokes, also Garda, Dungarvan, Waterford and Oldcastle, Meath)

6. Joe O'Sullivan
(Dingle, also UCD)

7. Tim O'Donnell
(Camp, also Dr Crokes)

8. Bob Stack
(Ballybunion)

9. Con Brosnan
(Moyvane)

10. Jackie Ryan
(Austin Stacks, also John Mitchels)

11. Miko Doyle
(Austin Stacks)

12. Eamonn Fitzgerald
(UCD, also Caherdaniel)

13. Ned 'Pedlar' Sweeney
(Kickhams, Dublin, also Austin Stacks)

14. John Joe 'Purty' Landers
(Austin Stacks)

15. John Joe Sheehy
(John Mitchels) Capt.

Subs: Paddy Whitty (John Mitchels); Sammy Locke (Kerins O'Rahillys); Micheál Ó Ruairc (John Mitchels); Denis 'Rory' O'Connell (Austin Stacks); James 'Bruddy' Quill (Finuge, also Kerins O'Rahillys); Paud O'Sullivan (Finuge); Jimmy Baily (Ballymacelligott, also Austin Stacks); Dan Joe Conway (Kerins O'Rahillys)

MONAGHAN (RUNNERS-UP)

1. Tommy Bradley
(Ballybay)

2. Tom Shevlin
(Carrickmacross)

3. Joe Farrell
(Castleblayney, also Garda, Dublin)*

4. Peter Duffy
(Ballybay)

5. Paddy Heeran
(Carrickmacross)

6. Paddy Kilroy
(Carrickmacross) Capt.

7. Jimmy Duffy
(Castleblayney)*

8. Peter Lambe
(Killanny)

9. Billy Mason
(Castleblayney)*

10. Mickey McAleer
(Monaghan Harps, also Army)

11. Christy Fisher
(Castleblayney)*

12. Sean O'Carroll
(Carrickmacross)

13. Peter McConnon
(Killeevan Sarsfields, also Army)

14. John Sexton
(Monaghan Harps, also Army)

15. Harry Brannigan
(Monaghan Harps, also Army, Kildare)

Subs: P.J. Duffy (Ballybay, also UCD) Played; Pat 'the Red Fella' McGrane (Clones) Played; Johnny McGuinness (Killanny); Joe Finnegan (Killeevan Sarsfields); Charlie McCarthy (Latton O'Rahillys); Mick McShane (Carrickmacross); Jack 'Rock' Treanor (Monaghan Harps, also Army)

* In 1930, the Castleblayney Faughs club did not affiliate so their players lined out with a number of different clubs.

1931

The art of GAA punditry was still very much in its infancy in the spring of 1931. Coverage of sport in the newspapers was slim and, in the national papers, there was usually a stronger emphasis on cricket, rugby, golf and even British motor racing than on GAA matters. Predictions about the likely destination of the Sam Maguire Cup were largely confined to the unscientific and less than impartial preferences of the GAA scribes in local newspapers.

The prospects of ultimate success for Kerry were widely acknowledged, particularly among the many Kerry publications which vied for readership in the county at the time. After the disappointment of the previous year's final, predictions were that Monaghan would probably go into footballing hibernation for a while. Cavan were tipped to re-emerge as Ulster kingpins. Mayo football was seen as being on an upward trajectory and hopes were high that they would soon be challenging for top honours. However, it was the old stalwarts, Kildare and Dublin, who were generally considered likely to be Kerry's most serious challengers.

In the Munster Championship, Kerry received a bye into the final. While the rest of the province battled it out for the right to challenge them, the men from the Kingdom spent the early summer in America, playing a series of exhibition games. One match, played at Yankee Stadium on 17 May, was attended by a crowd of over 62,000, a then record attendance for a GAA game.

Back home, Tipperary were showing real promise and they stormed through the Munster Championship with victories over Limerick (4-4 to 0-1), Waterford (0-7 to 0-0) and Cork (2-11 to 3-1). With players of the calibre of Connie Keane, Dick Power and Paddy Arrigan, Premier County supporters were beginning to harbour ambitions that they could topple the travel-weary men of the Kingdom. They were jolted into harsh reality, however, when the teams met at Clonmel on 9 August. Three first-half goals from Martin 'Bracker' O'Regan and another from Bob Stack put paid to Tipperary's chances as Kerry retained their title on a score of 5-8 to 0-2.

The big talking point of the 1931 Leinster campaign was the internal strife within the Dublin camp. In line with the practice in Dublin at the time, the team for their first round encounter with Louth was chosen by St Joseph's, county champions of 1930. There was no representation from the O'Toole's club, which had declined to make its players available. While Dublin beat Louth on a score of 5-6 to 1-6, not everyone was happy. A week later, O'Toole's overcame Erin's Hope in the replay of the 1931 county final and, as a result, O'Toole's now had charge of county team selection. Dublin's next championship engagement was against Wexford at Enniscorthy on 5 July when the team showed no fewer than ten changes from the side that had beaten Louth. A brilliant performance by Paddy McDonnell of O'Toole's was the key to a comfortable 4-3 to 1-3 victory.

Notwithstanding the evident disharmony, Dublin were looking good, with many tipping them for Leinster and perhaps All-Ireland honours. Their next outing was at Tullamore on 26 July, where they met a Westmeath team that had beaten Kilkenny by seven goals two months previously. What had been seen as a warm-up for the Leinster Final turned out to be a disaster for the Metropolitans. Outstanding performances from Tom Seery, Andy Geraghty, Jack Dunican and goalkeeper Seamus Bracken were key to Westmeath's stunning 2-4 to 1-4 victory.

On the other side of the Leinster draw, Kildare duly emerged to contest the second semi-final. The Lilywhites had been decidedly fortunate to escape with a one-point victory over Laois at Portlaoise on 25 May. It didn't help Laois that Har Browne had played in the Dublin Championship earlier the same day, while Jack Delaney lined out a day after suffering a bad hand injury. If this wasn't enough, former Cavan player J.P. Murphy scored a highly controversial goal for the Lilywhites.

A downpour at Navan on 7 June forced the abandonment of Meath's first clash with Offaly after just twenty minutes. When they met again three weeks later, the Meath men had a comfortable five-point win. For the third successive year, Kildare and Meath were now pitted against each other in the championship. In keeping with the pattern of their previous clashes, the sides drew first time out, with the Lilywhites once again taking the spoils in the replay.

The Leinster Final turned out to be something of an anticlimax, with Kildare coasting to a 2-9 to 1-6 victory over Westmeath. With veteran Paul Doyle in majestic form, the All-Whites took their sixth successive Leinster title, thereby equalling Wexford's 1913–1918 achievement. Despite their loss, Westmeath had succeeded in building on their Junior All-Ireland triumph and confidence was high that players such as Bracken, Dunican, Gavin, Seery and Smyth would soon deliver silverware at senior level.

Mayo supporters, including a contingent of what *The Connaught Telegraph* termed 'Soccerites' from Westport, travelled in vast numbers to see their favourites launch their 1931 campaign against Sligo at Tuam on 31 May. With impressive displays from Patsy Flannelly, Johnny Culkin and Mickey Moran, they won by seven points and so progressed to a semi-final encounter with Galway at Castlerea on 5 July. A crowd of almost 6,000 turned up at the Roscommon venue to witness an epic battle between these great rivals. Galway's Tommy 'Trixie' Leech was forced to retire through injury and thereafter Mayo forged ahead to win on a score of 3-5 to 1-4.

Although Roscommon had steamrolled past Leitrim in the second of the Connacht semi-finals, they were given little chance against Mayo when they met at Sligo on 9 August. An early goal from Jim Creighton gave the underdogs a tonic start, but they were unable to maintain the momentum and Mayo retained their title with a five-point victory.

The 1931 Ulster Championship maintained the proud tradition of excitement on, and off, the field. Donegal supporters were ecstatic when the county had a resounding nine-point victory over Antrim at Letterkenny on 10 May. With two months to prepare for their semi-final joust with Cavan, hopes were high that the team would be in peak condition for the big day. Unfortunately, there was to be no big day. At an Ulster Council meeting on 13 June, the referee reported Donegal for lining out forty minutes late against Antrim. The Council Chairman promptly reversed the result.

Having easily accounted for Down, Armagh staged something of a shock when they overcame Monaghan, 1-9 to 0-4, at Carrickmacross on 21 June. The Armagh County Board was strongly represented in Belfast two weeks later when Cavan met the reinstated Antrim in the second of the provincial semi-finals. While it was no surprise that Cavan won this battle, it turned out that this was very much the minor battle of the day.

When the final whistle was blown, an emergency meeting of the Ulster Council was convened in rooms at the grounds. By all accounts, this was a fiery affair as delegates argued over where to stage the Ulster Final. Eventually a vote was taken and, on a five to four majority, the meeting chose Breffni Park in Cavan as the venue.

In keeping with the precedent set in 1930, matters were not allowed to sit there. Armagh duly appealed to the Central Council. At a very long meeting held at Croke Park on Saturday 18 July, and under the chairmanship of GAA President Sean Ryan, it was finally decided to postpone the game by a week and refix it for … Dundalk! Cavan did not give in easily though; their price for conceding home advantage was that the All-Ireland semi-final between the Ulster champions and the Leinster champions would be played at Breffni Park.

There was a mass invasion of Dundalk on 30 August when Cavan and Armagh finally got down to the business of settling the 1931 Ulster Championship. The throw-in was delayed as sections of the huge crowd surged onto the pitch in what *The Anglo Celt* described as this 'famous and furious final'. Cavan emerged winners by a single point, 0-8 to 2-1, but the general view was that they were the far superior team. Once again, the man of the match was Cavan skipper Jim Smith, who broke Armagh hearts with his high fielding and surging runs.

After their great bid in the 1928 All-Ireland against the Lilywhites, many felt that home advantage would sway matters in Cavan's favour when the sides met at Breffni Park on 30 August. A Paddy Colleran goal helped Cavan to a five-point lead at the break and had the huge crowd buzzing. The second half saw a dramatic resurgence by the All-Whites, with Matt Goff outstanding at full-back and the left boot of Paul Doyle delivering the scores that propelled Kildare to yet another final.

On the same day at Tuam, Kerry were put to the pin of their collar before edging out Mayo on a score of 1-6 to 1-4. To the consternation of the huge Mayo contingent at the game, a late goal was disallowed because the ball was judged to have crossed the end line before ending up in the Kerry net.

THE FINAL – 27 SEPTEMBER

The fourth Kerry–Kildare final clash in six years created huge interest, not just in the participating counties, but throughout the country. Kerry were warm favourites to complete the three-in-a-row, but Kildare had shown impressive form in their championship run and were confident they could spoil the party.

Kerry's preparations suffered two major disruptions in the run-up to the final. Half-back Tim O'Donnell failed a fitness test on the Thursday before the match and the team was reshuffled, with Tim Landers brought back to man the number seven berth. In a further twist, the selectors dropped a bombshell in the dressing-room before the game when they announced the replacement of goalkeeper Johnny Riordan with Dan O'Keeffe. While it was generally agreed that Johnny had slipped out for a couple of quiet pints on the eve of the match, the official reason given for this decision was that he had 'broken training'.

The huge crowd of over 42,000 that turned up witnessed what was universally described as a fantastic exhibition of football. Kildare got off to a great start and Dermot Bourke had them in front after four minutes with a majestic point. The All-Whites put in a dazzling first-half display and were unfortunate not to lead at the break by a greater margin than three points as the teams went in at 0-7 to 0-4 in their favour. Their supremacy in this period was largely down to the efforts of their midfield pairing of Peter Waters and Paddy O'Loughlin.

After a series of astute half-time changes, the men from Kerry staged a remarkable second-half comeback. They proceeded to bombard the Kildare goalmouth and were it not for a series of spectacular saves by Martin Walshe they would have been out of sight with twenty minutes to go. They eventually levelled the scoring through Paddy Whitty but lost the initiative when Harry Burke put the Lilywhites back in front. It was Whitty who again came to Kerry's rescue with a brilliant point from over fifty yards out. It was neck and neck when Jackie Ryan gave Kerry the lead, but a fumble in the Kildare defence with five minutes remaining led to the only goal of the game from Paul Russell and Kerry were on the home straight. Despite the Trojan efforts of Jack Higgins and Bill Hynan to inspire a Kildare comeback, it was Ryan who closed out the scoring. Kerry had achieved the magical three-in-a-row on a final score of Kerry 1-11, Kildare 0-8.

FINAL STATISTICS

	Kerry	Kildare
Full-time:	1-11	0-8
Half-time:	0-4	0-7
Scorers:	J. Ryan 0-6 (0-4 frees)	P. Byrne 0-3 (0-1 free)
	P. Russell 1-0	H. Burke 0-3 (0-1 free)
	J.J. Landers 0-2	D. Bourke 0-1
	P. Whitty 0-2	P. Martin 0-1
	M. Doyle 0-1	
Attendance:	33,280	
Gate Receipts:	£3,863 (€4,905)	
Referee:	Tom Keating (Tipperary)	

FINAL MISCELLANY

- As a member of the Austin Stacks club, who were Kerry county champions, Joe Barrett was due to lead the county in the 1931 Championship. With what was seen as a gesture aimed at healing Civil War scars, he passed the honour to Moyvane's Con Brosnan, who had fought on the opposite side during the conflict.
- Kerry sub P.J. 'Peachy' Sullivan had won an All-Ireland Minor medal two weeks earlier.
- When Kildare beat Meath (1-5 to 0-5) in their Leinster semi-final replay at Croke Park on 2 August, it brought to an end a remarkable series of clashes between the two counties. This was the third successive year that they had met in the championship, a replay being required each year and the Lilywhites emerging victorious on each occasion.
- The official opening of the St Conleth's GAA Grounds in Newbridge took place on Sunday 10 May 1931. Owing to confirmation arrangements, the Bishop of Kildare and Leighlin, Most Rev. Dr Cullen, was unable to officiate and his place was taken by Pádraig Ó Caoimh, GAA General Secretary.

1931 — THE YEAR THAT WAS

- Spain was declared a republic on 14 April 1931.
- On 11 December, the British Commonwealth was formed.
- The Empire State Building, then the world's tallest building at 1,250 feet (381 metres), was opened in New York.
- On 5 September, the first edition of *The Irish Press* was published.

1931 TEAM LINE-OUTS

KERRY (WINNERS)

1. Dan O'Keeffe
(Kerins O'Rahillys)

2. Dee O'Connor
(Kilcummin, also Dr Crokes)

3. Joe Barrett
(Austin Stacks)

4. Jack Walsh
(Asdee)

5. Paul Russell
(Dr Crokes, also Garda, Dungarvan, Waterford and Oldcastle, Meath)

6. Joe O'Sullivan
(Dingle)

7. Tim 'Roundy' Landers
(Austin Stacks)

8. Bob Stack
(Ballybunion)

9. Con Brosnan
(Moyvane) Capt.

10. John Joe 'Purty' Landers
(Austin Stacks)

11. Miko Doyle
(Austin Stacks)

12. Eamonn Fitzgerald
(UCD, also Caherdaniel)

13. Jackie Ryan
(Austin Stacks, also John Mitchels)

14. Paddy Whitty
(John Mitchels)

15. Martin 'Bracker' O'Regan
(Austin Stacks)

Subs: Johnny Riordan (John Mitchels); Con Geaney (John Mitchels); Tim O'Donnell (Camp, also Dr Crokes); P.J. 'Peachy' Sullivan (Cahirciveen); Dan Spring (Kerins O'Rahillys); Tommy Barrett (Austin Stacks); James 'Bruddy' Quill (Kerins O'Rahillys, also Finuge); Ned 'Pedlar' Sweeney (Austin Stacks) was unavailable as a result of an injury received in a motor accident while in the US.

KILDARE (RUNNERS-UP)

1. Martin Walshe
(Kildare Round Towers) Capt.

2. Johnny Meaney
(Kildare Round Towers, also Dolphins, Dublin)

3. Matt Goff
(McKee Barracks, also Leixlip)

4. Frank Malone
(Caragh)

5. Patrick Miles
(Athy)

6. Jack Higgins
(Naas)

7. Bill Hynan
(Carbury)

8. Peter Waters
(Raheens)

9. Paddy O'Loughlin
(Rathangan)

10. Jimmy Maguire
(Naas)

11. Paddy Martin
(Rathangan)

12. Paddy Byrne
(Castledermot)

13. Harry Burke
(Naas, also Tullamore, Offaly)

14. Dermot Bourke
(Carbury, also Geraldines, Dublin)

15. Paul Doyle
(McKee Barracks, also Maddenstown and Suncroft)

Subs: J.P. Murphy (Army); Pat 'Darkie' Ryan (Milltown); Peter Pringle (Rathangan); Bill 'Squires' Gannon (Kildare Round Towers); Paul Matthews (Athy); Jack Hayes (Kildare Round Towers), team captain for the year, was unavailable through injury.

1932

The throw-in for the 1932 Championship took place on 10 April at Letterkenny in front of 1,000 spectators. Long before anyone thought of the qualifier system, the Super 8s, or any reform aimed at extending the season, Tyrone bowed out to Armagh on a scoreline of 1-5 to 1-4.

By the end of the month, Fermanagh, Down and Donegal would similarly exit the Ulster Championship before the summer had even begun.

There was nothing unusual in the manner of Fermanagh's departure from the competition – an outstanding performance by Monaghan's Christy Fisher was the deciding factor when the counties met on 17 April.

It was a different story in the cases of Down and Donegal. When Down played Antrim in both the Senior and Junior Championships in Belfast on 17 April, they decided to put all their championship eggs into the junior basket. They took the unusual step of 'demoting' eight of their senior team to play for their juniors, who duly beat Antrim by four points in the junior game. The 'promotion' of eight juniors to the senior team meant that the premier contest was a complete farce, with Antrim cruising to a 4-10 to 0-1 annihilation of the Mourne men.

A week later, Donegal travelled to Breffni Park to play Cavan. Whatever their prospects of springing a surprise might have been, these were well and truly scuppered on the morning of the game. Two of their players didn't travel and four more were injured in a motor accident on the way to the game. Cavan duly took full advantage of their weakened opposition and sauntered home, 8-7 to 1-6.

With Terry Coyle poacher-in-chief, the men from Breffni continued their impressive goal-scoring exploits when they beat Monaghan 8-8 to 2-6 in their semi-final clash at Belturbet on 29 May. After a comfortable win over Antrim, Armagh provided Cavan's Ulster Final opposition at Monaghan on 19 June. A crowd of over 11,000 packed into Oriel Park in expectation of a ding-dong battle. Unfortunately for Armagh, Jim Smith chose the day to deliver one of his greatest ever displays in the Cavan jersey. *The Irish Press* reported: 'Jim Smith was the cog of a nicely working football machine, and despite repeated efforts to knock him off his game, he not alone kept cool himself, but imparted his *sang froid* to the remainder of the team.'

Despite the best efforts of Jim McCullough, Eddie McMahon, John Vallely and goalkeeper Joe Houlihan, Cavan were full value for their 2-4 to 0-2 win.

Mayo, champions of the previous three years, were generally expected to retain the Connacht crown. Their first championship outing was a semi-final encounter with a Galway side that had hammered Roscommon 4-7 to 0-2 three weeks earlier. A huge Galway contingent travelled to Castlerea on 17 July, hopeful that their team's first-round performance and Mayo's recent exertions in the US might signal a changing of the guard. A goal in the first minute gave Galway the tonic start they needed but Mayo gradually began to assert their authority. The silken skills of Gerald Courell made all the difference as Mayo progressed to the Connacht Final on a score of 3-5 to 1-3.

Sligo overcame Leitrim, 1-7 to 1-3, on the opposite side of the draw and so progressed to meet Mayo in the final. Backboned by a number of outstanding performers such as Mick Kilcoyne, 'Click' Brennan and the Colleran brothers, the Sligo men had high hopes that they could topple their neighbours. When they met at Tuam on 7 August, they put up a great show, but first-half goals from Courell and Paddy Munnelly put Mayo on the road to victory. On a score of 2-6 to 0-7, they duly advanced to meet Cavan in the All-Ireland semi-final.

Aiming for a fourth All-Ireland title in a row, Kerry were considered virtually unbeatable and the only question was whether anyone could mount a serious challenge. They opened their account at Newcastlewest on 22 May with a comfortable 1-11 to 1-3 semi-final win over Limerick. This gave them over two months to prepare for their annual Munster Final outing.

Spurred on by the mighty George Comerford, Clare overcame Cork at Tralee on 15 May. On the same day at Clonmel, Tipperary had a goal to spare over a Waterford team which failed to register a score in the second half. At Limerick on 24 July, goalkeeper John Weston was the key man as Tipperary held out against Clare to advance to the provincial decider.

Marking the opening of the Davin Memorial Park in Clonmel, the Munster Final on 7 August between Kerry and Tipperary was expected to be a one-sided affair. True to form, the men from the Kingdom displayed all their old craft and combination as they coasted to a twelve-point victory. The margin would have been even bigger but for the usual heroics of Weston.

In Leinster, Kildare were bidding for their seventh successive provincial title, but their ascendancy was seen to be under threat. Many predicted that Laois or Meath were their most likely successors. Laois were well and truly removed from the equation when Davy Morris hit five goals in Wexford's runaway victory at Kilkenny on 22 May. Wexford now faced Kildare who had earlier beaten Louth with the help of three goals from Carbury's Dermot Bourke. When they met at Croke Park on 5 June, the Lilywhites got off to a dream start and were six points to the good early in the game. Wexford were not to be denied, however, and the inspirational Martin O'Neill led the charge as the Slaneysiders recovered to advance to the provincial final on a 2-8 to 2-5 scoreline.

It was a surprise that Dublin beat Meath at Newbridge on 29 May; it was a shock that their victory margin was eleven points. In atrocious weather conditions, the Meath men could make no impression on the Dublin defence, which had Paddy Hickey and debutant Gerry McLoughlin from Howth in top form. In the semi-final, Dublin faced Westmeath, easy winners over Offaly in the quarter-final. With Jack Dunican, Dinny Breen, Paddy Bracken and the lightning-fast Paddy Doyle on song, Westmeath kept in touch for most of the game but the Metropolitans eventually pulled away for a deserved five-point victory. Ned McCann was Dublin's outstanding performer, with Peter Synnott and Mick Keating also contributing handsomely.

Wexford took the field as favourites when they met Dublin in the Leinster Final at Croke Park on 7 August. After a particularly scrappy affair, they needed a last-minute point from the outstanding Nick Walsh to secure a replay.

Not even the absence through injury of star midfielder Jack Fane could account for Wexford's collapse in the replay. Dublin cantered to a ten-point victory, with Paddy McDonnell lord and master of all he surveyed. Leinster champions for the first time since 1924, the Metropolitans could now look forward to taking on champions Kerry for the right to contest the All-Ireland Final.

The All-Ireland semi-final double bill attracted a crowd of 21,000 to Croke Park on 21 August. The slippery conditions militated against good football but did not detract from the passion and excitement of the occasion. In the first game, Cavan and Mayo fought out a battle of attrition which saw the Ulster side poised for victory with just minutes to go. It was then that Gerald Courell, Mayo's main man throughout the season, turned on the style. He followed an opportunist goal with an outrageous point to put his team into the lead. As Cavan chased an elusive equaliser in the dying moments, Courell stepped in once again to rifle over the final nail in the Breffni coffin.

The second semi-final, between Kerry and Dublin, turned out to be an epic. This didn't seem likely at half-time when, amazingly, the sides were locked on a scoreline of 0-0 to 0-0. With Dublin playing into their favoured Railway End goal after the break, hopes were high that they could lower Kerry's colours. They moved ahead when Tom Dowd found the Kerry net. When the same player repeated the trick a few minutes later, they seemed to be home and hosed. To the consternation of Dublin's jubilant fans, this second goal was disallowed and Kerry were back in the frame. As the exchanges became more furious, a late goal from Paul Russell edged the Kingdom ahead. Dublin battled to the bitter end, but it was Kerry who won their ticket to the final on a score of 1-3 to 1-1.

THE FINAL — 25 SEPTEMBER

The football final of 1932 was played in wet and slippery conditions. Writing in *The Irish Press*, David Hogan acknowledged the verdict of the experts who seemed to agree that it was 'bad football'. As a spectacle, however, he judged it to be 'as thrilling an hour as any man or woman sat through'. Certainly, the see-saw nature of the exchanges suggests that, regardless of the quality of the play, this was a contest for the ages.

The game opened at a frantic pace, with Mayo bombarding the Kerry defence. Gerald Courell had them a point up after two minutes; Paddy Moclair doubled their lead after three, and Paddy 'Captain' Munnelly landed another point a minute later. Mayo supporters were delirious as their team seemed to have the men in green and gold on the rack. Gradually, however, Kerry began to assert themselves. With Johnny Walsh and the Landers brothers to the fore, they launched a series of attacks. Only the brilliance of Paddy Quinn, Tom Burke and teenager George Ormsby kept them at bay. The pressure finally paid off for Kerry in the tenth minute when, in a crowded goalmouth, Miko Doyle hit the equalising goal with a great left-footed drive. The game was now at fever pitch. Tim Landers and Moclair exchanged points to leave the scores level as half-time approached. It was Munnelly who broke the deadlock as he stretched to a Courell cross and fisted to the net. When referee Martin O'Neill sounded the half-time whistle the Connacht champions held the advantage: Mayo 1-4, Kerry 1-1.

On the resumption, Kerry brought a renewed intensity to their play. Midfielders Bob Stack and Johnny Walsh began to make inroads against Mayo's defence, while the switching of Tim Landers to corner-forward paid immediate dividends. He scored a goal and a point within minutes of the restart and proceeded to create numerous openings for his teammates. Kerry now took the upper hand and four unanswered points put them five clear with twelve minutes to go. Mayo responded and, after a period of intense pressure, 'Captain' Munnelly gave them hope with a well-taken goal. It was Kerry, however, who finished the stronger, Jackie Ryan closing the game out with the last point of the game to leave the final score Kerry 2-7, Mayo 2-4.

Kerry had now equalled Wexford's record of winning four titles on the trot. Already there was speculation that 1933 would see them extend their period of dominance. For now though, they were happy to bask in the glory of their achievement. Mayo supporters could console themselves in the knowledge that they had a very young team and that the big breakthrough could not be far away.

FINAL STATISTICS

	Kerry	Mayo
Full-time:	2-7	2-4
Half-time:	1-1	1-4
Scorers:	T. Landers 1-2	G. Courell 1-1 (0-1 free)
	M. Doyle 1-1	J. Forde 1-0
	J. Ryan 0-3 (0-3 frees)	P. Munnelly 0-2
	C. Brosnan 0-1	P. Moclair 0-1
Attendance:	24,816	
Gate Receipts:	£2,247 (€2,854)	
Referee:	Martin O'Neill (Wexford)	

FINAL MISCELLANY

- In the final, the ball was thrown in by Most Rev. Dr John Prenderville, Bishop of Zanzibar.
- Depending on the level of comfort sought, the price options for the final were 1/- (6.3 cent), 2/- (12.6 cent) or, for the then Premium Level (sideline seat), 2/6 (15.9 cent).
- Eamonn Fitzgerald, who had played on the winning Kerry teams in 1930 and 1931, was unavailable for much of 1932. He was representing Ireland at the Olympic Games in Los Angeles, where he finished fourth in the Triple Jump.

- Miko Doyle was only twenty-one years old when he collected his fourth senior All-Ireland medal in 1932.
- Mayo's disappointment at losing was compounded by the fuzzy radio reception available in the county. The *Evening Herald* reported: 'The match was broadcast but the reception in Ballina was poor.'

1932 – THE YEAR THAT WAS

- The 31st Eucharistic Conference took place in Dublin from 21–26 June. Coinciding with the 1,500th anniversary of the arrival of St Patrick, special legislation (The Eucharistic Congress [Miscellaneous Provisions] Act 1932) was enacted to facilitate the efficient management of traffic, catering and accommodation for the massive crowds descending on the capital. Congregations of 250,000 (men), 200,000 (women), 100,000 (children) and 1,000,000 (general) attended Mass in the Phoenix Park over the course of the five days.
- On 8 November, Franklin Delano Roosevelt was inaugurated as US president. He would go on to hold office for almost thirteen years.
- The general election in February 1932 led to the formation of the first Fianna Fáil government.
- On the day of the final, patrons could enjoy a special four-course lunch at Wynn's Hotel for 2/6 (15.9 cent).

1932 TEAM LINE-OUTS

KERRY (WINNERS)

	1. Dan O'Keeffe (Kerins O'Rahillys)	
2. Dee O'Connor (Kilcummin, also Dr Crokes)	3. Joe Barrett (Austin Stacks) Capt.	4. Jack Walsh (Asdee)
5. Paul Russell (Dr Crokes, also Garda, Dungarvan, Waterford and Oldcastle, Meath)	6. Joe O'Sullivan (Dingle, also UCD)	7. Paddy Whitty (John Mitchels)
8. Bob Stack (Ballybunion)		9. Johnny Walsh (Ballylongford)
10. Con Geaney (John Mitchels)	11. Miko Doyle (Austin Stacks)	12. Tim 'Roundy' Landers (Austin Stacks)
13. Jackie Ryan (Austin Stacks, also John Mitchels)	14. Con Brosnan (Moyvane)	15. John Joe 'Purty' Landers (Austin Stacks)

Subs: Bill 'Lang' Landers (Austin Stacks) Played; Bill Kinnerk (John Mitchels); Dan Ryan (Austin Stacks); Eamonn Fitzgerald (UCD, also Caherdaniel); Jackie Flavin (Moyvane, also Wolfe Tones, Galway); James 'Bruddy' Quill (Kerins O'Rahillys, also Finuge); Martin 'Bracker' O'Regan (Austin Stacks); Jack O'Connor (John Mitchels); Mick Healy (Austin Stacks).

Owing to injury, Tim O'Donnell was unavailable for selection.

MAYO (RUNNERS-UP)

1. Tom Burke
(Castlebar Mitchels)

2. Jack Gannon
(Erin's Hope, Dublin, also Belmullet)

3. Paddy Quinn
(Castlebar Mitchels)

4. P.J. 'Purty' Kelly
(Westport)

5. Tom Tunney
(Tuam Stars, Galway, also
Charlestown Sarsfields)

6. Seamus O'Malley
(Castlebar Mitchels, also Claremorris
and Ballinrobe)

7. George Ormsby
(Ballina Stephenites)

8. Mick Mulderrig
(Castlebar Mitchels, also Kiltimagh)
Capt.

9. Mickey Ormsby
(Ballina Stephenites)

10. Paddy 'Captain' Munnelly
(Crossmolina)

11. T.J. Hanley
(Ballina Stephenites and Army,
Dublin)

12. Patsy Flannelly
(Castlebar Mitchels)

13. Gerald Courell
(Ballina Stephenites)

14. Paddy Moclair
(Castlebar, also Ballina Stephenites)

15. Jim Forde
(Ballyhaunis)

Subs: Henry Kenny (Castlebar Mitchels, also Oughterard, Galway); Eddie Griffith (Claremorris); Sean Moran (Ballyhaunis, also St Grellan's, Galway); Bertie Frazer (Ballina Stephenites); John Egan (Castlebar Mitchels); Tom Grier (Ballycastle); Dick Munnelly (Crossmolina, also Ballina Stephenites)

Other Panel Members: Mickey Moran (Westport); Johnny Culkin (Ballina Stephenites); Phil Hoban (Westport, also Castlebar Mitchels); Hugh O'Brien (Ballina Stephenites); Jack Kenny (Claremorris)

1933

The only question being asked as the 1933 Championship got underway was whether the Kerry juggernaut could be stopped in its tracks as they sought an unprecedented five titles in a row. As usual, they sat out the early rounds of the Munster campaign as the other counties battled it out for the right to take on the Kingdom in the final.

On 14 May, fully three months before Kerry kicked a ball in the championship, Tipperary met Clare, while Cork played Waterford. It was no surprise that Tipperary eased to a nine-point victory over the Clare men at Limerick. In its match preview, *The Cork Examiner* extolled the virtues of the county's football team, while also proclaiming that the opposition to be offered by Waterford would 'not be very strong'. A couple of days later, after the sides had drawn 4-4 apiece, the same scribe concluded that 'Cork were unquestionably opposed by good talent from Waterford'. Having had to rely on a last-minute goal from Donal O'Sullivan to secure a draw, Cork made no mistake next time out, winning comprehensively on a score of 2-7 to 0-1. Waterford were left to bemoan the absence of star players Gough and Murphy, but there was no disputing the merit of Cork's win.

A barrage of first-half scores put Tipperary firmly on the road to victory when they met Cork at Clonmel on 23 July. Early goals from Dick Power and Dick Allen paved the way for a seven-point victory, and passage to a provincial showdown with Kerry.

Having dominated the championship for four years, Kerry were now routinely referred to as 'The Invincibles' in the sporting press. It was therefore no surprise that Tipperary's prospects of beating them in the Munster Final were regarded as negligible. The record shows that Kerry duly retained their provincial crown on a score of 2-8 to 1-4. This bald statistic does no justice to Tipperary's performance on the day. It was touch and go for most of the game, with the champions only pulling away in the closing stages. Kerry struggled to cope with Tipperary's Martin Shanahan and Connie Keane, both of whom enhanced their already stellar reputations.

In Ulster, the big story was Tyrone's march to the final for the first time ever. In a dour quarter-final encounter at Coalisland, they drew with Antrim. With both teams making several changes in personnel, the replay at Corrigan Park, Belfast, also ended level. In the face of Antrim's objections, and defying the rulebook, Tyrone refused to play extra time. Antrim did not insist on being awarded the game so the Ulster Council fixed a second replay for Omagh on 9 July. This time, Tyrone made no mistake and ran out 1-8 to 1-2 winners.

Next up for the Tyrone men was Fermanagh, who had six points to spare over a lacklustre

Monaghan in the first round. They met at Bundoran on 16 July where, after a titanic struggle, Clonoe's Mick O'Neill hit the winning point as Tyrone edged home, 1-4 to 1-3. With the county reaching its first ever Ulster Final, the sense of excitement was captured in the report of the *Strabane Chronicle*: 'Caps and other articles of headclothing must be scarce in Tyrone this week. Everything available went into the air when the long whistle sounded, and the proud clansmen of O'Neill carried their victors shoulder high from the pitch.'

When Cavan progressed to the Ulster Final with an easy nine-point win over Armagh, they were installed as overwhelming favourites to beat Tyrone in the decider. Tyrone's slim prospects were well and truly shattered just hours before the throw-in. There had been an ongoing dispute between the County Board and the Dungannon Clarkes club, and a move to drop some of its players from the team produced a swift response. The club's entire contingent stormed out of the Railway Hotel, thus depriving the team of five of its starting line-up and resulting in one of the most one-sided finals on record. Leading 5-8 to 0-1 at half-time, Cavan went on to record a resounding 6-13 to 1-2 victory.

Kildare looked to have booked their place in the Leinster semi-final when, with just two minutes to go, they led Laois by six points at Kilkenny on 28 May. Har Browne then netted for Laois after a great pass from Mick 'Tipper' Keating. This was followed by another goal, from Chris Delaney, on the stroke of time. Having escaped with a draw, Kildare finally negotiated this hurdle, winning 2-11 to 1-5 in the replay on 11 June, but the signs were that the Lilywhites were in serious decline.

Martin O'Neill led the way for Wexford when they outgunned Offaly, 4-4 to 1-3, at Croke Park on 7 May. This propelled them to a semi-final clash with Kildare on 2 July. On one of the hottest days of the year, the Yellow Bellies raced into an early lead and were five points to the good at the break. A magnificent fightback by the Lilywhites produced a footballing classic, with the result in doubt to the very end. Commentators agreed that the telepathic interplay between Martin O'Neill and Davy Morris was the deciding factor as Wexford repeated their 1932 success over the Lilywhites on a score of 2-8 to 1-8.

While Dublin were far superior to Meath for most of their quarter-final encounter at Drogheda on 11 June, they were fortunate to survive a series of onslaughts late in the game. Only for the wonderful defensive play of Ned McCann, Paddy Hickey and Gerry McLoughlin, it is likely that the Royals would have progressed to the semi-final.

Louth secured their first championship win in five years when they overcame Westmeath and so progressed to face Dublin in the second semi-final. Apart from the early exchanges, the Louth men were out of their depth, with Dublin cruising to a nine-point win, and a Leinster Final date with Wexford.

Played at Croke Park on 30 July, the provincial decider attracted a crowd of 16,000. Although the game was fought with vigour, and the outcome was uncertain throughout, this was a disappointing final. Dublin retained their title by a single point and their key to success lay in an impregnable defence in which Ned McCann and Paddy Hickey were again most prominent.

Cavan, All-Ireland champions 1933. Back (l–r): Seamus Gilheany (chairman), Willie Young, Jack Smallhorne, Dónal Morgan, Vincent McGovern, Mick Dinneny, J.J. (Jack) Clarke (secretary); middle (l–r): J.P. Murphy (manager), Paddy McNamee, Paddy Brady, 'Small' Tom O'Reilly, Willie Connolly, 'Big' Tom O'Reilly, Packy Devlin, Hughie O'Reilly, Jack Rahill, Michael O'Reilly (trainer); front (l–r): Tom Crowe, Louis Blessing, Packy Phair, Jim Smith (captain), Patsy Lynch, Terry Coyle, M.J. 'Sonny' Magee.

The first game in the Connacht Championship of 1933 saw Galway score 2-10 against a Roscommon team which failed to register a single score over the hour. It was difficult to gauge the merits of Galway's performance in this runaway victory, but there was universal agreement that Roscommon's fate would have been a whole lot worse but for the efforts of Tom Shevlin.

Galway duly negotiated the semi-final hurdle presented by Sligo at Castlerea on 2 July, romping home on a score of 4-8 to 0-4. As in Galway's previous game, Tom Shevlin gave another fine display – this time as match referee.

In the second Connacht semi-final at Tubbercurry, John 'Nipper' Shanley fired home a third-minute goal to give Leitrim a tonic start against Mayo. This was to be Leitrim's only score, however, with Mayo coasting to a twenty-four-point victory.

Bidding for a fifth successive Connacht title, Mayo were favoured to overcome Galway in the provincial final on 23 July. There was no lack of confidence among Galway's supporters, however, and they descended on Castlerea in their droves on that sunny morning. The almighty roar that accompanied the throw-in hadn't died down when veteran Mick Donnellan blasted the ball to the Mayo net. Galway continued to pile on the pressure against their strangely out-of-sorts opposition, and entered the break with a six-point lead. Mayo staged a frantic second-half resurgence and began to make inroads into Galway's lead. As the exchanges reached fever pitch, it was the defiance of Mick Connaire and Tadhg McCarthy at the heart of Galway's defence, and some inspired goalkeeping by Michael Brennan, that pulled the Tribesmen through, 1-7 to 1-5.

As for the Mayo verdict, *The Connaught Telegraph* certainly pulled no punches, claiming that some of the team hadn't kicked a ball for a month and calling for the 'weeding out of bad players'. Describing the team's lacklustre approach at the start of the game, it compared this to 'an exhibition by men on crutches'.

The first of the All-Ireland semi-finals, between Dublin and Galway, took place at Mullingar on 20 August. This time it was Galway's turn to concede a goal in the opening seconds as Dublin's Gerald Fitzgerald boxed home from close range. A succession of points from Brendan Nestor gave Galway the advantage and they went into the break with a three-point lead, 0-8 to 1-2. While they failed to register any score in the second half, another great defensive performance limited Dublin to just two points and the Tribesmen qualified for the final by the narrowest of margins.

Cavan met Kerry at Breffni Park in the second semi-final but home venue was generally not regarded as sufficient an advantage to knock the champions off their lofty perch. For fifty-five minutes of the game Kerry, inspired by Joe O'Sullivan, held the lead and seemed set to progress to the final. A neat point by M.J. 'Sonny' Magee was followed by a great goal from Vincent McGovern and now Cavan took the lead for the first time in the game. A last-ditch effort from Kerry's Bill Landers failed to find the target and the Cavan men held on for a famous victory. Unprecedented scenes followed as the jubilant crowd carried their heroes shoulder high from the pitch.

If Vincent McGovern grabbed the headlines for his winning goal, it was once again the commanding figure of Jim Smith who, more than any other player, dragged the men of Breffni over the line. In the words of *The Irish Press*, the Bailieboro native was 'the cynosure of all eyes'.

THE FINAL – 24 SEPTEMBER

Cavan were still seeking their first All-Ireland in 1933, and while the record books listed Galway as 1925 champions, that title had been awarded in the committee rooms after a series of objections and counter-objections. The final pairing was especially novel in that, for the first time, no Leinster or Munster team was involved. It generated enormous interest, with Cavan installed as favourites, largely on the basis of their semi-final victory over Kerry.

Newspaper reports highlighted the fact that the blue and white of Cavan significantly outshone the 'green and white' of Galway in the metropolis on the morning of the game. A record crowd of over 45,000 turned up in the drenching rain and were entertained by an enthralling contest, albeit one that could never be described as a classic. A clue as to why the standard of play was not of the highest order can be gleaned from the following passage in *The Anglo Celt* of 30 September: 'After six weeks of intense heat, and the sod as hard as iron, with almost all the grass burnt off, there was a terrific downpour of rain on Saturday which brought up a slime to the surface of the artificially constructed ground which made it almost impossible for the contestants to hold their feet …'.

Galway were first off the mark with Joe Kelleher pointing after four minutes. Cavan responded through 'Sonny' Magee, who levelled the scoring after seven minutes. Magee and Mick Higgins exchanged points and the sides were still level after twenty-two minutes even though Cavan had been in the ascendancy. The advantage then swung in the Cavan men's favour when a long-range effort from Jim Smith created confusion in the Galway defence and ended up in the back of the net. With Packy Devlin adding a further point and Vincent McGovern pouncing for an opportunist goal, Cavan took a commanding 2-3 to 0-2 lead into the break.

On the restart, Galway really came to life and veteran Mick Donnellan hit 1-1 to close the gap to a goal. It was touch and go for the next fifteen minutes but Cavan held out, Devlin striking the insurance point with only minutes to go. Their victory, on a scoreline of 2-5 to 1-4, was a first for an Ulster team and evinced an outpouring of joy never previously seen on Jones's Road.

On a momentous day for Cavan, there were many great performances. Tom and Hughie O'Reilly gave them midfield superiority. *The Anglo Celt* noted that wing-back Terry Coyle 'held up all invaders', while Packy Devlin and M.J. 'Sonny' Magee were the key men in the scoring department. However, hero among heroes was team captain Jim Smith. The *Irish Independent* of 25 September noted: 'Cool as a cucumber and slippery as an eel, he gave a serviceable display right through …'

While Galway did not play to the level they had hoped, impressive performances from Hugo Carey, Mick Connaire, Frank Fox and Dermot Mitchell suggested that All-Ireland glory was not far off. Their captain, and stalwart for many years, Mick Donnellan announced his retirement shortly after the game and would miss out on the county's golden era in the years that followed. The Donnellan contribution to Galway football would not end in 1933, however. Future generations of the Dunmore family would be central to no fewer than five All-Ireland successes.

FINAL STATISTICS

	Cavan	Galway
Full-time:	2-5	1-4
Half-time:	2-3	0-2
Scorers:	M.J. Magee 1-2	B. Nestor 1-1
	J. Smith 1-0	J. Kelleher 0-1
	P. Devlin 0-2	M. Higgins 0-1
	J. Smallhorne 0-1	M. Donnellan 0-1
Attendance:	45,188	
Gate Receipts:	£4,047 (€5,139)	
Referee:	Martin O'Neill (Wexford)	

FINAL MISCELLANY

- The radio commentary of Eamon de Barra was interrupted abruptly at half-time. A protester grabbed the microphone and announced to a startled nation: 'While this game is being played, men are on hunger strike in Mountjoy Prison. We would ask you to remember the Government, which is a so-called Republican Government, have men undergoing hunger strike.'
- This was the last final in which the Galway team wore green and white. Their fortunes improved dramatically the following year when they changed to their now familiar maroon jerseys.
- Cavan midfielder 'Big' Tom O'Reilly represented the county in the Minor, Junior and Senior Championships of 1933.
- Galway's goalkeeper, Michael Brennan, was also the netminder for the county's hurling team in 1933.

1933 – THE YEAR THAT WAS

- Adolf Hitler became German chancellor in January 1933. Within two months, the first concentration camp opened in Dachau.
- The property pages on All-Ireland day in 1933 advertised substantial four-bedroom houses in Clontarf for £975 (€1,238). These 'all mod con' homes came complete with 'electric light throughout'.
- After almost fourteen thirsty years, Prohibition in the United States was brought to an end in December 1933.
- When administering the sacrament of confirmation to over two hundred children at Ferrybank on 4 May, the Bishop of Ossory, Most Rev. Dr Collier, delivered a dire warning to the overflow congregation:

  Keep out of your homes these terrible papers, so corrupt in their influence to the young. I refer to the Sunday newspapers from across the water. I am afraid that the people living in towns and adjacent to them as are you, are in sad danger from the dirty rotten Sunday newspapers that are full of filth and dirt. There is nothing elevating or right for a Catholic in them. They are full of evil suggestions, so that you cannot come away with a clean mind after reading any of those dirty newspapers.

  Bishop Collier gave no indication to his flock as to how he was aware of the nature of the offending content.

- One of the most popular cigarette brands in the 1930s, Craven 'A', was promoted on the basis of its gentle effects on the smoker's throat. A regular newspaper advertisement contained the testimonial: 'I have smoked 50,000 CRAVEN 'A' ... and I have never had a sore throat.'

1933 TEAM LINE-OUTS

CAVAN (WINNERS)

1. Willie Young
(Cornafean)

2. Willie Connolly
(Cootehill, also Virginia)

3. Patsy Lynch
(Bailieboro)

4. Mick Dinneny
(Cornafean)

5. Terry Coyle
(Cavan Slashers)

6. Jim Smith
(Erin's Own, Kells, Meath, also Garda,
Bailieboro and Virginia) Capt.

7. Packy Phair
(Cornafean)

8. Hughie O'Reilly
(Cootehill, also Tullyvin)

9. 'Big' Tom O'Reilly
(Cornafean)

10. Dónal Morgan
(Cross, also Virginia)

11. Packy Devlin
(Killeshandra, also Croghan)

12. Jack Smallhorne
(Crosserlough, also Mountnugent)

13. Vincent McGovern
(Virginia)

14. Louis Blessing
(Cavan Slashers)

15. M.J. 'Sonny' Magee
(Drumlane, also Croghan and Cavan
Slashers)

Subs: Tom Crowe (Cavan Slashers) Played; 'Small' Tom O'Reilly (Mullahoran) Played; Eugene 'Sammy' Briody (Mullahoran); Paddy Brady (Castlerahan); Paddy McNamee (Cross, also Virginia and Lisnabuntry); Jack Rahill (Munterconnaught); Tom Brady (Cornafean)

GALWAY (RUNNERS-UP)

1. Michael 'Cussaun' Brennan
(Caltra-Ahascragh)

2. Hugo Carey
(Carna, also Galway Gaels and
Kickhams, Dublin)

3. Mick Connaire
(St Grellan's, also Kickhams, Dublin)

4. Dinny O'Sullivan
(Oughterard, also UCG)

5. Tommy Hughes
(Tuam Stars)

6. Tadgh McCarthy
(Galway Gaels, also An Chéad Cath)

7. Frank Fox
(Dunmore MacHales, also Galway
Gaels)

8. Martin Kelly
(Caltra-Ahascragh, also Garda, Dublin)

9. John 'Tull' Dunne
(St Grellan's)

10. Frank Burke
(Galway Gaels, also Clonbur and
Oughterard)

11. Brendan Nestor
(Dunmore MacHales, also Erin's
Hope, Dublin)

12. Mick Higgins
(Kilkerrin-Clonberne, also UCG)

13. Joe Kelleher
(St Grellan's)

14. Mick Donnellan
(Dunmore MacHales) Capt.

15. Dermot Mitchell
(Corofin, also Geraldines, Dublin)

Subs: Paddy Kelly (Tuam Stars); Eddie O'Toole (Oughterard); Mick Stewart (Tuam Stars); Bill Birrell (Tuam Stars); Frank Morris (Corofin); P.J. Morris (Corofin); Tommy 'Trixie' Leech (St Grellan's)

1934

The GAA was celebrating its Golden Jubilee in 1934. The Association was justifiably proud as it reflected on the enormous strides it had made in its first fifty years of existence. The level of participation in virtually every parish in the country, the popularity of the games and the impressive organisational structure all underpinned the GAA's status as the leading sporting organisation in the country. Only the Catholic Church rivalled it in terms of cultural importance.

Against this backdrop, and with many 'new' teams emerging as genuine contenders for All-Ireland glory, the 1934 Championship was one of the most eagerly awaited ever.

Champions Cavan had finally established themselves as the finest team in the land. Galway, 1933 runners-up, were highly regarded, but so too were their arch-rivals in Connacht, Mayo. In Leinster, Kildare seemed to be on the wane but Dublin were showing real promise while Meath and Louth had shown some evidence that they were on the rise. As always, Kerry were regarded as likely to fly the Munster flag and make a major push for ultimate honours.

The first game of Championship 1934, between Cavan and Tyrone, was played at Omagh on 29 April. With team captain Joe Henry Campbell in brilliant form, Tyrone kept Cavan in their sights for most of the game. They looked to have sprung the greatest ever shock when another Campbell, Seamus, forced the ball into the Cavan net on the stroke of full-time. The ensuing wild celebrations were short-lived, however, as the referee ruled that there had been an infringement, thus allowing Cavan to progress by the narrowest of margins. Ironically, it was Cavan who complained loudest after the game, with Chairman Seamus Gilheaney pulling no punches when he addressed his County Board the following week. He was irked that the daily newspaper reports on the game failed to mention that the pitch was only 120 yards by 75 yards; that four of Cavan's best players had to retire through injuries; that they had two goals disallowed … and that the referee was 'incompetent'. For the record, there was no 'C', let alone a 'CCC' or indeed a 'CCCC', when Mr Gilheaney made these pronouncements.

Cavan then headed off on an American tour, and when they returned home they faced Fermanagh, earlier victors over Donegal, in the provincial semi-final. Against a side backboned by the renowned McDonnell brothers from Derrylin, the champions were slow to assert their undoubted superiority. With a less than convincing performance, they qualified for the final on a score of 3-4 to 1-3.

On the other side of the draw in Ulster, Armagh and Monaghan qualified for the semi-final after comfortable victories over Antrim and Down respectively. Perhaps because a Monaghan victory was seen to be a foregone conclusion, the *Irish Independent* omitted to send a reporter to this semi-final. Its entire report on the game read: 'After a splendid exhibition of football, Armagh defeated Monaghan in the semi-final of the Ulster Senior Championship at Armagh, by 2-3 to 1-3.'

A surprise it may have been, but there was no disputing the merit of Armagh's win. If Jim McCullough and John Vallely were the twin architects behind this great win, the goalkeeping exploits of Joe Houlihan were also key to the victory. The scene was now set for Armagh to bridge a gap of more than thirty years since their last Ulster title.

There was little or no breeze in Armagh when the sides met on 29 July. However, the slope on the pitch at the Hope Estate conferred a significant first-half advantage on the home team after John Vallely chose to play 'downfield'. The advantage was short-lived, with the All-Ireland champions creating the chances that led to quick goals from Mick Dinneny and Louis Blessing. A seven-point half-time advantage translated into a comprehensive fifteen-point win. While it was a case of 'back to the drawing board' for Armagh, Cavan seemed stronger than ever and were now warm favourites to retain the Sam Maguire.

At a time when local newspapers routinely referred to counties by their nicknames, the *Leitrim*

The Dublin team which lost out to Galway in the 1934 Final. Back (l–r): Tom Brown (County Chairman), Paddy Hickey, Bobby Beggs, Johnny McDonnell, Mick Keating, Jim O'Shea, Mick Casey, Mick 'Ginger' O'Brien, Jackser Kavanagh (trainer); front (l–r): Mickey Wellington, Ned McCann, George Comerford, Willie Dowling, Des Brennan, Paddy Cavanagh, Frank 'Dizzer' Cavanagh, Michael 'Murt' Kelly. *Courtesy of Jimmy Wren.*

Observer reported that 'the Scutchers' (aka Leitrim) had elected not to contest the Senior Championship of 1934. In similar vein, the *Connacht Tribune* warned 'the Blazers' (Galway) against complacency in the lead-up to their semi-final clash with 'the Sheep Stealers' (Roscommon) at Castlerea on 17 June. While Galway emerged with a comfortable nine-point victory, Roscommon, with Tom Shevlin again starring, matched their opponents for much of the game.

The second of the Connacht semi-finals, involving Mayo and Sligo, took place at Tubbercurry on 8 July. Impressive combination play by Sligo's Mickey Gillen and Michael Snee created the opening for an early goal by Mick O'Dowd and this heralded scenes of wild jubilation among the vast local support. However, matters began to take their expected course as Patsy Flannelly and George Ormsby started to dominate at midfield. In blistering heat, Paddy Moclair (two) and Peter Laffey scored goals for Mayo as they ran out comprehensive winners, 3-7 to 1-3.

Castlerea hosted the Galway v Mayo provincial final on 22 July. Although Galway were reigning champions and had contested the All-Ireland Final of 1933, Mayo's league form was such that they were widely tipped to regain the title. A crowd of 16,000 travelled from far and wide in expectation of a classic. Most newspaper reports allude to the 'vigorous' nature of the exchanges, but one contribution in *The Connaught Telegraph* skipped the euphemisms and declared: 'A number of records went by the board at Castlerea on Sunday. A record crowd paid admission to make a record gate, and a record number of supporters never saw the game. A record number of spectators were on the field; it was a record rough game; and a record for bad football.'

One matter on which there was unanimous agreement was that Galway fully deserved their 2-4 to 0-5 victory. Martin Kelly and 'Tull' Dunne scored the winners' goals. However, it was an immaculate display from Hugo Carey that captured the headlines, while James Daly and Frank Fox were also in outstanding form.

A gale-force wind ensured that the opening tie of the Leinster Championship between Louth and Laois at Croke Park on 6 May was very much a 'game of two halves'. Louth held an eight-point advantage at the break, but such was the force of the elements that few in attendance gave them any chance of holding out for victory. Laois duly launched their expected comeback, but Louth kept their noses in front, largely thanks to the never-say-die defensive work by Mickey McKeon, Eugene Callan and Joe Hearty. A two-point win for the Wee County brought them to the semi-final against Wexford, earlier victors over Kildare. A Jack Fane goal gave Wexford the early advantage but Louth stormed back with goals from Sean Cullen (two), Tom 'Skinner' Caffrey and John Gartland. They won by ten points and so booked their place in the Leinster Final for the first time since 1918.

The opposite side of the Leinster draw saw Dublin and Meath progress to a semi-final meeting at Drogheda on 8 July. A speculative lob from Mickey Wellington in the dying seconds ended up in the Meath net and, against the run of play, Dublin were through to the provincial final. The *Meath Chronicle* certainly left its readers in no doubt as to which was the better team, referring to Dublin as 'the luckiest finalists in GAA history'.

Aside from making their All-Ireland breakthrough in 1936, Mayo dominated the National Football League in the 1930s, winning six titles in all. Back (l–r): Paddy 'Captain' Munnelly, George Ormsby, P.J. 'Purty' Kelly, Peter Laffey, Mick Raftery, Henry Kenny, Patsy Flannelly, Pat Cusack, Tom Burke, Paddy Quinn, Paddy Moclair; front (l–r): Jackie Carney, Paddy Collins, Tommy 'Danno' Regan, Gerald Courell, Jim 'Tot' McGowan, Jack Gannon, Josie Munnelly, Fr Eddie O'Hara (County Board President). *Picture courtesy of the* Western People.

It took three games to separate Dublin and Louth in the Leinster Final of 1934. The first two games were played at Croke Park, with Dublin again needing a last-minute goal to snatch a draw in the replay. Contrary to the rule, no extra time was played, the Leinster Secretary being 'aware of the attitude of the teams'.

In the lead-up to the second replay, 'Onlooker' in the *Drogheda Independent* reflected the hopes of Louth's supporters: 'Playing over familiar haunts, under native air, to the echo and cheer of their brother Gaels, Louth should have a good chance of ending the agony on this occasion.'

The third instalment took place at Drogheda on 19 August before a record crowd of 25,000, drawn from every corner of Ireland. In a tight game noted for the quality of the play, Dublin finally pulled through with a two-point win. Their outstanding performer was former Clare star George Comerford, whose scoring exploits laid the foundations for victory. Once again, the local newspaper was not convinced of the merit of Dublin's latest victory, with the *Drogheda Independent* proclaiming: 'No one, unless he is an out and out Dublin follower, would make the claim that Dublin were the better footballers.'

As expected, Kerry had little difficulty in emerging from Munster. No longer receiving a bye into the final, the men from the Kingdom had to negotiate three hurdles to secure provincial honours. They eased past Cork with nonchalant ease at Fermoy on 27 May. With Tim O'Donnell at his brilliant best, they followed this up with a nine-point semi-final win over Tipperary at Clonmel on 15 July.

Scoring four goals in a first-half blitz, Limerick showed impressive form in overcoming Waterford in the second Munster semi-final. Able to call on such talented players as Pat Lonergan, Tom Culhane and Matt Nunan, they were expected to pose problems for Kerry when they met in the provincial decider at Listowel on 29 July. Only a point behind at the break, Limerick finally succumbed to a barrage of scores from Willie Brick, John Joe Landers and Jackie Ryan, with Kerry winning 1-14 to 1-2.

The first of the All-Ireland semi-finals, between Galway and Cavan, took place at Tuam on 12 August. For years to come, this game would be known in Cavan football circles as 'The Tuam Fiasco'. Over two hours after the throw-in, the match ended in a three-point win for Galway (1-8 to 0-8) but the result attracted far less attention than the conditions in which the game was played. A crowd of 25,000, double the venue's capacity, turned up. Describing the chaotic overcrowding and constant pitch encroachment, the *Western People* reported: 'Scenes unparalleled in the history of the GAA were witnessed at Tuam on Sunday.' An interesting snapshot of the chaos was captured in *The Anglo Celt*: 'The enterprising proprietor of a horse-drawn lorry converted his vehicle to a temporary stand, charging 2/- each, but it was soon overcrowded, with the result that the wheels collapsed and the occupants got a short shrift "back to the land".'

The second semi-final, played at Tralee on 9 September, produced a major shock when Dublin completely dominated the game. In what was described as the 'swan song' of the great Kerry four-in-a-row team, they were well beaten by a slick Metropolitan combination, 3-8 to 0-6.

THE FINAL — 23 SEPTEMBER

There was a national newspaper strike in the period leading up to the Jubilee Final and this might have been expected to dampen somewhat public enthusiasm for the game. It is clear, however, that the regional press took up the slack so there was no shortage of coverage and informed opinion on the prospects of the two protagonists.

Dublin's impressive win over Kerry saw them widely tipped to win the title but Galway had been improving steadily over the previous two years and they were quietly confident that they could take the spoils. Both sides had a sprinkling of 'imported' talent at their disposal. Kerry natives Tadgh McCarthy and Mick Ferriter were key members of the Galway team while Dublin could call upon George Comerford and Mick Casey (both Clare), Mick Keating (Wicklow), Joe Colleran (Sligo), and Gearoid Fitzgerald, 'Murt' Kelly and Jim O'Shea (all Kerry).

When the big day arrived, Galway had a surprise in store for the 36,000 crowd in attendance. They discarded their traditional garb of white with green hoop for what would become their hallmark maroon and white. Starting with a flourish, and aided by a strong breeze, they hit the front courtesy of an early free from Brendan Nestor. Dublin hit back, however, and a Willie Dowling goal gave them the initiative. It was then that Mick Ferriter struck for two quick goals and Galway piled on the pressure as they carved out a five-point lead at the break.

As expected, Dublin launched a second-half comeback, and while they closed the gap at one stage to two points, their fate was sealed when Galway's Martin Kelly blasted the ball past Johnny McDonnell. At the end of what the *Connacht Tribune* described as 'The closest and greatest fight for All-Ireland honours in the history of the GAA', Galway emerged as champions on a scoreline of 3-5 to 1-9. That this was a game of the highest quality is clear from the newspaper reports in the following days. In a Galway team that had fifteen heroes, special credit was reserved for Dinny Sullivan, Frank Fox, midfielders Higgins and Dunne, and corner-forwards Ferriter and Nestor. For Dublin, goalkeeper McDonnell, the Cavanagh cousins, Beggs, Wellington and Keating were outstanding.

As the curtain came down on Championship 1934, there was a general acknowledgement that successive victories for Cavan and Galway pointed to a healthy new era, with a broader base of serious contenders. The question was whether the traditional powers of Kerry, Dublin and Kildare could reverse this trend in 1935.

FINAL STATISTICS

	Galway	Dublin
Full-time:	3-5	1-9
Half-time:	2-4	1-2
Scorers:	M. Ferriter 2-0	G. Comerford 0-6
	M. Kelly 1-2	W. Dowling 1-0
	J. Dunne 0-2	M. Kelly 0-1
	B. Nestor 0-1	M. Wellington 0-1
		M. Keating 0-1
Attendance:	36,113	
Gate Receipts:	£3,092 (€3,926)	
Referee:	Jack McCarthy (Kerry)	

FINAL MISCELLANY

- Long before the *The Sunday Game* came into existence, GAA supporters relied almost exclusively on newspaper reports for match analysis. In 1934, a summer newspaper strike, which lasted three months, starved followers of this lifeline. Even worse has been the impact on struggling researchers almost ninety years later!

- The *Connacht Tribune* of 28 July gave an interesting account of the lengths to which supporters went in order to attend the Connacht Final at Castlerea:

  They came in all kinds of vehicles – 'buses, trains, motor lorries, motor vans, traps, cars, farm carts, motor cars, motor bicycles and pedal bicycles. There were not enough vehicles to meet all requirements for I noticed three men on two bicycles on the road between Ballymoe and Castlerea. The two cyclists rode side by side. The third man, who must be the makings of an acrobat, stood upright between them, one foot on each carrier, his right hand on the shoulder of one cyclist and his left hand on the shoulder of the other. This enthusiastic trio had come from Oran, County Roscommon.

- Tipperary became All-Ireland Minor Football champions in 1934 without the inconvenience of having to play in the final. In the semi-final, they beat Mayo by ten points at Tralee on 9 September, while Dublin crushed Tyrone, 3-8 to 0-6, at Croke Park on the same day. Tyrone lodged an objection on the grounds that Dublin had fielded an overage player and, after investigation, the Metropolitans were disqualified. A subsequent objection by the Dublin County Board led to a statement from Tyrone that they 'were surprised to find three or four of their players illegal'. They promptly announced their 'withdrawal' from the championship and Tipperary were duly declared champions.

- Although Kerry failed to reach the 1934 decider, *The Kerryman* showed little evidence that there was anything approaching an inferiority complex within the county. Commenting on the victory of a Galway player who won the Long Kick Championship of Ireland with an effort of 49 yards 2 feet, it pointed out that the average Kerry junior would beat this mark. It went on to note that Miko Doyle was a 70-yard man.

1934 – THE YEAR THAT WAS

- Against trenchant Fine Gael opposition, the Dáil passed 'The Uniform (Restriction) Act' in March 1934. With the Blueshirt movement expanding its influence, the Act sought 'to restrict the wearing of or carrying of uniform, badges, banners and other such articles, and the use of military titles, to make certain provisions with a view to preventing breaches of the peace at public processions.'

- In 1934, the *Sunday Independent* routinely carried a commercial feature extolling the virtues of Tokalon Vanishing Skinfood, a product specially developed for women. Advising its target audience that usage guaranteed the early disappearance of blackheads, enlarged pores and other skin blemishes, the promotion went on to quote Mrs B., recently married to the son of an enormously rich manufacturer: 'You ask why did my husband choose me? Well, I used to be a typist in his father's office. I could not afford expensive frocks like all the other girls he used to go about with, but I always took the greatest care of my skin.' Unsurprisingly, Tokalon was her skin cream of choice, and Mr B. confided to his new wife that its beneficial effects were what triggered his enduring love, and his decision to propose marriage.

- In 1934, every class and shape of man aspiring to own a Shandon Hat was fully catered for by Cork-based outfitters, B. Gorman & Son. Their promotional blurb sought to entice prospective hat-owners with the assertion that: 'SHANDON HATS are made in wide brims for big men, in natty brims for modern young men; in low and medium qualities for men with slender purses; in better qualities for those who can afford them; and in various shades to match overcoats and suits.'

- After one of the most colourful and spectacular American manhunts ever, gangsters Bonnie Elizabeth Parker and Clyde Chestnut (Champion) Barrow ('Bonnie and Clyde') were ambushed and shot in Louisiana on 23 May 1934. They had been responsible for at least thirteen murders, nine of which were of police officers. Exactly two months later, notorious criminal John Dillinger met a similar fate.

1934 TEAM LINE-OUTS

GALWAY (WINNERS)

1. Michael 'Cussaun' Brennan
(Caltra-Ahascragh)

2. Hugo Carey
(Galway Gaels, also Carna Kickhams, Dublin)

3. Mick Connaire
(St Grellan's, also Kickhams, Dublin)

4. Dinny Sullivan
(Oughterard, also UCG and Wolfe Tones)

5. Tommy Hughes
(Tuam Stars)

6. Tadgh McCarthy
(An Chéad Cath, also Galway Gaels)

7. Frank Fox
(Dunmore MacHales, also Galway Gaels)

8. John 'Tull' Dunne
(St Grellan's)

9. Mick Higgins
(Kilkerrin-Clonberne, also UCG) Capt.

10. Dermot Mitchell
(Corofin, also Geraldines, Dublin)

11. Martin Kelly
(Caltra-Ahascragh, also Garda, Dublin)

12. Ralph Griffin
(Caltra-Ahascragh, also Kickhams, Dublin)

13. Mick Ferriter
(UCG, also Ballyferriter, Kerry)

14. P.J. McDonnell
(St Grellan's)

15. Brendan Nestor
(Geraldines, Dublin, also Dunmore MacHales)

Subs: Paddy 'Staff' Stevens (Corofin); Joe Kelleher (St Grellan's); James Daly (Galway Gaels); Frank Burke (Galway Gaels, also An Chéad Cath); Charlie Connolly (Tuam Stars, also Ballinasloe Mental Hospital and Tarmon, Roscommon)

DUBLIN (RUNNERS-UP)

1. Johnny McDonnell
(O'Tooles)

2. Mick Casey
(UCD)

3. Des Brennan
(Keatings)

4. Frank 'Dizzer' Cavanagh
(Dolphins)

5. Paddy Cavanagh
(Dolphins)

6. Ned McCann
(Geraldines)

7. Paddy Hickey
(Round Towers, Clondalkin)

8. Gearoid Fitzgerald
(Geraldines, also Sneem, Kerry)

9. Bobby Beggs
(St Joseph's, also Skerries Harps, Wolfe
Tones, Galway and Sean McDermotts)

10. Michael 'Ginger' O'Brien
(O'Tooles)

11. George Comerford
(Garda, also St Joseph's, Miltown
Malbay, Clare and Athy, Kildare)

12. Willie Dowling
(Round Towers, Clondalkin)

13. Mickey Wellington
(St Joseph's)

14. Michael 'Murt' Kelly
(Geraldines, also Beaufort, Kerry)

15. Mick Keating
(Garda)

Subs: Gerry McLoughlin (Beann Eadair); Peter Lambe (Garda, also Killanny, Monaghan); Paddy Perry (Garda, also Boyle, Roscommon); Peter Synnott (O'Tooles); Tom Dowd (Round Towers, Clondalkin)

Joe Colleran (Clanna Gael, also Curry, Sligo) was selected to line out. However, he was alleged to have played for another club under an assumed name. This raised doubts as to his eligibility and he was withdrawn from the team.

Jim O'Shea was unavailable for selection owing to injury sustained in the semi-final against his native Kerry.

1935

The big story in the run-up to the 1935 Championship was the absence of Kerry from the competition. At their annual convention, the County Board had voted to withdraw from national competition in protest at the treatment of republican prisoners. Although Kerry's dominance had dipped somewhat since 1932, the All-Ireland hopes of a number of counties rose on the back of this development.

If the race for the Sam Maguire Cup had opened up, the Munster Championship was very much a case of 'Hamlet without the Prince'. Since 1922, only Cork, in 1928, had broken Kerry's stranglehold on the provincial title. Cork's main rivals to fill the vacuum left by Kerry's absence were Tipperary, last winners of the title in 1922.

The opening game of the Munster Championship saw Clare beat Waterford by four points at Dungarvan on 12 May. This qualified the Banner County for a home semi-final encounter with Tipperary on 30 June. With Miltown Malbay garda George Comerford to the fore, the Clare men raced into an early three-point lead and looked set to spring a championship surprise. Templemore's Kieran Holland then began to exert a major influence on proceedings and this provided the launching pad for Tipperary's resurgence as they took the honours, 1-8 to 0-8. The decisive goal came from the boot of a Mullinahone native who gloried in the name Walter Scott, but who was known to all as 'Watty', presumably to distinguish him from the less well-known Scottish novelist of the same name!

Goals from Tim Cotter and William Lynch were the key scores when Cork defeated Limerick by five points in the other semi-final at Charleville on 26 May. The Rebels were very much the underdogs, however, when they faced Tipperary in the provincial showdown at Fermoy on 21 July. A final score of 2-8 to 1-2 suggests that the Dick Power-led Tipperary men were comfortable winners but, in reality, were it not for the brilliance of Tipperary's goalie, Jim Williams, Cork might have taken the spoils.

A great seven-point win over Roscommon at Tubbercurry on 12 May gave Sligo grounds for optimism as they prepared for a provincial semi-final joust with All-Ireland champions Galway. This turned out to be badly misplaced, with the Tribesmen hitting them for five goals when coasting to an easy 5-4 to 0-2 win at Castlebar on 2 June. If Galway's goal tally was impressive, it paled in comparison to Mayo's feat of finding the net no fewer than nine times against the unfortunate Leitrim in the second semi-final.

Over 26,000 people turned up at Roscommon on 21 July to see Galway defend their provincial crown against league champions Mayo. Predictions that Mayo would again need to be in goal-scoring form if they were to wrest the crown from the champions proved to be somewhat wide of the mark. On a score of 0-12 to 0-5, the Mayo men regained the title with a brilliant display of combination football. Noting the scenes of 'wild enthusiasm' which greeted the final whistle, *The Connaught Telegraph* reserved its highest praise for the contributions of Gerald Courell, Patsy Flannelly and George Ormsby to this great victory. Aside from the outstanding Mick Connaire, Galway's leading light was former Dublin star Bobby Beggs, whose ferocious duel with Josie Munnelly had the crowd enthralled throughout the game.

Carlow's victory over Wexford at Muine Bheag on 5 May was a huge surprise. That they out-gunned their neighbours by 5-7 to 1-6 was truly sensational. On a day when every man played his part, Tom 'Drakes' Walker shone like a beacon as the outstanding player in this famous victory. Carlow now faced Westmeath, earlier victors over Offaly, at Croke Park on 19 May. Despite the inclement conditions, they played out an exciting draw, with Walker once again in outstanding form. When they met again, at Portlaoise on 9 June, Carlow, despite the absence of Walker, held a seven-point half-time advantage and seemed set to advance to a quarter-final clash with Meath. The second half saw Dinny Breen, Jack Dunican and Andy Dunne take complete control for Westmeath as they cruised to a seven-point victory, 3-6 to 2-2.

In an effort to speed up the championship, the Leinster Council fixed the Meath–Westmeath quarter-final clash for Kells on Thursday 20 June, the feast of Corpus Christi. This, the first ever week-night fixture in the Senior Championship, attracted a large crowd, with gate receipts topping the £170 mark. Meath proved to be too strong for their neighbours and ran out 2-7 to 0-9 winners. Newspaper reports on the game highlight the performance of Westmeath's Matt Coleman. Having starred for the minor team in the curtain-raiser, he took the scoring honours in the senior match by notching four of the team's nine-point tally.

After the heartbreak of their three-game saga with Dublin the previous year, Louth made amends in their first-round clash at the newly-named Páirc Tailteann in Navan on 9 June. In a tight game, they beat the reigning champions 0-6 to 0-3, with Tom 'Skinner' Caffrey once again Dublin's tormentor-in-chief. Louth's semi-final clash with Meath at Croke Park on 14 July was one of the

Cavan, All-Ireland champions 1935. Back (l–r): Paddy McNamee, John Molloy, Eugene Finnegan, Terry Dolan, Mick Dinneny, James White, Willie Connolly, Ned O'Reilly, Jack Smallhorne, 'Big' Tom O'Reilly, Willie Young, Vincent McGovern, Joe Mitchell; front (l–r): Paddy Boylan, Dónal Morgan, 'Small' Tom O'Reilly, Jim Smith, Hughie O'Reilly, Packy Devlin, Louis Blessing, M.J. 'Sonny' Magee, Packy Phair.

best games of the year. It was touch and go throughout, with Louth pipping their neighbours with a last-minute 'wonder point' from student teacher J. Curran. Fielding an array of exotically nicknamed stars such as 'Boiler' McGuinness, 'Weasel' Browne, 'Buller' Rogers and 'Spog' Geraghty, Meath's quest to add another Leinster title to their sole success of 1895 was thwarted once again.

As expected, Kildare were comfortable winners over Laois when they met in the second of the Leinster semi-finals. Backboned by wily veterans Matt Goff, Jack Higgins and Paddy Martin, the Lilywhites showed flashes of their old 'machine-like play' as they progressed to their first provincial final in four years. As a footballing spectacle, the Leinster Final was a disappointment. As 'Gael' in the *Drogheda Independent* poetically observed, 'The cake, intelligently concocted and methodically prepared, failed to rise.'

Kildare took an early two-point lead and, after a dour tit-for-tat struggle, they held out for a narrow 0-8 to 0-6 victory. In an otherwise unremarkable game, the displays of Kildare's Matt Goff and Louth defender Jim Culligan were widely lauded. Ironically, Kildare's victory owed much to the dominance of midfielders Christy Higgins and team captain Paul Matthews, a native of Ardee.

It was predicted by many that Cavan's dominance in Ulster was at an end, especially after losing heavily to Monaghan in the Dr McKenna Cup final. These predictions seemed well founded when they struggled to get past Donegal in their first-round encounter at Bundoran on 9 June, having been held to a single point in the second half. Any extra confidence that this gave Monaghan in advance of their semi-final clash at Breffni Park on 30 June was utterly unfounded. An emphatic 2-12 to 0-1 victory propelled Cavan into the final against unlikely opponents, Fermanagh. The Ernesiders had needed replays to overcome Tyrone and Armagh to reach the decider and were hopeful that their Belturbet clash with the Cavan men could yield their first ever provincial title.

In a game that *The Anglo Celt* described as being more remarkable for its robustness than brilliance, Cavan held the upper hand throughout, winning 2-6 to 2-1. If 'Big' Tom O'Reilly was the key man for the winners, Fermanagh midfielder Jim McCullough was the outstanding player on view. His efforts, and those of Kinawley brothers Tommy and Eamon McDonnell, created many anxious moments for the Cavan men.

The first of the All-Ireland semi-finals saw Tipperary take on Cavan at Croke Park on 18 August. The Munster champions were quick to show that their provincial credentials were in no way tainted by virtue of Kerry's withdrawal from the championship. Inspired by Kieran Holland, they dominated much of the game, including a fifteen-minute spell when they scored six unanswered points. Cavan struggled to stay within striking distance and their prospects looked bleak as the game entered the dying seconds. It was then that Jim Smith once again came to their rescue when his powerful long-range effort was deflected to the Tipperary net by Hughie O'Reilly, leaving Cavan 1-7 to 0-8 winners. Tipperary's subsequent appeal to the Central Council, chiefly on the question of Jim Smith's eligibility, came to nought.

According to *The Irish Press*, the following Sunday saw 'Kildare's latest galaxy of stars outwit' the men from Mayo when they took the honours on a 2-6 to 0-7 scoreline. Goals in the opening minutes from Mickey Geraghty and Tom Keogh set the Lilywhites on their way, while veterans Jack Higgins and Matt Goff never gave an inch in their rock-solid defence. Despite the best efforts of Henry Kenny and Gerald Courell, Mayo struggled to respond to Kildare's lightning start. The experience would, however, prove to be a valuable one when they launched their 1936 championship campaign.

THE FINAL — 22 SEPTEMBER

The big talking point in the lead-up to the 1935 Final was the decision of the Kildare selectors to drop their regular goalkeeper, Athy's Pat 'Cuddy' Chanders. He was replaced by Naas clubman Jim Maguire, a former Armagh player who, by all accounts, had not previously played in goals. There was some speculation that this surprise decision might have an unsettling effect on the team, but supporters remained confident that the Sam Maguire was destined for the Short Grass County.

Unsurprisingly, the general view was that Kildare's decisive win over Mayo and Cavan's lucky escape against Tipperary justified the Lilywhites' favourites tag for the 22 September showdown. The view in Cavan, however, was that their semi-final performance was an aberration and that, but for 'The Tuam Fiasco' of 1934, they would now be lining up to take their third title in succession. It was against this backdrop that their followers travelled to Croke Park in far greater numbers than ever before. A record crowd of over 50,000, surpassing the 46,000 who had attended the Limerick–Kilkenny hurling decider three weeks previously, turned up on a day of glorious sunshine.

Right from the start, the Cavan men took the initiative. After a slick passing movement involving three of their forwards, 'Sonny' Magee put them in front within thirty seconds. While Mickey Geraghty hit the equaliser four minutes later, it was Cavan who proceeded to dominate for most of the first half. After hitting three points without reply, Paddy Boylan added a goal to give the Ulster champions a commanding lead. Despite a Tommy Mulhall goal for Kildare, Cavan maintained their advantage and another goal from Boylan left them with a commanding six-point lead at the break.

The Lilywhites needed a strong start to the second half if they were to give themselves a fighting chance. In the event, it was Cavan captain Hughie O'Reilly who drew first blood when he goaled within two minutes of the restart. The gap widened to ten points with twenty-five minutes to go, and while Kildare hit 1-3 without reply before the end of the game, Cavan were always firmly in control. They ran out convincing winners on a score of 3-6 to 2-5.

Cavan's transformation from their semi-final performance was the big talking point, especially as they were said to have had only twelve days' collective training. They held sway throughout the field, their top men being captain Hughie O'Reilly, corner-back Willie Connolly and forwards Paddy Boylan and 'Sonny' Magee. The two Tom O'Reillys, from Cornafean ('Big') and Mullahoran ('Small'), also received honourable mention in all the newspaper reports on the game.

Raheens man Peter Waters was widely acknowledged as Kildare's best performer. The Dowling brothers from Robertstown and Athy's Tommy Mulhall also impressed. Within the county, the controversy surrounding the choice of goalkeeper raged for years and was often quoted as the reason for the Lilywhites' demise. Whatever the merits or otherwise of the decision, contemporary reports confirm that Maguire acquitted himself very well and that he could not be faulted for any of Cavan's goals. While their supporters comforted themselves in the expectation that they would continue as a major footballing force, it would be another sixty-three years before the Lilywhites again lined out on All-Ireland day.

FINAL STATISTICS

	Cavan	Kildare
Full-time:	3-6	2-5
Half-time:	2-5	1-2
Scorers:	P. Boylan 2-0	J.J. Dowling 1-0
	T. O'Reilly 1-0	T. Mulhall 1-0
	M.J. Magee 0-3 (0-1 free)	M. Geraghty 0-2
	P. Devlin 0-1	P. Martin 0-2 (0-1 free)
	H. O'Reilly 0-1	P. Matthews 0-1
	J. Smallhorne 0-1	
Attendance:	50,380	
Gate Receipts:	£4,533 (€5,756)	
Referee:	Stephen Jordan (Galway)	

FINAL MISCELLANY

- Reporting on the Mayo–Galway Connacht Final, 'Green Flag' of *The Irish Press* was in no doubt as to the pre-eminence of Gaelic games when it came to sporting passion: 'They talk about Test fever or Cup-tie fever, but if any of these afflictions are half so virulent as the fever which gripped thousands of people on the little border town of Roscommon on Sunday, I'll certainly say, in the words of the Yankee, "Some disease, boy."'

- Commenting on Louth's thrilling win over Meath in the Leinster semi-final, *Drogheda Independent* columnist 'Gearoid' treated his readers to a musical account of Eddie Boyle's prowess: 'supporters saw six of the forwards bamboozle Louth's defence with a hand-passing symphony which, however, was overdone, and Boyle tore a hole in the ballad'.

- While Carlow's 5-7 against Wexford on 5 May was impressive, it wasn't the highest tally recorded at Muine Bheag that day. In the preceding minor hurling game, Kilkenny chalked up no fewer than seventeen goals and fourteen points against a Wicklow team which scored a single goal.

- According to the match preview in *The Irish Press* of Friday 20 September, Jim Smith, at 5'11", was the tallest player on the Cavan team. Three Kildare players, Matt Goff, Bill Mangan and Paul Matthews, were 6'2" tall.

1935 – THE YEAR THAT WAS

- At the direction of Benito Mussolini, Italy invaded Ethiopia on 22 October.
- On 10 June, Alcoholics Anonymous was founded in New York by William G. Wilson and Dr Robert Smith.
- On the recommendation of the 1932 Carrigan Commission Report, The Criminal Law Amendment Act of 1935 made the importation or sale of contraceptive devices illegal in Ireland. It also led, in the same year, to the Public Dance Halls Act. With the support of the three main political parties, the Gaelic League and the Catholic hierarchy, this sought to rid the country of the 'orgies of dissipation' associated with jazz and unregulated dances. In the years that followed, the Act had a devastating effect on Irish cultural traditions and music. As well as putting a stop to the targeted 'jazz' scene, the legislation had the effect of outlawing traditional music and dance gatherings.
- 1935 was a watershed year for industrial relations in Ireland. In April of that year, the Minister for Industry and Commerce, Seán Lemass, introduced legislation to provide for 'a week's annual holidays, with pay, for all workers in industry'.
- In 1935, life expectancy at birth in Ireland was 58.2 years for a male and 59.6 years for a female. The corresponding figures for 2019 were 80.8 years for males and 84.7 years for females.

1935 TEAM LINE-OUTS

CAVAN (WINNERS)

1. Willie Young
(Cornafean)

2. Willie Connolly
(Virginia, also Cootehill)

3. Jim Smith
(Erin's Own, Kells, Meath, also Garda, Bailieboro and Virginia)

4. Mick Dinneny
(Cornafean)

5. Terry Dolan
(Castlerahan)

6. 'Big' Tom O'Reilly
(Cornafean)

7. Packy Phair
(Cornafean)

8. Hughie O'Reilly
(Cootehill, also Tullyvin) Capt.

9. 'Small' Tom O'Reilly
(Mullahoran)

10. Dónal Morgan
(Virginia, also Cross)

11. Packy Devlin
(Croghan, also Killeshandra)

12. Jack Smallhorne
(Crosserlough, also Mountnugent)

13. Paddy Boylan
(Cavan Slashers)

14. Louis Blessing
(Cavan Slashers)

15. M.J. 'Sonny' Magee
(Croghan, also Drumlane and Cavan Slashers)

Subs: Paddy McNamee (Virginia, also Cross and Lisnabuntry); John Molloy (Cavan Slashers); Vincent McGovern (Virginia and UCD); Joe Mitchell (Bailieboro); James White (Gowna, also Clanna Gael, Dublin); Eugene Finnegan (Mountnugent); Ned O'Reilly (Cornafean); Patsy Lynch (Bailieboro)

Other Panel Members: John T. Sheridan (Mullahoran); Hugh Paddy O'Reilly (Gowna); Felix Traynor (Gowna); Vincent White (Gowna, also Clanna Gael, Dublin)

KILDARE (RUNNERS-UP)

1. Jim Maguire
(Naas)

2. Bill Mangan
(Round Towers, also Garda)

3. Matt Goff
(Leixlip, also Army Metro)

4. Jimmy Byrne
(Army Metro)

5. Peter Waters
(Raheens)

6. Jack Higgins
(Naas)

7. Frank 'Sambo' Dowling
(Robertstown, also Erin's Hope,
Dublin and Clanna Gael, Dublin)

8. Paul Matthews
(Athy) Capt.

9. Christy Higgins
(Naas)

10. Tommy Mulhall
(Athy)

11. Paddy Martin
(Rathangan, also Castledermot)

12. Paddy Byrne
(Castledermot)

13. Jim Joe Dowling
(Robertstown)

14. Mickey Geraghty
(Sarsfields)

15. Tom Keogh
(Garda, also Kildare Round Towers
and Portlaoise, Laois)

Subs: Jim Dalton (Clane) Played; Pat 'Cuddy' Chanders (Athy); Jim Fox (Athy); Bernard Dunne (Athy); John Crofton (Raheens); James Meaney (Army Metro)

1936

As the 1936 Championship season dawned, the list of serious title contenders was longer than usual. Reigning champions Cavan and their Ulster arch-rivals Monaghan remained formidable. Dublin and Kildare, beaten finalists of the previous two years, were considered most likely to carry Leinster's hopes in the latter stages of the competition. In Connacht, Mayo hoped to build on their provincial success of the previous year while Galway, backboned by most of their 1934 side, were still a force to be reckoned with. Kerry's decision to re-enter the championship after their 1935 sabbatical dampened Tipperary's hopes of retaining their Munster title and caused a stir among the All-Ireland contenders.

At Foynes on 24 May, Kerry launched their campaign with a routine 7-7 to 1-4 victory over Limerick. While they won emphatically, the Kerry men weren't particularly impressive, and were unable to win parity at midfield where Glin's Tommy Culhane ruled the roost for Limerick. The men from the Kingdom were even less impressive when they lined out in the semi-final against reigning provincial champions Tipperary at Limerick on 12 July. In what *The Irish Press* described as 'a slow motion game', Kerry looked hopelessly beaten at several stages of the proceedings. It took an inspirational display by the 'one man team' that was Miko Doyle to drag Kerry through to the Munster Final with just three points to spare.

Conceding 2-4 in the first half when they failed to register a single score, Cork were completely out of their depth when they faced Clare in the second semi-final. Against the backdrop of Kerry's stuttering form against Limerick and Tipperary, Clare supporters now harboured serious ambitions that they could add to their only previous title of 1917.

In the Munster Final, played at the Gaelic Grounds on 26 July, the Banner County featured George Comerford and Mick Casey, both of whom had lined out with Dublin in the 1934 All-Ireland Final. Also among their ranks were Railway Cup players Willie 'Terry' McMahon, John Burke, Tommy Hogan and Paddy Begley. Showing no hint of any inferiority complex, the Clare men led their rivals a merry dance in the opening stages and led by a point at the interval. The second half was an altogether different affair, however, as Kerry hit a succession of spectacular points. According to the *Irish Independent*, 'the man by the number board did his bending exercises at a pace to gratify the wishes of a drill instructor'.

Kerry duly proceeded to regain the Munster crown with a six-point victory. A feature of the game was the performance of teenager Joe Keohane at full-back but, once again, Miko Doyle was the outstanding performer on view.

The big question in Connacht was whether Mayo could build further on their impressive league form and their encouraging run in the 1935 Championship. Their first outing was at Ballina on 24 May when they swamped Sligo on a score of 5-6 to 0-4. In an otherwise uninteresting affair, the antics of Mayo's Tommy Regan brought some gaiety to the occasion. The *Ballina Herald* described how he 'headed the ball for about 10 yards in a solo run and simply mystified Devany of Sligo'.

Galway's footballers couldn't have been happy as they struggled to a three-point victory over Roscommon at Castlerea on 7 June. They were even less impressed when they returned to their changing room at a local restaurant after the game. A number of them had fallen victim to a pick-pocket while they were advancing to a Connacht Final rendezvous with Mayo. Bobby Beggs was suddenly cashless, while the unfortunate Frank Fox was missing 'a valuable pocket watch'.

In the final at Roscommon on 19 July, Mayo looked set to take the honours when they led by three points with only seconds to go. It was then that Dunmore's Brendan Nestor went on a dazzling solo run and, having eluded three Mayo defenders, launched a piledriver at Mayo's citadel. Despite Tom Burke's initial save, the ball appeared to cross the line and as the umpires stood motionless it was Nestor himself who grabbed the flag and signalled a goal. After much confusion and consultation,

The 1936 Mayo team that captured the county's first All-Ireland title. Back (l–r): Paddy Moclair, Patsy Flannelly, Tommy 'Danno' Regan, P.J. 'Purty' Kelly, Paddy Quinn, Paddy Brett, Tom Burke, Josie Munnelly, Jim 'Tot' McGowan; front (l–r): George Ormsby, Henry Kenny, Paddy 'Captain' Munnelly, Seamus O'Malley, Jackie Carney, Peter Laffey, Tommy Grier. *Picture courtesy of the* Western People.

Mayo captain Seamus O'Malley and Laois's Joe 'Rexie' McDonald lead their men in the 1936 pre-match parade. *Picture courtesy of the* Western People.

the score was let stand. When the teams returned to Roscommon on 2 August for the replay, Mayo made no mistake. They retained their title on a score of 2-7 to 1-4. Patsy Flannelly marked the occasion with the performance of his life, completely dominating the midfield exchanges alongside his partner, Henry Kenny.

Fresh from their early summer US tour, Cavan duly opened their Ulster campaign with a solid 1-8 to 2-1 semi-final victory over an Armagh side that failed to score until the dying minutes of the game.

On the other side of the draw, Down started with an impressive nine-point win over Tyrone on 14 June. Star of the show here was Annaclone's Dan Morgan who gave an exhibition of football. Monaghan presented the next challenge for Down, at Carrickmacross on 28 June, where the sides played out a thrilling draw. This time it was the turn of John, Tom and Dan O'Hare to retrieve the situation for Down after they had trailed by seven points. The replay proved to be something of a damp squib, however, as Monaghan powered home on a score of 4-9 to 0-4 at Newry on 12 July. The Farney men were very fortunate to secure a three-point home victory over Donegal in their semi-final clash at Carrickmacross on 26 July, with Mick Melly starring for Donegal.

The Ulster Final was played at Castleblayney on 9 August and Cavan took their sixth provincial title in a row with a 1-7 to 0-7 victory. The decisive goal was scored by Louis Blessing after a mix-up in the Monaghan defence. Cavan's outstanding player on the day was 'Big' Tom O'Reilly while Monaghan's Jack Crawley also turned in a brilliant performance.

While impressive, there was nothing earth-shattering about Offaly's 6-5 to 0-11 win over West-meath on 3 May. Their next fixture was a quarter-final clash with Dublin at Mullingar on 24 May, when their 0-8 to 1-3 victory certainly captured the headlines:

Irish Independent: 'Bombshell for Dublin'
The Irish Press: 'Offaly Astonish Dublin'

With Joe O'Connor leading the charge, Offaly thus qualified for a semi-final encounter with Laois. After a very impressive performance, they were considered unfortunate to lose out to the Laois men (4-5 to 3-4), for whom former Kildare player Tom Keogh was the star turn.

In a furious onslaught in the closing stages, Billy Shaw scored a brilliant solo goal for Meath as they just failed to close the gap in their quarter-final clash with Kildare at Mullingar on 7 June. Louth provided the semi-final opposition for Kildare at Navan on 5 July. The *Drogheda Independent* had a unique take on what it described as the largest assembly that ever gathered in Navan since the foundation of the GAA: 'a sea of heads on every side – old heads, big heads, small square heads, round heads, fat heads, lean heads, black heads, red heads, grey heads, white heads, and even a number of bald heads standing out in bold relief like yacht-sails on a sunlit bay.'

Despite the best efforts of Louth midfielders Jimmy Coyle and Jim McCullough, and an early goal from Jim McKevitt, the Lilywhites gradually took control. A goal from Paddy Martin and some magnificent point-scoring by Paddy Byrne paved the way for a 1-8 to 1-4 Kildare victory.

Scenes of unbounded joy greeted the final whistle when Laois beat Kildare in the Leinster Final. With a well-deserved 3-3 to 0-8 victory, the Laois men bridged a gap going back to 1889 since their

Heavily defeated by Mayo in the 1936 Final, Laois remained a strong footballing force for some years afterwards. This 1937 shot includes 'The Boy Wonder', Tommy Murphy, one of the most outstanding players the game has seen (middle row, fourth from right). *Image courtesy of the GAA Museum at Croke Park.*

previous provincial success. The report in *The Nationalist and Leinster Times* was crystal clear on two matters: every Laois man played brilliantly, and Jack Delaney was even better than brilliant. This victory meant that Laois corner-forward Tom Keogh had the unusual distinction of winning provincial titles with, and against, his native county in successive years.

The All-Ireland semi-finals saw Mayo pitted against Kerry while Laois took on champions Cavan. At Roscommon on 9 August, Mayo proved too strong for Kerry, with Patsy Flannelly and Henry Kenny once again lording it in midfield. Not alone did Flannelly score the decisive goal in this 1-5 to 0-6 victory, but, according to *The Irish Press*, 'The Castlebar man raced through the field like a greyhound.'

All-Ireland champions Cavan were expected to account for Laois in the other semi-final but they were in for a real surprise as they went down on a score of 2-6 to 1-5. Not for the first or last time, it was the four Delaney brothers from Stradbally, as well as their uncle, who powered their county to victory, with midfielder Bill the outstanding player on the field. The *Drogheda Independent* complimented Laois on winning this 'Brilliant Game', and attributed their success to a less than sophisticated brand of direct football: 'go for the ball, get it and kick it as far upfield as your strength will allow.'

Whatever about their playing style, no one could deny the merit of this victory nor the wild enthusiasm of Laois supporters as they carried their heroes shoulder-high when the final whistle sounded.

THE FINAL – 27 SEPTEMBER

The 1936 All-Ireland Final turned out to be one of the most disappointing in the history of the competition. Right from the start Mayo took the initiative, built up a commanding lead, and were never really threatened by a lacklustre Laois fifteen.

As had been the case all summer, the tone was set in midfield where the Castlebar duo of Patsy Flannelly and Henry Kenny were again outstanding. In fairness to Laois, Bill Delaney was far from fully fit. What *The Irish Press* had earlier reported as a minor training ground knock turned out to be a broken bone in his foot and this impeded the great man's efforts.

As the Mayo half-forward line of Carney, Grier and Laffey clicked into gear and began creating openings, it was Paddy Munnelly who capitalised with two first-half goals. The interval score stood at 2-5 to 0-2 and Laois needed a flying start to the second half to have any chance. In the event, it was Mayo who were again quickly out of the blocks and they were soon out of sight with further goals from Paddy Moclair and Josie Munnelly.

The game finished at 4-11 to 0-5 and commentators were unanimous in the view that Mayo had no weak links. *The Connaught Telegraph* went as far as saying that if there was such a thing as the 'perfect team', then Mayo was it. Particular credit was heaped on their impregnable defence which afforded so few opportunities to the Laois men.

After taking the Leinster title for the first time in forty-seven years and beating reigning champions Cavan in the semi-final, Laois were, understandably, bitterly disappointed. In modern-day parlance they had what might be described as 'a bad day at the office', but their subsequent record would show that this was a team of substance. Despite the result, it was acknowledged that they never gave up the fight, with the performances of Joe 'Rexie' McDonald, Paddy Swayne and Tom Keogh being widely lauded.

So, at the fourth time of asking, Mayo had finally reached the pinnacle. Given their subsequent successes, trials and tribulations in pursuit of All-Ireland glory, it is worth quoting the words of the then Minister for Justice and Ballina native, P.J. Ruttledge, who presented the winners' medals: 'If one thing more than anything else contributed to Mayo's victory, it is that defeat has never meant despair as far as the Mayo team is concerned. The wonderful perseverance that has prevailed in the county is the reason for the team's success.'

FINAL STATISTICS

	Mayo	Laois
Full-time:	4-11	0-5
Half-time:	2-5	0-2
Scorers:	P. Munnelly 2-1	B. Delaney 0-2
	P. Moclair 1-3	T. Keogh 0-1
	J. Munnelly 1-3	D. Douglas 0-1
	P. Flannelly 0-3	J. O'Reilly 0-1
	T. Grier 0-1	
Attendance:	50,168	
Gate Receipts:	£4,069 (€5,167)	
Referee:	Jack McCarthy (Kerry)	

FINAL MISCELLANY

- None of the twenty scores in the 1936 Final came from a free.
- On the night of Mayo's first All-Ireland win, team captain Seamus O'Malley and his friend John Smith travelled home to Claremorris in a hired car. The following morning, and without the benefit of any sleep, Seamus cycled to Meelickmore National School where he worked as a teacher. His pupils got an early chance to admire the magnificent Sam Maguire Cup – he had it securely tied to the handlebars of his bike when he arrived at the school.
- In the Minor Final, played on the same day, Louth overcame Kerry on a score of 5-1 to 1-8.
- Despite having starred against no less a man than Kerry's Miko Doyle in the semi-final, Mayo's Tom McNicholas lost his place for the final. A teacher based in Ballyjamesduff, County Cavan, his demotion was down to his inability to get the requisite two weeks off work for collective training in Castlebar.

- The winning Mayo team was trained by Dick Hearns and Garda Paddy Halpin. Hearns, who had previously played with the county, also represented Roscommon, Longford, Donegal, Cork and Dublin during his career. If that didn't prove his sporting prowess, he was also Irish Light-Heavyweight Boxing Champion on several occasions.
- While 1936 was a watershed year for the Mayo football team, it was not the first All-Ireland success for a Mayo footballer. In 1923, Mayo man P.J. O'Beirne lined out with the winning Dublin team.
- From the GAA Annual Congress held on 12 April:

  Cavan Proposal:
  Mr P. Reilly moved that both finalists in Senior Hurling and Senior Football, together with officials of the teams, be entertained at a banquet sponsored by the Central Council. Opposing the motion, L. Brady (Laois), said the winning of the championship was solace enough for any county.

  Antrim Proposal:
  Moved that all members of the GAA be forbidden to attend foreign dances under penalty of six months' suspension.
- *The Anglo Celt* of 18 July gave an account of the discussion at a County Board meeting on a recent fractious encounter between Cornafean and Templeport. When the referee reported Terry Cullen of Templeport for striking him, he tempered his remarks by acknowledging that Cullen later apologised. Springing to his fellow clubman's defence, a Mr Gallagher from Templeport argued that the referee had made a wrong decision, and that while Cullen grabbed the referee by the neck and 'gave him a shaking', he did not strike the man. The meeting was adjourned to allow for Cullen's attendance.

1936 – THE YEAR THAT WAS

- To the consternation of Chancellor Adolf Hitler, Black American athlete Jesse Owens won four gold medals at the Berlin Olympics. Hitler refused to shake his hand.
- After an army revolt under the direction of General Franco, the Spanish Civil War broke out on 18 July.
- The first Volkswagen Beetle was manufactured in 1936.
- In the 1930s, most of the country's regional newspapers offered readers advice on how to deal with the challenges of everyday life. Under the heading 'Household Hints', the *Kerry Champion* of 26 July 1936 proffered the following words of wisdom:

  For rusty kettles, add potato peelings to water, boil, and leave to stand until cold. Empty and rinse.

  Mildew can be removed from linen by soaping the marks when wet and covering them with powdered chalk, which should be rubbed in well.

Use both sides of the broom equally, to make it last longer.

The success of frying depends upon two things – having enough fat to completely cover the articles cooking in it, and having the fat smoking hot.

- A total of 2,376 students sat the Leaving Certificate examination in 1936. Of these, 1,469 were male and 917 female. Just over 63,000 students sat the Leaving Certificate in 2023.
- On 27 May, five days after Aer Lingus was registered as an airline, its first service began, between Baldonnell and Bristol. The capacity of the aircraft used was six passengers.

1936 TEAM LINE-OUTS

MAYO (WINNERS)

1. Tom Burke
(Castlebar Mitchels)

2. Jim 'Tot' McGowan
(Castlebar Mitchels)

3. Paddy Quinn
(Castlebar Mitchels)

4. P.J. 'Purty' Kelly
(Westport)

5. Tommy 'Danno' Regan
(Charlestown Sarsfields)

6. Seamus O'Malley
(Claremorris, also Castlebar Mitchels and Ballinrobe) Capt.

7. George Ormsby
(Ballina Stephenites, also Garda)

8. Patsy Flannelly
(Castlebar Mitchels)

9. Henry Kenny
(Castlebar Mitchels, also Oughterard, Galway)

10. Jackie Carney
(Ballina Stephenites, also Sean McDermotts, Dublin)

11. Tommy Grier
(Ballycastle)

12. Peter Laffey
(Foxford)

13. Josie Munnelly
(Crossmolina, also Castlebar Mitchels)

14. Paddy Moclair
(Castlebar Mitchels, also Ballina Stephenites) Vice Capt.

15. Paddy 'Captain' Munnelly
(Crossmolina)

Subs: Paddy Collins (Lacken); Liam Joyce (Claremorris); Paddy Brett (Balla); Tom McNicholas (Kiltimagh, also Erin's Hope, Dublin, Ballyjamesduff and Mountnugent, Cavan); Mick O'Malley (Louisburgh); Dick Winters (Ballycastle); Billy Mongey (Castlebar Mitchels); Gerald Courell (Ballina Stephenites)

LAOIS (RUNNERS-UP)

1. Tom Delaney
(Stradbally)

2. Joe Brennan
(Walsh Island)

3. Tom Delaney
(Stradbally)

4. Tim 'Sambo' O'Brien
(Graiguecullen)

5. Paddy Swayne
(Stradbally)

6. Joe 'Rexie' McDonald
(Graiguecullen) Capt.

7. Dan Walsh
(Castletown, also Army Metro)

8. Chris Delaney
(Stradbally, also Tullamore, Offaly and Garda)

9. Bill Delaney
(Stradbally)

10. Danny Douglas
(Portarlington, also Army)

11. Mick Delaney
(Stradbally)

12. Jack Delaney
(Stradbally)

13. Jim 'Tipper' Keating
(Graiguecullen)

14. Tom Keogh
(Portlaoise, also Kildare Round Towers and Crumlin Independents, Dublin)

15. John O'Reilly
(Ballybrittas)

Subs: Lee Moran (Army) Played; John 'Mallet' McDarby (Graiguecullen); Mick 'Cutchie' Haughney (Graiguecullen); Har Browne (Stradbally); Ger Feeney (Stradbally); Dick Rankins (Stradbally); Jim 'Sal' Slator (Graiguecullen)

1937

After their sterling displays in 1936, and their ongoing domination of the National League, Mayo were hotly tipped to retain their All-Ireland crown. Among the chasing pack, it was near neighbours Galway who were regarded as most likely to present the stiffest challenge. It was no surprise, therefore, that the Mayo camp was strongly represented when the Tribesmen lined out against Sligo in the Connacht semi-final at Castlerea on 13 June. It is hard to imagine that they learned a lot from this fractious affair which ended 3-1 to 0-2 in Galway's favour. The following paragraphs from *The Irish Press* gave a flavour of the chaos which marked the occasion:

> Play was inclined to be rough and at one stage two players were seen to come to blows. The crowd invaded the pitch, and things looked ugly when Father O'Dea, of Galway, interfered.
>
> Several players were struck and men with hurleys were seen to rush into the crowd. Some Galway priests and one Garda succeeded in restoring order. The official referee did not turn up and J. Farrell, of Roscommon, who acted as substitute, was 'booed' and had his rulings questioned several times.

The stage was now set for a re-run of the 1936 provincial decider, when Mayo prevailed after a replay. In its preview of the game, *The Connaught Telegraph* of 17 July stated that the competing teams would have an added incentive. It reported that 'those who are in a position to judge' were freely expressing the view that the winners in Connacht would take the All-Ireland crown. When the sides met the following day, Mayo started without the services of 'Purty' Kelly and were further handicapped during the game when Paddy Quinn, Tommy Grier and Josie Munnelly all suffered injuries. While they eventually prevailed, the result was in doubt until very late in the game. It was only after Peter Laffey fired a rasping shot to the Galway net in the dying minutes that Mayo supporters in the crowd of 15,000 could finally relax.

The Ulster Championship progressed along its by now familiar, and expected, course. At Enniskillen on 13 June, Cavan brushed aside the challenge of a game, but much lighter, Fermanagh fifteen. They followed this up two weeks later by cruising past Donegal, 2-12 to 1-4, in their semi-final encounter at Breffni Park on 27 June. A feature of this game was a return to the fold by veteran Jim Smith, who displayed all his old craft at the heart of Cavan's defence.

On the other side of the Ulster draw, Monaghan beat Tyrone by sixteen points and Armagh had ten points to spare over Down as they progressed to a semi-final clash at Armagh on 4 July. Having beaten the same opposition in the Dr McKenna Cup just weeks earlier, Monaghan were favourites, and, in the words of *The Anglo Celt*, 'were never more confident'. Within minutes of the throw-in, however, it became very obvious that their confidence was badly misplaced. As reported in the *Dundalk Democrat*, 'The Armagh forwards wove circles, squares and diamonds through the defence.'

In a totally one-sided affair, Armagh were easing up when Hughie O'Reilly blew the final whistle with twelve points separating the teams. Once again, John Vallely and Jim McCullough were outstanding for the winners but it was young Alf Murray, a future GAA President, who took most of the plaudits with a brilliant performance.

Such was the impact of Armagh's semi-final victory over Monaghan that even *The Anglo Celt* was, for once, moved to downplay Cavan's prospects of retaining the Ulster title. In the event, the men of Breffni produced one of their finest ever performances, snuffing out the Armagh threat in a 0-13 to 0-3 win at Castleblayney on 25 July. Showing no weak link, they captured their seventh successive provincial crown, securing an All-Ireland semi-final date with Mayo in the process.

In Munster, Kerry were again in dominant form. They blitzed Cork 6-7 to 0-4 in the opening round at Killarney on 13 June. This was despite the fact that they were short five of their original selection. Bill Dillon and Tim Landers were injured while, perhaps because they thought it unnecessary, Dublin-based 'Murt' Kelly and Gearoid Fitzgerald, as well as Mullingar resident Mick

The Cavan team which lost out to Kerry in the 1937 replay. Back (l–r): Rev. Tom Maguire (County Chairman), John Joe O'Reilly, Willie Young, Eugene Finnegan, Dan Kerrigan, Louis Blessing, Paddy Boylan, Paddy Smith, Hugh Smith (County Secretary); front (l–r): Vincent White, Packy Devlin, 'Big' Tom O'Reilly, Jim Smith, Mick Dinneny, Dónal Morgan, M.J. 'Sonny' Magee, Jack Smallhorne.

Ferriter, did not travel. Notwithstanding the scoreline, the match report in the following morning's *Cork Examiner* was at pains to point out that this 'did not reflect the merit of the Cork team's play.'

Tipperary, who had earlier edged out Waterford by two points, provided Kerry's opposition in the provincial semi-final at Mitchelstown on 11 July. A goal in the opening minutes by Mick Ferriter set the tone for what turned out to be something of a cakewalk, with Kerry cantering home on a score of 2-11 to 0-4.

After what they regarded as a disappointing semi-final draw with Limerick at Kilrush on 13 June, Clare made no fewer than six changes for the replay at Foynes two weeks later. Despite the best efforts of Limerick's Tom Culhane, the Banner County, with George Comerford and Joe Slattery outstanding, finally overcame Limerick's challenge and duly progressed to meet Kerry in the Munster Final.

Not for the first time, the provincial final, played at Limerick on 18 July, proved to be a total mismatch. A whirlwind start saw Kerry take an unassailable 2-7 to 0-0 lead into the break. From there, they sauntered through the second half, finally retaining their Munster crown on a score of 4-9 to 1-1.

The Leinster Championship of 1937 provided more than its quota of drawn matches. Wexford, Louth and Laois all needed two games before overcoming Carlow, Dublin and Offaly respectively.

In a tense clash quarter-final at Newbridge on 16 May, Offaly staged a late comeback as Harry Burke struck a point to snatch a draw with reigning champions Laois. This game marked the inter-county debut of sixteen-year-old 'Boy Wonder' Tommy Murphy, one of Gaelic football's all-time greats. In the replay at Athy two weeks later, the Offaly men, powered by Dick 'Boiler' Conroy and Joe O'Connor, were on the cusp of a famous victory with only two minutes remaining. Laois then pounced with two goals from Tom Keogh and Syd Harkins, paving the way for a semi-final clash with Kildare. This produced another victory for Laois on a 2-10 to 2-7 scoreline. *The Nationalist and Leinster Times* credited an outstanding display from 'the Boy Wonder' and John McDarby's 'cat among the pigeons' role for Laois's victory.

The big talking point on the other side of the Leinster draw was the clash between Dublin and Louth. The teams drew at Navan on 23 May when, with Dublin leading by a point, their full-back, Cork native Gerry O'Leary, was allegedly fouled at least three times as he tried to battle his way out of defence. When the referee eventually blew his whistle, he astounded all and sundry by awarding a free to Louth. With 'Skinner' Caffrey taking full advantage, the game duly went to a replay where, with a different referee, Louth emerged as four-point winners. In the semi-final, Louth trailed Wexford for forty-five minutes of the game, but a snap goal from Jimmy Coyle reversed their fortunes as they qualified for the Leinster Final.

In its Leinster Final report on the morning of 26 July, *The Irish Press* noted that expectations of a close struggle between Laois and Louth were 'far from realised'. In what it described as a 'Delaney day out', Jack, Bill, Chris and Mick all excelled, while 'Uncle Tom played a fine game at full-back'. If there was one note of concern in Laois's comprehensive 0-12 to 0-4 victory over the Wee County, it was the inordinate number of wides they chalked up over the hour.

Kerry and Laois met at Cork on 15 August when the game ended in a draw. With Laois hitting fourteen wides to Kerry's five, the star of the show was, once again, Graiguecullen teenager Tommy Murphy. Despite their superiority in the general run of play, Laois needed a last-minute point from Danny Douglas to force a replay. The teams met again at Waterford on 30 August where, yet again, Laois dominated for much of the game. However, it was the wily Kerrymen, with Ballylongford's Johnny Walsh in devastating form, who snatched victory with a late point from Mikey Lyne. Continuing the pattern of earlier matches, Laois were left to rue their inability to convert their scoring chances – this time they hit sixteen wides to Kerry's six!

With building work in Croke Park stalled because of a labour strike, the Cavan–Mayo semi-final was played before a packed house of 26,000 at Mullingar. The men of Breffni played second fiddle to champions Mayo for much of the game, but when brothers Tom and John Joe O'Reilly finally got into their stride, there was a complete reversal of fortunes. Late goals from 'Sonny' Magee and Louis Blessing gave Cavan a narrow 2-5 to 1-7 victory.

THE FINAL – 26 SEPTEMBER

Over the years, the All-Ireland football final has provided more than its share of high drama. The interventions of such as Edwin Carolan (1952), Mike Sheehy (1978), Seamus Darby (1982) and Stephen Cluxton (2011) have contributed hugely to the rich history of GAA folklore. The drawn final of 1937 ranks with these among the most dramatic in the annals of the game.

While the official attendance was 52,325, ground staff and gardaí removed the turnstiles forty minutes before the throw-in 'when confronted by a surging mass of people'. At least another 10,000 swarmed into the already packed stadium to witness an enthralling contest between the two best teams in the land.

John Joe Landers struck for two goals early in the game and Kerry held their advantage until the closing stages when Paddy Boylan netted for Cavan. The exchanges were frantic in the final minutes and the stadium erupted when Boylan manoeuvred the ball over the Kerry crossbar. With the scoreboard obscured by the milling crowd and the radio commentary announcing a Cavan point, half the nation was unaware that the referee had signalled a free to Kerry because Boylan had thrown the ball. It was only on returning home several hours later that many Cavan supporters, who hadn't waited to see the Cup presentation, discovered that their celebrations were premature. The match had ended in a draw.

Aside from the confusion and drama when the final whistle blew, the game was widely regarded as one of the greatest contests ever, with the standard of play of the highest order. Cavan captain Tom O'Reilly was outstanding, while on the Kerry side, it was his immediate opponent, Charlie O'Sullivan, who received top billing. Bill Myers was said to have played the game of his life in the Kerry defence while in attack the Landers brothers were up to their usual wizardry. Apart from O'Reilly, Drumkilly's Paddy Smith and goal scorer Boylan were others who came in for extra plaudits on a day when every man was a hero.

THE REPLAY – 17 OCTOBER

As is so often the case, the replay did not live up to the expectation that it would be another epic. Having previously won final replays against Kildare (twice) and Wexford, Kerry maintained this unblemished record with a 4-4 to 1-7 victory on 17 October. The sides were level at half-time and points from Packy Devlin and 'Sonny' Magee appeared to put Cavan in the driving seat. The next fifteen minutes saw Kerry hit 2-3 without reply and while Louis Blessing gave Cavan renewed hope when he netted with five minutes to go, John Joe Landers sealed their fate with a spectacular goal.

The game was a robust encounter and Cavan were handicapped by the loss of four men through injury. Despite the best efforts of Cornafean's Tom O'Reilly, Paddy Smith and Vincent White, they couldn't match the speed and guile of their opponents. Nobody denied Kerry's superiority. With Bill Dillon and Bill Kinnerk starring in defence, Kerry held sway at midfield where Sean Brosnan and Johnny Walsh were in control. Their forwards played with machine-like efficiency, with 'Purty' and 'Roundy' Landers once again to the fore. Perhaps their class was best captured by 'Sideliner' who reported in *The Irish Press*: 'Whether or not the Landers brothers actually invented football, there's certainly not much they don't know about it.'

After what Kerry people regarded as a 'five-year famine', the men from the Kingdom had reclaimed their place at the top of the footballing tree. Never ones to look back, the focus in the county now shifted to their prospects of dominating the game for the foreseeable future.

FINAL STATISTICS – DRAW

	Kerry	Cavan
Full-time:	2-5	1-8
Half-time:	2-0	0-4
Scorers:	J.J. Landers 2-1	P. Boylan 1-0
	T. Landers 0-1	M.J. Magee 0-3
	C. O'Sullivan 0-1	P. Devlin 0-2
	G. Fitzgerald 0-1	J. Smallhorne 0-1
	S. Brosnan 0-1	V. White 0-1
		L. Blessing 0-1
Attendance:	52,325	
Gate Receipts:	£4,730 (€6,006)	
Referee:	Mick Hennessy (Clare)	

FINAL STATISTICS — REPLAY

	Kerry	Cavan
Full-time:	4-4	1-7
Half-time:	1-0	0-3
Scorers:	T. O'Leary 2-0	L. Blessing 1-0
	T. Landers 0-4	M.J. Magee 0-3
	M. Doyle 1-0	P. Devlin 0-2
	J.J. Landers 1-0	V. White 0-2
Attendance:	51,234	
Gate Receipts:	£4,286 (€5,442)	
Referee:	Mick Hennessy (Clare)	

FINAL MISCELLANY

- The Royal Hotel in Howth was Kerry's base for the drawn match. On the weekend of the replay, the team stayed at Ross's Hotel in Dún Laoghaire. They spent the day before the game sightseeing in Glendalough.
- Tadhg Healy was also a member of the Kerry Minor team in 1937.
- Bill Myers, Tadhg Healy and Jimmy 'Gawksie' O'Gorman emulated their fathers (Jack, Con and Thady respectively) who won All-Ireland medals with Kerry in 1903.
- To take account of the extra expense associated with training the teams, the GAA Central Council awarded a grant of £350 (€444) to each of the Cavan and Kerry County Boards.
- Kerry midfielder Paddy Kennedy lined out in the drawn game just four days after the death of his father. On the Sunday before the replay, he suffered a dislocated shoulder playing for his club in a Kerry League match, and so was unavailable to play.
- Based in Bray, Cavan's Dan Kerrigan was on the Wicklow team that won the All-Ireland Junior Championship in 1936.
- From *The Irish Press* of Monday 18 October: 'An argument started in the goalmouth and immediately a Kerry fan jumped from his seat on the sideline, and ran about fifty yards unchallenged across the field to hit Finnegan, the Cavan full-back.'

1937 — THE YEAR THAT WAS

- The Constitution of Ireland (Bunreacht na hÉireann) came into force in 1937.
- Lowney's, Ford Main Dealers based in Clonakilty, boasted a complete range of new models at the West Cork Show on 13 July. A new car could be secured for the princely sum of £5 (€6.35) per month.
- On 27 August 1937, Dublin's first set of automatic traffic lights were brought into operation at the junction of Merrion Square and Clare Street.

- Just days before the drawn game, a group of ten boys and young men from Achill, aged between thirteen and twenty-three, perished when a fire engulfed the shed they were sleeping in at a potato farm in Kirknakillock, Scotland.
- 'We are on you but we cannot see you.' These words, spoken by Amelia Earhart on the morning of 2 July 1937, signalled the end of this extraordinary aviator's bid to fly solo around the world. She was officially declared dead on 5 January 1939.
- In Dublin's St Stephen's Green, a bronze equestrian statue of England's King George II was blown off its pedestal in an explosion on the morning of 13 May. Describing the scene, *The Irish Press* reported that 'the horse's hoof was blown a distance of 350 yards into York Street, where it struck a chimney stack.'

1937 TEAM LINE-OUTS — DRAW

KERRY

1. Dan O'Keeffe
(Kerins O'Rahillys)

2. Bill Kinnerk
(John Mitchels)

3. Joe Keohane
(John Mitchels, also Annascaul and Geraldines, Dublin)

4. Bill Myers
(Dr Crokes)

5. Bill Dillon
(Dingle)

6. Miko Doyle
(Austin Stacks) Capt.

7. Tadhg Healy
(John Mitchels)

8. Paddy Kennedy
(Kerins O'Rahillys, also Annascaul and Geraldines, Dublin)

9. Johnny Walsh
(Ballylongford)

10. Sean Brosnan
(Dingle, also Geraldines, Dublin)

11. Charlie O'Sullivan
(Kerins O'Rahillys, also Camp)

12. Gearoid Fitzgerald
(Sneem, also Geraldines, Dublin)

13. John Joe 'Purty' Landers
(Austin Stacks)

14. Tim O'Donnell
(Garda, also Camp and Dr Crokes)

15. Tim 'Roundy' Landers
(Austin Stacks)

Subs: Sean McCarthy (Knocknagoshel, also Austin Stacks) Played; Tim O'Leary (Killarney Legion); Mick Raymond (Kerins O'Rahillys); Bill Casey (Dingle, also Lispole); Mikey Lyne (Killarney Legion)

Other Panel Members: Michael 'Murt' Kelly (Beaufort, also Geraldines, Dublin); Dan Spring (Kerins O'Rahillys); Mick Ferriter (Ballyferriter); Brendan Reidy (Austin Stacks); Jer Carmody (Moyvane); Tom Murphy (John Mitchels); Con Geaney (Castleisland Desmonds, also John Mitchels); Jimmy 'Gawksie' O'Gorman (Austin Stacks); Michael O'Gorman (John Mitchels)

CAVAN

1. Willie Young
(Cornafean)

2. Eugene Finnegan
(Mountnugent)

3. Jim Smith
(Garda, also Erin's Own, Kells, Meath,
Bailieboro and Virginia)

4. Mick Dinneny
(Cornafean)

5. Bill Carroll
(Bailieboro, also Kingscourt)

6. 'Big' Tom O'Reilly
(Cornafean) Capt.

7. John Joe O'Reilly
(Cornafean, also Curragh, Kildare)

8. Paddy Smith
(Drumkilly, also Mullahoran)

9. James White
(Clanna Gael, Dublin, also Gowna)

10. Dónal Morgan
(Virginia, also Cross)

11. Packy Devlin
(Croghan, also Killeshandra)

12. Vincent White
(Clanna Gael, Dublin, also Gowna)

13. Paddy Boylan
(Cavan Slashers)

14. Louis Blessing
(Cavan Slashers)

15. M.J. 'Sonny' Magee
(Cavan Slashers, Croghan and
Drumlane)

Subs: Jack Smallhorne (Mountnugent, also Crosserlough) Played; Dan Kerrigan (Arva, also Bray Emmets, Wicklow) Played; Hugh Paddy O'Reilly (Gowna, also Clanna Gael, Dublin); Paddy McNamee (Virginia, also Cross and Lisnabuntry); 'Small' Tom O'Reilly (Mullahoran)

Other Panel Members: Packy Phair (Cornafean); Joe Mitchell (Bailieboro); Brendan Scanlon (Gowna); Michael Cully (Cornafean)

1937 TEAM LINE-OUTS – REPLAY

KERRY (WINNERS)

1. Dan O'Keeffe
(Kerins O'Rahillys)

2. Bill Kinnerk
(John Mitchels)

3. Joe Keohane
(John Mitchels, also Geraldines,
Dublin)

4. Bill Myers
(Dr Crokes)

5. Tim O'Donnell
(Camp, also Garda)

6. Bill Dillon
(Dingle)

7. Tadhg Healy
(John Mitchels)

8. Sean Brosnan
(Dingle)

9. Johnny Walsh
(Ballylongford)

10. Jackie Flavin
(Moyvane, also Wolfe Tones, Galway)

11. Charlie O'Sullivan
(Kerins O'Rahillys, also Camp)

12. Tim 'Roundy' Landers
(Austin Stacks)

13. John Joe 'Purty' Landers
(Austin Stacks)

14. Miko Doyle
(Austin Stacks) Capt.

15. Tim O'Leary
(Killarney Legion)

Subs: Tom 'Gega' O'Connor (Dingle) Played; Bill Casey (Dingle, also Lispole); Mick Raymond (Kerins O'Rahillys); Sean McCarthy (Knocknagoshel, also Austin Stacks); Eddie Walsh (Knocknagoshel); Paddy O'Brien (Kerins O'Rahillys).

Paddy Kennedy (Kerins O'Rahillys, also Annascaul and Geraldines, Dublin) was unavailable for selection because of injury.

Other Panel Members: Brendan Reidy (Austin Stacks); Con Geaney (Castleisland Desmonds, also John Mitchels); Michael 'Murt' Kelly (Beaufort, also Geraldines, Dublin); Gearoid Fitzgerald (Sneem, also Geraldines, Dublin); Dan Spring (Kerins O'Rahillys); Mick Ferriter (Ballyferriter)

CAVAN (RUNNERS-UP)

1. Willie Young
(Cornafean)

2. Eugene Finnegan
(Mountnugent)

3. Jim Smith
(Garda, also Erin's Own, Kells, Meath, Bailieboro and Virginia)

4. Mick Dinneny
(Cornafean)

5. Dan Kerrigan
(Arva, also Bray Emmets, Wicklow)

6. 'Big' Tom O'Reilly
(Cornafean) Capt.

7. John Joe O'Reilly
(Cornafean, also Curragh, Kildare)

8. Paddy Smith
(Drumkilly)

9. Vincent White
(Clanna Gael, Dublin, also Gowna)

10. Dónal Morgan
(Virginia, also Cross)

11. Packy Devlin
(Croghan, also Killeshandra)

12. Jack Smallhorne
(Mountnugent, also Crosserlough)

13. Paddy Boylan
(Cavan Slashers)

14. Louis Blessing
(Cavan Slashers)

15. M.J. 'Sonny' Magee
(Cavan Slashers, also Croghan and Drumlane)

Subs: 'Small' Tom O'Reilly (Mullahoran) Played; James White (Clanna Gael, Dublin, also Gowna) Played; Bill Carroll (Bailieboro, also Kingscourt) Played; Joe Mitchell (Bailieboro) Played; Hugh Paddy O'Reilly (Gowna, also Clanna Gael, Dublin)

Other Panel Members: Brendan Scanlon (Gowna); Paddy McNamee (Virginia, also Cross and Lisnabuntry); Packy Phair (Cornafean)

1938

With Kerry re-emerging, after a gap of five years, to take the 1937 title, there was more reason than ever for other counties to fear another period of dominance by the men from the south-west. Although they had to endure some close calls during the 1937 campaign, they had reached the summit with a very young team. The starting line-out in their victory over Cavan had no fewer than nine final debutants, suggesting that they were likely to be a serious force for years to come.

In the first round of the Munster Championship at Ennis on 29 May, the men from the Kingdom overwhelmed Clare (2-6 to 0-1), despite being short five first-choice players. Tipperary put up a more spirited effort in the semi-final but ultimately went down by six points.

After a hard-earned semi-final win over Limerick, it was Cork who progressed to face the Munster champions at Clonakilty on 7 August. In the build-up to this game, the local urban district council arranged a special reception for the Kerry team. A formal citation read: 'Occasions such as this contribute to unite us more closely in friendship and goodwill and to foster and kindle a better spirit in our people'.

Kerry responded to this generous welcome by going on the rampage and crushing the home team, 4-14 to 0-6. While Cork simply couldn't handle the skill, craft and power of their opponents, the GAA correspondent for *The Kerryman* was not convinced of the merit of this win against what he termed Cork's 'atrociously bad football'.

The All-Ireland semi-final pairings for 1938 were, for the first time, determined on the three-year rotation basis, which was in place until 2022. The inaugural pairings were Munster–Leinster and Connacht–Ulster. This meant that as Kerry strolled to yet another Munster title, they were keeping a watchful eye on developments in Leinster. The principal contenders there were Laois, aiming for their third successive provincial title, and the traditional kingpins, Kildare and Dublin. The latter two met in the quarter-final at Portlaoise on 29 May, with Kildare winning 4-7 to 3-5. While there was nothing extraordinary about this scoreline, the Lilywhites had held a sixteen-point advantage before Dublin launched a dramatic comeback. In the end, it was former Dublin and Clare great, Garda George Comerford, who steadied the Kildare ship as they progressed to a semi-final clash with Offaly.

Offaly had come through the earlier rounds with victories over Wexford (in a replay) and Longford. They were very fortunate to take the spoils against Longford. At a critical moment in the game, and after much soul-searching by the referee and his officials, Offaly's outstanding goalkeeper Jack Gibney was eventually adjudged to have prevented the ball from crossing the goal line. A common

thread in Offaly's victories was the terrific play of midfielder Tom O'Connor, a name that would feature prominently in Offaly successes decades later. O'Connor's immediate opponent against Longford was the outstanding Jimmy Hannify from Drumlish, another whose legacy would surface years later, when his son, also Jimmy, was central to Longford's 1960s breakthrough.

The Kildare–Offaly provincial semi-final at Carlow on 24 July opened in line with the general expectation that it would be a close affair. Offaly closed Kildare's two-point half-time advantage within minutes of the restart and an expectant crowd looked forward to a ding-dong battle to the end. Injury to Kildare's midfielder Christy Higgins saw Bob Martin enter the fray and the Ellistown man went on to dominate proceedings. He initiated attack after attack and, with the Kildare forward machine finding its rhythm, the Lilywhites powered to victory on a score of 4-8 to 0-6.

The other side of the Leinster draw also involved a replay, this time between Carlow and Wicklow. Thanks mainly to the wizardry of Tom 'Drakes' Walker, Carlow romped to a fourteen-point victory in the replay, so qualifying for a quarter-final joust with Meath at Croke Park on 3 July. Here, it was the better-balanced Meath who prevailed, 4-4 to 2-7, with Joe Loughran, Tony Donnelly and Ted Meade in outstanding form.

Fresh from their early summer sojourn in New York, Laois overcame Louth, 2-5 to 2-2, in their quarter-final clash at Croke Park on 3 July. In what was lauded as one of the best games in years, Jimmy Coyle was the inspiration as the Wee County looked like springing the shock of the year. With Louth in some disarray when ace forward Pat 'Babby' Byrne suffered an injury late in the game, brothers Bill and Jack Delaney combined to snatch a late victory for the Laois men.

The end of the championship road again looked in sight for Laois when they trailed a rampant Meath in the dying minutes of their 10 July semi-final clash. The simple ploy of moving Tommy Murphy was all that was needed, however, as the Graiguecullen teenager proceeded to engineer a Laois scoring spree which yielded 3-3 and brought the county to its third successive Leinster Final.

A panoramic view of the newly refurbished Croke Park prior to the throw-in for the Galway v Kerry Final (drawn match) of 1938. *Courtesy Gaelic Art.*

There were no heart palpitations for Laois supporters when it came to the provincial showdown with Kildare. A final scoreline of 2-8 to 1-3 hardly did justice to the superiority of the Laois men in what was one of the most disappointing Leinster Finals in years.

Unsurprisingly, there was yet another two-horse race between Mayo and Galway for provincial honours in Connacht. While Mayo had continued their monopoly of the National League with a fifth successive title, the general view was that they were showing signs of decline. Against that, Galway had shown steady improvement and the arrival of Clare's John Burke, as well as Kerry All-Ireland winner Jackie Flavin, strengthened the team considerably.

In the semi-final at Tuam on 19 June, Galway had eleven points to spare over Sligo but, according to *The Tuam Herald*, they were 'far from impressive'. One notable feature, however, was the performance of Corofin's Mickey Mannion. According to the *Irish Independent*: 'For the spectacular, the spotlight was taken by Mickey Mannion. This diminutive "bundle of tricks", by his safe handling and lightning acceleration, left the Sligo defenders bewildered at times.'

Mayo were aiming for their fourth title in a row when they faced Galway in the provincial final at Roscommon on 17 July. Before a crowd of 20,000, they seemed all set for victory after a dominant first-half display which saw them two points to the good at the break. However, as John Burke and 'Tull' Dunne proceeded to dominate the midfield exchanges, the Galway men got the upper hand. As described by the *Irish Independent*: 'Dunne drove ball after ball to the Mayo lines and as the pace grew hot the Mayo defenders wilted under a barrage that brought a succession of points.'

On a three-point winning margin, Galway were back in an All-Ireland semi-final, with high hopes that they could repeat their 1934 success.

The early rounds of the Ulster Championship produced what were regarded as entirely predictable results. Cavan and Armagh had easy wins over Fermanagh and Antrim respectively, so qualifying to meet in the semi-final at Armagh on 17 July. Provincial champions since 1931, Cavan were expected to negotiate this 'routine' hurdle with ease. Instead, they were, in the words of *The Irish Press*, 'out-manoeuvred by the strongest combination Armagh has ever produced'.

The foundation for this success was a watertight defence in which Joe Houlihan, Eddie McMahon and Eddie McLoughlin were outstanding.

The second of the Ulster semi-finals almost provided an even bigger shock, Monaghan escaping with a one-point victory over Donegal at Carndonagh.

Installed as match favourites for the final, Armagh were attempting to bridge a gap going back to 1902 since their last provincial success. When they lined out at home to Monaghan on 31 July, they opened well and held a deserved three-point half-time advantage. A second-half collapse saw them fail to raise a single flag as they went down on a score of 2-5 to 2-2. The *Irish Independent* captured the mood of the disappointed home supporters with the headline: 'Only The Twin Spires Of Armagh Cathedral Remained Unmoved.'

With construction of the Cusack Stand in Croke Park not yet completed, the first of the All-Ireland semi-finals, between Galway and Monaghan, took place at Mullingar on 14 August. This game was destined to go down in GAA history, regardless of what transpired on the pitch. It marked the first day of the distinguished broadcasting career of eighteen-year-old schoolboy Michael O'Hehir, who would go on to become 'the voice of the GAA' for decades to come. The game itself was a one-sided affair. With John Burke lording it at midfield, Galway held the upper hand throughout and had an easy 2-10 to 2-3 victory.

A week later, Croke Park hosted the second successive All-Ireland semi-final meeting between Kerry and Laois. This coincided with the official opening of the Cusack Stand, an occasion celebrated with much pomp by the great and the good of the political, religious and GAA fraternities.

In front of a record semi-final attendance, Laois started impressively. Playing against a stiff breeze, they were on level terms at the break and Kerry looked to be in real trouble. Play had hardly resumed when both Charlie O'Sullivan and 'Murt' Kelly struck goals for Kerry, giving Laois a mountain to climb. They responded magnificently, with Tom Delaney, Tommy Murphy and Dick Scully very much to the fore in this nail-biting struggle from which Kerry emerged with a two-point victory.

THE FINAL – 25 SEPTEMBER

Kerry and Galway clashed in an All-Ireland Final for the first time. The enthusiasm for this novel pairing was such that the increased capacity of the redeveloped Croke Park was tested to the limits. The previous record attendance (just over 52,000) was demolished when 68,950 passed through the turnstiles on 25 September. Over thirty bands applied to have the privilege of providing the match-day entertainment, and an early task of the Central Council was to whittle this down to four, one from each province.

The match, played under a broiling sun, was a classic. Describing it as 'an hour brim-full of soul-searching thrills and throbs', the *Irish Independent* adjudged the last five minutes to be 'the greatest minutes of the greatest football final ever played in Croke Park'.

For the second consecutive year, the final ended in a draw – Kerry 2-6, Galway 3-3. The Galway goals came from Brendan Nestor, Ned Mulholland and Ralph Griffin, while 'Purty' Landers and Tim O'Leary found the net for Kerry. There was controversy at the end of the game when the referee ruled that a point by Landers was struck after the final whistle had sounded.

THE REPLAY – 23 OCTOBER

Prior to 1938, there had been four drawn finals. Kerry had not alone played in each of these but had won all four replays. Most commentators at the time argued that this great replay tradition did not augur well for Galway's prospects.

When the sides met again, four weeks after the drawn encounter, the standard of play did not reach the same dizzy heights. The drama, however, was even more intense. A goal by Ralph Griffin and another from a deflected John Burke free put Galway in the ascendancy. As the game entered the dying minutes, and with the Tribesmen holding a four-point lead, referee Peter Waters signalled a free for Kerry. Before it could be taken, there was a pitch invasion by a mass of Galway supporters who mistakenly thought the final whistle had sounded. In the ensuing confusion many of the Kerry players, taking their cue from the crowd, left for the dressing-rooms. By the time a semblance of order was restored, some six minutes later, the game had restarted, but without a significant contingent of Kerry players, who were by now heading for the team hotel. They finished the game having used a total of nine substitutes, two of whom (Joe Keohane and 'Murt' Kelly), were not on the official list.

When the game finally ended, the Galway men had held on to win by three points, with the score at 2-4 to 0-7. The key to their success was the ability to convert the chances which came their way. With Brendan Nestor to the fore in attack, Mick Connaire and Bobby Beggs were outstanding in the centre of their defence. It was a particularly sweet win for Skerries man Beggs, a member of the Dublin side which lost the 1934 Final to Galway. Kerry, for whom Sean Brosnan was outstanding, were severely handicapped when midfielder Johnny Walsh had to retire with a dislocated shoulder. According to *The Irish Press* of 24 October, they had at least three-quarters of the play but they were incapable of translating this into superiority on the scoreboard. Much of the post-match comment focused on the fact that they had lost a replayed final for the first time, and questions were being asked as to whether the sun had finally set on their footballing dominance. It wouldn't take long to have these questions answered.

FINAL STATISTICS – DRAW

	Galway	Kerry
Full-time:	3-3	2-6
Half-time:	1-5	1-2

Scorers:	B. Nestor 1-1	T. O'Leary 1-1
	N. Mulholland 1-0	J.J. Landers 1-0
	R. Griffin 1-0	M. Doyle 0-2
	J. Flavin 0-1	P. Kennedy 0-2
	M. Kelly 0-1	T. McAuliffe 0-1
Attendance:	68,950	
Gate Receipts:	£6,166 (€7,829)	
Referee:	Tom Culhane (Limerick)	

FINAL STATISTICS — REPLAY

	Galway	Kerry
Full-time:	2-4	0-7
Half-time:	1-3	0-4
Scorers:	B. Nestor 0-4 (0-2 frees)	M. Doyle 0-3
	R. Griffin 1-0	S. Brosnan 0-3 (0-2 frees)
	J. Burke 1-0 (free)	C. O'Sullivan 0-1
Attendance:	47,581	
Gate Receipts:	£4,297 (€5,456)	
Referee:	Peter Waters (Kildare)	

FINAL MISCELLANY

- Kerry's Miko Doyle was unable to travel for the semi-final clash with Laois. He was suffering from a swollen face following the extraction of teeth.
- Although Mayo beat Galway in their National Football League encounter in early 1938, they subsequently forfeited the points because they fielded an 'illegal player'. George Ormsby was suspended for having earlier attended a soccer match in Sligo. An appeal to the GAA Central Council was lost, notwithstanding the fact that Ormsby was at the game while on duty as a member of An Garda Síochána.
- As both Roscommon and Leitrim opted out of senior competition, the Connacht championship of 1938 comprised exactly TWO games: Galway v Sligo and Galway v Mayo.
- Jackie Flavin won his second All-Ireland in a row in 1938 – the previous year he had lined out for his native Kerry in their victory over Cavan.
- When Donegal were pipped by Monaghan at Carndonagh on 10 July, it's doubtful that their supporters were hugely consoled by their Ulster Hurling Championship success in the curtain-raiser. They 'edged out' Cavan on a score of 8-3 to 0-0.
- Galway captain John 'Tull' Dunne became the county's football secretary in 1938. He would go on to hold this position for over forty years, during which time he also served on the Connacht Council and the GAA Central Council. He was coach and selector with many of Galway's

football successes. He also made time for a career as a top-flight referee and was in charge of the 1945 All-Ireland Final.

1938 – THE YEAR THAT WAS

- Within months of his inauguration as Ireland's first president, Douglas Hyde attended an international soccer match between Ireland and Poland. Following in the footsteps of George Ormsby, he duly fell foul of the ban on 'foreign games' and was promptly removed from his position as Patron of the GAA.
- On 12 March, and in defiance of the Treaty of Versailles, Austria was annexed by Germany.
- The ballpoint pen was invented by Laszlo Jozsef Biro in 1938.
- At the Catholic Truth Society Conference held at the Mansion House in Dublin on 22 June, the Bishop of Galway, Most Rev. Dr Browne, made a strong plea for more marriages. He condemned the attitude that marriage was a dangerous undertaking, only to be faced if one had ample income. He went on to assert that: 'In many so-called Catholic schools, education was concentrated on getting a girl a job, while it ignored the really serious and honourable work of her life, which was motherhood.'

1938 TEAM LINE-OUTS – DRAW

GALWAY

1. Jimmy McGauran
(Kilmore, Roscommon, also UCG and Wolfe Tones)

2. Mick Raftery
(Balla, Mayo, also UCG)

3. Mick Connaire
(St Grellan's, also Beann Eadair, and Sean McDermotts, Dublin)

4. Dinny Sullivan
(Oughterard, also UCG and Wolfe Tones)

5. Frank Cunniffe
(St Grellan's, also Beann Eadair, Dublin)

6. Bobby Beggs
(Wolfe Tones, also Skerries Harps, St Joseph's and Sean McDermotts Dublin)

7. Charlie Connolly
(Ballinasloe Mental Hospital, also St Grellan's and Tarmon, Roscommon)

8. John 'Tull' Dunne
(St Grellan's) Capt.

9. John Burke
(An Chéad Cath, also Labasheeda, Clare)

10. Jackie Flavin
(Wolfe Tones, also Moyvane, Kerry)

11. Ralph Griffin
(St Grellan's, also Ahascragh and Kickhams, Dublin)

12. Mick Higgins
(Wolfe Tones, also Kilkerrin Clonberne and UCG)

13. Ned Mulholland
(Wolfe Tones, also Kinnegad, Westmeath)

14. Martin Kelly
(Ahascragh, also Ardagh, Limerick)

15. Brendan Nestor
(Dunmore MacHales, also Geraldines and Erin's Hope, Dublin)

Subs: Mick Ryder (Tuam Stars); 'Small' Pat McDonagh (St Grellan's, also Tuam Stars and Kilconly); Mickey Mannion (Corofin); Eugene O'Sullivan (UCG); Paddy Kennedy (Ahascragh, also St Grellan's); John 'Connie' O'Connor (An Chéad Cath, also Dingle, Kerry); Jack Greaney (Dunmore MacHales); Johnny Casey (St Grellan's); Charlie Sullivan (Oughterard); Paddy Mitchell (Corofin)

KERRY

1. Dan O'Keeffe
(Kerins O'Rahillys)

2. Bill Kinnerk
(John Mitchels) Capt.

3. Joe Keohane
(John Mitchels, also Geraldines, Dublin)

4. Bill Myers
(Dr Crokes)

5. Bill Dillon
(Dingle)

6. Bill Casey
(Dingle, also Lispole)

7. Tom 'Gega' O'Connor
(Dingle)

8. Johnny Walsh
(Ballylongford)

9. Sean Brosnan
(Dingle, also Geraldines, Dublin)

10. Paddy Kennedy
(Kerins O'Rahillys, also Annascaul and Geraldines, Dublin)

11. Charlie O'Sullivan
(Kerins O'Rahillys, also Camp)

12. Tony McAuliffe
(Listowel Emmets)

13. John Joe 'Purty' Landers
(Austin Stacks)

14. Miko Doyle
(Austin Stacks)

15. Tim O'Leary
(Killarney Legion)

Subs: Bob Murphy (Moyvane); Eddie Walsh (Knocknagoshel); Mick Raymond (Kerins O'Rahillys); Michael 'Murt' Kelly (Beaufort, also Geraldines, Dublin); Ger Teahan (Kerins O'Rahillys, also Laune Rangers and Dingle); Martin 'Bracker' O'Regan (Austin Stacks); Paddy 'Bawn' Brosnan (Dingle)

1938 TEAM LINE-OUTS – REPLAY

GALWAY (WINNERS)

1. Jimmy McGauran
(Kilmore, Roscommon, also UCG and Wolfe Tones)

2. Mick Raftery
(Balla, Mayo, also UCG)

3. Mick Connaire
(St Grellan's, also Beann Eadair and Sean McDermotts, Dublin)

4. Dinny Sullivan
(Oughterard, also UCG)

5. Frank Cunniffe
(St Grellan's, also Beann Eadair, Dublin)

6. Bobby Beggs
(Wolfe Tones, also Skerries Harps and St Joseph's, Dublin)

7. Charlie Connolly
(Ballinasloe Mental Hospital, also St Grellan's and Tarmon, Roscommon)

8. John Burke
(An Chéad Cath, also Labasheeda, Clare)

9. John 'Tull' Dunne
(St Grellan's) Capt.

10. Jackie Flavin
(Wolfe Tones, also Moyvane, Kerry)

11. Ralph Griffin
(St Grellan's, also Ahascragh and Kickhams, Dublin)

12. Mick Higgins
(Wolfe Tones, also Kilkerrin Clonberne and UCG)

13. Ned Mulholland
(Wolfe Tones, also Kinnegad, Westmeath)

14. Martin Kelly
(Ahascragh, also Ardagh, Limerick)

15. Brendan Nestor
(Dunmore MacHales, also Geraldines and Erin's Hope, Dublin)

Subs: Mick Ryder (Tuam Stars) Played; 'Small' Pat McDonagh (St Grellan's, also Tuam Stars and Kilconly) Played; Mickey Mannion (Corofin); Eugene O'Sullivan (UCG); Paddy Kennedy (Ahascragh, also St Grellan's); John 'Connie' O'Connor (An Chéad Cath, also Dingle); Jack Greaney (Dunmore MacHales); Johnny Casey (St Grellan's); Paddy Mitchell (Corofin); Charlie Sullivan (Oughterard)

KERRY (RUNNERS-UP)

1. Dan O'Keeffe
(Kerins O'Rahillys)

2. Bill Kinnerk
(John Mitchels) Capt.

3. Paddy 'Bawn' Brosnan
(Dingle)

4. Bill Myers
(Dr Crokes)

5. Bill Dillon
(Dingle)

6. Bill Casey
(Dingle, also Lispole)

7. Tom 'Gega' O'Connor
(Dingle)

8. Johnny Walsh
(Ballylongford)

9. Sean Brosnan
(Dingle)

10. Paddy Kennedy
(Kerins O'Rahillys, also Annascaul
and Geraldines, Dublin)

11. Charlie O'Sullivan
(Kerins O'Rahillys, also Camp)

12. Tony McAuliffe
(Listowel Emmets)

13. Martin 'Bracker' O'Regan
(Austin Stacks)

14. Miko Doyle
(Austin Stacks)

15. Tim O'Leary
(Killarney Legion)

Subs: John Joe 'Purty' Landers (Austin Stacks) Played; Joe Keohane (John Mitchels, also Geraldines, Dublin) Played; Michael 'Murt' Kelly (Beaufort, also Geraldines, Dublin) Played; Joe Sheehy (John Mitchels) Played; Eddie Walsh (Knocknagoshel) Played; Ger Teahan (Kerins O'Rahillys, also Laune Rangers and Dingle) Played; Bob Murphy (Moyvane) Played; Con Geaney (John Mitchels, also Castleisland Desmonds) Played; Mick Raymond (Kerins O'Rahillys) Played

1939

As Galway set out on the 1939 campaign with hopes of retaining their All-Ireland crown, there was a widespread view that their greatest challenge would come from within their own province. Their victory over Mayo in 1938 had come as a major surprise and the Mayo men were eager for another tilt at the title-holders. Opinion was divided as to which of the two would prevail, with little confidence that the only remaining contender for provincial honours, Sligo, would make any impression. According to the *Irish Independent*, Sligo 'went into serious training' in advance of their semi-final clash with the Mayo men, so it was a major disappointment when they could only muster 0-2 to Mayo's 2-10 when they met on 25 June.

When the Connacht Final took place at Roscommon on 16 July, a crowd which was estimated by some to be in the order of 25,000 created havoc for the stewards on duty. The start of the game was delayed by thirty minutes and there was ongoing spectator encroachment throughout. The chaos was described in the *Irish Independent* thus: 'It took thirty minutes to get the Connacht Senior Football Final started, and it would have taken the Gardaí, plus the Army, in order that the game could be finished.'

Two brilliant goals from team captain Paddy Moclair set Mayo on their way. With two minutes to go they were completely on top when matters finally came to an abrupt head. *The Irish Press* captured the scene: 'The referee had placed the ball for a free to Galway when four or five thousand people crowded on to the playing pitch, and for an hour or more pandemonium reigned. There were isolated bouts of fisticuffs, wild scampers from end to end of the field, and in fact it was like Bedlam let loose ...'

With the score standing at 2-6 to 0-3 in Mayo's favour, the match was finally abandoned at 7pm. When the Connacht Council formally awarded the game to Mayo the following week, its Chairman, Paddy Kilduff, made the novel suggestion that the Roscommon County Board should in future consider the use of turnstiles, 'even if this meant renting them for the occasion'.

The Munster Championship followed a familiar pattern. Kerry were given a bye into the final while the remaining counties battled it out for the right to become the proverbial lambs to the slaughter. In the quarter-final at Ennis on 14 May, Clare and Limerick provided plenty of drama when they played out an exciting draw. The replay at Lahinch on 18 June was a complete anticlimax, however, with Clare, inspired by Sean Guinane, emerging as seventeen-point winners. Two weeks later, Clare's run came to a halt when they lost out to Tipperary, earlier winners over Cork, at Limerick. The key to this success for the Premier County was another outstanding performance by netminder Jim Williams.

Kerry, All-Ireland champions, 1939. *Image courtesy of the GAA Museum at Croke Park.*

As was widely expected, Kerry had no difficulty in beating Tipperary in the final and so took their fourth successive provincial title. This was a particularly proud day for reigning county champions, Dingle, home club of an impervious half-back line of Tom 'Gega' O'Connor, Bill Casey and Bill Dillon.

There was a peculiar scoreline in the opening game of the Leinster Championship. At Longford on 14 May, the home team scored an impressive tally of 0-17, edging out neighbours Westmeath, who scored 4-4, by a single point. Having taken an early eight-point lead Longford were fortunate to survive, but it seems they didn't learn much from this experience. In their next game, against Carlow, they allowed a seven-point advantage to slip, before finally escaping with a two-point win. Their luck ran out in their next engagement, however, with 'Sacker' Furlong and 'Locky' Quinn starring in Wexford's narrow win over the midlanders.

Wexford were now through to the semi-final where they faced a confident Louth side, fresh from an impressive four-point win over Dublin. With Paddy Cluskey, Eddie Boyle and Eugene Callan having sparkled against the Metropolitans, Louth were hotly tipped to overcome the Wexford challenge. The Wee County's prospects were not helped by the fact that two of their top men, Callan and Jimmy Coyle, had played for Sean McDermotts in the Croke Park curtain-raiser, the Dublin County Final. At the end of a neck-and-neck struggle, a goal from Gusserane's Tom Somers, with the last kick of the game, swung the result in Wexford's favour, 1-7 to 0-7.

It was a shock when Meath edged out Laois by two points at Mullingar on 4 June. This victory came after Willie O'Brien pounced for a goal in the dying moments. Meath's semi-final opponents were Kildare, who had beaten Offaly 2-11 to 1-1, in a game that saw John Crofton in brilliant form for the Lilywhites.

There was a general sense of bewilderment in the air when the referee blew the final whistle at the end of the Meath–Kildare semi-final clash at Drogheda on 9 July. The *Irish Independent* reported: 'The senior match will be talked about for many moons to come, for at the end of the game the majority of the spectators were just as uncertain as to who had won as they were at the beginning as to who would win.'

The controversy arose when Meath's Jack Cummins fisted the ball into the Kildare net after the referee had blown for an infringement. The umpire didn't raise any flag and the game continued on. It was only on seeing the Meath players being carried shoulder-high from the pitch that the crestfallen Lilywhites realised the goal had been awarded and their championship journey had come to an end. Tony Donnelly was Meath's star player in this 2-10 to 2-8 victory.

Few would have predicted in early summer that Wexford and Meath would grace Croke Park on

Kerry captain Tom 'Gega' O'Connor is chaired off the field following his side's 1939 win over Meath. 'Gega' was appointed captain when his Dingle clubmate, Sean Brosnan, was the victim of a severe bout of flu in the days before the game. *Image courtesy of the GAA Museum at Croke Park.*

Leinster Final day; *The Irish Press* went so far as to say that they had 'wrecked the form book'. While Meath's surprise victories over Laois and Kildare had been impressive, the prevailing view was that Wexford, with their much stronger footballing tradition, would win out.

If the sides failed to deliver a footballing classic when they met at Croke Park on 30 July, there was certainly no shortage of tension and drama. It was tit-for-tat for over three-quarters of the game, but then Meath went on a typical scoring spree, notching four late points to take the spoils on a score of 2-7 to 2-3.

Winning only their second ever Leinster title, and after a gap of forty-four years, this was an epic breakthrough for the Royal County. Celebrations were temporarily subdued, however. Having played the 'game of his life', Tommy 'Boiler' McGuinness was stretchered off, unconscious, only seconds before full-time. Aside from the 'Boiler', Joe Loughran, Tony Donnelly and Mattie Gilsenan were the chief architects of this famous win.

The Ulster Championship saw Cavan steamroll their way to the final, beating Tyrone (4-11 to 1-2) and Donegal (5-12 to 0-4) in the process. Elsewhere, Monaghan needed a last-gasp point from John Loughman to escape with a draw in their semi-final clash with Armagh. Inspired by Jim McCullough, Armagh made no mistake in the replay and ran out easy winners on a score of 1-6 to 0-2.

The crowd that turned up to see Cavan play Armagh in the final in Castleblayney on 6 August was such that newspaper reporters had the unenviable task of describing a game which they couldn't see. Noting the presence of numerous stewards, *The Anglo Celt* bemoaned the fact that these were mostly 'of the ornamental variety'. There were repeated pitch encroachments, and efforts to control the heaving masses were said to resemble 'trying to force the contents of the half-pint into the naggin'.

Fully two and a half hours after the throw-in, and with Cavan holding a two-point lead, there were still fifteen minutes to go. It was just before 7pm when the referee concluded that all prospects of completing the game had evaporated and the match was abandoned.

The rematch was fixed for Croke Park the following Sunday as a curtain-raiser for the Kerry–Mayo semi-final. Leading 1-4 to 0-1 at half-time, Armagh's prospects looked bright, but they failed to register a single score in the second half, eventually losing on a score of 2-3 to 1-4.

The first of the All-Ireland semi-finals, between Kerry and Mayo, was a dour affair and ended level at 0-4 each. Claiming that their players had been 'disabled in bunches', the Mayo County Board threatened not to field for the replay. In the event, the sides met for a second time on 10 September when early goals by Dan Spring and Charlie O'Sullivan set the tone for an emphatic 3-8 to 1-4 Kerry victory.

The second semi-final saw Meath overwhelm Cavan, 1-9 to 1-1. This was a brilliant all-action team performance which left the Cavan men floundering from the word go. *The Irish Press*, having already adjudged Tommy McGuinness's Leinster Final display as his greatest ever, decreed that the Boiler's latest performance had surpassed even that.

THE FINAL – 24 SEPTEMBER

In the early weeks of September 1939, the eyes of the world were fixed firmly on the outbreak of war in Europe. Locally, however, it was the first-time championship clash of Kerry and Meath that grabbed the attention of the nation. Kerry were installed as hot favourites to regain the title, but the commentary in the media in the lead-up to the game suggests there was no hint of an inferiority complex among Meath's GAA fraternity.

Apart from their outstanding tradition, Kerry's tag as favourites was also based on their perceived superiority in the physical stakes. Perhaps this was best encapsulated by the fact that their full-back line had an average height of just under 6'2", while the opposing Meath full-forward line averaged 5'8". The semi-final replay with Mayo had given Kerry the chance the settle on their best fifteen, while Meath felt it necessary to make three changes to the team that had beaten Cavan.

In order to avoid a clash of colours, Kerry took the field in the red and white of county champions Dingle. Their prospects took a major blow when their captain, Sean Brosnan, cried off because of illness. His place on the team was taken by the experienced 'Murt' Kelly, while 'Gega' O'Connor took over the captaincy. An early point by Kelly was followed by a Dan Spring goal and Kerry seemed to be on their way. However, Meath eventually settled down, and with 'Boiler' McGuinness and Christy O'Reilly to the fore, they fought back to level the scoring by half-time. Their captain, Mattie Gilsenan, hit a brilliant goal after racing through the Kerry defence just before the break.

On the resumption, Kerry again took the initiative and they held a five-point lead after Spring scored a goal and a point in quick succession. Were it not for the brilliance of Hughie McEnroe in the Meath goals, Spring would have achieved the rare feat of scoring an All-Ireland hat-trick. The teams slugged it out for the remainder of the game, with frees being awarded by the minute. Meath closed the gap when Jim Clarke hit a great goal past O'Keeffe. In a helter-skelter finish, Joe Keohane cut off a last-minute Meath attack to save the day for Kerry.

The modern formality of presenting a man-of-the-match award was a long way off in 1939. There is little doubt, however, that if such an award were in vogue at the time, then Dan Spring would have been its recipient. He was a constant thorn in the side of the Meath defence and his 2-2 from play was a huge contribution in such a low-scoring era. Elsewhere, Kerry's half-back line of Dillon, Casey and Walsh was outstanding while their midfield pairing of Paddy Kennedy and 'Gega' O'Connor held sway for much of the hour.

Christy O'Reilly was widely regarded as Meath's best performer on the day. McEnroe, McGuinness and the Donnelly brothers were also superb, while Mattie Gilsenan led from the front and brought them back into contention with his spectacular goal.

Kerry's 1939 victory brought them to within two of Dublin in the All-Ireland roll of honour and the consensus was that they wouldn't be waiting too long to finally close the gap completely.

FINAL STATISTICS

	Kerry	Meath
Full-time:	2-5	2-3
Half-time:	1-2	1-2
Scorers:	D. Spring 2-2	M. Gilsenan 1-0
	M. Kelly 0-2	J. Clarke 1-0
	T. Landers 0-1 (0-1 free)	T. Donnelly 0-3 (0-3 frees)
Attendance:	46,828	
Gate Receipts:	£3,726-4-2 (€4,731)	
Referee:	Jimmy Flaherty (Offaly)	

FINAL MISCELLANY

- Giving an account of the traffic going through Navan on the day of the 1939 Final, the *Meath Chronicle* reported: 'Twenty-six buses passed through the Square in Navan on the way to the match between 10 o'clock and 1.15 p.m. on Sunday. Between the same hours, 214 motor cars passed and eleven motor cycles. Thousands made the journey on push bicycles and we saw two well-known members of Bohermeen C.C. on a tandem.'
- Under the heading 'An Inspiring Scene', the *Chronicle* also reported that, before departing from Randalstown that morning, each member of the Meath team blessed himself with holy water provided by Mrs Daly who was in charge of catering.
- When the abandoned Ulster Final between Cavan and Armagh was replayed in Croke Park on 13 August, the GAA Central Council awarded a compensation grant of £400 (€508) to the Ulster Council.
- In its wisdom, *The Irish Times* commissioned poet Patrick Kavanagh to write a feature article to capture the atmosphere of Ireland's most popular sporting event. For the princely fee of one guinea (€1.33), Kavanagh treated readers to a novel, and occasionally comical, description of events. He commented: 'Some of the emblems worn show originality, but generally they denote a lack of aesthetic sensibility in the followers of the GAA. Cheap, tawdry and vulgar. I saw a fellow wearing on his lapel a red and white doll that would be of school-going age if it was flesh and blood.'
- On the day of the final, the Galway Senior Hurling Final was also played, with Castlegar taking the honours against Clarenbridge on a score of 9-1 to 8-2.
- While worldwide attention was focused on Adolf Hitler in September 1939, the Führer was a distant second as a topic of conversation in the village of Carrickshock. All the headlines there were reserved for local hero Jimmy Kelly, who struck Kilkenny's winning point against Cork in the famous 'Thunder and Lightning' Hurling Final.

1939 — THE YEAR THAT WAS

- On 1 September, Germany, having occupied Czechoslovakia and signed pacts with Italy and the USSR, invaded Poland. Two days later, Britain and France declared war on Germany. The deadliest conflict in human history would claim more than 50 million lives over the next six years.
- The Irish government responded swiftly to developments in Europe. Legislation was introduced on 2 September to deal with what was referred to as 'the Emergency'. This provided for a system of rationing and it lasted until 1946. The terms of this legislation contained some interesting features, while the extent to which people went to circumvent its provisions were often extreme:
  - There was a limit of 1 lb (454 grams) of sugar per person per week. (Nowadays, health experts recommend no more than 210 grams per week.)
  - Certain individuals qualified for an increase in the coupon allowance for clothing. For example, a vet qualified for 110% of the basic allowance while actors could claim up to 135% of standard. At the top of this league were expectant mothers and postulants, who could claim 178% of the basic allowance.
  - One resourceful individual got herself into 'hot water' when she received a court fine for serving watered-down turf mould as tea to her unsuspecting customers.
- 1939 saw the release of two of Hollywood's greatest cinema classics, *Gone with the Wind* and *The Wizard of Oz*.
- A popular recommendation for the treatment of a range of ailments was an ointment called 'Zam-Buk'. This versatile concoction was advertised as a quick cure for 'Hard & Soft Corns, Eczema, Pimples (Acne), Impetigo, Rashes, Abscesses, Ulcers, Poisoned Wounds, Bad Legs, Scalp Troubles, Piles, Burns, Scalds, Cuts, Bruises etc.'

1939 TEAM LINE-OUTS

KERRY (WINNERS)

1. Dan O'Keeffe
(Kerins O'Rahillys)

2. Bill Myers
(Dr Crokes)

3. Joe Keohane
(John Mitchels, also Geraldines, Dublin)

4. Tadhg Healy
(John Mitchels)

5. Bill Dillon
(Dingle)

6. Bill Casey
(Dingle, also Lispole)

7. Eddie Walsh
(Knocknagoshel)

8. Paddy Kennedy
(Kerins O'Rahillys, also Geraldines, Dublin and Annascaul)

9. Tom 'Gega' O'Connor
(Dingle) Capt.

10. Jimmy 'Gawksie' O'Gorman
(Austin Stacks)

11. Michael 'Murt' Kelly
(Beaufort, also Geraldines, Dublin)

12. Johnny Walsh
(Ballylongford)

13. Charlie O'Sullivan
(Kerins O'Rahillys, also Camp)

14. Dan Spring
(Kerins O'Rahillys)

15. Tim 'Roundy' Landers
(Austin Stacks)

Subs: Tony McAuliffe (Listowel Emmets); Martin McCarthy (Castleisland Desmonds); Mick Raymond (Kerins O'Rahillys); Johnny Moriarty (Dingle); Jim 'Bawn' Fitzgerald (Kerins O'Rahillys); Martin 'Bracker' O'Regan (Austin Stacks); Mikey Lyne (Killarney Legion)

Chosen to captain the team, Sean Brosnan of Dingle fell victim to flu in the days before the match and was unable to line out.

MEATH (RUNNERS-UP)

1. Hughie McEnroe
(Kells, also Moynalty, Oldcastle and Kilbeg)

2. Paddy Beggan
(Oldcastle)

3. Tommy 'Boiler' McGuinness
(Kilmessan, also Navan Gaels, Navan Parnells and Skryne)

4. Pat 'Red' Donnelly
(Kilmessan, also Skryne)

5. Ted Meade
(Castletown)

6. Christy O'Reilly
(Duleek)

7. Jim Kearney
(Oldcastle)

8. Matt O'Toole
(Skryne)

9. Joe Loughran
(Kilmessan, also Donaghmore)

10. Mattie Gilsenan
(Moynalty) Capt.

11. Tony Donnelly
(Kilmessan, also Skryne and Donaghmore)

12. Jim Clarke
(Duleek)

13. Willie O'Brien
(Duleek)

14. Jack Cummins
(Castletown)

15. Kevin Devin
(Oldcastle)

Subs: Hughie Lynch (Oldcastle) Played; Mark Clinton (Kells) Played; Kevin Johnson (Skryne); Jack Synnott (Donaghmore); Dick Cassidy (Kells); Willie Clynch (Navan Gaels); Bill Halpenny (Syddan); Frank Nulty (Ballinlough); Christy Coleman (Duleek)

1940

The Munster Championship of 1940 started on 19 May, when there were no fewer than three games played. Without the luxury of direct entry into the provincial final, Kerry lined out against Limerick at Glin where they recorded an easy 4-9 to 1-2 quarter-final win. On the same day at Mitchelstown, Tipperary beat Cork 2-7 to 1-5 in the second quarter-final.

The first of the Munster semi-finals, between Waterford and Clare, also took place on 19 May, and this proved to be a classic 'game of two halves'. Waterford looked home and hosed with a 1-5 to 0-0 half-time lead, but with Paddy Begley in outstanding form, Clare fought their way back into the game. A late goal from Paddy Fitzpatrick gave them a replay, but they were no match for the Waterford men when the sides met again on 30 June. Declan Goode was the star as Waterford secured a Munster Final berth with a five-point winning margin.

The second Munster semi-final proved to be something of a cakewalk for Kerry as they overcame Tipperary on a score of 4-8 to 1-5. Despite not having been tested in their opening games, Kerry were overwhelming favourites when they lined out against Waterford in the Munster Final at Walsh Park on 21 July. Against a strong breeze, and facing into the sun, the Kerry men found themselves three points in arrears at the break. It was a different story after the changeover, however, with Sean Brosnan scoring 1-4 and leading the charge as Kerry cruised to a seven-point victory.

In Ulster, champions Cavan almost bit the dust in their quarter-final clash with Antrim at Corrigan Park on 23 June. They led by eleven points at the break but, with George Watterson and Kevin Armstrong in inspirational form for Antrim, they were fortunate to hold out for a draw, 0-12 to 3-3. There was no mistake by the Breffni men in the replay, however, as they romped to a 6-14 to 0-4 victory. Responding to suggestions that Cavan had been overenthusiastic in piling on the scores, *The Anglo Celt* asserted that: 'no relaxation can be condoned'.

Donegal, shock winners over Armagh, provided Cavan's semi-final opposition at Bundoran on 14 July. On a pitch described by *The Anglo Celt* as 'spacious but peculiarly graded', the Cavan men were made to fight every inch of the way before securing the win with a three-point victory. On what was regarded as an emerging force in Gaelic football, Donegal's top men were Hudie Beag Gallagher and Mick Melly.

Trailing 2-2 to 0-1 at half-time, Down's prospects against Monaghan in the second semi-final looked bleak in the extreme. A dramatic second-half turnaround was topped by a late equaliser from Dan McConville, giving the Mourne men home advantage in the replay. Outstanding displays by goalkeeper Jimmy McLoughlin, Tom McCann, Terry McCormack, John McClorey and the Carr brothers from Warrenpoint laid the foundations for a famous Down win, 0-8 to 1-3, and progression into their first ever Ulster Senior Final. It was a day of bitter disappointment for Monaghan, and particularly for Jack Crawley and Vincent Duffy, both of whom were outstanding on the day.

The return to the fold of Brother Michael Lynch, who now joined his Downpatrick clubmate, Brother William O'Boyle, on the team, was seen as a great boost to Down's prospects against Cavan in the provincial final. The verdict on the game was that Down acquitted themselves well, and that a fifteen-point defeat did not accurately reflect the quality of their performance. For all their speed and slick movement, they simply didn't have enough guile and experience to match the scoring platform created by Cavan's midfield powerhouse of John Joe and Tom O'Reilly.

Sligo were on the verge of creating a major shock when they led Mayo by three points with seconds to go in their Connacht semi-final clash on 30 June. They looked to have the game sewn up when they were awarded a close-in free, but this failed to meet the target and the ball was cleared to Mayo's Mick O'Malley who found the net with a rasping shot. Having escaped by the proverbial skin of their teeth, Mayo went on to win the replay two weeks later, largely thanks to a brilliant two-goal performance by Paddy Moclair.

Moclair's absence from the Mayo team in the provincial final was a major body blow, and the experienced Galway side, with Bobby Beggs in commanding form, took full advantage. A man-of-the-match performance by Henry Kenny was not enough to stem the tide, and Galway were full value for their 1-7 to 0-5 victory. The quality of the fare on view can be gauged from the report in the *Irish Independent* which described the game as 'probably the most uninteresting Connacht final ever staged on the Roscommon pitch'.

When Dublin pipped Louth, 1-9 to 2-5, in their Leinster quarter-final clash at Navan on 18 May, the dramatic headline in *The Irish Press* read: 'Dublin's Home-Brew Too Much For Louth'. This was a reference to the county's new, if only temporary, policy of limiting its selection to Dubliners.

The Metropolitans' next outing was a semi-final tilt at Meath who had earlier beaten Longford 3-11 to 1-7. They met at Newbridge on 7 July, where Meath emerged with a six-point victory, but only after a battle that *The Irish Press* labelled as 'little better than a maul'. Describing the conduct of the crowd, it went on: 'They encroached on the pitch, refused to move and whatever little of the game that was not already spoiled by rough tactics and consequent super-abundance of free kicks was pretty effectively wrecked by the fans, who, on occasion, even took part with the players in bouts of fisticuffs.'

On a day when quality football was at a premium, Tony Donnelly and Mattie Gilsenan of Meath and Dublin's Gerry McLoughlin and Peter O'Reilly were the leading lights.

Laois and Offaly had no difficulty in overcoming Wexford and Kildare respectively, to reach the second semi-final in Leinster. When they met at Athy on 14 July, Offaly were quick to seize the initiative. With Joe O'Connor in outstanding form and Bill Mulhall blotting out the threat posed by Tommy Murphy, they were poised to cause a major upset. What the *Irish Independent* termed 'a six minute scoring cyclone' saw Laois clock up 2-4, and a stunned Offaly were out of the championship.

The Leinster Final at Croke Park on 28 July was a very robust affair, with 'a good deal of temper displayed'. After just six minutes of play Laois were six points to the good but, showing greater stamina, Meath began to make inroads on the scoreboard. The dismissal of Bill Delaney (Laois) and Joe Loughran (Meath) seemed to unsettle Laois the most and their lead continued to slip. The Meath men finished with a flurry of unanswered points from Kevin Devin and Tony Donnelly (two), to retain their title on a three-point margin.

The All-Ireland semi-finals were played as a double header at Croke Park on 18 August. For the first of these, between Galway and Meath, the ball was thrown in by John Cusack, son of Michael, one of the founders of the GAA. The game itself was something of an anticlimax, with John Dunne and newcomer Joe Duggan lording it at midfield for Galway as they raced into an early lead. When Meath lost their captain, Tony Donnelly, through injury their prospects took a nosedive. They rallied somewhat in the second half, but a fortuitous goal by John Burke finally settled the issue in Galway's favour.

In the second semi-final, Paddy Smith was the key man as Cavan took the initiative and, in the words of the *Irish Independent*, 'led Kerry a merry dance' until well into the second half. Then Kerry, without reaching their usual standards, forced their way back into the game with two fortuitous goals from 'Gawksie' O'Gorman putting them on the road to a five-point victory.

An interesting footnote to these semi-final clashes was a comment in *The Kerryman* on the eve of the final: 'Galway did some training for the semi-final with Meath. Kerry did none for Cavan. Kerry has never trained for a semi-final (except for Mayo last year).'

THE FINAL – 22 SEPTEMBER

The final of 1940 was one of the most eagerly awaited ever. The clash of Kerry and Galway saw the title-holders of the previous two years pitted against each other. Kerry had an added incentive in that their defeat by Galway in 1938 was their first ever loss in a replayed final. Now was the time to avenge that defeat. Also, victory would bring their title haul to fourteen, and put them level with Dublin on the all-time roll of honour.

With World War II now into its second year, the country was beginning to feel the effects of the petrol restrictions and there was an assumption that this would have a major impact on the attendance. In the event, a crowd of 68,824 turned up, making it the second highest (after 1938) to attend a final.

Heavy overnight rain meant that conditions were far from ideal, with heavy ground and a greasy ball contributing to what *The Irish Press* described as a 'robust, rugged game'. Referee Seamus Bourke of Kildare had a torrid time trying to control the play and awarded a total of sixty-two frees, with the scheduled sixty minutes extending to seventy-three. The unsavoury nature of the exchanges was captured by 'the Recorder' in the *Irish Independent*: 'There was too much holding and pushing of players, and that some were too ready to use their fists revealed a lack of spirit calculated to create a bad impression on the vast majority of the large crowd who would wish to have the game played in a sporting manner without bitterness or rough and unfair tactics which should be foreign to the Gaelic field.'

Right from the throw-in, there were intermittent bouts of fisticuffs. The game was fully sixteen minutes old before 'Gega' O'Connor finally broke the scoring deadlock with a point for Kerry. After Dan Spring added to their tally, Galway began to make inroads and they took the lead when Joe Duggan burst through the Kerry defence to score a magnificent goal.

Galway held a two-point lead (1-2 to 0-3) at half-time and Kerry's cause was not helped when team captain Spring was forced to retire through injury. His replacement, Paddy 'Bawn' Brosnan, was quick to make an impact, scoring a point immediately after his introduction. It was a dour war of attrition for the remainder of the game and the sides were locked on level terms with only seconds to go. This was when Charlie O'Sullivan produced a touch of magic and hit the point that edged Kerry over the line, 0-7 to 1-3.

Amid all the focus on the poor quality of play and the rancour between the teams, there was unanimous praise for the performances of a select few. Galway goalkeeper Jimmy McGauran played brilliantly and his full-back cover of Mick Raftery, Mick Connaire and Dinny Sullivan were magnificent. Elsewhere, Joe Duggan and Brendan Nestor presented a constant threat to Kerry. For the victors, Joe Keohane and Tadhg Healy were outstanding in defence. Others to shine were Eddie Walsh, Charlie O'Sullivan and particularly Sean Brosnan, who lorded proceedings at midfield.

There were many 'inquests' after the 1940 Final, with much criticism of the time taken to complete the match. Among neutrals, the consensus was that victory could have gone either way. Such were the conditions on the day that it would be difficult to predict the prospects of either team for 1941. As it turned out, each would get the chance to set the record straight twelve months later.

FINAL STATISTICS

	Kerry	Galway
Full-time:	0-7	1-3
Half-time:	0-3	1-2
Scorers:	C. O'Sullivan 0-2	J. Duggan 1-0
	M. Kelly 0-2 (0-2 frees)	B. Nestor 0-1 (0-1 free)
	S. Brosnan 0-1	J. Dunne 0-1 (0-1 free)
	T. O'Connor 0-1	J. Burke 0-1
	D. Spring 0-1	
Attendance:	60,824	
Gate Receipts:	£5,226 (€6,652)	
Referee:	Seamus Bourke (Kildare)	

FINAL MISCELLANY

- From *The Kerryman* of Saturday 21 September: 'Mass will be celebrated at 6.00am in St John's Church, Tralee on Sunday, for the benefit of those travelling by the 6.45am train to the All-Ireland.'

- The *Sunday Independent* of 22 September reported that football enthusiasts in New York were so anxious to find out the result that they went to the enormous expense of arranging a transatlantic phone call to Dublin in the minutes after the game.

- *The Cork Examiner* reported on the GAA Central Council meeting of 27 July 1940: 'Requests for a postponement from August 18, owing to the All-Ireland pilgrimage to Knock, of the All-Ireland Senior Football semi-finals fixed for the same date at Croke Park, were turned down with regret at the meeting of the Central Council in Dublin, on Saturday. The Council, however, expressed their willingness, if necessary, to forego the broadcast of the matches.'

- When Geraldines beat Sean McDermotts (2-5 to 1-6) in the Dublin County Final at Croke Park on 23 June, Ignatius Levey was the only Dublin man on the field. After the game, four of the vanquished Sean McDermotts team travelled to Portlaoise to play their second game of the day. Joe O'Connor and Paddy McIntyre lined out for Offaly, while Bob Martin and Willie Ryan played for Kildare in their quarter-final clash.

- At the Connacht Final at Roscommon on 21 July, a minute's silence was observed in memory of recent All-Ireland winners Patsy Flannelly (Mayo) and Frank Fox (Galway). Both had died at a young age in the previous months. They had competed against each other not just on the football field, but also on the athletics front. They had alternated as Connacht sprint champion in the 1930s. The name Frank Fox remains a familiar one in Galway GAA circles; the county senior football trophy is named in his honour.

- Wartime shortages meant restrictions on newspaper coverage in 1940, but this hardly explains the meagre reports of the *Irish Independent* on the Ulster semi-finals played on 14 July. Four very short paragraphs were deemed sufficient to tell the story of both games.

1940 – THE YEAR THAT WAS

- At the age of sixty-five, Winston Churchill became British prime minister for the first time on 23 July.
- The Vichy regime in France signed an armistice with Germany on 22 June.
- The prehistoric cave paintings in Lascaux, France were discovered in September 1940.
- The German Luftwaffe began its blitzkrieg (the 'Blitz') over London on 7 September 1940, resulting in the deaths of over 40,000 civilians over the following eight months.

1940 TEAM LINE-OUTS

KERRY (WINNERS)

1. Dan O'Keeffe
(Kerins O'Rahillys)

2. Bill Myers
(Dr Crokes)

3. Joe Keohane
(John Mitchels, also Geraldines, Dublin)

4. Tadhg Healy
(John Mitchels)

5. Bill Dillon
(Dingle)

6. Bill Casey
(Dingle, also Lispole)

7. Eddie Walsh
(Knocknagoshel)

8. Sean Brosnan
(Dingle, also Geraldines, Dublin)

9. Johnny Walsh
(Ballylongford)

10. Jimmy 'Gawksie' O'Gorman
(Austin Stacks)

11. Tom 'Gega' O'Connor
(Dingle)

12. Paddy Kennedy
(Kerins O'Rahillys, also Geraldines, Dublin and Annascaul)

13. Michael 'Murt' Kelly
(Beaufort, also Geraldines, Dublin)

14. Dan Spring
(Kerins O'Rahillys) Capt.

15. Charlie O'Sullivan
(Kerins O'Rahillys, also Camp)

Subs: Paddy 'Bawn' Brosnan (Dingle) Played; Mick Raymond (Kerins O'Rahillys); Jim 'Bawn' Fitzgerald (Kerins O'Rahillys); Tony McAuliffe (Listowel Emmets); Sean McCarthy (Knocknagoshel)

GALWAY (RUNNERS-UP)

1. Jimmy McGauran
(UCG, also Kilmore, Roscommon and Wolfe Tones)

2. Mick Raftery
(UCG, also Balla, Mayo)

3. Mick Connaire
(St Grellan's, also Beann Eadair, Dublin)

4. Dinny Sullivan
(Oughterard, also Wolfe Tones)

5. Frank Cunniffe
(St Grellan's, also Beann Eadair, Dublin)

6. Bobby Beggs
(Wolfe Tones, also Skerries Harps, St Joseph's and Sean McDermotts, Dublin)

7. Charlie Connolly
(St Grellan's, also Tuam Stars and Tarmon, Roscommon)

8. John 'Tull' Dunne
(St Grellan's)

9. Joe Duggan
(Annaghdown)

10. Jackie Flavin
(Wolfe Tones, also Moyvane, Kerry)

11. John Burke
(An Chéad Cath, also Labasheeda, Clare)

12. Jarlath Canavan
(Tuam Stars, also Geraldines, Dublin)

13. Mick Higgins
(Kilkerrin Clonberne, also Wolfe Tones)

14. Ned Mulholland
(Wolfe Tones, also Kinnegad, Westmeath)

15. Brendan Nestor
(Dunmore MacHales, also Geraldines, Dublin)

Subs: Johnny Casey (St Grellan's); 'Small' Pat McDonagh (Kilconly, also Tuam Stars and St Grellan's); Paddy Mitchell (Corofin, also UCG); Con McGovern (UCG, also Drumlish, Longford); John 'Connie' O'Connor (An Chéad Cath, also Dingle, Kerry)

1941

With everyday life throughout Europe severely disrupted as the war intensified, it was an outbreak of foot-and-mouth disease that caused havoc with the GAA championships in the summer of 1941. Munster and Leinster were most affected and it became necessary for the GAA Central Council to intervene in order to ensure the timely completion of the All-Ireland series.

In football, the biggest disruption was in Leinster and it was an ever-improving Carlow who would suffer most in the ensuing fixtures chaos. In front of over 8,000 wildly enthusiastic home supporters, they started their campaign impressively on 18 May, when they beat Laois on the peculiar scoreline of 3-4 to 3-1. The foundation for this surprise win lay at midfield, where the brilliant Luke Kelly got the upper hand on no less a man than Tommy Murphy.

Exactly fifty years before Meath and Dublin treated the GAA world to a footballing epic, Carlow and Wexford also needed to lock horns four times before a winner emerged. Carlow may have been underdogs when they first met at Dr Cullen Park on 8 June, but it took a last-gasp equaliser by Wexford's Jack Murphy to force a replay. There was further stalemate at Wexford Park two weeks later in a game that saw 'Jimma' Rae score 2-3 for Carlow, while Jack Murphy hit 1-4 for the Wexford men.

For the third instalment of this saga at Croke Park on 20 July, Carbury's John Joe Malone took over the refereeing duties from his clubmate, Seamus Bourke. He decreed that extra time would be played when the teams remained level after sixty minutes. A goal from Bennie Underwood seemed to swing the pendulum in Wexford's favour but, once again, Rae came to Carlow's rescue with three late points.

They met for the fourth time seven days later when, amazingly, there was nothing close about the proceedings as the Carlow men stormed to an emphatic 2-8 to 0-3 victory. A monopoly of midfield possession courtesy of Jim Morris and Luke Kelly provided the platform for Rae, Micky Byrne, John Doyle and the irrepressible Tom 'Drakes' Walker to engineer the scores that brought an end to this incredible saga. While vanquished, Wexford had contributed enormously to one of the real highlights of the season, and such as Jim 'Sacker' Furlong, Tom Somers, Billy Howlin and Bennie Underwood had shown that they were players of the highest order.

Carlow were now through to the Leinster Final for the first time in their history. With the benefit of five tough games behind them, they had good reason to believe they could progress further, with *The Nationalist and Leinster Times* correspondent declaring: 'I cannot see Carlow being beaten on their present form.'

Carlow were scheduled to meet Dublin in the provincial final. The Metropolitans had escaped with a draw in the first round against Louth, before a late Matt Fletcher goal swung the replay in their favour. They were indebted to Fletcher once again when he scored two goals in their one-point victory over Kildare in the semi-final.

As the protagonists readied themselves for the Leinster Final showdown, the Minister for Agriculture ruled that certain designated counties could not participate in the championship until three weeks after the latest foot-and-mouth outbreak. Along with Kilkenny and Tipperary, Carlow was such a county. It was then that the Leinster Council stepped in and nominated Dublin to represent the province in the All-Ireland semi-final against the Munster champions. Carlow would get to play in the Leinster Final in due course and, if they won this, they would qualify directly for the All-Ireland Final if Dublin were to win their semi-final encounter.

The clash of Clare and Cork at Ennis on 25 May didn't seem to generate much interest. The game received no coverage in the *Irish Independent*, while the full report in *The Irish Press* read: 'Clare, 1-8: Cork, 1-3, In the Munster Championship at Ennis yesterday, Clare defeated Cork.'

This didn't give Kerry much of an insight into the opposition as they prepared to face the Clare men in the Munster Final at Limerick on 20 July. They need not have worried, however, as they coasted to an easy 2-9 to 0-6 victory, with Charlie O'Sullivan and Michael 'Murt' Kelly the key men in the scoring stakes.

It was Tyrone who grabbed most of the headlines in the Ulster Championship. In their opening game, they survived a four-goal onslaught from Armagh to hold out for a draw, 1-17 to 4-8. The replay at Coalisland on 6 July witnessed an amazing turnaround with the game ending on a 3-13 to 0-1 scoreline in favour of Tyrone. A one-point victory over Down in the semi-final brought them to only their third ever provincial final.

On the opposite side of the draw, Cavan were expected to make their routine progression through to the final. Against Monaghan at Breffni Park on 6 July, they found themselves 2-2 to 0-0 in arrears after just five minutes of play. With the alarm bells ringing loudly in their ears, the Breffni men responded with a flurry of scores, and entered the half-time break with a

The cover of the 1941 football final programme.
Image courtesy of the GAA Museum at Croke Park.

two-point lead, going on to record a solid five-point victory. As was the case in 1940, Cavan had to fight all the way before finally overcoming Donegal at Bundoran, so qualifying for the provincial showdown with neighbours Tyrone.

The lead-up to the Ulster Final was not without controversy. When the game was fixed to be played at Armagh on 3 August, Cavan appealed to the GAA Central Council for a change of venue on account of the difficulty of getting players, officials and supporters to Armagh in light of the wartime border regulations recently introduced. The appeal was rejected, and the Cavan County Board convened a special meeting days before the game, finally deciding: 'to fulfil the fixture at Armagh and to request a postponement to 10th August … the committee insist that in order to safeguard the personal interests of players, officials and followers that the necessary regulations governing the admission of citizens of Eire to Northern Ireland be strictly complied by the obtaining of travel permits and that the cost of same on behalf of the team and officials be borne by the Ulster Council under the heading of travel expenses'.

The Anglo Celt pleaded with the Cavan players 'to rise to the annoying occasion' and, with only a dozen of their supporters in attendance, they did this in some style. With John Joe and Tom O'Reilly lording it at midfield, and Paddy Boylan playing the game of his life in attack, the Breffni men powered to a 3-9 to 0-5 victory.

Reigning champions Galway retained their Connacht title with victories over Mayo and Roscommon. They were tested to the full in both games and were particularly fortunate to hold out against Roscommon in the provincial final. A feature of this encounter was the outstanding defensive performance of schoolboy Bill Carlos, who was launching his illustrious career in the Roscommon colours.

While the All-Ireland semi-final pairings had now been determined, there were still, uniquely, five teams left in the championship. Carlow could only sit on the sidelines and watch their All-Ireland prospects play out as Dublin clashed with Kerry on 10 August. In what *The Irish Press* described as a 'dour and dogged' affair, a late free from 'Murt' Kelly glanced off the upright and fell over the bar to give Kerry an unlikely 0-4 to 0-4 draw. The replay took place the following Sunday in Tralee and, as so often with Kerry, they turned on the style and stormed to a 2-9 to 0-3 victory. At one fell swoop, therefore, they dashed the All-Ireland hopes of two counties in one day. The Leinster Final was delayed until November, by which time it had lost much of its attraction, and Dublin outscored Carlow at Dr Cullen Park, 4-6 to 1-4.

The second semi-final saw Galway and Cavan meet on 17 August at Croke Park. This turned out to be very one-sided with the Cavan defence under pressure all through. They didn't, as had been expected, dominate at midfield where Charlie Connolly gave an exhibition for the Tribesmen in this 1-12 to 1-4 victory.

THE FINAL – 7 SEPTEMBER

After their disappointing performance against Kerry in the previous year's final, Galway were well and truly motivated to turn the tables as they prepared to face the same opposition in the 1941 showdown. For Kerry, there was the prospect of taking their third successive title and, in the process, overtaking Dublin on the list of All-Irelands won.

The impact of the restrictions associated with what was known as 'The Emergency' was really beginning to bite in 1941. Compared to previous years, there was generally a significant fall-off in the match attendances that year. When over 45,000 people turned up at Croke Park on 7 September, the real mystery was how, with such severe restrictions on travel, so many contrived to attend. The consensus was that bicycles solved the transport problem, the *Irish Independent* noting: 'They came city-wards, five and six abreast, along the roads from the mountains of Wicklow, the pastures of Westmeath and the plains of Kildare.'

As the crowd waited anxiously for the game to begin, it was noted that the supporters of Kerry and Galway did not embrace the national policy of neutrality. When GAA President Paddy McNamee threw in the ball, it was helter-skelter from the word go. While the first half was acknowledged as being the equal of anything ever seen in an All-Ireland final, there was no shortage of robust exchanges, with *Irish Independent* social diarist Gertrude Gaffney amusingly noting: 'We could hardly have stood the excitement had it been unbroken by the spills that gave us breathing space, while St John Ambulance men rushed to the fallen gladiators and limbs were massaged into new activity.'

At the end of one of the most enthralling half-hours in All-Ireland history, the sides were level at 0-4 each. On the resumption, Galway forced the pace and were two points to the good within minutes. The turning point came ten minutes into the second half when 'Gega' O'Connor latched on to a pass from 'Gawksie' O'Gorman and sent a rasper to the Galway net. Urged on by John Dunne and Bobby Beggs, Galway responded manfully but Kerry's midfield dominance, where Sean Brosnan and Paddy Kennedy excelled, ultimately decided the issue in favour of the Kingdom.

While Kerry won, 1-8 to 0-7, Galway contributed handsomely to this footballing epic. In a team of heroes, special credit was accorded to Kerry corner-back, Bill Myers. Confined to bed due to illness the day before the game, he lined out at the request of the selectors and delivered one of his finest ever performances in the Kerry jersey. Dingle clubmates 'Gega' O'Connor and 'Bawn' Brosnan were the chief architects in an impressive forward division, while Joe Keohane was spectacular at full-back.

Suffering their second successive All-Ireland Final defeat, this was a major disappointment for Galway. Apart from Dunne and Beggs, Joe Duggan and John Burke performed heroically. Else-where, their full-back line trio of Mick Raftery, 'Small' Pat McDonagh and Dinny Sullivan were said to have marked their much-vaunted Kerry full-forward line so tightly that they might as well have been handcuffed to them.

An eventful season had come to an end like so many before and since, with Kerry as All-Ireland champions. Asked many years later about the formula for Kerry's footballing successes of eighty years earlier, Dingle legend Paddy 'Bawn' Brosnan gave this pithy response: 'In our day, we had a few farmers, a few fishermen, and a college boy to take the frees.'

FINAL STATISTICS

	Kerry	Galway
Full-time:	1-8	0-7
Half-time:	0-4	0-4
Scorers:	T. O'Connor 1-2	J. Dunne 0-3 (0-2 frees)
	M. Kelly 0-2 (0-1 free)	J. Burke 0-3 (0-2 frees)
	J. O'Gorman 0-2	E. Mulholland 0-1
	P. Brosnan 0-1	
	J. Walsh 0-1	
Attendance:	45,512	
Gate Receipts:	£3,541-10-7 (€4,506)	
Referee:	Peter McKenna (Limerick)	

FINAL MISCELLANY

- In attendance at the All-Ireland Final was the Canadian high commissioner, Mr J.D. Kearney. Acknowledging that the Kerry–Galway clash was a wonderful game, he went on to express a preference for hurling, having watched his first ever game in the code when the minors of Cork and Antrim met in the curtain-raiser. It clearly wasn't the closeness of the scoring which enthralled the commissioner – Cork won 13-8 to 1-2.
- Owing to the foot-and-mouth restrictions, the Munster Hurling Final, between Cork and Tipperary, was not played until after the All-Ireland Final. In the meantime, Cork were chosen to represent the province in the All-Ireland series and they duly won the Liam MacCarthy Cup on 28 September, beating Dublin 5-11 to 0-6 in the final. Then the Rebels fell to Tipperary, 5-4 to 2-5, in the Munster Final on 26 October, leaving them in the unique position of being All-Ireland title-holders, but not provincial champions.
- Thousands who attended the final at Croke Park on 7 September relied on peat-fuelled trains to get to Dublin. As an extreme example of the nationwide excitement generated by this match, Dundalk natives Michael Halpenny (aged twenty-one) and Fred Harty (twenty-three) cycled on a tandem from Killarney to Dublin.
- Under the heading 'Changed Menu', the *Irish Independent* of 8 September noted: 'One of the wartime changes noted during the match was the absence of sweets and fruit in the baskets of the refreshment vendors. They replaced these commodities by bottles of minerals. They are even less elegant in manipulation, with the froth steaming out of them, than the traditional and now defunct orange.'
- Aside from native sons, a number of counties were represented when Galway took to the field for the 1941 Final: Mayo (Mick Raftery); Dublin (Bobby Beggs); Kerry (Dan Kavanagh); Longford (Jimmy Hannify); Clare (John Burke); Roscommon (Jimmy McGauran).
- Future Irish international soccer player, Mick Martin, won a Leinster title with Dublin in 1941.

He was later suspended from the GAA for playing soccer and he only received his winners' medal some thirty years later.

1941 – THE YEAR THAT WAS

- Germany's two-year siege of Leningrad began on 22 June.
- A number of German bombs were dropped in Ireland during the war. On 31 May, twenty-eight lives were lost when four bombs fell on Dublin's North Strand.
- On 7 December, 350 Japanese aircraft bombed Pearl Harbor on Hawaii, killing over 2,400 people. This precipitated America's entry into the war.
- First-time director Orson Welles brought *Citizen Kane,* one of the great film classics, to the cinema in 1941.
- A toothpaste brand called 'Phillips' Dental Magnesia' was widely advertised in national and local newspapers in 1940. Accompanied by a caption of a clearly happy couple lighting up, the promotion of this delightful product came with a guarantee of removing the dreaded 'smokers' fur', a rough woolly feeling in the mouth caused by cigarette smoking. As an added incentive, daily use was sure to deliver 'a sweet mouth to give new zest to smoking'.

1941 TEAM LINE-OUTS

KERRY (WINNERS)

1. Dan O'Keeffe
(Kerins O'Rahillys)

2. Bill Myers
(Dr Crokes)

3. Joe Keohane
(John Mitchels, also Geraldines, Dublin)

4. Tadhg Healy
(John Mitchels)

5. Bill Dillon
(Dingle) Capt.

6. Bill Casey
(Dingle, also Lispole)

7. Eddie Walsh
(Knocknagoshel)

8. Sean Brosnan
(Dingle, also Geraldines, Dublin)

9. Paddy Kennedy
(Kerins O'Rahillys, also Geraldines, Dublin and Annascaul)

10. Johnny Walsh
(Ballylongford)

11. Tom 'Gega' O'Connor
(Dingle)

12. Paddy 'Bawn' Brosnan
(Dingle)

13. Jimmy 'Gawksie' O'Gorman
(Austin Stacks)

14. Michael 'Murt' Kelly
(Beaufort, also Geraldines, Dublin)

15. Charlie O'Sullivan
(Kerins O'Rahillys, also Camp)

Subs: Tim 'Roundy' Landers (Austin Stacks) Played; Mikey Lyne (Killarney Legion) Played; Jimmy Pierce (Annascaul, also John Mitchels); Tom Lawlor (Ardfert); Sean McCarthy (Knocknagoshel, also Austin Stacks); Ger Teahan (Kerins O'Rahillys, also Laune Rangers and Dingle); Tony McAuliffe (Listowel Emmets); Jackie Falvey (Kerins O'Rahillys)

GALWAY (RUNNERS-UP)

1. Jimmy McGauran
(UCG, also Kilmore, Roscommon and Wolfe Tones)

2. Mick Raftery
(Balla, Mayo, also UCG)

3. 'Small' Pat McDonagh
(Tuam Stars, also Kilconly and St Grellan's)

4. Dinny Sullivan
(Oughterard, also Wolfe Tones)

5. Frank Cunniffe
(Garda, Fermoy, also St Grellan's and Beann Eadair, Dublin)

6. Bobby Beggs
(Wolfe Tones, also Skerries Harps, St Joseph's and Sean McDermotts, Dublin)

7. Joe Duggan
(Annaghdown and UCG)

8. Charlie Connolly
(St Grellan's, also Tuam Stars and Tarmon, Roscommon)

9. Dan Kavanagh
(UCG, also Dr Crokes, Kerry and Dingle, Kerry)

10. Jimmy Hannify
(Wolfe Tones, also Drumlish, Longford)

11. John 'Tull' Dunne
(St Grellan's) Capt.

12. Jarlath Canavan
(Tuam Stars, also Geraldines, Dublin)

13. Ned Mulholland
(Wolfe Tones, also Kinnegad, Westmeath)

14. 'Big' Pat McDonagh
(Rossaveal)

15. John Burke
(An Chéad Cath, also Labasheeda, Clare)

Subs: Pierce Thornton (Furbo, also UCG) Played; Johnny Casey (St Grellan's); Jackie Flavin (Wolfe Tones, also Moyvane, Kerry); Paddy Mitchell (Corofin, also UCG); John 'Connie' O'Connor (An Chéad Cath, also Dingle); Liam Kitt (Castleblakeney)

1942

The footballers of Carlow had made big headlines in the 1941 campaign. Their four-game saga against Wexford was followed by a disappointing exit from the All-Ireland series without even getting the chance to battle for provincial honours. Far from retreating into the shadows, they were destined to grab even more headlines as the 1942 Championship unfolded.

Their journey started on 10 May, when they travelled to Kilkenny for their first-round clash with Wexford. After the previous year's marathon, there was huge interest in this game, but fuel rationing restricted the numbers who could travel to the game. According to *The Nationalist and Leinster Times*, 'people who would not dream of covering the distance other than in a motor car a year ago are now talking in terms of ponies, horses, bikes and tandems.'

With Wexford forced to line out without two of their top men, Jim 'Sacker' Furlong and Peter Hayes, Carlow repeated their 1941 victory and duly progressed to a semi-final joust with Offaly. The Offaly men had started out with a two-point victory over Kildare in their preliminary-round clash, before going on to pulverise Laois, 6-5 to 2-7, at Portlaoise on 24 May. This was a game that saw former Kildare star Harry Burke terrorise the Laois defence with a man-of-the-match performance.

A thrill-a-minute game between Carlow and Offaly at Athy on 14 June produced a draw, but there was even more excitement, and controversy, when they met again at Portlaoise the following Sunday. Offaly were handicapped by the fact that two of their best players, Paddy McIntyre and Joe O'Connor, had played in the Dublin Championship earlier in the day. With ten minutes to go, Carlow were leading by six when the referee mistakenly blew the final whistle. He quickly realised his mistake when the pitch was invaded by incensed Offaly supporters. However, he failed in his efforts to restart the game as the Offaly players refused to continue. The Leinster Council awarded the match to Carlow, while Offaly received a six-month suspension for their refusal to finish the game.

On the opposite side on the Leinster draw, Dublin made a faltering start. They were extremely fortunate to escape with a draw in their first-round clash with Longford at Mullingar on 10 May. Ironically, it was the free-taking brilliance of Longford man Tommy Banks that kept Dublin alive even though they were completely outplayed. There was no mistake in the replay, however, as Dublin romped to a fifteen-point victory, thus progressing to a semi-final encounter with Meath. Despite the fact that Meath had the better of the exchanges generally, this clash saw the Metropolitans emerge one-point victors, 3-5 to 1-10. Echoing the frustration of the county's disappointed supporters, the *Meath Chronicle* proclaimed: 'We find ourselves at a complete loss to advance any explanation for this defeat.'

In what was a drab, low-standard Leinster Final played at Athy on 19 July, the final score read 0-8 to 0-6 in Dublin's favour. This was not the end of the story, however. At a meeting of the Leinster Council eight days later, Kildare GAA official Joe Fox gave evidence that he had seen Dublin's Jimmy Joy enter the rugby grounds of North Kildare on 26 April. The title was duly awarded to Carlow and they held this honour for fully twenty-four hours when the ruling was reversed at an emergency meeting of the Central Council. It seems that Mr Fox was not an 'official member' of the GAA Vigilance Committee and so his evidence could not be accepted.

Not for the first, or last, time, Kerry were installed as early favourites to take the All-Ireland. Success would see them emulate the four-in-a-row records of the great Wexford (1914–1918) and Kerry (1929–1932) teams of the past. Instead of getting a bye into the provincial decider, they found themselves in the unusual position of having to play three teams, Clare, Tipperary and Cork, on their way to the title. They won these games with ease, finding the net three times in each. For the first time in their illustrious history, Kerry had won the Munster Championship for the seventh successive year.

Galway, All-Ireland finalists of the previous two years, launched their 1942 campaign against Leitrim on 21 June at Mohill, with a resounding 4-9 to 1-2 semi-final victory. The other side of the draw saw a Bill Carlos-inspired Roscommon surprise Mayo in their quarter-final clash at Tuam on 14 June. An easy win over Sligo in the second semi-final paved the way for a second successive Roscommon–Galway Connacht Final. The sides met at Ballinasloe on 19 July before a crowd of over 10,000 and played out a thrilling encounter, with Galway holding out for the narrowest of wins (2-6

A rare action shot from the 1942 Final which saw Dublin defeat Galway. Dublin players featured (l–r) are Paddy 'Beefy' Kennedy, Brendan Quinn and Peter O'Reilly. (Unidentified Galway player is tackling Paddy Kennedy.)
Image courtesy of Jimmy Wren.

to 3-2). A notable feature of this game was the performance of Roscommon's Donal Keenan who played havoc with the Galway defence.

The Ulster Championship began on 31 May at the Athletic Grounds when Armagh defeated a depleted Tyrone team on a scoreline of 3-4 to 0-0. Their semi-final clash with Down at Newcastle on 5 July ended in disarray. With Down leading by a point, an encroachment onto the pitch by spectators brought the game to an abrupt conclusion. The Ulster Council refixed the game for the following Sunday and Down took the honours with a four-point win to reach the provincial final.

Almost inevitably, Down's Ulster Final opposition was presented by Cavan who had swept past Donegal in the second semi-final. Paddy Boylan and Joe Stafford each scored a hat-trick as Cavan hit the net no fewer than seven times in this one-sided affair. Against the backdrop of the travel difficulties associated with the 1941 Final, the Ulster Council fixed the showdown for Dundalk on 19 July. Noting that there had 'never been so many bicycles seen on the streets', the *Dundalk Democrat* wrote glowingly about the atmosphere in the town on the morning of the game. On a perfect day for football, and on a pitch manicured to within an inch of its life, the game turned out to be a bitter disappointment. Cavan took charge from the throw-in and cruised to a 5-11 to 1-3 victory over the hapless Mourne men.

If the Breffni men were superior in every position, it was centre half-back John Joe O'Reilly who commanded the greatest adulation. He was, in the words of the *Dundalk Democrat*, 'the embodiment of physical fitness, and a grand footballer in every sense, towered above all'.

The eagerly awaited All-Ireland semi-final between Dublin and Cavan did not live up to expectations. The game was played at Croke Park on 2 August, where the combination of inclement weather and ongoing travel restrictions meant that a crowd of just over 8,000 turned up. A goal directly from a fifty by Paddy 'Beefy' Kennedy set Dublin on their way and they were six points to the good with only minutes to go. A goal from T.P. O'Reilly came too late for Cavan and the game petered out with Dublin qualifying for the final on a score of 1-6 to 1-3.

The second semi-final between Galway and Kerry was a vastly superior display of quality football, with victors Galway immediately installed as favourites to take the Sam Maguire Cup. After a tense struggle, the Tribesmen managed to overcome a Kerry team that began to falter as the game wore on. The final score was 1-3 to 0-3, with all of Kerry's scores coming from placed balls. There had been a degree of unrest in the Kerry camp when Sean Brosnan was surprisingly dropped, a decision that led to the withdrawal of fellow Dingle men Paddy 'Bawn' Brosnan and Bill Casey from the team. Bemoaning the absence of the Dingle trio, as well as the inter-county retirement of Bill Dillon, *The Kerryman* declared: 'we had not the material to fill the gaps'.

THE FINAL — 20 SEPTEMBER

The stage was now set for a Dublin–Galway showdown. It had been eight years since Dublin's last appearance in a final when they had lost to Galway in the 1934 decider. Bobby Beggs and Mick Connaire were the only survivors from that final but now Beggs was back wearing the colours of his native county. While nineteen years had elapsed since Dublin had last won the title, Galway had featured prominently in recent championship campaigns. They took the title in 1938 but were beaten in the finals of 1940 and 1941. They were now facing the possibility of an unprecedented hat-trick of losses.

Previews of the game invariably pointed to Galway's advantage in the physical stakes; they were said to weigh in at an average of nearly a stone heavier than Dublin. Notwithstanding this, there was a quiet confidence among the Metropolitans, whose game was based on speed and agility. When the big day arrived, damp conditions and a slippery ball seemed to give Galway a further advantage, but this theory proved unfounded.

Galway got off to a strong start and held a three-point half-time lead. However, they looked vulnerable in defence and they couldn't come to grips with the midfield play of Joe Fitzgerald and Mick Falvey, both Kerry men. As the second half progressed, the superior fitness levels of the Dublin team began to translate onto the scoreboard. In a tense, and sometimes fractious, struggle they pulled away to win by two points. In winning their first final since 1923, they now had fifteen titles, drawing level with Kerry in the process.

Apart from their midfield superiority, the launching pad for this win was Dublin's powerful half-back line where the outstanding Peter O'Reilly was flanked by Brendan Quinn and Sligo native Paddy Henry. As usual, Tommy Banks led the scoring, with Jimmy Joy and Matt Fletcher also seen to good effect.

Galway were left to rue their overreliance on the traditional 'catch and kick' approach, something which was totally unsuitable in the slippery conditions. Only Mick Connaire, 'Small' Pat McDonagh and the Thornton brothers were able to reproduce their semi-final form. Losing three finals in a row was a major blow to a county that had spent ten years in the limelight. As the championship season closed, few could have predicted that they would have to wait more than a decade before they would again be dining at the top table.

FINAL STATISTICS

	Dublin	Galway
Full-time:	1-10	1-8
Half-time:	1-6	1-3
Scorers:	T. Banks 0-6 (0-5 frees)	S. Thornton 0-4
	P. O'Connor 1-1	J. Casey 1-0
	J. Joy 0-2	M. Fallon 0-2
	M. Fletcher 0-1	P. Thornton 0-1
		J. Flavin 0-1
Attendance:	37,105	
Gate Receipts:	£2,635-4-2 (€3,346)	
Referee:	Sean Kennedy (Donegal)	

FINAL MISCELLANY

- A notable feature of the 1942 decider was the number of players from outside the competing counties who were involved:

  Dublin: Joe Fitzgerald (Kerry); Mick Falvey (Kerry); Jimmy Joy (Kerry); Jack Murphy (Kerry); Paddy Henry (Sligo); Tommy Banks (Longford); Colm Boland (Westmeath); Caleb Crone (Cork)

  Galway: Dan Kavanagh (Kerry); Jackie Flavin (Kerry); Johnny Clifford (Kerry); Jimmy McGauran (Roscommon)

- Two sets of clubmates were in opposition in the 1942 Final. Joe Fitzgerald, Jimmy Joy and Paddy Henry (Dublin) and Frank Cunniffe and Jarlath Canavan (Galway) all played with the Geraldines club in Dublin. Another Dublin club, Sean McDermotts, was represented by Bobby Beggs and Tommy Banks (Dublin) and Mick Connaire (Galway).
- Three of the four midfielders who lined out in the 1942 Final, Joe Fitzgerald, Mick Falvey (Dublin) and Dan Kavanagh (Galway), were all from the west Kerry Gaeltacht.
- Skerries native Bobby Beggs won his first All-Ireland medal as a Dublin player in 1942, having previously been on the Metropolitan side that lost to Galway in the 1934 Final. In the interim, he had played for Galway and was a key member of their 1938 winning side. He was on the losing Galway teams in 1940 and 1941.
- Joe Duggan was one of a number of Galway players on the losing sides of 1940, 1941 and 1942. His son Jimmy was a member of the Galway teams that lost the finals of 1971, 1973 and 1974. Jimmy did have the consolation of playing a starring role as an eighteen-year-old in Galway's 1966 triumph.
- Brothers Pierce and Sean Thornton had lined out with Galway's hurlers in their All-Ireland semi-final defeat to Cork on 26 July.
- In 1942, the four provincial finals were played on the same day, 19 July. Unusually, all reigning champions – Kerry, Galway, Dublin and Cavan – retained their titles.
- Dublin full-back Paddy 'Beefy' Kennedy had played at full-forward in the hurling final against Cork.

1942 – THE YEAR THAT WAS

- On 20 January, leading members of the Nazi regime met at the Wannsee Conference to discuss the logistics of implementing what they called the 'Final Solution to the Jewish Question' through death camps such as Auschwitz.
- The first nuclear reactor capable of producing electricity was completed by Italian scientist Enrico Fermi on 2 December.
- Humphrey Bogart and Ingrid Bergman were the stars of cinema classic *Casablanca*.

1942 TEAM LINE-OUTS

DUBLIN (WINNERS)

1. Charlie Kelly
(Peadar Mackens)

2. Bobby Beggs
(Sean McDermotts, also Skerries
Harps and Wolfe Tones, Galway)

3. Paddy 'Beefy' Kennedy
(Peadar Mackens)

4. Caleb Crone
(Air Corps)

5. Paddy Henry
(Geraldines)

6. Peter O'Reilly
(St Mary's, Saggart)

7. Brendan Quinn
(Parnells)

8. Mick Falvey
(Civil Service, also Dingle, Kerry)

9. Joe Fitzgerald
(Geraldines, also An Ghaeltacht, Kerry)

10. Jimmy Joy
(Geraldines, also Laune Rangers,
Kerry)

11. Paddy Bermingham
(St Mary's, Saggart)

12. Gerry Fitzgerald
(St Mary's, Saggart)

13. Matt Fletcher
(Peadar Mackens)

14. Paddy O'Connor
(St Mary's, Saggart)

15. Tommy Banks
(Sean McDermotts)

Subs: Frank Ryan (Clanna Gael); Jack Murphy (Civil Service); Sean Healy (Clanna Gael); Sean Moriarty (Civil Service, also Castlegregory, Kerry); Mick Richardson (Pioneers); Colm Boland (Geraldines); Tommy McCann (Parnells); Joe Delaney (Peadar Mackens)

GALWAY (RUNNERS-UP)

1. Jimmy McGauran
(UCG, also Kilmore, Roscommon and Wolfe Tones)

2. Frank Cunniffe
(St Grellan's, also Beann Eadair,
Dublin and Garda)

3. Mick Connaire
(Sean McDermotts, Dublin, also St
Grellan's)

4. 'Small' Pat McDonagh
(Tuam Stars, also Kilconly and St
Grellan's)

5. Joe Duggan
(Annaghdown and UCG)

6. Johnny Casey
(St Grellan's)

7. Tom Sullivan
(Oughterard)

8. Dan Kavanagh
(UCG, also Dr Crokes, Kerry and
Dingle, Kerry)

9. Charlie Connolly
(St Grellan's, also Tarmon, Roscommon
and Tuam Stars) Capt.

10. Johnny Clifford
(An Chéad Cath, also St Mary's
Cahirciveen, Kerry)

11. Mick Fallon
(Dunmore MacHales, also Cavan
Slashers, Rathnew, Wicklow and St
Grellan's)

12. Jarlath Canavan
(Tuam Stars, also Geraldines, Dublin)

13. Jackie Flavin
(Wolfe Tones, also Moyvane, Kerry)

14. Pierce Thornton
(UCG, also Furbo)

15. Sean Thornton
(UCG, also Furbo)

Subs: Ned Mulholland (Wolfe Tones, also Kinnegad, Westmeath) Played; Sean Walsh (An Chéad Cath, also Charlestown Sarsfields, Mayo) Played; 'Big' Pat McDonagh (Rossaveal); Paddy Fitzgerald (UCG, also Dunmore MacHales); Mick Cassidy (Kilconnell); John 'Connie' O'Connor (An Chéad Cath, also Dingle, Kerry)

1943

In 1943, wartime shortages and travel restrictions continued to impact everyday life in Ireland. However, attendances at inter-county GAA matches were no longer being hugely affected. Whether it was the emergence of new contenders for national titles, growing radio and newspaper coverage, or the age-old attraction of local rivalries, the games were now more popular than ever. Cars, buses and trains may have been generally off-limits, but supporters remained undaunted and the trusty bicycle filled the void as the primary means of transport for the country's original football fanatics.

In Leinster, Louth qualified for a quarter-final meeting with All-Ireland champions Dublin when they beat Meath 2-10 to 1-8 at Drogheda on 2 May. Despite the brilliance of Meath's Jim Clarke, the Louth forwards, with Peter Corr in scintillating form, created the openings which paved the way for this victory. It was midfielder Jim Thornton who was the chief architect of the Wee County's surprise win, 1-6 to 1-5, over the Metropolitans at Drogheda on 30 May. According to the *Drogheda Independent*, Thornton 'gave as fine a display throughout the hour as was ever seen on a Gaelic field'.

Next up for the Wee County were Offaly, who had pipped Longford by two points after a ding-dong battle at Tullamore on 6 June. Louth emerged with a three-point victory over the men from the Faithful County, but only after a controversial penalty incident. Walsh Island's Dick Gorman, playing brilliantly in goals for Offaly, seemed to be fouled at least three times as he attempted to break free from the inrushing forwards. To his astonishment, and to that of the huge Offaly contingent in attendance, the referee's whistle signalled a penalty for Louth. Gorman made yet another fantastic save from Corr's effort but Jimmy Coyle punched the rebound to the net for the winning goal.

On the other side of the Leinster draw, Laois had made light work of Kildare, 4-8 to 1-10, before going on to pip Carlow by two points in their semi-final encounter at Athy on 27 June. In what *The Irish Press* described as a 'game of a hundred thrills', it was once again the magic of Tommy Murphy which swung the pendulum in Laois's favour as they ran out 3-8 to 3-6 winners.

The Leinster Final, played at Croke Park on 25 July, saw the form book thrown out the proverbial window as Louth crushed favourites Laois, 3-16 to 2-4. Their first Leinster title since 1912 was inspired by the brilliant Corr, whose 'wizardry had the Laois backs mesmerised', according to *The Irish Press*. The diminutive wing-forward contributed no less than 1-8 to his side's total.

Louth had not contested an All-Ireland semi-final for over thirty years and, as it turned out, their opponents in the semi-final had to go back twenty-eight years to their last appearance at the same stage of the competition. Roscommon, who had shown real promise in recent years, outgunned

Cavan, runners-up to Roscommon in the 1943 Final.

Leitrim, 2-13 to 1-3, to reach the Connacht Final. Facing a new-look Galway outfit which had earlier overwhelmed Mayo, the Roscommon men made up for recent narrow failures with a deserved six-point win. While Frankie Kinlough and Donal Keenan were Roscommon's key men in this breakthrough victory, Galway's Charlie Connolly was the outstanding player on view.

The Leinster and Connacht campaigns may have produced their share of surprises but it was in Munster that the shock of the season took place. Cork led Kerry a merry dance in their semi-final clash at Cork on 6 June and would have won handsomely but for their erratic shooting. As it was, Kerry needed a last-minute equaliser from Tarbert man Pat Holly to force a draw. The presumption that this result was only a wake-up call for the Kingdom proved unfounded, with Cork, largely through the efforts of Eamonn Young, edging the replay on a score of 1-5 to 1-4. In the Munster Final Cork overcame a stubborn Tipperary outfit by three points at Fermoy on 25 July, with Clonakilty's Jim Aherne scoring the decisive goal. Once again, Young was the chief inspiration behind Cork's win, while Miah Murphy was also outstanding.

There were no major surprises in the Ulster Championship where the traditional powers, Cavan and Monaghan, emerged once again to contest the provincial final. Cavan had an easy semi-final win, 4-10 to 1-3, over Tyrone, while Monaghan had impressive victories over Armagh and Antrim.

According to *The Anglo Celt*, the sense of anticipation in the lead-up to the Ulster Final could be gauged from the fact that the outcome was 'being discussed with relish in the bogs, meadows, factories, shops and everywhere fans congregate'.

The final was played at Breffni Park on 1 August, in what the *Dundalk Democrat* described as 'appalling weather conditions which completely ruled out any decent football, making fielding and shooting almost impossible and damped the bright spirits of Ulster enthusiasts'.

While Cavan held sway at midfield through the efforts of Simon Deignan and Fonsie Comiskey, Monaghan gave as good as they got and had outstanding players in Peter McCarney, Leo Burns and Belfast-based George Hughes. In the end, Cavan's greater experience was the telling factor as they retained their Ulster crown on a score of 2-3 to 0-5. While Joe Stafford and T.P. O'Reilly found the net for the Cavan men, it was Paddy Smith who was the real star of the show.

The Roscommon–Louth and Cavan–Cork semi-finals were the first ever championship encounters

'Big' Tom O'Reilly leads the Cavan team against Roscommon on All-Ireland day 1943.

between these counties. The first semi-final, between Roscommon and Louth, was played in atrocious conditions but, despite this, the teams served up a game of high quality in which the scoring was close throughout. The consensus was that the more direct approach of Roscommon was more suited to the conditions and they held out for a four-point victory, the clinching goal coming from Frankie Kinlough in the dying minutes. In its report on the game, the *Drogheda Independent* noted that: 'Several Roscommon players wore gloves and had their boots specially spiked for the occasion. They held their feet on the slippery sod much better than the Louth men.'

The Cavan–Cork game attracted a crowd in excess of 30,000 but the standard of play was a disappointment. An early Jim Cronin goal gave Cork the advantage but when Cavan switched Tom O'Reilly to midfield, he proceeded to dictate the run of play. Joe Stafford was again on the mark with a goal for Cavan, who held on to win by the slimmest of margins, 1-8 to 1-7.

THE FINAL — 26 SEPTEMBER

When Roscommon and Cavan met on 26 September, a crowd of 68,023, then the second highest ever, turned up to see this novel championship encounter. Roscommon, playing in their first ever decider, were considered underdogs against a county that had been in the first rank of contenders for over a decade.

The first half saw Cavan justify their tag as favourites and they led 1-4 to 0-3 at the break. Joe Stafford was yet again on target, finding the net with a spectacular effort in the opening minutes.

The second half was a different story as Roscommon, with Liam Gilmartin and Eamon Boland dominating the midfield exchanges, staged a great comeback. A Jimmy Murray goal set the scene for a grandstand finish, with a late point from John Joe O'Reilly securing a draw for Cavan. When the referee, Peter McKenna of Limerick, called the sides together to propose extra time, he was met with deaf ears and Central Council was then obliged to make arrangements for a replay.

THE REPLAY — 10 OCTOBER

The replay took place on 10 October and saw a reduced, but still commendable, attendance of over 47,000. Despite the slippery conditions, the standard of play was high. Roscommon dominated the early proceedings, so much so that one newspaper described the first half as 'a crick in the neck towards the Cavan goals'. The scoring took on a peculiar pattern and at half-time Roscommon led 2-2 to 2-0.

The second half saw the men from the west blossom and take their first ever title amid some of the most extraordinary scenes ever witnessed in an All-Ireland final. About midway through the half there was an exchange of blows between a number of players, and Cavan's Joe Stafford was sent to the line. From then on, the game is said to have gone from bad to worse and it ended with gardaí, and spectators, flooding the field. *The Irish Press* described the scene as one of the umpires attempted to signal a Roscommon point:

> Two or three Cavan men tried to impede him, and he was knocked down, but got up and signalled the point, which was registered by the score board man. The referee (P. Mythan [*sic*], Wexford) moved in to the goal-mouth, where he was struck and knocked down by a Cavan player. In a second or two, (a) portion of the crowd, which was on the move towards the exits, rushed on to the pitch and the referee was again knocked down. He managed to get the game restarted, but immediately blew full-time, picked up the ball and started for the Hogan Stand, from which he received an ovation. He had, however, only gone a few yards when he was surrounded by a small section of the players and spectators, some of whom aimed blows at him, one or two of which took effect.

Amid all of this chaos, Roscommon were ecstatically celebrating their first All-Ireland Senior title.

The full-time score of 2-7 to 2-2 seemed incidental amid all that was happening. There was no denying that the man of the match was centre-back Bill Carlos. He was simply imperious throughout. Others who starred for Roscommon included Jimmy Murray, Donal Keenan, Frankie Kinlough and midfielder Liam Gilmartin. As so often before, brothers Tom and John Joe O'Reilly were Cavan's outstanding players, with honourable mention also for Paddy Boylan, Paddy Smith and Joe Stafford, who, prior to his sending off, had shown to very good effect.

Roscommon had made the fairytale journey from junior ranks to a senior All-Ireland title in a few short years and the big question was whether the momentum could be sustained into 1944. Jimmy Murray and his men were about to provide an emphatic answer to this question.

FINAL STATISTICS – DRAW

	Roscommon	Cavan
Full-time:	1-6	1-6
Half-time:	1-4	0-3
Scorers:	P. Murray 0-3	J. Stafford 1-3
	J. Murray 1-0	S. Maguire 0-1
	D. Keenan 0-2 (0-1 free)	J.J. O'Reilly 0-1 (0-1 free)
	L. Gilmartin 0-1	P. Smith 0-1 (0-1 free)
Attendance:	68,023	
Gate Receipts:	£5,314 (€6,764)	
Referee:	Peter McKenna (Limerick)	

FINAL STATISTICS – REPLAY

	Roscommon	Cavan
Full-time:	2-7	2-2
Half-time:	2-2	2-0
Scorers:	D. Keenan 0-5 (0-5 frees)	J. Stafford 1-0
	F. Kinlough 1-1	P. Boylan 1-0
	J. McQuillan 1-0	T. O'Reilly 0-1 (0-1 free)
	P. Murray 0-1	J.J. O'Reilly 0-1 (0-1 free)
Attendance:	47,193	
Gate Receipts:	£3,848-11-7 (€4,887)	
Referee:	Paddy Mythen (Wexford)	

FINAL MISCELLANY

- In the wake of the 1943 replay, the GAA Central Council deemed it necessary to deal with what it called a number of 'incidents' which occurred during the game. Four Cavan players, Tom O'Reilly, Joe Stafford, T.P. O'Reilly and Barney Cully, were summoned to Croke Park on Friday 22 October. Shortly after midnight, the following statement was issued to the press:

  The Council decided, after hearing representatives from Cavan, on the following sentences – Stafford has been suspended until 10th October 1944; T.P. O'Reilly suspended for nine months from the date of the match: Tom O'Reilly suspended until 10th October 1944. In view of Mr Bernard Cully having intimated that he had resigned from membership of the Association, the Council declared him ineligible for membership for a period of ten years from October 10th, 1943.

  The referee, Paddy Mythen, had reported that Cully had knocked him down with a blow. In 1945, when Cavan next appeared in the final, the ever durable Barney was in his customary corner-back position, having had his membership reinstated. He went on to collect a winners' medal in 1948.

- Any description of the 1943 replay would be incomplete without providing a little balance from the Cavan perspective. *The Anglo Celt* of 16 October reported:

  > The most vivid recollection I shall carry of the replay in Croke Park, last Sunday, between Cavan and Roscommon, for the All-Ireland football final, is that while under the code no active Gael is permitted to witness a rugby match, the "tackling" of that imported game was used to such effect by two of the Connacht men in the second half against Stafford, the Breffni deadly-shooting full-forward, when in possession of the ball at his opponent's goal, with every likelihood of a point, or possible goal, that he was rendered absolutely helpless by two attackers, one of the foulers gripping him firmly around the knee while pulling him backwards, and this at the most critical period of the game – and then the thought flashed through my mind what I would have done to shake myself free under similar circumstances.

- Established by Éamon de Valera, *The Irish Press* newspaper 'occasionally' lapsed into 'Fianna Fáil' mode when reporting on national events. This tendency was taken to a new level in its report on the Connacht Final on the morning of 19 July. A paragraph, in bold print, midway through the detailed match report, read: 'Among the first to congratulate the winners was Mr. G. Boland, Minister for Justice, who, with his three sons, travelled specially to be present at the final.' At the time, Mr Boland was a Fianna Fáil TD for the Roscommon constituency.

- From 8 July 1928 to 11 July 1943, Kerry were unbeaten in the Munster Championship. The 1935 title went to Tipperary, but only after Kerry had withdrawn from the competition.

- Antrim provided some real shocks in the hurling championship of 1943. Having beaten Galway, 7-0 to 6-2, at Corrigan Park, they stunned Kilkenny with a 3-3 to 1-6 semi-final win, before losing heavily to Cork in the final. One of Antrim's outstanding players was Kevin Armstrong, a man who would go on to a forge a distinguished football career.

- *The Anglo Celt* commented on the relative ease with which Cavan were able to make their way to Enniskillen for their Ulster semi-final game with Tyrone: 'The Cavan team experienced little difficulty in surmounting the Border regulations. A list of players and officials had been supplied beforehand to the District R.U.C. Inspector and when the party arrived at the frontier, the list was checked, in and out, by the officials. Cyclists also had an easy passage, some of them not being even questioned.'

- When Laois and Kildare met on 16 May, two spectators were alleged to have '… refused to obey the instructions of the stewards, used insulting language, and sat on the grass in front of the sideline seats'. The Leinster Council duly prosecuted the obstreperous pair, each of whom was fined four shillings, with eighteen shillings in costs.

1943 – THE YEAR THAT WAS

- At Listowel District Court in August 1943, tailor James Lynch from Lixnaw was fined five shillings (32 cent) for breaching the Emergency Regulations governing men's suits – he had made jackets with more than the stipulated number of pockets.

- Jacques Cousteau and Emil Gagnan invented scuba diving equipment in 1943.

- At a meeting in Ennis on 6 June, Taoiseach Éamon de Valera compared the prospects of a coalition government involving Fine Gael, the Labour Party and the Farmers' Party with the practice of tying two goats together with a stick:

  'Tied together in this way, the goats have not the same mind. One wants to go over the fence, the other to stay down; the result is that the stick joining them gets stuck in the fence and they go nowhere. And isn't it much worse if you have three goats tied together on the brush handle?' he asked, amid tumultuous laughter.

- Among the many magic potions advertised extensively in the regional newspapers of the 1940s, 'Bile Beans' was perhaps the most prominent. This was despite the fact that a US court had ruled the product a fraud some forty years earlier. Said to contain substances from a previously unknown vegetable, the product was marketed under the name of a fictitious chemist known as Charles Forde. An extract from a promotion in *The Anglo Celt* of 10 July reads:

  Taken regularly, Bile Beans gently but surely remove all hindrance to slimness, cleansing and toning the system, improving health in every way. Here is no finer tonic-laxative than these purely vegetable Bile Beans; no easier or safer means to youthful slenderness and the radiant health that goes with it.

- The Battle of Stalingrad, the bloodiest in the history of warfare, ended on 2 February 1943. After five months of intense and brutal fighting, the Russian army finally overcame the German 6th Army and the Italian 8th Army to secure control of this strategically important city. Over 1.2 million perished in what is generally regarded as the turning point in the European theatre of war.

1943 TEAM LINE-OUTS — DRAW

ROSCOMMON

1. Frank Glynn
(Tarmon)

2. Larry 'Pop' Cummins
(Tarmon)

3. J.P. 'Doc' O'Callaghan
(Tarmon)

4. Bill Jackson
(Tarmon)

5. Brendan Lynch
(Oran, also Ballinaheglish and Army)

6. Bill Carlos
(Tarmon, also Ballintober and Garda)

7. Bill Heavey
(Fuerty, also St Patrick's)

8. Eamon Boland
(Tarmon, also Strokestown and Lees, Cork)

9. Liam Gilmartin
(St Patrick's, also Ballymurray and Sean McDermotts, Dublin)

10. Phelim Murray
(St Patrick's and UCD)

11. Jimmy Murray
(St Patrick's) Capt.

12. Donal Keenan
(Elphin and UCD)

13. Derry McDermott
(Mantua)

14. Jack McQuillan
(St Patrick's, also Ballyforan)

15. Frankie Kinlough
(Castleisland Desmonds, Kerry, also Moore)

Subs: Hugh Gibbons (Strokestown); Harry O'Connor (Ballinameen, also Elphin); Bill Kinlough (Moore); Brian O'Rourke (Tarmon and UCG); Jim Brennan (St Patrick's); Tommy Conry (Elphin); Owensie Hoare (St Coman's)

CAVAN

1. Des Benson
(Croghan)

2. Eugene Finnegan
(Mountnugent)

3. Barney Cully
(Arva and UCD)

4. Peter Paul Galligan
(Cornafean)

5. Gerry Smith
(Kill)

6. 'Big' Tom O'Reilly
(Cornafean)

7. Simon Deignan
(Army, also Mullagh and Civil Service)

8. John Joe O'Reilly
(Curragh, Kildare, also Cornafean)

9. Mick Higgins
(Mountnugent, also Kilnaleck and Oliver Plunketts, Louth)

10. Donal Morgan
(Virginia, also Cross)

11. Paddy Smith
(Mullahoran, also Drumkilly)

12. T.P. O'Reilly
(Belturbet and UCD, also Templeport and Ballyconnell)

13. Paddy Boylan
(Sean McDermotts, Dublin, also Cavan Slashers)

14. Joe Stafford
(Sean McDermotts, Dublin, also Killinkere and Arva)

15. Seamus Maguire
(Cornafean)

Subs: John Willie Martin (Army, also Templeport); Brendan Kelly (Bailieboro); Tom Cahill (Cavan Slashers); Harry Rodgers (Arva); John Keogan (Crubany); Willie Fitzpatrick (Cornafean); Patsy Clarke (Knockbride); Gerry Darcy (Cavan Slashers)

1943 TEAM LINE-OUTS — REPLAY

ROSCOMMON (WINNERS)

1. Frank Glynn
(Tarmon)

2. Larry 'Pop' Cummins
(Tarmon)

3. J.P. 'Doc' O'Callaghan
(Tarmon)

4. Bill Jackson
(Tarmon)

5. Brendan Lynch
(Oran, also Ballinaheglish and Army)

6. Bill Carlos
(Tarmon, also Ballintober and Garda)

7. Owensie Hoare
(St Coman's)

8. Eamon Boland
(Tarmon, also Strokestown and Lees, Cork)

9. Liam Gilmartin
(St Patrick's, also Ballymurray and Sean McDermotts, Dublin)

10. Phelim Murray
(St Patrick's and UCD)

11. Jimmy Murray
(St Patrick's) Capt.

12. Donal Keenan
(Elphin and UCD)

13. Derry McDermott
(Mantua)

14. Jack McQuillan
(St Patrick's, also Ballyforan)

15. Frankie Kinlough
(Castleisland Desmonds, Kerry, also Moore)

Subs: Harry O'Connor (Ballinameen, also Elphin); Hugh Gibbons (Strokestown); Bill Kinlough (Moore); Brian O'Rourke (Tarmon and UCG); Peter Connellan (Strokestown); Tommy Conry (Elphin); Jim Brennan (St Patrick's)

Bill Heavey was unavailable due to injury

CAVAN (RUNNERS-UP)

1. Des Benson
(Croghan)

2. Eugene Finnegan
(Mountnugent)

3. Barney Cully
(Arva and UCD)

4. Peter Paul Galligan
(Cornafean)

5. Gerry Smith
(Kill)

6. 'Big' Tom O'Reilly
(Cornafean)

7. John Joe O'Reilly
(Curragh, Kildare, also Cornafean)

8. Simon Deignan
(Army, also Mullagh and Civil Service)

9. T.P. O'Reilly
(Belturbet and UCD, also Templeport and Ballyconnell)

10. Donal Morgan
(Virginia, also Cross)

11. Paddy Smith
(Mullahoran, also Drumkilly)

12. Mick Higgins
(Mountnugent, also Kilnaleck and Oliver Plunketts, Louth)

13. Paddy Boylan
(Sean McDermotts, Dublin, also Cavan Slashers)

14. Joe Stafford
(Sean McDermotts, Dublin, also Killinkere and Arva)

15. Harry Rodgers
(Arva)

Subs: John Keogan (Crubany) Played; Brendan Kelly (Bailieboro); John Willie Martin (Army, also Templeport); Tom Cahill (Cavan Slashers); Seamus Maguire (Cornafean); Willie Fitzpatrick (Cornafean); Josie Greenan (Cavan Slashers); Peter Donohoe (Kilnaleck)

1944

THE CHAMPIONSHIP

As Roscommon set out on their 1944 campaign it was clear that they would have to surmount some serious obstacles if they were to retain their crown. Galway were seen as their strongest challengers in Connacht. Cavan, beaten finalists in 1943, were again regarded as likely contenders. Elsewhere, the big question was whether Cork could remain at the helm in Munster and keep traditional kingpins, Kerry, at bay. The Leinster Championship was likely to be highly competitive, with any one of six counties deemed capable of taking the provincial crown. It was seen as doubtful, however, if any of these could launch a serious challenge for All-Ireland honours.

If Roscommon's prospects in Connacht seemed to receive a boost when a rejuvenated Mayo put hot favourites Galway to the sword on 18 June, they came back down to earth when star defender, Larry 'Pop' Cummins, suffered a broken leg in a challenge match against Westmeath just a week before their first championship outing. At Boyle on 9 July, they needed a Jack McQuillan goal to salvage a draw against a Sligo side that had the McMorrough brothers in sparkling form. In the replay two weeks later, Sligo were superior for much of the game, but Roscommon eventually got the upper hand, Eamon Boland and Hugh Gibbons playing starring roles.

The scene was now set for a Roscommon–Mayo provincial showdown. They met at Tuam on 6 August. Based on their performance against Galway, and Roscommon's recent lacklustre displays, the Mayo men were generally fancied to prevail. While the game was close early on, Roscommon gradually began to recapture their All-Ireland form of 1943, and pulled away midway through the second half. Winning on a score of 2-11 to 1-6, it was the midfield supremacy of Boland and Liam Gilmartin that was their trump card. For a disappointed and disappointing Mayo, goalkeeper Tommy Byrne, Tommy Hoban and, as usual, Sean Flanagan, were outstanding.

In Ulster, 2 July was a very busy championship day. Monaghan had a close encounter with the home team when they met at Armagh, finally emerging 3-7 to 3-3 winners.

On the same day, Down beat Tyrone, 3-4 to 0-4, at Belfast. This game was closer than the winning margin suggests. Down goalkeeper John O'Hare came to their rescue when a Willie McKenna scorcher seemed certain to find the net, while Mick King was in the breach to repel a succession of Tyrone attacks. The second game in Belfast that day saw Cavan, with no fewer than eight newcomers, overcome Antrim on a score of 1-4 to 0-2. Among the debutants, future Tánaiste, John Wilson from Mullahoran, gave an outstanding display at left corner-back.

The first of the Ulster semi-finals saw Vincent Duffy star as Monaghan pipped Down, 1-5 to

Having been knocking on the door for a number of years in the early 1940s, the men from Carlow finally won the Leinster Championship in 1944. Back (l–r): Ted Joyce, Jim Archbold, Paddy Farrell, Paddy O'Sullivan, Jim Morris, Seamus Corcoran, Brian O'Rourke, John Doyle, Jim Hughes, Chris Maher, Johnny Lawler, Johnny Darcy, John Brady. Front (l–r): Luke Kelly, John 'Buller' Moore, 'Jimma' Rae, John 'Pim' Quinlan, Michael Byrne, Andy Murphy, Willie Hosey, Joe Brennan, Mattie Doyle, Peter 'Peenie' Whelan. *Courtesy Gaelic Art.*

1-4, at Belfast on 9 July. There was nothing close about the outcome of the second semi-final, as Cavan cantered away from Donegal, 5-9 to 2-3, at Omagh on 16 July. Top scorer for the winners was Crubany's Larry Murphy, who scored 2-1, including a spectacular effort when he flung himself full-length to fist the ball to the Donegal net.

The Ulster Final was played at Clones on 30 July in front of a crowd of 13,000 which, according to *The Anglo Celt*, was 'composed chiefly of cyclists from the contending counties, as well as from the adjoining Northern areas'.

The grounds had been newly revamped for the occasion but there was much angst when the admission charge was increased from one shilling (6 cent) to two shillings (12 cent). Monaghan controlled proceedings for three-quarters of the game but then Cavan's guile and experience took over as they held out for a 1-9 to 1-6 victory. Much of the credit for their win was put down to the half-forward line of Tony Tighe, Mick Higgins and Larry Murphy, with John Joe O'Reilly and Simon Deignan also to the fore. Reading the match report in *The Anglo Celt*, it is difficult to imagine how Monaghan managed to lose this game. No fewer than twelve of their team – Mulligan, McCarney, Rice, Brennan, Duffy, McDonald, Finnegan, McGrath, McCarville and McCormack and two McCooeys – were described as 'outstanding'.

If Cork were focusing on Kerry as the chief obstacle to retaining their Munster title, then they were not reckoning with Tipperary. At Clonmel on 18 June, they struggled to come to terms with the

Roscommon full-back J.P. 'Doc' O'Callaghan (on right) outjumps Kerry's Johnny Clifford as O'Callaghan's team mates Bill Carlos (centre) and Phelim Murray (7) await developments. *Image courtesy Colm Hennelly.*

midfield mastery of William 'Bunny' Lambe and Michael Cahill, ending up on the wrong end of a 1-9 to 1-3 scoreline. As expected, Kerry sauntered through the other side of the draw to tee up a provincial final clash against Tipperary at Limerick on 9 July. Reports of this game highlight Tipperary's total dominance at midfield, with Lambe and Cahill again in sparkling form. Against a backline marshalled by the outstanding Dick Winters, the Kerry forwards were a disappointment. However, their defence, with Keohane, Healy and Brosnan excelling, was rock solid. In a low scoring war of attrition, Kerry regained their crown, 1-6 to 0-5.

The Leinster Championship provided an early shock. While Carlow had been showing steady improvement, they surprised everyone but themselves by holding Kildare to a draw at Athy on 14 May. They went one better two weeks later at home when they had nine points to spare over the Lilywhites. Their championship journey continued with successive wins over Laois (2-8 to 2-3) and Wexford (5-7 to 3-6). Notwithstanding the team's goal-scoring exploits, it was their own goalkeeper, John 'Pim' Quinlan, who won most plaudits in these victories.

On the opposite side of the Leinster draw, Dublin had a narrow win over Meath before coming from eight points down to pip Louth in their quarter-final clash at Croke Park on 18 June. Their semi-final opponents were Longford, who had Jimmy Hannify to thank for their earlier win over Offaly in a game in which, *The Irish Press* declared, 'good football was out of the question'. Dublin went into this game as the hottest of favourites but they struggled throughout, finally snatching the winning point through Mick Falvey with the last kick of the game.

Over 15,000 people, mostly Carlow supporters, packed into Athy's Geraldine Park for the Leinster Final on 30 July. *The Nationalist and Leinster Times* described the 'never-ending stream of cyclists and horse drawn vehicles', further noting that 'bikes were parked in every available place, and even stabling found for the horses'.

Although Dublin took an early lead and held a four-point advantage at the break, they were under constant pressure at midfield, where Carlow's Jim Morris and Luke Kelly were imperious. This advantage translated into a succession of scores in the second half as the men from Carlow deservedly took the laurels, and their first provincial title, on a score of 2-6 to 1-6. Heroes all, the players were carried shoulder high as their ecstatic supporters went wild at the sound of the final whistle. Aside from Morris and Kelly, others picked out for special mention included team captain

Led by Knockcroghery's Jimmy Murray, the Roscommon team of 1944 parade before their showdown with Kerry.
Image courtesy of the GAA Museum at Croke Park.

Peter 'Peenie' Whelan, John 'Buller' Moore, 'Jimma' Rae, John Doyle and team trainer Jack Dundon.

The first of the All-Ireland semi-finals, between Roscommon and Cavan, took place at Croke Park on 20 August. There was no repeat of the close affairs of 1943, as the Roscommon men cantered to a 5-8 to 1-3 victory. The platform for this win was provided by midfielders Gilmartin and Boland, while the Roscommon forwards ran riot, with goals coming from Gibbons (two), Kinlough, Nerney and McQuillan. While Cavan could point to the absence of Joe Stafford, Barney Cully and Tom O'Reilly as a result of happenings in the 1943 Final, their problems seemed to be more deep-rooted. *The Anglo Celt* went so far as to suggest that 'not a few psychologists are endeavouring to fathom the problem'.

The Kerry–Carlow encounter saw the attendance record for a semi-final broken for the second consecutive week. Despite playing into a stiff breeze in the first half, Kerry held a one-point advantage at the break, 2-1 to 0-6. A goal from a deflection extended their lead to five points, and the result seemed a foregone conclusion. The Carlow men fought back gallantly, however, and points from Doyle (two) and Moore closed the gap to a single point. While Kerry held on to win 3-3 to 0-10, they were widely considered to have had all the luck. Brilliant defending by Eddie Walsh, Joe Keohane and Tadhg Healy saved the day for the Kingdom against luckless Carlow. Aside from conceding two very soft goals, the Leinster champions were deprived of the services of the outstanding Luke Kelly, who was injured early in the game.

THE FINAL – 24 SEPTEMBER

The sense of anticipation in the run-up to the 1944 Final was unprecedented. Roscommon had matured into one of the finest teams ever to grace the game, but nobody expected they would have an easy time against a resurgent Kerry. When the big day arrived, it was clear from early on that all attendance records would be smashed. At a time when transport restrictions were at their most severe, the official attendance of 79,245, ten thousand more than the 1938 record, was a truly astonishing figure. Even more impressive was the fact that when the gates closed over an hour before throw-in, many who had made the long trek to Dublin missed out on one of the greatest ever finals. As *The Irish Press* reported, 'Thousands saw what will be ranked as one of the most exciting finals ever, a grim, dogged, rugged game, robust and rapid, but yet displaying the ready sportsmanship of two great teams. They saw what thousands of others wished in vain to see.'

Those missing out didn't have the consolation of watching the highlights later on *The Sunday Game*, but, as always, the radio commentary of Michael O'Hehir brought the excitement of the game into every household in the country.

After a titanic battle Roscommon, having led 1-4 to 1-2 at the break, retained their title on a scoreline of 1-9 to 2-4. It was widely considered that this was a victory for youth over experience. The sides had been level on several occasions when Roscommon's pace and stamina began to give them the edge as the game entered the final quarter. The *Irish Independent* gave this succinct analysis of what separated the two teams: 'While Kerry had greater craft, they had not the youth of their opponents. Physically, both teams were magnificent sets of men. The Roscommon players, however, were better served by their youth and this gave them that extra bit of speed that enabled them to evade the traps and snares of their crafty opponents.'

Reports on the game were unanimous in crediting Kerry for putting up a magnificent battle in their bid to regain the title. Despite being hampered by a foot injury, Paddy 'Bawn' Brosnan was outstanding, while Michael 'Murt' Kelly and Dinny Lyne were said to have operated with 'machine like movement'. Teak-tough defenders Joe Keohane and Martin McCarthy tried everything to stem the Roscommon tide, but eventually had to give way to the Donal Keenan orchestrated forward division of Roscommon. As so often previously, central defenders 'Doc' O'Callaghan and Bill Carlos led by example as the Rossies marched to their second successive title. The final whistle witnessed unprecedented scenes of joy among Roscommon supporters. Their exuberance carried on into the night, as *The Irish Press* noted the following morning: 'Roscommon men and women were dancing on O'Connell Bridge last night. Watched by a smiling but startled Dublin audience, they jigged and reeled to the accompaniment of street musicians' Irish pipes.'

Although there was disappointment for Kerry, the consensus was that they had turned a corner and were well and truly on the way back. Surely Cork, the upstarts of 1943, could be discounted? The Kingdom could instead focus on the important task of spoiling Roscommon's three-in-a-row ambitions.

FINAL STATISTICS

	Roscommon	Kerry
Full-time:	1-9	2-4
Half-time:	1-4	1-2
Scorers:	D. Keenan 0-6 (0-5 frees)	D. Lyne 1-0
	F. Kinlough 1-1	E. Dunne 1-0
	J. Murray 0-1	P. Kennedy 0-2 (0-1 free)
	L. Gilmartin 0-1	B. Dillon 0-1
		M. Kelly 0-1
Attendance:	79,245	
Gate Receipts:	£6,476-9-6 (€8,223)	
Referee:	Paddy Mythen (Wexford)	

FINAL MISCELLANY

- The great throng that converged on Dublin for the final prompted the *Irish Independent* to note that 'The city's unpreparedness for such huge numbers was evidenced in the groups who walked the streets all night for want of sleeping accommodation.'
- When Louth lost out to Dublin in their Leinster semi-final encounter at Croke Park on 18 June, they brought on a talented teenager for his championship debut. Brendan O'Dowda would go on to become a renowned tenor. His grandson, Callum, became an Irish international soccer player.
- When Cavan played Donegal in the Ulster semi-final at Omagh on 16 July, the *Derry People* noted: 'As a tribute to the visiting teams from the Twenty-Six Counties, the Tricolour was flown from a prominent position in the grounds'.
- The Tipperary team that lost out to Kerry in the Munster Final included no fewer than seven members of the Army. They were Jim Williams, Dick Sleator, John Larkin, Chris Sullivan, William 'Bunny' Lambe, Pat O'Neill and Tom Ryan.
- On the eve of the Leinster Final which was played at Athy, the Dublin County Board relied on the *Evening Herald* to notify its players and subs where to assemble in advance of their journey to south Kildare. They were to meet outside McBirney's on Aston Quay at 12.00 noon. WhatsApp was a long way off in 1944.
- Acknowledging the county's designation as the Onion County, many of Carlow's fervid supporters were seen sporting scallions for colours on the day of their Leinster Final clash with Dublin.

1944 – THE YEAR THAT WAS

- Under the code name 'Operation Overlord', Allied troops landed on the beaches of Normandy on 6 June – D-Day.
- On 23 February, children's allowance, now called child benefit, was introduced in Ireland.
- In May 1944, Iceland voted to sever its ties with Denmark. It formally became a republic on 17 June.
- An article on the front page of the *Sunday Independent* of 17 December 1944:

  ### DRINKING AMONGST WOMEN AND GIRLS

  The lounge bars which were springing up in cities and towns were meant to cater specially for women and girls, said Rev. P. Doherty S.J., Dublin, Assistant Director, Pioneer Total Abstinence Association, preaching at Thurles Cathedral. It would be very tragic indeed if women and girls were to turn away from the high calling of womanhood and trample underfoot the splendid traditions of the Irish Catholic women of the past.

- At a time when product advertising was a standard feature on the front page of the national newspapers, page one of the *Irish Independent* on Thursday 21 December 1944 included the following bargain enticement to those stocking up for their Christmas dinner:

Turkeys (any weight)	2/6 per lb
Fat Geese	1/9 per lb
Chickens	1/9 per lb
Best Rabbits	1/8 each

  It seems doubtful that anyone spending £2 on a 16lb hen turkey in 1944 would have bothered to specify 'free range' or 'organic'.

1944 TEAM LINE-OUTS

ROSCOMMON (WINNERS)

1. Owensie Hoare
(St Coman's)

2. Bill Jackson
(Tarmon, also St Brigid's)

3. J.P. 'Doc' O'Callaghan
(Tarmon)

4. Jack Casserly
(Four Roads)

5. Brendan Lynch
(Oran, also Ballinaheglish and Army)

6. Bill Carlos
(Tarmon, also Ballintober and Garda)

7. Phelim Murray
(St Patrick's and UCD)

8. Eamon Boland
(Strokestown, also Tarmon and Lees, Cork)

9. Liam Gilmartin
(Sean McDermotts, Dublin, also Ballymurray and St Patrick's)

10. Frankie Kinlough
(Castleisland Desmonds, Kerry, also Moore)

11. Jimmy Murray
(St Patrick's) Capt.

12. Donal Keenan
(Elphin and UCD)

13. Hugh Gibbons
(Strokestown and UCG)

14. Jack McQuillan
(St Patrick's, also Ballyforan)

15. John Joe Nerney
(Boyle)

Subs: Derry McDermott (Mantua) Played; Gerry Dolan (St Coman's); Johnny Briens (St Patrick's); Peter Connellan (Strokestown); Frank Glynn (Tarmon); Mattie Heavey (St Patrick's, also Four Roads); Paddy Beisty (Mantua, also Elphin); Paddy 'Dickie' Hanley (Tarmon)

KERRY (RUNNERS-UP)

1. Dan O'Keeffe
(Kerins O'Rahillys)

2. Tadhg Healy
(John Mitchels)

3. Joe Keohane
(John Mitchels, also Geraldines)

4. Tim 'Timineen Deas' Brosnan
(Dingle)

5. Bill Dillon
(Dingle)

6. Martin McCarthy
(Castleisland Desmonds)

7. Eddie Walsh
(Knocknagoshel)

8. Paddy Kennedy
(Kerins O'Rahillys, also Geraldines, Dublin and Annascaul)

9. Sean Brosnan
(Dingle, also Geraldines, Dublin)

10. Johnny Clifford
(St Mary's, Cahirciveen, also An Chéad Cath, Galway)

11. Jackie Lyne
(Killarney Legion)

12. Paddy 'Bawn' Brosnan
(Dingle) Capt.

13. Dinny Lyne
(Killarney Legion)

14. Michael 'Murt' Kelly
(Beaufort, also Geraldines, Dublin)

15. Eddie Dunne
(John Mitchels)

Subs: Dan Kavanagh (Dr Crokes, also Dingle and UCG) Played; Johnny Walsh (Ballylongford) Played; Derry Burke (Castleisland Desmonds); Jimmy 'Gawksie' O'Gorman (Austin Stacks); Bill Casey (Dingle, also Lispole); Eddie Condon (Valentia); William 'Bruddy' O'Donnell (John Mitchels)

1945

At its Annual Congress on Easter Sunday 1945, the GAA voted to introduce a new rule whereby a ball going over the sideline would be kicked back into play, rather than by the traditional throwing method. The change, which was seen as a major deterrent to the practice of wilfully kicking the ball over the line, first saw the light of day in two games on Sunday 29 April.

At Enniscorthy, Wicklow hardly broke sweat when beating Kilkenny, 3-10 to 0-2. On the same day, the game between Longford and Westmeath at Mullingar was a much tighter affair, with the home team snatching a draw through a late point from their outstanding captain, Maurice Dunne. A week later, and now with the benefit of home advantage, Longford edged past their neighbours on a score of 1-10 to 2-6, and so progressed to meet Offaly in the quarter-final at Mullingar on 10 June. Through a combination of erratic shooting by their forwards and a solid Offaly defence in which dual player Jimmy Kelly shone, Longford bowed out of the championship at the wrong end of a 3-4 to 1-6 scoreline.

Offaly's next assignment was against Meath in the provincial semi-final at Portlaoise on 24 June. The Royal County had intially beaten Louth, before taking two games to finally overcome Dublin in the quarter-final. A peculiar aspect of the replay was that while Meath were generally perceived to have been very lucky to be on level terms at the end of the hour, they ran riot in extra time and romped home with a nine-point victory. Based on this scintillating half hour of play by the Meath men, the general view was that Offaly's prospects of advancing to the provincial final were bleak in the extreme.

For generations, Offaly footballers have paid scant regard to the exalted reputations of opposing teams. This was seldom more evident than on Sunday 24 June in Mullingar. They tore the form book to shreds with a display of no-nonsense, direct football that had the Meath men reeling from the first minute. While their six-point victory was based on a brilliant all-round performance, the star of the show was Billy Adams who, according to *The Irish Times*, 'gave a spectacular exhibition of fielding and used his speed and delightful swerve to full effect.'

On the opposite side of the Leinster draw, Kildare avenged their 1944 defeat at the hands of Carlow with a deserved 2-13 to 2-10 win over the home team at Dr Cullen Park on 6 May. Much of the credit for this unexpected result was attributed to their solid defence, in which the Geraghty brothers and goalkeeper Tommy Malone were outstanding. Their defence was much less impressive three weeks later when an emerging Wexford side hit them for five goals. A measure of Wexford's

Cork captain Tadhg Crowley with the Cup at Glanmire Station after his team's 1945 victory over Cavan. *Image courtesy of the GAA Museum at Croke Park.*

superiority can be gleaned from the fact that match reports all asserted that their goal tally would have been double this but for the acrobatic brilliance of Kildare netminder Malone.

Wexford's semi-final opposition was provided by Laois who had pipped Wicklow, 2-10 to 2-8, at Carlow on 17 June. At Nowlan Park on 1 July, they continued with their goal-scoring exploits, overcoming the Laois men 4-5 to 1-11. With Bill Delaney maintaining his outstanding championship form, Laois could have won the day, but some woeful shooting by their forwards proved to be their downfall. At the other end of the field, Des O'Neill, Paddy Keogh and Nicky Rackard rarely put a foot wrong, while defenders Willie Goodison, Ger Kavanagh and Jackie Culleton were rock-like in defence for Wexford.

The clash of Offaly and Wexford in the Leinster Final was a novel affair. It had been 1925 when Wexford last achieved provincial success, while this was only the second ever Leinster Final appearance for the Faithful County – they had lost out to Dublin by ten points in the 1907 decider. Played before a crowd of 10,000 at Portlaoise on 22 July, the game proved to be a major disappointment as Wexford ran out convincing 1-9 to 1-4 winners. While Goodison, Culleton, John 'Suck' Morris and Dermot Clancy were the key men for the Model County, the outstanding feature of the match was the titanic battle between Offaly full-back Jimmy Kelly and future Wexford hurling colossus Nicky Rackard. In what might be described in boxing parlance as a 'split decision', the Offaly man was generally regarded as having shaded matters.

After many years of dominance by Cavan, with the occasional Monaghan interruption, the Ulster Championship seemed to open up on the afternoon of Sunday 24 June. After a gap of eight years, Fermanagh returned to the senior ranks and started their campaign by overwhelming Monaghan 4-13 to 0-5 at Enniskillen, with Lisnaskea's Tommy Durnien in majestic form. On the same day, Armagh showed their credentials with a resounding 3-13 to 0-2 victory over Tyrone. A ding-dong semi-final battle at Clones on 8 July saw Fermanagh edge past Armagh by the slimmest of margins, 2-4 to 1-6. Coming from nowhere, the Ernesiders had seriously impressed on their way to what was only their third ever provincial final appearance.

In a game that marked Derry's first appearance in the Senior Championship, they faltered badly against a lacklustre Donegal at Letterkenny on 10 June. Despite the best efforts of Jack Convery, Roddy Gribbin and Mickey McNutt, the Derry men weren't yet equipped for the hurly-burly of the senior game.

Donegal's semi-final opponents were traditional kingpins Cavan, who had managed to overcome Antrim and Down in the earlier rounds, but not with the ease expected. Against Donegal, however, the men of Breffni turned on the style to win by a staggering twenty-point margin, 6-12 to 2-4. While little could be gleaned from this one-sided affair, Cavan were expected to ease past Fermanagh in the Ulster Final. They duly obliged with a 4-10 to 1-4 victory. Top rating in this game went to

There were huge celebrations when the Cork team returned home after their 1945 success. *Image courtesy of the GAA Museum at Croke Park.*

Cavan's Mick Higgins who, according to the *Irish Independent*, 'played the roles of defender, attacker, and link man in between; both departments with distinction.'

Reigning Munster champions Kerry had their first championship outing of the year when they met Limerick in the semi-final on 10 June. Although they emerged winners on an impressive score-line of 5-8 to 2-7, the game was in the balance until the final ten minutes. Limerick's sterling performance was largely down to the efforts of legendary hurlers Mick Mackey, Dick Stokes and Jackie Power. The second semi-final saw Cork pip Tipperary by one point in an entirely mediocre encounter at Dungarvan on 24 June. In light of Cork's subsequent progress in the championship, it is interesting to note that *The Cork Examiner* described this robust encounter as 'Not over productive of good football.'

The general presumption was that Kerry would have little difficulty in the final, especially as it was fixed for Fitzgerald Stadium, Killarney. Cork strengthened their team with the introduction of Clare man Mick Tubridy and hurling star Jack Lynch into their attack. Also, P.A. 'Weesh' Murphy returned to his familiar full-back position. These changes paid rich dividends in a game that saw the Rebels lead from start to finish, finally taking the honours on a score of 1-11 to 1-6. Cork supporters celebrated deliriously after this shock win, but it was an entirely different mood that hung over the Kerry camp. Under the banner headline 'Untrained Men Lost Us Title', *The Kerryman* sympathised with the thousands who had cycled 'twenty, thirty and forty miles', only to emerge 'disgusted, dazed and stunned' from Fitzgerald Stadium.

With Kerry and Carlow losing their respective provincial titles, the pattern continued in Connacht where Roscommon fell at the semi-final stage when Mayo beat them 2-8 to 1-6 at Sligo on 8 July. It was veteran Henry Kenny who led the charge for Mayo, capping a brilliant all-round performance with what *The Irish Press* described as a 'wonder goal'. As a result of this great win, the Mayo men were duly installed as favourites to overcome Galway in the provincial decider. The Tribesmen had other ideas, however, and they raced into a six-point lead within ten minutes of the throw-in. In a real 'backs to the wall' battle in the closing stages, and with Dinny Sullivan defiant at full-back for Galway, they held out for a two-point win, and so qualified to meet Cork in the first of the All-Ireland semi-finals.

The game between Galway and Cork at Croke Park on 12 August provided plenty of thrills for the attendance of over 33,000. Cork had to line out without their inspirational full-back, 'Weesh' Murphy, who was unable to travel on account of the death of his brother. Another absentee from the Munster Final win was Tadgh O'Driscoll who had recently had a finger amputated following an accident. Despite these losses, the Cork men took an early six-point lead with goals coming from Derry Beckett and Fachtna O'Donovan. Galway fought back valiantly but the Cork defence was up to the challenge, with goalkeeper Moll O'Driscoll making a number of brilliant saves. Winning on a scoreline of 2-12 to 2-8, the Leesiders now awaited the outcome of the second semi-final, between Cavan and Wexford, and their first All-Ireland Final appearance since 1911.

When Cavan and Wexford met on 19 August, it was widely expected that the Ulstermen would prevail with something to spare. This did not discourage supporters of the two counties, however, and a record semi-final crowd of over 44,500 turned up. The game was a very disappointing affair which Cavan won on a score of 1-4 to 0-5. The consensus was that their victory margin should have been much greater but their failure to convert numerous scoring chances left the result in doubt until the final whistle. During the course of the game they hit no fewer than nineteen wides as against seven for Wexford, with the deciding score from Joe Stafford being described in *The Irish Press* as 'a masterpiece'.

THE FINAL – 23 SEPTEMBER

One of the main talking points in the lead-up to the final was how the teams would cope with the revised, mid-championship, interpretation of the hand-pass rule. All but the fisted pass was now outlawed and referee John Dunne of Galway made it very clear in the days before the game that the rule would be applied rigidly. It was widely believed that Cavan's style of play would suffer more under the new interpretation, but they remained slight favourites to hold the upper hand. A curious aspect of the newspaper predictions was that they all invariably referenced 'Cavan's guile versus Cork's dash' in contrasting the respective styles of play.

As the day of the big game approached, interest throughout the country was at fever pitch and a huge crowd was expected. As it turned out, Sunday 23 September dawned to appalling weather conditions, with early morning wind, rain, thunder and lightning putting paid to any prospects of a record-breaking attendance.

While the weather had improved somewhat by the time play got underway, the slippery sod meant that conditions were far from ideal. It was a major blow to Cavan's prospects when star player Mick Higgins had to cry off through injury. They scored the first point of the game but Mick Tubridy had a goal for Cork after five minutes when he was put through by Derry Beckett. It was touch and go for the rest of the first half, with Cork holding a two-point advantage after thirty minutes. There was major controversy when Cavan's Simon Deignan sent the ball crashing to the Cork net on the stroke of half-time. With the umpire signalling a goal, and Michael O'Hehir's radio commentary 'confirming' the score, the referee decreed that the half-time whistle had blown, so denying the lead to the men of Breffni.

Cork edged further in front early in the second half but they were under severe pressure as Cavan launched attack after attack. Only for some very poor shooting, Cavan would likely have closed the gap. The final nail in their coffin was an opportunist goal by the elusive Beckett with minutes remaining. The final score was 2-5 to 0-7 as Cork took their first title since 1911. Star forward Derry Beckett and man of the match Eamonn Young, both sons of 1911 Cork players, had extra reason to celebrate. It was also a special day for Jack Lynch who, having played for the hurlers from 1941 to 1944, won his fifth senior All-Ireland medal in succession.

While Cavan could bemoan their wayward shooting, the Cork defence, in which 'Weesh' Murphy and Tadhg Crowley were outstanding, suffocated many of their moves. Cork had the edge at midfield while their forwards, especially Beckett, Tubridy and Lynch, were very efficient. Joe Stafford was the main threat for Cavan, while their half-back line of John Wilson, John Joe O'Reilly and Paddy Smith was universally lauded.

FINAL STATISTICS

	Cork	Cavan
Full-time:	2-5	0-7
Half-time:	1-4	0-5
Scorers:	D. Beckett 1-2 (0-1 free)	J. Stafford 0-3 (0-2 frees)
	M. Tubridy 1-2	T.P. O'Reilly 0-2
	H. O'Neill 0-1	T. Tighe 0-1
		P. Donohoe 0-1 (0-1 free)
Attendance:	67,329	
Gate Receipts:	£5,558-11-6 (€7,058)	
Referee:	John Dunne (Galway)	

FINAL MISCELLANY

- Cavan's Simon Deignan, a key member of the team that lined out against Cork in the final, had refereed the Munster Final between Cork and Kerry on 8 July.
- A feature of the 1945 decider was the number of fifties conceded. While Cork had two, *The Anglo Celt* made the confusing assertion that 'Cavan forced ten fifties (four in the first half and five in the second).'
- Newspaper advertisements appearing in the days after the 1945 Final proclaimed: 'The National Stadium, Croke Park was disinfected with Jeyes Fluid.'
- No fewer than eight members of Cork's 1945 panel were from the Clonakilty club. The Cavan panel included eleven former pupils of St Patrick's College in Cavan town.
- Future Taoiseach Jack Lynch won his only All-Ireland football medal in 1945. He won hurling medals in 1941, 1942, 1943, 1944 and 1946, becoming the first man to win six successive medals. His achievement was finally equalled by a number of Dublin footballers in 2020.
- In 1945, Cavan's teenage midfielder, Tony Tighe, was almost lost to a career in soccer. He was offered a professional contract by Glasgow Celtic.

1945 – THE YEAR THAT WAS

- As World War II drew to a close, the United States dropped atomic bombs on the Japanese cities of Hiroshima (6 August) and Nagasaki (9 August), resulting in well over 100,000 deaths.

- In 1945, American Export Airlines commenced a tri-weekly service between New York and Foynes. The one-way fare was £130 (€165).
- When Most Rev. Dr MacNamee, Bishop of Ardagh and Clonmacnoise, visited Ferbane in June 1945 to administer the sacrament of confirmation, his major concern seemed to be the dangerous practice of 'doing servile work on Sundays'. According to the *Offaly Independent*, Dr MacNamee declared that 'this commandment had been so seriously violated that he had found it necessary to speak very strongly about it … it was particularly shocking to see them engaged on the bogs at turf … it was utterly wrong and perverse.'

    Dr MacNamee went on to remind his congregation that there was only one operation for which permission could be grudgingly given by the parish priest, and that was where the hay crop was in danger of ruin owing to the state of the weather.
- Éamon de Valera, Ireland's Taoiseach and Minister for External Affairs, created controversy and hit the international news headlines in May 1945. The furore was caused when, after the death by suicide of Adolf Hitler, the Taoiseach, as reported by *The Irish Press*, 'called on Dr. Hempel, the German minister … to express his condolences'. Two weeks later, de Valera was hailed as a national hero when his response to Winston Churchill's criticism of Ireland's neutrality was broadcast on Radio Éireann. When he entered Dáil Éireann the following day, the entire house rose to accord the Taoiseach a standing ovation. If all this adulation was not enough, Mr de Valera was promptly elected a Freeman of the Borough of Sligo.
- On 14 June 1945, the people of Ireland cast their votes in the first ever presidential election. A present-day electorate might be surprised to discover what were then considered to be the essential virtues of an aspiring candidate. The official election blurb for Fine Gael candidate, Sean Mac Eoin, included the following: 'The President is the First Citizen of the State and, as such, he should be typical of the best of Irish manhood.'

1945 TEAM LINE-OUTS

CORK (WINNERS)

1. Michael 'Moll' O'Driscoll
(Clonakilty)

2. Dave Magnier
(Fermoy)

3. P.A. 'Weesh' Murphy
(Bere Island)

4. Caleb Crone
(Air Corps)

5. Paddy Cronin
(Fermoy)

6. Tadhg Crowley
(Clonakilty) Capt.

7. Din O'Connor
(Millstreet, also Dromtarriffe)

8. Fachtna O'Donovan
(Clonakilty)

9. Eamonn Young
(Army, also Dohenys)

10. Ned 'Togher' Casey
(Clonakilty, also Macroom)

11. Humphrey O'Neill
(Clonakilty)

12. Mick Tubridy
(Army, also Kilrush Shamrocks, Clare)

13. Jack Lynch
(Civil Service, also St Nicholas)

14. Jim Cronin
(Collins Barracks, also Milltown-
Castlemaine, Kerry)

15. Derry Beckett
(St Finbarr's)

Subs: Jim Aherne (Clonakilty); Sean Linehan (St Nicholas); Paddy O'Grady (Fermoy); Mick Finn (Clonakilty); Des Cullinane (Clonakilty); Paddy Healy (Clonakilty); Sean Cavanagh (Commercials); Brendan Murphy (Bere Island); Dave Roche (Fermoy)

CAVAN (RUNNERS-UP)

1. Brendan Kelly
(Bailieboro)

2. 'Big' Tom O'Reilly
(Cornafean) Capt.

3. Peter Paul Galligan
(Cornafean)

4. Barney Cully
(Arva)

5. John Wilson
(Mullahoran)

6. John Joe O'Reilly
(Curragh, Kildare, also Cornafean)

7. Paddy Smith
(Stradone, also St Mary's, Granard,
Longford and St Mary's, Ardee,
Louth)

8. Tony Tighe
(Mountnugent, also Castlerahan and
Clones, Monaghan)

9. Simon Deignan
(Army, also Mullagh and Civil Service)

10. T.P. O'Reilly
(Templeport, also Ballyconnell and
Belturbet)

11. Alphonsus 'Fonsie'
Commiskey
(Mullahoran)

12. Jack Boylan
(Mullahoran)

13. Joe Stafford
(Killinkere, also Arva and Clanna
Gael, Dublin)

14. Peter Donohoe
(Kilnaleck, also Mountnugent and
Banba, Dublin)

15. P.J. Duke
(Stradone and UCD)

Subs: John Willie Martin (Templeport); P.A. O'Reilly (Templeport); Owen Roe McGovern (Swanlinbar, also Clanna Gael, Dublin); Tom Casserly (Bailieboro); Connie Kelly (Mountnugent, also Oldcastle, Meath); Dessie Reilly (Stradone); Phil 'Gunner' Brady (Mullahoran, also Garda, Cork and Bailieboro)

Mick Higgins (Mountnugent) was injured and unavailable for selection.

1946

The championship of 1946 provided more than its share of controversy and heated debate.

Unusually, all four provincial winners from 1945 lost their titles. On 2 June, All-Ireland champions Cork fell when Kerry beat them by four points before a crowd of 15,000 at Killarney. The scoreline of 1-8 to 1-4 does little justice to the drama that unfolded. With two evenly matched teams going hammer and tongs, Cork's defence contrived to 'score' 1-1 for Kerry in a three-minute spell early in the second half – the 'own point' being the result of Caleb Crone's unfortunate attempt to fist the ball away from the danger zone. Despite a late rally, they had dug themselves into too deep a hole and the heroic efforts of Jim Cronin to retrieve the situation came to nought. For Kerry, Jackie Lyne was in outstanding form while Ger Teahan was described by *The Irish Press* as being 'in one of his greatest moods' and 'was the idol of the Kerry crowd'.

Anyone who thought Kerry would now cruise to the Munster title hadn't reckoned with the strong challenge Clare would present. The men from the Kingdom were led a merry dance in the first half of their clash at Ennis on 7 July. They trailed by five points at the break and, after a pulsating second half, needed last-minute scores from Lyne and Paddy Burke to scrape a two-point victory. There were no such heroics from Waterford in the final, as Kerry ran out comprehensive fourteen-point winners.

In Ulster, Cavan got off to a flying start with an emphatic 8-13 to 1-3 victory over Tyrone at Omagh on 23 June. This was after easing up somewhat in the second half – they led 7-7 to 0-1 at half-time! On the same day at Clones, Donegal had a surprise five-point win over Monaghan to tee up a provincial semi-final clash with Cavan. When they met at Omagh on 7 July, however, Donegal suffered a similar fate to Tyrone. They trailed 3-5 to 0-0 at half-time and eventually suffered a humiliating twenty-point defeat. In the second of the Ulster semi-finals, Antrim, having already disposed of Derry, showed very impressive form in beating Armagh by nine points on 15 July.

The final was played at Clones on 21 July where, against all predictions, Antrim took their first title since 1913 with a 2-8 to 1-7 victory. The foundations for their success were based on a lightning start which saw them five points ahead after just three minutes' play. Reports on the game highlighted the dazzling play of their half-forward line of Sean Gibson, Kevin Armstrong and Frank McCorry. Midfielders Sean Gallagher and Harry 'Red Dog' O'Neill also impressed while corner-forward Joe McCallin capped a fine display with two crafty goals.

The opening game of the Connacht Championship took place at Carrick-on-Shannon on 26

May where the local side were utterly overwhelmed as Sligo ran out 6-10 to 0-6 winners. Mayo provided Sligo's semi-final opposition at Ballina on 23 June where, in torrential conditions, Joe Gilvarry inspired the Mayo men to a three-point win. Reigning provincial champions Galway fell to Roscommon on 16 June in a game that saw Phelim Murray produce an outstanding midfield display while scoring five points in a 0-7 to 0-4 victory.

The Mayo v Roscommon provincial final clash at Ballinasloe on 21 July was a truly extraordinary affair. The dramatic events were vividly captured in the opening paragraph of the following day's *Irish Independent*: 'The referee consulting two goal-umpires; the excited crowd on tenterhooks awaiting their decision; the exultant Roscommon captain, J Murray, raising the green flag after the official had at first refused to do so, and finally the score being hesitatingly set up on the board; that was the scene of absolute confusion which preceded the awarding of a goal, scored by Jimmy Murray, which paved the way for his side's one point victory – 1-4 to 0-6 – over Mayo in the Connacht Senior football final at Duggan Park, Ballinasloe yesterday.'

This apparent victory for Roscommon was not the end of the story, however. After a series of objections and counter-objections, the Connacht Council, following a three-hour debate and on a seven to six majority, finally accepted the referee's report and ordered a replay. This time Roscommon made no mistake and ran out emphatic 1-9 to 1-2 winners in a game which saw Bill Carlos give an outstanding performance.

The Leinster Championship opener saw Kildare and Carlow finish level, 2-3 each, in a dour affair at Athy on 5 May. The following Sunday, Kildare edged the tie by a single point when, as in the drawn game, a Bob Martin goal proved to be the crucial score.

The Lilywhites were very much the outsiders when they met reigning champions Wexford in the semi-final clash at Carlow on 16 June. Expectations were met when they trailed by eight points at half-time. In keeping with their reputation for 'consistent inconsistency', they staged a remarkable comeback and won the game by two points to reach their first provincial decider in eleven years. Dublin and Laois were considered the strongest teams on the other side of the draw and when they met at Athy on 19 May, the Laois men won, 1-3 to 0-5, largely thanks to the brilliance of Tommy Murphy. Laois progressed to the final with narrow wins over both Offaly and Louth.

The final at Croke Park on 14 July drew a record crowd of 27,353 and saw Tommy Murphy once again inspire his team to victory. Apart from the excellence of his defensive play, he scored no fewer than eight points in a 0-11 to 1-6 victory. His contribution was described in *The Irish Press* the following morning: 'If ever a man carried his team to victory Tommy Murphy … did it in capital style at Croke Park yesterday.'

The novel meeting of Antrim and Kerry in the first of the All-Ireland semi-finals created its own share of controversy. A late goal by Batt Garvey was the deciding score as Kerry emerged 2-7 to 0-10 winners, but the real story of this clash was Antrim's objection on the grounds of Kerry's rough play. In lodging their objection, the Antrim County Board listed a litany of injuries to eight of their players, claiming that Kerry had employed 'brutal methods' against them. On a vote, the objection was lost and Kerry proceeded to contest the final.

In the second semi-final, Roscommon were somewhat fortunate to edge past Laois on a final score of 3-5 to 2-6. A great block by Gerry Dolan in the dying minutes saved Roscommon's bacon in a game where, once again, Tommy Murphy was in majestic form.

THE FINAL – 6 OCTOBER

The 1946 decider was fixed for 22 September but, in an unprecedented move, and with just three days to go, the Central Council of the GAA took the decision to postpone the game for two weeks. After one of the wettest summers on record, the change released at least 50,000 additional volunteers to add to the half million already committed to the national 'Save the Harvest' emergency campaign.

The most notable footballing consequence of the postponement was that Kerry's Bill Casey, suspended after his exploits in the semi-final against Antrim, was now eligible to play. Any perceptions that Casey's return to the fold would swing the pendulum firmly in Kerry's favour were quickly dispelled when referee Bill Delaney threw in the ball on 6 October. Roscommon immediately took control throughout the field and Kerry seemed powerless against their relentless pressure. With only minutes to go Roscommon led by six points and their captain, Jimmy Murray, left the field temporarily to have blood wiped from his face, allegedly in order to 'look right' for the presentation. It was then that Kerry's Paddy Kennedy really began to exert his influence. He launched an attack that led to a goal from Paddy Burke, setting up a grandstand finish in the process. The deafening excitement that greeted Burke's goal had hardly died down when 'Gega' O'Connor lobbed a high ball into the Roscommon goalmouth. Backs and forwards scrambled furiously for possession but the ball ended up in the Roscommon net and the teams were level. A helter-skelter finish, which included six minutes of added time, failed to break the deadlock in what was one of the most exciting All-Ireland Final finishes ever witnessed.

THE REPLAY – 27 OCTOBER

The replay three weeks later saw Roscommon, understandably, installed as warm favourites to capture the title they had last held in 1944. Kerry had other ideas, however, and this time they never let Roscommon out of their sights. No more than two points separated the teams for most of the game and the scores were level with four minutes to go. Just when it looked like extra time would be required, Kerry introduced Gus Cremin. He had captained the team in the drawn match but had been dropped for the replay. Playing very solidly since his introduction, he now embellished his performance with a magnificent long-range point and Kerry were ahead with only seconds to go. Before the stroke of full-time a 'Gega' O'Connor free was fielded by Roscommon goalkeeper Gerry Dolan who was then unceremoniously bundled into the net by the inrushing forwards. The score was let stand and Kerry took their thirteenth title on a score of 2-8 to 0-10. This put them at the top of the All-Ireland roll of honour, a position they have held ever since.

FINAL STATISTICS — DRAW

	Kerry	Roscommon
Full-time:	2-4	1-7
Half-time:	0-1	1-5
Scorers:	Tom O'Connor 1-2 (0-2 frees)	D. Keenan 0-4 (0-4 frees)
	P. Burke 1-1	J.J. Fallon 1-1
	B. Garvey 0-1	F. Kinlough 0-2
Attendance:	75,771	
Gate Receipts:	£6,190-18-8 (€7,871)	
Referee:	Bill Delaney (Laois)	

FINAL STATISTICS — REPLAY

	Kerry	Roscommon
Full-time:	2-8	0-10
Half-time:	0-4	0-6
Scorers:	Tom O'Connor 1-4 (0-4 frees)	D. Keenan 0-7 (0-7 frees)
	P. Burke 1-0	J.J. Fallon 0-2
	B. Garvey 0-2	J. McQuillan 0-1
	P. Kennedy 0-1	
	G. Cremin 0-1	
Attendance:	65,661	
Gate Receipts:	£5,503 (€6,987)	
Referee:	Paddy Mythen (Wexford)	

FINAL MISCELLANY

- Kerry had four different captains during their successful 1946 campaign: Eddie Dowling, Bill Casey, Gus Cremin and Paddy Kennedy.
- For both the draw and the replay, the ball was thrown in by Dr Redmond Prenderville, Bishop of Perth. He had lined out with the winning Kerry team in the 1924 Final.
- Both teams had a novel mascot for this final. Roscommon had a wild Irish hare while Kerry had a duck, fully attired in green and gold.
- The *Irish Independent* of 19 September described Roscommon's daily regime in preparation for the 1946 Final:

  8.30: Rise

  9.30: Breakfast

  10.30: Walk

12.45: Sponging and towelling

1.30: Dinner

3.30: To St Coman's Park for limbering, free exercises, hurdling, sprinting, place-kicking and general tactics

5.30: Baths and attention to injuries

6.30: Tea

8.00: Short walk

9.45: Supper

10.30: Retire

- Two extracts from *The Irish Press* of Monday 7 October:

  – A Kildare contingent on the Hogan Stand had a portable radio with them and they had the unusual experience of watching the game and, at the same time, listening to the broadcast on Radio Eireann.

  – The midday Aer Lingus plane from Shannon had a party of 18 from Limerick who, after attending the game, returned home last night.

1946 – THE YEAR THAT WAS

- The Nuremburg War Crimes Tribunal completed its deliberations in October 1946. Eleven of the twenty-one accused were sentenced to death by hanging.
- The United Nations was established on 26 June, with fifty states signing up.
- The Republic of Yugoslavia was formed under the leadership of General Tito on 15 August.
- The bikini made its official debut in 1946.
- From the business pages of the *Irish Independent* of 5 October:

  Applications are invited from men aged 35 to 45 years for the position of Chief Accountant to Aer Rianta and its subsidiaries.

  Having met the gender and age parameters, prospective applicants are then wowed by the prospect of receiving a salary of 'not less than £800 per annum'.

1946 TEAM LINE-OUTS — DRAW

KERRY

1. Dan O'Keeffe
(Kerins O'Rahillys)

2. Dinny Lyne
(Killarney Legion)

3. Joe Keohane
(John Mitchels, also Geraldines, Dublin)

4. Paddy 'Bawn' Brosnan
(Dingle)

5. Teddy O'Connor
(Dr Crokes)

6. Bill Casey
(Dingle, also Lispole)

7. Eddie Walsh
(Knocknagoshel)

8. Gus Cremin
(Ballydonoghue) Capt.

9. Dan Kavanagh
(Dr Crokes, also Dingle)

10. William 'Bruddy' O'Donnell
(John Mitchels)

11. Paddy Kennedy
(Kerins O'Rahillys, also Geraldines, Dublin and Annascaul)

12. Batt Garvey
(Dingle, also Geraldines, Dublin)

13. Jackie Lyne
(Killarney Legion)

14. Paddy Burke
(Milltown/Castlemaine)

15. Tom 'Gega' O'Connor
(Dingle)

Subs: Eddie Dowling (Ballydonoghue) Played; Brendan Kelliher (Keel) Played; Ger Teahan (Dingle, also Laune Rangers and Kerins O'Rahillys); Jackie Falvey (Kerins O'Rahillys); Frank O'Keeffe (John Mitchels); Charlie O'Connor (Castleisland Desmonds); Tom Long (Dingle); Mossie Moore (Dingle); Nick O'Donoghue (John Mitchels); Teddy O'Sullivan (Killarney Legion)

ROSCOMMON

1. Gerry Dolan
(St Coman's)

2. Bill Jackson
(Tarmon)

3. Jack Casserly
(Four Roads)

4. Owensie Hoare
(St Coman's)

5. Brendan Lynch
(Oran, also Ballinaheglish and Garda)

6. Bill Carlos
(Tarmon, also Ballintober and Civil Service)

7. Tom Collins
(Crossmolina, Mayo, also Croghan)

8. Phelim Murray
(St Patrick's and UCD)

9. Eamon Boland
(Tarmon, also Strokestown and Lees, Cork)

10. Frankie Kinlough
(Castleisland Desmonds, Kerry, also Moore)

11. Jimmy Murray
(St Patrick's) Capt.

12. Donal Keenan
(Elphin and UCD)

13. Jack McQuillan
(St Patrick's)

14. John Joe Fallon
(Strokestown, also Bornacoola, Leitrim)

15. John Joe Nerney
(Boyle)

Subs: Vinny Beirne (Tibohine, also Frenchpark) Played; J.P. 'Doc' O'Callaghan (Tarmon); Derry McDermott (Mantua); Hugh Gibbons (Strokestown); Mattie Heavey (St Patrick's, also Four Roads); Jim Quinn (St Coman's); Frank Cox (Boyle); Timmy J. Lynch (Keadue, also Boyle); Des Boyd (Croghan); Johnny Briens (St Patrick's)

1946 TEAM LINE-OUTS — REPLAY

KERRY (WINNERS)

1. Dan O'Keeffe
(Kerins O'Rahillys)

2. Dinny Lyne
(Killarney Legion)

3. Joe Keohane
(John Mitchels, also Geraldines, Dublin)

4. Paddy 'Bawn' Brosnan
(Dingle)

5. Jackie Lyne
(Killarney Legion)

6. Bill Casey
(Dingle, also Lispole)

7. Eddie Walsh
(Knocknagoshel)

8. Paddy Kennedy
(Kerins O'Rahillys, also Geraldines, Dublin and Annascaul) Capt.

9. Teddy O'Connor
(Dr Crokes)

10. Jackie Falvey
(Kerins O'Rahillys)

11. Tom 'Gega' O'Connor
(Dingle)

12. Batt Garvey
(Dingle, also Geraldines, Dublin)

13. Frank O'Keeffe
(John Mitchels)

14. Paddy Burke
(Milltown/Castlemaine)

15. Dan Kavanagh
(Dr Crokes, also Dingle)

Subs: Gus Cremin (Ballydonoghue) Played; Brendan Kelliher (Keel); William 'Bruddy' O'Donnell (John Mitchels); Ger Teahan (Dingle, also Laune Rangers and Kerins O'Rahillys); Mick Finucane (Ballydonoghue); Teddy O'Sullivan (Killarney Legion); Tom Long (Dingle)

Other Panel Members: Charlie O'Connor (Castleisland Desmonds); Mossie Moore (Dingle); Nick O'Donoghue (John Mitchels)

ROSCOMMON (RUNNERS-UP)

1. Gerry Dolan
(St Coman's)

2. Bill Jackson
(Tarmon)

3. Jack Casserly
(Four Roads)

4. Owensie Hoare
(St Coman's)

5. Brendan Lynch
(Oran, also Ballinaheglish and Garda)

6. Bill Carlos
(Tarmon, also Ballintober and Civil Service)

7. Tom Collins
(Crossmolina, Mayo, also Croghan)

8. Phelim Murray
(St Patrick's and UCD)

9. Eamon Boland
(Tarmon, also Strokestown and Lees, Cork)

10. Frankie Kinlough
(Castleisland Desmonds, Kerry, also Moore)

11. Jimmy Murray
(St Patrick's) Capt.

12. Donal Keenan
(Elphin and UCD)

13. Jack McQuillan
(St Patrick's)

14. John Joe Fallon
(Strokestown, also Bornacoola, Leitrim)

15. John Joe Nerney
(Boyle)

Subs: Vinny Beirne (Tibohine, also Frenchpark) Played; J.P. 'Doc' O'Callaghan (Tarmon); Derry McDermott (Mantua); Hugh Gibbons (Strokestown); Mattie Heavey (St Patrick's, also Four Roads); Jim Quinn (St Coman's); Des Boyd (Croghan); Timmy J. Lynch (Keadue, also Boyle); Frank Cox (Boyle); Johnny Briens (St Patrick's)

1947

At the prompting of Clare's Canon Michael Hamilton, and to mark the centenary of the Great Famine, the GAA took the momentous decision to stage the 1947 Football Final in New York. The prospect of playing in such an exotic location generated enormous interest among the principal contenders, and record match attendances reflected tremendous grassroots enthusiasm for the project.

Reigning champions Kerry made a serious statement of intent when they lined out against Clare at Limerick on 6 July. Unlike in previous years, it was clear they had already commenced collective training when they swamped the unfortunate men from the Banner on a score of 9-10 to 0-4. It was Frank O'Keeffe who took the scoring honours with a three-goal salvo. Noting the huge score chalked up, the *Irish Independent* report on the game observed that: 'The scoreboard manipulator . . . had one of the busiest afternoons of his life.'

On the same day in Fermoy, Cork were far from impressive when beating Tipperary 2-3 to 1-2. Interestingly, their outstanding performer was Kerry native James 'Jas' Murphy.

When Cork and Kerry met at the Athletic Grounds on 27 July, a new record Munster Final crowd of 32,000 attended the game. Thousands more struggled in vain to gain entry and the gates were locked almost two hours before the throw-in. It was a day of sweltering heat and many reports provide vivid accounts of people collapsing and requiring medical attention. Some enterprising hawkers ran a profitable trade of selling empty orange boxes to patrons straining to get a glimpse of proceedings. In contrast to the stifling conditions, the major talking point was the appalling condition of the pitch, which was completely waterlogged after recent heavy rains.

Notwithstanding the challenges presented, the teams served up one of the greatest ever Munster showdowns. Excitement was at fever pitch throughout. As Cork's Jim Ahern lined up to take a second-half penalty, Kerry full-back Joe Keohane placed his foot on the ball while appealing the decision with referee Simon Deignan. With the ball now firmly embedded in the sodden ground, Ahern's kick was miscued and Dan O'Keeffe made an easy save. The real turning point came in the closing minutes, however, when Frank O'Keeffe, repeating his semi-final heroics, hit a screamer to the Cork net, leaving Kerry winners on a score of 3-8 to 2-6.

In Leinster, champions Laois held off the Kildare challenge, 2-7 to 1-8, when they met in front of a crowd of 20,000 at Tullamore on 22 June. Holding a commanding eight-point lead early in the second half, the Laois men seemed to be sauntering to an easy victory when the Sarsfields duo of Mickey Geraghty and Paddy 'Boiler' White inspired a remarkable comeback. Laois required two

The Cavan team of 1947, winners of the only All-Ireland Final played outside the country. Back (l–r): Eunan Tiernan, T.P. O'Reilly, 'Big' Tom O'Reilly, Peter Donohoe, Tony Tighe, John Wilson, Phil 'Gunner' Brady; middle (l–r): John McGeough (trainer), Willie Doonan, Terry Sheridan, Val Gannon, Simon Deignan, Columba McDyer, P.J. Duke, Hughie O'Reilly (team manager); front (l–r): Hughie Smyth (Secretary, County Board), Joe Stafford, Owen Roe McGovern, John Joe O'Reilly (captain), Edwin Carolan, Paddy Smith, Patsy Lynch (Chairman, County Board). *Image courtesy of the GAA Museum at Croke Park.*

late points from Cork-based newcomer Dom Murray to finally get over the line, and so advance to a semi-final.

Here they faced Offaly, who had shown well in defeating Carlow 2-6 to 1-3 at Portlaoise on 11 May. Many expected this to be a close encounter but Offaly failed to ignite, and fell to a twenty-two point defeat, 5-11 to 0-4. Although it is difficult to assess Laois's true worth on the basis of this win, Jim Sayers, Mick 'Cutchie' Haughney, Bill Delaney and goal-poacher Stephen 'Faun' Hughes were very impressive.

On the other side of the Leinster draw, it was Meath who came powering through with impressive wins over Wicklow (5-7 to 2-3), Westmeath (1-8 to 0-5) and Louth (0-9 to 0-4). One of the highlights of Meath's run was Peter McDermott's performance against Wicklow when he hit four spectacular goals.

The Leinster Final at Croke Park on 20 July saw the previous record attendance of 29,351 consigned to history as 41,631 paid to see the much anticipated clash of Laois and Meath. In a game where they showed no weak link, Meath produced a spectacular performance as they ran out 3-7 to

1-7 winners. Their forwards were particularly impressive, with McDermott scoring 2-3 as he continued his great run of form.

Roscommon, All-Ireland runners-up in 1946, had little difficulty in retaining their Connacht title. In turn, they overcame Mayo (1-10 to 0-4) and Leitrim (1-9 to 0-3) before meeting Sligo in the final. Sligo's semi-final victory over Galway was a major shock, the highlight of which was an outrageous score from stalwart Tom Dunleavy, who struck a sixty-five-yard free over the bar. The final was something of a cakewalk for Roscommon as the Murray brothers wreaked havoc with the Sligo defence, the game ending on a 2-12 to 1-8 scoreline. As is often the case when a team suffers a big defeat, it was the losers' goalkeeper who was their shining light – Brendan Wickham saved his team from total annihilation with an outstanding display.

There were four draws in the 1947 Ulster Championship. Tyrone and Fermanagh could not be separated when they met at Irvinestown on 8 June, but Tyrone pulled through by two points in the replay the following Sunday. They also needed a replay before accounting for Armagh (2-5 to 1-4), thus advancing to the semi-final against Cavan. The Breffni men had themselves required a replay before overcoming Monaghan by two points. Home advantage counted for little when Tyrone fell by fifteen points to Cavan at Dungannon on 6 July.

As expected, Cavan's provincial final opponents were Antrim, who had easily accounted for Donegal and Down on their way to the decider. In a reversal of the previous year's result, Cavan came

Homecoming of all homecomings. Greeted by their ecstatic supporters, the Cavan team parades through the town's Casement Street in the aftermath of the historic 1947 triumph. *Image courtesy of the GAA Museum at Croke Park.*

out on top, 3-4 to 1-6, before a crowd of 34,000 at Clones on 20 July. The basis for Cavan's success was a blistering start which saw them eleven points up inside as many minutes. Peter Donohoe led the scoring charge while, according to the *Irish Independent*, Mick Higgins and T.P. O'Reilly were 'lambasting' the Antrim lines. Any hopes of a revival by the Glensmen were dealt a fatal blow when Kevin Armstrong was forced to retire through injury.

If the Polo Grounds factor was responsible for the upsurge in match attendances throughout the 1947 campaign, the dial moved to an entirely new level when it came to the All-Ireland semi-finals. On 3 August, a crowd of just over 60,000 turned up to see Cavan and Roscommon do battle in what was a rerun of the 1943 decider. This broke the previous semi-final record of 51,275 who watched Roscommon and Laois in 1946. It was a hectic, hard-hitting game which saw Cavan emerge winners, 2-6 to 0-6. With what *The Irish Press* described as a 'million-dollar goal', engineered by Tony Tighe and finished by Peter Donohoe, Cavan grabbed the early initiative. Injuries saw the early departure of Roscommon's Bill Carlos, Jimmy Murray and Tom Collins and they suffered further misfortune when a brilliant Jack McQuillan goal was disallowed in the second half. The result was finally settled when, further embellishing a brilliant performance, Tony Tighe found the Roscommon net with a rasping shot in the dying minutes.

It took precisely seven days for the new semi-final attendance record to be overtaken. Just under 66,000 flocked to headquarters to see the eagerly awaited clash of Kerry and Meath. Predictions that a classic was on the cards proved wide of the mark. Kerry simply overwhelmed Meath, and booked their place in the final on a score of 1-11 to 0-5. The introduction of Eddie Dowling for the injured Paddy Kennedy had a huge impact on the game as the Ballydonoghue man proceeded to dominate the midfield exchanges. Any hopes of a Meath resurgence were finally dashed when William 'Bruddy' O'Donnell sent a daisy-cutter past the outstretched Kevin Smyth late in the game.

THE FINAL – 14 SEPTEMBER

More than seventy years after the historic Polo Grounds final of 1947, it is difficult to comprehend the pioneering nature of what was achieved. In the lead-up to the game, GAA General Secretary Pádraig Ó Caoimh spent several weeks in New York attending to every organisational detail. At home, his wife, Peg, filled the chief liaison role in dealing with the various parties which sought advice and support in relation to the upcoming adventure.

The journey to New York was undertaken through a combination of air and sea travel. A twenty-nine-hour flight, and the essential refuelling stops, may seem extreme from the vantage point of the twenty-first century. As we reflect on the contrast with modern air travel it is even more interesting to consider the experience of those who travelled by ship. These weary travellers reached their destination in five days, the same time it took for Neil Armstrong and his fellow-astronauts to reach the moon in 1969.

The game itself provided more than its share of exciting and quality play, notwithstanding the sweltering heat and condensed dimensions of the rock-hard pitch. To complete the hardships for the warriors from Cavan and Kerry, the centre of the field was adorned by an elevated baseball pitcher's mound.

In the extreme heat and humidity, Kerry made a lightning start. Batt Garvey and the imperious Eddie Dowling scored early goals to give their team an eight-point lead. Cavan's response was to move Mick Higgins and Tony Tighe to midfield. At the same time, the unfortunate Dowling landed heavily on the baseball mound and had to leave the field. Cavan now began to make inroads into Kerry territory and goals from Higgins and Joe Stafford gave them a one-point advantage at the break, 2-5 to 2-4.

In the second half, Peter Donohoe proceeded to give an exhibition of place kicking. He ended up with a tally of eight points as Cavan marched to a 2-11 to 2-7 victory. Apart from Donohoe's scoring feat, Cavan's success was based on the brilliance of their half-back line of Deignan, O'Reilly and Duke and a man-of-the-match performance from New York native Mick Higgins. Nothing of Kerry's much vaunted reputation was lost in this epic encounter. In defence, the Lyne brothers and Eddie Walsh played brilliantly while their best attacker, and scorer-in-chief was, once again, the redoubtable 'Gega' O'Connor.

The sequel to the game involved an exhibition game where the counties combined to challenge a local selection. The teams eventually arrived home in early October, having completed the greatest adventure in GAA history.

FINAL STATISTICS

	Cavan	Kerry
Full-time:	2-11	2-7
Half-time:	2-5	2-4
Scorers:	P. Donohoe 0-8 (0-6 frees)	Tom O'Connor 0-5 (0-5 frees)
	M. Higgins 1-2	E. Dowling 1-0
	J. Stafford 1-0	B. Garvey 1-0
	C. McDyer 0-1	P. Kennedy 0-1
		Teddy O'Connor 0-1
Attendance:	34,941	
Gate Receipts:	£38,000 (€48,250)	
Referee:	Martin O'Neill (Wexford)	

FINAL MISCELLANY

- The *Irish Independent* reported on the morning of 15 September: 'The biggest radio audience of the GAA and Radio Eireann was chalked up last night, when almost every household in the country gathered about the loud speaker to hear Michael O'Hehir's commentary on the match. Carried by landline from the Polo Grounds, New York, and by transatlantic cable, and broadcast from Dublin, Athlone and Cork transmitters, the commentary was heard quite plainly in this country.'

- A film of the final was made by Winick Films Corporation, under the supervision of the General Secretary of the GAA, Pádraig Ó Caoimh, for the National Film Institute. *The Irish Press* noted that: 'The film will be flown to Ireland by Constellation plane and will be shown in Dublin cinemas on Saturday. After Dublin, Kerry and Cavan cinemas will be the first to be served.'

- Reporting from New York, Anna Kelly advised readers of *The Irish Press*: 'There is no shortage of food or drink in this dog's house, hot dog, frankfuerters, cheese, ham, sandwiches, beer, minerals, milk, ice cream, mounted sticks, coca cola, chewing gum, candies, all plentiful. Pennants of the Kerry and Cavan teams are also selling and gramophone records of Mr. de Valera's speech on Partition on last St. Patrick's Day. It is also in book form, with his photo, at two dollars each.'

This report, and those of Arthur P. Quinlan, also of *The Irish Press*, were made possible by the co-operation of the United Press and Commercial Cables in New York, London and Dublin. Readers were informed:

> Our reports were radioed direct from the Polo Grounds to the New York offices of United Press, and then transmitted to Dublin via London … The story behind the appearance of the pictures is one of split-second timing and break-neck rush. As Associated Press experts in London watched the first picture come from the machine a fast car stood outside the building with its engine running. In four minutes a transmitter was pulsing out the picture to The Irish Press process room in Dublin. The other four pictures followed (five appeared in our later additions) and the last was in Dublin before 2.00 a.m. Fleet Street was professionally excited about the Irish newspaper enterprise.

- Cavan half-forward Columba McDyer was a busy man in September 1947. Days before travelling to New York where he became the first Donegal man to collect an All-Ireland medal, he travelled to Ballina in Mayo where he married his fiancée, Peggy, a union that would extend for well over half a century, until he died in 2001, the week of the Football Final.

- Supporters of Cavan and Roscommon who attended the All-Ireland semi-final clash on 3 August not only arrived early but, it seems, were a very thirsty lot. *The Irish Press* described the scene in the city centre on the day before the game:

> Reckoned at over 15,000, Saturday's influx played havoc with the stocks of public houses, already seriously affected by the abnormal tourist trade the previous week.
>
> By 6.30 stout was off, whiskey non-existent; within an hour beer and cider had disappeared, sherry and port depleted, and at 9 o'clock, one out of every two houses within walking distance of O'Connell Bridge had closed, sold out completely.

- So newsworthy was the imminent Polo Grounds game with Kerry that *The Anglo Celt* of 6 September transferred much of its usual coverage to the front page, under the heading 'ON

THEIR WAY TO U.S.A.'. The adjacent column gave details of an equally important event. This was an account of the prosecution of father and son, John and Michael McBride, from Castleblayney in relation to the alleged attempt to export seven turkeys. Under the banner headline 'MONAGHAN TURKEYS', readers were told that the case was dismissed on the basis that there was corroborating local evidence that Mrs McBride had reared the turkeys and there was no question of intention to export.

1947 – THE YEAR THAT WAS

- On 15 August 1947, India was partitioned into the independent states of India and Pakistan.
- The Dead Sea Scrolls were discovered at Qumran in Palestine.
- The carbon-dating technique was discovered in 1947.
- Addressing the July 1947 meeting of the Gaelic League in Dublin, Ceallacháin MacCárthaigh told delegates that of the 30,000 who emigrated from Ireland in 1946, 20,000 were girls. Of these, 14,000 were under fifteen years of age.

1947 TEAM LINE-OUTS

CAVAN (WINNERS)

1. Val Gannon
(Mullahoran)

2. Willie Doonan
(Cavan Harps, also Cavan Slashers)

3. Brian O'Reilly
(Mullahoran)

4. Paddy Smith
(Stradone, also St Mary's, Granard, Longford and St Mary's, Ardee, Louth)

5. John Wilson
(Mullahoran)

6. John Joe O'Reilly
(Curragh, Kildare, also Cornafean) Capt.

7. Simon Deignan
(Army, also Mullagh and Civil Service)

8. Phil 'Gunner' Brady
(Mullahoran, also Garda, Cork and Bailieboro)

9. P.J. Duke
(Stradone and UCD)

10. Tony Tighe
(Mountnugent, also Castlerahan and Clones, Monaghan)

11. Mick Higgins
(Mountnugent, also Kilnaleck and Oliver Plunketts, Louth)

12. Columba McDyer
(Cavan Slashers, also Glenties, Donegal)

13. Joe Stafford
(Arva, also Sean McDermotts, Dublin and Killinkere)

14. Peter Donohoe
(Mountnugent, also Kilnaleck)

15. T.P. O'Reilly
(Ballyconnell, also Templeport, Belturbet and Banba, Dublin)

Subs: Edwin Carolan (Mullagh and UCD); John Joe Cassidy (Arva, also Banba, Dublin); Owen Roe McGovern (Swanlinbar, also Clanna Gael, Dublin); Eunan Tiernan (Templeport); Brendan Kelly (Bailieboro)

Other Panel Members: 'Big' Tom O'Reilly (Cornafean); 'Small' Tom O'Reilly (Mullahoran); Dan Deneher (Mullahoran); Jim Deignan (Mullagh); Terry Sheridan (Killinkere)

KERRY (RUNNERS-UP)

1. Dan O'Keeffe
(Kerins O'Rahillys)

2. Dinny Lyne
(Killarney Legion) Capt.

3. Joe Keohane
(John Mitchels, also Geraldines,
Dublin)

4. Paddy 'Bawn' Brosnan
(Dingle)

5. Jackie Lyne
(Killarney Legion)

6. Bill Casey
(Dingle, also Lispole)

7. Eddie Walsh
(Knocknagoshel)

8. Eddie Dowling
(Ballydonoghue)

9. Teddy O'Connor
(Dr Crokes)

10. Teddy O'Sullivan
(Killarney Legion)

11. Dan Kavanagh
(Dr Crokes, also Dingle)

12. Batt Garvey
(Dingle, also Geraldines, Dublin)

13. Frank O'Keeffe
(John Mitchels)

14. Tom 'Gega' O'Connor
(Dingle)

15. Paddy Kennedy
(Kerins O'Rahillys, also Geraldines,
Dublin and Annascaul)

Subs: William 'Bruddy' O'Donnell (John Mitchels) Played; Mick Finucane (Ballydonoghue) Played; Tim 'Timineen Deas' Brosnan (Dingle) Played; Ger Teahan (Dingle, also Laune Rangers and Kerins O'Rahillys) Played; Tom Long (Dingle); Gerald O'Sullivan (Killarney Legion); Sean Keane (Kerins O'Rahillys)

1948

Anyone who anticipated that 1948 would witness something of an anticlimax in the aftermath of the New York experience of 1947 need not have feared. Interest in the games continued to grow and this was reflected in attendance figures at venues throughout the country. The list of pretenders to the All-Ireland title had widened, so that in addition to recent winners Cavan, Kerry, Cork and Roscommon, counties such as Louth, Meath and Antrim harboured serious ambitions.

It was away from the playing pitches that the prospects of one of the 'sleeping giants' emerged from the chasing pack. With the bad weather putting paid to any involvement in the previous National League campaign, an unfit and untrained Mayo team had suffered an ignominious home defeat to Roscommon in the first round of the 1947 Championship. Having later quit the team in total frustration, star player Sean Flanagan was coaxed by teammate Eamonn Mongey to travel to Tralee for a November league match. Against all the odds, Mayo acquitted themselves very well against Kerry and shortly afterwards its Dublin-based players issued an open letter to the County Board. This letter, signed by Flanagan, Mongey, Pádraig Carney, Tom Langan and Liam Hastings, was published in *The Connaught Telegraph* and the *Western People* on 29 November. With what can only be described as the most eloquent, yet forceful, display of GAA player power ever, they galvanised the county into a fundamental reassessment of their whole approach and laid the foundations for what was to become Mayo's second golden era.

The opening games of the 1948 Ulster Championship were played on 6 June, a day on which the entire country was saturated by a torrential downpour. In Belfast, the match between Antrim and Donegal survived until early in the second half when referee John Vallely of Armagh had no option but to call a halt to proceedings as the pitch deteriorated into a quagmire. Antrim, who had led by five points when the first game was abandoned, made no mistake the second time around, with a convincing ten-point winning margin. In the semi-final, they brought the hand-passing technique to a new level as they easily accounted for a Tyrone side that had schoolboy star Iggy Jones in its ranks.

Without being overly impressive, All-Ireland champions Cavan had five-point wins over both Down and Monaghan on their way to the provincial showdown with Antrim. When the sides met at Clones on 25 July, a crowd of 32,000 was brought to its feet when, against the run of play, Antrim's Joe McCallin scored an equalising goal with fifteen minutes to go. It was then that Peter Donohoe moved up a gear and propelled Cavan to another Ulster title with a series of magnificent scores.

Cavan, All-Ireland champions 1948. Back (l–r): Tony Tighe, Brian O'Reilly, Victor Sherlock, Des Benson, T.P. O'Reilly, Peter Donohoe, John Joe Cassidy, Mick Higgins, Patsy Lynch (chairman); front (l–r): P.J. Duke, Willie Doonan, Edwin Carolan, John Joe O'Reilly (captain), Simon Deignan, Phil 'Gunner' Brady, Paddy Smith, Joe Stafford.

If Donohoe won the plaudits for his scoring exploits, the performance of Cavan captain John Joe O'Reilly was universally acknowledged as his greatest ever in an illustrious career.

In Leinster, champions Meath were deemed fortunate to get past a resilient Westmeath when they met at Mullingar on 2 May. Their luck ran out in the semi-final, however, when a goal in added time from Stephen White gave Louth the narrowest of victories (2-6 to 2-5). An interesting postscript to this encounter was the humble apology which an over-zealous *Drogheda Independent* reporter later offered to Meath supporters for his description of their team's performance. Having been accused of penning a totally one-sided account of the match, the Drogheda scribe later acknowledged the truth of this allegation, his only excuse being the fact that he 'was completely carried away by Louth's success'.

On the opposite side of the draw in Leinster, Offaly started impressively as they overwhelmed Kildare, 5-5 to 1-8, at Portlaoise on 9 May. They seemed to be continuing on the upward graph as they led Wexford by ten points early in the second half of the quarter-final clash at Carlow on 6 June. Their prospects looked even more secure when Wexford's leading player, Willie Goodison, received his marching orders. Amazingly, it was Wexford who took inspiration from the sending off and they proceeded to make inroads into Offaly's apparently insurmountable lead. With two goals in the dying seconds from Jimmy Rogers, Wexford pulled off an amazing victory, 4-6 to 3-8, and so advanced to the provincial semi-final.

Next up for Wexford was a Carlow team which, once again inspired by the midfield mastery of Luke Kelly and Jim Morris, had already accounted for Laois. If Wexford's comeback against Offaly was impressive, their semi-final resurgence against Carlow was borderline miraculous. Having trailed from the first minute of the game, they snatched victory when Gusserane's Paddy Kehoe fired home a goal in time added on, giving them a one-point victory, and a Leinster Final date with the Wee County.

In keeping with the pattern of earlier games, the story of the Leinster Final was of yet another comeback. With Billy Kelly hitting two early goals, Wexford completely dominated the first half. However, they were held scoreless after the break, while Louth gave an exhibition of scoring, going on to win 2-10 to 2-5. It was the performances of Pat Markey, Frank Fagan and sprint champion Kevin Connolly that provided the springboard for Louth's second-half recovery.

Kerry's opening game in the 1948 Championship saw them come up against Clare at Bally-longford on 4 July. The venue was chosen to coincide with the opening of a week-long carnival in the town. Fresh from an emphatic twenty-point win over Limerick, the Clare men were quietly confident that they could mount a serious challenge. They acquitted themselves well until midway through the second half when the Kerry scoring machine, and Batt Garvey in particular, moved into top gear. The final score was 6-6 to 1-8.

Mayo, 1948 Runners-Up. Back (l–r): Gerald Courell (trainer), Billy Kenny, Paddy Prendergast, Tom Acton, Tommy Byrne, Pat McAndrew, Tom Langan, Peter Quinn, Johnny Gilvarry; front (l–r): Eamonn Mongey, Peter Solan, Pádraig Carney, Joe 'Joko' Gilvarry, John Forde, Sean Flanagan, Sean Mulderrig, Jackie Carney (trainer). *Picture courtesy of the* Western People.

In the Munster Final, Kerry's challengers were Cork, fresh from a solid nine-point win over Tipperary. A crowd of well over 50,000 turned up at Fitzgerald Stadium on 25 July to witness what turned out to be a titanic struggle between these two great rivals. In its account of the match the following day, *The Irish Press* described it as 'a game in a million'. The early exchanges were extremely robust. Cork's Tadhg Crowley and Kerry's William 'Bruddy' O'Donnell were given their marching orders by referee Bill Delaney (Laois) after a bout of fisticuffs in the opening minutes. Tempers calmed down somewhat after that and Kerry, aided by a stiff breeze, edged into a three-point half-time lead. Cork played brilliantly after the break but, just as it seemed they might close the gap, 'Gega' O'Connor scored a superb goal to propel the Kingdom to a 2-9 to 2-6 victory.

Over in Connacht, Mayo's emergence from the doldrums saw them hit four goals in each of their victories over Leitrim and Sligo. Their provincial final opponents were Galway who had a two-goal win over Roscommon. When the sides met on 18 July, Mayo took early control of proceedings and looked set for a comfortable win. A late goal from Jarlath Canavan and a magnificent point from wing-back Tom Sullivan gave the Tribesmen a second bite of the cherry. Sullivan went on to give a man-of-the-match performance in the replay, an equally close affair, with the scores level at the end of normal time. Eventually, it was the scoring exploits of Pádraig Carney which swung the game in Mayo's favour – he scored 0-9 as they regained the provincial crown on a 2-10 to 2-7 scoreline.

All-Ireland champions Cavan were firm favourites to overcome the challenge of Louth in their semi-final encounter on 22 August. If ever the cliché 'a game of two halves' described a match, this was a prime example. Cavan simply overwhelmed Louth in the first half and, with Mick Higgins giving a masterclass, they led 1-10 to 0-1 at the break. In the second half, however, it was Louth who took control. They launched attack after attack and hit four quick-fire goals, two coming from the boot of Mick Hardy. They missed many more opportunities, including one at the death which would have levelled the game, before finally going down by a three-point margin. The foundation for Cavan's progress to their second successive All-Ireland Final was their outstanding midfield partnership of 'Gunner' Brady and Victor Sherlock.

While Mayo had won many admirers with their impressive run in Connacht, their clash with Kerry was regarded as the true acid test of their progress. When they met at Croke Park on 29 August, not even their most optimistic supporters could have imagined the footballing lesson they were about to deliver to the aristocrats of the game. Taking the lead within ten seconds of the throw-in, they were relentless throughout as they outran, outmuscled and outwitted their much vaunted opponents. The final score was 0-13 to 0-3, with Kerry failing to register a score in the second half as they fell to one of their biggest ever championship defeats. Mayo had no weak link in a never to be forgotten performance, but the displays of Pat McAndrew, Pádraig Carney and Eamonn Mongey were the real highlights of this epic performance.

THE FINAL — 26 SEPTEMBER

The All-Ireland Final of 1948 was one of the most eagerly awaited in the history of the championship. Enthusiasts from each county were easily persuaded that they had strong grounds for optimism. As reigning champions, and with an array of household names in their line-out, Cavan could feel confident that they would perform well on the day. On the other hand, in the aftermath of their disastrous 1947 campaign, Mayo's renewed concentration on speed, stamina and teamwork was beginning to pay rich dividends. Nobody who saw their semi-final annihilation of Kerry could suggest that it was a flash in the proverbial pan.

One thing was immediately apparent as Sunday 26 September dawned. A near gale-force wind, gusting from behind the Canal goals in Croke Park, was about to play havoc with the biggest game of the year. Whatever impact the weather would have on the run of play, it made little difference to the enthusiasm of the travelling hordes. By 9.00am, a long weary-eyed queue had already formed on Jones's Road; the sideline was packed to capacity by 12.15pm and the authorities were obliged to close the gates at 1.40pm. According to *The Irish Press*, this left 'a solid mass of queued humanity milling around the approaches'. Best estimates suggest that over 25,000 would-be patrons had travelled in vain, precipitating the by now annual barrage of demands to increase the stadium's capacity.

It was Cavan who had wind advantage in the first half and, as in the semi-final against Louth, they took full advantage. They held a 3-2 to 0-0 lead at half-time, their goals coming from the bang-in-form Tony Tighe (two) and Victor Sherlock. While their advantage seemed more than sufficient to ensure victory, they had been guilty of missing numerous chances to extend their lead. In addition, Mayo centre half-back Pat McAndrew was in brilliant form and his constant intercessions cut off many scoring opportunities.

Cavan suffered a blow early in the second half when John Joe O'Reilly, their inspirational captain, had to retire through injury. Undaunted, his teammates continued to press their advantage and when Mick Higgins hit their fourth goal, the gap rose to twelve points. It was now Mayo's turn to adopt an all-out attacking strategy and the game was turned on its head. Tom Acton scored two goals before a penalty from Pádraig Carney left three points between them. Remarkably, Mayo hit the next three points and, against all the odds, the sides were level at 4-4 each. The pace was now frantic. With only minutes to go, it was Cavan's ace free taker, Peter Donohoe, who broke the deadlock when he pointed a free into the swirling wind. There were gasps of astonishment when referee Jimmy Flaherty blew the long whistle. While Cavan's joy was unbounded, Mayo's crestfallen supporters were convinced that there was insufficient time added on.

If the Polo Grounds final has generated more headlines over the years than any other, the 1948 decider has to be one of the most extraordinary ever. In appalling conditions, the men from Cavan and Mayo served up a classic. Cavan were fortunate, but deserving, winners. Their defence was solid, with O'Reilly, P.J. Duke and replacement Owen Roe McGovern particularly prominent. The strength of their midfield pairing of Brady and Sherlock was a great launching pad for their forward division. Apart from the outstanding Tony Tighe, who scored two vital goals, Mick Higgins and Joe Stafford made key contributions.

Understandably, Mayo were bitterly disappointed but they could take great heart from the fantastic progress of such a young and skilful team. The GAA world had not seen the last of Sean Flanagan and his ambitious disciples.

FINAL STATISTICS

	Cavan	Mayo
Full-time:	4-5	4-4
Half-time:	3-2	0-0
Scorers:	T. Tighe 2-0	T. Acton 2-0
	P. Donohoe 0-4 (0-4 frees)	P. Carney 1-1 (0-1 free)
	V. Sherlock 1-1	P. Solan 1-0
	M. Higgins 1-0	S. Mulderrig 0-2 (0-1 free)
		E. Mongey 0-1
Attendance:	74,645	
Gate Receipts:	£6,129-9-0 (€7,783)	
Referee:	Jimmy Flaherty (Offaly)	

FINAL MISCELLANY

- On the eve of the final, *The Irish Press* profiled the thirty players lining out. Twenty-six were under 6' in height.
- From *The Anglo Celt* of Saturday 25 September: 'As will be seen by advt. on another page, no person will be admitted to the Cavan dressing-rooms at Croke Park on Sunday except those in possession of official badges.'
- According to *The Irish Press* on Monday 27 September, one-third of those who turned up for the final failed to gain admission. It commented that 'so far as appearances go, not even a sardine could be infiltrated into GAA Headquarters when the Cavan versus Mayo match began.' It further noted that 'although it was raining at noon, Croke Park sidelines were packed full with cap and colour wearing partisans, as oblivious to the climate as if the venue was Honolulu.'
- Cavan midfielder Victor Sherlock had played with Meath from 1945 to 1947.
- In 1948, Pádraig Carney became the first man to score a penalty in an All-Ireland Final.

1948 – THE YEAR THAT WAS

- Mahatma Gandhi was assassinated by a Hindu fanatic on 30 January.
- The Jewish state of Israel was established on 14 May.

- The microwave oven was invented in 1948.
- On Saturday 1 April 1948, American vice-presidential candidate Senator Glenn Taylor was arrested and charged in Birmingham, Alabama. His crime: breaking the peace by using a Black entrance, instead of a White entrance, when attending a youth conference.
- Described as a 'nicely situated' house on 1.5 acres, 'Knocksedan', a ten-bedroom detached residence on Shrewsbury Road, Ballsbridge, sold for £13,000 in September 1948.

1948 TEAM LINE-OUTS

CAVAN (WINNERS)

1. Des Benson
(Croghan)

2. Willie Doonan
(Cavan Harps, also Cavan Slashers)

3. Brian O'Reilly
(Mullahoran)

4. Paddy Smith
(Stradone, also St Mary's, Granard, Longford and St Mary's, Ardee, Louth)

5. P.J. Duke
(Stradone and UCD)

6. John Joe O'Reilly
(Curragh, Kildare, also Cornafean)
Capt.

7. Simon Deignan
(Army, also Mullagh and Civil Service)

8. Phil 'Gunner' Brady
(Mullahoran, also Garda, Cork and Bailieboro)

9. Victor Sherlock
(Kingscourt, also Gypsum Rovers, Meath and Scotstown, Monaghan)

10. Tony Tighe
(Mountnugent, also Castlerahan and Clones, Monaghan)

11. Mick Higgins
(Oliver Plunketts, Louth, also Mountnugent and Kilnaleck)

12. John Joe Cassidy
(Arva, also Banba, Dublin)

13. Joe Stafford
(Killinkere, also Arva and Sean McDermotts, Dublin)

14. Peter Donohoe
(Mountnugent, also Banba, Dublin and Kilnaleck)

15. Edwin Carolan
(Mullagh and UCD)

Subs: Owen Roe McGovern (Swanlinbar, also Clanna Gael, Dublin) Played; Barney Cully (Arva); T.P. O'Reilly (Ballyconnell, also Templeport and Belturbet); John Wilson (Mullahoran); Terry Sheridan (Killinkere); Paul Fitzsimons (Maghera); Val Gannon (Mullahoran); Seamus Morris (Arva, also Cornafean)

MAYO (RUNNERS-UP)

1. Tommy Byrne
(Castlebar Mitchels)

2. Peter Quinn
(Ballina Stephenites, also Ardnaree
Sarsfields)

3. Paddy Prendergast
(Dungloe, Donegal, also Ballintubber)

4. Sean Flanagan
(Ballaghaderreen and UCD)

5. John 'Denny' Forde
(Ballina Stephenites, also Ardnaree
Sarsfields) Capt.

6. Pat McAndrew
(Crossmolina and UCG)

7. Johnny Gilvarry
(Killala)

8. Eamonn Mongey
(Civil Service, also Castlebar Mitchels)

9. Pádraig Carney
(Swinford and UCD, also Castlebar
Mitchels and Charlestown Sarsfields)

10. Billy Kenny
(Claremorris and UCG, also Treaty
Sarsfields, Limerick)

11. Tom Langan
(Garda, Dublin, also Ballycastle)

12. Joe 'Joko' Gilvarry
(Killala)

13. Tom Acton
(Ballina Stephenites)

14. Peter Solan
(Castlebar Mitchels and UCG, also
Islandeady)

15. Sean Mulderrig
(Corballa, Sligo, also Ballina
Stephenites)

Subs: Mick Flanagan (Castlebar Mitchels and UCD); Liam Hastings (Louisburgh and UCD, also Westport and Sarsfields, Kildare); Paddy Gilvarry (Killala); Michael 'Pop' McNamara (Mayo Abbey); Henry Dixon (Mayo Abbey, also Claremorris); Josie Munnelly (Castlebar Mitchels); Paddy Jordan (Ballina Stephenites, also Ballaghdereen); Seamus Daly (Castlebar Mitchels)

1949

Cavan's quest for a third successive All-Ireland title began on 5 June when they met a youthful Tyrone side at Breffni Park. As a contest, this was a total mismatch, as Cavan romped to a 7-10 to 1-7 victory. On the same day, Antrim beat Derry 5-9 to 1-6, thus setting up a semi-final tilt with the reigning champions. When they met at Corrigan Park on 26 June, Cavan seemed well on their way to the final as they led by eleven points with only minutes remaining. Antrim staged a great comeback and had reduced the gap to four points when Brian McAteer sent the ball crashing to the Cavan net. Unfortunately for Antrim, referee John Vallely of Armagh called back play and awarded them a free kick instead. The comeback was stalled and Cavan held on for a 3-7 to 2-6 victory.

Armagh provided the opposition for Cavan in the provincial final. They had shown good form in overcoming Monaghan and Donegal in the earlier rounds. Their win over Monaghan was a close shave, however, needing a spectacular goal from Art O'Hagan in the dying minutes to pull through.

The Ulster Final was held at Clones on 31 July, where a superbly fit Armagh side threw down the gauntlet, putting the champions to the pin of their collar for the full hour. In the end, Cavan stumbled over the line, 1-7 to 1-6, thanks largely to a very fortuitous Peter Donohoe goal. The big talking point from this game was the majestic performance of Armagh midfielder Bill McCorry. Another to impress was defender Paddy O'Neill, who succeeded in subduing a succession of Cavan's much-vaunted forwards.

Championship shocks are most pronounced when one of the great traditional powers of the game is felled by a so-called minnow. In the echelons of Gaelic football, no county sits higher than Kerry, and Clare's 3-7 to 1-8 victory over the Kingdom at Ennis on 19 June ranks as one of the biggest shocks in championship history. Despite what was later described as a lethargic performance, Kerry looked to be in control as they led with three minutes to go. Capitalising on the midfield dominance of brothers Dick and Vincent Bradley, Clare then laid siege on the Kerry goal, with Noel Crowley and Pat Crohan engineering three late goals to snatch victory for the Banner County. The report in the *Kerry Champion* on this, Clare's first ever championship victory over the Kingdom, gave an amusing account of the death of Kerry football, describing a 'Post Mortem' in which such diverse characters as 'Dr. Man in The Street', 'public prosecutor', 'Mr. Selector' and 'Dr. Investigator' all gave evidence.

The second Munster semi-final, between Cork and Tipperary at Clonmel on 10 July, saw the Cork men progress with a four-point victory. Apart from a three-goal haul for Cork's Donie O'Donovan, this game is remembered for an attack on the referee after the final whistle. In its matter-of-fact

High King: Meath defender Kevin McConnell is lifted in celebration by jubilant supporters after the county's first ever All-Ireland title in 1949. Kevin's son, Kevin junior, also played with Meath in the 1970s, while his grandson, Ross McConnell, was a member of Dublin's 2011 All-Ireland winning squad. *Image courtesy of the National Library of Ireland.*

description of the scene, the *Irish Independent* reported: 'Though he received a number of kicks, Mr Sullivan was, fortunately, not seriously injured.'

Thankfully, the provincial decider, played in Limerick on 24 July, was a much calmer affair, with O'Donovan again very much to the fore in Cork's 3-6 to 0-7 victory.

In Connacht, Mayo's resurgence continued as they started their campaign with a 2-10 to 1-9 win over Roscommon. This game was played at Ballymote on 5 June, before an attendance of 13,000. In the semi-final, it was Sligo who fell victim to the Mayo machine, conceding seven goals as they lost by twenty-nine points. Peter Solan was in devastating form for Mayo, giving a masterclass of forward play and scoring no less than 5-2 in the process.

In the second of the Connacht semi-finals, Leitrim sprang a major surprise with a 3-3 to 1-7 win over Galway at Carrick-on-Shannon on 12 June. Pete Dolan, Leo McAlinden and Eugene Boland were the leading lights in this famous victory which gave Leitrim a provincial final date with Mayo at Roscommon on 10 July.

Despite the Trojan defensive efforts of Leitrim's Sean Rutledge, Jimmy Gill and John Heslin, Mayo had it all their own way in a comfortable 4-6 to 0-3 Connacht Final victory. Pádraig Carney had an outstanding game, and provided a continuous supply of ball to the Mayo forward division where, once again, Peter Solan was in devastating scoring form.

Eyes on the prize: Meath full-back Paddy O'Brien (wearing number 3) gets ready to contest for a ball in the 1949 All-Ireland Final against Cavan, watched by his colleague Micheál O'Brien (left) and Cavan's Tony Tighe (number 10). *Image courtesy of the National Library of Ireland.*

In terms of All-Ireland titles, the twenty years prior to 1949 had been a lean one for Leinster counties. Dublin's win in 1942 was the province's only success in that period and there was little evidence that anything was about to change. Unimpressive preliminary round victories for Dublin, Meath and Westmeath, over Longford, Kildare and Carlow respectively, were consistent with recent championship fare in the province. Meath's second outing was against Wexford at Croke Park on 12 June, when they progressed to the semi-final on the extraordinary scoreline of 0-14 to 4-0.

Meath's next opponents were Louth and this semi-final clash provided some of the summer's best entertainment. It took three games, the second of which went to extra time, before Meath finally emerged victorious, 2-5 to 1-7. This saga saw the teams' fortunes ebb and flow, with many players turning in heroic performances. The Meath triumvirate of Brian Smyth, Peter McDermott and Frankie Byrne performed consistently well throughout. For Louth, Tom Mulligan, Jim Quigley, Jim McDonnell, Ray 'Gu' Mooney and future Galway All-Ireland winner Frank Stockwell were always to the fore.

On the opposite side of the Leinster draw, Westmeath followed up their preliminary-round victory over Carlow with a surprise win over Laois at Tullamore on 29 May. Two Rosemount clubmen, Ned Martin and Johnny Ward, found the Laois net in this enthralling game, which was played in front of almost 15,000 spectators.

The men who captured Meath's first All-Ireland title, 25 September 1949. Back (l–r): Paddy O'Brien, Matty McDonnell, Charlie Smyth, Larry McGuinness, Paddy Dixon, Kevin Smyth, Des Taaffe, Thomas Farrelly, Bill Halpenny, Jim 'Red' Meehan, Johnny Bashford; front (l–r): Jim Kearney, Paddy Connell, Micheál O'Brien, Frankie Byrne, Kevin McConnell, Seamie Heery, Brian Smyth, Christo Hand, John Meehan, Peter McDermott, Pat Carolan, Paddy Meegan. *Courtesy Gaelic Art.*

It was back to Tullamore for Westmeath on 10 July, when they faced Offaly in the provincial semi-final before a crowd of 20,000. This drab affair, which ended in a draw, was brightened only by the impressive play of John Kinahan in the Offaly half-forward line and Westmeath sharpshooter Peter Molloy. The quality of the fare was not much better in the replay the following Sunday, when Westmeath, with Jimmy Greally and J.J. Flynn in control at midfield, progressed to the Leinster Final on a score of 0-8 to 1-2. Aside from being the outstanding player on view, Rhode's Paddy Casey scored the late consolation goal for the Offaly men.

Appearing in only their second ever Leinster Final, Westmeath were unfortunate in coming up against a powerful and ever-improving Meath outfit. The men from the Royal County won easily, 4-5 to 0-6, in a game where Seamie Heery delivered a defensive masterclass. The winning margin left little doubt as to the merit of this win, but it belied the progress that was being made by footballers of the Lake County. There were high hopes that with talented players such as Jack Carbery, Peter Woods, Johnny Lyng and Johnny Ward at its disposal, a Leinster title could not be far off. In the event, it would be another fifty-five years before Westmeath would break their provincial duck.

The first of the All-Ireland semi-finals, between Meath and Mayo, produced yet another championship surprise. Mayo had followed through on their impressive 1948 form and were expected to have something to spare over an inexperienced Meath. Once they survived an early onslaught from Mayo, Meath settled down and were full value for their 3-10 to 1-10 win. According to the *Irish Independent* of 15 August, every member of the Meath team 'played splendidly', but Paddy O'Brien and Frankie Byrne were operating on a different level. With so many of their key men out of sorts, this was a big disappointment for Mayo, but hopes remained high that this young group were far from finished.

A crowd of 50,000 turned up the following Sunday to see if Cork could topple Cavan from their perch. In a whirlwind start, and with Con McGrath dictating the pace, the Rebels took an early four-point advantage. Slowly but surely, Cavan began to make inroads and had narrowed the gap to a single point at the break. In the second half, Simon Deignan played a blinder, and with strong support from John Joe O'Reilly and P.J. Duke, led Cavan to an emphatic 1-9 to 2-3 victory.

THE FINAL — 25 SEPTEMBER

The fact that the All-Ireland Final was being contested by adjoining counties created a frenzied enthusiasm in the run-up to the game. Adding spice to the occasion was Cavan's bid for a third title on the trot. Prior to 1949, only three counties, Kerry (twice), Wexford and Dublin had managed to win three successive football titles. Compared to relative newcomers Meath, Cavan had a highly experienced team which had played in the finals of 1943, 1945, 1947 and 1948, winning the latter two. It was no surprise, therefore, that they were installed as hot favourites to retain the title.

The late 1940s was an era when the notion of discretionary income was an alien concept for most Irish citizens. This was no impediment, however, when it came to the magnetic pull of All-Ireland fever. In 1949, the recent problems of congestion at the final were more acute than ever. The bare statistic that there was a new attendance record of just under 80,000 does not tell the full story. The *Irish Independent* of Monday 26 September gives a real flavour of the scene: 'An hour before the start of the major match, there was the strange spectacle of a solid stream of people moving away from the grounds, back to the city centre … quite a number who surged into the grounds gave up the struggle in the heat and congestion, and were fortunate to be able to fight a way out again.'

From the moment Kerry's Dan Ryan threw in the ball, it was clear that this season of shocks was about to witness yet another, on this, the biggest day of the footballing calendar. Meath took control from the start and suffocated Cavan's every attempt to develop their normal, free-flowing game. They were masters in virtually every sector of the field, with their speed and stamina propelling them into an early lead. Their half-time advantage was a modest four points (0-7 to 0-3), but, even then, Cavan's prospects seemed remote.

A common thread in the various match reports was Meath's superiority at midfield, a sector which Cavan's Phil 'Gunner' Brady and Victor Sherlock had dominated in all their previous outings that season. Jim Kearney, a survivor from the 1939 Final, had been recalled for this game and defied the label 'veteran' with a brilliant performance. His partner, Paddy Connell, played his greatest ever game in the Meath jersey. In describing his flawless performance *The Irish Press* noted: 'if he dropped one ball in the hour, it escaped my notice.'

Using this midfield supremacy as a launching pad, Meath continued to control the game. Such was their grip that all of Cavan's six points were scored from frees. Even when Mick Higgins scored a brilliant goal to narrow the gap to two points, the Meath men were able to reassert their authority. Late scores from Frankie Byrne and, fittingly, Connell, closed off the game and Meath took their first title on a score of 1-10 to 1-6.

Every Meath player was a hero in this, their first All-Ireland win. Brian Smyth played a real captain's part, his incessant scheming creating havoc for a Cavan defence which also struggled with the speed and guile of Byrne and Peter McDermott. If Paddy Dixon was singled out as the star defender, it was because the task facing him, in the form of one Mick Higgins, was the most daunting.

Cavan had fought valiantly but could not match Meath's exceptional play. Their best performer on the day was P.J. Duke at wing-back. While the era of All-Ireland glory had not yet ended for Cavan, this Stradone legend had played his last championship match. Sadly, he passed away the following May after a short illness.

FINAL STATISTICS

	Meath	Cavan
Full-time:	1-10	1-6
Half-time:	0-7	0-3
Scorers:	F. Byrne 0-4 (0-4 frees)	P. Donohoe 0-6 (0-6 frees)

B. Smyth 0-3	M. Higgins 1-0
B. Halpenny 1-0	
P. Connell 0-1	
P. Meegan 0-1	
M. McDonnell 0-1	

Attendance:	79,460
Gate Receipts:	£7,057-11-3 (€8,961)
Referee:	Dan Ryan (Kerry)

FINAL MISCELLANY

- The *Meath Chronicle* had little doubt but that 'pedigree' was a vital factor in the county's first ever All-Ireland success. Commenting on Paddy Connell's performance, it noted: 'Through O'Connell's veins runs the football blood of the Coles, and that blood told on Sunday.'
- From the *Meath Chronicle*, reporting on a novel gesture by Aer Lingus after the 1949 Final: 'Taking the victorious All-Ireland team for a spin over their own county was, this year, an innovation, and it is likely that it will become an annual practice.'
- In the All-Ireland Camogie Final of 1949, Dublin's Kathleen Cody scored an incredible 6-7 in her side's 8-7 to 4-2 victory over Tipperary. She went on to win a total of seven All-Ireland medals, before retiring in her mid-twenties to become a nun with the Holy Faith Order.
- Legendary GAA commentator Mícheál Ó Muircheartaigh made his broadcasting debut, *as Gaeilge*, at the Railway Cup final on St Patrick's Day 1949. He was nineteen years old.
- There was an enthusiastic response to a fundraising drive launched by the Westmeath County Board to help finance the county's extended championship run. The Board was particularly gratified to receive a generous donation from Athlone Town FC.

1949 – THE YEAR THAT WAS

- At the instigation of the inter-party government led by Fine Gael's John A. Costello, the twenty-six counties formally became the Republic of Ireland at midnight on 17 April 1949, thus terminating the state's membership of the British Commonwealth.

  To mark the occasion, a number of celebratory events were organised throughout the country. These included:

  - A twenty-one gun salute on O'Connell Bridge at one minute past midnight.
  - Solemn High Mass celebrated by the Archbishop of Dublin in the Pro-Cathedral and attended by the President as well as members of the government, the judiciary and the diplomatic corps.
  - Fireworks in the Phoenix Park.
  - A ceilidhe in Dublin Castle, attended by President Sean T. O'Kelly.

- Neither hurling nor Gaelic football attracted the biggest crowd of the year to Croke Park in 1949. The front page of *The Irish Press* of Monday 27 June reported: 'Into a page of Irish history marched 80,000 men and women through Dublin Streets, yesterday, to Croke Park, where, in the hushed silence of the vast stadium, they knelt for Benediction before a gold and white altar to celebrate the Golden Jubilee of the Pioneer Total Abstinence Association.'
- With one of the main aims being to act as a deterrent to Russian expansion in Europe, twelve nations signed the NATO treaty on 14 April. The alliance committed its members to democracy and the peaceful resolution of conflict, while it also introduced the concept of collective defence.
- Ireland refused to join the alliance because of its sovereignty claims over the Six Counties.
- Under the direction of Mao Zedong, The People's Republic of China was proclaimed on 1 October.
- As Meath and Cavan battled it out for All-Ireland honours at Croke Park on 25 September, the members of Clontarf Gun Club captured the Dublin Inter-Club Championship in the final shoot of the season in Raheny.

1949 TEAM LINE-OUTS

MEATH (WINNERS)

1. Kevin Smyth
(Naas, Kildare, also Kells Harps)

2. Micheál O'Brien
(Skryne)

3. Paddy 'Hands' O'Brien
(Sean McDermotts, Dublin, also Skryne)

4. Kevin McConnell
(Syddan, also Castletown)

5. Seamie Heery
(Rathkenny)

6. Paddy Dixon
(Ballivor)

7. Christo Hand
(Sean McDermotts, Dublin, also Ardcath)

8. Paddy Connell
(Moynalty, also Sean McDermotts, Dublin)

9. Jim Kearney
(Oldcastle)

10. Frankie Byrne
(Clanna Gael, Dublin, also Navan Parnells and Navan O'Mahonys)

11. Brian Smyth
(Skryne) Capt.

12. Matty McDonnell
(Ballinlough)

13. Paddy Meegan
(Syddan)

14. Bill Halpenny
(Syddan)

15. Peter McDermott
(Young Irelands, Cushinstown, also Donaghmore and Navan O'Mahonys)

Subs: Pat Carolan (Kilmainhamwood) Played; Des Taaffe (St Mary's, Bettystown, also St Dympna's, Dublin); Larry McGuinness (Nobber); Johnny Bashford (Drumree); John Meehan (Fordstown); Jim 'Red' Meehan (Fordstown, also Naomh Mhuire, Drogheda, Louth); Thomas Farrelly (Syddan); Charlie Smyth (Westerns, Dublin, also Oldcastle)

CAVAN (RUNNERS-UP)

1. Seamus Morris
(Arva, also Cornafean)

2. James McCabe
(Mullahoran, also Ballinagh and
Banba, Dublin)

3. Paddy Smith
(St Mary's, Ardee, Louth, also
Stradone and St Mary's, Granard,
Longford)

4. Owen Roe McGovern
(Clanna Gael, Dublin, also
Swanlinbar)

5. P.J. Duke
(Stradone and UCD)

6. John Joe O'Reilly
(Curragh, Kildare, also Cornafean)
Capt.

7. Simon Deignan
(Civil Service, also Army and
Mullagh)

8. Phil 'Gunner' Brady
(Garda, Cork, also Mullahoran and
Bailieboro)

9. Victor Sherlock
(Kingscourt, also Gypsum Rovers,
Meath and Scotstown, Monaghan)

10. Tony Tighe
(Mountnugent, also Castlerahan and
Clones, Monaghan)

11. Mick Higgins
(Oliver Plunketts, Louth, also
Mountnugent and Kilnaleck)

12. John Joe Cassidy
(Banba, Dublin, also Arva)

13. Joe Stafford
(Clanna Gael, Dublin, also Killinkere
and Arva)

14. Peter Donohoe
(Banba, Dublin, also Mountnugent
and Kilnaleck)

15. Edwin Carolan
(Mullagh and UCD)

Subs: T.P. O'Reilly (Ballyconnell, also Templeport and Belturbet); Willie Doonan (Cavan Harps, also Cavan Slashers); Brian McNamara (Belturbet); Bartle 'Batty' McEnroe (Castlerahan); Rory O'Connor (Bailieboro); Paddy Wall (Ballinagh); James McEnroe (Kill); Des Maguire (Cornafean, also Oldcastle, Meath); Johnny Cusack (Lavey); Paul Fitzsimons (Maghera)

1950

Players faced a new challenge at the outset of the 1950 Championship. Passes from the hand were now only allowed using the closed fist. The opening rounds in particular saw many instances of a forward celebrating a deftly executed 'goal', only to be blown up by referees eager to demonstrate just how well they had adapted to the application of the new rule. In a very painful example of 'once bitten, twice shy', these incidences dwindled rapidly as the championship progressed.

Champions Meath, who had so impressed when beating Cavan in the 1949 decider, were regarded as the leading contender. Their expectations were dampened somewhat, however, when they played Cavan in the League Final at Croke Park on 4 June. In what was Meath's first defeat in twenty-five games, Cavan impressed in taking the honours, 2-8 to 1-6. This reopened the debate as to which of these neighbouring football powers had the brighter championship prospects for 1950.

It didn't take Meath long to settle back into their winning ways. On 18 June, they had a facile 6-8 to 0-3 victory over Wicklow. Their provincial semi-final encounter with Wexford on 2 July was an altogether different matter. Meath played second fiddle throughout, the consensus being that Wexford had at least three-quarters of the play. It was only their appalling efforts to kick the ball over the bar which prevented the underdogs from registering a famous win. They struck countless wides in the second half, and eventually lost by two points. Rory Deane, who had been moved from the half-forward line to midfield, was largely responsible for Wexford's territorial dominance.

On the other side of the Leinster draw, Kildare showed good form in ousting Dublin (2-11 to 1-9) and Offaly (2-5 to 1-6), with midfielder Jim 'Dealers' Daly their key player. The Lilywhites' semi-final opponents were Louth, who had only progressed after benefitting from a series of Carlow blunders in their quarter-final clash. On 25 June, Louth progressed to face Meath in the Leinster Final after winning a scrappy encounter, scoring 1-10 to Kildare's 1-8.

The Leinster Final was a repeat of the previous year's three-game saga. Those anticipating another close contest were not disappointed. The teams drew, 1-3 apiece, when they met at Croke Park on 23 July. Supporters of both sides were upset that the game was blown up early and all newspaper accounts expressed frustration, with the *Drogheda Independent* reporting: 'Reason for the depression was the startling blunders of the referee who specialised in unforgiveable errors. Yes, the gentleman in charge of the whistle gave the impression of having but one ambition in life – getting out of Croke Park as quickly as possible!'

The replay on 6 August, complete with a new referee, was described by the *Irish Independent* as

Louth's Tom Conlon (3) and Mayo's Tom Langan vie for possession during the 1950 decider. *Image courtesy of the GAA Museum at Croke Park.*

having 'a thrill for every second of the hour'. On a sweltering day, the game was played at a frantic pace, the lead changing hands a number of times. It was Louth who took the honours, 3-5 to 0-13, with Nicky Roe scoring the winning point from a free in the dying seconds. Many reports commented that Louth showed greater stamina and that towards the end several Meath players lay prostrate, apparently suffering from exhaustion. For Louth, goalkeeper Sean Thornton and full-back Tom Conlon got the major credit for keeping Meath goalless while Roe, Stephen White and Hubert Reynolds were their star forwards. Meath may have lost their title but their reputation was untarnished, with defenders Paddy O'Brien and Seamie Heery as well as midfielders Des Taaffe and Paddy Connell all giving outstanding displays.

Down in Munster, Kerry were out to avenge their shock 1949 defeat at the hands of Clare when they met at Tralee on 18 June. Amazingly, Clare again controlled proceedings for most of the game and Kerry looked dead and buried as it drew to a close. With a goal from D.J. McMahon and a Teddy O'Sullivan point, Kerry clawed their way back to level the score: Kerry 1-6, Clare 2-3. The replay took place, in appalling weather conditions, on 16 July. This time Kerry piled on the pressure and ran out 6-6 to 2-4 winners.

On the same day, the weather conditions played havoc with the second semi-final between Cork

As per the custom at the time, Mayo captain Sean Flanagan pays due respect to the Bishop of Kilmore, Dr Austin Quinn. *Picture courtesy of the* Western People.

and Tipperary. With the aid of a gale-force wind, Tipperary led 0-3 to 0-0 at half-time, but Cork, inspired by their midfield pairing of Con McGrath and Noel Fitzgerald, cruised to a 3-5 to 0-3 victory.

The Cork Athletic Grounds hosted the provincial decider on 30 July and attracted a crowd of 25,000. Cork were very much in the driving seat but, with ten minutes to go, Kerry's veteran full-forward Dan Kavanagh hit two goals within a minute to propel his team to a 2-5 to 1-5 win.

The first game in the Ulster Championship of 1950 saw stylists Antrim adapt to the new fisted-pass rule to great effect when they trounced Derry, 5-10 to 0-5, at Corrigan Park. While the *Irish Independent* was effusive in its praise of Antrim's performance, and particularly that of newcomer Frank Dunlop, it was less than impressed by the quality of the opposition: '"NC", to use the abbreviation, will suffice for Derry's performance' – presumably meaning 'no comment'.

Cavan's pursuit of four Ulster titles in a row started impressively at Coalisland on 11 June, where they went on a veritable scoring spree in beating Tyrone 8-7 to 0-3. It is interesting that while Cavan's dominance was absolute in this totally one-sided encounter, it was Tyrone centre half-back Tommy Campbell who was universally acclaimed man of the match. Cavan and Antrim were now pitted against each other in the first of the provincial semi-finals. Before an attendance of over 20,000 at

Clones on 2 July, Cavan advanced 1-12 to 2-6 but largely on the back on Antrim's misfortune. They were forced to line out without star forward Sean Gibson; lost their two staunchest defenders (Alec Quinn and Paddy 'Cocker' Murray) early in the second half; conceded a dubious goal; and, just for good measure, missed two sitters as the match came to a close.

Cavan's opponents in the provincial final were Armagh who had impressed in their victories over Monaghan and Down. A big factor in their progress was the free-taking exploits of Gerry O'Neill, who struck eight points against Monaghan and followed this up with a further five against Down. With Armagh bidding for their first Ulster title since 1903, they were rank outsiders when they faced the men of Breffni before a crowd of over 30,000 at Clones on 26 July. In one of the major upsets in championship history, they proceeded to outspeed, outplay and outlast their opponents. Bill McCorry and Art O'Hagan were imperious at centre-field while scorer-in-chief Gerry O'Neill was again in sparkling form. There were scenes of unbounded joy when referee Mick McArdle blew the final whistle with the scoreboard reading 1-11 to 1-7 in Armagh's favour.

The fruits of the player-inspired renaissance in Mayo's football fortunes would finally be realised in 1950. The latest step on the road to glory had been to change the method of appointing the team captain. Instead of the honour going to the nominee of the county champions, the innate leadership qualities of Sean Flanagan were recognised and he was given the role. Soon asserting himself, the Ballaghaderreen man issued a diktat that members of the County Board were to keep their distance from the team until Mayo were champions.

Mayo's prospects did not appear too rosy, however, to those who turned up at the newly opened Tuam Stadium on 16 July to see them battle it out against Roscommon for the Connacht title. Mayo had received a bye into the final while their opponents had shown less than impressive form when ousting Galway (0-10 to 1-4) and Sligo (0-10 to 1-5). The final contained little quality football, and while Mayo ran out 1-7 to 0-4 winners they were far from impressive, many commentators discarding their All-Ireland prospects. The consensus was that but for the performance of Mick Mulderrig, who scored 1-3, Roscommon would have prevailed.

The stage was now set for two novel All-Ireland semi-final pairings. Mayo and Armagh had never previously met in the championship, while the most recent meeting of Kerry and Louth had been the 1909 All-Ireland Final when Kerry won, 1-9 to 0-6. Louth had gained a measure of revenge in 1910 when the sides were due to meet in that year's final. Owing to a dispute in relation to transport arrangements for their supporters, Kerry refused to travel and Louth were awarded the title, their first.

When Mayo and Armagh met at Croke Park on 13 August, the 50,000 in attendance were treated to an anticlimax of the highest order. The final scoreline of 3-9 to 0-6 in Mayo's favour doesn't really do justice to their superiority. Were it not for the brilliance of goalkeeper Liam McVeigh and full-back Sean Quinn, Armagh would most likely have lost by over twenty points. Mayo showed no weak links in this game, with Billy Kenny, Eamonn Mongey and Pádraig Carney dictating the play, while Tom Langan's two goals were taken with his usual aplomb.

A week later, the second semi-final, between Kerry and Louth, was an epic encounter. Not just the closeness of the exchanges, but the quality of play, had commentators in raptures. In a game that many suggested didn't deserve to have a loser, Louth edged home, 1-7 to 0-8. A huge factor in their victory was the performance of goalkeeper Sean Thornton, who was labelled 'superman' in the *Drogheda Independent* match report. He made numerous brilliant saves and one in the first half brought 'the house down'. Every player on the field contributed to this thrill-a-minute battle but Louth's Jack Regan and Frank Reid came in for special mention. For Kerry, Paddy 'Bawn' Brosnan and Donie Murphy gave faultless displays while Jackie Lyne had a brilliant game despite playing with the handicap of a broken finger.

THE FINAL – 24 SEPTEMBER

In the lead-up to the final, neutral pundits were reluctant to make a definite prediction as to the likely winners. Indeed, one newspaper report suggested that it would be foolhardy to do so. Mayo were certainly seen as an ever improving team but little was learned about their progress in their facile semi-final win over Armagh. On the other hand, while Louth had impressed when beating Kerry, they lacked what the *Sunday Independent* coined as that 'frozen asset', Croke Park experience.

Sunday 24 September was a damp, windy day and it is hardly surprising that luck, or the lack of it, would play a role in determining the destination of the title. When referee Simon Deignan blew the final whistle at 4.52pm that day, Mayo were champions on a score of 2-5 to 1-6, with all three goals coming from defensive lapses in the slippery conditions.

Playing with the aid of the breeze, Louth were quickly off the mark, Nicky Roe pointing after just thirty seconds of play. At this point Mayo took the initiative and scored 1-3 without reply, Peter Solan scoring a rather fortuitous goal. They were then dealt a cruel blow when centre half-forward Billy Kenny, who was in outstanding form, suffered a badly broken leg and had to retire. Kenny gestured defiantly to his teammates as he was carted off but his departure had an unsettling effect on Mayo. Louth stormed back into contention and led at the interval, 1-4 to 1-3, their goal coming from Nicky Roe after a mix-up in the Mayo defence.

While their half-time lead looked far from a comfortable one, Louth continued to force the pace. The *Irish Independent* reported that they controlled the game for three-quarters of the hour. They were still in the driving seat when, with twelve minutes to go, Mick Flanagan latched on to a loose ball and fisted to the net from close range to put Mayo back into the lead. Louth made desperate efforts to close the gap but Sean Flanagan stopped them in their tracks as Mayo held out for a famous win.

This was a final that would not go down in history for the quality of the play, but for sheer dogged-ness on the part of both teams it had few equals. There was no denying the merit of Mayo's victory but Louth could reasonably argue that, with a little more fortune, they could have prevailed.

On this historic day for Mayo, when they bridged a fourteen-year gap to take their second title, it was their captain who led the way, not just with his powerful defensive play but for the manner in which he rallied the team when the pressure was on. Apart from Flanagan, Eamonn Mongey was said to have played the game of his life at centre-field while corner-back John Forde crowned a magnificent career with a brilliant performance. For Louth it was a case of 'so near, yet so far'. Some of the players would go on to climb the Everest of Gaelic football; others would finish their careers without that elusive All-Ireland medal. On this day of bitter disappointment, their half-back line of Boyle, Markey and McArdle never flinched. Elsewhere, it was the performance of Nicky Roe, scorer of 1-5, which won most of the Louth plaudits.

FINAL STATISTICS

	Mayo	Louth
Full-time:	2-5	1-6
Half-time:	1-3	1-4
Scorers:	M. Flanagan 1-0	N. Roe 1-5 (0-3 frees)
	P. Solan 1-0	J. McDonnell 0-1
	E. Mongey 0-2	
	M. Mulderrig 0-2	
	J. Gilvarry 0-1	
Attendance:	76,174	
Gate Receipts:	£6,524-19-9 (€7,929)	
Referee:	Simon Deignan (Cavan)	

FINAL MISCELLANY

- Eamonn Mongey (Mayo), Sean Thornton (Louth) and referee Simon Deignan played with the same club in 1950 – Civil Service (Dublin).
- From a preview in *The Irish Press* in the build-up to the 1950 decider: 'My impression, having watched both teams in training, is that neither relies too much on the work done in the camps. Overtraining has become such a bogey that neither will endanger themselves by it.'
- On the eve of the 1950 Final, the *Drogheda Independent* GAA correspondent was salivating at the prospect of the meal to be served at the following night's team reception in Clery's Restaurant: 'The Menu for this function makes mighty tasteful reading. We will start off with "hors d'Oevres", drift into "Créme a la Ardee", have a spot of "Grilled Clogherhead Plaice with Hollandaise Sauce", plough through Roast Chicken, Irish Ham, Baked Cooley Potatoes (spuds to you, bud), open our belts for jelly and cream with vanilla ices, and polish off a darned good feed with coffee, and, I hope, whiskey a la Sam Maguire.'

1950 – THE YEAR THAT WAS

- With the support of the USSR, North Korea invaded South Korea, leading to the outbreak of the Korean War.

- Secondary school teachers were on the campaign trail for salary increases in May 1950. For teachers with a pass degree on the maximum of the scale, they were negotiating from the following bases: Married – £650; Single – £320; Women – £300.
- In July 1950, the government released a bill with a view to alleviating the general shortage of housing. The scheme was aimed at housing in the price bracket £1,000 to £2,000, and the deposit required ranged from £50 to £100. A qualifying house could have a maximum floor space of 1,400 sq. ft. A state grant of up to 27.5% would be made against the house cost. With the scheme primarily aimed at white-collar workers, agricultural labourers were specifically excluded.
- At a circuit court hearing in Longford, a local man presented an unusual defence in a 'breach of promise' case brought against him by a neighbour. The thirty-seven-year-old defendant agreed that he had promised to marry the woman, but he demanded a warranty that she was no more than forty-one years of age. The woman said she was astonished to find out that her birth certificate showed her age as forty-six, and this after she had made the marriage arrangements through the local parish priest. Finding against the defendant, the judge awarded damages of £100.

1950 TEAM LINE-OUTS

MAYO (WINNERS)

1. Billy Durkin
(Swinford)

2. John 'Denny' Forde
(Ardnaree Sarsfields, also Ballina Stephenites)

3. Paddy Prendergast
(Dungloe, Donegal, also Ballintubber)

4. Sean Flanagan
(Ballaghaderreen and UCD) Capt.

5. Peter Quinn
(Ardnaree Sarsfields, also Ballina Stephenites)

6. Henry Dixon
(Claremorris, also Mayo Abbey)

7. John McAndrew
(Crossmolina, also Ballina Stephenites and Castlebar Mitchels)

8. Pádraig Carney
(Swinford, also Castlebar Mitchels and Charlestown Sarsfields)

9. Eamonn Mongey
(Castlebar Mitchels, also Civil Service)

10. Mick Flanagan
(Castlebar Mitchels and UCD)

11. Billy Kenny
(Claremorris and UCG, also Treaty Sarsfields, Limerick)

12. Joe 'Joko' Gilvarry
(Killala)

13. Mick Mulderrig
(Ballina Stephenites)

14. Tom Langan
(Garda, also Ballycastle)

15. Peter Solan
(Castlebar Mitchels and UCD, also Islandeady)

Subs: Sean Wynne (Air Corps, also Ballina Stephenites); Mick Caulfield (Aghamore); Sean Mulderrig (Ballina Stephenites); Joe Staunton (Louisburgh); Tom Acton (Ballina Stephenites); Paddy Irwin (Lacken); Tom Byrne (Castlebar Mitchels); Liam Hastings (Sarsfields, Kildare, also Westport and Louisburgh)

LOUTH (RUNNERS-UP)

1. Sean Thornton
(Civil Service, also Cooley Kickhams)

2. Mick 'Huckle' Byrne
(St Bride's)

3. Tom Conlon
(Stabannon Parnells, also
Drumconrath, Meath) Capt.

4. Jim Tuft
(Dundalk Young Irelands)

5. Sean Boyle
(St Mary's, Ardee, also Cooley
Kickhams)

6. Paddy Markey
(St Mary's, Ardee)

7. Paddy McArdle
(St Mary's, Ardee, also
O'Raghallaighs)

8. Jack Regan
(Dundalk Gaels, also Sheelagh
Emmets)

9. Frank Reid
(Dundalk Gaels, also Dowdallshill)

10. Jimmy McDonnell
(Darver Volunteers)

11. Nicky Roe
(St Mary's, Ardee)

12. Stephen White
(Dundalk Young Irelands, also
Cooley Kickhams and Mountbellew-
Moylough, Galway)

13. Roger Lynch
(Geraldines)

14. Hubert Reynolds
(Dundalk Gaels, also Oliver Plunketts)

15. Mickey Reynolds
(Stabannon Parnells)

Subs: Ray 'Gu' Mooney (St Mary's, Ardee) Played; Mickey McDonnell (Darver Volunteers) Played; Jack Bell (St Mary's, Ardee); Peadar Smith (Oliver Plunketts); John 'Boiler' Morgan (Dundalk Young Irelands); Patsy 'Bunny' Byrne (Stabannon Parnells)

1951

Mayo's defence of their All-Ireland crown began at Ballymote on 24 June when they accounted for Sligo, 3-7 to 1-5. Even though they were without the services of Carney, Prendergast, Wynne and McAndrew, Mayo selector Gerald Courell managed, in the words of *The Sligo Champion*, to 'fill the gaps with bushes that the Sligomen could not fell'.

Not even the outstanding performances from 'Big Tom' Dunleavy, Ned Durcan, Paddy Kennedy and Fintan Quigley were enough to knock the champions out of their stride.

With Sean Purcell and Liam Hanniffy showing brilliant form in their semi-final win over Roscommon on 1 July, there was much speculation that Galway might now be ready to put a stop to Mayo's gallop. However, their youthful team proved no match for the All-Ireland champions when they met at Tuam on 15 July. Mayo took an early eight-point lead and sauntered to a sixteen-point victory in what the *Irish Independent* described as 'one of the poorest Western finals on record'. Tom Langan gave a virtuoso performance at full-forward while Paddy Prendergast gave an outstanding display at the other end of the field. Galway were a huge disappointment and were it not for the brilliance of their goalkeeper Jack Mangan, they would, in the words of the *Connacht Tribune*, have suffered a 'cricket score defeat'.

The Munster semi-finals of 1951 were completely one-sided affairs which did little for either victors or vanquished. On 24 June, Cork, with former Tipperary star Mick Cahill notching 4-1, strolled to a seventeen-point win over a Clare side that had been expected to put up stern resistance. The following Sunday, it was Kerry's turn to inflict a seventeen-point defeat; Waterford were the unfortunate victims in a game where they conceded no fewer than five goals.

The Munster Final was played, in broiling heat, at Killarney on 15 July, where Kerry came out on top, 1-6 to 0-4. It took a late goal by Dermot Hannafin to seal victory for the Kingdom in what the *Irish Independent* described as a 'grim struggle'. It reported that: 'There was no fancy work for the hour, and there was nothing dainty about the tremendous goalmouth melees which occurred from time to time.'

Star of the game was Paddy 'Bawn' Brosnan, who gave a flawless display at full-back, while Jackie Lyne and Donie Murphy were also to the fore. For Cork, the evergreen 'Weesh' Murphy and Mick Cahill were outstanding.

Three drawn games meant that the Leinster Championship was a long-drawn-out affair. The first of these was at Portlaoise on 20 May when the Longford–Carlow clash ended in stalemate. While

The Mayo team which retained the title in 1951. Back (l–r): J. Quinn, E. Quinn (brothers of Rev. Peter Quinn), Paddy Jordan, Mick Loftus, John 'Denny' Forde, Joe 'Joko' Gilvarry, Tom Langan, Paddy Irwin, John McAndrew, Dr Jimmy Laffey (County Chairman), Henry Dixon, Liam Hastings, Mick Mulderrig, Gerald Courell (trainer), Pat Conway (County Board Treasurer); front (l–r): Willie Casey, Jackie Carney (trainer), Sean Wynne, Mick Flanagan, Eamonn Mongey, Sean Mulderrig, Peter Quinn, Pádraig Carney, Sean Flanagan (captain), Paddy Prendergast, Jimmy Curran, Joe Staunton. *Picture courtesy of the* Western People.

Longford had a comfortable six-point win in the replay the following Sunday, the big story that day was the tragedy of five Carlow supporters losing their lives in a car crash near Kinnegad on the way home from the game in Mullingar.

Longford's next outing was against Laois at Tullamore on 3 June. A brilliant comeback display by Tommy Murphy put Laois in the driving seat as Paddy Peacock, Des Connolly and Brendan McWey did the scoring damage in a comprehensive 1-12 to 2-2 victory for the Laois men.

Wexford needed a hotly disputed goal to force a draw with Westmeath before going on to win the replay on 10 June, largely thanks to the performance of teenager 'Packo' Sheehan. Their semi-final encounter with Laois was an uninspiring affair, with *The Irish Press* describing the contest as one 'abounding in fumbling, mis-kicks and apparent wides'. Apart from the outstanding play of Laois midfielders Seamie Mulhall and Morgan Fitzpatrick, there was nothing in their performance to suggest that they had any real prospect of taking provincial honours.

Reigning champions Louth advanced to the Leinster semi-final with a late goal from Togher's Paddy Butterly in their 2-9 to 2-6 win over Kildare at Croke Park on 27 May. Here they once again faced Meath who had impressed when outscoring Dublin by three points at Drogheda on 3 June.

When these neighbours met at Croke Park on 8 July they produced the third draw of the Leinster campaign. Remarkably, these sides had also ended level in 1949 (twice) and 1950. There was still little between them when they resumed hostilities on 22 July, Meath winning 0-7 to 0-6.

It was generally expected that Laois would struggle against Meath in the Leinster Final but few could have anticipated the scale of the disaster that would befall them. In one of the poorest show-downs on record, Meath met little resistance in a 4-9 to 0-3 annihilation of their hapless opposition, with Jim Reilly and Frankie Byrne creating havoc for a beleaguered Laois defence.

In Ulster, Donegal survived the sending off of midfielder Joe Carroll, and the absence of star player Antoin Rodgers, to hold Antrim to a draw at Letterkenny on 3 June. Despite an outstanding display by the returning Rodgers two weeks later, Antrim progressed thanks to a last-minute point from a free by Joe McCallin.

In the provincial semi-final, Antrim faced reigning Ulster champions Armagh, who had over-come Tyrone with a workmanlike 1-13 to 2-3 victory on 17 June. When they met at Coalisland on 1 July, Armagh led 0-5 to 0-1 with the game well into the second half. From there on, however, it was Antrim all the way as they proceeded to score 1-7 without reply. The outstanding Joe McCallin accounted for 1-4 of their total.

On the other side of the Ulster draw, Cavan had a solid eight-point win over Down while Monaghan fell to Derry by a single point at Magherafelt on 24 June. According to *The Anglo Celt*, a contributing factor to Monaghan's defeat was 'the peculiar layout of the pitch'.

The Ulster Final was played, in ideal conditions, at Clones on 29 July. Here, the men from Breffni conspired to lose a game they could have won by a comfortable margin. Hitting wide after

Mayo's Tom Langan (left) challenges Meath's Paddy 'Hands' O'Brien (with ball) for possession during the 1951 decider while Meath captain Seamie Heery keeps Joe Gilvarry at bay. *Picture courtesy of the* Western People.

wide, they never managed to open the gap that their share of possession merited. The more economic play of the Antrim men paid off at the death when Ray Beirne scored the winning point in a 1-7 to 2-3 victory.

The first of the All-Ireland semi-finals took place at Croke Park on 12 August and saw champions Mayo do battle with a Kerry outfit which had been less than inspirational in taking the Munster crown. Against all predictions, it was Kerry who ruled the roost for most of the game and Mayo needed 1-2 in added time to salvage a draw. As so often in the past, it was the brilliance of Paddy 'Bawn' Brosnan and Jackie Lyne that was Kerry's inspiration. The replay on 9 September saw Mayo's Mick Flanagan assume the mantle of hero as he rifled home two magnificent goals in their 2-4 to 1-5 victory. John D. Hickey, who would go on to report brilliantly to generations of GAA followers in the *Irish Independent*, colourfully described how Flanagan 'administered the solar plexus blows in the form of two goals'.

When Meath played Antrim at Croke Park on 19 August, they led 2-6 to 0-1 ten minutes into the second half. Taking the foot off the proverbial pedal, they slipped from this apparently secure position and when Pat O'Hara burst through in the last minute to hit a piledriver into the Meath net, it looked as though a replay would be needed. However, to the consternation of Antrim players and supporters, referee Simon Deignan called back play and awarded a free for a foul on O'Hara. The resulting point was scant consolation as the Meath men pulled through on a score of 2-6 to 1-7.

THE FINAL – 23 SEPTEMBER

Opinion was divided as to whether Mayo or Meath would prevail in the 1951 decider. Mayo were reigning champions and were appearing in their third final in four years. Meath, backboned by their 1949 heroes, had beaten Mayo in their four most recent clashes, including the 1950–51 League Final. Few disputed that these were the two best teams in the land, each fielding an array of household names.

A crowd of over 78,000 packed into Croke Park on Sunday 22 September in anticipation of a classic. Their expectations were not realised, however, as Mayo took a grip on proceedings and completely blotted out the Meath challenge.

Playing with the advantage of a strong breeze, Meath eased into an early three-point lead. Mayo full-forward Tom Langan then showed all his old wizardry when he evaded three defenders before blasting the ball into the roof of the net. Meath then suffered a real body blow when Christo Hand, who was having the game of his life, had to retire through injury. Their woes continued when a speculative lob from Joe 'Joko' Gilvarry ended up in the Meath net. With Mayo entering the break with a one-point lead and wind advantage to come, Meath's prospects seemed bleak in the extreme.

Limiting the opposition to a single point in the second half, Mayo turned on the style. Gaining the upper hand in every sector, they began to pick off their scores and were not flattered by their eventual five-point winning margin, 2-8 to 0-9.

No player contributed more to Mayo's success than Pádraig Carney, who was generally adjudged to have been the outstanding player on view. The *Irish Independent* gave great credit to the entire Mayo defence, with Henry Dixon coming in for special mention. When it came to doling out the plaudits to Mayo's forwards, however, *The Irish Press* really surpassed itself. It reported that Meath had no answer to 'the mighty Carney, the wily Langan, the flying Mick Flanagan, the elusive Gilvarry, the penetrating Mulderrig and the striving Irwin'.

Many attributed Meath's listless performance to the fact that their minds were firmly focused on their imminent League Final engagement with New York at the Polo Grounds. In preparation for their departure on 25 September, they had been vaccinated in the weeks before the final and questions were asked as to whether this impacted performance. The view expressed in the *Meath Chronicle* was clear: 'Training and vaccinations are ill bedfellows.'

As regards individual performances, Christo Hand was exonerated from any blame, while others mentioned favourably in dispatches included Kevin McConnell, Peter McDermott, Paddy Dixon, Micheál O'Brien and Kevin Smyth. As usual, John D. Hickey of the *Irish Independent* was very direct in his assessment of the Meath men's performance, suggesting that 'nothing short of mass hypnotism could explain the almost astonishing mediocrity of most of them'.

Meath and Mayo were undoubtedly the leading football powers as the sun set on Championship 1951. Mayo, now holders of three titles, could reasonably look forward to many more years of glory. Meath supporters, on the other hand, would be hopeful that their sole (1949) title would soon be added to on the roll of honour. Few could have anticipated that, more than seventy years later, Mayo would still be waiting for their fourth success while Meath would have brought their All-Ireland tally to seven.

FINAL STATISTICS

	Mayo	Meath
Full-time:	2-8	0-9
Half-time:	2-3	0-8
Scorers:	P. Carney 0-5 (0-5 frees)	P. Meegan 0-2
	J. Gilvarry 1-1	P. McDermott 0-2
	T. Langan 1-0	C. Hand 0-1
	E. Mongey 0-1	J. Reilly 0-1
	P. Irwin 0-1	M. McDonnell 0-1
		F. Byrne 0-1 (0-1 free)
		D. Taaffe 0-1
Attendance:	78,201	
Gate Receipts:	£9,334-11-0 (€11,852)	
Referee:	Bill Delaney (Laois)	

FINAL MISCELLANY

- In the decades after their 1951 success, the 'Mayo curse' was routinely quoted as the reason for the county's failure to recapture the Sam Maguire Cup. It was claimed that a priest in Foxford was unhappy at the team's failure to show due respect to a passing funeral cortège. The story went that, as punishment, he determined that the county would not win the title again until all members of the team had gone to their eternal reward. Although Mayo lost eleven finals between 1951 and 2021, and the last survivor Paddy Prendergast passed away in 2021, not even their most superstitious supporters would attribute their record to the infamous 'curse'.

- At the time, the GAA had a strict cap on the number of medals awarded to the winning team. The rules were relaxed many years later and, as a result, Mayo subs Willie Casey, Paddy Jordan and Mick Loftus finally collected their medals in 2006, fifty-five years after the final. The experience of forwards Mick Mulderrig and Peter Solan was only slightly better. Having been dropped for the final, they subsequently received their medals through the post.

- Mayo half-back Peter Quinn, who had been ordained a priest the previous December, retired from football immediately after the 1951 success. At a function in Bray, he was presented with the match ball by renowned GAA commentator Michael O'Hehir. Fr Quinn brought the ball with him when he embarked on his journey to the Philippines where he would work as a missionary for many years.

- Mayo's Joe 'Joko' Gilvarry captained Blackrock College to victory in the 1942 Leinster Schools Senior Cup final.

- Listing the occupations of players in its preview of the 1951 Final, the *Meath Chronicle* told its readers that there were no fewer than seven farmers on the Meath team.

- Mayo's great team of 1950–51 may well hold the record for most current or future medical doctors on an All-Ireland team. Its medicine men included:

  Pádraig Carney
  Billy Kenny
  'Joko' Gilvarry
  John McAndrew
  Mick Loftus

- There was something of a stand-off between Radio Éireann and the GAA in the aftermath of the 1951 Final. The cost associated with transporting Michael O'Hehir, Ireland's pre-eminent commentator, to New York for the following week's League Final in New York was £240. The radio authorities expected the GAA to foot the bill. When this request was refused, the assignment went to Irish-American John 'Lefty' Devine. The reaction of the listening public resulted in this being Mr Devine's one and only radio broadcast. Michael O'Hehir continued as before, and eventually brought no fewer than ninety-nine All-Ireland finals to his devoted fan base.

1951 – THE YEAR THAT WAS

- 1951 witnessed one of the most controversial episodes in Irish social history, when the Minister for Health, Dr Noel Browne, was pressured into resigning because of opposition by the Catholic hierarchy to his proposed 'Mother and Child' health scheme.
- Between August 1950 and November 1951, a total of 269 houses were connected to the electricity grid in Cong, County Mayo.
- At the June meeting of the Laois Hurling Board it was decided, 'by a very small majority', that women should henceforth pay for the privilege of attending local games. Arguing for the change, Chairman Jack Conroy said: 'Girls are always able to find plenty of money for other amusements, such as dances, and for the luxuries necessary in the preparation for such functions.'
- The UNIVAC (Universal Automatic Computer), the world's first commercial computer, was put into use by the US Census Bureau in June 1951.

1951 TEAM LINE-OUTS

MAYO (WINNERS)

1. Sean Wynne
(Air Corps, also Ballina Stephenites)

2. John 'Denny' Forde
(Ardnaree Sarsfields, also Ballina Stephenites)

3. Paddy Prendergast
(Dungloe, Donegal, also Ballintubber)

4. Sean Flanagan
(Ballaghaderreen and UCD) Capt.

5. Joe Staunton
(Louisburgh)

6. Henry Dixon
(Claremorris, also Mayo Abbey)

7. Peter Quinn
(Ardnaree Sarsfields, also Ballina Stephenites)

8. Eamonn Mongey
(Civil Service, also Castlebar Mitchels)

9. John McAndrew
(Crossmolina, also Ballina Stephenites and Castlebar Mitchels)

10. Paddy Irwin
(Garda, also Lacken)

11. Pádraig Carney
(Swinford, also Castlebar Mitchels and Charlestown Sarsfields)

12. Sean Mulderrig
(Westerns, Dublin, also Ballina Stephenites)

13. Mick Flanagan
(Castlebar Mitchels)

14. Tom Langan
(Garda, Dublin, also Ballycastle)

15. Joe 'Joko' Gilvarry
(Killala)

Subs: Liam Hastings (Sarsfields, Kildare, also Westport and Louisburgh) Played; Paddy Jordan (Ballina Stephenites, also Ballaghaderreen); Mick Mulderrig (Ballina Stephenites); Peter Solan (Castlebar Mitchels, also Islandeady); Mick Loftus (Crossmolina); Willie Casey (Ballina Stephenites); Jimmy Curran (Claremorris, also St Vincent's, Meath); Padraig Doherty (Ballina Stephenites); Christy Hegarty (Castlebar Mitchels)

MEATH (RUNNERS-UP)

1. Kevin Smyth
(Naas, Kildare, also Kells Harps)

2. Micheál O'Brien
(Skryne)

3. Paddy 'Hands' O'Brien
(Sean McDermotts, Dublin, also Skryne)

4. Kevin McConnell
(Syddan, also Castletown)

5. Seamie Heery
(Rathkenny) Capt.

6. Connie Kelly
(Oldcastle, also Mountnugent, Cavan)

7. Christo Hand
(Sean McDermotts, Dublin, also Ardcath)

8. Des Taaffe
(St Dympna's, Dublin, also St Mary's, Bettystown)

9. Paddy Connell
(Sean McDermotts, Dublin, also Moynalty)

10. Frankie Byrne
(Navan O'Mahonys, also Clanna Gael, Dublin, and Navan Parnells)

11. Matty McDonnell
(Ballinlough)

12. Paddy Meegan
(Syddan)

13. Brian Smyth
(Skryne)

14. Jim Reilly
(Dunboyne)

15. Peter McDermott
(Navan O'Mahonys, also Young Irelands, Cushinstown and Donaghmore)

Subs: Paddy Dixon (Ballivor) Played; Danny McNamara (Ballinabrackey); Bob Ruske (Dunboyne); Larry McGuinness (Nobber); Pat Carolan (Kilmainhamwood); Aidan Foran (Longwood)

1952

Mayo's first hurdle in the defence of their All-Ireland title was their clash with Sligo in the newly named Fr O'Hara Park, Charlestown on 22 June. Although the champions were forced to line out without some of their established stars, few believed Sligo had any real prospects of victory. Spurred on by 'Big' Tom Dunleavy, Barney Oates and Nace O'Dowd, the Sligo men gave as good as they got for three-quarters of the game. It was only in the latter stages that Mayo, chiefly through the brilliance of Pádraig Carney, edged ahead, winning on a 0-9 to 0-6 scoreline. Such was the quality of Carney's play that *The Connaught Telegraph* confessed to struggling for 'adjectives to adequately describe his superlative skills'.

The second semi-final, between Roscommon and Galway, brought much in terms of thrills but was devoid of any quality football. Roscommon's outstanding performer was Eamon Boland, while Peadar Kearns got the decisive goal in their 1-6 to 1-5 victory. As ever, Sean Purcell was Galway's leading light with brothers Harry and Ned Keogh also to the fore.

When Mayo met Roscommon in the provincial final at Castlebar on 13 July they were unbackable favourites. Unfortunately for them, Roscommon failed to read the script and proceeded to dole out an eight-point hammering (3-5 to 0-6) to the champions. The big talking point after the game was not the sensational result itself, rather the incredible performance of Gerry O'Malley in the number six shirt for Roscommon. Brilliantly supported by fellow half-backs Batt Lynch and Frank Kelly, the Brideswell man delivered a real tour de force from start to finish.

The throw-in for the 1952 Leinster Championship took place at Mullingar on 4 May, when Longford upset the odds by beating Kildare, 3-8 to 0-5. While Seamus Greene was their main star, a feature of Longford's win was the performance of their full-forward, Jimmy O'Brien. Having last played for the county four years previously, and now a member of the County Board, he was their scorer-in-chief as he played havoc with the Kildare defence. Longford's impressive run continued when they beat Offaly by two points at Cusack Park on 8 June, Vincent Tierney hitting the winning scores. Their semi-final opponents were Meath, who had already accounted for Dublin. What seemed to be the whole of Longford travelled to Mullingar on 29 June where their heroes put Meath to the pin of their collar before losing out, 1-9 to 0-9. The deciding Meath goal was a piledriver from Brian Smyth who had only recently come out of retirement.

The other side of the draw in Leinster threw up the apparently inevitable opposition for Meath in the provincial final. On 1 June at Croke Park, Louth were less than impressive when beating

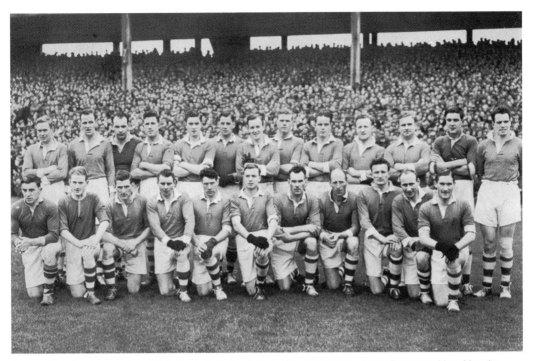

Cavan, All-Ireland champions 1952. Back (l–r): Paul Fitzsimons, Tony Tighe, Peter Donohoe, Liam Maguire, Brian Gallagher, Victor Sherlock, Tom Hardy, Bartle 'Batty' McEnroe, Aidan Corrigan, Edwin Carolan, Simon Deignan, Vincent Clarke, James McCabe; front (l–r): John Sheridan, Terry Keogan, Des Maguire, Seamus Morris, Johnny Cusack, Seamus Hetherton, Phil 'Gunner' Brady, Mick Higgins (captain), Paddy Carolan, John Joe Cassidy, Brian 'Phildy' O'Reilly.

Wexford by four points in their quarter-final game. It was a different story, however, when they faced Carlow in the semi-final on 22 June. Playing scintillating football, and with Jack Regan and Paddy Behan in top form, they had a facile 3-11 to 0-4 win.

Meath and Louth produced yet another nail-biting encounter when they met in the provincial final at Croke Park on 13 July. It was Meath who prevailed, 1-6 to 0-8, with Brian Smyth coming to their rescue once again as he found the net in a third successive championship game. Paddy O'Brien reproduced his brilliant form of 1949 while teenager Brendan Maguire gave what the *Meath Chronicle* described as 'an electrifying exhibition' at midfield. The general view was that Meath's victory would have been more emphatic but for the defiant efforts of Louth's outstanding half-back line of Mick McDonnell, Paddy Markey and Paddy McArdle.

Although Cavan beat Down at Newcastle on 15 June by thirteen points, their performance did not give much cause for optimism as regards their All-Ireland prospects. In the words of *The Irish Press*: 'The Cavan candle is still burning, but the wick is getting very short.' They were more impressive when they ousted Antrim, 3-6 to 2-6, at Clones on 13 July, with veterans Mick Higgins and 'Gunner' Brady leading the way.

Monaghan, having accounted for Derry and Armagh, provided the Ulster Final opposition. A

Far left: The cover of the 1952 football final programme. *Image courtesy of the GAA Museum at Croke Park.*

Left: The cover of the 1952 football final replay programme. *Image courtesy of the GAA Museum at Croke Park.*

pitch invasion late in their semi-final clash with pre-match favourites Armagh had almost cost the Farney men their place in the final.

At Breffni Park on 27 July, Cavan regained the Ulster title on a score of 1-8 to 0-8, largely thanks to the scoring accuracy of J.J. Cassidy and a brilliant goal from Edwin Carolan. It was a close call and, but for some wayward shooting, Monaghan might have prevailed on a day when John Rice, Hughie McKearney, brothers Paddy and Ollie O'Rourke and the Moyna twins, Tommy and Mackie, all performed heroically.

After Cork overcoming Tipperary, and Kerry having four points to spare over Waterford, the stage was set for the seemingly inevitable Cork–Kerry Munster Final. Cork had recently won the National League and Kerry had shown poor form all year, and so it was the Leesiders who were installed as favourites. The form book held good and Cork, with the Cronin brothers in outstanding form, romped to a 0-11 to 0-2 victory. It was a dismal display by Kerry and only Paddy 'Bawn' Brosnan emerged with his reputation intact. *The Cork Examiner* report on the game was perhaps the first and only time in GAA history when the term 'inferiority complex' was used in describing a Kerry football team.

The first of the All-Ireland semi-finals saw Meath and Roscommon do battle at Croke Park on 3 August. Before a crowd of over 42,000, which included Hollywood legend Gene Kelly, Meath took the spoils, 1-6 to 0-7, after a dour struggle. The *Meath Chronicle* provided a colourful description of how Roscommon's ambitions 'were impaled on Meath's doggedness'. Peter McDermott and Connie Kelly were their top performers. Ironically, it was Meath-based Eamon Boland who was Roscommon's outstanding player on the day.

After their emphatic victory over Kerry, Cork were brimful of confidence when they lined out against Cavan in the second semi-final on 17 August. In its match preview, *The Cork Examiner* warned its readers: 'The tiny seedling of diffident hope has produced a sturdy stalk which in the last few weeks I suspect has blossomed into a florid bloom of over-confidence.'

It was underdogs Cavan who took the early initiative and set the pace of the game with a whirl-wind start. Cork eventually began to settle and a goal by Tom Moriarty gave them a two-point half-time advantage. With ten minutes to go, Cork goalkeeper Danno Keeffe saved a penalty and Tom Moriarty found the Cavan net directly from the resultant clearance. The gap was now four points and the result seemed a foregone conclusion. However, the Cavan forwards turned in an incredible closing ten minutes, scoring five points without reply to snatch victory and a place in the final against neighbours Meath. Reports of the game were unanimous on two matters: firstly, the game was one of the best seen at Croke Park in years, and secondly, Mick Higgins was at his brilliant best throughout the game.

THE FINAL — 28 SEPTEMBER

The Maguire family from Cornafean was the centre of attention in the run-up to the 1952 Final. Having moved from Cavan to Oldcastle in Meath, brothers Des and Liam continued to play for Cavan, while their teenage brother, Brendan, had starred at midfield in Meath's great championship run. Whichever team won, the Maguire household was bound to experience bittersweet memories of All-Ireland day.

When Sunday 28 September arrived, it heralded what was almost certainly the worst weather ever witnessed for a football final. The downpour of Arctic rain which lashed the capital throughout the morning prompted the following headline in *The Anglo Celt*: 'Cavan and Meath Draw But Jupiter Pluvius Won.'

Much to the disappointment of the thousands who had braved the Croke Park elements from noon onwards, the authorities took the unprecedented step of postponing the minor final between Cavan and Galway.

Against all the odds, the two senior teams proceeded to serve up a thrilling contest in the appalling conditions. The only sour note was struck when the exchanges got somewhat out of hand towards the end of the first half. In a comment piece in *The Irish Press*, Liam MacGabhann complained: 'A greasy ball is valid excuse enough for a missed pass but a punch in the stomach doesn't offset that error. 64,000 people besides the referee took notes of the players who became pugilistic – and there was no need to write them down.'

Mr MacGabhann, who absolved only Cavan's Mick Higgins and Meath's Brendan Maguire as bringing a hint of 'cool discipline' to proceedings, does not appear to have been given any forum for his views on the replay two weeks later.

Whatever about the borderline nature of some of the 'tackling', all match reports were *ad idem* on one point: this was a brilliant contest in the most testing of conditions.

In a game that ended level, Meath scoring 1-7 to Cavan's 2-4, none of the goals scored generated as much debate as Cavan's 'miracle' equaliser. Describing Edwin Carolan's effort from an impossible angle, Tony Myles in *The Irish Press* wrote: 'Two minutes before referee Sean Hayes blew the final whistle, at Croke Park yesterday, a ball landed on the flagpole on the extreme right of the Meath goal. The Meath backs, and most of the 64,200 spectators, thought it had gone wide, but Edwin Carolan, the Cavan left half-forward, knew otherwise. He followed it, the wind blew it back, and the next thing we saw was Carolan's kick from the end line strike the far upright, bounce back over the crossbar, and Cavan were in the running again for the All-Ireland replay on October 12.'

If Carolan was Cavan's saviour on the day, most of the credit for their survival to a replay belonged to veterans 'Gunner' Brady, Tony Tighe and their brilliant leader, Mick Higgins. For Meath, eighteen-year-old Brendan Maguire won most of the plaudits while centre-back Connie Kelly played brilliantly. Ironically, having received a heavy knock early in the match, Kelly had no memory of the game.

THE REPLAY — 12 OCTOBER

The replay took place two weeks later, and although conditions were much improved on the drawn game, the weather was of the late autumn variety. At the end of yet another pulsating encounter, Cavan took the honours on a 0-9 to 0-5 scoreline.

The big difference between the sides was the overall brilliance of Mick Higgins. Apart from hitting no fewer than seven points of Cavan's total, the skipper inspired his teammates with an outstanding performance. Brian O'Reilly was another to shine, while Victor Sherlock, hampered somewhat by a hand injury in the drawn game, produced a real tour de force at centre-field. The result was a disappointment for Meath on a day when Paddy O'Brien gave what was possibly his best ever performance in the Meath jersey. Others to impress for the Meath men were newcomer Declan Brennan and Dunboyne's Jim Reilly.

Cavan had now captured their fifth All-Ireland title while Meath had but one success to their credit. Anyone predicting the relative success rate of these counties over the next number of decades could hardly have foreseen the dramatic change of fortunes that would transpire.

FINAL STATISTICS — DRAW

	Cavan	Meath
Full-time:	2-4	1-7
Half-time:	1-2	0-5
Scorers:	T. Tighe 1-0	P. Meegan 0-4 (0-2 frees)
	J.J. Cassidy 1-0	P. McDermott 1-1
	M. Higgins 0-1	J. Reilly 0-1
	V. Sherlock 0-1	M. McDonnell 0-1
	P. Fitzsimons 0-1	
	E. Carolan 0-1	

	Attendance:	64,200

Attendance: 64,200
Gate Receipts: £8,696-9-6 (€11,042)
Referee: Sean Hayes (Tipperary)

FINAL STATISTICS — REPLAY

	Cavan	Meath
Full-time:	0-9	0-5
Half-time:	0-3	0-2
Scorers:	M. Higgins 0-7 (0-7 frees)	P. McDermott 0-2
	T. Tighe 0-1	J. Reilly 0-1
	J. Cusack 0-1	M. McDonnell 0-1
		D. Taaffe 0-1
Attendance:	62,515	
Gate Receipts:	£8,152-11-5 (€10,352)	
Referee:	Sean Hayes (Tipperary)	

FINAL MISCELLANY

- Cavan's celebrations after their 1952 victory became subdued when news emerged, within weeks of the final, that John Joe O'Reilly, perhaps the county's greatest ever player, had passed away at the young age of thirty-three.
- The honour of throwing in the ball for the 1952 Final was given to the Papal Nuncio, Most Rev. Dr Gerald O'Hara.
- After his footballing days were over, Meath's Bartle 'Batty' McEnroe concentrated his efforts on building up one of Europe's finest herds of Aberdeen Angus cattle. There were many comments about his association with a papal bull when, in 1963, he had the distinction of becoming the first All-Ireland medal winner to sell a bull, named the Duke of Liss, to His Holiness Pope John XXIII.

1952 — THE YEAR THAT WAS

- In the aftermath of the 1952 Budget, the *Sunday Independent* of 6 April described the growing sense of shock and dismay at the measures introduced by Fianna Fáil's Sean McEntee. It reported: 'Ever since their return to office last June, Ministers have been vying with each other in threatening the public with fiscal whips and scorpions. They have been chanting in chorus that the nation is living beyond its means and warning the public to prepare for spurning delights and living laborious days. Bad news, indeed, had certainly been promised, but the promise was fulfilled in a measure few expected.'

   Through a combination of reductions in food subsidies and tax increases, the minister raised a total of £15 million (€18.8 million). Increased prices resulting from the changes included:

Pint of stout:	1/3 (8 cent)
Gallon of petrol:	3/6 (22 cent)
Cigarettes:	2/4 (15 cent) for 20
Butter:	3/10 (24 cent) per lb.

- Following the death of her father, King George VI, Queen Elizabeth II ascended to the throne of the United Kingdom in February 1952. This was shortly before Cavan took their last (to date) All-Ireland title.

- One of the most popular cars on the market in the 1950s was the Ford Anglia. In the week of the 1952 Final, the *Irish Independent* ran an advertisement proclaiming that this 'all mod cons' saloon could be had for £386 ('ex works').

- A combination of industrial pollution and high-pressure atmospheric conditions led to the 'Great Smog of London' from 5 to 9 December 1952. Bringing the city to a virtual standstill, it was responsible for the deaths of at least 8,000 citizens.

1952 TEAM LINE-OUTS — DRAW

CAVAN

1. Seamus Morris
(Cornafean, also Arva)

2. James McCabe
(Banba, Dublin, also Mullahoran and Ballinagh)

3. Phil 'Gunner' Brady
(Bailieboro, also Mullahoran and Garda, Cork)

4. Des Maguire
(Oldcastle, Meath, also Cornafean)

5. Tom Hardy
(Mullahoran and UCD)

6. Liam Maguire
(Garda, also Cornafean and Oldcastle, Meath)

7. Brian 'Phildy' O'Reilly
(Mullahoran)

8. Victor Sherlock
(Kingscourt, also Gypsum Rovers, Meath and Scotstown, Monaghan)

9. Paul Fitzsimons
(Maghera)

10. Seamus Hetherton
(Munterconnaught)

11. Mick Higgins
(Bailieboro, also Kilnaleck, Mountnugent and Oliver Plunketts, Louth) Capt.

12. Paddy Carolan
(Mullagh)

13. John Joe Cassidy
(Banba, Dublin, also Arva)

14. Tony Tighe
(Castlerahan, also Mountnugent and Clones, Monaghan)

15. Edwin Carolan
(Mullagh)

Subs: Simon Deignan (Mullagh, also Army and Civil Service); Bartle 'Batty' McEnroe (Castlerahan); Johnny Cusack (Lavey); Aidan Corrigan (Fr Griffin's, Galway, also Milltown, Galway); Brian Gallagher (Cootehill); Peter Donohoe (Banba, Dublin, also Mountnugent and Kilnaleck); Terry Keogan (Bailieboro); Vincent Clarke (Clanna Gael, Dublin, also Knockbride)

MEATH

1. Kevin Smyth
(Naas, Kildare, also Kells Harps)

2. Micheál O'Brien
(Skryne)

3. Paddy 'Hands' O'Brien
(Sean McDermotts, Dublin, also Skryne)

4. Kevin McConnell
(Syddan, also Castletown)

5. Patsy McGearty
(Ballivor)

6. Connie Kelly
(Oldcastle, also Mountnugent)

7. Christo Hand
(Sean McDermotts, Dublin, also Ardcath)

8. Brendan Maguire
(Oldcastle, also Cornafean, Cavan)

9. Des Taaffe
(St Dympna's, Dublin, also St Mary's, Bettystown)

10. Paddy Connell
(Moynalty, also Sean McDermotts, Dublin)

11. Brian Smyth
(Skryne)

12. Paddy Meegan
(Syddan) Capt.

13. Matty McDonnell
(Ballinlough)

14. Jim Reilly
(Dunboyne)

15. Peter McDermott
(Navan O'Mahonys, also Young Irelands, Cushinstown and Donaghmore)

Subs: Owenie O'Sullivan (Kilbride); Paddy Dixon (Ballivor); Pat Carolan (Kilmainhamwood); Sean O'Brien (Skryne); Declan Brennan (Duleek); Jim Duff (Syddan); Tom O'Brien (Skryne); Peter McKeever (Rathkenny); Ned Durnin (Donaghmore).

1952 TEAM LINE-OUTS — REPLAY

CAVAN (WINNERS)

1. Seamus Morris
(Cornafean, also Arva)

2. James McCabe
(Banba, Dublin, also Mullahoran and Ballinagh)

3. Phil 'Gunner' Brady
(Bailieboro, also Mullahoran and Garda, Cork)

4. Des Maguire
(Oldcastle, Meath, also Cornafean)

5. Paddy Carolan
(Mullagh)

6. Liam Maguire
(Garda, also Cornafean and Oldcastle, Meath)

7. Brian 'Phildy' O'Reilly
(Mullahoran)

8. Victor Sherlock
(Kingscourt, also Gypsum Rovers, Meath and Scotstown, Monaghan)

9. Tom Hardy
(Mullahoran and UCD)

10. Seamus Hetherton
(Munterconnaught)

11. Mick Higgins
(Bailieboro, also Kilnaleck, Mountnugent and Oliver Plunketts, Louth) Capt.

12. Edwin Carolan
(Mullagh)

13. John Joe Cassidy
(Banba, Dublin, also Arva)

14. Tony Tighe
(Castlerahan, also Mountnugent and Clones, Monaghan)

15. Johnny Cusack
(Lavey)

Subs: Paul Fitzsimons (Maghera) Played; Simon Deignan (Mullagh, also Army and Civil Service); Bartle 'Batty' McEnroe (Castlerahan); Aidan Corrigan (Fr Griffin's, Galway, also Milltown, Galway); Brian Gallagher (Cootehill); Peter Donohoe (Banba, Dublin, also Mountnugent and Kilnaleck); Terry Keogan (Bailieboro); Vincent Clarke (Clanna Gael, Dublin, also Knockbride); John Sheridan (Killinkere)

MEATH (RUNNERS-UP)

1. Kevin Smyth
(Naas, Kildare, also Kells Harps)

2. Micheál O'Brien
(Skryne)

3. Paddy 'Hands' O'Brien
(Sean McDermotts, Dublin, also Skryne)

4. Kevin McConnell
(Syddan, also Castletown)

5. Tom O'Brien
(Skryne)

6. Connie Kelly
(Oldcastle, also Mountnugent, Cavan)

7. Christo Hand
(Sean McDermotts, Dublin, also Ardcath)

8. Brendan Maguire
(Oldcastle, also Cornafean, Cavan)

9. Des Taaffe
(St Dympna's, Dublin, also St Mary's, Bettystown)

10. Declan Brennan
(Duleek)

11. Brian Smyth
(Skryne)

12. Paddy Meegan
(Syddan) Capt.

13. Matty McDonnell
(Ballinlough)

14. Jim Reilly
(Dunboyne)

15. Peter McDermott
(Navan O'Mahonys, also Young Irelands, Cushinstown and Donaghmore)

Subs: Owenie O'Sullivan (Kilbride); Paddy Dixon (Ballivor); Pat Carolan (Kilmainhamwood); Sean O'Brien (Skryne); Ned Durnin (Donaghmore); Jim Duff (Syddan); Peter McKeever (Rathkenny); Paddy Connell (Moynalty, also Sean McDermotts, Dublin); Patsy McGearty (Ballivor)

1953

Cavan's return to the All-Ireland summit in 1952 had been something of a surprise and many doubted their ability to match the championship 'big guns' of Mayo, Meath and Kerry as the 1953 campaign got underway. Before they could test themselves in the heat of Croke Park battle, however, they first had to go through the routine of the Ulster Championship. Monaghan presented their first hurdle and the men of Breffni duly put them to the sword, 2-7 to 0-2, on 21 June. In the semi-final, they had a convincing six-point victory over Tyrone after a tumultuous encounter. Describing the exchanges after Cavan's 'Gunner' Brady had received his marching orders, the *Irish Independent* wrote: 'The Tyrone player who unleashed a right uppercut, delivered with the fluency of which any boxer would have been proud, at Mick Higgins shortly afterwards, was lucky not to follow Brady.'

Goalmouth action from the 1953 Final which saw luckless Armagh lose out to Kerry. In the background, referee Peter McDermott from Meath keeps a close eye on proceedings. Twelve months later, the 'man with the cap' would return to Croke Park to captain his team to victory over … Kerry! *Image courtesy of the GAA Museum at Croke Park.*

Since the mid-1960s the number contesting the throw-in has been confined to four players. This shot from the 1953 Final between Kerry and Armagh gives a sense of the 'free-for-all' potential. *Image courtesy of the GAA Museum at Croke Park.*

On the other side of the draw, it was Armagh who progressed to the Ulster Final. A surprise win over Antrim at Lurgan on 21 June was followed by an emphatic 12 July trouncing of Derry in Belfast. Full-forward Art O'Hagan was in devastating form as the Orchard County clocked up 4-11 to Derry's 1-5.

The final took place in Belfast on 26 July where, against all the odds, Armagh dethroned the All-Ireland champions with a well-deserved 1-6 to 0-5 win. On a day that saw a rare combination of thunder, lightning, rain and sunshine, Armagh set their stall out early and, having played against the wind, held a one-point lead at the break. With centre half-back Pat O'Neill turning in a storming performance in the second half and O'Hagan, Joe Cunningham and Brian Seeley tormenting the Cavan defence, they pulled away for a fully merited win. Cavan's traditional machine-like combination play was notably absent in this final and were it not for the heroics of goalkeeper Seamus Morris the margin of defeat would have been greater.

Armagh had now won the right to contest the All-Ireland semi-final against the champions of Connacht. Reigning champions Roscommon had their first outing against Galway at Tuam on 5 July. In wet and windy conditions they deservedly won this semi-final encounter on a score of 4-4 to 0-3. The other semi-final saw Sligo put in a spirited performance against Mayo before finally losing out, 2-6 to 1-6. A feature of this game was the performance of the Sligo full-back line of Ray Tully, Frank White and one Ted Nealon, who would later go on to achieve national prominence as a political commentator.

In a continuous downpour, over 30,000 patrons turned up at St Coman's Park on 19 July to see Roscommon and Mayo re-enact their 1952 provincial final clash. Roscommon retained their title on a score of 1-6 to 0-6. Their goal was a rasping effort from Michael Shivnan that took a deflection off Mayo full-back and star man Willie Casey, on its way to the back of the net. An interesting sequel to this game was Mayo's unsuccessful objection to Roscommon's victory. Their argument: five of the Roscommon team were born outside the county.

After their embarrassing loss to Cork in 1952, Kerry's prospects received a fillip when Ned Roche, John Cronin, Tom Moriarty and Sean Kelly all declared for their native county. In the semi-final, they hammered Clare at Ennis, 6-10 to 0-2, with Paudie Sheehy responsible for 3-3 of their total. Perhaps the best measure of Kerry's superiority was the fact that Clare's goalkeeper Michael Garry, although beaten six times, had an outstanding game.

Cork progressed to the final but only after a stuttering 1-7 to 1-5 win over Waterford. In describing the quality of the play in this encounter the *Irish Independent* observed: 'If you have ever seen novice skaters on an ice rink you will be able to form a good mental picture of the trend of affairs in the Munster Senior Football semi-final yesterday.'

In an absolute downpour at Killarney on 19 July, Kerry took the Munster title on a score of 2-7 to 2-3. Leading by five points at the break, their rock-like defence gave Cork few opportunities to close the gap in the second half. Despite ending up on the losing side it was Cork's high-fielding centre-back, Paddy O'Driscoll, who was the game's outstanding performer.

In Leinster, reigning champions Meath had their first championship outing on 24 May against Dublin at Navan. When the sides had met in the league in March the Meath men were well and truly hammered, 3-13 to 2-3. With Dublin going on to take the league title and playing spectacular football in the process, Meath's championship prospects did not look good. Great things were expected of Dublin's much-vaunted forward division but the Meath defence, in which Kevin Lenehan, Jim Reilly and Ned Durnin were outstanding, provided the inspiration for a famous win, 2-6 to 2-5.

In the semi-final, Meath met Louth for what was an incredible ninth year in a row. In keeping with the pattern of previous years, this was yet another close affair, with the Wee County edging it, 1-7 to 1-6, Jimmy McDonnell hitting the winning point.

Having accounted for Laois and Offaly, Wexford emerged to meet Louth in the provincial final on 26 July. Louth were raging-hot favourites, so much so that the *Drogheda Independent* preview was at pains to warn against the dangers of overconfidence. Although they managed to overcome the Wexford men, 1-7 to 0-7, the difference between the sides being a second-half goal scored by Hughie O'Rourke, they were less than impressive. While Tom Conlon, Pat Markey and Stephen White were their standout players, it was commonly agreed that Wexford's Rory Deane was the real star of the show.

The first of the All-Ireland semi-finals was played on 9 August and, after a scrappy, uninspiring encounter, Armagh had a single point to spare over Roscommon, thus reaching the All-Ireland Final for the first time in their history.

This was a game in which neither set of forwards impressed, the hour producing no fewer than twenty-seven wides. Top billing in this encounter went to Art O'Hagan, whose second-half display

Above: Kerry captain James 'Jas' Murphy lifts the Sam Maguire Cup after the 1953 victory over Armagh. *Image courtesy of the GAA Museum at Croke Park.*

Below: Kerry defenders Ned Roche (number 3) and John Cronin (number 6) have matters under control in this action shot from the 1953 Final. *Image courtesy of the GAA Museum at Croke Park.*

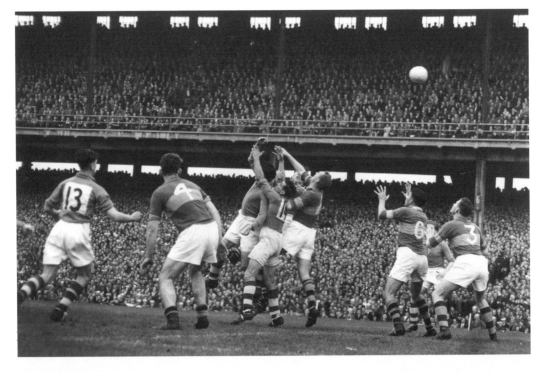

suggested that his first period of inactivity was a ruse to create a feeling of false security in the Roscommon rear-guard.'

Kerry were forced to line out without a number of their first-choice fifteen when they faced Louth in the second semi-final on 23 August. One of their absentees was former Cork player Tom Moriarty. The Munster Council's decision to reinstate him from suspension was overruled by Central Council, thus depriving the Kingdom of his services. Peculiarly, although Moriarty had served his six months' suspension for playing rugby the previous February, the unfortunate man fell foul of a separate rule that confined reinstatement to the period between 1 January and Easter Sunday.

Undeterred by all of this, Kerry took the initiative and led by 3-1 to 0-5 at the break despite having played against the breeze. The result seemed a foregone conclusion but Louth launched a great second-half revival. It was the introduction of Kevin Connolly that made all the difference. Wearing an unnumbered jersey, and officially described as 'Kevin McArdle', this clerical student gave a brilliant exhibition of football, almost singlehandedly closing the gap. John D. Hickey informed his readers: 'I doubt if there was ever a back who pulled on a boot who could have countered all the attributes of the Louth man.'

Kerry eventually held out for a five-point win and much of the credit for this went to defenders James 'Jas' Murphy and John Cronin.

THE FINAL – 27 SEPTEMBER

A big talking point in the week leading up to the 1953 Final was the decision of the Kerry selectors to demote team captain Paudie Sheehy to the substitutes' bench. A complication here was the fact that Paudie's father, John Joe, himself an All-Ireland winning captain, was part of the selection committee. Many felt that this decision, coupled with the enforced absence of Tom Moriarty, might not bode well for the county's prospects.

It's not known exactly how many people turned up at Croke Park on 27 September to see first-time finalists Armagh take on the might of Kerry in the All-Ireland showdown. The official attendance was a then record of 85,155. Several thousand more gained entry and more again were turned away at the turnstiles. What is known is that those who attended were privileged to witness one of the most keenly contested, skilful and sporting finals on record.

The opening minutes of the game did not augur well for a classic as Armagh seemed stage-struck and Kerry began to weave their magic. Points from Jim Brosnan and Tadhgie Lyne gave them an early lead but gradually the Ulstermen began to settle down. Gerry O'Neill opened their account from a free and this was followed by a goal from midfielder Mal McEvoy, who was having the proverbial 'stormer'. With play reaching the highest standards, the teams fought tooth and nail for the remainder of the half which ended with Armagh holding a one-point advantage, 1-3 to 0-5. The brilliance of the spectacle was captured by John D. Hickey the following morning: 'Speed of action, magnificent kicking and fielding of inspiring grandeur, combined to merit the first half being quoted as would a text-book on the game.'

Armagh suffered a blow just before half-time when their goalkeeper, Eamon McMahon, had to retire through injury. Playing a blinder, he had saved what looked like three certain goals for Kerry. Further misfortune followed early in the second half when their classy wing-back and team captain, Seán Quinn, also had to go off injured. Despite these setbacks, Armagh continued to take the game to Kerry.

Largely due to the efforts of Tadhgie Lyne and John Joe Sheehan, the men from the Kingdom held a two-point lead with only six minutes remaining. Armagh's hopes rose when they were awarded a penalty after Kerry goalkeeper Johnny Foley was adjudged to have handled the ball on the ground inside the small parallelogram. This was taken by Bill McCorry, so often a hero for his county, who could only watch in despair as his shot flew past the outside of the post.

Armagh seemed to lose their momentum after this miss and Kerry added further scores before finally taking the honours on a score of 0-13 to 1-6.

Kerry had now moved their All-Ireland tally to seventeen while Armagh, who had contributed so much to this classic final, would wait nearly fifty years to finally reach the footballing Holy Grail. Aside from McMahon, Quinn and McEvoy, they had many heroes on the day, with the full-back line of Gene Morgan, Jack Bratton and John McKnight outstanding.

While chief scorers Sheehan and Tadhgie Lyne were lauded as key to Kerry's success, they also had outstanding performers in defence. Top billing went to Ballylongford's Colm Kennelly while Donie Murphy and John Cronin made major contributions. Cronin's performance was all the more remarkable given that he played much of the game with a broken nose. As a foretaste of what was to come, a young Sean Murphy turned in a great second-half performance against Armagh's danger man, McEvoy.

After what was a relative 'famine' for Kerry, who had waited seven years to regain the crown, they were now hopeful that order could be restored and that 1954 would see a continuation of their dominance. Time would tell if these expectations were well founded.

FINAL STATISTICS

	Kerry	Armagh
Full-time:	0-13	1-6
Half-time:	0-5	1-3
Scorers:	J.J. Sheehan 0-3	M. McEvoy 1-2
	T. Lyne 0-5 (0-2 frees)	G. O'Neill 0-2 (0-1 free)
	J. Brosnan 0-3	J. Cunningham 0-1
	T. Ashe 0-1	B. Seeley 0-1
	J. Lyne 0-1	
Attendance:	85,155	
Gate Receipts:	£10,904-9-1 (€13,846)	
Referee:	Peter McDermott (Meath)	

FINAL MISCELLANY

- The referee for the final, Peter McDermott, had been on the All-Ireland-winning Meath team of 1949 and would go on to lead the Royal County to further success in 1954. This remarkable feat of winning an All-Ireland medal after having refereed a final was also achieved by Cavan's Simon Deignan and Waterford hurler Vin Baston.

  Deignan refereed the 1950 Final between Mayo and Louth and later lined out on the winning 1952 team. Baston refereed the 1945 Final between Tipperary and Kilkenny, later starring for his county in their 1948 success over Dublin.

- Kerry's 1953 win coincided with the fiftieth anniversary of their first title in 1903. Among the guests at their jubilee banquet in Killarney was Joe Rafferty, captain of the Kildare team which had lost out in that three-game epic fifty years earlier. Bemoaning what he regarded as a deterioration in standards, he implored the Gaels of Kerry to help do away with that 'rotten practice of hand to toe'.

- When Dublin won the National Football League title in 1953, their goalkeeper was Tony O'Grady (Air Corps). The other fourteen members of the team were from the St Vincent's club.

- Mayo won the Minor Championship of 1953, beating Clare 2-11 to 1-6 in the final. Their captain that year was student priest Sean Freyne who, in the absence of permission from the authorities at Maynooth College, missed the final. The Toureen native went on to become a renowned theologian, and was appointed a professor at Trinity College, Dublin.

- Kerry's John Cronin was carrying on a family tradition when he won an All-Ireland with Kerry in 1953. His brother Jim was a member of Cork's victorious team in 1945.

- Meath and Louth met in the championship in all nine seasons from 1945 to 1953. They drew four times; there was a one-point victory on five occasions; twice there was a two-point victory, and twice the winning margin was three points. Meath won the 'series', five wins to four.

1953 – THE YEAR THAT WAS

- On 29 May, New Zealander Edmund Hillary and Sherpa mountaineer Tenzing Norgay became the first men to reach the summit of Mount Everest. There was much controversy in the aftermath of this achievement, with contradictory claims as to which man was first to reach the top. A statement by Tenzing proclaiming 'We reached the summit almost together' did little to clarify matters.

- At ceremonies in Dublin, Maynooth and Moynalty over the weekend of 20–21 June, a total of seventy-eight priests were ordained.

- Inclement conditions on 26 July led to a fall-off in the number participating in the annual pilgrimage to Croagh Patrick. Just over 60,000 made the climb, a drop of 10,000 compared to the previous year.

- The GAA ban on foreign games was the subject of much heated public debate in the lead-up to the Association's Annual Congress on Easter Sunday 1953. The refusal of the Limerick County Board to allow its members to participate in a parade which included members of the rugby, soccer and hockey fraternities had precipitated an avalanche of disapproving correspondence to the national newspapers.

In his presidential address to Congress, Vincent O'Donoghue pulled no punches when rejecting any criticism. He said: 'Make no mistake about it, in Ireland today a relentless struggle is being waged unceasingly between the ideologies of Gaelicism and Anglicisation. All the forces of modern pagan materialism are straining ruthlessly to utterly destroy the Irish way of life and the brunt of the defence against alien aggression is borne by the GAA.'

Mr Donoghue was very clear as to the prime culprits in all of this. As reported in the *Irish Independent*, 'With the venom only equalled by their brazen effrontery, he said, every Anglo-phile scribe, posing as a freedom lover, every tub-thumping champion of what he is pleased to call "broad mindedness" in sport, with the sound and fury of outraged indignation raves at the abominable tyranny of the narrow-minded GAA.'

1953 TEAM LINE-OUTS

KERRY (WINNERS)

1. Johnny Foley
(Kerins O'Rahillys)

2. James 'Jas' Murphy
(Kerins O'Rahillys, also Garda and St Nicholas, Cork) Capt.

3. Ned Roche
(Collins Barracks, Cork, also Knocknagoshel)

4. Donie Murphy
(Killarney Legion, also Clann na Gael, Kilkenny)

5. Colm Kennelly
(Ballylongford)

6. John Cronin
(Collins Barracks, also Milltown/Castlemaine)

7. James 'Mixie' Palmer
(Killarney Legion, also Sneem and Dunhill, Waterford)

8. Sean Murphy
(Geraldines, Dublin and UCD, also Camp and Dingle)

9. Dermot Hanafin
(Castleisland Desmonds)

10. Jim Brosnan
(Moyvane)

11. John Joe Sheehan
(Castleisland Desmonds, also Killarney Legion and Firies)

12. Tadghie Lyne
(Dr Crokes)

13. Tom Ashe
(Dingle)

14. Sean Kelly
(Civil Service, also Kilcummin)

15. Jackie Lyne
(Killarney Legion)

Subs: Gerald O'Sullivan (Killarney Legion, also St Mary's, Cahirciveen); Jerome O'Shea (St Mary's, Cahirciveen); Paudie Sheehy (John Mitchels and UCC); Brendan O'Shea (Ardfert, also Dingle); Mick Brosnan (Moyvane and UCC); Bobby Buckley (Clounmacon and UCC, also Kenmare); Mick Murphy (Kerins O'Rahillys, also Dingle)

ARMAGH (RUNNERS-UP)

1. Eamonn McMahon
(Clan na Gael)

2. Gene Morgan
(Crossmaglen Rangers)

3. Jack Bratton
(Armagh Harps)

4. John McKnight
(Killeavy and UCD, also Aodh
Ruadh, Donegal and Belturbet Rory
O'Moores, Cavan)

5. Frank Kernan
(Crossmaglen Rangers)

6. Pat O'Neill
(Keady Michael Dwyers)

7. Seán Quinn
(Sarsfields, also Sean McDermotts,
Dublin) Capt.

8. Mick O'Hanlon
(Cullyhanna)

9. Mal McEvoy
(Killeavy)

10. Joe Cunningham
(Armagh Harps)

11. Brian Seeley
(Clan na Gael)

12. Bill McCorry
(Wolfe Tones, Lurgan)

13. Pat Campbell
(Armagh Harps)

14. Art O'Hagan
(Keady Michael Dwyers)

15. Gerry O'Neill
(Middletown Eoghan Rua, also
Aghagallon Shamrocks, Antrim)

Subs: Gerry Wilson (Armagh Harps) Played; Gerry Murphy (Keady Michael Dwyers) Played; Joe O'Hare (Ballymacnab) Played; Gerry McStay (Clan na Gael); Johnny McBreen (Killeavy); Pat McCreesh (Crossmaglen Rangers); Pat Murphy (Crossmaglen Rangers); Isaac Henderson (Clan na Gael)

1954

Not that it made much difference to Kerry, but the Munster Championship of 1954 was contested by just four teams, Limerick and Clare both opting out. The semi-finals were both played on 4 July. In very wet and blustery conditions, and in front of a very small crowd, Kerry had no difficulty in disposing of the Waterford challenge, 3-10 to 1-2. It was a different story at the Cork Athletic Grounds where Tipperary looked like creating a sensation when they led the home team by nine points at the interval. In the second half, however, dual player Josie Hartnett took matters in hand and rifled home two goals as Cork ran out 3-11 to 2-7 winners.

The Munster Final saw Kerry take their fortieth provincial title with a resounding 4-9 to 2-3 victory. This was a ferociously physical affair, with several match reports noting that the ball was an incidental feature of the game. The launching pad for this win was the brilliance of their wing-backs Colm Kennelly and Sean Murphy, while Bobby Buckley lorded over matters at centre-field.

In Connacht, reigning champions Roscommon came down to earth with a bang when they met league champions Mayo at Castlebar on 13 June. With twenty-seven minutes gone, Roscommon had yet to register a score while Mayo, playing champagne football, had chalked up 2-5. Key men for Mayo were forwards Dan O'Neill and Tom Langan who were both in devastating form. One of the ironies of this encounter was that the star of Mayo's impregnable defence was Eddie Moriarty, a Roscommon-born garda who was stationed in Mayo.

Mayo were now spoken of as strong contenders for All-Ireland honours, with many suggesting another title was a formality. Unfortunately for them, Galway had not read the script and the Tribesmen duly sprang the shock of the summer with a 2-4 to 1-5 victory at Tuam on 4 July. Hit by injuries, the Galway selectors were forced to field a somewhat experimental fifteen. The decision to play Sean Purcell at full-back worked like a dream. Purcell proceeded to give an exhibition of football and repelled a succession of opponents as he inspired his team to a famous victory.

In the second of the Connacht semi-finals, Leitrim's Packie McGarty burst past four defenders before ramming a piledriver to the Sligo net in the dying minutes of their clash in Carrick-on-Shannon on 27 June. This paved the way for a hectic finish which saw Joe Masterson grab the winning point for the Sligo men at the death.

In the Connacht Final in Tuam on 18 July, Sligo almost forced a draw in the dying seconds. When Mick Gaffney got a fist to a high lobbing ball in the Galway goalmouth, Jack Mangan's desperate efforts to prevent it from crossing the line were hotly debated. The scene was described in the *Irish*

Independent: 'Confusion followed for a couple of minutes as players, umpire and referee and some over curious spectators held an impromptu debate, marked by gesticulations which reminded one of an excited Frenchman.'

Making a decision which almost had 'J.J.' of *The Sligo Champion* in tears, the referee awarded a free out and Galway were champions, 2-10 to 3-4. Almost inevitably, Purcell was again the standout performer, with great support from Tom 'Pook' Dillon and the Meath-born sprint champion, Mick Hanley. Nace O'Dowd gave another sterling display for Sligo, with strong support from Mick and Paddy Christie and the ever-reliable Frank White.

Roscommon were not the only provincial title-holders to bow out ignominiously in 1954. At Drogheda on 23 May, Louth were well and truly trounced by Dublin. Jim Crowley and Ollie Freaney were the brightest among a galaxy of stars as the Metropolitans coasted to a 0-11 to 0-2 victory. Not for the first or last time, the expectations created by Dublin came to nought when they were dumped out of the championship by Offaly at Portlaoise. The Offaly men reversed a seven-point interval deficit with some sparkling football in the second half. With goals from Sean Kinahan and Mick Furlong and outstanding performances from Paddy Casey, Paddy Fenlon and Christy Carroll, Offaly

Goalmouth action from the 1954 Final, which saw an ageing Meath side spring a surprise on reigning champions Kerry. *Image courtesy of the GAA Museum at Croke Park.*

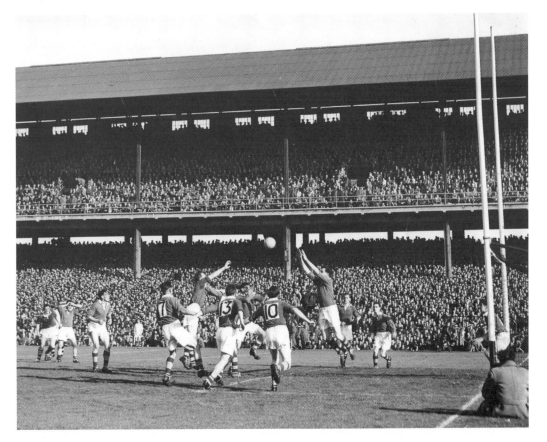

fully deserved their victory and their place in the Leinster Final.

On the other side of the Leinster draw, a last-gasp point from Davy Dalton gave Kildare the narrowest of wins in their second replay with league finalists Carlow. The Lilywhites' semi-final opponents were Meath who had scraped past Wicklow courtesy of a point from Paddy Meegan in the ninth minute of time added on in their preliminary round clash. One of the real highlights of this game was the outstanding display of Wicklow defender Joe Timmons.

In the semi-final, Meath entered the fray against Kildare with their full-forward line manned by players who had come out of inter-county retirement. Paddy Meegan, Brian Smyth and Peter McDermott all contributed handsomely to their deserved six-point victory but it was their goal-keeper Patsy McGearty who was the game's outstanding performer. Meath followed this victory with a comprehensive semi-final win over Longford on 11 July. This game witnessed one of the best individual displays of the championship, with Meath right half-back Kevin 'Gus' Lenehan giving an exhibition of skill, speed and power.

The stage was now set for the Offaly–Meath showdown, with many tipping newcomers Offaly to overcome the Royal veterans. They met at Croke Park on 25 July and while Meath had the edge on the general run of play it was still close at the break – Meath 1-4, Offaly 0-4. The big turnaround took place early in the second half when Meath's star midfielder Tom Duff suffered a broken leg. His replacement was the wily Peter McDermott, who wove all his old magic over proceedings. Within minutes, Meath had stretched their advantage to ten points. Offaly rallied and late goals from Paddy Casey and Sean Kinehan reduced the final gap to three points.

Contrary to what the scoreline might suggest, this was a comfortable win for Meath. Full-back Paddy O'Brien was at his imperious best, while McDermott was the chief architect in a forward line where Mícheál Grace and Tom Moriarty starred. For Offaly, brothers Paddy and Mick Casey put in a great hour while Christy Carroll continued his semi-final form with an outstanding display.

In the Ulster Championship, Derry got the better of Down, 4-11 to 3-4, at Newcastle on 13 June. A week later, Armagh edged out Antrim, 1-8 to 1-6, after Art O'Hagan had given them the lead with a goal in time added on. Describing the scene as the Orchard County clung on, *The Irish Press* noted: 'If all the dogs in Belfast perked their ears around five o'clock yesterday you couldn't really blame them. It was just 4,000 Armagh fans in Casement Park giving vent to 4,000 whistles in an attempt to get referee Carr to sound full-time.'

With Mal McEvoy on majestic form, Armagh had little difficulty overcoming Derry, 1-12 to 1-6, in the semi-final at Casement Park on 4 July.

Cavan, having already accounted for Monaghan, had just three points to spare over Tyrone in the second semi-final. Looking comfortable for much of the hour, the Breffni men had to withstand a frantic Tyrone comeback that was inspired by the outstanding play of Frankie Donnelly and Jack Taggart.

The Ulster Final was played at Clones on 25 July. Cavan scored 1-3 without reply in the first eight minutes, their goal a result of a speculative lob from Gerry Keys. With Victor Sherlock and Tom Maguire dominating at centre-field, it was an uphill struggle for the reigning champions as Cavan pulled through, 2-10 to 2-5. To their credit, however, Armagh battled to the end and had outstanding performers in Jack Bratton and the McKnight brothers.

The first of the 1954 semi-finals was played at Croke Park on 1 August, when Meath beat Cavan by a single point. The national newspapers were in agreement that the better team won. The *Meath Chronicle* shared this view, and the opening lines of its match report gave the following succinct description of proceedings: 'A quite unexpected third quarter blitzkrieg which engulfed the enthusiasm of their supporters; a daring gamble brilliantly brought off by Paddy O'Brien, who played the cleverest game of his spectacular career; a dazzling display of attacking football by Tom O'Brien until he sustained a broken collar bone; a delightful goal by Brian Smyth – these were the chief features of the big match and Meath's 1-5 to 0-7 victory over Cavan.'

The report in *The Anglo Celt* adopted a slightly different stance, proclaiming that: 'Meath won altogether against the run of play.'

The second of the All-Ireland semi-finals saw reigning champions Kerry, minus the suspended Ned Roche, beat Galway, 2-6 to 1-6, in an extraordinary affair at Croke Park on 15 August. What *The Irish Press* described as a 'leg weary, clumsy handed' Galway team were given a drubbing in the first half. The boot was on the other foot after the break, however, as the Tribesmen, inspired by Billy O'Neill, dominated every facet of play and were unfortunate to come up short in a pulsating finish. Such was the extent of the second-half turnaround that John D. Hickey in the *Irish Independent* proclaimed that an inexperienced spectator could be forgiven for concluding that the teams had swopped jerseys at the interval.

THE FINAL – 26 SEPTEMBER

Given the county's remarkable All-Ireland record, and that they were reigning champions, it's hardly surprising that Kerry were widely tipped to retain their title. As for Meath, they had been considered fortunate to survive in several of their earlier games and, with the exception of Mick Dunne of *The Irish Press*, neutral pundits doubted that luck could carry them through against the might of the Kingdom. The GAA had introduced severe restrictions on collective training earlier in the year and Dunne identified this as tilting the balance in Meath's favour.

In what was widely regarded as one of the most disappointing finals in memory, Kerry were overwhelmed, 1-13 to 1-7, by a much fitter and more determined Meath fifteen. The immediate reaction in the Kingdom was that the recently imposed restrictions on full-time collective training had dealt a mortal blow to their prospects. As all but one of its players were living in the county, this gave Meath a significant advantage over Kerry, who had ten players living outside the Kingdom. Heated debate on the issue was not confined to the sports pages; the 'Letters to the Editor' columns were kept busy for weeks afterwards.

This excerpt from the *Meath Chronicle* of 11 September suggests that Meath's advantage in the fitness stakes may not have been great: 'The Meath selectors have decided on a light training programme for the Royal County team in preparation for the forthcoming all-Ireland senior football final against Kerry. The first exercise took place in Páirc Tailteann, Navan, on Wednesday of last week. Probably there will be two or three sessions next week. None of the players is laying off work, even during the week preceding the big match. No training fund is being established.'

Right from the throw-in, Meath set the tone for the game. Even though he won the toss, their captain, Peter McDermott, elected to play against the elements. Kerry's confused defenders lined out at the wrong end of the ground. There was further confusion when the game finally got underway, with a small dog invading the pitch, before being summarily dismissed by referee Simon Deignan.

Meath proceeded to build up a solid lead but John Joe Sheehan scored a goal for Kerry just before the break, giving them a one-point advantage at half-time. It was largely one-way traffic in the second half as Meath, with their blend of youth and experience, pulled away for a comfortable victory, and their second title. It was ironic that Meath's goal was scored by Kerry native Tom Moriarty.

The 'old guard' of McDermott, Smyth, the O'Briens and Meegan led by example, with the last-mentioned having cut short his honeymoon to line out. Among the younger brigade, Kevin Lenehan and Ned Durnin were superb, but top billing went to Micheál Grace who, according to Padraig Puirséal in *The Irish Press*, 'gave an exhibition that he may yet equal, but certainly can never surpass.'

The consensus was that Meath's was a fifteen-man victory, while Kerry 'stars' were thin on the ground. Their outstanding performer was wing-forward Paudie Sheehy, who never gave up the fight. The rest of the forward division showed only flashes of their true form, but a breakthrough against the ever-alert Patsy McGearty proved beyond them. Elsewhere, Garry O'Mahony, John Cronin, James 'Mixie' Palmer and Tom Moriarty were Kerry's best. Kerry's Tom Moriarty and his Meath namesake both came from the village of Castlegregory.

Aside from the general agreement that the 1954 Final had fallen short as a spectacle, there was also a widespread view that neither Meath nor Kerry were likely to be in the shake-up for honours in the foreseeable future. No fewer than five of Meath's most experienced men had flagged their intention to retire. It was not a spate of retirements which called Kerry's prospects into doubt; only the usual air of despondency which hangs in the air after a final defeat. Of course, if there was one county which could resurrect itself from the footballing doldrums, it would be the men from the south-west.

FINAL STATISTICS

	Meath	Kerry
Full-time:	1-13	1-7
Half-time:	0-7	1-5
Scorers:	P. Meegan 0-5 (0-4 frees)	T. Lyne 0-4 (0-1 free)

T. Moriarty 1-2	J.J. Sheehan 1-1
B. Smyth 0-3	J. Brosnan 0-2
M. McDonnell 0-2	
P. McDermott 0-1	

Attendance: 75,275
Gate Receipts: £9,613-7-0 (€12,206)
Referee: Simon Deignan (Cavan)

FINAL MISCELLANY

- Meath's outstanding full-back Paddy O'Brien was a very doubtful starter for the final, suffering an illness in the lead-up to the game. John D. Hickey of the *Irish Independent* remarked: 'I saw the Sean McDermott's man on Friday and doubted his assurance that he would play – he looked entirely unfitted for such a test after having been tormented all week by a carbuncle on the back of his neck.'

  The concerns about O'Brien's fitness reached crisis proportions among Meath supporters at the half-time break in the Minor Final. An urgent request was made over the public address system for Paddy Dixon, full-back on the 1949 team, to go to the Meath dressing-room and the rumour spread that he was to fill the full-back berth.

  It transpired that goalkeeper Patsy McGearty had travelled to Dublin with Dixon and had left his playing gear in the boot of his car.

- Glorying in his prediction of Royal County success, the chief GAA correspondent with the *Meath Chronicle* certainly didn't hold back in his match report of 2 October: 'Like 99.99 per cent of the daily and Sunday newspaper critics, our Kerry friends made the mistake of not so much exaggerating Kerry's abilities, but of grossly underestimating Meath's. Having to eat their own words must have given these same critics, by the way, a right good dose of indigestion.'

- In the All-Ireland hurling semi-final played at Croke Park on 8 August, Nicky Rackard, who had scored 5-4 in the Leinster Final against Dublin, struck for 7-7 in Wexford's 12-17 to 2-3 victory over Antrim. Having given the Rathnure man the sporting headlines, the *Irish Independent* continued: 'the only other point worth mentioning is the splendid goalkeeping of Antrim's McMullan – yes, even with twelve unstoppable goals against him.'

- To avoid a clash of colours, Kerry wore the Cavan blue in the final against Meath. The referee, Cavan's Simon Deignan, was attired in white. Writing in *The Irish Press*, Benedict Kiely commented on an amusing diversion when 'the ball dropped smack into the referee's hands, and the great Simon looked around for one hesitant, bewildered moment (confused by all those blue jerseys) before he realised that he should hop the ball, not kick it.'

- When Kerry lost out to Meath in the 1954 decider, Ballylongford's Colm Kennelly lined out as a wing-back. On a tough day for the Kennelly family, his younger brother, Brendan, was on the minor team beaten by Dublin. Brendan's football career was relatively short-lived (he did line out for the senior team against Wexford in the 1957 League), but he went on to distinguish himself as a poet and academic.

- On the Sunday after losing the senior final, Kerry won the All-Ireland Junior title. While 'P.F.' gave due credit in his *Kerryman* column the following week, he expressed one grave reservation: 'It seems to me a mistake to play Culloty in this company. He is only a boy and it is unfair to put him in among men. If this policy is persevered with, this young lad, who has a promising career, may be ruined and his club should stop the practice.' The 'boy' in question would annex his first senior All-Ireland medal twelve months later, and his fifth Celtic Cross fifteen years after that.

1954 — THE YEAR THAT WAS

- On the Sunday before the 1954 showdown, the Pioneer Total Abstinence Association organised a pilgrimage to Knock. A crowd of over 50,000 non-drinkers made the journey.

   Just as a mass of pioneers was descending on Knock, visitors returning to the US were being enticed by Cork firm Woodford Bourne Ltd to take home, tax free, a five-bottle pack of John Jameson Whiskey. Equivalent to one American gallon, and delivered on board the liner exiting Cobh, this special offer was priced at £3.10.0 (€4.44).

- The likelihood of a Fianna Fáil/Fine Gael coalition at any time in the future seemed extremely remote in 1954. After being escorted by a mile-long procession of cars from Foxford, Taoiseach Éamon de Valera attended an election rally in Ballina on 2 May. Noting the opposition's unfounded expressions of confidence, he said: 'Fine Gael, after winning a few by-elections, became so puffed up in the Dáil that they seemed too big for their seats. They were like pricked balloons after the North Mayo by-election and also after the South Galway by-election, we may see them like pricked balloons again after this election.'

- On 6 May 1954, Britain's Roger Bannister became the first man to run a mile in less than four minutes. The current record is 3:43.13, set by Hicham El Guerrouj of Morocco in 1999.

1954 TEAM LINE-OUTS

MEATH (WINNERS)

1. Patsy McGearty
(Ballivor)

2. Micheál O'Brien
(Skryne)

3. Paddy 'Hands' O'Brien
(Sean McDermotts, Dublin, also
Skryne)

4. Kevin McConnell
(Syddan, also Castletown)

5. Kevin Lenehan
(Duleek)

6. Jim Reilly
(Dunboyne)

7. Ned Durnin
(Donaghmore)

8. Paddy Connell
(Sean McDermotts, Dublin, also
Moynalty)

9. Tom O'Brien
(Skryne)

10. Micheál Grace
(Kells Harps)

11. Brian Smyth
(Skryne)

12. Matty McDonnell
(Ballinlough)

13. Paddy Meegan
(Syddan)

14. Tom Moriarty
(Kilcloon, also Castlegregory, Kerry
and Starlights, Wexford)

15. Peter McDermott
(Navan O'Mahonys, also
Donaghmore and Young Irelands,
Cushinstown) Capt.

Subs: John Clarke (Kells Harps); Billy Rattigan (Dunshaughlin); Frankie Byrne (Navan O'Mahonys, also Navan Parnells, and Clanna Gael, Dublin); Gerald Smith (Kells Harps); Bernard Flanagan (Kells Harps); Larry O'Brien (Dunshaughlin); Patsy Ratty (Navan O'Mahonys); Dick Mee (Trim); Paddy Brady (Navan O'Mahonys); James Farrell (Trim)

Tom Duff (Syddan) was unavailable for selection because of a broken leg sustained in the Leinster Final against Offaly.

KERRY (RUNNERS-UP)

1. Garry O'Mahony
(John Mitchels)

2. James 'Mixie' Palmer
(Killarney Legion, also Sneem and
Dunhill, Waterford)

3. Ned Roche
(Collins Barracks, Cork, also
Knocknagoshel)

4. Donie Murphy
(Killarney Legion, also Clann na
Gael, Kilkenny)

5. Sean Murphy
(Camp and UCD, also Geraldines,
Dublin and Dingle)

6. John Cronin
(Collins Barracks, Cork, also
Milltown/Castlemaine)

7. Colm Kennelly
(Ballylongford)

8. John Dowling
(Kerins O'Rahillys) Capt.

9. Tom Moriarty
(Clonakilty, Cork, also Austin Stacks
and Dohenys, Cork)

10. Bobby Buckley
(Clounmacon and UCC, also
Kenmare)

11. John Joe Sheehan
(Castleisland Desmonds, also Killarney
Legion and Firies)

12. Paudie Sheehy
(John Mitchels)

13. Jim Brosnan
(Moyvane)

14. Sean Kelly
(Civil Service, also Kilcummin)

15. Tadghie Lyne
(Dr Crokes)

Subs: Jackie Lyne (Killarney Legion); Jerome O'Shea (St Mary's, Cahirciveen, also Erin's Hope, Dublin and UCD); Gerald O'Sullivan (Killarney Legion, also St Mary's, Cahirciveen); Eddie Dowling (Ballydonoghue); Brendan O'Shea (Ardfert, also Dingle); Mick Murphy (Kerins O'Rahillys, also Dingle); Daniel O'Sullivan (Churchill); Gerry Stack (Listowel Emmets); Tom Ashe (Dingle); Dermot Dillon (Dingle)

1955

Over the years, there have been many great footballing campaigns and standout finals in the race for the Sam Maguire Cup. Among these, 1955 always features prominently in any historic review of the championship. At a time of unprecedented interest in Gaelic games, this was the year that saw the beginning of what was to become one of the keenest and most enduring rivalries in football.

The early rounds of the Leinster Championship saw Westmeath, Louth and Kildare record one-point wins over Wicklow, Longford and Wexford respectively. League champions Dublin began their campaign with a twelve-point win, 3-9 to 0-6, over Carlow at Newbridge. The Carlow men held the upper hand for much of this game, with Eamonn Kehoe, Paddy Delaney and Paddy Metcalf all excelling. Were it not for great defensive work by Jim Lavin and long kick specialist Mick Moylan, the victory margin would have been much slimmer. Offaly, with Croghan brothers Paddy and Mick Casey to the fore, beat Louth by five points to tee up a semi-final joust with the Metropolitans.

In sweltering heat at Portlaoise on 10 July, Dublin had just three points to spare over an Offaly team that had to line out without their talisman, Paddy Casey. They thus progressed to their first provincial final in twelve years. Their stars were Des 'Snitchie' Ferguson and Jim Crowley, who, according to Mick Dunne in *The Irish Press*, 'sailed into the air and pulled down high balls with damaging efficiency.'

This was one of the rare occasions when Kevin Heffernan was held in check as Offaly full-back Kevin Scally continued his brilliant form from the Louth game. He formed part of a very solid Offaly defence in which Noel Magee, Dickie Conroy and Peter Nolan shone.

On the other side of the Leinster draw, All-Ireland champions Meath progressed in similar manner to their 1954 campaign. They escaped with a draw against Kildare at Croke Park on 29 May and needed extra time to pip the Lilywhites by a point in the replay. Mitchel Cogley, veteran reporter with the *Irish Independent*, described the replay as one which 'will rank with the finest ever played at Croke Park.' A feature of this game was the brilliant play of Meath's Matty McDonnell who had the game of his life.

Next up for the champions were rank outsiders Westmeath. Against all the odds, and with Brian Kavanagh lording matters at centre-field, the Meath men were put to the pin of their collars as they scraped home with a single point to spare. The *Irish Independent* reported that while Meath had no outstanding performer, they didn't have any weaknesses either. Westmeath's top men were Paddy

Flanagan, Jack Lyster and late replacement Paddy 'Butcher' McCormack. Special credit went to Paddy Dunne, who performed heroically despite lining out with a broken thumb.

The Leinster Final, played on 24 July, was a repeat of the League Final when Dublin crushed Meath by twelve points, 2-12 to 1-3. While Dublin were firm favourites to win, not many expected their winning margin to be anything close to the league decider. What transpired was an even more emphatic victory: 5-12 to 0-7. Mitchel Cogley opined that: 'Never in the history of the game have the reigning champions been so humbled.'

Every Dublin player was on song. If Norman Allen was outstanding at centre-back and Jim Crowley in total control at midfield, it was undisputed that Kevin Heffernan was the real star. Apart from scoring two brilliant goals, he tormented the Meath defence for the hour. With only Matty McDonnell shining for the losers, this was the end of an era for a Meath team that brought so much glory to the county.

Such was the quality of Dublin's display on that July day that Mick Dunne was prompted to write: 'Unless the form explodes they must win the Sam Maguire Cup in September.'

The Connacht Championship provided more than its share of shocks in 1955. When provincial champions Galway met Roscommon at Castlebar on 19 June, they were overwhelming favourites

The Dublin team that lost out to Kerry in their famous 1955 showdown. Back (l–r): Ollie Freaney, Paddy O'Flaherty, Jim McGuinness, Jim Crowley, Mick Moylan, Jim Lavin, Terry Jennings, Joe Brennan, Kevin Heffernan, Jimmy Gray, Peter O'Reilly (team trainer); front (l–r): Johnny Boyle, Cyril Freaney, Cathal O'Leary, Norman Allen, Mossy Whelan, Nicky Maher, 'Danno' Mahony (captain), Sean Manning, Billy Monks, Padraig 'Jock' Haughey, Des 'Snitchie' Ferguson. *Sportsfile.*

to progress to the semi-final. Instead of the expected victory, they found themselves at the end of a 1-6 to 0-3 drubbing. In deplorable weather conditions, Roscommon's midfield pairing of Eamonn Donoghue and Seamus Scanlon provided the platform for a victory that boosted the ambitions of the rest of the province. Roscommon continued their championship march two weeks later when they had an easy 1-8 to 0-4 win over Sligo. Donoghue was again in sparkling form.

When Mayo played Leitrim in a quagmire at Markievicz Park on 26 June, they had their expected comfortable win, coasting to a 3-11 to 0-9 victory. It was John Nallen and former Dublin minor Brendan McLoughlin who set the tone at midfield as they progressed to the provincial final. A feature of this game was the brilliance of Leitrim's Packie McGarty who, by common consent, was the best player on view.

It was a case of youthful Roscommon against the veterans of Mayo when they met at Tuam on 17 July. Against most predictions, Mayo not only won the game, they annihilated Roscommon on a score of 3-11 to 1-3. Their victory was widely attributed to the craft and brains of their more experienced players, with Tom Langan, Paddy Prendergast, Eddie Moriarty and the Flanagans, Sean and Mick, all outstanding. There were few crumbs of consolation for Roscommon but, as always, Gerry O'Malley gave it everything. Reporting in *The Irish Press*, Mick Dunne wrote: 'with every kick of the ball he justified the £40 plane fare back from Denmark.'

Reigning champions Cavan were once again favourites to emerge from Ulster. They started their campaign against Antrim on 19 June at Breffni Park and found themselves two goals in arrears after just ten minutes. The returning Kevin Armstrong was their tormentor-in-chief during this period, but gradually the champions began to take control. They restricted Antrim to just a single point for the remainder of the game and had six points to spare at the end. In a forward division which *The Anglo Celt* described as 'not sparking on all plugs', top billing went to one 'Sean Smith', the undercover name allotted to clerical student Seamus Hetherton.

Cavan's next opponents were Donegal, who, inspired by Frank Brennan, had overcome Monaghan in their quarter-final clash. The Breffni men were very fortunate to escape with a two-point victory when they met at Clones on 10 July. With two injured players, Jimmy 'Cookie' Boyle and Jackie McDermott, lining out for Donegal, their task became more challenging and many felt this made all the difference in a very close game. Defenders Phil 'Gunner' Brady and Hubert Gaffney were the key men for Cavan as they progressed to yet another provincial decider.

The other side of the Ulster draw saw an up-and-coming Derry side reach their first ever provincial final by virtue of impressive wins over Tyrone and Armagh. Veterans Frankie Niblock and Roddy Gribbin were central to these victories, but the real ace in their pack was midfielder Jim McKeever, who was fast being recognised as one of the finest players in the game.

They met Cavan in the final at Clones on 31 July in what was a particularly scrappy encounter, with no fewer than sixty-five frees awarded over the hour. It was Cavan who prevailed on a score of 0-11 to 0-8, with veteran Peter Donohoe notching eight. Apart from Donohoe, Cavan owed their victory to goalkeeper Seamus Morris, who made a number of terrific saves, including from a penalty by Charlie 'Chuck' Higgins. Jim McDonnell had a great game at wing-back for Cavan while Derry's best were McKeever and Roddy Gribbin.

Niall O'Dea and Eugene Doherty were the main men for Tipperary when they overcame Clare, 1-10 to 0-7, in the Munster Championship first-round tie at rain-soaked Limerick on 12 June. Playing six of their 1953 All-Ireland minor runners-up, Clare put up a great show, with Sean Liddy and Eddie Cotter their best performers. Cork were Tipperary's opponents in the provincial semi-final when they had a comfortable 2-8 to 0-7 win. Johnny Creedon was the hero of the hour, hitting 2-2 in a man-of-the-match performance.

The second semi-final, between Kerry and Waterford, was an utterly one-sided affair, Kerry cruising to a 3-7 to 0-4 victory. John Dowling and Tom Moriarty were the key men as Kerry progressed to their traditional Munster Final showdown with neighbours Cork.

They met at Killarney on 24 July, where Cork matched their much-vaunted opponents in every department except point taking. They hit a total of seventeen wides, eventually losing out by two points. The Kerry forwards were vastly more efficient than their counterparts, with Paudie Sheehy and Tadhgie Lyne accounting for nine of their points. If these two were the cream of the Kerry forward division, their stars in defence were James 'Mixie' Palmer, Donie Murphy and Jerome O'Shea, who is said to have played the game of his life. For Cork, Paddy Harrington (father of future Major golf champion Pádraig) and Nealie Duggan controlled the midfield exchanges for much of the game, while in an otherwise disappointing forward line, two-goal Jim Donovan was best.

An unusual feature of the 1955 Championship was that both semi-finals went to a replay. Kerry and Cavan could not be separated when they served up a thrilling encounter on 14 August. The quality on display was captured by John D. Hickey: 'never did so many players in one match so distinguish themselves in one all too short hour.'

Kerry started smartly and built up a four-point lead at the break. Then it was Cavan's turn to take control, with Victor Sherlock and Gerry Keys dominating at midfield and a youthful Tom Maguire playing brilliantly at centre-back. With just a minute to go, Cavan held a two-point advantage and looked set to record one of the greatest ever comeback victories. It was then that a brilliant cross from teenager Johnny Culloty found its way to Tadhgie Lyne, who blasted it to the net. Before the cheering had abated, Keys lofted a long-range equaliser just as referee Peter McDermott sounded the long whistle.

Such was the interest in the double header of replays on 11 September that over 71,000 people turned up at Croke Park. As so often when it came to a replay, Kerry showed no mercy in crushing Cavan on a 4-7 to 0-5 scoreline. Kerry's man of the hour was a rejuvenated John Cronin, while their forwards played havoc with the Cavan defence, with Johnny Culloty the most conspicuous. Having stayed the pace in the first half, Cavan virtually collapsed after the break and only wing-backs Jim

McDonnell and Hubert Gaffney seemed immune from the general air of lethargy within their ranks.

The first instalment of the Dublin v Mayo semi-final attracted over 60,000 to Croke Park on 21 August. In treacherous conditions, and against all predictions, Mayo outpaced and outplayed the opposition for much of the game. Two late points from Ollie Freaney and Nicky Maher gave a decidedly lucky Dublin a second bite of the cherry. One of the highlights of this game was a 'miraculous' save by Owen Roe O'Neill from Dublin's Kevin Heffernan.

The replay was no less exciting, with Dublin taking the honours by the narrowest of margins, 1-8 to 1-7. Commentators were in agreement that the principal reasons for Dublin's victory were the performances of Rush native Jim McGuinness at centre-field and St Vincent's Mossy Whelan at wing-back.

In what was to be the swansong for many of Mayo's golden generation, top honours went to Eddie Moriarty, Willie Casey, Jimmy Curran and the irrepressible Sean Flanagan.

THE FINAL – 25 SEPTEMBER

Prior to 1955, Kerry and Dublin had last clashed in an All-Ireland Final in 1924 when Kerry put a stop to Dublin's four-in-a-row bid. This reversed the result of the 1923 showdown when Dublin had got the better of the men from the Kingdom. Notwithstanding these earlier encounters, it is the 1955 meeting that represents the genesis of a rivalry that has continued for generations.

The mid-1950s saw interest in both hurling and football rise to unprecedented levels. The imminent clash of Dublin and Kerry brought enthusiasm to a new level and there was never any doubt that the Croke Park attendance record would be broken. Bringing added spice to the occasion was the fact that, for the first time in their history, the Dublin selection was an entirely native one. The only men born outside the county, Denis 'Danno' Mahony (Cork), Des Ferguson (Down) and Jim Crowley (New York), had been well and truly Dublin reared.

Many of the predictions for the game focused on Dublin's demolition of Meath in the Leinster Final, seemingly taking the view that their two-game struggle with Mayo was something of an aberration. The Irish Press preview on the day before the match was typical. Top reporters Mick Dunne and Padraig Puirséal were joined by Mayo captain Tom Langan and Cavan skipper Phil Brady in analysing the prospects of the respective teams. Each gave an emphatic vote of confidence to the Metropolitans, with Dunne predicting a minimum of a five-point margin. Of course, with his usual sprinkling of humility, 'P.F.' in The Kerryman had a different view when forecasting a Kerry win: 'We hear much talk of Dublin's greatness. City folk always talk big … In regard to the Dublin seniors this year I feel like the man from Missouri. You got to show me. There is nothing in Dublin's record which should cause us undue worry.'

When match day arrived, a huge crowd converged on Dublin and, as widely predicted, the attendance represented a new record for any sporting event in Ireland. Apart from the 87,107 official patrons, several thousand more gained 'unofficial' admittance.

Aided by a strong breeze in the first half, Kerry grabbed the initiative which they would hold throughout the game. Their marked superiority in the air posed severe problems for the Dublin forward division, which most had predicted would sway the result. While every one of the Kerry team contributed handsomely to their three-point victory, most praise was reserved for their outstanding defence. Jerome O'Shea, Sean Murphy and 'Mixie' Palmer came in for special mention, while Ned Roche did much to blunt the threat posed by Kevin Heffernan.

It is testimony to Dublin's great never-say-die spirit that they remained in contention right to the finish. The excitement towards the end of the game was described in the *Irish Independent*: 'Greater hours there have been, but a more titanic last four minutes not even those whose memories are coloured by the passage of time could conjure up.'

Apart from their rock-solid defence, Kerry captain John Dowling was inspirational. If Tadhgie Lyne was the scoring hero of the hour for the Kingdom, Paudie Sheehy and teenager Johnny Culloty were no less impressive.

Dublin's outstanding performer on the day was Jim Crowley, first at centre-back and later at midfield. 'Danno' Mahony and Johnny Boyle also acquitted themselves well, but this was a day when many of their stars failed to shine. They couldn't have known it at the time, but in some respects this loss was the foundation for outstanding success in the future. Kevin Heffernan, their key player, and ultimately the most influential figure ever in Dublin GAA, would later acknowledge that the lessons from 1955 shaped his thinking as he set about building the county into a football superpower.

FINAL STATISTICS

	Kerry	Dublin
Full-time:	0-12	1-6
Half-time:	0-5	0-3
Scorers:	T. Lyne 0-6 (0-4 frees)	O. Freaney 1-3 (1-2 frees)
	J. Brosnan 0-2	J. Boyle 0-2
	J. Dowling 0-1 (fifty)	K. Heffernan 0-1
	P. Sheehy 0-1	
	M. Murphy 0-1	
	J.J. Sheehan 0-1	
Attendance:	87,102	
Gate Receipts:	£10,677-19-6 (€13,558)	
Referee:	Willie Goodison (Wexford)	

FINAL MISCELLANY

- Describing the inability of Roscommon's forwards to hit the target in their Connacht Final clash with Mayo at Tuam on 17 July, John D. Hickey of the *Irish Independent* observed: 'the losers' forwards made scoring seem a "black art" of which they were entirely innocent.'

- Kerry's Jim Brosnan was based in the United States and only arrived back in Ireland to join the team's preparations five days before the final.
- Kevin Heffernan's innovative roving approach confused defences that year. He took his cue from how Don Revie was operating at centre-forward for Leeds United in the English League at the time. The traditional view was that Heffernan wasn't 'playing fair'!
- 1953 medallist and one of the real stars of Kerry's Munster Final win over Cork was full-back Donie Murphy (Killarney Legion). Within weeks of that victory he was diagnosed with tuberculosis and his footballing career came to an abrupt end. Although confined to his hospital bed as the Kingdom annexed the 1955 title, he got to take a sip from the Sam Maguire Cup when his teammates paid him a visit shortly after the game.
- A restaurant strike meant that there were no dining services on the train bringing the Kerry team to Dublin for the 1955 Final. The *Sunday Independent* reported that Kerry trainer Dr Eamon O'Sullivan arranged to have sandwiches prepared to meet the needs of his hungry charges on their long journey. The report went on: 'But whoever cut the sandwiches forgot it was a day of abstinence and the ham sandwiches had to remain uneaten.'

1955 – THE YEAR THAT WAS

- On 1 December, African American Rosa Parks was arrested for violating Alabama's segregation laws. She had refused to give up her bus seat to a white passenger.
- Among the many tours to Lourdes advertised in the *Sunday Independent* of 13 February 1955, the official pilgrimage of the Dublin Archdiocese, a ten-day land and sea trip, was priced at thirty-seven guineas (€49.32). Alternatively, pilgrims could travel by air on a seven-day all-in package for the princely sum of £29-10-0 (€37.45). A special feature of this option, which came complete with a priest as spiritual leader, was that: 'Air stewardess serves meals free of charge.'
- A specially-convened meeting of the Football Association of Ireland held on 15 October decided to proceed with the playing of an international match against communist Yugoslavia. The decision went against the wishes of the Department of Justice and Dublin Archbishop Dr John Charles McQuaid, who took exception to the Association's failure to consult with him before arranging the fixture.

1955 TEAM LINE-OUTS

KERRY (WINNERS)

1. Garry O'Mahony
(John Mitchels)

2. Jerome O'Shea
(St Mary's, Cahirciveen, also Erin's
Hope, Dublin and UCD)

3. Ned Roche
(Collins Barracks, Cork, also
Knocknagoshel)

4. James 'Mixie' Palmer
(Killarney Legion, also Sneem and
Dunhill, Waterford)

5. Sean Murphy
(Geraldines, Dublin and UCD, also
Camp and Dingle)

6. John Cronin
(Collins Barracks, Cork, also
Milltown/Castlemaine)

7. Tom Moriarty
(Clonakilty, Cork, also Austin Stacks
and Doheny's, Cork)

8. John Dowling
(Kerins O'Rahillys) Capt.

9. Dinny O'Shea
(Kerins O'Rahillys)

10. Paudie Sheehy
(John Mitchels)

11. Tom Costello
(Duagh)

12. Tadhgie Lyne
(Dr Crokes)

13. Johnny Culloty
(Killarney Legion)

14. Mick Murphy
(Geraldines, Dublin, also Kerins
O'Rahillys and Dingle)

15. Jim Brosnan
(Moyvane)

Subs: John Joe Sheehan (Castleisland Desmonds, also Killarney Legion and Firies); Gerard O'Sullivan (Killarney Legion, also St Mary's, Cahirciveen); Bobby Buckley (Clounmacon, also Kenmare); Dan McAuliffe (Duagh); Colm Kennelly (Ballylongford); Dermot Dillon (Duagh); Ned Fitzgerald (St Mary's, Cahirciveen); Jim 'Bawn' Fitzgerald (Kerins O'Rahillys); Donal 'Marcus' O'Neill (St Mary's, Cahirciveen)

Donie Murphy (Killarney Legion) was unavailable for selection due to illness.

DUBLIN (RUNNERS-UP)

1. Paddy O'Flaherty
(Beann Eadair)

2. Denis 'Danno' Mahony
(St Vincent's) Capt.

3. Jim Lavin
(St Vincent's)

4. Mick Moylan
(St Vincent's)

5. Mossy Whelan
(St Vincent's)

6. Jim Crowley
(St Vincent's)

7. Nicky Maher
(St Vincent's)

8. Jim McGuinness
(St Maur's)

9. Cathal O'Leary
(St Vincent's)

10. Des 'Snitchie' Ferguson
(St Vincent's, also Gaeil Colmcille,
Meath)

11. Ollie Freaney
(St Vincent's)

12. Johnny Boyle
(Air Corps, also Clanna Gael and
Suncroft, Kildare)

13. Padraig 'Jock' Haughey
(St Vincent's)

14. Kevin Heffernan
(St Vincent's)

15. Cyril Freaney
(St Vincent's)

Subs: Terry Jennings (St Vincent's); Billy Monks (St Margaret's); Marcus Whelan (St Vincent's); Joe Brennan (Na Fianna); Jimmy Gray (Na Fianna)

Norman Allen (St Vincent's) underwent an appendix operation in the lead-up to the game and was unavailable for selection.

1956

As the 1956 Championship got underway, the people of Kerry had good reason to feel optimistic. Having contested each of the previous three All-Ireland Finals, and having won two of these, the county was firmly re-established at the top of the football pyramid. However, an exhibition match against their 1955 All-Ireland Final victims, Dublin, at the Polo Grounds in New York on 3 June, proved a sobering experience. In front of a crowd of over 25,000 their confidence received something of a jolt when the Metropolitans swamped them, 3-12 to 1-4. Many commentators suggested that maybe Dublin had finally got the measure of the men from the south-west and looked forward to a late summer showdown between the two.

On the same day that Kerry were being put to the sword by Dublin, Tipperary overcame Clare in the Munster Championship, thus qualifying for a semi-final tilt with the Kingdom. For

The men from Tyrone who brought the county its first provincial title in 1956. Back (l–r): Hugh Donnelly, John Joe O'Hagan, Dermot McCloskey, Tommy Campbell, Sean Donnelly, Donal Donnelly, Hugh Kelly, Brian McSorley, Paddy Corey, Jim McAleer, Frank Higgins, Jackie Taggart, Pat Donaghy, Thady Turbett; front (l–r): J. Casey (team official), Mickey Kerr, Paddy Quinn, Mickey Quinn, Eddie Devlin, Patsy Devlin, unknown (team mascot), Jody O'Neill, Jim Devlin, Iggy Jones, Frankie Donnelly. *Courtesy Gaelic Art.*

Galway captain Jack Mangan, lifting the Sam Maguire Cup after his team's victory over Cork. *Image courtesy of the GAA Museum at Croke Park.*

the umpteenth time, Tipperary owed their victory to the brilliance of goalkeeper Tony Newport. Expectations of a rout when Kerry and Tipperary met in the semi-final were off the mark as the Kingdom struggled to an unexciting 3-7 to 3-2 victory. In an otherwise forgettable encounter, this game marked the championship debut of one Mick O'Connell from Valentia. This master craftsman would go on to fashion a footballing career that many assert has no equal in the history of the game.

As Kerry progressed to the provincial final, arch-rivals Cork did likewise on the same day with a 0-12 to 0-1 demolition of Waterford. It was difficult to gauge the merit of Cork's victory as Waterford, apart from man of the match Tom Cunningham, put up little resistance. A particularly worrying feature of Cork's performance was their poor marksmanship, as they shot twenty-five wides over the hour.

The word 'incredible' is the only one which adequately describes the Kerry v Cork clash in the Munster Final on 15 July. In the words of the *Irish Independent*, 'It was an amazing game from the start and the ending was even more remarkable than the beginning.'

Cork dominated in every sector for every minute of the game. They led 0-6 to 0-0 at the break, by which time they had amassed a total of eleven wides. They proceeded to kick wide after wide in the second half, their final tally being one higher than in the semi-final. Having had two goals and a point disallowed, struck the upright three times and watched Kerry goalkeeper Donal 'Marcus'

The Master: Sean Purcell, regarded by many as the greatest player the game has seen, was the key man as Galway bridged an eighteen-year gap to take the 1956 title. *Image courtesy of the GAA Museum at Croke Park.*

O'Neill save what seemed four certain goals, the Cork men held a slender three-point advantage with less than a minute to go. With the last play of the game, the burly Jim Brosnan gathered the ball fifty yards out from the Cork goal. He burst through a series of would-be tackles before slamming the ball to the net for a dramatic equaliser and salvation for the Kingdom.

Kerry had home advantage for the replay in Killarney two weeks later before a crowd of over 36,000, an increase of 12,000 on the drawn encounter. In another tight finish a goal from John Cronin brought Kerry level with only minutes to go, but this time Cork had time to respond and Niall Fitzgerald hit the last point for Cork in a famous 1-8 to 1-7 victory. Ironically, Castleisland-born Eric Ryan was the key man for Cork, with Denis Bernard following up on his man-of-the-match exploits in the drawn game with another outstanding performance. Once again goalkeeper O'Neill came to Kerry's rescue on a number of occasions, while Mick O'Connell showed flashes of his undoubted brilliance.

If Kerry's elimination from the Munster Championship was a surprise then Dublin's capitulation at the hands of Wexford at Carlow on 24 June was in the seismic shock category. Although Kevin Heffernan, Jim Crowley and Marcus Wilson were all absent from the Dublin line-up, there was no denying the merit of Wexford's great win. Their defence, ably marshalled by Sean Turner, was outstanding, while Paddy Kehoe and Paco Sheehan were their leaders in attack. One peculiar incident from this game was the departure to the sideline of Des 'Snitchie' Ferguson. Many thought he had been sent off but he returned to the fray, explaining later that his 'sabbatical' was prompted by frustration at a number of refereeing decisions.

Wexford's provincial final opponents were Kildare. A most fortuitous goal by Ned Treacy was the difference when the Lilywhites beat Louth on 20 May. Lady Luck, and the brilliant Larry McCormack, were to the fore when they edged out Longford in the quarter-final on 20 June. It was McCormack again, together with fellow half-backs Paddy Gibbons and Miko Doyle, who led the way as the Lilywhites overcame Offaly in the semi-final at Portlaoise on 1 July. The performance of

Ballymore's Peter Mooney was particularly commendable – he was suffering under the handicap of a broken big toe.

Pundits were divided as to the likely victors when Wexford and Kildare met in the Leinster Final on 22 July. Wexford, with dual player Paddy Kehoe and John Ryan in top form, started in whirlwind fashion and held a commanding five-point lead midway through the first half. They then began to concede needless frees, and with Seamie Harrison on free-taking duty, the Lilywhites began to close the gap. The second half became something of a procession, with McCormack, Jim Clarke, Paud Moore and team captain Davy Dalton starring as Kildare pulled away to win 2-11 to 1-8.

The 1956 pattern of provincial championship shocks continued in Ulster. Cavan seemed to be on course for yet another title after taking care of Antrim (3-15 to 2-4) and Armagh (1-9 to 1-5). The great combination play of brothers Brian and Charlie Gallagher was a feature of these Cavan wins.

An up-and-coming Tyrone team had a comfortable six-point win over Derry in the quarter-final at O'Neill Park on 3 June. With Frankie Donnelly and Jody O'Neill starring in attack and Mick McIlkenny and Mick Cushenan controlling midfield, Derry were fighting a losing battle throughout. Next up for Tyrone were the men from Monaghan and, against all predictions, they progressed to their first Ulster Final since 1941. Once again, Carrickmore's Frankie Donnelly was in brilliant form but the real star of the show was Jody O'Neill. As so often in the past, Monaghan relied heavily on the Herculean work of John Rice, but not even his great efforts could stem the tide.

Tyrone were underdogs when they lined out against Cavan in the Ulster Final at Clones on 29 July. Certainly, tradition was not on their side. Not alone were they yet to win a provincial crown, they had never previously beaten Cavan in a senior championship game. What happened on the day was described by Tom Cryan in *The Irish Press*: 'The skies opened up after half an hour at Clones yesterday – and so did amazing Tyrone. They revelled in the downpour and proceeded to pulverise pre-match favourites, Cavan, with a display of fast, lively football that brought them their first ever Ulster senior football title and sent their thousands of supporters delirious with excitement.'

Quite simply, Tyrone dominated completely and were not flattered by their ten-point victory, 3-5 to 0-4. Patsy Devlin and Jody O'Neill provided a constant supply of ball to a rampant forward division in which Iggy Jones, Frank Higgins and Jackie Taggart excelled. Even when Cavan threatened the Tyrone goal they met a staunch defence, behind which goalkeeper Thady Turbett was outstanding. History was made and, for the first time, a Tyrone senior team would play at Croke Park.

As happened in the other three provinces, champions Mayo failed to retain the Connacht title. There was no hard luck story about their exit from the championship – Galway hammered them, 5-13 to 2-5, at Castlebar on 17 June. Based on this display, many were now tipping Galway as serious contenders for All-Ireland glory. They consolidated this growing confidence in their prospects with an easy 1-9 to 0-2 win over Roscommon in their next game. Once again, this was very much a team performance, though the *Irish Independent* couldn't resist some poetic descriptions of standout performers. It referred to 'the Horatio-like effectiveness of full-back Gerry Daly' and 'the lordly magnificence of midfielder Mattie McDonagh'.

Sligo, who overcame Leitrim in the second semi-final, were Galway's next victims as the Tribesmen steamrolled their way to the provincial title. The final score was 3-12 to 1-5 in a game that saw Sean Purcell give an exhibition of football. Amazingly, Galway's journey to the title was achieved without making a single positional switch or substitution during the campaign.

With new champions in all four provinces, the stage was now set for an intriguing battle for ultimate honours. In a season of many shocks, most commentators were reluctant to make predictions; those who did invariably plumped for Galway.

The clash of Cork and Kildare on 5 August was described by Padraig Puirséal in *The Irish Press* as: 'The poorest senior football semi-final I have watched for many a day.'

Not to be outdone, the ever-colourful John D. Hickey of the *Irish Independent* reported: 'After having watched Cork, victors by 0-9 to 0-5, and Kildare maltreat a football in the All-Ireland senior semi-final at Croke Park yesterday, my uppermost emotion is to give profound thanks that it was not a draw.'

This was a free-ridden and often tempestuous affair. Cork were much superior but still failed to impress. They continued their extraordinary squandermania in front of goals, amassing twenty-one wides over the hour. Their best performers were in defence, where Paddy Harrington and Dan Murray were on song, while their midfield pairing of Sean Moore and Eric Ryan held sway throughout. The profligacy of the Cork forwards and the agility of Kildare goalkeeper Dessie Marron saved the Lilywhites from annihilation. An indication of Kildare's lack of firepower can be gleaned from the fact that all their scores came from Seamie Harrison frees.

Based on their hugely impressive run in Connacht, Galway were overwhelming favourites when they lined out against first-time Ulster champions Tyrone in the second semi-final on 12 August. A doubtful starter for the Tribesmen was centre-back Jack Mahon, who had chipped a bone in his elbow a week before the game. Not alone did he line out, Mahon gave an outstanding display and was probably the main difference between the sides as Galway recorded a two-point win, 0-8 to 0-6.

Facing a stiff breeze in the first half, Tyrone were just three points behind at the break. Unfortunately for them, the wind died down after a rain shower when they emerged after the break. They made a valiant effort to close the gap in the second half while their defence, in which full-back Jim Devlin was outstanding, kept a tight rein on Galway's attack. Goalkeeper Thady Turbett and wing-back Sean Donnelly performed heroically, while speed merchant Iggy Jones was a constant threat up front.

Apart from Mahon, goalkeeper Jack Mangan was key to this success while Frank Evers did Trojan work at midfield. In what was now a well-established pattern, Sean Purcell produced yet another tour de force. Galway's tag as favourites for All-Ireland glory was severely dented after this close-run affair and Cork's prospects received a corresponding boost.

THE FINAL — 7 OCTOBER

Immediately after the Galway v Tyrone semi-final, the GAA announced the postponement of the final on account of a polio outbreak in Cork. The most immediate beneficiary of the postponement was Cork's Waterford-born goalkeeper, Paddy Tyers, who now had time to recover from an operation for appendicitis. The extra weeks' training gave the teams the opportunity to be in peak condition. An interesting contrast with present-day training schedules can be gleaned from the wonder at the time that the Galway players had 'no fewer' than thirty-nine training sessions between June and October.

As the big day approached, opinion was evenly divided as to who the likely winners would be. Neither side was deemed to have shown good form in their semi-final games. Galway had struggled to edge past Tyrone, while Cork had beaten Kildare in what was adjudged to be one of the poorest games in years.

As it turned out, the semi-finals gave no taste of what was to come on 7 October. In damp and greasy conditions, Galway and Cork served up one of the really great finals. Padraig Puirséal of *The Irish Press* described how, from the moment referee Peter McDermott ('resplendent in canary yellow') threw in the ball, the game produced thrill after thrill, even surpassing the excitement of the epic Wexford v Cork hurling decider two weeks earlier. The match was lauded not only for the quality of the play, but for the exemplary sportsmanship shown.

In the early stages, Galway held the upper hand, with Frank Stockwell in particular creating havoc. His combination play with fellow clubman Sean Purcell led directly to two first-half goals, which left the westerners with a seemingly comfortable six-point lead at the break. When they tacked on two points early in the second half it looked like the writing was on the wall for Cork. Mirroring the performance of their hurlers against Wexford, the Leesiders then embarked on an incredible comeback.

Padraig Puirséal reported that 'these Leeside footballers in Munster blue drove home score after score amidst a mounting delirium of excitement, till there was only a point between them with five minutes to go.'

With Denis 'Toots' Kelleher finding the net twice and Johnny Creedon adding another goal, the game was well and truly in the melting pot. In the pulsating dying moments of the game it was Galway's 'terrible twins', Purcell and Stockwell, who steadied the ship once again with the clinching scores in a dramatic 2-13 to 3-7 victory.

In a game that had everything, there were many outstanding displays. Stockwell's 2-5 was a scoring record that stood for decades. Purcell shone on the biggest stage and the third of the Tuam contingent, Jack Mangan, performed heroically. At centre-back, Jack Mahon showed no ill effects from the chipped elbow he carried into the game. Teenager Mattie McDonagh gave the first of his many great All-Ireland displays. John D. Hickey reserved special praise for corner-back Tom 'Pook' Dillon: 'A raw-boned farmer, almost as broad as he is long, he was the sheet anchor of the full line'.

Although Cork were naturally disappointed with the result, they had contributed enormously to an epic final and had many brilliant performers. A feature of their play was the vast improvement on earlier games by their forward division. Niall Fitzgerald and goalscorers Kelleher and Creedon were outstanding. Offaly native Sean Moore had a great game at midfield while the two Paddys, O'Driscoll and Harrington, were magnificent in defence.

Galway had brought an eighteen-year All-Ireland famine to an end but Cork would have to wait a little longer. Within twelve months, however, they would be back knocking on the door in their quest to emulate their 1945 predecessors.

FINAL STATISTICS

	Galway	Cork
Full-time:	2-13	3-7
Half-time:	2-6	0-6
Scorers:	F. Stockwell 2-5	D. Kelleher 2-1
	S. Purcell 0-3 (0-2 frees)	E. Ryan 0-3 (0-3 frees)
	G. Kirwan 0-2	J. Creedon 1-0
	J. Coyle 0-2	N. Fitzgerald 0-2
	F. Evers 0-1	T. Furlong 0-1
Attendance:	70,772	
Gate Receipts:	£9,208-17-6 (€11,693)	
Referee:	Peter McDermott (Meath)	

FINAL MISCELLANY

- Cork achieved an unwelcome double in 1956 – they were beaten in both the football and hurling finals.
- Cork supporters travelling to the 1956 Final could avail of an 'all-in' train package. For £2 (€2.54), they could have a reserved seat, lunch on the way to Dublin and 'high tea' on their journey home.
- Antrim won the 1956 Senior Camogie Championship. In the semi-final they beat Dublin, title-holders for the previous eighteen years.
- When the famed Rhode club joined forces with the local parochial committee to raise funds, it decided to host the biggest seven-a-side tournament ever staged in Ireland. Under the inspiring leadership of parish priest Fr William Dowling, the organising committee spared no expense when deciding to present what *The Gaelic Weekly* advertised as nine 'new' portable radio sets to the winning team. Almost thirty clubs from across the midlands signed up, and huge crowds turned up to see dozens of the country's leading players do battle for the precious transistors.

1956 — THE YEAR THAT WAS

- Ronnie Delany became a national hero when he won a gold medal in the Olympic 1,500-metre Final in Melbourne on 1 December.

- A new scheme of five-bedroomed houses on Nutley Lane, Ballsbridge was launched over the June Bank Holiday of 1956. Priced from £3,500, an attractive financing package could be secured (for 'suitable buyers'), with monthly mortgage repayments amounting to £14.08 (€17.88).

- A photograph of the Minister for Finance, Gerard Sweetman, as he 'enjoys a cigarette before going into the Dáil' to deliver his budget statement, appeared on the front page of the *Irish Independent* of 9 May 1956. He was heavily criticised for increasing the price of twenty cigarettes from 2/5 to 2/10 (€0.18). On 12 October 2021, Minister Paschal Donohoe didn't raise an eyebrow when he decreed that smokers would henceforth have to pay €15 for their twenty a day.

1956 TEAM LINE-OUTS

GALWAY (WINNERS)

1. Jack Mangan
(Tuam Stars, also Kickhams, Dublin) Capt.

2. Sean Keeley
(St Grellan's)

3. Gerry Daly
(Garda, also St Grellan's)

4. Tom 'Pook' Dillon
(Ahascragh, also Westerns, Dublin)

5. Jack Kissane
(An Chéad Cath, also Ballydonoghue, Kerry)

6. Jack Mahon
(Dunmore MacHales)

7. Mick Greally
(Ballygar)

8. Frank Evers
(Garda, also Tuam Stars)

9. Mattie McDonagh
(Ballygar, also Erin's Hope, Dublin)

10. Jackie Coyle
(Ballygar)

11. Sean Purcell
(Tuam Stars)

12. Billy O'Neill
(An Chéad Cath, also Carrigtwohill, Cork)

13. Joe Young
(An Chéad Cath, also St Vincent's, Dublin)

14. Frank Stockwell
(Tuam Stars, also Dundalk Young Irelands)

15. Gerry Kirwan
(St Grellan's, also Eastern Command)

Subs: Aidan Swords (Fr Griffin's, also Charlestown Sarsfields, Mayo) Played; Joe O'Neill (An Chéad Cath); Joe Lowney (Fr Griffin's); Liam Mannion (Corofin); Seamus Colleran (Tuam Stars); Cyril Kelly (Tuam Stars); Tom McHugh (Clonbur, also Caherlistrane, Oughterard and Ballinacor, Wicklow)

CORK (RUNNERS-UP)

1. Paddy Tyers
(Lees)

2. Paddy O'Driscoll
(Garda, also Russell Rovers)

3. Donal O'Sullivan
(Lees) Capt.

4. Dan Murray
(Macroom and UCC)

5. Paddy Harrington
(Garda, Dublin, also Ardgroom)

6. Denis Bernard
(Doheny's and UCC)

7. Mick Gould
(Macroom)

8. Sean Moore
(Glenview, also Castlebar Mitchels, Mayo)

9. Eric Ryan
(Garda, also Macroom)

10. Denis 'Toots' Kelleher
(Millstreet)

11. Nealie Duggan
(Lees, also Urhan and St Patrick's)

12. Paddy Murphy
(Dromtarriffe and UCC)

13. Tom Furlong
(St Michael's)

14. Niall Fitzgerald
(Collins Barracks, also Macroom)

15. Johnny Creedon
(Macroom)

Subs: Eamonn Goulding (St Nicholas) Played; Denis Murphy (St Finbarr's); Bernie O'Sullivan (Garnish); Dermot O'Sullivan (UCC); Liam Power (Mitchelstown); Donal Herlihy (Glanmire); Mick Lynch (Lees)

1957

With All-Ireland champions Galway due to play the winners of Roscommon and Mayo in the provincial semi-final, their manager, 'Tull' Dunne, travelled to Roscommon on 9 June to assess the prospective opposition. Having watched a particularly dull and uninspiring encounter, which Roscommon edged on a score of 0-7 to 0-6, he left without a care in the world. Apart from the by now usual brilliance of Gerry O'Malley, nothing he saw suggested that Roscommon would worry his charges.

When the sides met at St Coman's Park on 30 June, his confidence was fully justified as Galway ran out 0-13 to 0-7 winners. Their victory was hard won, however. With Roscommon trailing by five points at half-time, they moved O'Malley to join Des Dockery at midfield and their dominant play began to pay rich dividends against a seriously stretched Galway defence. Goalkeeper Aidan Brady and centre-back Batt Lynch were in fine form for the challengers and Galway relied heavily on the shooting boots of Sean Purcell and Sean Kirwan to hold out for victory.

The second Connacht semi-final, played at Carrick-on-Shannon on 23 June, saw Leitrim qualify for their first provincial showdown since 1949 when they overcame Sligo, 1-8 to 2-1. Leitrim's task had been made all the easier when Sligo's star player, Nace O'Dowd, withdrew owing to an injury sustained in a club match three days beforehand. Sligo were doubly unfortunate in that, apart from O'Dowd's absence, they had to contend with the brilliance of Leitrim's Packie McGarty. He was simply too hot to handle, despite the best efforts of Ray Tully and Harry O'Dowd in the Sligo defence. Eddie Rowley and Columba Cryan were other Leitrim forwards to impress, while defenders Josie Murray and Frank Quinn were in fine fettle. On a bitterly disappointing day for Sligo, Mick and Paddy Christie were their strongest performers.

Galway were the hottest of hot favourites to retain their provincial crown when they faced Leitrim in the decider at the newly opened Pearse Park on 14 July. Amazingly, despite playing with wind advantage in the first half, they led by a mere two points, 0-4 to 0-2, at the break. However, any hopes of a shock win for the underdogs were well and truly dashed in the first ten minutes of the second half when Purcell, Frank Stockwell and Joe Young all found the net and put the champions into an unassailable lead. Galway proceeded to dominate matters for the rest of the game and ran out emphatic 4-8 to 0-4 winners. Notwithstanding their impressive scoring tally, the real foundation for their victory was an outstanding half-back line of Jack Kissane, Jack Mahon and man of the match Mick Greally. Only McGarty and Cathal Flynn made any real impression in Leitrim's attack. Elsewhere, Leo Heslin was their best defender, while Tom Colreavy and Noel Blessing also impressed.

Louth, 1957 champions. Back (l–r): Jim McArdle (injured), Dan O'Neill, Jackie Reynolds, Jim 'Blackie' Judge, Tom Conlon, Ollie Reilly, Alfie Monk, Barney McCoy, Mickey Flood, Sean Óg Flood, Aidan Magennis, Jim 'Sogger' Quigley (trainer); front (l–r): Stephen White, Frank Lynch, Kevin Beahan, Seamie O'Donnell, Dermot O'Brien, Peadar Smith, Patsy Coleman, Jimmy McDonnell, Sean Cunningham, Jim Roe, Jim 'Red' Meehan.

Galway had now negotiated their way to the All-Ireland semi-final where they would face the challenge of the Munster champions. The big question was whether this would be the 1956 All-Ireland runners-up Cork, or the traditional aristocrats Kerry. This question was well and truly answered on 2 June when, in what still ranks as one of the greatest ever championship shocks, mighty Kerry were beaten by Waterford.

It seems that Kerry suffered a serious bout of overconfidence both before and during this game. With five of their players failing to travel, they were reduced to just sixteen men on the day, one being journalist Jo Jo Barrett who was drafted in when they arrived in Waterford. When the game got underway, they began to exert their apparent superiority, but when Waterford hit two second-half goals, the men from the Kingdom were incapable of responding. With the game in the melting pot as the seconds ticked away, Waterford's brilliant centre-back, Tom Cunningham, advanced up the field and launched what proved to be the winning point.

There was deep and lengthy soul-searching in Kerry after this game but it would be unfair to discard Waterford's victory as undeserved. Apart from Cunningham, they had heroes throughout the field, with Gerry McCarthy, Billy Kirwan, Noel Power and Kerry-born Georgie White all outstanding. Few on the Kerry team came through with their reputations intact but one who escaped any criticism was making his championship debut at wing-back. His name: Mick O'Dwyer. From this humble beginning, the Waterville man would go on to forge what is perhaps the greatest career in inter-county football.

Waterford's prize for this unlikely victory was a Munster Final showdown with a Cork team which had ousted Clare, 1-7 to 0-3, at Limerick on 9 June. The poor quality of the play in this second semi-final was such that the *Irish Independent*'s John D. Hickey expressed optimism for Waterford's prospects in the final. He further described how the utter boredom of the occasion 'caused me to yawn as often as if I had not slept for days'.

It was one of the coldest days of the summer when Cork and Waterford met at Thurles on 21 July in what was generally acknowledged as one of the worst provincial finals in years. As expected, there was no giant-killing act this time, with Cork running out easy winners, 0-16 to 1-2. The gallant individual efforts of such as Seamus Power, Mick O'Connor, Billy Kirwan and Jimineen Power were no match for Cork's teamwork. Reports on the game had little to say about the general run of play, focusing instead on the robust nature of the exchanges, and expressing wonder that nobody got marching orders from referee Jackie Lyne.

Predicting the outcome of the 1957 Leinster Championship was not an easy task. Since 1953, four different counties had won the title and there was no clear front-runner. Reigning champions Kildare had been less than impressive in the league campaign, losing all of their games. They opened their championship account against Offaly at Portlaoise on 19 May, cruising to an emphatic 2-10 to 1-3 victory. This qualified them for a semi-final encounter with Louth who had firstly accounted for Carlow on 5 May, and followed this up with victory over Wexford at Croke Park on 26 May. The Wee County win against Wexford saw them reverse a five-point half-time deficit to canter home, 1-12 to 0-9. Star of the show here was Ardee's Kevin Beahan, who was described in *The Irish Press* as

Cork, 1957 runners-up. Back (l–r): Mick Gould, Paddy O'Driscoll, Tim O'Callaghan, Dennis Bernard, Joe O'Sullivan, Eric Ryan, Sean Moore, Donal O'Sullivan, Colm O'Shea, Paddy Harrington, Eamonn Young (trainer); front (l–r): Finbarr McAuliffe, Niall Fitzgerald, John Joe Hinchion, Tommy Furlong, Denis 'Toots' Kelleher, Nealie Duggan, Dan Murray, Liam Power, Mick McCarthy, Eamonn Goulding. *Image courtesy of GAA Museum at Croke Park.*

'by long chalks the most polished and effective footballer on the field'.

The much-anticipated clash of Kildare and Louth proved to be a major anticlimax. Louth, with the returning Jimmy McDonnell of Darver Volunteers in brilliant form, crushed the Lilywhites on a score of 5-8 to 1-9. Indeed, were it not for a series of outstanding saves by Kildare goalie Dessie Marron, the gap would have been much greater. Apart from the mercurial McDonnell, who scored 3-3, Dan O'Neill, Kevin Beahan, Alfie Monk and Dermot O'Brien played some great football. In addition, Louth now possessed a half-back line of Patsy Coleman, Jim McArdle and Stephen White which was being spoken of as among the best in the business. Many predicted that this could be the launching pad for something special.

The opposite side of the Leinster draw saw Dublin and Wicklow emerge to contest the second semi-final. The principal feature of Wicklow's great run was the outstanding play of Gerry O'Reilly, Jim Rogers and Dublin native John Timmons. Their quarter-final win over Meath was a dramatic one. First, Harry Fay found the net at the end of an inspirational run by full-back Pat Roche. Then Timmons waltzed through the defence and hit the winning goal in the dying minutes.

Wicklow's fairytale summer came to an abrupt end at Newbridge on 23 June when Dublin beat them comfortably, 3-9 to 0-9. The foundation for Dublin's victory was the midfield pairing of Jim Crowley and Paddy Downey. They completely dominated matters for the hour, and provided a steady supply of ball to their lively forward division where Johnny Boyle, Cathal O'Leary and Des 'Snitchie' Ferguson took full advantage. This was a major setback for Wicklow football at a time when their star seemed to be on the rise. In Timmons, Rogers, O'Reilly, Dermot Kavanagh and goalkeeper Andy Phillips, they undoubtedly had the nucleus of a good team; the big question was whether they could build on this.

If the Leinster Championship campaign of 1957 produced more than its share of dull games, the final between Dublin and Louth at Croke Park on 7 July was a classic. Playing before a crowd of over 30,000 in challenging weather conditions, the teams served up a thrilling, if sometimes over-robust, encounter. Dublin held the upper hand early in the game and extended their two-point half-time advantage to four shortly after the resumption. Thereafter, Louth began to take control and piled on score after score before finally emerging victors on a score of 2-9 to 1-7.

The game was played at a frantic pace and newspaper reports all suggest that Dublin began to run out of steam towards the end. Jimmy McDonnell was once again to the fore for the Wee County, scoring both their goals. After being dominated by Jim Crowley and Paddy Downey in the first half, Louth's midfield pairing of Dan O'Neill and Kevin Beahan turned things around in the second half, and this paved the way for some sparkling play by their forwards. Dublin's late efforts to bridge the gap perished on the rock that was Louth's full-back Tom Conlon, who was imperious.

Penning the sporting obituary of the Metropolitans, Padraig Puirséal noted in *The Irish Press* that 'it must have been obvious that a great era in Dublin football has come to an end'. How Kevin Heffernan and his teammates reacted to this assertion would become clear the following year.

With Tyrone having emerged as first-time Ulster champions in 1956, there was speculation that another rising power, Derry, could follow suit in 1957. They underlined their championship credentials with a 4-14 to 0-8 annihilation of Antrim at Ballinascreen on 9 June. This eighteen-point win would have been even greater but for the heroic display of Antrim full-back Alec Quinn.

Derry's next game, against Cavan at Dungannon on 7 July, was expected to be their real acid test. In terms of possession, they started well in this game, but they failed to make much of an impression on the scoreboard. Cavan led 1-4 to 0-2 at the break, their goal a brilliant volley from midfielder Mick Lynch. After the restart, Derry began to respond to the promptings of their outstanding centre half-back, Jim McKeever, and gradually clawed their way back into contention. A Roddy Gribbin goal closed the gap further and the match ended in a welter of excitement, with Sean O'Connell hitting Derry's winning point seconds before the final whistle sounded.

As expected, Tyrone negotiated their way through the opposite side of the draw, thereby setting up a novel provincial final pairing with neighbours Derry. Their journey to the final was not without incident. Their quarter-final clash with Armagh was an extremely fractious affair, at the end of which referee John Wilson of Cavan needed to be escorted from the field fully half an hour after he blew the final whistle. Tyrone's 2-9 to 3-5 victory only came after they received a controversial last-minute free which Frankie Donnelly converted. Their semi-final encounter with Donegal was far from the expected cakewalk, with Jim Gallagher turning in a magnificent performance as Donegal looked set to defy the odds. Tyrone ultimately prevailed, 3-5 to 2-3, largely thanks to the brilliance of Eddie Devlin.

The Ulster Final, between Tyrone and Derry, was the first since 1912 that didn't feature either Cavan or Monaghan. This unique encounter attracted a crowd of over 36,000 to Clones on 28 July. At the end of the first half, Tyrone held a three-point lead and the game seemed to be heading to its expected conclusion. The Derry men then proceeded to launch a powerful comeback which put Tyrone's crown in jeopardy. Reports on the game were *ad idem* on one thing: Tyrone's 1-9 to 0-10 escape was firmly down to the triumvirate of Eddie Devlin, Jody O'Neill and Mick Cushenan. Derry performed heroically and showed that they were a coming team. Jim McKeever was their outstanding performer in a game that saw a youthful Sean O'Connell show glimpses of what he was to contribute to his county over the next two decades.

The first of the All-Ireland semi-finals saw a rerun of the previous year's final when Galway and Cork met at Croke Park on 11 August. With Galway continuing their great form of 1956 as well as capturing the league title, and Cork hampered by the absence of a number of their first-choice players, everything pointed to another All-Ireland Final appearance for the Connacht men. Over 40,000 people saw a thrilling encounter, which Cork won by the narrowest of margins, 2-4 to 0-9. Dubbed the 'executioner' by *The Cork Examiner*, midfielder Eric Ryan stole the show. Apart from laying on his team's two goals and dominating the skies, he hit the last two points to give Cork their ticket to their second successive final.

A week later, almost 61,000 patrons turned up to see Louth and Tyrone battle it out for the right to face Cork in the final. If the quality of play was not of the highest standard, there was compensation in the form of the keenness of the contest. Tyrone dominated the early exchanges and led by three points after fifteen minutes. Spurred on by midfielders Dan O'Neill and Kevin Beahan, Louth then came to life and led by a single point at the break. The signs were ominous for Tyrone when the outstanding Jody O'Neill suffered an injury which was to hamper his performance for the rest of the game. With Dermot O'Brien, Jimmy McDonnell and Jim Roe opening up the Tyrone defence, Louth began to pick off their scores, before running out 0-13 to 0-7 winners.

THE FINAL – 22 SEPTEMBER

Prior to 1957, Cork and Louth had never previously met in either the championship or the league. Having lost to Galway in the 1956 Final, Cork were hungry to make amends and take their first title since 1945. If they had endured a relatively barren period, it was nothing in comparison to the experience of the Wee County. Their last All-Ireland success had been in 1912 when they beat Antrim in the final. The closest they had got in the meantime was in 1950 when they lost at the final hurdle to the great Mayo team of that era.

In the lead-up to the 22 September showdown, there was much comment on the teams' contrasting styles. Cork were the bigger, more physical outfit. Louth's forte was their speed and craft and their preparations received a boost when local Ardee electrician William Wright erected 'floodlights', in the form of a series of 200 watt bulbs, for training purposes.

A crowd of almost 73,000 turned up to witness one of the most eagerly awaited finals ever. One who almost didn't make it was Louth captain Dermot O'Brien. He didn't travel with the team because he had to get an extra injection that morning for a shoulder injury sustained in the semi-final and consequently was locked out of the ground, arriving just ten minutes before throw-in. As he was pleading with stewards to let him in, he could hear his name being called out over the tannoy, requesting him to go to the Louth dressing-room without delay!

It was a game of see-saw fortunes as the sides had alternating periods of dominance. A late Sean Cunningham goal edged Louth into a two-point lead, which they defended to the final whistle. On a score of 1-9 to 1-7, they set a record by bridging a gap of forty-five years since their last title.

That Cork played brilliantly and looked likely winners for most of the hour was scant consolation. They held the upper hand, 1-4 to 0-5, at the break and they pulled further ahead early in the second half. It was then that some judicious changes by the Louth selectors began to shift the balance of power. Swopping midfielder Kevin Beahan and wing-forward Seamie O'Donnell benefitted both players, but the real clincher was the move of Stephen White to centre half-back. The Young Irelands star proceeded to deliver a footballing exhibition, creating plenty of openings for a rampant forward division. Close on White's heels for the man-of-the-match accolade was veteran full-back Tom Conlon. Former Meath player Jim 'Red' Meehan was the man in the breach as Louth repulsed Cork's last desperate onslaught in the dying seconds.

The consensus was that while Louth were worthy champions, Cork had been decidedly unlucky. Despite great performances from a number of their players, notably Eric Ryan, Liam Power, Tommy

Furlong and Niall Fitzgerald, it was a case of so near, and yet so far away. The result meant that a host of the county's greatest football servants would leave the stage without the coveted All-Ireland medal. It is seldom that a team that could boast such talent as Nealie Duggan, 'Toots' Kelleher, Paddy O'Driscoll and Paddy Harrington is denied the ultimate footballing reward.

It would be another generation before Cork's long-suffering aficionados would finally get a well-deserved day in the sunshine. Just as Cork football went into the shade for a prolonged period, Louth faded even further from the limelight. They hardly raised their head above the championship parapet for over fifty years, and when they finally did, it would be in the most heartbreaking of circumstances.

FINAL STATISTICS

	Louth	Cork
Full-time:	1-9	1-7
Half-time:	0-5	1-4
Scorers:	S. Cunningham 1-1	D. Kelleher 0-3
	J. Roe 0-3 (0-2 frees)	T. Furlong 1-0
	K. Beahan 0-3	E. Ryan 0-2 (0-2 frees)
	D. O'Neill 0-1	N. Duggan 0-1
	S. O'Donnell 0-1	N. Fitzgerald 0-1
Attendance:	72,732	
Gate Receipts:	£8,472-12-9 (€10,758)	
Referee:	Patsy Geraghty (Galway)	

FINAL MISCELLANY

- The question of who would captain Louth in the final remained open until the eve of the game. The man chosen, Dermot O'Brien, later had a highly successful career as a professional musician.
- Louth players Dan O'Neill and Seamie O'Donnell were natives of Mayo and had both won National Football League medals with their native county in 1954.
- Teenager Frank Lynch, a key player in Louth's march to glory in 1957, was unavailable for their Leinster Championship contest with Wexford on 26 May. The game clashed with the annual sports day of his school, St Mary's, Dundalk.
- Former star player Jim 'Sogger' Quigley, who was trainer and selector with the 1957 team, was widely regarded as the key man in Louth's success. He ceased his involvement with the team early in 1958 when he was inexplicably omitted from the party which travelled to the US to play New York.
- If Kerry man Micksie Palmer was confused when he lined out at full-forward for Waterford in the 1957 Munster Final against Cork, he could be excused. The referee was Jackie Lyne, a former Kerry teammate, who sported a number 4 Kerry jersey.

1957 – THE YEAR THAT WAS

- The European Economic Community (EEC) was established with the signing of the Treaty of Rome on 25 March.
- On 4 October, the USSR launched Sputnik, the first artificial satellite, into space.
- On 6 March, Ghana, formerly the British colony of the Gold Coast, secured its independence.
- In the summer of 1957, a local priest and some of his parishioners organised a boycott of Protestant-owned businesses in Fethard-on-Sea, County Wexford. The boycott began when the mother of children of a mixed marriage refused to bring them up as Catholics, as the Rev. Father Stafford, with the support of his bishop, had instructed.
- In 1957, almost 60,000 people, or 2% of the population, left Ireland. This was a continuation of the trend established throughout the 1950s. The decade saw an annual average of 45,000 emigrating, corresponding to 80% of the average number born in the country twenty years earlier.
- A baby boy, born in Castleisland on 26 February 1957, received national attention when he weighed in at 16 lb. Charlie Nelligan returned to the spotlight in the 1970s and 1980s, winning seven All-Ireland medals for Kerry as one of the greatest goalkeepers the game has known.

1957 TEAM LINE-OUTS

LOUTH (WINNERS)

1. Sean Óg Flood
(Dundalk Young Irelands, also Ballinagh, Cavan)

2. Ollie Reilly
(Hunterstown Rovers)

3. Tom Conlon
(Stabannon Parnells, also Drumconrath, Meath)

4. Jim 'Red' Meehan
(Naomh Mhuire, Drogheda, also Fordstown, Meath)

5. Patsy Coleman
(St Mary's, Ardee)

6. Peadar Smith
(Oliver Plunketts)

7. Stephen White
(Dundalk Young Irelands, also Cooley Kickhams and Mountbellew-Moylough, Galway)

8. Kevin Beahan
(Sean McDermotts, Dublin, also St Mary's, Ardee)

9. Dan O'Neill
(St Dominic's, also Castlebar Mitchels, Mayo and Naomh Mhuire, Drogheda)

10. Seamie O'Donnell
(Cooley Kickhams, also Ballaghaderreen, Mayo, Westerns, Dublin and Navan O'Mahonys, Meath)

11. Dermot O'Brien
(St Mary's, Ardee, also Navan O'Mahonys, Meath)

12. Frank Lynch
(Geraldines)

13. Sean Cunningham
(Dundalk Young Irelands)

14. Jimmy McDonnell
(Darver Volunteers, also St Joseph's)

15. Jim Roe
(St Mary's, Ardee)

Subs: Alfie Monk (Naomh Mhuire, Drogheda, also St Patrick's, Meath); Mickey Flood (Dundalk Young Irelands); Barney McCoy (St Mary's, Ardee); Aidan Magennis (St Mary's, Ardee); Jim 'Blackie' Judge (Newtown Blues, also Oliver Plunketts); Jackie Reynolds (Oliver Plunketts, also Newtown Blues)

Other Panel Members: Tom Carroll (Dundalk Young Irelands); Paddy Butterly (Stabannon Parnells); Noel Loughran (St Dominic's); Bertie Dullaghan (Dundalk Gaels); Paddy Cheshire (Dundalk Gaels)

Jim McArdle (Roche Emmets, also Dundalk Young Irelands and Stabannon Parnells) was on the team for the championship but a knee injury forced him to miss the final. Donegal native Cormac Breslin missed the final too because he had relocated to London for work after the Leinster Final.

CORK (RUNNERS-UP)

1. Liam Power
(Mitchelstown)

2. Mick Gould
(Macroom)

3. Dennis Bernard
(Dohenys)

4. Dan Murray
(Macroom and UCC)

5. Paddy Harrington
(Garda, Dublin, also Ardgroom)

6. Paddy O'Driscoll
(Garda, also Russell Rovers)

7. John Joe Hinchion
(Canovee, also Millstreet)

8. Sean Moore
(Glenview)

9. Eric Ryan
(Garda, also Macroom)

10. Joe O'Sullivan
(Urhan)

11. Niall Fitzgerald
(Collins Barracks, also Macroom)

12. Tommy Furlong
(St Michael's)

13. Eamonn Goulding
(St Nicholas)

14. Nealie Duggan
(Millstreet) Capt.

15. Denis 'Toots' Kelleher
(Millstreet)

Subs: Finbarr McAuliffe (Waterville, Kerry, also Castletownbere) Played; Tim O'Callaghan (Macroom); Donal O'Sullivan (Lees); Mick McCarthy (St Finbarr's); Colm O'Shea (Adrigole, also Clanna Gael, Dublin); Pat Woods (St Finbarr's); Dermot O'Donovan (Bandon)

1958

As the 1958 Championship got underway, the race for the Sam Maguire Cup was, as was usual in the 1950s, wide open. Louth, Galway, Kerry and Meath had taken the previous four titles. Tyrone and Derry seemed to be on the up, while Cork and Dublin still harboured ambitions that recent near-misses could be converted into outright success.

An early championship exit was the fate of many counties in that pre-back-door era, and unfortunate Longford were first to bite the dust when they suffered an eleven-point defeat at the hands of Meath at Mullingar on 27 April. With Dinny Donnelly and future Galway star Mick Garrett controlling midfield for Meath, the result was never in doubt. It didn't take the Meath men long to make their own departure from the championship; they were at the wrong end of a 1-12 to 2-7 scoreline when they played Dublin at Drogheda on 1 June. This was a game which ended in a welter of excitement as Meath desperately chased the goal that would have given them the spoils. Their efforts were repulsed time and again by a tenacious Dublin defence in which Marcus Wilson, Jim Crowley and Johnny Boyle excelled. The man-of-the-match accolade in this encounter belonged to Meath wing-back Micheál Grace, while Willie McGuirk, Jim Ryan and Dom O'Brien also performed heroically. Dublin went on to secure their Leinster Final spot when beating Carlow by five points on 22 June. A major talking point after this game was the decision of the Carlow selectors not to introduce the brilliant Ned Doogue until late in the game.

On the opposite side of the Leinster draw, Offaly started in whirlwind fashion by beating Laois, 7-8 to 3-5, at Newbridge on 11 May. This game was a personal triumph for former defender Peter Nolan, who hit an incredible 4-3 of his side's total. Offaly followed this up with a one-point victory over National League runners-up, Kildare, on 1 June. A feature of this game was the play of two of the youngest men on the field. Offaly sub Paddy McCormack was outstanding when introduced while Kildare's teenage centre-back, Mick Carolan, gave the first of his many majestic displays in the white jersey. Offaly's impressive run came to a halt at Croke Park on 29 June when they were well beaten by All-Ireland champions Louth. Alfie Monk and Frank Lynch were the key men in a rampant Louth forward division.

The Dublin v Louth Leinster Final took place at Navan on 20 July before a crowd of nearly 28,000. Although Dublin won by only five points, they were vastly superior and, but for the efforts of Louth goalkeeper Sean Óg Flood, this would have been a complete rout. Former Wicklow player John Timmons was outstanding for the Metropolitans and Sean 'Yank' Murray was his very able assistant at midfield. Elsewhere, it was Jim Crowley who once again reached the dizzy heights, *The Irish Press* commenting: 'their superb centre half-back, Jim Crowley was in invincible form. A player of great and yet ever-growing brilliance.'

In Connacht, Mayo easily accounted for Sligo at Charlestown on 15 June in a game that marked the final chapter in the long and illustrious inter-county career of Sligo veteran Mick Christie. In the semi-final, Mayo held the advantage in the first twenty minutes of their clash with Galway at Tuam on 29 June. It was then that, in the words of *The Irish Press*, 'The wily brain and the flashing foot of Sean Purcell' took control. He bamboozled the Mayo defence, scoring 2-3 in yet another man-of-the-match performance as Galway ran out nine-point winners.

In the second of the Connacht semi-finals, Leitrim had two points to spare over a Roscommon team that had staged a brilliant fightback and had looked set for victory. The day was saved for Leitrim when the inimitable Packie McGarty took control and carried his team to victory. Cathal Flynn and Columba Cryan were also to the fore as Leitrim qualified for their second successive Connacht Final against Galway.

The final was played at Roscommon on 13 July. Galway were hot favourites to retain their title and

The 1958 pre-match parade, with Jim McKeever leading the men from Derry and Kevin Heffernan captaining Dublin. *Image courtesy of the National Museum of Ireland.*

This great action shot from the 1958 Final shows Dublin's Johnny Joyce (wearing 14) and Derry's Hugh Francis Gribbin (right) contesting for the ball. *Image courtesy of the GAA Museum at Croke Park.*

thus become the first holders of the Nestor Cup. Their expectations seemed on course in the first half when, against a stiff breeze, Frank Stockwell and Dublin native Joe Young scored two great goals. Undaunted, Leitrim came roaring back and it was neck and neck all the way to the final whistle before Galway finally emerged winners on a 2-10 to 1-11 scoreline. To a man, the Leitrim players performed heroically and won the hearts of friend and foe alike. Amazingly, McGarty surpassed all previous displays of brilliance in the green and gold of Leitrim. The national newspapers agreed that he was the best player in the land but the *Leitrim Observer* knew better, anointing him 'the greatest forward the game has produced'. It was another day of disappointment for McGarty and his teammates, among whom Leo Heslin, Josie Murray, Tony Hayden, Cathal Flynn and teenager Jim O'Donnell were outstanding.

In Munster, Cork were bidding to take the provincial crown for the third year in a row. They opened their account at Fermoy on 29 June, where they faced a Waterford side that had been less than impressive when beating Clare in the quarter-final. Although Cork won, 1-11 to 1-4, theirs was a lacklustre performance, with only midfielder Eric Ryan and defender Paddy O'Driscoll playing up to form. Waterford didn't have enough players of the calibre of Tom Bermingham, Matty Lonergan and goalkeeper Sean Ormond to put up a serious challenge.

On the same day that Cork were qualifying for the Munster Final, Kerry and Tipperary met in the other semi-final at Thurles. Having failed miserably in the campaigns of 1956 and 1957, Kerry continued their dismal championship form, requiring a very late intervention from Mick O'Dwyer to stumble into the final on a score of 1-6 to 0-7. All newspaper reports on the game acknowledged that Tipperary were the better team on the day. Kerry's prospects of escaping from the footballing doldrums were considered negligible, with one local newspaper commenting: 'so poor were Kerry that the mere thought of the Munster Final against Cork on Sunday week, is too depressing to be entertained.'

When the teams met at the Cork Athletic Grounds on 13 July, Kerry did what nobody had predicted: they pulverised Cork into submission. On top in every sector for the full hour, they ran out easy winners, 2-7 to 0-3. Scorer-in-chief was twenty-year-old Garry McMahon, son of the playwright Bryan, who hit 2-2 of Kerry's total. Brothers Sean and Seamus Murphy were both outstanding as Kerry progressed to the All-Ireland semi-final stage for the first time in three years.

The form of reigning Ulster champions Tyrone had slipped somewhat in the run-up to the championship. Completely outclassed by Kildare in a notoriously robust league semi-final, they had moved down the pecking order in betting odds for the provincial crown. Before an attendance of 15,000, they met Armagh at Dungannon on 22 June where they recovered much of their old poise, emerging 1-9 to 0-10 winners as Frankie Donnelly and Iggy Jones got the decisive scores. Their return to form was only temporary, however, and they were well and truly outgunned, 1-9 to 0-2, by a youthful Down side at Lurgan on 6 July. Such was the Mourne men's dominance that there were only eight minutes left in the game when Tyrone managed to record their first score.

On the opposite side of the draw in Ulster, old foes Cavan and Monaghan met at Clones on 15 June. After an hour of substandard fare, the game ended in a draw, 0-7 each, with Cavan being especially fortunate to get a second chance. When the sides met at Breffni Park two weeks later, the quality of play was no better. In the words of the *Monaghan Argus*, 'The standard of play was little above zero.'

Worse still, the behaviour of a large section of the crowd was deplorable. The sides were level at 1-5 each at the end of sixty minutes but referee Liam Friel of Antrim was prevented from playing extra time by an angry mob who took exception to some of his decisions. The sides met for the third time at Belfast a week later where, in contrast to their earlier clashes, they served up a magnificent contest. Cavan had a well merited five-point win after withstanding a great Monaghan revival that was inspired by the brilliant John Rice.

This propelled Cavan to a semi-final encounter with Derry, who had already accounted for Antrim. Their clash at Clones on 13 July was notable for one main reason: the brilliance of Derry's Jim McKeever. While Derry's winning margin was a modest four points, in reality they were vastly superior and fully deserved their passage to a novel provincial decider against Down.

When they met at Clones on 27 July, Down's prospects suffered a major blow even before the teams togged out. Due to a misunderstanding about travel arrangements, key defender George Lavery wasn't in Clones. When the game got underway, Derry took the initiative immediately and held the upper hand throughout a generally disappointing game. Their four-point winning margin, 1-11 to 2-4, didn't reflect their dominance over a Down team that fell well short of its best form. Once again, Jim McKeever was the outstanding player on view, with Brendan Murray, Charlie Higgins and goalkeeper Patsy Gormley also contributing handsomely to this maiden Ulster title. While Down were understandably disappointed, they had shown great promise and players such as James McCartan, Pat Rice, Leo Murphy and Paddy Doherty were clearly on the road to stardom.

Dublin and Galway were considered to be evenly matched in the run-up to their semi-final encounter on 17 August. Many thought that the withdrawal, through injury, of Dublin's Johnny Boyle would tilt the balance in favour of the Tribesmen in what was certain to be a tight affair. A tight affair it was: Ollie Freaney hit Dublin's winning point from a free with the last kick of the game. The victory laurels could have gone either way and indeed Galway looked likely winners until early in the second half when Dublin's 'Yank' Murray and John Timmons began to monopolise midfield proceedings. Two great goals, both scored by their outstanding forward, Johnny Joyce, brought Dublin back into the game before Freaney hammered the final nail into Galway's coffin. The Connacht champions were decidedly unlucky not to force a draw as, for the second successive year, a late free precipitated their championship exit.

The general expectation was that Kerry would provide Dublin's opposition in the final – Derry were being quoted at 3/1 for their clash with the Kingdom. These odds looked justified when Kerry took an early four-point lead after a Tadhgie Lyne free sailed all the way, untouched, into the Derry net. Undaunted, the Derry men launched an impressive comeback and carried a two-point lead into the break. The second half was largely a story of Kerry's profligacy while Derry took full advantage of their limited opportunities. When referee Mick McArdle of Louth blew the final whistle, Derry were ahead, 2-6 to 2-5, and were through to their first ever final. Kerry's disappointment was all the more acute in light of their tally of seventeen wides as against four for the Derry men.

Once again, Jim McKeever had a big role to play in Derry's win, while Patsy McLarnon, 'Wee' Tommy Doherty, Hugh Francis Gribbin and Sean O'Connell were also superb. The outstanding player on the field was Kerry's Jerome O'Shea, while Valentia's Mick O'Connell was at his elegant best when moved to midfield.

THE FINAL – 28 SEPTEMBER

With Derry bidding for their first title and Dublin aiming to bridge a sixteen-year gap since their last, the 1958 decider generated enormous interest. Hot favourites Dublin were reigning league champions, and their team included eight survivors from the 1955 Final. Most previews of the game typically opted for a Dublin victory but carried a caveat that Derry, under McKeever's inspirational leadership, were capable of springing a surprise.

Despite crowd restrictions due to construction work at Croke Park, more than 73,000 crammed into the stadium for this novel encounter. As the clock ticked down towards throw-in time, there was a minor scare in the Dublin dressing-room. Wing-forward Paddy Farnan was delayed in the throngs heading to the game and arrived with only minutes to spare. Before the day was out, his tardiness would be fully forgiven after he scored a spectacular, and decisive, goal for the Metropolitans.

The records show that Dublin won on a score of 2-12 to 1-9, and so chalked up their sixteenth All-Ireland title. Their victory was not as comprehensive as the scoreline suggests, however, and a Johnny Joyce goal in time added on flattered the new champions.

Derry started strongly and wing-forwards Sean O'Connell and Dinny McKeever were in devastating form. The threat they presented was negated when Dublin switched Cathal O'Leary and Johnny Boyle and the Metropolitans proceeded to build up a four-point lead at the break.

Although there was no doubting Dublin's overall superiority, the game was still in the melting pot ten minutes into the second half when Owen Gribbin hit an equalising goal for Derry. Despite playing second fiddle at centre-field, Dublin's forward machine began to create the openings for the scores which pulled them clear.

While Farnan's goal was a real turning point, the biggest thorn in the side for Derry was the diminutive Pádraig 'Jock' Haughey, whose speed and scheming were a constant threat. Dublin also had good reason to be thankful to defenders Joe Timmons and the ever-reliable Jim Crowley. Their goalkeeper, Howth's Paddy O'Flaherty, had a brilliant hour and made several crucial saves.

With a performance that would later be acknowledged with being honoured as Footballer of the Year, Jim McKeever was the outstanding player on view. His midfield partner, Phil Stuart, also had a great game. Elsewhere, defenders Hugh Francis Gribbin, Colm Mulholland, 'Wee' Tommy Doherty and especially Peter Smith performed heroically for the Derry men.

Derry were disappointed with the result, but looked forward to building on their breakthrough and perhaps going one step further in 1959.

With Dublin's victory, one of the most talented groups of players ever assembled finally got their All-Ireland reward. It had been a long and frustrating journey for Kevin Heffernan and his comrades-in-arms. Many speculated that perhaps time had caught up with this team and that they would not again feature on the All-Ireland stage. As history would later show, Heffernan himself had no intention of leaving any stage, and he would go on to make an imprint on the game that has few equals.

FINAL STATISTICS

	Dublin	Derry
Full-time:	2-12	1-9
Half-time:	0-8	0-4
Scorers:	O. Freaney 0-7 (0-6 frees)	S. O'Connell 0-5 (0-2 frees)
	K. Heffernan 0-3	O. Gribbin 1-1
	P. Farnan 1-1	B. Mullan 0-1
	J. Joyce 1-0	D. McKeever 0-1
	John Timmons 0-1 (fifty)	J. McKeever 0-1
Attendance:	73,371	
Referee:	Simon Deignan (Cavan)	

FINAL MISCELLANY

- The opening paragraph of Mick Dunne's match report in *The Irish Press* on Monday 29 September read: 'From this day forth sing not of the pretty girls in Dublin's Fair City. Henceforth let the metropolis be noted, not for the beauty of its daughters, but for the precision and devastating scoring power with which it equips its footballing forwards.'
- Future Republic of Ireland soccer manager Martin O'Neill attended the 1958 Final as a six-year-old. His two brothers, Gerry and Leo, came on as second-half substitutes for Derry.
- The St Vincent's club had special reason to celebrate the 1958 double All-Ireland success. Kevin Heffernan led the senior team while Des Foley captained the minor side in the county's victory over Mayo. In a single day, no fewer than eighteen members of the club won All-Ireland medals.

Senior: Kevin Heffernan

Jim Crowley

Marcus Wilson

Mossy Whelan

Lar Foley

Cathal O'Leary

Pádraig Haughey

Ollie Freaney

Des Ferguson

Paddy Farnan

Johnny Joyce

Christy Leaney

Minor: Des Foley

Noel Fox

Mick Kissane

Jackie Gilroy

Simon Behan

Paddy Behan

- Derry half-forward Dinny McKeever was back in Croke Park for the 1993 Final, when he was a selector with All-Ireland winners Derry.
- Dublin's Johnny Boyle started his football career with Suncroft in Kildare. He captained the Lilywhites at minor level for three consecutive years, and lined out with the senior team in 1952. An all-round sportsman, he won six caps with the Irish basketball team.

1958 — THE YEAR THAT WAS

- In the 1950s, the national newspapers routinely published the detailed Lenten Regulations as issued by the country's Catholic bishops. In 1958, Dublin's Archbishop McQuaid gave instructions that only one full meal could be consumed on 'fast' days. He then reiterated his ruling that attendance at the 'Protestant University of Trinity College' would constitute a mortal sin.
- Mao Zedong's ill-fated Great Leap Forward was launched in 1958. The plan to transform China from an agrarian economy into a communist society failed miserably, and led to the deaths of tens of millions in the resultant famine.
- In May 1958, the Minister for Education, Jack Lynch, announced that the requirement for women teachers to retire on marriage was to be revoked. It would be another fifteen years before a similar ban for civil servants would be removed.

1958 TEAM LINE-OUTS

DUBLIN (WINNERS)

1. Paddy O'Flaherty
(Beann Eadair)

2. Lar Foley
(St Vincent's)

3. Marcus Wilson
(St Vincent's)

4. Joe Timmons
(St Mary's, Saggart, also Annacurra,
Wicklow)

5. Cathal O'Leary
(St Vincent's)

6. Jim Crowley
(St Vincent's)

7. Johnny Boyle
(Clanna Gael, also Air Corps and
Suncroft, Kildare)

8. John Timmons
(St Mary's, Saggart, also Annacurra,
Wicklow and Sean McDermotts)

9. Sean 'Yank' Murray
(Skerries Harps, also Na Fianna)

10. Pádraig 'Jock' Haughey
(St Vincent's)

11. Ollie Freaney
(St Vincent's)

12. Des 'Snitchie' Ferguson
(St Vincent's, also Gaeil Colmcille,
Meath)

13. Paddy Farnan
(St Vincent's)

14. Johnny Joyce
(St Vincent's)

15. Kevin Heffernan
(St Vincent's) Capt.

Subs: Mossy Whelan (St Vincent's) Played; Paddy Downey (St Brigid's); Brendan Morris (Na Fianna); Joey Brennan (Na Fianna); Christy Leaney (St Vincent's); Tony Gillen (Clanna Gael); Dermot McCann (Erin's Isle)

DERRY (RUNNERS-UP)

1. Patsy Gormley
(Claudy)

2. Patsy McLarnon
(Newbridge)

3. Hugh Francis Gribbin
(Newbridge)

4. 'Wee' Tommy Doherty
(Lavey)

5. Patsy Breen
(Desertmartin)

6. Colm Mulholland
(Lavey)

7. Peter Smith
(Ballinderry)

8. Jim McKeever
(Ballymaguigan, also Leicester Young Irelands,
Leicestershire and RGU Downpatrick, Down) Capt.

9. Phil Stuart
(Ballinderry)

10. Sean O'Connell
(Ballerin Sarsfields)

11. Brendan Murray
(Ballerin Sarsfields)

12. Dinny McKeever
(Ballymaguigan)

13. Brian Mullan
(Ballerin Sarsfields)

14. Owen Gribbin
(Newbridge)

15. Charlie 'Chuck' Higgins
(O'Donovan Rossa, Magherafelt)

Subs: Paddy Gribbin (Newbridge) Played; Leo O'Neill (Kilrea Pearses) Played; Gerry O'Neill (Kilrea Pearses) Played; Harry Cassidy (Bellaghy Wolfe Tones); Willie Cassidy (Bellaghy Wolfe Tones); Tom Scullion (Bellaghy Wolfe Tones); Seamus Young (Ballymaguigan); Liam Mulholland (Bellaghy Wolfe Tones); 'Long' Tommy Doherty (Newbridge)

1959

All-Ireland champions Dublin opened their 1959 campaign on 24 May at Portlaoise where they lined out against lowly Carlow. Based on the quality of their play against Wexford in the opening round, the GAA correspondent in *The Nationalist and Leinster Times* was adamant that the underdogs would prevail. While this ambitious prediction didn't come to pass, Dublin were made to work hard before finally emerging with a four-point win, 1-11 to 2-4. Ollie Freaney's free-taking was the main difference between the teams. Carlow had stars in Paaks Connolly, Brendan Hayden and the outstanding Ned Long, of whom *The Nationalist* reported: 'It was most disheartening to see Ned Long play his heart and lungs out and then see his forwards stand around as though horror stricken that he should present them with the ball'.

Dublin's Leinster semi-final opponents were Louth, who had earlier survived late goals from Kieran O'Malley and Ned Treacy in a very tight 1-13 to 3-6 win over Kildare. Once again it was the boot of Freaney that came to Dublin's rescue, his last-minute point securing a replay against a gallant Louth outfit. It was a completely different story when the sides met again at Navan on 26 July, as Dublin's forwards ran amok in the second half. Feeding off their brilliant teenage midfielder Des Foley, they piled on the scores and romped home on a score of 3-14 to 1-9.

On the other side of the Leinster draw, Laois started their campaign against Wicklow at Athy on 3 May. Although Wicklow were without a championship win since 1949, they started this game as favourites. However, they couldn't match a rampant Laois, for whom Noel Delaney, Fintan Walsh and Liam Doran were outstanding. A feature of this game was a brilliant man-of-the-match performance by Wicklow's Gerry O'Reilly.

Laois were again underdogs when they met Offaly at Portlaoise on 17 May. This was an epic struggle, with Laois grabbing a late equaliser through ace sharpshooter Jack Kenna. Centre-back Mick McDonald was the key man for Laois while replacement goalkeeper Larry Fox made a number of saves that were described by Peadar O'Brien in *The Irish Press* as being in 'the near-miracle bracket'. Offaly could thank midfielders Charlie Wren and Willie Bryan for doing most to give them a second bite of the cherry.

The replay at Tullamore on 7 June fell well short of the standard of the drawn game. Two factors contributed to this: a gale-force wind blowing directly down the field, and the absence through injury of several of Offaly's key players. Laois were comfortable 3-8 to 0-10 winners in a game that had Jack Kenna and Noel Delaney as the outstanding performers.

Mick O'Connell leads his Kerry team in the 1959 All-Ireland Final parade. *Image courtesy of the GAA Museum at Croke Park.*

Longford presented the provincial semi-final opposition for Laois. The Longford men had surprised both Westmeath and Meath to qualify for this, a most unlikely semi-final pairing. For once, Laois were favourites, and they didn't disappoint, running out 2-9 to 0-8 winners. Despite having to line out without star forward Jack Kenna, Laois were never in danger of losing. Noel Delaney, Liam Doran, Teddy Delaney, Bob Miller and goalkeeper Paddy Bracken were all in fine fettle. While Laois were by far the better balanced team, it was a Longford player who gave the performance of the day: midfielder Jim Harold was unbeatable in the air.

Dublin were strongly favoured to overcome Laois when the sides met in the Leinster Final at Tullamore on 2 August. Their prospects looked far from certain when two goals from Mick Phelan propelled Laois into a five-point half-time lead. However, as they had done in the semi-final against Louth, the Metropolitans really opened up in the second half and won comfortably, 1-18 to 2-8. Star of the show was centre-back Cathal O'Leary, while twenty-year-old Mickey Whelan, a late addition to the team, contributed 1-3 to Dublin's tally. The winning margin would have been much wider but for a series of great saves by Laois goalkeeper Paddy Bracken.

As Leinster champions, Dublin were scheduled to meet their Munster counterparts in the All-Ireland semi-final. The general expectation was that this would be Kerry, whose opening game was in the semi-final against Tipperary at Killarney on 5 July. Tipperary's already slim prospects were dealt a body blow on the eve of the game when Johnny Ryan, scorer of two goals in their win over

Waterford, was forced to cry off with a hand injury. Kerry asserted their superiority from the first minute and, without ever moving out of second gear, ambled to a facile 1-15 to 1-2 win. While this was a generally lethargic affair, reports on the game were agreed on one matter: Kerry captain Mick O'Connell was majestic in everything he did.

The second Munster semi-final saw Cork overpower Clare, 4-9 to 1-7, but their winning margin did not reflect the general run of play. Clare were going well until a series of defensive lapses saw them concede 3-2 within a five-minute period. Despite the gallant efforts of Paddy Downes, Tom Mangan and Frank Kennedy, they could make no inroads on the scoreboard. Cork supporters were not exactly brimming with confidence after this game where only Paddy Harrington and goalkeeper Liam Power played up to expectations.

Unsurprisingly, Kerry were favourites for their Munster Final clash with Cork at Killarney on 2 August. For once, Cork's difficulties lay in defence rather than in their previously much-maligned forward division. However, Kerry's forwards, feeding off a constant supply from Seamus Murphy and the incomparable O'Connell, scored at ease in a solid 2-15 to 2-8 victory. Dan McAuliffe, Jim Brosnan and Dave Geaney were their most prominent attackers. For Cork, veteran Paddy O'Driscoll, who had been coaxed out of retirement, Tom Furlong and former Waterford star George White performed heroically.

At Lurgan on 31 May, Armagh produced one of the shocks of the year when they dumped 1958 All-Ireland finalists Derry out of the championship. Although Derry were without Patsy Gormley, Phil Stuart and Sean O'Connell, there was no denying the merit of Armagh's victory. With John McKnight playing a blinder and Jimmy Whan, Mal McEvoy and Felix McKnight to the fore, Derry were completely overwhelmed.

Next up for Armagh was Cavan, a county without a provincial title since 1955, a gap they had last experienced over forty years previously. The men of Breffni had shown promise in their first-round victory over Donegal and there were hopes that they could build a successful team around such as Gabriel Kelly, Con Smith and the Gallagher brothers, Brian and Charlie. Controversy surrounded their drawn encounter at Castleblayney on 5 July, when referee Pat Rooney blew the final whistle with three minutes left on the clock. Bertie Watson, scorer of two great goals, was Armagh's hero on the day. The replay at Clones two weeks later was also clouded in controversy. Cavan won by two points but not without the benefit of a hotly disputed goal from Jim Brady late in the game. A highlight of this game was the great battle, with honours even, between two outstanding players, Cavan's Charlie Gallagher and Armagh full-back John McKnight.

On the opposite side of the Ulster draw, Down and Tyrone progressed to a semi-final encounter at Belfast on 12 July. Down had built on their earlier promise when they ousted Antrim, 4-9 to 1-3, in searing heat at Newcastle on 14 June. Their ace forward Sean O'Neill had to sit out this game after suffering an insect bite while golfing the previous day. Also missing for much of the game was Antrim midfielder Hugh O'Kane, who had to retire early owing to the intense heat. Tyrone's path

Mick O'Connell raises the Cup after Kerry's 1959 victory over Galway. 'Sam' would spend a lonely night on his own – he was left behind in the dressing-room and only retrieved the following day. *Image courtesy of the GAA Museum at Croke Park.*

to the semi-final saw Jody O'Neill star in their five-point victory over a disappointing Monaghan on 21 June.

At Casement Park on 12 July, Down and Tyrone drew, 1-6 each, in a thrilling contest that reached fever pitch in the dying minutes. There was no repeat of the drama in the replay two weeks later when Down had eleven points to spare at the end of a dreary, uncompetitive affair.

If tradition were to be the deciding factor in the Ulster Final then everything pointed to a Cavan victory. They were chasing provincial title number forty-four, while the Mourne men had yet to break their duck. When they met at Clones on 9 August, it was obvious within five minutes of the throw-in where the title was headed. With a brand of blistering combination play, Down overwhelmed the Cavan men and coasted to the easiest of victories, 2-16 to 0-7. The highly talented Down forward division showed no mercy, while a defence backboned by Leo Murphy and James McCartan was virtually impenetrable. Cavan's fifteen-point defeat would have been even greater but for the heroic efforts of Gabriel Kelly, Jim McDonnell and Charlie Gallagher.

In Connacht, Galway were aiming to secure their fourth title in a row, a feat only Mayo had previously achieved in the province. They started their journey at Salthill on 21 June, where they comfortably overcame Roscommon, 0-12 to 0-4, in the first of the semi-finals. On the same day at Markievicz Park, Mayo had to fight every step of the way to overcome a gallant Sligo outfit, thereby qualifying to meet Leitrim in the second semi-final. It was a Joe Corcoran goal, against the run of play, which set Mayo on the road to a flattering six-point win over a luckless Sligo.

A strong downfield wind completely dictated the run of play when Leitrim and Mayo met at Roscommon on 12 July. At half-time, Leitrim had played with wind advantage and led 2-6 to 0-0. Although they only scored a single point in the second half, they still progressed to their third successive final by limiting Mayo's tally to 2-5. Two goals from Ivan McCaffrey and a towering display by Willie Casey were not enough to bridge the gap for a largely out-of-sorts Mayo fifteen. Predictably, Packie McGarty was once again Leitrim's kingpin, with Mick Mullen, Columba Cryan and Joe Dolan lending strong support.

The Connacht Final took place at Sligo on 9 August. Having come so close against Galway in the previous year's final, Leitrim were quietly confident that they could bridge the gap going back to 1927, when they were last Connacht champions. Galway persuaded Frank Stockwell to come out of retirement for this game and the renewal of his partnership with his old schoolmate Sean Purcell meant trouble for Leitrim. Serious trouble. The telepathic interplay of the 'Terrible Twins' had Galway out of sight within minutes of the throw-in. Indeed, were it not for the outstanding play of Leitrim netminder Jackie Gallagher, the Tribesmen's 5-8 to 0-12 victory would have been much bigger. Aside from Purcell and Stockwell, Galway had impressive performances from Paddy Dunne, Jack Kissane and Michael 'Hauleen' McDonagh. Although it was ultimately in vain, Leitrim fought tenaciously in the second half, with Cathal Flynn, Eddie Duffy, Tom Hayden and Bernie Doyle particularly prominent.

The All-Ireland semi-final on 16 August between great rivals Kerry and Dublin was summarised by John D. Hickey in the *Irish Independent* thus: 'Although the passage of time hallows memories, causes one to rate good matches great and great matches epic, I have no doubt that yesterday's majestic All-Ireland Senior semi-final at Croke Park, in which Kerry defeated Dublin, the All-Ireland title-holders, by 1-10 to 2-5, was the best, most enthralling and the most incident-packed football encounter that I have ever seen.'

Hickey was not alone in according such status to this match – all reports confirm it was exceptionally exciting, played to the highest standard. Based on the footballing artistry of Mick O'Connell, Kerry were able to build up a solid lead and Dublin's cause seemed hopeless when they lost both Paddy O'Flaherty and Cathal O'Leary through injury in the first half. O'Leary's return to the fold in the second half heralded one of the great football comebacks and goals from 'Jock' Haughey and Ollie Freaney left the minimum between the sides. Almost inevitably, it was O'Connell who broke the siege and Kerry held out in a welter of excitement. The Kerry half-back line of Sean Murphy, Kevin Coffey and Mick O'Dwyer played brilliantly, as did forwards Tom Long and Paudie Sheehy.

A week later, the second semi-final saw newcomers Down take on Galway in front of almost 63,000 spectators. The Mourne men failed to show their earlier dash and method as they succumbed to what *The Cork Examiner* described as the 'studied, effortless exhibition of leadership' of Sean Purcell. The final score was 1-11 to 1-4, with a classy goal from Sean O'Neill being the only evident spark of Down's undoubted potential. Great work by Jack Kissane and Jack Mahon in Galway's defence meant that Down's forward division failed to reproduce the cohesive teamwork that was the hallmark of their Ulster campaign.

THE FINAL – 27 SEPTEMBER

Kerry's form in the Munster Championship was so impressive that many pundits had begun tipping them for All-Ireland glory long before their impressive semi-final victory over Dublin. Nonetheless, Galway were considered likely to present a formidable challenge in their imminent showdown. Andy Croke in his *Sunday Independent* preview went so far as to opt for the Tribesmen as likely victors. Certainly, Kerry's favourites' tag in no way dimmed interest in the contest, with almost 86,000 cramming into the revamped Croke Park on 27 September.

The general view that the game would be a classic turned out to be well wide of the mark. Even though their expected midfield dominance did not materialise, Kerry were on top in every other sector and they ran out comfortable 3-7 to 1-4 winners. Despite playing into the wind they took the lead after just fifteen seconds through a John Dowling point and had Galway under pressure throughout. A goal by Frank Evers kept Galway on level terms at the break but the floodgates opened in the second half. Dan McAuliffe hit two goals and substitute Garry McMahon scored another within seconds of being brought on. Thereafter, the game was played out at a pedestrian pace to its inevitable conclusion.

Reporting on the lacklustre nature of the contest, some newspapers opined that the only winners were the thousands outside the ground who had failed to gain admission. In reality, those who were present witnessed what is almost certainly the greatest individual performance in All-Ireland Final history. Newspaper extracts describing Sean Murphy's incredible performance are included elsewhere in these pages but suffice to say that the 1959 decider is invariably referred to as 'The Sean Murphy Final'.

The other two members of Kerry's half-back line, Kevin Coffey and Mick O'Dwyer, were also outstanding. Full-back Niall Sheehy was unfazed by the challenge presented by Sean Purcell, while his brother Paudie was his usual scheming, elusive self at the other end of the field. Tom Long and John Dowling were voted by many as next in line to Murphy in the performance stakes, while Tadhgie Lyne, married the previous day, made an impressive return to the team, though it has to be acknowledged that O'Connell suffered a heavy blow early on and this hampered his movement. Aside from centre-field, Galway struggled to hold their own, but Jack Mahon, Jack Kissane and Joe Young were defiant to the end.

FINAL STATISTICS

	Kerry	Galway
Full-time:	3-7	1-4
Half-time:	0-5	1-2
Scorers:	D. McAuliffe 2-2	S. Purcell 0-3 (0-1 free)
	G. McMahon 1-0	F. Evers 1-0
	T. Lyne 0-2 (0-1 free)	J. Young 0-1
	J. Dowling 0-2	
	M. O'Dwyer 0-1	
Attendance:	85,897	
Referee:	John Dowling (Offaly)	

FINAL MISCELLANY

- Kerry captain Mick O'Connell travelled home to Valentia Island on the evening of the big game, completing the final leg of the journey by rowing a currach from the mainland. As his teammates went about their celebrations back in Dublin, a central character was missing. The Sam Maguire Cup had been left behind in the Kerry dressing-room.

- It's unlikely that any All-Ireland Final player ever was showered with superlatives such as landed on Sean Murphy in the wake of his astonishing display in this decider:

    – *Irish Independent*: 'Sean Murphy had what must have been his greatest hour. I cannot recall his once being beaten for a ball; he popped up to achieve rescue work in the most unlikely places ...'

    – *The Cork Examiner*: 'so great was Murphy's contribution to this win that it must surely be remembered as "his" Final.'

    – *The Irish Press*: 'For the brilliance of this 27-year-old native of Camp sparkled unforgettably ... like a rare jewel among stones.'

    – *The Kerryman*: 'Man of the match was, without doubt, Sean Murphy. He has played many great games for his county. Sunday's display surpassed them all.'

    – *Connacht Tribune*: 'Sean Murphy was in devastating form ...'

- Playing in goals for Kerry, Johnny Culloty joined a select band of players who won senior All-Ireland medals as a goalkeeper and as an outfield player. Others who achieved this feat included Larry 'Hussey' Cribbin (Kildare) and Owensie Hoare (Roscommon). Cavan's 1933 and 1935 goalkeeper, Willie Young, lined out at full-forward on their 1928 losing team. Galway's John Kennedy was not available for the 1959 Final. A clerical student, he did not manage to get the necessary clearance to leave the seminary for the game.

- The 'new' Hogan Stand at Croke Park was officially opened on Sunday 7 June 1959. The occasion also witnessed what *The Cork Examiner* described as the 'classical, impudent hurling genius' of Christy Ring, whose tally of 4-5 in Munster's Railway Cup Hurling Final victory over Connacht failed dismally to reflect the true quality of the Cloyne man's performance.

1959 — THE YEAR THAT WAS

- After a lifetime at the forefront of Irish political life, seventy-six-year-old Éamon de Valera retired from active politics and became Ireland's third President. Having spent a total of over twenty-one years in his role as president of the Executive Council and later Taoiseach, 'Dev' would go on to serve a further fourteen years as head of state.
- After the brutal suppression of a Tibetan uprising by Chinese troops, the country's spiritual and political leader, the Dalai Lama, was forced to escape into exile in India. From here, he would spend decades advocating for a free Tibet.
- The first female recruits to An Garda Síochána were appointed on 9 July 1959. The Dáil debates on the admission of women to the force included one notable contribution: 'while recruits should not be horsefaced, they should not be too good looking; they should just be plain women and not targets for marriage.'
- Hawaii became the fiftieth US state in 1959.

1959 TEAM LINE-OUTS

KERRY (WINNERS)

1. Johnny Culloty
(Killarney Legion)

2. Jerome O'Shea
(St Mary's, Cahirciveen)

3. Niall Sheehy
(John Mitchels)

4. Tim 'Tiger' Lyons
(Castleisland Desmonds, also Cordal)

5. Sean Murphy
(Geraldines, Dublin and UCD, also Camp and Dingle)

6. Kevin Coffey
(Clanna Gael, Dublin, also Beaufort and Dundalk Young Irelands)

7. Mick O'Dwyer
(Waterville)

8. Mick O'Connell
(Valentia, also Waterville)

9. Seamus Murphy
(Camp, also Lispole)

10. Dan McAuliffe
(Duagh)

11. Tom Long
(Dr Crokes, also An Ghaeltacht)

12. Paudie Sheehy
(John Mitchels)

13. Dave Geaney
(Castleisland Desmonds)

14. John Dowling
(Kerins O'Rahillys)

15. Tadghie Lyne
(Dr Crokes)

Subs: Garry McMahon (Listowel Emmets) Played; Jack Dowling (Castlegregory); Moss O'Connell (St Brendan's, Abbeydorney); Tom Collins (Ardfert); Paddy Hussey (Dingle)

Jim Brosnan was injured in the semi-final and was unavailable for the final.

GALWAY (RUNNERS-UP)

1. Jimmy Farrell
(Ballygar)

2. Jack Kissane
(An Chéad Cath, also Ballydonoghue, Kerry)

3. Sean Meade
(St Grellan's, also Aodh Ruadh, Donegal)

4. Mick Greally
(Ballygar)

5. Mick Garrett
(Tuam Stars, also St Vincent's, Meath)

6. Jack Mahon
(Dunmore MacHales)

7. Seamus Colleran
(Tuam Stars)

8. Frank Evers
(Garda, also Tuam Stars)

9. Mattie McDonagh
(Ballygar)

10. Joe Young
(An Chéad Cath, also St Vincent's, Dublin)

11. Sean Purcell
(Tuam Stars) Capt.

12. Michael 'Hauleen' McDonagh
(Tuam Stars)

13. Mick Laide
(Fr Griffin's and UCG, also Ballymacelligott, Kerry)

14. Frank Stockwell
(Tuam Stars, also Dundalk Young Irelands)

15. John Nallen
(Tuam Stars, also Crossmolina, Mayo, Trim, Meath and Castlerahan, Cavan)

Subs: Paddy Dunne (Fr Griffin's) Played; Sean Keeley (St Grellan's); Brendan Glynn (Dunmore MacHales); John Donnellan (Dunmore MacHales); Mick Reynolds (Tuam Stars, also Ballaghaderreen, Mayo and St Wilfred's, Manchester); Andy O'Connor (Dunmore MacHales); Liam Mannion (Corofin)

Jackie Coyle (Ballygar) and John Kennedy (Tuam Stars) were unavailable for selection.

1960

Anyone placing a bet on the likely destination of the Sam Maguire Cup in 1960 would have received long odds on a new name being added to the roll of honour. Down had broken the mould by winning their first Ulster title in 1959 and followed this up with National League success in the spring of 1960. However, the championship was a different proposition and Down's below par performance in their 1959 semi-final clash with Galway suggested that ultimate honours were unlikely in the short term. Their predecessors as champions in Ulster, Derry, had fallen down the pecking order and they were not regarded as serious contenders. The traditional powers of Kerry and Dublin, champions of the previous two years, were viewed as favourites to contest the final. Of the rest, Galway retained a strong contingent from their 1956 team and rumour had it that they had an impressive crop of talented players coming through.

In the mid-1950s, under the guidance of Maurice Hayes, Down created a comprehensive ten-year development strategy. The plan was a simple one in concept: to win the Sam Maguire Cup. The hard work was in implementation. A fundamental overhaul in approach to planning, organising, training and playing was seen as essential if this aim was to be realised. If the ambition seemed audacious to some, Hayes was nothing if not confident and competent; he knew that more of the same was a guarantee of failure.

After their successful league campaign earlier in the year, the Mourne men opened their championship account with a less than impressive win over Antrim, 0-14 to 1-4, in Belfast on 12 June. This gave them a semi-final date with Monaghan, for whom Seamus McAllister, Jim Byrne, Mick Ashe and Danny O'Brien had been outstanding in their quarter-final win over Tyrone.

The Down–Monaghan semi-final was played in atrocious weather conditions at Dungannon on 10 July. It was a tight affair until well into the second half when, despite the appalling conditions, the Down machine, with Leo Murphy inspirational, began to kick into gear. While their ten-point winning margin was impressive, it belies the fine showing by Monaghan who had great performers in John Rice, Bennie Toal, Jim O'Hanlon and especially their goalkeeper, John McKenna.

It was Cavan who emerged from the other side of the Ulster draw. After beating Donegal 1-10 to 1-0, they had all the luck when they held out for a draw against a Fermanagh side which had the athletic P.T. Treacy, Mick Brewster, Jim Cassidy and the Maguires in sparkling form. In the replay on 26 June, three goals from full-forward Seamus Conaty put paid to Fermanagh's gallant bid. While Conaty was to the fore again in the semi-final against Derry, scoring two goals in an

Down, All-Ireland champions 1960. Back (l–r): James McCartan, John McAuley, Joe Lennon, Jarlath Carey, P.J. McElroy, Eamonn Lundy, Leo Murphy, Dan McCartan, Sean O'Neill, Kevin O'Neill, Pat Rice, Eddie Burns, Pat Fitzsimons, Kieran Denvir; front (l–r): John Haughian, Eamonn McKay, Patsy O'Hagan, Paddy Doherty, Kevin Mussen, George Lavery, Tony Hadden, Breen Morgan, Seamus Kennedy, Eamonn Clements, James Fitzpatrick. *Image courtesy of the GAA Museum at Croke Park.*

impressive 3-6 to 0-5 victory, Jim McDonnell was their outstanding performer.

The final, played at Clones on 31 July, attracted a crowd of 33,000 to see if the traditional kingpins could reverse the 1959 result against the same opposition. For their third successive championship game, Down found themselves playing in a downpour. This didn't stop them from opening at a blistering pace and they were two goals to the good after just two minutes. Cavan didn't fold, however, and clawed themselves back to level the scoring early in the second half. The chief architect of this comeback was the brilliant Con Smith, who, according to *The Anglo Celt*, gave 'perhaps his greatest display in the county jersey.'

Not for the first, or last, time it was Down's half-forward line of Sean O'Neill, James McCartan and Paddy Doherty that swung matters in favour of the Mourne men, with Doherty pouncing on a loose ball to grab a vital goal late in the game.

At Mullingar on 1 May, Longford eliminated Meath, 0-9 to 0-8, from the Leinster Championship for the second consecutive year. While Rogie Martin struck the winning point, Jim Harold was the big difference between the sides in what could be euphemistically termed an 'uncompromising affair'. Meath full-back Martin Quinn was described as being in his element in a game where, according to the *Meath Chronicle*, 'no mercy was shown where tackling and charging were concerned.'

While unhappy with some of the tactics employed by the Longford players, the *Chronicle* deserves full credit for adding some balance in its match report: 'We are not suggesting that Meath was represented by fifteen alabaster saints.'

Longford now prepared to face Dublin in the provincial quarter-final at Mullingar on 29 May. The

Down's triumph in 1960 was not just a first for the county, it was the first time the Cup would cross the border into the Six Counties. To mark this momentous occasion, the team were guests of President Éamon de Valera at Áras an Uachtaráin the day after the final.*Image courtesy of the National Library of Ireland.*

Longford Leader headline cautiously proclaimed: 'Dublin can be Beaten.' Unfortunately for Longford, they encountered a Dublin team that could do no wrong on the day as they blasted their way to an astounding 10-13 to 3-8 victory. Johnny Joyce grabbed all the headlines with a tally of 5-3 to his credit. Despite the heavy defeat, a number of Longford players acquitted themselves very well, with Larry Gillen, Noel Dodd, Billy Morgan and Mickey Bracken all showing to good effect.

In the provincial semi-final, Dublin faced Offaly at Portlaoise on 26 June. It had taken a last-minute goal by Charlie Wren, playing his second game of the day, to edge the Offaly men past Carlow in their quarter-final game in Newbridge on 15 May.

Mindful of the concession of 3-8 to Longford, the Dublin selectors undertook a major revamp of their defence for the Offaly game. Offaly too showed a number of changes, the most significant brought about by the emigration of Peter Nolan to New York. Reshuffle or no reshuffle, the Metropolitans remained firm favourites when the sides faced off at Portlaoise on 26 June. In blazing sunshine, and in front of a wildly partisan attendance of 18,000, the Offaly men set about dismantling Dublin's newly fashioned defence. In a comprehensive 3-9 to 0-9 victory, their goals came from Donie Hanlon and Peter Carey. In what was a wonderful all-round performance, the highlight of the game was Offaly's second goal, scored by Hanlon after a sweeping movement involving Sean Ryan, Tommy Cullen, Sean Foran and Tommy Green.

On the opposite side of the Leinster draw, Louth needed a late Jackie Reynolds goal to overcome Wicklow on 22 May. Their semi-final opponents were Westmeath, deserving winners over Kildare in a game that saw teenage corner-forward George Kane playing a blinder, and scoring 2-5 in the process.

At Navan on 3 July, Westmeath completely failed to capitalise on the constant stream of possession supplied by centre-back Mick Moran and their centre-field pairing of Mick Carley and Ned 'Dinger' Bruer. Remarkably, none of Westmeath's starting forwards, nor any of the three subs introduced, managed to register a score over the sixty minutes. With Ollie Reilly, Frank Lynch and Patsy Coleman excelling, Louth progressed to the Leinster Final, but not even the usually optimistic *Drogheda Independent* was impressed, proclaiming that: 'Louth did not shape like champions.'

Torrential rain in the minutes before the throw-in ruined any prospect of a classic when Louth and Offaly met in the Leinster Final on 31 July. It was a momentous day for Offaly who took their first provincial title, 0-10 to 1-6, but otherwise this was a largely forgettable affair. Had referee Brian Smyth of Meath not adopted a lenient approach with the whistle, it's likely that a number of players would have been enjoying their second shower of the day long before full-time.

Despite the narrow margin, Louth were magnanimous in defeat, and few at Croke Park that day could deny Offaly their big breakthrough. It was an especially emotional occasion for the veterans of their 1954 defeat, Sean Foran, Mickey Brady and Mick Casey, the burly blacksmith from Rhode.

In Munster, Kerry eased their way into the provincial final with a comfortable eight-point victory over Tipperary. Match reports suggest that the winning margin would have been double this but for the outstanding displays of Tipperary full-back Leo Dooley and veteran goalkeeper Tony Newport.

Elsewhere, Waterford sprang a major surprise when they edged out Cork (1-9 to 0-11) in their semi-final clash at Lismore on 10 July. *The Cork Examiner* noted the 'air of nonchalance' that pervaded its team's ranks, but acknowledged fully the merit of Waterford's victory. The foundation for this Déise success lay in a rock-solid full-back line, where the powerful Mick Prendergast was flanked by Marcus Dingley and Jimineen Power. Another to impress was Waterford's diminutive wing-back Tom Power, who was described in *The Cork Examiner* as 'this bundle of energy in the off-white beret.'

From a footballing perspective, the Munster Final was a major disappointment, with Kerry rarely moving above second gear as they outscored Waterford, 3-15 to 0-8. While Waterford fought gallantly, and Tom Power had yet another stormer, they couldn't come to grips with the superior class of the Kingdom. In a team which had no weak link, the *Irish Independent* said that Mick O'Connell 'lorded it through the second half when he often appeared to be talking to the ball so obediently did it follow his dictates.'

In Connacht, favourites Galway had London-based Frank Evers to thank for their two-point victory over Mayo in the first round at Castlebar on 12 June. Ironically, former Galway player Aidan Swords was Mayo's outstanding performer on the day.

Galway's next engagement was against Sligo at Tuam on 26 June, when, according to the *Connacht Tribune*, they 'fumbled' their way to the Connacht Final, on a score of 1-8 to 1-3. Veteran Sean Purcell, with 1-6, was top scorer against a stubborn Sligo defence in which goalkeeper Noel Mullaney gave the performance of his life.

Despite the absence, through injury, of London-based Packie McGarty, Leitrim progressed to their fourth successive Connacht Final when they beat Roscommon, 2-8 to 1-6, at Sligo on 19 June. The performance of Ballinamore's Seamus Brogan grabbed all the headlines after this game. Having monopolised midfield proceedings, he suffered a bad facial injury and had to leave the field. As Roscommon began to make serious headway in the second half, Brogan returned to the fray and proceeded to inspire his county.

The provincial showdown at Sligo on 10 July was an anticlimax, with John D. Hickey of the *Irish Independent* noting: 'From start to finish the standard was quite in harmony with the weather conditions – both were positively miserable.' In a game of few highlights, Galway were gifted an own goal and an own point, as they won through on a 2-5 to 0-5 scoreline.

The first All-Ireland semi-final, played at Croke Park on 7 August before an attendance of 37,000, saw Kerry edge out Galway, 1-8 to 0-8. While not a classic, this was a thrilling encounter, with the result in doubt to the end. A wonderful performance from Galway's Sean Purcell wasn't enough to break the resistance of a Kerry defence in which Kevin Coffey, Tim 'Tiger' Lyons and goalkeeper Johnny Culloty were outstanding. With what by now had become a standard acknowledgement, Mitchel Cogley of the *Irish Independent* noted that Mick O'Connell 'proceeded to give one of his greatest displays'.

There was a huge sense of anticipation in the lead-up to the second semi-final between Down and Offaly. Neither county had previously contested a final and this novel pairing drew a crowd of over 64,000 on 21 August. All newspaper reports of this game, which ended in a draw, describe it as an 'epic' that neither side deserved to lose. There was one other matter of common agreement: the penalty awarded to Down in the dying minutes, and which was duly scored by Paddy Doherty, should, instead, have been a free out for Offaly. The replay on 11 September attracted an even bigger crowd, over 68,000. As in the drawn game, Offaly held a solid half-time lead but the Mourne men fought back and reached their first final by a two-point margin, 1-7 to 1-5, with James McCartan their top man.

THE FINAL – 25 SEPTEMBER

While Down were seeking their first All-Ireland in the 26 September showdown, Kerry were aiming for a record twentieth championship title. This intriguing clash captured the imagination of the nation and the scramble for tickets was at fever pitch. A then record attendance of 87,768 saw the game, and many thousands more remained outside the stadium when the gates closed an hour before throw-in.

Down took the early initiative and were a point to the good inside three minutes, courtesy of corner-forward Tony Hadden. A majestic long-range effort by Mick O'Connell two minutes later levelled matters and it was neck and neck for the remainder of the first half, with Down holding a two-point advantage, 0-7 to 0-5, at the break.

A Kerry surge brought the teams level within five minutes of the restart with Mick O'Connell and Seamus Murphy finding the target. After nearly ten minutes of stalemate, and with both teams missing chances to pull clear, it was Down's star performer James McCartan who finally broke the deadlock. His forty-yard effort caught the Kerry defence off guard and finished in the back of the net. Within a minute, McCartan started a movement which ended up with Paddy Doherty being felled inside the Kerry square. Doherty himself blasted the resultant penalty past Johnny Culloty and Down were on the home stretch. Despite Kerry's best efforts, they were held in check by a staunch Down defence, while sharpshooter Doherty rounded matters off with the last three points of the game. When John Dowling blew the final whistle the score stood at 2-10 to 0-8. Croke Park erupted amid scenes of jubilation never previously witnessed at that historic venue.

The players who brought the Sam Maguire Cup across the border for the first time were, to a man, lauded as heroes. While James McCartan was singled out as the man of the match, reports at the time were effusive in their praise for Down's invincible full-back line of George Lavery, Leo Murphy and Pat Rice. Team captain Kevin Mussen achieved footballing immortality as the first man to lead a team from the Six Counties to All-Ireland glory.

While Kerry suffered their worst ever final loss in 1960, they were, as always, gracious in defeat. No one doubted that they would return again and again to the top table and the performances of O'Connell, O'Dwyer and the Sheehys suggested that they would not have to wait too long. For the moment, however, the laurels rested with the Mourne men and time would tell whether they could go on to enhance their legacy.

FINAL STATISTICS

	Down	Kerry
Full-time:	2-10	0-8
Half-time:	0-7	0-5
Scorers:	P. Doherty 1-5 (1-0 penalty, 0-4 frees)	T. Lyne 0-4 (0-4 frees)
	J. McCartan 1-1	M. O'Connell 0-2
	T. Hadden 0-2	J. O'Connor 0-1
	J. Lennon 0-1 (0-1 free)	Seamus Murphy 0-1
	S. O'Neill 0-1	
Attendance:	87,768	
Referee:	John Dowling (Offaly)	

FINAL MISCELLANY

- Kerry's John Dowling picked up an injury on the morning of the game after 'jokingly tussling' with teammate Jerome O'Shea. In the *Irish Independent*, correspondent John D. Hickey described how Dowling 'cut an extraordinary figure' as he limped around in the pre-match parade.

- Former Meath great and All-Ireland referee Peter McDermott joined the Down backroom team in an advisory capacity prior to the semi-final replay with Offaly.
- Both Down goals were scored at the Canal End. The county's colours were hoisted on to the top of one of the posts after the game.
- An indication of the scramble for tickets for the 1960 Final can be gleaned from an advertisement taken out by a Tyrone man in the *Armagh Observer*. In exchange for ten match tickets, a three-and-a-half acre 'farm' was on offer.
- For the first time, there was an allocation of six complimentary tickets to forty players – twenty from each county.
- Down's ace marksman Paddy Doherty previously played soccer professionally with Lincoln City.

1960 – THE YEAR THAT WAS

- The President of Ireland, Éamon de Valera, only managed to get to the game at half-time. He had an earlier engagement relating to the Tercentenary of St Vincent de Paul and St Louise de Marillac.
- John F. Kennedy defeated Richard M. Nixon in the US presidential election of 1960. Kennedy took 49.72% of the popular vote, as against 49.55% for Nixon.
- In November 1960, the country was thrown into a state of shock when nine Irish soldiers, serving with the UN in the Congo, were ambushed and massacred by Baluba militiamen.

1960 TEAM LINE-OUTS

DOWN (WINNERS)

1. Eamonn McKay
(Dundrum)

2. George Lavery
(Kilwarlin)

3. Leo Murphy
(Kilkeel, also Dundrum and St Bronagh's, Rostrevor)

4. Pat Rice
(Castlewellan)

5. Kevin Mussen
(Clonduff, also O'Donovan Rossa, Antrim) Capt.

6. Dan McCartan
(Glenn, also Tullylish)

7. Kevin O'Neill
(Newry Mitchel)

8. Joe Lennon
(Aghaderg, also St Patrick's, Meath)

9. Jarlath Carey
(Ballymartin, also Dundrum)

10. Sean O'Neill
(Newry Mitchel)

11. James McCartan
(Glenn, also Tullylish)

12. Paddy Doherty
(Ballykinlar, also Loughinisland)

13. Tony Hadden
(Newry Shamrocks)

14. Patsy O'Hagan
(Clonduff)

15. Breen Morgan
(Annaclone)

Subs: Kieran Denvir (Kilclief) Played; Eamonn Clements (Banbridge); P.J. McElroy (Leitrim, also Glenn); John Haughian (Longstone); John McAuley (St Bronagh's, Rostrevor); Eamonn Lundy (Dromara, also Bryansford); Eddie Burns (Newry Shamrocks); Seamus Kennedy (Glenn); Pat Fitzsimons (Kilclief); James Fitzpatrick (Loughinisland)

KERRY (RUNNERS-UP)

1. Johnny Culloty
(Killarney Legion)

2. Jerome O'Shea
(St Mary's, Cahirciveen)

3. Niall Sheehy
(John Mitchels)

4. Tim 'Tiger' Lyons
(Castleisland Desmonds, also Cordal)

5. Sean Murphy
(Geraldines, Dublin, also Camp and UCD)

6. Kevin Coffey
(Clanna Gael, Dublin, also Beaufort and Dundalk Young Irelands, Louth)

7. Mick O'Dwyer
(Waterville)

8. Mick O'Connell
(Valentia, also Waterville)

9. Jerdie O'Connor
(Ballydonoghue)

10. Seamus Murphy
(Camp, also Lispole)

11. Tom Long
(Dr Crokes, also An Ghaeltacht)

12. Paudie Sheehy
(John Mitchels)

13. Garry McMahon
(Listowel Emmets)

14. John Dowling
(Kerins O'Rahillys)

15. Tadghie Lyne
(Castleisland Desmonds)

Subs: Jack Dowling (Castlegregory) Played; Dan McAuliffe (Duagh) Played; Bernie O'Callaghan (Moyvane); Jim Brosnan (Moyvane); Timmy O'Sullivan (Castleisland Desmonds)

1961

Down's 1960 All-Ireland triumph was hugely significant in more ways than one. Their achievement of being the first county to bring the Sam Maguire Cup across the border made all the headlines, and was a source of tremendous pride to the GAA fraternity in the Six Counties. Down's arrival on the scene also witnessed a change in the general attitude to what constituted the most effective style of play. With a game plan more focused on combination play rather than a reliance on individual talent, they brought a new glamour to the game and set the template for more scientific team preparation.

The Mourne men had won many admirers throughout the country and they were hotly tipped to repeat their first championship success in 1961. It was, however, acknowledged that several hurdles stood in the way of retaining the title, not least within their own ultra-competitive province. First opposition in the queue came in the form of Fermanagh, one of only two counties in Ulster without a provincial title. The sides met at Newry on 11 June where the expected cakewalk failed to materialise. Down won, 0-12 to 0-7, after a most fractious encounter that saw members of the Fermanagh team requiring the protection of Down players and officials when a section of the crowd rushed onto the field at the final whistle. Down's renowned forward machine made little headway against a resolute Fermanagh defence in which the full-back line of Jim Collins, Hugh Flanagan and the imperious Sean Maguire gave nothing away. With Mick Brewster and Joe Goodwin winning the midfield battle for the Ernesiders, Down needed defenders Leo Murphy, George Lavery and Pat Rice in top form to carry the day for the champions.

Down's semi-final opponents were Derry, who themselves had been fortunate to escape with a two-point win over Tyrone, with an opportunist goal from Seamus Devlin giving them the edge. At Casement Park on 2 July, over 20,000 people turned up to see what would be an epic encounter, at the end of which Down had withstood a great Derry comeback to win, 2-12 to 1-10. Playing brilliant football from the start, with Jarlath Carey their star man, they took a six-point lead into the break. However, with Jim McKeever switching to midfield, and his brother Dinny and Willie O'Kane storming into the game, Derry fought back and closed the gap to within two points. In a helter-skelter finish, the Down men turned on the afterburners to pull away in the final minutes.

Down's opponents in the Ulster Final were Armagh, who had started their campaign at Lurgan on 4 June with an easy five-point win over a Cavan team whose display was described by Peadar O'Brien of *The Irish Press* as 'pathetically feeble'. Armagh's main man in this win was Johnny McGeary, who lorded proceedings at midfield. McGeary was again Armagh's star when they trounced Monaghan,

Offaly, All-Ireland runners-up, 1961. Back (l–r): Greg Hughes, Peter 'Peenie' Dunne, Mick Casey, Charlie Wrenn, Phil O'Reilly, Sean Ryan, Mickey Brady, Frank Higgins, Frank Weir, Sean Foran; front (l–r): Larry Fox, Donie Hanlon, Har Donnelly, Tommy Greene, Willie Nolan, Tommy Cullen, Peter Daly, Sean Brereton, Paddy McCormack, Johnny Egan, Peter O'Reilly (trainer). *Sportsfile.*

5-9 to 0-5, at Dungannon on 25 June. His midfield partner, Gene Larkin, and half-backs Des Harney, Danny Kelly and Harry Hoy were also in fine fettle. Reports on the game all acknowledged the gallant efforts of Monaghan's Seamus Mulligan who turned in a storming display.

The Ulster Final at Casement Park on 23 July was a particularly hectic encounter. Armagh were on top in the first half and were full value for their five-point lead at the break. It was then that the Down selectors made the decision to introduce James McCartan, who had failed a fitness test prior to the game. The results of this change were immediate as Down steadily whittled away at Armagh's lead. They were three points in front when, in the final seconds, a piledriver from Johnny McGeary looked to have found its way through a crowded goalmouth and levelled the scores. When Cavan referee Liam Maguire ruled that the ball had not crossed the line there was uproar, and when he blew the final whistle seconds later, he needed an escort to the sanctuary of the dressing-rooms.

In Munster, Cork and Kerry duly progressed to their expected Munster Final showdown at the Athletic Grounds on 16 July. Cork had been very fortunate that teenager Mick Burke was on hand to fist home the decisive goal in the semi-final battle with Tipperary. Kerry's semi-final victory over Clare was a different story as they won easily on the unusual score of 1-13 to 1-0. Peculiarly, Kerry were behind after twenty minutes of the game when Matt Fitzpatrick hit Clare's only score of the hour.

Kerry were hot favourites when they travelled to Cork on 16 July but with Tom Connolly, Vincie Barrett and the O'Sullivan brothers, Con, Paddy and Stevie, playing great football, it was the men in the red jerseys who dominated. Kerry's saviours were Kevin Coffey, Mick O'Dwyer and, inevitably,

Action from the 1961 decider between Down and Offaly, a game which attracted the all-time record attendance of 90,556. *Sportsfile.*

Mick O'Connell. *The Cork Examiner* described O'Connell's performance as one of 'sheer splendour' and bemoaned Cork's misfortune that only a brilliant equalising point by the Valentia man had denied them the title.

In the days after the drawn game, much was written about the likely course of the replay. Those with Kerry leanings feared that the county was going downhill while their Cork counterparts spoke of the pride that had been restored. All agreed that, while the outcome was uncertain, a footballing classic was in the offing. The recall by Kerry of John Dowling to the full-forward berth changed everything. He proceeded to terrorise the Cork defence and was the chief architect in one of the most one-sided games of the year. Kerry romped home, 2-13 to 1-4, and they were promptly installed as favourites for All-Ireland glory.

Galway were fancied to complete an unprecedented six-in-a-row in Connacht and they started out with a four-point win over Mayo at Tuam on 11 June. Their key men were full-back Sean Meade and newcomer John Keenan, but the general view of their performance was that it didn't augur well for their championship ambitions. Leitrim presented Galway's next opposition at Ballinamore on 25 June and, after an impressive start that saw them take a five-point lead, they fell apart as Pat Donnellan, John Keenan and Sean Purcell led Galway to a seven-point victory. As always, Packie McGarty was in great form for Leitrim while defenders Jack Faughnan and Tom Colreavy also stood out.

By virtue of a less than impressive win over Sligo at Charlestown on 18 June, Roscommon qualified to play Galway in the provincial final. When they met at Castlebar on 9 July, the Tribesmen were firm favourites and matters seemed to be going according to plan until Eamonn Curley was switched to midfield for Roscommon. He dominated proceedings for the remainder of the game, while brothers Don and Des Feely created all sorts of problems for the Galway defence. Despite the heroic efforts of Galway's John Donnellan, it was Roscommon who finally edged it, their winning point coming from Tony Kenny with just twenty seconds to go.

The big question in Leinster was whether Offaly, first-time champions in 1960, could repel the likely challenges of Dublin and Louth as they sought to retain their provincial crown. The men from the Faithful County crossed their first hurdle with a routine five-point win over Carlow at Newbridge on 11 June. In that pre health and safety era, a crowd of over 20,000 packed into St Conleth's, prompting *Nationalist and Leinster Times* reporter James O'Rourke to write: 'For the first time in my life I wished I was a sardine. For a sardine, at least, would have had room to move.'

Offaly's Har Donnelly was in great scoring form but their top performer was Sean Brereton who played a blinder. Their victory would have been of the 'cakewalk' variety but for the Trojan efforts of Carlow's Eddie 'Cran' Hogan, Eddie Walker and goalkeeper Joe Nolan.

The Offaly men might have expected to face Louth in the semi-final but the Wee County came a cropper at a bitterly cold Croke Park on 28 May when Kildare beat them, 4-7 to 2-5. With Clogherinkoe's Pat Tyrrell in fine scoring form and the Carbury duo of Pat 'Archie' Moore and Pat Cummins on song, not even the best efforts of Kevin Beahan and Frank Lynch could turn the tide in Louth's favour. Kildare's impressive win turned out to be another false dawn, however, as the Lilywhites slumped to a twelve-point defeat to Offaly in their Portlaoise semi-final on 2 July. They had no answer to the powerful play of Sean Ryan, and Offaly's full-back line of Paddy McCormack, Greg Hughes and John Egan suffocated their every attack. On what one newspaper described as a 'Black Day for the All-Whites', only Pa Connolly, Mick Carolan, Pat Cummins and substitute John Joe Walsh made any impression.

With their Leinster Final place firmly secured, Offaly now watched on as Dublin and Meath prepared to do battle for the right to face the champions. Meath had overcome Longford by a single point while Dublin's forward machine had sprung into action with a nine-point win over Wexford. On a day when Paddy Holden and Cathal O'Leary led the charge for Dublin, Wexford's Martin Óg O'Neill had the distinction of scoring all of his side's 1-7 total.

Although Dublin were favoured to overcome the Meath challenge in the semi-final, few could have envisaged the one-sided nature of what was to ensue. After an uneventful first half, Dublin proceeded to bore holes in the Meath defence and ran out 4-14 to 1-7 winners in a game that saw Mickey Whelan, John Timmons and newcomer Simon Behan play starring roles.

The stage was now set for the widely anticipated showdown between Dublin and Offaly. The comprehensive nature of the Metropolitans' victory over Meath prompted many to forecast Offaly's demise. When they met at Portlaoise on 23 July, Dublin's acclaimed attackers were completely stymied by a brilliant defence led by Mickey Brady, Greg Hughes and Paddy McCormack. The final score was 1-13 to 1-8 in favour of Offaly, with Mick Casey getting the decisive goal early in the game.

The first of the All-Ireland semi-finals saw Down play Kerry on 9 August in what was a repeat of the 1960 decider. Within a minute of the throw-in, Sean O'Neill hit a rocket into the back of the Kerry net. While the men from the Kingdom fought back gallantly and had drawn level by half-time, Down were in the ascendancy throughout the field. Inspired by the McCartan brothers, George Lavery, Joe Lennon and ace marksman Paddy Doherty, they pulled away to win convincingly, 1-12 to 0-9. With only 'Tiger' Lyons, Jerome O'Shea and goalkeeper Johnny Culloty playing up to form, Kerry had to give way to what was clearly a far superior team.

The second semi-final saw the novel clash of Offaly and Roscommon, with the Leinster champions hotly tipped to reach their first ever final. Whatever about the prospects of an Offaly win, few would have predicted how comprehensive their victory would be. Having played against the elements on a wet and windy day, they trailed by just one point at the break. The second half was something of a formality, with Roscommon failing to register a score as the Offaly men cruised to a 3-6 to 0-6 victory. The basis of this win was a rock-solid defence, each member of which held the upper hand on his immediate opponent. Their midfielders, Sean Ryan and Sean Brereton, provided a steady stream of openings for a forward division in which two-goal hero Tommy Greene was outstanding. Contrary to some of the post-match comments in the press, this was not quite the swansong for Gerry O'Malley and his men. They would return to Croke Park for another bid at All-Ireland glory in 1962.

THE FINAL — 24 SEPTEMBER

While Down had developed a reputation for having the slickest forward division in the game, Offaly's clam-like defence was widely regarded as the best in the land. Pre-match analysis typically concluded that success would depend on whether the Faithful rearguard could hold the Mourne scoring machine in check. All of this speculation, and the unique final pairing, created more interest than ever in the 1961 All-Ireland Final. The official record shows an attendance of 90,556, a figure exceeded neither previously nor since. This was long before all-ticket arrangements were introduced and best estimates indicate that a further 30,000 people turned up at Croke Park on 24 September in the vain hope of gaining entry.

When the teams raced onto the pitch the stadium erupted in an incredible cacophony of noise. The players didn't seem to be unsettled by this electric atmosphere as they produced an epic, incident-packed first half. Down's captain Paddy Doherty hit the first point within forty seconds of the throw-in. Then it was Offaly's turn. Goals in quick succession from Mick Casey and Peter Daly pushed them into an unlikely six-point lead. Down responded in dramatic fashion. Goals courtesy of Sean O'Neill, Tony Hadden and a gravity-defying effort from James McCartan gave them a 3-3 to 2-3 half-time advantage.

The second half of the game was not for the purists. The play was ragged and many hard knocks were given and taken. Despite clocking up eighteen wides to Offaly's five, Down did just enough to hold out for victory on a score of 3-6 to 2-8. Many argued that the result might have been different if the referee had awarded a penalty when Tommy Greene was set upon by three Down defenders early in the second half. The consensus, however, was that Down's victory was merited, with Offaly likely to be their biggest threat in 1962.

And so the Sam Maguire Cup made the return journey across the border. Once again, Down's brilliant half-forward trio of O'Neill, McCartan and Doherty featured prominently in accounts of how the game was won. Jarlath Carey gave a great display at centre-field while Dan McCartan and an injury-hampered Pat Rice were stalwart defenders. For Offaly, their full-back line stood firm, with Greg Hughes having one of his finest outings. Mickey Brady, Sean Brereton, Tommy Cullen and Har Donnelly also performed well on this, the biggest stage of all. With such a young team, and having put their county on the footballing map, they had good reason to be optimistic about the future. Alas, it would take ten years before the Faithful County would reach the Holy Grail, by which time all except Paddy McCormack and Greg Hughes would have retired their inter-county boots.

FINAL STATISTICS

	Down	Offaly
Full-time:	3-6	2-8
Half-time:	3-3	2-3
Scorers:	J. McCartan 1-1	M. Casey 1-0
	S. O'Neill 1-1 (0-1 free)	P. Daly 1-0
	B. Morgan 1-0	H. Donnelly 0-6 (0-6 frees)
	P. Doherty 0-2	T. Cullen 0-1
	T. Hadden 0-2	S. Brereton 0-1
Attendance:	90,556	
Referee:	Liam Maguire (Cavan)	

FINAL MISCELLANY

- When Cavan lost to Armagh at Lurgan on 4 June, it was the first time since 1915 that they were beaten in the first round of the championship.
- *The Glasgow Herald*, apparently in expectation of a caustic report, dispatched a young journalist to Dublin to witness the 1961 Final between Down and Offaly. What came back was probably one of the finest objective assessments of Irish and GAA culture. Having described the bone-crunching nature of the exchanges and the sportsmanship of players and supporters alike, the awe-stricken scribe had some words of advice for his fellow countrymen. He wrote: 'for the most noisy of the patrons of the Rangers and Celtic football clubs, I recommend a visit to Croke Park, at All-Ireland Football time. They will find it, I hope, a shattering, humbling

experience, from which they would come back better, rather than battered men. No swearing, no bitterness. Just all good, honest, noisy, boisterous sportsmen together. And jolly company.'

- The 1961 Final marked a turning point in TV coverage of Gaelic Games in Northern Ireland. UTV rushed film back to Belfast for late-night broadcast. The BBC also covered the game, with Derry midfielder Jim McKeever in the commentary box.

1961 – THE YEAR THAT WAS

- Russian cosmonaut Yuri Gagarin became the first person in space on 12 April.
- Telefís Éireann went on the air for the first time on 31 December.
- Long before the arrival of the popular 'Agony Aunt' features in Sunday newspapers, the *Sunday Independent* gave its readers access to the sage advice of one Fr Lucius McLean, O.P.M. One young woman wrote to ask whether she should break off her engagement with her boyfriend because of the fact that on some occasions they had rather overstepped the mark in giving and receiving signs of affection. She was assured by Fr McClean that what had happened so far had been the outcome of foolishness rather than a display of malice. Once they had settled the matter with God, they could expect to deal with their difficulty successfully and they could look forward to being happily married.

1961 TEAM LINE-OUTS

DOWN (WINNERS)

1. Eamonn McKay
(Dundrum)

2. George Lavery
(Kilwarlin)

3. Leo Murphy
(Kilkeel, also Dundrum and St Bronagh's, Rostrevor)

4. Pat Rice
(Castlewellan)

5. Patsy O'Hagan
(Clonduff)

6. Dan McCartan
(Glenn, also Tullylish)

7. John Smith
(Ballykinlar)

8. Jarlath Carey
(Dundrum, also Ballymartin)

9. Joe Lennon
(Aghaderg, also St Patrick's, Meath)

10. Sean O'Neill
(Newry Mitchels)

11. James McCartan
(Glenn, also Tullylish)

12. Paddy Doherty
(Ballykinlar, also Loughinisland)
Capt.

13. Tony Hadden
(Newry Shamrocks)

14. P.J. McIlroy
(Leitrim, also Glenn)

15. Brian Morgan
(Annaclone)

Subs: Kevin O'Neill (Newry Mitchels) Played; Gerry McCashin (Ballykinlar); Kevin Mussen (Clonduff, also O'Donovan Rossa, Antrim); Eamonn Lundy (Dromara, also Bryansford); John Haughian (Longstone)

OFFALY (RUNNERS-UP)

1. Willie Nolan
(Clara)

2. Paddy McCormack
(Rhode)

3. Greg Hughes
(Kinnegad Westmeath, also Cloghan
and Gaeil Colmcille, Meath)

4. Johnny Egan
(Kickhams, Dublin, also Doon)

5. Phil O'Reilly
(Tullamore)

6. Mickey Brady
(Edenderry)

7. Charlie Wrenn
(Air Corps, also St Mary's)

8. Sean Brereton
(Walsh Island, also Clonbullogue)

9. Sean Ryan
(St Monica's, London, also Doon)

10. Tommy Cullen
(Edenderry)

11. Peter Daly
(Tullamore and Military College)

12. Tommy Greene
(Daingean)

13. Mick Casey
(Rhode)

14. Donie Hanlon
(Gracefield)

15. Har Donnelly
(Air Corps, also Athlone)

Subs: Frank Weir (Gracefield) Played; Sean Foran (Edenderry) Played; Frank Higgins (Gracefield) Played; Peter 'Peenie' Dunne (St Mary's); Larry Fox (Tullamore); Christy Carroll (Edenderry)

1962

Having followed up their maiden Ulster title of 1959 with successive All-Irelands in 1960 and 1961, the footballers of Down were widely predicted to remain at the top of the pile for some time to come. Many believed that they would emulate the feats of the great Wexford and Kerry teams of the past, and so stretch their All-Ireland run to four. Certainly, their prospects for 1962 seemed bright. Offaly had made great strides and seemed best placed to dethrone the champions. Dublin and Galway had recently produced very promising minor teams but the transition to senior would likely require more time. While Kerry had maintained their dominance in Munster, they had fallen short on the national stage and seemed set for an extended period in the doldrums.

It was against this backdrop that a confident Down set out on their championship campaign. They opened their account against Fermanagh at Irvinestown on 1 July. Despite the best efforts of their tenacious opposition, for whom Vincent Greene, Jim Cassidy and the elusive P.T. Treacy starred, Down produced a scintillating display as they romped to an eleven-point victory. The chief talking point after this game was the mercurial brilliance of Sean O'Neill.

Two weeks later Down overcame Tyrone by six points with an efficient, rather than brilliant, performance. Tony Hadden set them on the road with an early goal while it was the turn of the second O'Neill brother, Kevin, to play the starring role. Tyrone's veteran goalkeeper Thady Turbett made numerous fine saves, while one Peter Harte was their goal scorer.

Down were now safely into the Ulster Final where they faced a resurgent Cavan. The men from Breffni had battled it out with Armagh in the quarter-final before emerging 3-8 to 2-2 winners. In a game that most reports described as a 'brawl', it was merely incidental that three players were ordered off. With ongoing pitch incursions the second half took fifty-one minutes to complete as matters descended into total chaos. This battle marked the arrival on the scene of Cavan teenager Ray Carolan, who gave a towering display at midfield.

Matters were less fractious when Cavan overcame Antrim by four points in a scrappy semi-final at Casement Park on 8 July. Short three first-choice players, Cavan needed its full-back line of Gabriel Kelly, P.J. McCaffrey and Mickey Brady in top form to keep the Antrim scoring threat at bay. Elsewhere, Carolan and Tom Lynch held sway at midfield while Antrim's best were Liam Hamill, Jim McCorry and Patsy Grogan.

Cavan welcomed the return of Charlie Gallagher, Hugh Barney O'Reilly and team captain Jim McDonnell for the provincial final clash with Down. However, in addition to these experienced

The cover of the 1962 football final programme. *Image courtesy of the GAA Museum at Croke Park.*

players, their line-out included seven of their successful junior side. Two of the team, Ray Carolan and Jimmy Stafford, were teenagers who had played at schools' level just months previously.

Against what many regarded as one of the greatest ever teams, Cavan were seen as no-hopers. Nonetheless, a record crowd of over 40,000 turned up at Casement Park on 29 July, with Cavan supporters in a distinct majority. The game was even enough for the first fifteen minutes – and then the deluge arrived. It was not the expected deluge though; it was the underdogs who proceeded to pulverise the champions into submission. They had the game well and truly wrapped up long before the final whistle. Every Cavan man played like his life depended on the outcome, and Down couldn't break free of their suffocating grasp.

Down assigned five different players in an effort to subdue Carolan and Tom Lynch at midfield, but they all suffered the same fate: abject failure. Newcomer Stafford had a dream debut, scoring two goals and making a third. The half-back line of Tony Morris, Tom Maguire and Jim McDonnell were feted for their achievement of taming what was perhaps the most potent half-forward line in the history of the game.

In their shock defeat, few of the Down team impressed but Leo Murphy, Pat Rice and the ever-reliable Sean O'Neill could hold their heads high.

It was Sligo who made many of the headlines in the Connacht Championship of 1962. In the opening round at Charlestown on 10 June, they escaped with an unlikely draw against Mayo when substitute Ed Johnson found the net seconds before full-time. Two weeks later they went one better, with a one-point victory in the replay at Markievicz Park. Outstanding performances by Sean Sexton, Padraig Kilgannon, Gerry O'Connor, Paddy Christie and the classy Mickey Kearins paved the way to a semi-final encounter with provincial champions Roscommon.

Just when they seemed set to qualify for an all too rare Connacht Final appearance, the Sligo men were dealt a sucker punch when a last-gasp goal by Cyril Mahon gave Roscommon victory by the narrowest of margins, 3-6 to 1-11.

Roscommon were pitted against Galway in the provincial decider at Castlebar on 22 July. The Tribesmen had overcome Leitrim in their semi-final when a returning Sean Purcell hit two goals in yet another man-of-the-match performance. If this game belonged to Purcell, the final itself was owned by Roscommon veteran Gerry O'Malley. In the words of Donal Carroll of *The Irish Press*, 'His

Away from his busy life as a dual player and Kinsealy farmer, Des Foley finds time to relax. He subsequently added to his schedule when he was elected to Dáil Éireann. *Image courtesy of the National Library of Ireland.*

was a masterly exhibition of the true captain's role, an unforgettable piece of sheer generalship.'

Roscommon's prospects had seemed doomed, but when O'Malley moved to midfield early in the second half, the pendulum swung in their favour. The final nails in Galway's coffin were hammered in by brothers Don and Des Feely who got the winning scores in their 3-7 to 2-9 victory. As well as making a number of vital saves, Roscommon goalie Aidan Brady hit the headlines when he contrived to break the crossbar early in the second half. Another to feature prominently was full-back John Oliver Moran who managed to limit the scoring threat posed by Sean Purcell.

Reigning champions Offaly, who were favoured to retain the Leinster title, were drawn to play the winners of Carlow and Kilkenny in the quarter-final. When these neighbours met at Nowlan Park on 29 April, they produced one of the most ill-tempered games of the year, with fists and boots flying with abandon. With the excellent Tim Wilson notching nine points for the Kilkenny men, the result was much closer than had been predicted. It was the class of Brendan Hayden, who scored 3-7, that was the big difference in Carlow's 3-12 to 2-12 victory.

Offaly's ragged performance against the Carlow men on 20 May didn't augur well. Although they advanced with a five-point victory, their forwards put in a lacklustre display. Were it not for the great work of an inspired Paddy McCormack, and the midfield pairing of Larry Coughlan and Sean Brereton, they could have been taking the championship exit door. Their form hadn't improved greatly when they faced Kildare in the semi-final at Croke Park on 1 July. True, the All-Whites had shown up well in their wins over Wexford (5-12 to 1-6) and Meath (0-8 to 0-6) but they were not seen as likely to dethrone the champions. Within two minutes of the throw-in, Pat 'Archie' Moore sent a screamer to the Offaly net and this set the tone for the game. Tigerish defending by Jimmy Cummins, Toss McCarthy and Danny Flood choked the Offaly scoring threat while Mick Carolan was lord and master at midfield. With Pat Cummins, Kieran O'Malley and 'Archie' Moore cutting through the Offaly defence, a shock result seemed inevitable. But for the exertions of Paddy McCormack, John Egan and Tommy Cullen, Kildare would have been out of sight. With the champions in a seemingly hopeless situation, Mick Casey and Tommy Furlong scrambled two late goals and, Houdini-like, Offaly were through to the Leinster Final.

The opposite side of the draw saw Laois and Dublin win their way through to the semi-final. Laois started their journey against Longford at Tullamore on 6 May. Liam Doran, Tom Browne and Fintan Walsh provided the platform for Jack Kenna and two-goal hero Eddie Dunne to clock up the vital scores in their five-point win. From there, Laois had to contend with the robust challenge of Westmeath on 27 May. With Mick Carley, George Kane and Paddy Cooney in great form for the opposition, Laois needed goalkeeper Pat Bracken and scorer-in-chief Jack Kenna at their best to escape with a two-point win.

Dublin's passage to the semi-final came on the back of a one-point win over Louth at Tullamore on 3 June. Mick Gartland and Johnny Woods gave the Wee County a decided midfield edge and Dublin had to rely heavily on Paddy Holden, Christy Kane and goalie Paschal Flynn to limit scoring damage. It was veteran Kevin Heffernan's brilliant goal that ultimately got them over the line, 1-8 to 0-10. Dublin also had a narrow escape in their semi-final clash with Laois, where they played second fiddle for most of the game as Ballyboughal's Leo Hickey came to their rescue with a number of vital interceptions. Tom Browne was once again the outstanding player on the pitch and Laois looked set for a famous win until John Timmons hit two magnificent points to guide Dublin into the final.

A Leinster Final record attendance of just under 60,000 flocked to Croke Park on 15 July for the eagerly anticipated clash of Dublin and title-holders Offaly. They were treated to an enthralling contest as both teams left behind their earlier indifferent form. Dublin raced into a five-point lead inside seven minutes but Offaly, with the help of a tonic goal from Tommy Cullen, battled back to hold the lead at half-time. The enforced departure of two of Dublin's best performers, Tom Howard and Des McKane, looked ominous. Instead, the arrival of Johnny Joyce and Paddy Farnan heralded a new spirit within the team and they proceeded to dominate for the remainder of the game, going on to win 2-8 to 1-7. Top billing went to the magnificent Cathal O'Leary, while Joyce, Noel Fox and newcomer Eamonn Burgess were also outstanding. As Offaly's three-in-a-row ambitions were shattered by Dublin's second-half blitz, their top performers were all in defence, Greg Hughes, Paddy McCormack and Charlie Wrenn being most impressive.

The result of every game in the Munster Championship went according to expectations. In a rough and tumble affair at Clonmel on 27 May, Waterford had eight points to spare over a Tipperary side that failed to register a single score in the second half. The classiest players on view were Waterford's Tom Power and Ben Coughlan, though Tipperary's Gus Danagher also gave a great display. It was a different ball game for the Déise when they met Kerry in the semi-final at Listowel on 24 June. The Kingdom ran out easy winners, 2-18 to 2-6, with the three Sheehy brothers, Paudie, Niall and Sean Óg, all contributing handsomely. Dave Geaney, Dan McAuliffe and Tom Long led the way in the scoring stakes, with Waterford goalkeeper Sean Ormonde saving his side from an even bigger defeat.

The second semi-final saw Cork register their expected easy win over Clare at Buttevant on 17 June. Downplaying the significance of Cork's win, *The Cork Examiner* gave this pithy description of their opposition: 'Clare were crude, unimaginative, but strong.' The *Examiner* then went on to acknowledge that Clare corner-back Tom Mangan was the best defender on the field, with the man-of-the-match accolade firmly belonging to Cork's Gene McCarthy.

The Athletic Grounds' showdown between the traditional rivals was a disappointment in more ways than one. That the game was one of the most one-sided finals ever (Kerry 4-8, Cork 0-4) was incidental. The real story was one of a fractious affair that saw violent scenes on the pitch matched by equally outrageous behaviour by sections of the crowd. Sods, stones and even bottles were thrown at Kerry players during the game, with their outstanding goalkeeper, Johnny Culloty, particularly fortunate to avoid serious injury.

As for the play itself, the result was clear after just five minutes as Kerry bored holes in the Cork defence. With Dan McAuliffe, Tom Long and speed merchant Dave Geaney on song, even the gallant efforts of Johnny Flynn and Paddy Harrington failed to stem the tide. Kerry's rock-solid defence revelled in the robust exchanges while Mick O'Connell gave a masterclass which he embellished with what John Barrett of *The Irish Press* described as 'one of the greatest goals I have ever seen'. Cork's shining light in this disaster was once again Rosscarbery's Gene McCarthy, who continued the great form he had shown throughout the championship.

The first of the 1962 All-Ireland semi-finals, between Dublin and Kerry, proved to be a major anticlimax. The Kerry men simply ran riot in the first half and were home and hosed at the break when they led 2-9 to 0-3. Superior throughout the field, and with Tom Long, 'Tiger' Lyons and Mick O'Connell playing brilliantly, Kerry produced their best performance in years. Cantering home to a 2-12 to 0-10 victory, they installed themselves as firm favourites to take the title. With only Cathal O'Leary, Paddy Holden and Noel Fox impressing for Dublin, many commentators predicted a prolonged barren period for the men in blue.

The second semi-final saw hot favourites Cavan leave their shooting boots at home as they crashed to a two-point (1-8 to 1-6) defeat to Roscommon. Under the inspiring leadership of their captain, Gerry O'Malley, the Roscommon men were vastly more efficient in every facet of play. Midfielder Bernie Kyne and substitute George Geraghty were others to star for the winners, while only Cavan's half-back line of Tony Morris, Tom Maguire and team captain Jim McDonnell impressed.

THE FINAL – 23 SEPTEMBER

In the week before the 1962 Final, Dublin bookmaker Terry Rogers was offering 2/1 on Roscommon to take the title. Compared to Kerry's highly impressive victory over Dublin, the Roscommon men needed a share of luck before scraping past Cavan in their semi-final. Further, with an array of household names in their line-up, and generations of tradition behind them, nobody was predicting anything other than a twentieth title for the Kingdom. Any prospect Roscommon had of mounting a serious challenge rested firmly on the shoulders of their captain, Gerry O'Malley. After sixteen years in the county jersey, this footballing colossus had almost single-handedly dragged his county into the All-Ireland Final. The general sentiment throughout the GAA world was that, if ever a man deserved an All-Ireland medal, Gerry O'Malley was that man.

One absentee from the Kerry team for the final was outstanding corner-back Donie O'Sullivan, who had been so impressive in the semi-final. Studying for the priesthood, he was back in Maynooth College, and so unavailable, before the end of September. As for Roscommon, they almost had to do without the services of midfielder John Kelly, who needed to have two 'troublesome' teeth removed on the Friday evening before the match.

Kerry's chief mentor for this game was Dr Eamon O'Sullivan, who had guided the county to so many successes in the past. Roscommon had Jimmy Murray, captain of their All-Ireland sides of the 1940s, at the helm. When the teams ran onto the pitch on 23 September, Roscommon were led by their talisman O'Malley. Kerry's captain was Sean Óg Sheehy, one of three brothers on the team and son of Kerry legend, John Joe, who was now a selector. Also running onto the pitch that day with Kerry was their seven-year-old mascot, one Denis 'Ogie' Moran, later to accumulate no fewer than eight All-Ireland medals with the county, including one as team captain.

Within thirty-four seconds of the throw-in, Kerry already had one hand firmly grasped on the cup. Latching on to a long-range free from Mick O'Connell, Listowel's Garry McMahon fisted the ball to the back of the Roscommon net. They thus took a lead which wasn't threatened for the rest of the game. A goal from a penalty by Roscommon's Don Feely late in the first half put a hint of respectability on the scoreboard but their cause was a hopeless one. Trailing by seven points at the break, and with O'Malley struggling with an injury, there was no way back for the Connacht champions.

The game, described in the *Irish Independent* as 'undistinguished, unexciting, cheerless and insipid', limped to its inevitable conclusion, with a final score of Kerry 1-12, Roscommon 1-6.

Generally efficient throughout the field, those who shone brightest for Kerry were Culloty in goal, defenders 'Tiger' Lyons and Mick O'Dwyer, the immaculate O'Connell at centre-field and the brilliant Tom Long in attack. For Roscommon, it was what would nowadays be termed a bad day at the office. They only managed to register a single score from play. O'Malley's early injury and subsequent departure was a severe blow, but it is uncertain whether even he at his best could have roused the team out of its slumbers. Eamonn Curley was a revelation, while Ronnie Creaven, Bernie Kyne, Tony Whyte and Don Feely did most to limit the damage.

Over half a century after the 1962 decider, by 2023, Kerry had gone on to win eighteen more All-Irelands – thirty-eight in total – and had contested another thirteen finals. Roscommon, on the other hand, had only made a single appearance on All-Ireland day when, in 1980, they got to within three points of … Kerry.

FINAL STATISTICS

	Kerry	Roscommon
Full-time:	1-12	1-6
Half-time:	1-8	1-1
Scorers:	M. O'Connell 0-7 (0-7 frees)	Don Feely 1-5 (1-0 penalty, 0-5 frees)
	G. McMahon 1-0	J. Kelly 0-1
	T. O'Sullivan 0-2	
	P. Sheehy 0-2	
	T. Long 0-1	
Attendance:	75,771	
Referee:	Eamonn Moules (Wicklow)	

FINAL MISCELLANY

- Kerry's 1962 victory meant that they were the first county to amass twenty All-Ireland titles in either football or hurling.
- Scoring a goal after just thirty-four seconds gave Garry McMahon a record that lasted until 2020, when Dublin's Dean Rock found the Mayo net after just twelve seconds.
- On St Patrick's Day 1962, Dublin's Des Foley won Railway Cup medals with Leinster in both hurling and football.
- On 23 September 1962, Edinburgh-born John McKay, aged ninety-two, settled down at his daughter's residence in Ballybough to watch the first football final to be televised live. Though primarily a soccer man, he had a particular interest in the proceedings – his expert hands had crafted the magnificent Sam Maguire Cup over thirty years earlier.

1962 – THE YEAR THAT WAS

- In what became known as the Cuban Missile Crisis, the world was on the brink of nuclear war when Russian leader Nikita Khrushchev installed missiles with atomic warheads in Cuba with the capability of reaching the United States. After some astute military manoeuvring, US president John F. Kennedy managed to diffuse matters.
- On 6 July, Gay Byrne presented the first edition of *The Late Late Show* on Telefís Éireann.
- In 1962, the GAA sold the rights to televise the All-Ireland semi-finals and finals (hurling and football) to Telefís Éireann. The exorbitant fee involved was £10 (€12.70).

1962 TEAM LINE-OUTS

KERRY (WINNERS)

1. Johnny Culloty
(Killarney Legion)

2. Seamus Murphy
(Camp, also Lispole)

3. Niall Sheehy
(John Mitchels)

4. Tim 'Tiger' Lyons
(Castleisland Desmonds, also Cordal)

5. Sean Óg Sheehy
(John Mitchels) Capt.

6. Noel Lucey
(Glenbeigh/Glencar, also Air Corps)

7. Mick O'Dwyer
(Waterville)

8. Mick O'Connell
(Valentia, also Waterville)

9. Jimmy Lucey
(Glenbeigh/Glencar)

10. Dan McAuliffe
(Duagh)

11. Timmy O'Sullivan
(Castleisland Desmonds)

12. Jerry O'Riordan
(Glenbeigh/Glencar)

13. Garry McMahon
(Listowel Emmets)

14. Tom Long
(Dr Crokes, also An Ghaeltacht)

15. Paudie Sheehy
(John Mitchels)

Subs: Jo Jo Barrett (Austin Stacks) Played; Kevin Coffey (Clanna Gael, Dublin, also Beaufort and Dundalk Young Irelands, Louth) Played; Seamus Roche (John Mitchels); Pat Aherne (Ballymac-elligott); Dave Geaney (Castleisland Desmonds)

ROSCOMMON (RUNNERS-UP)

1. Aidan Brady
(Elphin)

2. John Joe Breslin
(St Brendan's, also Erin's Hope, Dublin and Na Fianna)

3. John Lynch
(Tuam Stars, Galway, also Loughglynn and Michael Glaveys)

4. John Oliver Moran
(Sean McDermotts, Dublin, also Moore and Clann na nGael)

5. Ronnie Creaven
(Sean McDermotts, Dublin, also Padraig Pearses)

6. Gerry O'Malley
(St Brigid's, also St Patrick's)

7. Gerry Reilly
(Newtown Blues, Louth also Rooskey/St Barry's, Strokestown and Trim, Meath)

8. Bernie Kyne
(Padraig Pearses, also St Faithleach's and Clonbur, Galway)

9. John Kelly
(Elphin and UCG)

10. George Geraghty
(Garryowen, London, also St Croan's)

11. Eamonn Curley
(Padraig Pearses, also Bailieboro, Cavan)

12. Tony Whyte
(Clann na nGael)

13. Don Feely
(St Brigid's)

14. Cyril Mahon
(Roscommon Gaels)

15. Des Feely
(St Brigid's)

Subs: Tom Turley (Padraig Pearses) Played; Tony Kenny (Clann na nGael) Played; P.J. Shine (Clann na nGael); Brian Mitchell (St Brigid's, also St Aidan's); Seamus Keane (Creggs, also United Stars); Richard 'Dickie' Beirne (Shannon Gaels, Croghan); Peter Watson (Clann na nGael); Christy Grogan (St Croan's); Mickey Kenny (Oran)

1963

When Kerry's trainer, Dr Eamonn O'Sullivan, addressed the heaving masses in Tralee on the night after their 1962 triumph, he made a modest prediction. While acknowledging that his charges were no longer a young team, he envisaged being on the same podium in September 1964 when the Kingdom would be celebrating their third successive title. It is not known precisely how other counties reacted to this bold prediction. It is likely, however, to have given some extra motivational ammunition to team mentors in such as Cork, Down, Roscommon, Galway and, who knows, perhaps even Dublin.

Continuing their impressive form of the previous year, Kerry started 1963 by adding the League (Home) title to their All-Ireland crown. (At the time the 'Home' winners played New York in the final proper, but this game was yet to take place.) Their first outing in the championship was at Listowel on 23 June against a Tipperary team that had already accounted for Clare. Largely due to the efforts of Liam Connolly, John Keating, Gus Danagher, and an opportunist goal from Michael 'Babs' Keating, the Tipperary men found themselves in the unusual position of leading the champions early in the second half. Having decided to rest Tom Long for this seemingly routine assignment, the Kerry selectors now pleaded with him to tog out and join the fray. With his introduction, Kerry finally began to put the foot on the pedal and pulled away for an emphatic sixteen-point victory.

The second semi-final was a complete mismatch. Without the services of star player Monty Guiry, Waterford were out of their depth and had but a single point on the scoreboard before late goals from Tom Kirwan and Paddy Walsh reduced Cork's winning margin to thirteen points. Such was the ease with which Cork won this game that it was difficult to gauge their prospects against Kerry. There was no doubt, however, that this new-look outfit would travel to Killarney on 14 July, confident that they could spring a surprise.

When Millstreet's Willie O'Leary scored Cork's third goal midway through the second half of the Munster Final, he moved his team four points clear. With Kerry's grip on the provincial crown beginning to look a little precarious, they moved up the gears and produced what *The Cork Examiner* described as eight minutes of 'football sorcery'. Led by the brilliant Mick O'Dwyer, the Kerry forwards went on a scoring spree, with the champions retaining their title on a 1-18 to 3-7 scoreline. Apart from the performances of old reliables such as O'Dwyer, Coffey, O'Connell and Long, Kerry's stars included Pat Griffin and Frank O'Leary. Eighteen-year-old Griffin, who had previously lined out for Kildare, was widely acclaimed as an up-and-coming Mick O'Connell. O'Leary, who

Des Foley leads the Dublin team in the 1963 pre-match parade. An outstanding player, Foley holds the distinction of having played inter-provincial football before making his inter-county championship debut. He is the only player to have won Railway Cup medals in both hurling and football on the same day. *Image courtesy of the GAA Museum at Croke Park.*

previously played with both Westmeath and Mayo, almost missed out on his Kerry debut. He was rushed to hospital on the day before the game and was scheduled to undergo surgery. When this was postponed by a couple of days, he was allowed to go to see the game. This wasn't enough for the doggedly determined veterinary surgeon. He duly took his place on the team and contributed handsomely to their victory.

Sligo had been the hard-luck story of the 1962 Connacht Championship. Their semi-final exit at the hands of Roscommon was very much against the run of play. This was their chance to make amends since another semi-final joust with Roscommon was on the cards. The only hurdle to cross was the formality of beating Leitrim at Markievicz Park on 9 June. The Leitrim men were in no mood to accommodate and, with a display of unrelenting pressure, they dumped Sligo out of the championship. Jim Lynch, Josie Murray and Jackie Faughnan defended heroically while Fergus O'Rourke (older brother of future Meath star Colm) gave Leitrim the lion's share of midfield possession. Up front, veterans Packie McGarty and Cathal Flynn led the way once again. Having earlier been labelled 'dark horses' for the provincial crown, this was a major setback for Sligo, with only Jimmy Killoran and Mickey Kearins performing to expectations.

Leitrim's giant-killing exploits didn't end there. In atrocious conditions at Sligo on 23 June, they had a fully merited 1-8 to 1-3 win against reigning Connacht champions Roscommon. With

Action from the 1963 showdown between Dublin and Galway. *Image courtesy of the GAA Museum at Croke Park.*

the sides level at half-time, and Leitrim facing the elements in the second half, it was another outstanding performance by centre-back Josie Murray that was the key to this success. Cathal Flynn was in great scoring form, converting the chances created by such as Tom Grey and Kevin McGowan. Roscommon were but a pale shadow of the team that had reached the All-Ireland Final the previous September, and only Gerry O'Malley and Tony Whyte could be satisfied with their contribution.

Leitrim's Connacht Final opponents were Galway, who had beaten Mayo by five points in a lacklustre affair at Castlebar on 16 June, to reach their eighth successive provincial decider. While the Tribesmen were clear favourites, Leitrim had sprung two major championship surprises and hoped that they could now atone for the final defeats inflicted by Galway in the four years to 1960. It didn't take long on a blustery day at Castlebar on 14 July for any such hope to evaporate. Galway dominated from start to finish, led by twelve points at the break, and had clocked up 4-11 to Leitrim's 1-6 when referee Mick Loftus blew the long whistle. Monaghan-born Mick Garrett was Galway's captain and he celebrated his twenty-fifth birthday with a man-of-the-match performance at centre-field, with Tuam Stars clubmate Mick Reynolds in support. The team's impressive performance was tempered somewhat by Leitrim's failure to rise to the occasion. The shining exception to the general malaise within their ranks was centre-back Josie Murray, who produced a brilliant performance for the third successive game.

The big question in Ulster was whether Cavan could keep up the momentum from the previous year or whether Down could re-emerge after their 1962 hiccup. The Mourne men put down a serious marker at Newry on 9 June when they trounced Monaghan, 6-11 to 1-3. Even without the services of James McCartan and Paddy Doherty, their forwards ran riot, with Sean O'Neill starring as Val Kane and Jack Fitzsimmons created opening after opening in the Monaghan defence. An encouraging aspect of this win was the performance of newcomer Tom O'Hare, a man who would go on to fashion a reputation as one of the finest defenders of his generation.

Down's form dipped somewhat when they met Armagh in the semi-final on 7 July. They were anything but impressive as they negotiated their way to a four-point win in this war of attrition against a dogged Armagh fifteen, for whom Jimmy Whan and Tom McCreesh battled gallantly.

The second Ulster semi-final involved Cavan and Donegal, neither of which had shown much form in their quarter-final wins over Derry and Fermanagh respectively. Other than the local Donegal press, few pundits were prepared to opt for anything other than a comfortable win for the men of Breffni. After all, Cavan had appeared in more finals than any other county, while Donegal had never even qualified for a provincial decider.

For Donegal people, it was a case of unbounded joy at Clones on 14 July as they swept Cavan off their feet to record an emphatic 4-5 to 0-6 victory. If every Donegal player was a hero, none contributed more than centre half-forward Sean Ferriter, who had the game of his life. Feeding off a solid supply of ball from midfielders Frank McFeely and P.J. Flood, Ferriter orchestrated the Donegal attack where Harry Laverty, scorer of 2-3, took most advantage. Aside from corner-backs Gabriel Kelly and Jimmy Stafford, Cavan were way below form and there was no argument with Donegal's clear superiority on the day.

Expectations were high that the provincial decider would be a classic. Instead, the 35,000 people who travelled to Breffni Park on 28 July witnessed one of the worst finals in years. Whether or not it was stage fright, Donegal simply never got off the starting blocks. They failed to score in the first half and were fortunate to be just six points in arrears at the break. Without ever showing anything approaching their hallmark efficiency, Down romped to an easy 2-11 to 1-4 victory. Their outstanding performer was wing-back Patsy O'Hagan, who turned in a faultless hour. A notable contribution in their forward division came from Val Kane, who had lined out for the county's minors earlier in the afternoon. It says much about Donegal's display that their top men were in defence, where Bernard Brady, Sean O'Donnell, Paul Kelly and brilliant goalkeeper Seamus Hoare stood out.

Newspaper reports on the Leinster quarter-final clash between Dublin and Meath at Croke Park on 2 June make for very interesting reading. The focus was not so much that this was a poor game or that Dublin had managed to scrape through on a score of 2-6 to 2-5. Instead, it was a clear prediction that Dublin's championship prospects were practically non-existent. John Barrett of *The Irish Press* described them as 'The weakest Dublin football team I have ever seen play a championship game'. John D. Hickey of the *Irish Independent* commented: 'Neither side even remotely resembled a team capable of winning a provincial title, never mind an All-Ireland crown.'

The view seems to have been that, in the midst of a fog of mediocrity, the efforts of the Foley brothers and the injury-hampered Paddy Holden were sufficient to tip the balance against a Meath side on which only Martin Quinn and Bertie Cunningham impressed.

With Kildare showing serious form in their victory over Louth on 9 June, they were widely fancied to overcome the Metropolitans in the semi-final. Predicting Dublin's demise, the *Sunday Independent*'s Andy Croke opined that since the All-Whites had cast off their earlier reluctance to train they were much more formidable. In Kildare, optimism was high that stalwarts such as Danny Flood, Mick Carolan and Pa Connolly could lead the county into a long-overdue appearance in the Leinster Final. Unfortunately for Kildare, newly appointed Dublin selector Kevin Heffernan had a brainwave. He persuaded Des 'Snitchie' Ferguson to come out of retirement after a number of years' absence. The consequences were dramatic, as Ferguson was the central figure in their five-point win that advanced them into the provincial decider.

Laois and Offaly contested the second of the Leinster semi-finals the following Sunday. Offaly had been less than inspiring in accounting for a disappointing Longford in the quarter-final, while Noel Delaney had spearheaded an early blitz when Laois overcame Carlow at Athy on 26 May. Unexpectedly, Offaly sharpshooter Tommy Greene did not travel from London for this game and Laois were never seriously threatened in his absence, winning 2-7 to 0-9.

Des Foley had broken his wrist in the Kildare game, so Dublin were without him for their Leinster Final clash with Laois. If this gave a confidence boost to Laois, it was short-lived. Their powerful midfielder Fintan Walsh suffered an ankle injury in a club match just days before the game and, clearly unfit, he didn't last the pace. With Tom Browne giving Laois the edge at midfield, the game looked in the balance at the break, as Dublin led by just three points even though they were playing with wind advantage. On the resumption, it was 'Snitchie' Ferguson who once again unlocked the opposition defence to set up a more comfortable victory than the 2-11 to 2-9 scoreline suggests.

Galway were given little chance of toppling Kerry when they met in the first of the All-Ireland semi-finals on 4 August. Trailing by five points early in the second half, their prospects looked bleak. Their shining light all afternoon had been Pat Donnellan, and when the Dunmore man fisted the ball to the Kerry net the whole Galway team seemed to come alive. Kerry were hanging on by their fingernails with less than two minutes to go. In a tense finish, Seamus Leydon hit three points for the Tribesmen to give them an unexpected place in the final.

Championship surprises weren't finished there. Dublin, underdogs as in every previous round, turned in a solid performance to record a comprehensive 2-11 to 0-7 win over Down in the second semi-final. Reports on this game invariably focused on the ill-tempered nature of this no-holds-barred contest. Surprise was expressed that Waterford referee Con Crowley was so lenient, even when a man was kicked while lying on the ground. Amid all the carnage, it was Dublin's outstanding half-back line of Des McKane, Paddy Holden and Mick Kissane that laid the foundations for victory, with Holden having what John D. Hickey described as 'a truly remarkable hold on the game.' Down presented feeble opposition and, with only Joe Lennon playing well for the full hour, many took the view that Down would now return into football obscurity.

THE FINAL – 22 SEPTEMBER

The story goes that US president John F. Kennedy was in something of a quandary in the lead-up to the 1963 decider. Having recently been awarded the title of 'Freeman' in both Dublin and Galway, the unfortunate man didn't know which county to support. Whatever interest America's thirty-fifth president might have had in the game, the clamour for All-Ireland tickets was, as usual, at fever pitch. In addition to the over 87,000 who attended the game, the growing ownership of television sets meant that a record audience got to see the game.

In this, their fifth championship game of the year, Dublin were favourites for the first time. Having previously had to line out without such stalwarts as Paddy Holden, Paschal Flynn and Des Foley, they now had their full complement available. This was seen as giving them a clear advantage over the young Galway team.

While there were no assertions that the game was a classic, it was lauded for the fitness and speed on display. It also broke the pattern of unsavoury play evident in other games during that year's championship. The bare facts show that Dublin won, 1-9 to 0-10, after staging something of a resurrection in the second half. Behind this headline summary lies the reality that the Metropolitans capitalised on their limited chances, while Galway's forwards went on a bout of incredible squandermania.

Galway were well on top in the first half and their prospects seemed to improve when Dublin centre-back Paddy Holden had to retire with a head injury. Unfortunately for them, Holden's replacement, Paddy Downey, went on to play a stormer. Allied to this, Galway's profligacy in front of goal meant they held a mere two-point advantage at the break even though they had generally dominated the play.

When Brendan Quinn and Kevin Heffernan decided to switch Mickey Whelan to midfield at the start of the second half, the pendulum began to swing in Dublin's favour. Not alone did Whelan's constant probings create havoc for Galway, his arrival signalled a transformation in the performance of Des Foley. Where Galway's Mick Garrett and Mick Reynolds had earlier ruled the midfield roost, Dublin were now in the ascendancy. The big turning point came in the ninth minute of the second half. A well-taken line ball from Brian McDonald arrived in a crowded goalmouth as the inrushing Gerry Davey and Noel Fox stretched to connect, with the final touch to the net being credited to Davey.

Galway still had plenty of chances but their continued failure to convert was their downfall. Of their forwards, only Mattie McDonagh reached top form. Although it was an unsatisfactory day for

Pat Donnellan, Seamus Leydon and Cyril Dunne, it may be that it was the experience gained in this cauldron that steeled all three to the reach such dizzy heights in the following years. Elsewhere, their defence was generally sound, with Noel Tierney in exceptional form.

With only three of the 1958 team on board, Dublin had come from nowhere to take the crown. Ireland's fledgling television station had not yet come up with the man-of-the-match concept; if it had the then equivalent of Colm O'Rourke, Pat Spillane and Ciaran Whelan would have needed extra time to decide which of Leo Hickey or Mickey Whelan was most deserving.

FINAL STATISTICS

	Dublin	Galway
Full-time:	1-9	0-10
Half-time:	0-4	0-6
Scorers:	M. Whelan 0-5 (0-4 frees)	M. McDonagh 0-5
	G. Davey 1-0	C. Dunne 0-2 (0-2 frees)
	J. Timmons 0-2 (0-1 free)	J. Keenan 0-2
	D. Ferguson 0-1	S. Leydon 0-1
	B. McDonald 0-1	
Attendance:	87,106	
Referee:	Eamonn Moules (Wicklow)	

FINAL MISCELLANY

- Dublin's Des Foley achieved a rare distinction when leading his county to glory in 1963. He had also captained the Dublin minor team which took All-Ireland honours in 1958.
- In assessing where the blame lay for the fractious All-Ireland semi-final between Dublin and Down, *The Cork Examiner* speculated that: 'A Solomon with field glasses might apportion the overall blame for this regrettable exhibition of poor sportsmanship.'
- When Carlow beat Kilkenny in the first round of the Leinster Championship of 1963, Brendan Hayden accounted for 3-7 of their total.
- On the night of Dublin's 1963 success, the skyline resembled that of Halloween. *The Irish Press* reported that the Dublin Fire Brigade was called into action to deal with over forty bonfires around the county.
- Matters were more muted in Galway, however. In the days after the game, Sean Purcell organised a game between the 1956 team and the vanquished team of 1963. According to Jack Mahon's account of this encounter, things 'turned sour towards the 1963 team and some unnecessary abuse was directed at them from elements of the crowd'.

1963 – THE YEAR THAT WAS

- The assassination of the US president, John F. Kennedy, in Dallas on Friday 22 November evoked stunned reactions around the globe.

- When George Wallace became governor of Alabama in January 1963, his acceptance speech included the line 'segregation now, segregation tomorrow, and segregation forever!'
- In April 1963, there was concern expressed at the ballooning cost of land in Dublin when £9,750 was paid for ten acres of residential land in Howth.
- Judging by newspaper coverage, the well-being of Pope John XXIII was clearly a matter of serious concern for the people of Ireland. *The Irish Press* carried the following front-page headlines:

> Monday 27 May: 'Pope's Serious Relapse'
>
> Tuesday 28 May: 'Pope Improves, Still Weak'
>
> Wednesday 29 May: 'Pope Serene After Crisis'
>
> Thursday 30 May: 'Pope Improves Slightly'
>
> Saturday 1 June: 'Pope Emerges From Coma But Crisis Not Over'
>
> Monday 3 June: 'Pope Is Sinking Slowly'
>
> Tuesday 4 June: 'Holy Father Dies After Days of Suffering'

1963 TEAM LINE-OUTS

DUBLIN (WINNERS)

1. Paschal Flynn
(St Mary's, Saggart)

2. Leo Hickey
(Ballyboughal)

3. Lar Foley
(St Vincent's)

4. Bill Casey
(Na Fianna)

5. Des McKane
(St Vincent's)

6. Paddy Holden
(Clanna Gael)

7. Mick Kissane
(St Vincent's)

8. Des Foley
(St Vincent's)

9. John Timmons
(Sean McDermotts, also St Mary's,
Saggart and Annacurra, Wicklow)

10. Brian McDonald
(Synge Street, also St Coman's,
Roscommon and Castlebar Mitchels,
Mayo)

11. Mickey Whelan
(Clanna Gael, also St Vincent's)

12. Gerry Davey
(Clanna Gael)

13. Simon Behan
(St Vincent's)

14. Des 'Snitchie' Ferguson
(St Vincent's, also Gaeil Colmcille,
Meath)

15. Noel Fox
(St Vincent's)

Subs: Paddy Downey (St Brigid's) Played; Frank McPhillips (Inchicore Hibernians); Christy Kane (Clanna Gael); Aidan Donnelly (Clanna Gael); Eamonn Breslin (Ballyfermot Gaels, also Inchicore Hibernians); Pat Synnott (Clanna Gael); Sean Lee (St Anne's); Sean 'Blackie' Coen (St Vincent's)

GALWAY (RUNNERS-UP)

1. Michael Moore
(Menlough)

2. Enda Colleran
(Mountbellew-Moylough)

3. Noel Tierney
(Milltown)

4. Sean Meade
(St Grellan's, also Aodh Ruadh,
Donegal)

5. John Bosco McDermott
(Williamstown, also Dunmore
MacHales)

6. John Donnellan
(Dunmore MacHales, also
Carrantryla)

7. Martin Newell
(Fr Griffin's and UCG)

8. Mick Garrett
(Tuam Stars, also St Vincent's, Meath)
Capt.

9. Mick Reynolds
(Tuam Stars, also Ballaghaderreen,
Mayo and St Wilfred's, Manchester)

10. Cyril Dunne
(St Grellan's)

11. Mattie McDonagh
(Ballygar)

12. Pat Donnellan
(Dunmore MacHales)

13. John Keenan
(Dunmore MacHales, also
Carrantryla)

14. Sean Cleary
(Ballygar)

15. Seamus Leydon
(Dunmore MacHales, also Nemo
Rangers, Cork)

Subs: Brian Geraghty (Oughterard) Played; Tom Farrell (Ballygar); Sean Brennan (Milltown); Sean Keeley (St Grellan's); Sean 'Scan' Concannon (Milltown)

1964

'By far the best money spent by the Galway GAA in many moons was the fare home for Mairtín Newell from Germany.' This was the verdict of the *Connacht Tribune* when summarising the Galway v Sligo Connacht semi-final of 21 June 1964. In a game that saw the Tribesmen's half-time lead of nine points whittled away by the wizardry of Sligo's Mickey Kearins, it was the ever-astute Newell who steadied the ship as Galway crossed the line with just three points to spare. While the Connacht champions had negotiated their first championship hurdle of the year, and players such as Newell, Noel Tierney and Cyril Dunne had come up trumps, doubts still remained as to whether they had the temperament to exploit their undoubted talent.

The opposite side of the draw in Connacht looked like it was about to produce a major surprise when Leitrim led Roscommon in the closing stages of their clash at Carrick-on-Shannon on 7 June. Not for the first time, it was the redoubtable Gerry O'Malley who came to his county's rescue. Not listed in the original panel, he togged out at half-time and set up the equaliser when he entered the fray late in the game. The teams remained deadlocked when they again met two weeks later at Roscommon. Amid all sorts of confusion, and against the earlier directive of the Connacht Council, no extra time was played. Back in Carrick-on-Shannon the following Sunday, Roscommon made no mistake as they cantered to a 5-9 to 1-10 victory. Two goals each from P.J. Watson and Cyril Mahon and outstanding defending by Brendan O'Connor were the highlights for Roscommon.

With three games under their belt, confidence was high in Roscommon that their battle-hardened troops could make a serious onslaught on the provincial title. Such notions were well and truly shattered, however, when they fell comprehensively to Mayo in the semi-final at Castlebar on 5 July. Not even the best efforts of Roscommon's outstanding centre-back George Geraghty could stem the tide of attack after attack by the Mayo forward division in which Mick Connaughton, Frank McDonald and Davy Doris were rampant.

Amazingly, when Galway played Mayo in the Connacht Final on 19 July, it was the first time in thirteen years that these great rivals had clashed in the provincial decider. The level of interest in the game was unprecedented, with a record crowd of over 30,000 cramming into Tuam Stadium in anticipation of a classic. Instead, they were treated to a footballing exhibition by the men in maroon as they proceeded to crush Mayo, 2-12 to 1-5. According to the *Connacht Tribune*, they were 'ticking over like a well-oiled machine', while Mick Dunne of *The Irish Press* was convinced that they would 'make a tremendous bid for the Sam Maguire Cup'.

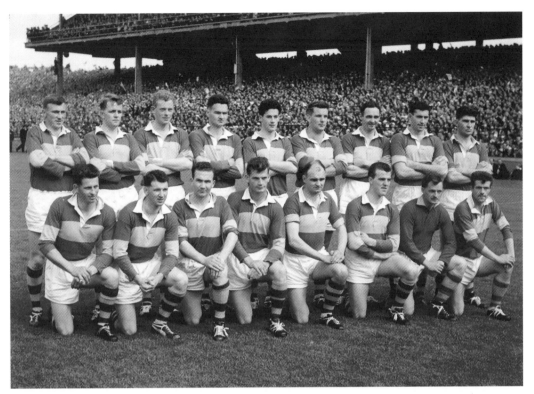

Kerry, beaten by Galway in the 1964 Final. Back (l–r): Donie O'Sullivan, Mick Morris, Paud O'Donoghue, Mick O'Connell, Pat Griffin, Frank O'Leary, Brian Sheehy, Mick Fleming, Mick O'Dwyer; front (l–r): Tom Long, Seamus Murphy, Jo Jo Barrett, Jerdie O'Connor, Niall Sheehy, Denis O'Sullivan, Johnny Culloty, Pete Hanley. *Image courtesy of the National Library of Ireland.*

Although they didn't show a weak link, Galway particularly benefitted from the inspired play of goalkeeper Johnny Geraghty, midfielder Mick Reynolds and the bewildering movement of a forward division in which Sean Cleary and Christy Tyrrell were outstanding. Willie Casey and Joe Langan were Mayo's best on this day of bitter disappointment for a county without a provincial title since 1955.

In 1964, the prize for winning the Connacht title was an All-Ireland semi-final date with the champions of Leinster. Galway would have expected to capture the provincial crown. They would also have expected a rematch with Dublin, their conquerors in 1963. The Metropolitans started obligingly with a hard won, but deserved, 1-14 to 1-5 victory over Carlow at Newbridge on 24 May. Mick Nolan and Eddie Walker had created plenty of problems for the champions until the Dublin half-back line of Des McKane, Paddy Holden and Noel Fox settled into their stride and closed off the scoring threat.

A delegation of Dublin selectors travelled to Tullamore the following Sunday to size up their semi-final opposition as Laois and Westmeath battled it out. They spent most of the hour assessing how to deal with the combination play of Westmeath's forwards and penetrate a solid defence, built around the masterful Mick Carley. With Westmeath leading by nine points at the break and still seven ahead with just minutes to go, the result looked a foregone conclusion. Repeating the act of grand larceny perpetrated by Jack Kenna the previous year, Laois again came with a late flourish as two Noel Delaney goals in the dying embers of the game dumped a luckless Westmeath out of the championship.

In a game that Mitchel Cogley of the *Irish Independent* labelled as not having a single memorable moment, Dublin got the better of Laois, 0-8 to 1-2, in their semi-final clash at Tullamore. Although Dublin were the better side, Laois had a justifiable claim for a late penalty denied when Sean Price was felled in the goalmouth.

The second of the Leinster semi-finals saw neighbours Meath and Louth do battle at Croke Park on 28 June. Meath's path had been an easy one, with a very subdued Kildare offering only token resistance in the quarter-final. The performances of the three Quinn brothers had been a revelation in this game which the Royal County won by ten points. Louth were unimpressive in their first-round win over Wexford but they turned on the style when beating Offaly, 1-9 to 1-4. The great play of midfielders Mick Gartland and Val Murphy and the attacking threat posed by Liam Leech, Mick 'Muckle' McKeown and Gerry Clifford suggested that Louth might well have the measure of Meath.

When the sides met at Croke Park on 28 June, they served up a great game before 32,000 spectators. A replay looked on the cards when Louth's Kevin Beahan scored an equalising goal with just two minutes remaining. Not to be denied, however, Meath responded with late points from Dave Carty and Paddy Mulvany as they advanced to their first Leinster Final since 1955.

Memories of the 1955 Leinster Final, when Dublin destroyed Meath, were high on the agenda in the lead-up to the 1964 decider. It was Dublin who now carried the tag of favourites, but nobody was predicting a rout of 1955 proportions. They were all wrong. A rout it was, only this time the boot was very much on the Meath foot. The final score of 2-12 to 1-7 didn't fully reflect Meath's superiority as they dictated the play from start to finish. With Jack Quinn and Peter Moore in charge at midfield, and Dinny Donnelly, Bertie Cunningham and the tigerish 'Red' Collier leading the defence, the Meath forwards were given plenty of opportunities to show their wares. Ollie Shanley, Jimmy Walsh and former Laois star Tom Browne took full advantage as the Royals booked their semi-final slot with Galway. As so often in the past, Paddy Holden was Dublin's top performer while Brian McDonald put in a great hour.

The Munster Championship opened with two games on 14 June. In a drab affair at Dungarvan, Cork had their expected easy semi-final win over Waterford. The chief scorers in their 2-8 to 1-2 victory were Willie O'Leary, J.J. Murphy and the industrious Paul Sullivan. On the same day in Limerick, Tipperary had a single point to spare over Clare after a very scrappy encounter. This was a game that Clare could have won but for some very poor shooting. While Tipperary forwards Gus Danagher, John O'Donoghue and 'Babs' Keating were in fine fettle and accounted for most of their team's scores, the top performer on the day was Clare's Tom Mangan, first at centre-back and later at midfield.

Tipperary were now through to a semi-final date with reigning champions Kerry, but few gave them much chance of springing a surprise. When they met at Thurles on a miserably wet day, there

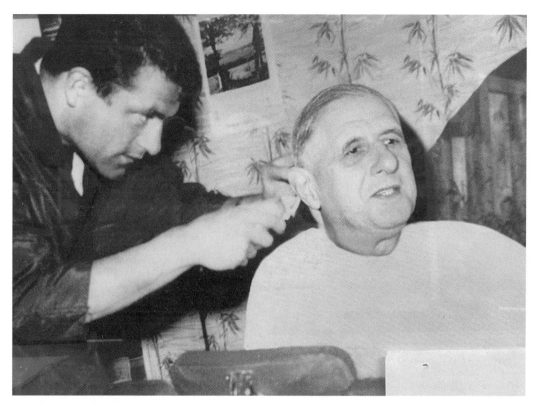

When General Charles de Gaulle resigned as French president in 1969, he travelled to Ireland for a well-earned holiday. The highlight of his six-week break was having his hair trimmed by Kenmare's Pete Hanley, a member of Kerry's 1964 All-Ireland panel. *Image courtesy of Pete Hanley.*

was no upset to the form book as the Kingdom eased home, 1-14 to 1-7, with Bernie O'Callaghan their scorer-in-chief. Tipperary did, however, give their supporters grounds for optimism. The displays of such as Patsy Dawson, Patsy Conway, John Keating and Gus Danagher suggested that they might soon make a breakthrough.

All of this meant that Cork and Kerry would, once again, contest the provincial showdown. When they met on a wet and miserable day at the Cork Athletic Grounds on 19 July, Kerry were clear winners, 2-11 to 1-8. The newspaper reports on this game paint a vivid picture of the difference in the standards expected of the two counties. That Kerry won pulling up, and never looked in any danger, paled into insignificance in the context of what was perceived as a performance well short of All-Ireland standard. Only a handful of their players merited praise, with Niall Sheehy their outstanding performer, while Mick Fleming, Jerdie O'Connor and Paud O'Donoghue were generally solid. On the other hand, even though Cork were comprehensively outplayed, the result was deemed to represent real progress for the county. Newcomers Flor Hayes and Johnny Carroll were a great boost to their forward division. The consensus was that, with time, and building a team around such as Mick Bohane, Gus Harrington, Con O'Sullivan and Willie O'Leary, Cork could again become a major footballing force. For Kerry, their strategic time frame was much more short term: an All-Ireland semi-final date with the champions of Ulster the following month.

The draw for the Ulster Championship had joint favourites, Down and Cavan, on opposite sides and few would have betted against this great rivalry being renewed in the final. Cavan started out on 14 June with a nine-point win over a weak Derry combination that had to line out without three of their selected players. The game, which started twenty-seven minutes late, was played in atrocious conditions, the only highlight being a virtuoso performance from Cavan's Ray Carolan. Two weeks later, Cavan clinched their place in the provincial final when they overcame Donegal, 1-9 to 0-7, at Irvinestown. With eight different Donegal players recording wides, they could, and perhaps should, have won this game. As it was, the usual masterclass from Carolan and an impressive performance by former Leitrim player Jimmy O'Donnell swung matters in the Cavan men's favour.

Down had their share of good fortune as they manoeuvred their way to the Ulster Final. In a six-point win over Monaghan at Ballybay on 21 June, their cause was helped in no small way by the Farney men's tally of nineteen wides over the hour. Their two-point victory over Antrim on 5 July had more than a tinge of good luck. Antrim, with midfielders Danny Dougan and Des McNeill in the ascendancy, and Jimmy Ward, Jim McCorry and Tony McAtamney defending heroically, held the upper hand for much of the game. But for the shooting boots of Paddy Doherty and a controversial goal from James McCartan, the championship curtain would have dropped for the Mourne men.

If good fortune was the key to Down's journey to the provincial final, complacency was their downfall in the decider. In what Donal Carroll of the *Irish Independent* described as 'a free riddled, pull-and-drag monstrosity', Down seemed to be sauntering to another title until Cavan hit them for 2-3 inside five minutes. Substitute Peter Prichard from Bailieboro was hardly on the field when, combining with his former teacher Jimmy O'Donnell, he rattled the Down net. He repeated the dose two minutes later. In a helter-skelter finish, the Breffni men held out for a three-point win that had looked highly improbable only fifteen minutes earlier.

The first of the All-Ireland semi-finals took place on 9 August and saw Galway beat Meath, 1-9 to 0-10, in a game that could have gone either way. Showing greater speed and combination play than their physically bigger opponents, Galway needed late scores from Mick Reynolds and Sean Cleary to guide them home. The highlight of the game was a magnificent performance from Galway full-back Noel Tierney. Johnny Geraghty and Enda Colleran were others to shine against a Meath team that had Pat Reynolds and Jack Quinn in top form.

Expectations of a close game in the second semi-final between Kerry and Cavan were seriously wide of the mark. Showing no weak links, Kerry simply coasted to the final, 2-12 to 0-6. Cavan's cause was not helped by the fact that talisman Ray Carolan carried a leg injury into the game, but it's doubtful whether Carolan at his best could have put a dent in Kerry's dominance.

THE FINAL – 27 SEPTEMBER

Kerry had two notable absentees when they lined out against Galway in the 1964 decider. Bernie O'Callaghan hadn't yet recovered from an operation for appendicitis, while clerical student Tony Barrett followed in the 1962 footsteps of Donie O'Sullivan and returned to Maynooth College before the end of September. Despite these losses, neutral commentators remained broadly divided as to the likely outcome of the game. All agreed it would be a tight affair, with the typical 'down to the wire' metaphor liberally invoked.

The reality was very different. From start to finish, Galway held the upper hand against a strangely out-of-sorts Kerry. The final score was 0-15 to 0-10, but this scarcely captures the extent of Galway's superiority. In a team of stars, none shone more brightly than team captain John Donnellan. Cyril Dunne struck nine points, three from play, and completely exorcised the ghosts of 1963. Johnny Geraghty and Mattie McDonagh were others to come in for special mention, but this was a team without a weakness, and whose intelligent combination play brought football to a new level. In the words of *The Cork Examiner*, 'the day of space devouring kicking is gone'.

Kerry never got into their stride. The decision to select Mick O'Connell at half-forward, rather than his familiar midfield berth, didn't work. A further decision to introduce the still recuperating O'Callaghan late in the game was seen as an act of desperation, suggesting that Kerry's traditional cool head approach was absent on the day. Not even strong performances from Denis O'Sullivan and Niall Sheehy, together with wing-forward Pat Griffin, could lift the team out of its general air of despondency.

More than anything else, the final of 1964 will always be remembered for the general sense of gloom which descended in its wake. Within minutes of accepting the trophy, thereby realising his life's ambition, John Donnellan was told that his father, Mick, had passed away during the game. It then emerged that Mick Higgins, captain of Galway's 1934 heroes, had died while watching the game on television. Within days, it was Kerry's turn to mourn when selector Tom Spillane died suddenly. A man steeped in every aspect of Kerry GAA, he left a wife and four young children. It took another generation for the full extent of his legacy to Kerry to become apparent. His three sons, Pat, Mick and Tom, collected a total of nineteen All-Ireland medals, more than any other family in the history of the game.

FINAL STATISTICS

	Galway	Kerry
Full-time:	0-15	0-10
Half-time:	0-7	0-3
Scorers:	C. Dunne 0-9 (0-7 frees)	M. O'Connell 0-7 (0-5 frees)
	S. Leydon 0-2	P. Griffin 0-2
	J. Keenan 0-1	M. O'Dwyer 0-1 (0-1 free)

	M. McDonagh 0-1
	C. Tyrrell 0-1
	S. Cleary 0-1
Attendance:	76,498
Referee:	Jimmy Hatton (Wicklow)

FINAL MISCELLANY

- At a time when the ban on foreign games was rigidly policed, many diehards took exception to Dublin's Eamonn Breslin when he headed the ball to the net against Laois at Croke Park on 1 November. In his first game as an inter-county referee, Kildare's Seamus Aldridge had no hesitation in confirming the validity of the score.
- *The Irish Press* marvelled at the physique of the Meath team that won the Leinster title. It reported: 'New Leinster champions Meath are undoubtedly the biggest football side to come out of the province in years, with an average weight of 12 stone 10¾ lbs. and an average height of 5ft. 10½ ins.'
- Johnny Geraghty's understudy as Galway goalkeeper was eighteen-year-old Frank McLoughlin. He was drafted in for Geraghty's clubmate Michael Moore, who was unavailable after being recalled to the seminary.
- As a measure of dedication to refereeing duties, it would be hard to surpass the commitment of future GAA President Dr Mick Loftus. While in New York, he learned that he had been appointed to referee the Minor Final between Offaly and Cork. At his own expense, he crossed the Atlantic to take charge of the game.

1964 – THE YEAR THAT WAS

- Having been found guilty of an anti-government conspiracy, Nelson Mandela was given a life sentence. He was released in 1990, after serving almost twenty-six years in prison.
- Cassius Clay (Muhammad Ali), later honoured as the Sportsman of the Century, beat Sonny Liston on 25 February to become World Heavyweight Boxing Champion.
- Taking America by storm, and having attracted a viewing audience of 73 million on *The Ed Sullivan Show*, The Beatles held the top five positions on the US Billboard Top Forty singles in April 1964.
- The Criminal Justice Act eliminated the death penalty in Ireland for all but the murder of gardaí, diplomats and prison officers. It would be another twenty-six years before capital punishment would be removed altogether from the statute books.

1964 TEAM LINE-OUTS

GALWAY (WINNERS)

1. Johnny Geraghty
(Mountbellew-Moylough, also Kilkerrin-Clonberne and Fr Griffin's)

2. Enda Colleran
(Mountbellew-Moylough)

3. Noel Tierney
(Milltown)

4. John Bosco McDermott
(Dunmore MacHales, also
Williamstown)

5. John Donnellan
(Dunmore MacHales, also
Carrantryla) Capt.

6. Sean Meade
(St Grellan's, also Aodh Ruadh,
Donegal)

7. Martin Newell
(Fr Griffin's)

8. Mick Garrett
(Tuam Stars, also St Vincent's, Meath)

9. Mick Reynolds
(Tuam Stars, also Ballaghaderreen,
Mayo and St Wilfred's, Manchester)

10. Cyril Dunne
(St Grellan's)

11. Mattie McDonagh
(Ballygar)

12. Seamus Leydon
(Dunmore MacHales, also Nemo
Rangers, Cork)

13. Christy Tyrrell
(Mountbellew-Moylough)

14. Sean Cleary
(Ballygar)

15. John Keenan
(Dunmore MacHales, also Carrantryla)

Subs: Frank McLoughlin (St Jarlath's College, Tuam, also Dunmore MacHales); Kieran O'Connor (Fr Griffin's); Tommy Sands (Ballygar, also Fr Griffin's); Pat Donnellan (Dunmore MacHales); Brian Geraghty (Oughterard); Tommy Keenan (Dunmore MacHales); Michael Coen (Killererin)

KERRY (RUNNERS-UP)

1. Johnny Culloty
(Killarney Legion)

2. Mick Morris
(John Mitchels)

3. Niall Sheehy
(John Mitchels)

4. Paud O'Donoghue
(Ballylongford)

5. Denis O'Sullivan
(Kerins O Rahillys)

6. Seamus Murphy
(Camp, also Lispole)

7. Jerdie O'Connor
(Ballydonoghue)

8. Mick Fleming
(Currow and UCC, also St Finbarr's,
Cork and Bishopstown, Cork)

9. Donie O'Sullivan
(Clanna Gael, Dublin, also Spa and Dr
Crokes)

10. Pat Griffin
(Glenbeigh/Glencar, also Clonakilty,
Cork)

11. Mick O'Dwyer
(Waterville)

12. Mick O'Connell
(Valentia, also Waterville)

13. Frank O'Leary
(St Mary's, Cahirciveen, Multyfarnham
College, Westmeath and Mayo)

14. Tom Long
(Dr Crokes, also An Ghaeltacht and
Erin's Hope, Dublin)

15. Jo Jo Barrett
(Austin Stacks)

Subs: John McCarthy (Ballylongford) Played; Kevin Coffey (Clanna Gael, Dublin, also Beaufort and Dundalk Young Irelands, Louth) Played; Bernie O'Callaghan (Moyvane) Played; Vincent Lucey (Laune Rangers, also Glenbeigh/Glencar); Derry O'Shea (John Mitchels); Pete Hanley (Kenmare Shamrocks); Tim O'Sullivan (Castleisland Desmonds); Dom O'Donnell (John Mitchels); John Burke (Milltown-Castlemaine); Brian Sheehy (John Mitchels)

1965

When reporting on Mayo's easy 2-13 to 1-6 win over Roscommon in the provincial quarter-final of 1965, Michael O'Connell of *The Connaught Telegraph* wrote: 'Leaving the pitch, the question of how Mayo would fare against Galway was being asked on all sides. Mindful of what happened last year, people were not too quick to commit themselves.'

The Irish Press and *Irish Independent* also expressed reservations about Mayo's prospects against the reigning All-Ireland champions. Perhaps the doubts had to do with a less than spectacular performance against a below-par Roscommon outfit, for which only Tony Whyte and Eamonn Curley were up to form. Maybe it was down to the fact that only Mick Ruane, P.J. Loftus, Cormac Hanley and debutant Ray Prendergast hit the highs on a team that kicked sixteen wides over the hour. Whatever the reason, this was a very unfortunate case of the collective 'jumping the gun' – Sligo, and one Mickey Kearins, stood between Mayo and a Connacht Final meeting with the champions.

Sligo had opened their campaign on 20 June, but their 4-12 to 0-6 win over Leitrim didn't seem to register any alarm bells in Mayo. Superior in every department, Sligo's star against Leitrim was centre-forward Danny McHugh, who bagged 2-5 of their total. When it came to the semi-final on 4 July, McHugh was forced to cry off after the death of his father that morning. Everything was going according to plan for Mayo when they led by nine points early in the second half. Their problem was that Sligo, to a man, simply wouldn't relent and they proceeded to embark on the mother and father of all comebacks. With Kearins leading the charge, the Sligo men converted the nine-point deficit into a three-point victory, 2-11 to 2-8, and the irony was that the decisive goal was scored by Bill Shannon, a native of Mayo. As for Kearins, this extract from the *Western People* gives us a flavour of his performance: 'Prompting and probing, weaving and moving, alert and confident, he was as elusive as a slippery eel and had the whole defence guessing every time he touched the ball.'

The mood in Mayo after this game can be gauged from the response of County Secretary Johnny Mulvey when asked for his view: 'What I thought is not printable!'

Sligo were now into the Connacht Final against a Galway team that was having its first championship outing of the year. When they met at Tuam on 31 July, Sligo led by seven points towards the end of the first half and a shock result was very much on the cards. It was then that Mattie McDonagh began to exert serious influence on proceedings and, with strong support from John Donnellan, John Keenan and Christy Tyrrell, led Galway back into contention and, ultimately, to a narrow three-point victory. One of the highlights was Sligo's first goal, engineered by Mickey

Kearins, and finished with aplomb by Danny McHugh. So, after just one game, Galway were back in the All-Ireland semi-final where they would be pitted against the champions of Ulster.

As had become the pattern in recent seasons, Cavan and Down were expected to slog it out to see who would be the Ulster standard-bearers for 1965. Down started out on 13 June with a runaway victory, 3-13 to 1-6, against Tyrone. The day belonged to Paddy Doherty, who had a personal tally of 2-7 as the Mourne men fought back from an early five-point deficit. They were much less impressive in their semi-final win over Antrim at Newry on 4 July when they were fortunate to get through, 0-10 to 1-5.

The real talking points, on and off the field, of the 1965 Ulster Championship emerged from the opposite side of the draw. When Cavan's Ray Carolan was declared unfit to start, the tag of favourites swung even more in Donegal's direction before they met at Ballybofey on 20 June. The Breffni men found themselves six points down at the break and the time had come to take a gamble on Carolan. This paid immediate dividends in the form of midfield supremacy and ultimately paved the way for Charlie Gallagher to hit the equaliser with the last kick of the game.

In the replay two weeks later at Breffni Park, it was the turn of Donegal to force a rematch when Pauric McShea escaped the clutches of the Cavan defence to fire over the equaliser. Despite the entreaties of referee Jimmy Martin from Tyrone, Donegal did not reappear for extra time. Cavan claimed victory on account of Donegal's refusal to continue. After three hours' deliberation, the Ulster Council voted, ten to eight, that the game be again replayed, with Cavan retaining home advantage.

The third game was yet another close affair. Donegal seemed to be on their way to a famous victory but Charlie Gallagher and Seamus McMahon both scored in the last minute to swing the result in Cavan's favour, 0-9 to 0-8. A review of the respective local newspapers (the national newspapers were on strike that summer) gives a sense of the acrimony arising from this three-game saga. There was even a suggestion that Donegal would appeal the result on the grounds that Cavan wing-back Donal O'Grady was ineligible to play since he lived in Meath, the county of his birth. This threat was described in *The Anglo Celt* as an attempt to win by a 'Technical Knock Out'. For its part, the *Donegal Democrat* confined itself to a pithy heading: 'Robbed, Not Beaten, At Breffni.'

Elsewhere, Monaghan, short several regulars, were underdogs in their first-round game against Fermanagh at Irvinestown on 6 June. Their task seemed to become an impossibility when, having already lost their goalkeeper Harry McAree, a 'sizzling' clash of heads led to the departure of Seamus McElroy and Seamus Mulligan as well as Fermanagh's Ray Dundas. They escaped complete disaster a few minutes later when yet another collision involving two of their players, John McArdle and Danny Hughes, led to a hold-up in play, before both were allowed to continue. Against all the odds, the Monaghan men proceeded to take control of the game and progressed to the quarter-final with a 2-12 to 1-5 victory.

Monaghan's good fortune ended when they came up against a Jimmy Whan-inspired Armagh fifteen which qualified for the semi-final against Cavan with a 3-7 to 1-9 victory. When Armagh

Johnny Geraghty, goalkeeper on Galway's great three-in-a-row team, shows the agility that won him the reputation as one of the finest netminders ever to play the game. *Sportsfile*.

met Cavan at Clones on a miserable, wet day in the second semi-final, they were at the wrong end of a 1-10 to 0-4 scoreline, and they failed to raise any flag in the second half.

After all the excitement of the earlier rounds, the Ulster Final was a disappointing affair that saw Down regain the title with a 3-5 to 1-8 victory. In this undistinguished and hard-hitting game, it was Down's ability to take their limited scoring chances that was the difference between the sides. Sean O'Neill (two) and Paddy Doherty were Down's goalscorers while Charlie Gallagher was on the mark for Cavan. All-Ireland champions Galway would be the next hurdle for Down as they sought to recapture the glory days of 1960–61.

The fact that fewer than 1,000 patrons turned up at Limerick on 13 June, to see Kerry go through the motions in the Munster semi-final against Clare, tells everything about the expected result. Clare failed to replicate their impressive form from the previous round as Kerry overwhelmed them. Their cause was not helped by infighting over team selection but, regardless of personnel, they were never going to topple the Kingdom. The final score of 9-10 to 0-4 reflected the gulf between the two teams.

The prelude to Cork's semi-final game saw Limerick dispose of Waterford, 4-10 to 0-6, with hurling stars Eamon Cregan and Bernie Hartigan, together with Mick Tynan and Pat Murphy, to the fore. Despite this sixteen-point win, *The Irish Press* concluded that Limerick 'failed to impress' and their semi-final prospects against Cork were all but dismissed. Maybe such comments lulled Cork into a false sense of security but, for whatever reason, they were simply no match for Limerick when they met at Killarney on 20 June. Goals from Cregan and Tynan and a wonderful performance by team captain Tony Fitzgerald were the key to this success. Limerick were now in their first provincial decider since 1896, a year in which they had won their second All-Ireland title.

The Munster Final produced the expected result, Kerry eventually pulling away for a nine-point win, 2-16 to 2-7. That Kerry were deserving winners was undisputed, but Limerick performed gallantly and indeed led by five points at the break. Kerry's traditional craft and guile showed in the end, with such as Jo Jo Barrett, Denis O'Sullivan and Vincent Lucey leading the charge.

The real story of the 1965 Leinster Championship was the arrival on the scene of a highly talented Longford team. When they lined out against Offaly in the first round at Mullingar on 2 May, their record against the Faithful County was one championship win in the previous twenty-seven years. Having undergone an intensive training regime under the direction of Cavan's Mick Higgins and Down's Joe Lennon, they overcame hot favourites Offaly, 1-5 to 0-5. But for the outstanding play of P.J. McIntyre, Offaly's defeat would have been much heavier against a well-balanced outfit whose top men were Terry McGovern, Brendan Barden and Bobby Burns.

It was very much a case of Laois shooting themselves in the foot when it was their turn to take on the Longford men at Mullingar on 6 June. They had pleaded, successfully, with the Leinster Council to have the game postponed so that their full-forward Noel Delaney could make it home from Boston. What they didn't seem to realise was that the extra week allowed Longford's Bobby Burns to serve out his one-month suspension. Naturally, Burns proceeded to torment Laois and was one of the key men, along with Jimmy Flynn, Jackie Devine and John McCowell, in leading his county into a surprise provincial semi-final appearance.

With Leinster champions Meath next in line, Longford's fairytale journey was surely about to come to an end. Or was it? In what *The Cork Examiner* described as 'the greatest Gaelic football upset in years', Longford continued their giant-killing exploits with a thoroughly deserved 2-8 to 1-7 victory. Goals from Sean Murray and Mickey Burns set Longford on their way and the *Longford Leader* included these in their list of candidates for man of the match. Others picked out for special mention were John Donlon, Jimmy Hannify, Jimmy Flynn, Bobby Burns, Larry Gillen and Brendan Gilmore, before the clearly ecstatic scribe finally plumped for Brendan Barden as 'Numero Uno'.

The opposite side of the Leinster draw went very much along predictable lines. Kildare had easy wins over Wicklow and Carlow to progress to the semi-final against Dublin, comfortable winners over Wexford. Curiously, the newspaper headlines covering their respective quarter-final victories labelled both Kildare and Dublin as 'unimpressive'. When it came to their semi-final clash, Dublin were so beset by injuries that the Lilywhites were strongly tipped to advance. In the event, Dublin cruised to a 1-11 to 0-5 victory, with John Timmons playing a blinder, and scoring seven points in the process.

The record books show that Dublin took the Leinster crown on a score of 3-6 to 0-9. This bare statistic does not do justice to Longford's contribution to a great game, the result of which could have been so different. Forced by injuries to use two substitutes within the first six minutes, Longford then had to endure a missed penalty and the concession of one of the softest goals imaginable. With every man playing his part, they fought gallantly to the end but simply couldn't close the gap against the Des Foley-inspired Metropolitans.

The first of the All-Ireland semi-finals saw Kerry and Dublin battle it out at Croke Park on 8 August. Dublin were first off the mark and were five points to the good before Kerry registered a score. Maintaining the advantage, and holding a two-point lead at the break, Dublin seemed well positioned for victory. The introduction of Mick O'Dwyer into the Kerry forward division changed the whole flow of the game as he proceeded to make and take the scores that finally saw Kerry home, 4-8 to 2-6.

There was no goal fest when Galway and Down met in the second semi-final on 22 August. In a dogged war of attrition, the Tribesmen battled their way through for a narrow, but deserved, win. As the scoreline of 0-10 to 0-7 suggests, this was a game in which defences were on top. To the fore was Galway's captain, Enda Colleran, who time and again thwarted the Down attack as he led his team to their third consecutive final.

THE FINAL – 26 SEPTEMBER

Prior to 1965, the last time the same two counties had met in successive finals was in 1940 and 1941, when Kerry beat Galway in both years. Galway had put a stop to Kerry's championship gallop in both 1963 and 1964, so it is no surprise that this latest encounter was expected to generate more than the usual quota of competitive tension. In the event, the nature of the exchanges turned out to be off the scale, when measured against even the most robust of championship finals. Mitchel Cogley of the *Irish Independent* penned the following: 'It was a rough-and-tumble, catch-as-catch-can final, virtually devoid of the game's skills, and will hold no worth-while memories. A line in the record books.' Framing his report against the backdrop of an unprecedented television audience, complete with its international dimension, Mick Dunne of *The Irish Press* referred to the game as 'an embarrassment'.

That Galway won, 0-12 to 0-9, was widely regarded as merely incidental to the main story. Not that this would have worried Enda Colleran and his men as they became the first Galway team to win successive titles.

Galway's day started with the bad news that Mick Reynolds, suffering from tonsillitis, would be unable to start. He was replaced by Mick Garrett who, despite having been on the long-term injury list, turned in a highly commendable performance. It was universally agreed that Galway were the better team. In contrast to their Kerry counterparts, they had a forward division whose combination play and speed regularly left the opposition defences floundering.

From the moment John Keenan fisted Galway into the lead after three minutes, they were in front all the way. Kerry did narrow the gap to a single point early in the second half but Galway responded by relocating Pat Donnellan to mark Mick O'Connell, where the Dunmore stalwart proceeded to harry the Kerry man out of the limelight. This restored the balance of power, paving the way for the Tribesmen to ease to victory.

After so many robust, and indeed dangerous, challenges early in the game it was something of a surprise that, late in the game, referee Mick Loftus invoked the ultimate sanction against Galway's John Donnellan and Kerry's Derry O'Shea after a relatively innocuous altercation. John 'Thorny' O'Shea was later given the opportunity to keep his brother company in the dugout when he too received his marching orders in the dying minutes. An editorial in the *Sunday Independent* of 3 October likened the sendings-off to 'killing lambs and letting the ravening wolves escape'.

Bertie Donohoe, writing under the pen name 'JBD' in the *Connacht Tribune*, adopted a novel approach when rating the performances of the players on the victorious team. Allocating grades as in college exams, all fifteen of Galway's warriors received First Class Honours. A perfect score of 100 was reserved for just two players: goalkeeper Johnny Geraghty and wing-back Martin Newell.

None of the Kerry players were accorded anything approaching First Class Honours in the numerous post mortems conducted within the county. Johnny Culloty and the defence generally were deemed competent, while O'Connell's brilliance was universally acknowledged, even by those bemoaning his inclination to take time out occasionally. The forward division found itself in the line of fire from all sides including, incredibly, from team trainer and County Chairman Dr Jim Brosnan: 'There isn't a forward who can kick a ball from forty yards out with any degree of accuracy. That's the trouble.' Dr Jim went further: 'The trouble is that we haven't got them. You've got to have bricks and mortar to build. We haven't got the raw material.'

Four years later, no fewer than seven of this team would form the backbone of the side which would deliver Kerry's twenty-first title.

FINAL STATISTICS

	Galway	Kerry
Full-time:	0-12	0-9
Half-time:	0-7	0-4
Scorers:	C. Dunne 0-4 (0-4 frees)	B. O'Callaghan 0-6 (0-5 frees)
	S. Leydon 0-3	M. O'Connell 0-2 (0-2 frees)
	P. Donnellan 0-2 (0-2 frees)	M. O'Dwyer 0-1
	J. Keenan 0-2	
	M. Garrett 0-1	
Attendance:	77,735	
Referee:	Mick Loftus (Mayo)	

FINAL MISCELLANY

- This was the first year that the number of players contesting the throw-in was limited to the four midfielders.
- Members of the Kerry County Board took grave umbrage when the *Sunday Independent* described the approach of one of their players thus: 'we shall not specify the county to which one man belongs, but he went around like a roaring lion, seeking whom he could devour.'
- After this notoriously tough final, Galway captain Enda Colleran was greeted with a chorus of booing when he asked for the customary three cheers for the losing team. Colleran stood his ground, however, and insisted that the vanquished Kerry team be accorded due respect.
- Writing in *The Connaught Telegraph*, former Mayo footballer Joe McFadden had an interesting view on the use of substitutes: 'The substitute rule is being shamefully abused. It was introduced so that an injured player could be replaced during the course of a game. It was not intended that men could be taken off just because they were having an off day.'
- When Cavan and Donegal drew in the Ulster quarter-final at Ballybofey on 20 June the replay was to take place the following Sunday. However, *The Anglo Celt* explained that since Donegal brothers Brendan and Frank McFeely would be attending the enthronement of their uncle as Bishop of Raphoe, it became 'necessary to put the game back a further week'.

1965 – THE YEAR THAT WAS

- At 195 feet (59.5 metres) high, Dublin's Liberty Hall was the tallest building in Ireland when it was completed in 1965.
- In January 1965, Taoiseach Seán Lemass travelled to Belfast to meet Northern Ireland prime minister Terence O'Neill. This was the first such meeting since Ireland was partitioned in 1922.
- Giving an account of a Dublin society wedding in October 1965, the *Sunday Independent* provided its readers with details of the fashion on view and of the elegant surroundings for the reception. However, the bold headline above a photo of the bridal party left no doubt as to the most significant feature of the event. It read: 'A honeymoon in Canary Islands…'
- Irish pole vault champion Liam Gleeson suffered an unusual misfortune at the final of the Munster Track and Field Championships at Cobh on 11 July. Having already secured the title, he set his sights on a new Irish record height. Just at the end of his run-up, a stray dog flashed across the back of the pit, forcing the unfortunate Gleeson to abandon his effort. Understandably upset, the Roscrea man gently asked: 'Who owns that ****ing dog?!'

1965 TEAM LINE-OUTS

GALWAY (WINNERS)

1. Johnny Geraghty
(Mountbellew-Moylough, also Kilkerrin-Clonberne and Fr Griffin's)

2. Enda Colleran
(Mountbellew-Moylough) Capt.

3. Noel Tierney
(Milltown)

4. John Bosco McDermott
(Dunmore MacHales, also Williamstown)

5. John Donnellan
(Dunmore MacHales, also Carrantryla)

6. Sean Meade
(St Grellan's, also Aodh Ruadh, Donegal)

7. Martin Newell
(Fr Griffin's)

8. Pat Donnellan
(Dunmore MacHales)

9. Mick Garrett
(Tuam Stars, also St Vincent's, Meath)

10. Cyril Dunne
(St Grellan's)

11. Mattie McDonagh
(Ballygar)

12. Seamus Leydon
(Dunmore MacHales, also Nemo Rangers, Cork)

13. Christy Tyrrell
(Mountbellew)

14. Sean Cleary
(Ballygar)

15. John Keenan
(Dunmore MacHales, also Carrantryla)

Subs: Mick Reynolds (Tuam Stars, also Ballaghaderreen, Mayo and St Wilfred's, Manchester) Played; Greg Higgins (Tuam Stars); Tommy Sands (Ballygar); Tommy Keenan (Dunmore MacHales); Brian Geraghty (Oughterard); Jimmy Glynn (Corofin)

KERRY (RUNNERS-UP)

1. Johnny Culloty
(Killarney Legion)

2. Donie O'Sullivan
(Clanna Gael, Dublin, also Spa and Dr Crokes)

3. Niall Sheehy
(John Mitchels)

4. Mick Morris
(John Mitchels)

5. Seamus Murphy
(Camp, also Lispole)

6. Paud O'Donoghue
(Ballylongford)

7. Jerdie O'Connor
(Ballydonoghue)

8. Denis O'Sullivan
(Kerins O'Rahillys)

9. Mick O'Connell
(Valentia, also Waterville)

10. Vincent Lucey
(Laune Rangers, also Glenbeigh/Glencar)

11. Pat Griffin
(Glenbeigh/Glencar, also Clonakilty, Cork)

12. Derry O'Shea
(John Mitchels)

13. Bernie O'Callaghan
(Moyvane)

14. Mick O'Dwyer
(Waterville)

15. Jo Jo Barrett
(Austin Stacks)

Subs: Dave Geaney (Castleislands Desmonds) Played; John 'Thorny' O'Shea (John Mitchels) Played; Tim Sheehan (Kilcummin); Mick Fleming (Currow and UCC, also St Finbarr's, Cork and Bishopstown, Cork); Seanie Burrows (John Mitchels); John Burke (Milltown-Castlemaine); Jimmy Lucey (Glenbeigh/Glencar); Teddy Bowler (Glenbeigh/Glencar); Seamus Mac Gearailt (An Ghaeltacht, also Gaoth Dobhair, Donegal)

1966

As the 1966 Championship got underway, few would have questioned Galway's status as the finest team in the land. True, they had been pipped in the League Final (Home) by an ever-improving Longford, but who could match the Tribesmen when it came to the white heat of championship battle? Kerry, Dublin and Down had all gone into reverse. Meath, Longford and newly crowned Under-21 champions Kildare were making waves, but none seemed capable of preventing Galway from becoming only the fourth county to capture three titles in a row.

With an easy twelve-point win over Leitrim, Roscommon set the scene for a semi-final clash with the champions at Castlebar on 26 June. On a day of torrential rain, Galway had a solid, if unspectacular, nine-point victory. There were widely expressed reservations about the overall quality of their display but, against this, there was unanimity on one point. After putting his injury problems behind him, Pat Donnellan had emerged as an outstanding midfield playmaker. Pitted against a succession of the best that Roscommon could throw at him, the Dunmore dynamo was master of all he surveyed.

Galway now awaited the winners of the Mayo v Sligo replay at Castlebar the following Sunday. If a ten-point haul by Sligo's Mickey Kearins was the highlight of the drawn game, it was a hat-trick of goals from corner-forward Mick Ruane that captured the headlines in a 4-7 to 3-7 replay win for Mayo.

It was back to Castlebar again for the provincial final on 17 July. The story of this game is really one of lost opportunity for Mayo. Gaining a stranglehold at midfield through Joe Langan and Mick Connaughton, they had Galway under constant pressure. A goal from Achill's M.J. Ruddy early in the second half put them four points to the good, but instead of kicking on they seemed to become overanxious and fluffed a number of further scoring opportunities. Hitherto unable to make any inroads against an outstanding Mayo defence, Galway began to chip away at the lead before Liam Sammon struck the killer blow with the winning point in time added on.

The result was a bitter disappointment for Mayo on a day when they had so many outstanding performers. Vincent Nally, Johnny Carey, Ray Prendergast and the classy John Morley defended brilliantly. Mayo owned midfield, and Ruddy, Joe Corcoran and Mick Ruane were a constant threat to the Tribesmen. Without getting anywhere near their usual standard, Galway's perseverance and guile got them through. Solid, if not spectacular in defence, they could thank Sammon, Cyril Dunne, Seamus Leydon and newcomer Jimmy Duggan for eking out this fortunate win.

Galway's Enda Colleran leads his team to their historic three-in-a-row in 1966. Colleran's talents as a player and a leader were recognised when he was chosen as right corner-back on the Team of the Century and the Team of the Millennium. *Image courtesy of the GAA Museum at Croke Park.*

Victory for Galway in Connacht gave them an All-Ireland semi-final joust with the Munster champions. While Kerry were heading for their ninth successive provincial title, many commentators were suggesting that Cork were ready to break the sequence. The ease with which they beat Clare (3-11 to 0-4) at Ennis on 15 May made it difficult to assess their true capabilities. They did look impressive, however, and their goal tally would have been much greater but for the brilliance of Clare goalkeeper Alfie Howley. Thus advancing to the provincial semi-final against Limerick, the Cork men exacted full revenge for their surprise loss to the same opposition twelve months previously. Behind by a point at the interval, they really opened up in the second half and romped home, 5-10 to 1-8.

Having overcome Waterford, 3-8 to 2-3, in the quarter-final, Tipperary faced Kerry in the second semi-final at Killarney on 26 June. In Sean Kearney, Patsy Dawson and Jim McCormack, they could boast one of the best half-back lines in the country, and with Paddy O'Connell and 'Babs' Keating on board, they harboured realistic ambitions of toppling the champions. Early in the game, Tipperary had a distinct edge as Stephen McCormack and Kildare man Peter Archibald took control at midfield. The prospect of a shock result was quickly dispelled, however, when Kerry shifted Mick O'Connell to his customary position. O'Connell proceeded to spray pass after pass to an eager forward division that clocked up an impressive 3-16 against Tipperary's 2-6.

Killarney was also the venue for the Munster showdown on 17 July. The crowd of over 25,000 which turned up in ideal conditions looked forward to what many predicted would be a classic. Tense and exciting it was; but it was no classic. In one of the scrappiest Munster Finals ever, there was, in the words of *The Cork Examiner*, 'an undercurrent of ill feeling between certain opponents'.

Matters came to a head late in the second half when Kerry's Seamus Mac Gearailt was sent off after reacting to a heavy tackle. This was Cork's cue to go on the offensive and they pulled clear with goals from Johnny Carroll and an unfortunate deflection from the otherwise outstanding Kerry full-back, Paud O'Donoghue. It was a case of too little, too late when Tony Barrett goaled for Kerry as the Cork men held on for a 2-7 to 1-7 victory. Even *The Cork Examiner* acknowledged that they were a shade lucky to regain the crown, but there was no denying their spirit and unflinching determination. In what was very much a team effort, Cork's outstanding performer was goalkeeper Billy Morgan, a man who would go on to transform the county's football standing in the decades ahead.

It was widely believed that the 1966 race for honours in Leinster would be one of the keenest in years. Champions Dublin and their predecessors Meath were bound to feature, while Longford had been making huge strides and Kildare had a highly talented pool of young players at its disposal. The campaign began on 1 May when Wexford beat Wicklow comfortably and Westmeath had four points to spare over Carlow. They may have needed the introduction of Mick Carley to pull clear of a dogged Carlow outfit, but the Westmeath men were never in any danger when they overwhelmed Laois, 2-12 to 1-5, at Tullamore on 5 June. Wing-backs Christy Corroon and Mick Murphy were the stars in a defence that held Laois scoreless in the second half, while Carley and Dom Murtagh gave them control at midfield throughout.

Westmeath's win over Laois gave them a rare semi-final appearance where they were pitted against neighbours Meath. The Royals had put Wexford to the sword, 4-15 to 0-3, in a totally one-sided affair at Croke Park on 15 May, with Tony Brennan accounting for 3-2 of their total. It was more of the same when they lined out against the Westmeath men at Croke Park on 26 June. After just twenty minutes, Meath had chalked up 1-9 while Westmeath had yet to register a score. Thereafter, it was a matter of damage limitation for Westmeath. With converted midfielder Tom Finneran exerting a big influence on the game, they managed to keep a look of respectability on the scoreboard through the accurate boot of Pat Buckley and a well-taken Dessie Dolan goal. In the end, Meath won, 2-14 to 1-8, and they were back in the Leinster Final. While they looked strong all round, their true worth had still not been fully tested.

There was an early shock on the opposite side of the Leinster draw. In front of a crowd of 20,000 at Navan on 8 May, Louth had a fully merited six-point win over recently crowned league champions, and hot favourites, Longford. Showing great determination and skill, the Wee County held the upper hand throughout the field, and crucially at midfield, where Mick 'Muckle' McKeown and Harry Donnelly ruled the roost. Frank Lynch, Leslie Toal, Liam Leech and Benny Gaughran all contributed handsomely to this great victory, which advanced Louth to a quarter-final clash with Dublin.

Home advantage turned out to be of little value to injury-hampered Louth when the sides met at Drogheda on 12 June. They never recaptured their earlier form and crashed to an eight-point defeat against a rampant Dublin team that had John Timmons in vintage form.

Elsewhere, it took two games to separate Kildare and Offaly as they battled for the right to meet Dublin in the second semi-final. It was the Lilywhites who were fortunate to survive the first game, a dramatic late point from Pa Connolly saving their bacon. They made no mistake in the replay, however, as Jack Donnelly and Kevin Kelly led the scoring in an impressive five-point win. Even more impressive was their 3-9 to 2-5 win over Dublin in the semi-final on 10 July, with Pat Dunney scoring three memorable goals. In atrocious weather conditions, they produced an exhibition of football such that they were being universally hailed as 'the' emerging force in the game. They had a brilliant midfield pairing in Mick Carolan and Tommy Carew. If Ollie Crinnigan, Joe McTeague, Pat Nally and Jimmy Cummins formed an impregnable defence, their forward division, built around the mighty Pa Connolly, would cause havoc against any opposition.

All of this promise was to be tested severely when the All-Whites lined out against Meath in the provincial final on 24 July. Within ten minutes of the throw-in, Meath had raced into a 1-4 to 0-1 lead, 'Red' Collier initiating the move that saw Ollie Shanley fire a daisy-cutter to the Kildare net. Seven points behind at the break, the Lilywhites launched a great second-half comeback and a late Tommy Walsh goal closed the gap to a single point. Seconds later, a Jimmy Cummins sideline kick was fielded by Jack Donnelly, who was hauled to the ground as he bore down on goal. A simple free and come back for the replay? Absolutely not! Referee John Dowling ruled that his whistle had signified the end of the game *before* Donnelly gained possession. Meath celebrated a hard-earned win; Kildare were crestfallen and, for the second championship game in a row, referee Dowling required an escort to his dressing-room.

Meath's outstanding performers in this close-run affair were Pat Reynolds and Ollie Shanley, with Jack Quinn, 'Red' Collier, Peter Moore and Noel Curran also hitting the high notes. For Kildare's young team, Jimmy Cummins, Joe Doyle, Mick Carolan, Pat Mangan and Jack Donnelly were their top men on a day that would come to be regarded as the genesis of a saga of recurring misfortune.

Despite beating Tyrone by eleven points in the quarter-final on 12 June, Ulster champions Down were far from impressive. A real positive, however, was the arrival on the scene of one of Down's greatest ever players, one Colm McAlarney. They again struggled in the semi-final on 10 July, before escaping with a 0-9 to 0-5 win over Antrim. Felix Quigley and Jackie Fitzsimons were their top men against a disjointed team whose manager, Sean Gallagher, had resigned just days before the game. Antrim's defeat would have been far greater but for an inspired performance by goalkeeper George Eagleson.

Fermanagh, and specifically P.T. Treacy, made all the headlines on the opposite side of the Ulster draw. Profiting from some great combination play with Mickey Brewster, Treacy notched 2-4 in their five-point win over Monaghan on 5 June. Three weeks later, a further haul of 2-4 by Treacy helped Fermanagh overcome Armagh, and so progress to their first provincial semi-final since 1945. On a miserably wet day, every man contributed to this great win. Apart from Treacy and Brewster, Bennie Murphy, Noel McClurg, Vincie Greene and Tommy Gallagher were outstanding.

Fermanagh's semi-final opponents were Donegal, who had hit five goals in their seven-point win over Cavan. With Cavan three points in front at the break, it was Mickey McCloone who created the openings for Donegal's great comeback. McCloone was again the arch-schemer when they steamrolled their way past Fermanagh, 4-17 to 1-8, at Dungannon on 17 July.

Such was the level of interest in the Down v Donegal Ulster Final of 1966 that, in order to accommodate the expected record crowd, the Antrim County Board installed an additional 4,000 seats at Casement Park. With the match being shown live on BBC television, the attendance was 20,000 below expectations. If this was a disappointment, the game itself was a free-infested shambles. In the view of Mick Dunne of *The Irish Press*, the standard of play was such that it would have shamed two junior club teams. The result was a two-point, 1-7 to 0-8, win for Down who now collected their sixth title in eight years. Donegal's forward division was well below par and could make no headway against a defence that had Leo Murphy, Dan McCartan and especially Tom Morgan on song. For a Donegal team that lined out with the obviously injury-hampered Sean Ferriter, their best were goalie Seamus Hoare and brilliant defender Bernard Brady.

Not having to face Kerry in the All-Ireland semi-final may have been something of a confidence booster for Galway as they attempted to qualify for their fourth successive final. They got a rude awakening, however, when Eamon Moules threw in the ball for their encounter with Cork on 7 August. With midfielder Mick Burke leading the way, Cork really put it up to the champions. This great contest was in the balance all through, with Cyril Dunne notching the scores that eventually got the Tribesmen over the line, 1-11 to 1-9. Also, were it not for the agility of goalkeeper Johnny Geraghty, who twice foiled Cork's Niall Fitzgerald, Galway's three-in-a-row ambitions would have gone up in smoke.

Two weeks later, Meath produced an astonishing second-half display as they converted a three-point deficit into an emphatic ten-point victory over Down. While the Mourne men were far from impressive, there was no disputing the quality of Meath's performance. Peter Moore was in control at midfield, while Gerry Quinn and Noel Curran tortured the Down defence. Meath's great strength was in defence, where full-back Jack Quinn was imperious, while wing-back Pat Reynolds fully justified Andy Croke's description of him in that day's *Sunday Independent*: 'close as mustard plaster and twice as hot to handle'.

THE FINAL – 25 SEPTEMBER

That Galway were playing in their fourth successive final might have been expected to give them the tag of hot favourites for the title. However, their stuttering wins over Mayo and Cork and Meath's emphatic victory over Down changed the general perception of the likely outcome. Many pundits were now predicting a Meath victory. Some believed that the decision of Galway's selectors to replace John Donnellan with Colie McDonagh would have an unsettling effect on the team. It was Donnellan's magnanimous address to his teammates in the days before the game that eliminated any such danger. Galway were short of neither confidence nor motivation when they took to the field on 25 September.

A travel mishap on the way to the game and a timing mix-up that resulted in the team having to return to the dressing-room after their initial entrance probably didn't help Meath. Playing against a stiff breeze, their usual whirlwind start was notably absent as they, inexplicably, struggled throughout the first half. A leg injury suffered by Ollie Shanley blunted their attack. Galway held a commanding 1-6 to 0-1 lead at the break and the result was a foregone conclusion. A minor rally by the Meath men in the second half gave the scoreboard a better complexion but, in reality, they were no match for the champions on the day.

Winning by 1-10 to 0-7, Galway were universally lauded for the quality of their play and achieving the three-in-a-row milestone. The *Connacht Tribune* was effusive: 'The best drilled, best trained and best equipped football machine in the country came to Croke Park on Sunday and with a dazzling display murdered the Meath myth.'

In a team that had no weak link, full-back Noel Tierney was majestic. Goalkeeper Johnny Geraghty kept a clean sheet for the third successive final. Enda Colleran led by example. Pat Donnellan and teenager Jimmy Duggan combined brilliantly at midfield. Goalscorer Mattie McDonagh was the central figure in a fast-moving attack that had John Keenan and Seamus Leydon creating havoc for the Meath defence.

History would later show that this was a great Meath team but the 1966 Final was a big setback. 'Red' Collier had a good game, even though he was pitted against the elusive Leydon. Jack Quinn confirmed his status as one of the great full-backs while Peter Moore's class stood out. Their forward division struggled against Galway's vice-like grip, but Noel Curran created all sorts of problems for the Tribesmen.

In the wake of the final, there were widespread predictions of a record equalling four-in-a-row for Galway. Some suggested that Meath would struggle to reach the top unless they went back to square one. If a lot can happen in a week of politics, so too can a year in football transform a county's fortunes.

FINAL STATISTICS

	Galway	Meath
Full-time:	1-10	0-7
Half-time:	1-6	0-1
Scorers:	M. McDonagh 1-1	M. O'Sullivan 0-2 (0-2 frees)
	J. Keenan 0-3	N. Curran 0-2
	C. Dunne 0-3 (0-3 frees)	O. Shanley 0-2
	S. Leydon 0-1	T. Brennan 0-1

	S. Cleary 0-1
	L. Sammon 0-1
Attendance:	71,569
Referee:	Jimmy Hatton (Wicklow)

FINAL MISCELLANY

- Meath half-back Pat Reynolds had the misfortune of being involved in a minor road accident on the way to the final.
- The great achievements of Tyrone's footballers in recent times contrast with the county's standing in 1966. After their defeat by Down on 12 June, Mick Dunne of *The Irish Press* was content to describe their efforts as 'the most feeble I have ever seen from a Tyrone team'. Donal Carroll of the *Irish Independent* was more colourful: 'Tyrone were unbelievably bad. Their defence never inspired confidence, midfield operated on one wing, and their forwards were as inept a bunch as one would see in a month of Sundays'.
- The leading scorer in a championship campaign typically plays with one of the All-Ireland finalists, or at least one of the provincial title-holders. In 1966, the leading marksman was Fermanagh's P.T. Treacy. Even though his county were eliminated in the Ulster semi-final, Treacy chalked up an impressive tally of 4-12.
- In 1966, Wicklow's Jimmy Hatton became the ninth man to referee both the hurling final and the football final in the same season. The men who had previously taken charge of both finals in the same year were:

    Dan Fraher (Waterford) – 1892
    J.J. Kenny (Dublin) – 1895
    John McCarthy (Kilkenny) – 1900, 1903
    M.F. Crowe (Limerick) – 1905, 1909, 1913
    Willie Walsh (Waterford) – 1921
    Patsy Dunphy (Laois) – 1922
    Jim Flaherty (Offaly) – 1939
    John Dowling (Offaly) – 1960

1966 – THE YEAR THAT WAS

- Nationwide commemorations to mark the Golden Jubilee of the 1916 Rising reached saturation point in 1966. A military parade on Easter Sunday was attended by 900 veterans of the Insurrection and a crowd of over 200,000. Conspicuous by their absence on the GPO viewing stand were Fine Gael and Labour leaders, Liam Cosgrove and Brendan Corish, as well as President de Valera's opponent in the imminent election, Tom O'Higgins.
- There were no casualties when an IRA explosion brought Nelson's Pillar on O'Connell Street

crashing to the ground on 8 March 1966. Public reaction to the event was relatively light-hearted; there was even a report that President Éamon de Valera rang *The Irish Press* to suggest they use the headline 'British Admiral Leaves Dublin By Air'.

- Arising out of one of the worst cases of bungling ineptitude in British history, there was a catastrophic collapse of a colliery spoil tip in the Welsh mining village of Aberfan in Wales on 21 October 1966. When, after heavy rains, 140,000 cubic yards of spoil slid down a hill into the village, it engulfed numerous buildings, including the local junior school. The death toll was 144, of whom 116 were children.

- In England, the 4-2 victory of Alf Ramsey's charges over West Germany in the soccer World Cup Final prompted unprecedented scenes of celebration. It also precipitated a huge upsurge of interest in the game in Ireland. The majesty of Brazil's winning team of 1970, and the 1971 lifting of the GAA ban on 'foreign games', further eroded the status of Gaelic football as the pre-eminent national pastime. Equilibrium was restored after Kevin Heffernan led Dublin out of the wilderness in 1974, and Kerry's Mick O'Dwyer took up the gauntlet twelve months later.

1966 TEAM LINE-OUTS

GALWAY (WINNERS)

1. Johnny Geraghty
(Mountbellew-Moylough, also Kilkerrin-Clonberne and Fr Griffin's)

2. Enda Colleran	3. Noel Tierney	4. John Bosco McDermott
(Mountbellew-Moylough) Capt.	(Milltown)	(Dunmore MacHales, also Williamstown)

5. Colie McDonagh	6. Sean Meade	7. Martin Newell
(Fr Griffin's)	(St Grellan's, also Aodh Ruadh, Donegal)	(Fr Griffin's)

8. Pat Donnellan	9. Jimmy Duggan
(Dunmore MacHales)	(Corofin, also Claremorris, Mayo)

10. Cyril Dunne	11. Mattie McDonagh	12. Seamus Leydon
(St Grellan's)	(Ballygar)	(Dunmore MacHales, also Nemo Rangers, Cork)

13. Liam Sammon	14. Sean Cleary	15. John Keenan
(Fr Griffin's, also Salthill-Knocknacarra)	(Ballygar)	(Dunmore MacHales, also Carrantryla)

Subs: John Donnellan (Dunmore MacHales, also Carrantryla) Played; Frank McLoughlin (Dunmore MacHales); Tommy Sands (Ballygar); Christy Tyrrell (Mountbellew-Moylough); Mick Reynolds (Tuam Stars, also Ballaghaderreen, Mayo and St Wilfred's, Manchester); Tommy Keenan (Dunmore MacHales)

MEATH (RUNNERS-UP)

1. Sean McCormack
(Nobber, also Kilmainhamwood and Kingscourt, Cavan)

2. Dinny Donnelly	3. Jack Quinn	4. Peter Darby
(Skryne)	(Kilbride)	(Trim)

5. Pat 'Red' Collier	6. Bertie Cunningham	7. Pat Reynolds
(St Patrick's)	(Ballivor)	(Walterstown)

8. Tom Browne	9. Peter Moore
(Enfield, also O'Dempseys, Laois and Emo, Laois)	(Ballinabrackey)

10. Tony Brennan	11. Murty O'Sullivan	12. David Carty
(Enfield, also Castleblayney Faughs, Monaghan and Dunderry)	(Kilbride)	(Skryne) Capt.

13. Gerry Quinn	14. Noel Curran	15. Ollie Shanley
(Kilbride)	(Dunshaughlin, also Thomas Davis, Dublin)	(Duleek, also Trim)

Subs: Jack Fagan (Killallon) Played; Mick White (Rathkenny) Played; Martin Quinn (Kilbride) Played; Paddy Cromwell (Skryne); Jim Carolan (Kilmainhamwood); Paddy Mulvany (Skryne); Vincent Foley (Duleek); Larry Kearns (Seneschalstown); Mick Mellett (Martinstown); Jimmy Walsh (Drumree); Michael Lynch (Skryne); Mick O'Brien (Walterstown); James Fagan (Killallon)

1967

'I'll walk barefooted from Pearse Stadium if Mayo are beaten by Galway on Sunday'. This was the pledge made by *Connaught Telegraph* GAA correspondent Sean Rice in his preview of the provincial semi-final which took place on 25 June 1967. Rice was in a minority of exactly one; the overwhelming view was that Galway would advance with ease. After all, Mayo hadn't impressed in their first-round win over Sligo, and home venue would surely be worth a few points to the Tribesmen.

Mr Rice probably did a jig when the referee called curtains on this game. If he did, his shoes and socks remained firmly in place as Mayo tore the champions to shreds with an exhilarating display, romping home on a score of 3-13 to 1-8. This was their first championship win over Galway since 1952 and it rekindled hopes that Mayo's glory days were back. For their part, Galway looked weary after their prolonged stay at the top. Only the brilliant John Keenan caused problems for Mayo. The midfield mastery of P.J. and Willie Loftus was the foundation for Mayo's win, but they had quality in every sector of the field. Ray Prendergast and John Morley backboned a solid defence while Joe Corcoran and Seamus O'Dowd, scorer of a spectacular goal, tormented Galway throughout.

Leitrim emerged as Mayo's opponents in the Connacht Final after a dramatic end to their game with Roscommon on 11 June. With time almost up, and Leitrim clinging to a two-point lead, Roscommon were awarded a fourteen-yard free. Referee Mick Loftus signalled to Dermot Earley that this was the last kick of the game. A piledriver found its way to the back of the Leitrim net and Roscommon supporters went wild as the umpire raised the green flag. Joy was short-lived, however, with referee Loftus judging that Leitrim goalie Mick McTiernan had gotten a hand to the ball. Not having being scored directly from the kick, the score was disallowed and it was Leitrim's turn to celebrate.

Mayo were overwhelming favourites when they lined out against Leitrim in the Connacht Final at Tuam on 16 July. Winning the toss, and electing to play with the near gale-force wind, they got off to a flying start, clocking up a total of 1-12 in the first half. Matters didn't improve for Leitrim after the break as Mayo, on a score of 4-15 to 0-7, bridged a twelve-year gap since their last provincial title. Such was the one-sided nature of the game that Mayo seemed to have no weak link, while it is telling that goalkeeper McTiernan was Leitrim's best performer. Leitrim's Packie McGarty, universally acknowledged as the county's greatest ever player, was lining out in his sixth, and last, Connacht Final. After a lifetime of service, he would end his career without that elusive provincial medal.

In Leinster, reigning champions Meath opened their account against Louth at Croke Park on 21

Meath, All-Ireland champions of 1967. Back (l–r): Bertie Cunningham, Paddy Mulvany, Noel Curran, Peter Moore, Jack Quinn, Mattie Kerrigan, Ollie Shanley, Pat Reynolds; front (l–r): Tony Brennan, Terry Kearns, Peter Darby, Sean McCormack, Mick White, Pat 'Red' Collier, Mick Mellett. *Image courtesy of the GAA Museum at Croke Park.*

May. After a hesitant start, the Meath men took control, eventually progressing to the semi-final with a twelve-point win. While Meath's half-back line of 'Red' Collier, Bertie Cunningham and Pat Reynolds were again outstanding, the real star of the show was full-forward Noel Curran, who scored 2-5 of Meath's total.

Meath's surprise opponents in the provincial semi-final were Westmeath, who had shocked Dublin at Tullamore on 11 June. A late goal from Tommy Dolan had given them a one-point lead, and despite Dublin's frantic efforts, they couldn't manage to close the gap. Ironically, the mastermind behind this victory was Brendan Quinn, a man who had played with Dublin in their 1942 All-Ireland success, and was trainer of their 1963 All-Ireland winning team.

Without ever really showing their best form, Meath overcame the Westmeath challenge, 0-12 to 0-6, at Tullamore on 9 July. The basis for this victory was a very solid defence, in which Collier was the outstanding figure.

The second of the Leinster semi-finals saw Offaly play Longford at Croke Park on 2 July. Offaly had had an easy passage along the way, beating Wicklow on 18 June. A last-minute point from Sean Murray had given Longford a second chance against a Kildare side that had Jack Donnelly in

Tenacious wing-back, and great favourite of Meath supporters, Pat 'Red' Collier launches himself in an effort to prevent Cork's Bernie O'Neill from making a clearance during the 1967 All-Ireland Final. *Image courtesy of the GAA Museum at Croke Park.*

majestic form. They duly took full advantage with an impressive five-point win in the replay. Offaly were sufficiently concerned about the form being shown by such as Longford's Jimmy Hannify, Jackie Devine and Brendan Barden that they put out an SOS for Cyprus-based Larry Coughlan. Their investment paid rich dividends as Coughlan was a key man in his county's three-point victory. If Coughlan's contribution was crucial, the performance of the outstanding Tony McTague was the real highlight of the hour.

The Leinster Final on 23 July saw Meath, aided by the breeze, build up a six-point half-time lead. This was whittled down to a single point with ten minutes to go, and Offaly seemed primed for victory. In a frantic finish, the Meath men held out for a two-point win. As had become something of the norm for Meath, their win was built on the strength of their defence. Jack Quinn caught ball after ball while the bustling Collier did a great job in limiting McTague's effectiveness.

The big question in Munster was whether Cork could build on their previous year's success, or if Kerry could return to claim the crown that they regarded as rightly theirs. As expected, neither had much difficulty in negotiating their way through to the final. In their respective semi-finals, Cork had seven points to spare over Clare while the Kingdom cruised to an eleven-point win over Limerick. Cork supporters were especially encouraged by the displays of Mick Burke and Denis Coughlan at midfield, while Johnny Carroll was brilliant in attack. As for Kerry, their form was hard to assess, but Pat Griffin's display was so impressive that John D. Hickey was moved to compare him to Mick O'Connell. An interesting aside to Kerry's win over Limerick was that the biggest cheers of the day were reserved for Limerick goalkeeper Bobby Walsh, who executed a series of incredible saves.

The Munster Final took place at the Cork Athletic Grounds on 16 July. On the face of it, Cork's single point victory, 0-8 to 0-7, would suggest near parity in the run of play. In reality, Cork were superior in every sector, and for the entire game. Profligacy in front of goal, so long the bane of Cork football, was the reason for the closeness of the scoring. The performances of Mick Burke, Eamonn Ryan and Billy Morgan were Cork's trump cards, while full-back Seanie Burrows was the only Kerry player to enhance his reputation.

In Ulster, nobody expected much of a change from the recent pattern of Down and Cavan battling it out for provincial honours. Down started out with a 3-9 to 1-10 win over Derry at Newry on 11 June. The traditional cliché about a blend of youth and experience was seldom more evident than in this Down side. Their decisive goal was scored by veteran James McCartan who had only returned from the US the previous day. The performances of John Murphy, Colm McAlarney and Peter Rooney, minors from the previous year, augured well for the future.

The Cork team which pipped Cavan in the 1967 semi-final. Back (l–r): Bernie O'Neill, John O'Mahony, Con O'Sullivan, Jerry Lucey, Mick Burke, Flor Hayes, Kevin Dillon, Frank Cogan; front (l–r): Eamonn Ryan, Mick O'Loughlin, Brian Murphy, Billy Morgan, Denis Coughlan, Johnny Carroll, Eric Philpot. *Image courtesy of the GAA Museum at Croke Park.*

Down followed this up with an impressive 2-8 to 2-5 semi-final win over Donegal at Clones on 2 July. Amazingly, this game started without any linesmen on duty. Returning to the fold after completing his law exams, Sean O'Neill was the star turn while McAlarney continued to build on his great promise. This was a big disappointment for Donegal, who for some years now had been threatening to make the big breakthrough.

On the opposite side of the draw, Cavan had Ray Carolan and Charlie Gallagher to thank for their quarter-final win over Antrim on 18 June. Despite the great efforts of their star midfielder Tony McAtamney, Antrim had no answer to the Cavan pair's inspired play. In the semi-final, Cavan met a Tyrone side that had earlier accounted for Fermanagh and Monaghan. Although they monopolised possession and seemed destined for victory from early on, the Cavan men were left bewildered as Ciaran McIlduff, Niall Timlin and Peter Harte all found the net for Tyrone. Eventually, Cavan steadied the ship and pulled through by four points. The sending off of goalkeeper Jim McCallin was a body blow for Tyrone and this, more than anything, swung the game back in Cavan's favour.

The *Sunday Independent* of 23 July was in no doubt as to the destination of the Ulster title. While acknowledging the undoubted talent of Cavan centre-back Ray Carolan, Andy Croke concluded that 'not even six Ray Carolans' could stem the tide against the Down forward machine. It's not known if any of this provided motivational fodder in the Cavan dressing-room before the game, but the heading in the *Irish Independent* the next day read: 'Carolan Shines in Cavan Win'.

Strange to relate, Cavan not only beat the reigning champions, 2-12 to 0-8, but the scoreline did scant justice to their superiority. They played inspired football, with every man contributing handsomely. Apart from the peerless Carolan, John Joe O'Reilly and Charlie Gallagher stood out against a bedraggled Down fifteen.

The stage was now set for the championship run-in. Cavan would take on Cork while Meath and Mayo would meet in the second semi-final. Each of the four could harbour realistic ambitions of ultimate success but, by virtue of their victory over Galway, Mayo were marginal favourites to annex the Sam Maguire Cup.

Thanks to a one-point win over Cavan at Croke Park on 6 August, Cork were first to book their place in the All-Ireland Final. A scoreline of 2-7 to 0-12 might suggest that the losers had the lion's share of possession and that Cork were fortunate to take the spoils. True, the Cork men were the beneficiaries of two soft goals but, with the inevitable exception of *The Anglo Celt*, all newspaper reports concluded that they were deserving winners. There was also a consensus that Mick Burke was their key man in this victory, though Frank Cogan ran him a close second. For their part, Cavan were not totally downhearted. There was a strong sense of optimism that success could be built around such talent as Gabriel Kelly, Ray Carolan, Steve Duggan and Charlie Gallagher.

Just three weeks before their semi-final clash with Meath, Mayo suffered a cruel blow when their inspiring captain, John Morley, was struck down with appendicitis, and had to undergo an operation. They seemed to make light of Morley's absence, however. Having trailed by a goal at the break, they eased into the lead and looked set to book their place in the final. It was then that Meath cut loose with a barrage of scores, including two goals, inside a three-minute spell. A TV blackout meant that this scoring spree was missed by the national viewing audience, and Meath were on the home strait when coverage was restored. Meath's final tally of 3-14 (against Mayo's 1-14) brought back memories of their similar tour de force against Down in the previous year's semi-final.

As usual, Meath's defence was rock solid, but most of the plaudits went to their rampant forward division, with the half-forward combination of Tony Brennan, Mattie Kerrigan and Mick Mellett particularly impressive. With Mayo's forwards being kept on a tight rein, they never played with the same fluency as in their Connacht campaign. Also, their selectors didn't help their cause a lot. They introduced the clearly unfit Morley into the game at the expense of the industrious Johnny Farragher. In an exercise of extraordinarily muddled thinking, they reinstated a clearly bemused Farragher all of four minutes later.

THE FINAL – 24 SEPTEMBER

As was the case with Mayo before their semi-final, Cork's All-Ireland Final preparations were badly disrupted. Three weeks before the game, ace corner-forward Johnny Carroll fell from a ladder and fractured his wrist. Meath had already been installed as favourites to take the title, but Carroll's absence was considered by many as giving the Rebels an almost impossible task. Matters nearly got worse for Cork days before the final when corner-back John O'Mahony had a lucky escape in a road accident.

When Tipperary's John Moloney set the game in motion on 24 September, Cork, with the aid of the breeze, began to monopolise the play. However, they were soon struggling under two handicaps. Firstly, their forwards seemed obsessed with manoeuvring the ball close to the Meath goals before shooting and this limited their scoring return. Secondly, their outstanding Mick Burke was injured in a fall after colliding with 'Red' Collier and, visibly in pain, he was not a force thereafter. Even with a meagre return of four points in the first half, the Cork men held a three-point advantage at the break, Meath's solitary point arriving in the twenty-seventh minute.

On the resumption, Meath did what Meath teams do. Nonchalantly, they began to pile on points from distance, with one brilliant score by Noel Curran sailing over from an acute angle, the Dunshaughlin man seemingly not bothering to eye up the target. When Terry Kearns got on the end of a Mattie Kerrigan centre to flick the ball to the Cork net, Meath were in full control. Cork now began to stage a serious comeback. Three pointed frees from Con O'Sullivan reduced the gap to the minimum and the game was in the melting pot again.

Late points from Kearns and Curran finally settled matters in Meath's favour as they went on to capture their third All-Ireland crown, on a score of 1-9 to 0-9. This was not by any means a classic final and the standard of play did not reach the dizzy heights. For Meath, however, it was sweet success after previous disappointments, particularly their failure in the 1966 Final. Their defence came up trumps once again, with Mick White and Bertie Cunningham both magnificent. Elsewhere, third midfielder Ollie Shanley did Trojan work while Kearns, moved from midfield to the forty, was their top scorer. Bridging a gap of thirteen years, the victory celebrations in Meath went on for a long time, and with great gusto.

After their hurlers had succumbed to Kilkenny three weeks previously, this was another bitter pill for Cork supporters to swallow. While many believed that the performances of Jerry Lucey, Frank Cogan, Mick O'Loughlin, Eric Philpott and the ever-reliable Billy Morgan pointed to better days ahead, it would take them another six years to reach the Holy Grail.

FINAL STATISTICS

	Meath	Cork
Full-time:	1-9	0-9
Half-time:	0-1	0-4
Scorers:	T. Kearns 1-2	C. O'Sullivan 0-3 (0-3 frees)
	N. Curran 0-2	E. Philpott 0-3 (0-1 free)
	M. Mellett 0-2	F. Hayes 0-1
	P. Mulvany 0-2	M. O'Loughlin 0-1
	T. Brennan 0-1 (0-1 free)	B. O'Neill 0-1
Attendance:	70,343	
Referee:	John Moloney (Tipperary)	

FINAL MISCELLANY

- Meath's starting team in the final had the distinction of representing fifteen different clubs.
- The *Irish Independent* of 23 September was effusive in its admiration for Meath's Noel Curran: 'considering that he scarcely ever gets more than three club games per year, his progress is indeed remarkable.' Noting Curran's loyalty to the Dunshaughlin club, the report concluded that were he attached to a Dublin side he would be able to participate regularly in club games, and that 'he would not have it for a drawer full of medals'.
- As champions, Meath toured Australia the following March to play a series of games against teams representing the AFL. In addition to their £5,000 share of gate receipts and a £1,000 grant from the GAA Central Council, a fundraising raffle generated an impressive £14,000.
- In what became an annual tradition, both of the final teams were guests of RTÉ at Donnybrook the following morning to view a videotape of the game.
- Although hundreds gained free entry to the 1967 Final by climbing over barriers at the Canal End of the ground, many would-be patrons missed out when the gates were closed shortly after 3pm. Answering questions about the general confusion, GAA General Secretary Seán Ó Síocháin opined that, on account of 'distribution difficulties', there was little likelihood of all-ticket finals ever being introduced.

1967 — THE YEAR THAT WAS

- The world's first human heart transplant was carried out in Cape Town by Dr Christiaan Barnard. His pioneering patient, Dr Louis Washkansky, survived just eighteen days before succumbing to pneumonia.
- The Six-Day War, which saw Israel in battle with Egypt, Jordan and Syria, began on 5 June.
- The Minister for Education, Donogh O'Malley, caused consternation among his cabinet colleagues when he addressed a dinner of the National Union of Journalists on 10 September. Without having consulted with the Minister for Finance, Jack Lynch, he announced the introduction of free secondary education.
- The first independent computer in Ireland began operation at Shannon Airport.
- Outstanding poet, but less than outstanding Gaelic footballer, Patrick Kavanagh from Inniskeen, died on 30 November.
- A pile-up at the twenty-third fence during the Aintree Grand National caused consternation among TV commentators when a 100/1 'unknown and unnamed' outsider averted the carnage and left the entire field in its wake. Perhaps it was his attention to detail, honed over decades of commentary on Gaelic games, that allowed Michael O'Hehir to inform the millions of viewers worldwide that 'Foinavon' was destined to capture the 1967 version of the world's greatest steeplechase.

1967 TEAM LINE-OUTS

MEATH (WINNERS)

1. Sean McCormack
(Nobber, also Kingscourt, Cavan, and Kilmainhamwood)

2. Mick White
(Rathkenny)

3. Jack Quinn
(Kilbride)

4. Peter Darby
(Trim) Capt.

5. Pat 'Red' Collier
(St Patrick's)

6. Bertie Cunninghan
(Ballivor)

7. Pat Reynolds
(Walterstown)

8. Peter Moore
(Ballinabrackey)

9. Terry Kearns
(St Vincent's)

10. Tony Brennan
(Enfield, also Castleblayney Faughs, Monaghan and Dunderry)

11. Mattie Kerrigan
(Summerhill)

12. Mick Mellett
(Martinstown)

13. Paddy Mulvany
(Skryne)

14. Noel Curran
(Dunshaughlin, also Thomas Davis, Dublin)

15. Ollie Shanley
(Duleek, also Trim)

Subs: Paddy Cromwell (Skryne); Ollie Geraghty (Duleek, also Mattock Rangers, Louth); Martin Quinn (Kilbride); Peter Black (Bellewstown); Mick O'Brien (Walterstown); Austin Lyons (Summerhill); David Carty (Skryne); Jimmy Walsh (Drumree); Pat Rooney (Kilbride); Pat Bruton (Kilbride); Murty O'Sullivan (Kilbride); Gerry Quinn (Kilbride)

CORK (RUNNERS-UP)

1. Billy Morgan
(Nemo Rangers)

2. Brian Murphy
(Crosshaven)

3. Jerry Lucey
(Naomh Abán)

4. John O'Mahony
(Kanturk)

5. Frank Cogan
(Nemo Rangers)

6. Denis Coughlan
(St Nicholas) Capt.

7. Kevin Dillon
(Clonakilty)

8. Mick Burke
(Mitchelstown)

9. Mick O'Loughlin
(Kanturk, also Bishopstown)

10. Eric Philpott
(UCC, also St Finbarr's and Bandon)

11. Gene McCarthy
(St Finbarr's and Air Corps)

12. Bernie O'Neill
(Adrigole)

13. Eamonn Ryan
(Glenville and UCC)

14. Con O'Sullivan
(Urhan, also Bishopstown)

15. Flor Hayes
(Clonakilty)

Subs: Johnny Carroll (Dohenys) Played; Jimmy Dowling (Urhan) Played; J.J. Murphy (Clanna Gael, Dublin, also Urhan) Played; Jerry O'Sullivan (St Nicholas); John Crowley (Dohenys); Tom Bermingham (Grange, also Kill, Waterford, Fermoy and Bantry Blues)

1968

THE CHAMPIONSHIP

It is an occasion of great pride, and celebration, when a county makes the breakthrough to take provincial honours for the first time. The 1950s had, in quick succession, seen Tyrone, Derry and Down emerge from the shadows in Ulster, while Offaly had arrived with a bang to take the 1960 Leinster title. The big story of the 1968 Leinster Championship was the arrival of Longford at football's top table. Although they had captured the league title in 1966, they had, until now, fallen just short when it came to the heat of championship battle.

By 1968, Longford were a talented and cohesive group and held high ambitions as they prepared for their championship opener against Dublin at Tullamore on 2 June. With full-forward Mick Hopkins in fine form, Longford emerged with a three-point win, but this did not impress Mick Dunne of *The Irish Press*. He wrote: 'they cannot be satisfied with their performance in this game which glaringly spotlighted the poverty-stricken state to which Dublin have slumped.'

Longford's next engagement was in the semi-final against All-Ireland champions Meath, who had earlier overcome Westmeath, 1-11 to 1-7. Apart from their highly successful Australian venture earlier in the year, Meath had been showing very patchy form and this was to continue at Mullingar on 7 July. Right from the throw-in, Longford set the pace, while Meath's traditional fighting qualities were notably absent. Repeating their 1965 victory over the Royals, Longford progressed to the Leinster Final with a 0-12 to 0-7 win.

The opposite side of the draw saw Laois overcome Wexford by six points on 28 April. They followed this up with a 1-12 to 0-7 win over Carlow at Athy on 12 May when their half-back line of Tom Walsh, Gabriel Lawlor and Kieran Brennan excelled. In the words of Mick Dunne, this victory gave Laois the 'dubious' privilege of a quarter-final clash with Kildare. In similar vein, the *Sunday Independent* described Kildare as 'a different side altogether this year', before dismissing Laois's prospects of victory. Naturally, when they met at Carlow on 9 June, Laois steamrolled the Lilywhites out of the championship. Early goals from Tom Dunne, Mick Fennell and teenager John Lawlor set them on their way to a comprehensive 3-9 to 0-9 victory.

Also on 9 June, Offaly easily overcame Louth, 0-11 to 0-6, in a game which the *Dundalk Democrat* described as 'a shambles of a contest'. In selecting their team, the Louth selectors had included the Newtown Blues duo of Frank Clarke and Liam Leech. Both men had earlier written to the County Board to signal that they had 'retired for the time being' and neither travelled. The whole situation generated a lot of aggravation among clubs and board officers in the lead-up to the game. The

Longford were a very strong footballing force in the mid-1960s, becoming Leinster Champions in 1968. This photograph shows the Longford team that won the National Football League title in 1966. Back (l–r): Mickey Burns, Terry McGovern, Jimmy Hannify, Mick Hopkins, John Donlon, Seamus Flynn, Jimmy Flynn, Bobby Burns; front (l–r): Sean Donnelly, Sean Murray, Brendan Barden, Larry Gillen, Brendan Gilmore, John Heneghan, Jackie Devine. *Courtesy Gaelic Art.*

County Board meeting on the following evening was, to say the least, a fractious affair.

Offaly's provincial semi-final opponents were neighbours Laois. A crowd of over 30,000 crammed into O'Connor Park on 30 June, where Laois continued their great run with an emphatic five-point victory. Their defence was again outstanding, with top honours going to Kieran Brennan and Tom Walsh, while their goalkeeping captain, Paddy Bracken, was unbeatable.

This paved the way for a novel Leinster Final pairing of Laois and Longford at Croke Park on 21 July. While Longford had shown more impressive form in recent seasons, the quality of Laois's play in their run to the final gave their supporters grounds for optimism. This was rudely shattered as Longford eased into the lead in the first half, before exploding with a barrage of scores after the break and romping home, 3-9 to 1-4. Taking their first senior provincial title on this historic day, Longford had heroes throughout the pitch. Mick Dunne of *The Irish Press,* himself a disappointed Laois man, was in no doubt as to the key to this victory: 'Nowhere was this slick teamwork more noticeable than in the menacing foraging and tantalising combination of Jimmy Hannify, Jackie Devine, Mick Hopkins and Sean Donnelly.'

For Laois, seeking their first Leinster title since 1946, this was a bitter pill to swallow, especially since Eddie Mulhall and Seamus Fleming had dominated the midfield exchanges. Their defeat was widely attributed to lack of big match experience, but the question was whether they could maintain their momentum and get that experience.

Down in Munster, Cork were confident that they could build on their 1967 All-Ireland Final experience and capture their third successive provincial crown on their way to even greater things. In their first outing, they faced Clare in the semi-final at Ennis on 16 June. This was meant to be a cakewalk after Clare earlier struggled to a most unimpressive victory over Waterford in the first round. Instead, Cork were decidedly lucky to escape from Ennis with a single-point win, the decisive score coming from Con O'Sullivan in the second minute of injury time. Clare midfielder Pat McMahon, scorer of 1-3, played a stormer, while Senan Downes, Martin McInerney and Michael Chambers were others to make life difficult for the Cork men. The robust nature of the play in this game was captured by Kerry native Tom O'Riordan, who reported in the *Irish Independent*: 'there was far too much wild kicking, not always in the direction of the ball, and an over use of fists and elbows.'

The second of the Munster semi-finals saw Kerry overcome Tipperary, 0-17 to 2-7, at Clonmel on 22 June. With the return from self-imposed exile of Mick O'Connell, Seamus Murphy and Mick O'Dwyer, Kerry seemed to have turned a corner. The acid test, however, would be their showdown with Cork on 14 July at Killarney. With the aid of a strong breeze, Cork were 2-3 to 0-2 ahead after just seven minutes and the three-in-a-row seemed very much on the cards. Then O'Connell proceeded to strike three glorious long-range frees between the posts, and Kerry were back in business. A point behind at the break, the Kingdom took complete control in the second half, winning 1-21 to 3-8. For Kerry, a particularly gratifying feature of this game was the play of newcomers Brendan Lynch and Eamonn O'Donoghue. However, Gerry McCarthy in *The Irish Press* was clear that the basis for this latest victory was best described in just two words: Mick O'Connell.

With Mayo finally breaking their hoodoo in 1967, the big question in Connacht was whether they could maintain dominance over arch-rivals Galway. Their first championship outing was against a Sligo team that had beaten Leitrim by eleven points in a one-sided affair on 2 June. Although Sligo had reached the league semi-final and could boast that in Mickey Kearins they had perhaps the best forward in the country, Mayo were still expected to progress to the provincial decider when they met at Castlebar on 23 June. Neither side impressed in the first half, which ended on level terms, but with Sligo having had wind advantage. The second half was a disappointment all round, as Sligo failed to score and Mayo trundled along to a five-point win.

The second Connacht semi-final was contested by Galway and Roscommon. The teams ended level when they met at Ballinasloe on 16 June. Commenting that Galway had done enough in this game 'to lose two or three matches', John D. Hickey in the *Irish Independent* described their survival as being in the nature of a miracle. Ironically, it took a last-second point by Roscommon's George Geraghty to bring the game to a replay.

Galway were a transformed team when they met for the second time at Roscommon on 14 July. With a devastating second-half display, they pulled back a four-point deficit and progressed to the final on a score of 2-8 to 1-9. A highlight of the game was a scorcher to the Roscommon net by Seamus Leydon midway through the second half. Apart from Leydon, Galway's top performers were Mattie

Kerry's Mick O'Connell has a firm grasp of the ball in this action shot from the 1968 decider. *Image courtesy of the National Library of Ireland.*

McDonagh and John Keenan, while Ronnie Creaven and Tony Whyte shone for Roscommon.

Just seven days after their victory over Roscommon, Galway lined out in the provincial final against Mayo at Castlebar. They served up a footballing classic, with the Tribesmen edging matters on a score of 2-10 to 2-9. There were many great displays in this ding-dong battle, but none came close to matching that of Dunmore's John Keenan. He scored a goal and seven points, mostly from prodigious distances, but this statistic doesn't fully reflect his true contribution. Combining brilliantly at midfield with Jimmy Duggan, Keenan had the game of his life.

Apart from Keenan, the general view was that there were a number of outstanding performers on both sides. It seems, however, that Sean Rice of *The Connaught Telegraph* took a different view. His (non) report on the game read as follows:

> I refuse.
>
> I refuse to become involved in any analytical chaos born out of the confused minds of Mayo's footballers on Sunday.
>
> When the Mayo players decide to grow up, to become men, to show some signs of determination in their play and their approach, I shall be glad to report their games.
>
> Until then I simply refuse.

Once again, Cavan and Down were considered to be the chief contenders for the Ulster crown. Cavan were reigning champions but Down had shown impressive form when taking the league title.

The Cavan men opened their account on 16 June against Antrim where, despite a ten-point victory, they were distinctly unimpressive. Antrim's pairing of Alastair Scullion and Brian Whitney ruled the midfield roost throughout, and it needed a couple of fortuitous goals to swing matters Cavan's way.

Cavan's next outing was against neighbours Monaghan, who had needed two bites of the cherry before finally getting the better of a luckless Fermanagh. In the first game, Fermanagh midfielders Vincent Greene and Sean McGrath provided a steady stream of scoring opportunities, but their forward division failed to take advantage and Monaghan survived by the skin of their proverbial teeth. Next time out it was a point-scoring fest by Tommy McCudden and Sean Woods that earned the Monaghan men their semi-final tilt with the reigning champions.

Predictions that Monaghan would prove a handful for Cavan when they met at Clones on 7 July proved to be very wide of the mark. They could only muster five points against Cavan's 1-11 and *The Irish Press* was in no doubt as regards the reason for this collapse: 'Blame Monaghan's attack for this ignominious walloping'.

On the opposite side of the Ulster draw, Down started their campaign on 9 June against Derry at

This iconic photograph features Kerry's Mick O'Connell (centre) and Down's Sean O'Neill (left), two of the greatest exponents of the game, vying for possession in the 1968 Final. *Image courtesy of the GAA Museum at Croke Park.*

Ballinascreen. The Derry men adopted an uncompromising approach and in a free-infested encounter that saw four players sent to the line, Down escaped with a two-point victory. In the semi-final at Breffni Park on 30 June, Down had no difficulty swotting aside Donegal, 2-14 to 0-8. Despite its one-sided nature, a feature of the game was the battle royal between the respective midfield pairings: Colm McAlarney and Jim Milligan of Down and the Donegal combination of Sean Ferriter and Declan O'Carroll.

A crowd of 35,000 turned up at Casement Park on 28 July to see Down, playing in their eleventh successive Ulster Final, take on reigning champions Cavan. The Mourne men were firm favourites, with Andy Croke of the *Sunday Independent* concluding that only a miracle could save Cavan from following the lead of Meath, Cork and Mayo, who all failed to retain their provincial crown. However remote the prospects of a miracle might have been, they had become non-existent when Ray Carolan suffered a serious knee injury in a club match just two weeks before the game. Inspired by the classy John Murphy, who gave a real tour de force when moved to midfield, Down duly took the honours on a 0-16 to 1-8 scoreline. While this was a comprehensive win, Down's performance was patchy. Major doubts remained as to whether they could achieve the necessary consistency to capture their third All-Ireland crown.

Longford made their bow at the semi-final stage of the All-Ireland Championship when they lined out against Kerry at Croke Park on 4 August. Without two of their star players, Jimmy Flynn and Sean Murray, their prospects might have been completely dismissed against such exalted opposition. But such had been the quality of their play in the Leinster campaign that nobody, least of all Kerry, took them for granted.

At the end of a thrilling encounter, Kerry emerged victorious on a score of 2-13 to 2-11. By common consent, this was a great game and one which could have gone either way. Longford raced into an early lead but Kerry responded magnificently and looked likely winners when they led by nine points shortly after the break. Then it was Longford's turn to regain the initiative. Jimmy Hannify moved out to midfield where he made an immediate impact. A brilliant goal from Tom Mulvihill was followed by another, from a penalty, by Jackie Devine and Longford were suddenly in the lead. It was then that Mick O'Connell stepped up another gear and, with what John D. Hickey described as 'the calculation of a computer', he laid on the equalising point for Mick O'Dwyer. In a grandstand finish, it was the boot of Brendan Lynch that finally got Kerry over the line.

The second semi-final, between Down and Galway, attracted over 50,000 to Croke Park on 18 August. After a largely uneventful first half, most notable for the brilliance of Tom O'Hare, Down had pulled five points clear and looked comfortable. Within six minutes of the restart, however, the teams were level. First, a speculative long-range effort by Jimmy Duggan found its way into the Down net. Then Cyril Dunne was on hand to hammer the ball home after Danny Kelly had parried a penalty taken by John Keenan. With the outcome in the balance, the ever-reliable Sean O'Neill capitalised on a half-chance created by Peter Rooney and sent the ball crashing to the Galway net.

Down were home and hosed and could look forward to renewing hostilities in the final with the mighty Kingdom.

THE FINAL – 22 SEPTEMBER

The term 'mouth-watering' is one often used to give a sense of the level of anticipation and excitement in the lead-up to major sporting contests. Judging by the vast newspaper coverage prior to the 1968 Final, such a description would hardly do justice to the hyperbole that this game generated. Generations of success for Kerry contrasted sharply with Down's recent arrival at the football summit. This, and their markedly different styles of play, contributed to its being one of the most eagerly awaited finals in years.

Based largely on recent form, most commentators plumped for a Down victory. However, Kerry had a history of emerging from their occasional periods of hibernation and springing an All-Ireland Final surprise for some unsuspecting hot favourite. A strong start was seen as the key to victory, and Down had their supporters in dreamland within minutes of the throw-in. Sean O'Neill started it all when he lofted the opening point a mere thirteen seconds into the game. Minutes later he followed this up with one of *the* great All-Ireland goals. When Peter Rooney's effort for a point rebounded off the upright, O'Neill was in like a light to connect with the dropping ball which went flying past a startled Johnny Culloty. Still not finished, O'Neill's next contribution was to send a piledriver which Culloty could only parry into the path of the inrushing John Murphy, who duly dispatched the leather to the back of the Kerry net.

This astonishing start saw the Mourne men enter the break with a 2-7 to 0-5 lead. Kerry's prospects seemed hopeless. In the second half, they fought back gallantly and though they began to cut the arrears, the gap was too great. Brendan Lynch's last-minute goal from a fourteen-yard free cut the deficit to two points but, in truth, the result was a foregone conclusion long before that.

Few disputed that Down fully deserved this, their third title of the decade. If O'Neill was the real ace in the pack, they had quality throughout the team. The combination of the experienced men from 1960–61 and their young lions gave them the perfect balance. As for Kerry, the big question was whether their appearance in the final represented a one-off for a once-great power, or whether this was just the first step on the road to further glory. Twelve months later, they would deliver a very loud and clear answer to this question.

FINAL STATISTICS

	Down	Kerry
Full-time:	2-12	1-13
Half-time:	2-7	0-5
Scorers:	S. O'Neill 1-2	B. Lynch 1-2 (1-1 frees)
	J. Murphy 1-0	M. O'Dwyer 0-5

P. Doherty 0-5 (0-2 frees)   P. Griffin 0-3

T. O'Hare 0-2 (0-2 fifties)   M. O'Connell 0-2

P. Rooney 0-2   D.J. Crowley 0-1

J. Milligan 0-1

Attendance: 71,294

Referee: Mick Loftus (Mayo)

FINAL MISCELLANY

- The Down players were less than impressed by the engraving stamped on the back of their 1968 All-Ireland medals. The designation 'Kerry v Down' was seen as failing to give due precedence to the winning team.
- Tyrone won the All-Ireland Junior Championship of 1968. The team was captained by Art McRory, a man who went on to give distinguished service to his county, including managing the senior teams that reached the All-Ireland Finals of 1986 and 1995.
- Down's Sean O'Neill was unquestionably the outstanding player of 1968. Writing in the *Gaelic Weekly*, Eugene McGee gave his take on the Newry man's status:

  Rarely can the choice of Footballer of the Year be so obvious as in 1968. Since January 28, when the playing season opened with the meeting of Down and Meath at Newry, Sean O'Neill has dominated senior intercounty football to an extent seldom achieved in any amateur team game.

  His dominance was realised in a manner that was anything but dramatic, no flamboyancy, no showmanship and above all no exulting over less talented colleagues and opponents.

- Down captain Joe Lennon, one of the most influential coaching figures in the history of the game, donated the 1968 Final match ball to the Biafran famine relief effort.

1968 – THE YEAR THAT WAS

- In a year of unprecedented political unrest, US civil rights activist Martin Luther King was assassinated on 4 April. Four weeks later, leading Democratic nominee for the presidency, Robert Kennedy, died of bullet wounds suffered in the wake of his California primary victory.
- As part of its investigations into boys' reform schools, the Kennedy Committee visited Daingean Reformatory on Ash Wednesday 1968. When queried about the circumstances associated with the corporal punishment of boys, the school manager, Fr William McGonagle, replied 'openly and without embarrassment' that punishment was applied to the buttocks with a leather. When asked why he allowed boys to be stripped naked for punishment, he replied, 'in a matter-of-fact way', that he considered it was more humiliating when it was administered in that fashion.
- On 20 August 1968, the Soviet Union led 500,000 Warsaw Pact troops in an invasion of

Czechoslovakia in order 'to crack down on reformist trends in Prague'.

- During the 200 Metres medal ceremony in the Olympic Stadium in Mexico City on 16 October, African Americans Tommie Smith and John Carlos, who wore human rights badges and were shoeless, but wearing black socks, each raised a black-gloved fist during the playing of 'The Star-Spangled Banner'. They were promptly suspended from the US team. Australian Peter Norman, the silver medallist, who had worn a human rights badge in support of his fellow athletes, was also reprimanded by his country's Olympic authorities.

1968 TEAM LINE-OUTS

DOWN (WINNERS)

1. Danny Kelly
(RGU Downpatrick)

2. Brendan Sloan
(Atticall)

3. Dan McCartan
(Tullylish, also Glenn)

4. Tom O'Hare
(Mayobridge, also Clonduff)

5. Ray McConville
(Kilclief)

6. Willie Doyle
(Leitrim)

7. Joe Lennon
(St Patrick's, Meath, also Aghaderg)
Capt.

8. Jim Milligan
(Dunsford, also Ardglass)

9. Colm McAlarney
(Leitrim, also Castlewellan)

10. Mickey Cole
(St Bronagh's, Rostrevor)

11. Paddy Doherty
(Ballykinlar, also Loughinisland)

12. John Murphy
(Newry Shamrocks)

13. Peter Rooney
(St Peter's, Warrenpoint)

14. Sean O'Neill
(Newry Mitchels)

15. John Purdy
(Tullylish)

Subs: Larry Powell (Newry Shamrocks) Played; George Glynn (Castlewellan, also Kilconly, Galway and Kilbride, Meath) Played; Dickie Murphy (Saul); Pat McAlinden (Newry Shamrocks); Val Kane (Newry Mitchels); Hilary McGrath (St Bronagh's, Rostrevor); Eugene Treanor (Newry Shamrocks); Mickey Daly (St Bronagh's, Rostrevor)

KERRY (RUNNERS-UP)

1. Johnny Culloty
(Killarney Legion)

2. Seamus Murphy
(Camp, also Lispole)

3. Paud O'Donoghue
(Ballylongford)

4. Seanie Burrows
(John Mitchels)

5. Denis O'Sullivan
(Kerins O'Rahillys)

6. Mick Morris
(John Mitchels and UCC)

7. Donie O'Sullivan
(Spa, also Dr Crokes and Clanna
Gael, Dublin)

8. Mick Fleming
(Currow and UCC, also St Finbarr's,
Cork and Bishopstown, Cork)

9. Mick O'Connell
(Valentia, also Waterville)

10. Brendan Lynch
(Beaufort and UCC)

11. Pat Griffin
(Glenbeigh/Glencar, also Clonakilty,
Cork) Capt.

12. Eamonn O'Donoghue
(Ballylongford)

13. Tom Prendergast
(Keel, also Forestry College, Wicklow,
Sean Mac Cumhaills, Donegal and
Ballingeary, Cork)

14. Din Joe Crowley
(Rathmore)

15. Mick O'Dwyer
(Waterville)

Subs: Seamus Mac Gearailt (An Ghaeltacht, also Gaoth Dobhair, Donegal) Played; Pat Moynihan (Gneeveguilla) Played; Josie O'Brien (Kerins O'Rahillys); Dom O'Donnell (John Mitchels); Mícheál Ó Sé (An Ghaeltacht); Tim Sheehan (Kilcummin); P.J. McIntyre (Kenmare Shamrocks, also St Rynagh's, Offaly); Mike O'Sullivan (Glenbeigh/Glencar); Teddy Bowler (Glenbeigh/Glencar); Declan Lovett (Ardfert)

1969

THE CHAMPIONSHIP

In the 1960s, Kerry football was in a state of relative famine. In every decade since 1920, no county had bettered Kerry in terms of All-Ireland successes. The 1960s were different, however. To date, Down and Galway had each accumulated three titles, while the men from the south-west had to suffer the 'indignity' of being confined to just one. After their comprehensive defeat to Down in 1968, there was a genuine fear in Kerry that their glory days might be gone forever. It was against this backdrop, and with no small degree of trepidation, that the Kingdom embarked on their 1969 championship campaign.

Kerry's first outing was a semi-final encounter with Waterford, who had needed two games to overcome a 'Babs' Keating-inspired Tipperary fifteen. Despite an early setback which saw Pa Walsh find the net for Waterford, the game settled down to its expected pattern, and Kerry eased to a comfortable 1-18 to 2-7 victory. But for the efforts of Waterford defenders Tom Brady and substitute Wally Connors, the winning margin would most likely have been far greater.

In the second of the Munster semi-finals, Clare were decidedly unfortunate to go into arrears in the dying minutes when Eric Philpott goaled for Cork. Even then they were close to rescuing matters, but a brilliant save by Billy Morgan decided the issue in Cork's favour, 2-4 to 1-5.

On 20 July, the eyes of the world were firmly focused on Apollo 11 as Neil Armstrong and Edwin 'Buzz' Aldrin became the first humans to step onto the surface of the moon. Of course, Cork and Kerry supporters had much more important matters on their minds on that momentous day. The Athletic Grounds hosted the by now annual Munster Football Final confrontation between these two great rivals. While Andy Croke of the *Sunday Independent* confidently predicted a Cork victory, it seems he didn't reckon with the ability of Mick O'Connell and Din Joe Crowley to soar even higher than Messrs. Armstrong and Aldrin. Monopolising midfield proceedings, they provided a steady stream of scoring opportunities for a hungry forward division that took full advantage. The final score of 0-16 to 1-4 didn't fully reflect Kerry's dominance. Newspaper reports suggest that the gap between the sides might have been twice as big but for the superhuman performance of Cork goalkeeper Billy Morgan.

Kerry were now through to the semi-final of the All-Ireland series, where they would face the Connacht champions. It came as little surprise to anyone in the world of football that this boiled down to either Mayo or Galway. In their semi-final clash with Leitrim on 22 June, Mayo cruised to a 6-13 to 1-8 victory. The performance of corner-forward John Nealon, scorer of four goals, was the highlight of an otherwise drab affair.

Iron Man on a Mission: Offaly's Paddy McCormack (right) closes in on Mick O'Connell of Kerry during the windswept 1969 decider. After his team's three-point defeat, the 'Iron Man from Rhode' announced his retirement from inter-county football. Three years later, he occupied the full-back berth on the All-Star team and was the holder of two All-Ireland medals. *Image courtesy of the GAA Museum at Croke Park.*

Roscommon may have harboured high ambitions after they accounted for Sligo, 2-12 to 1-6, in their quarter-final clash on 15 June. If so, they were in for a very rude awakening when they came up against Galway at Ballinasloe on 6 July. With a performance that John D. Hickey of the *Irish Independent* described as 'unbelievably bad', they only managed to register a single point as they fell to a seven-point defeat. Peculiarly, despite this ignominious defeat, Roscommon's Ronnie Creaven vied for the man-of the-match rating alongside Galway's Jimmy Duggan and Noel Colleran.

The Connacht Final attracted a crowd of over 25,000 to Pearse Stadium on 20 July, where Galway and Mayo fought tooth and nail, before a late point from Joe Corcoran gave Mayo a second bite of the cherry. If Corcoran was Mayo's saviour, John Keenan was Galway's outstanding performer.

When the replay took place at Castlebar on 3 August, Galway were handicapped by the absence of Enda Colleran and Colie McDonagh, both of whom were suffering from influenza. Mayo took full advantage and were deserving winners, 1-11 to 1-8, after an enthralling encounter. Their star man was half-forward Des Griffith, who proved a real handful for no less a man than Pat Donnellan, his own first cousin. Elsewhere, defenders Ray Prendergast, Johnny Carey and John Morley ensured that the Galway scoring threat was kept in check. Galway's best performers were in defence, where both Jack Cosgrove and Liam O'Neill emerged with their reputations enhanced.

The drawn-out nature of the Leinster Championship can be gauged from the fact that Wicklow made their exit on 27 April, exactly three months before the provincial final. Wicklow's victors, Carlow, were in championship action again on 11 May, when they finished on level terms with Wexford in a dogged affair. Jack Berry, who scored six points, was Wexford's saviour in a match that saw them reduced to fourteen men when substitute John Quigley was ordered to the line within sixty seconds of entering the fray. At Croke Park three weeks later, the Wexford men scraped a two-point win in what Padraig Puirséal of *The Irish Press* described as a 'comedy of errors'. When Wexford returned to headquarters seven days later to face provincial champions Longford, their prospects seemed bleak in the extreme. Turning the form book on its head, however, they overwhelmed the Longford men and advanced to the semi-final with a well-deserved win, 3-5 to 1-8. Fitter and sharper throughout the field, the key to their success lay in an outstanding midfield pairing of Joe Foley and Andy Merrigan.

With Tony McTague in scintillating form, Offaly brushed aside the Westmeath challenge on 29 June, and so qualified to meet Wexford in the provincial semi-final. While the Offaly men duly progressed to the final on a score of 3-9 to 2-10, they were made to fight every inch of the way by a tough, but talented, Wexford fifteen. Despite a great marking job by John Quigley, McTague was to the fore once again, and his spectacular goal late in the game finally settled the issue. One of the big talking points after this game was the leniency with which referee Pat Hughes of Louth dealt with a number of 'unseemly outbursts'.

The general view was that Meath would probably emerge from the opposite side of the Leinster draw, but they came a cropper at the first hurdle against Kildare on 25 May. The Lilywhites looked the team of all talents as they coasted to a 2-16 to 1-11 victory. While Mick 'Butcher' Mullins scored two great goals, the real star of the show was midfielder Jack Donnelly. In the *Irish Independent*, John D. Hickey declared that, notwithstanding Mick O'Connell's recent performances, 'I rate Jack Donnelly's as the finest demonstration of midfield expertise seen at Croke Park for years.'

Next up for the Lilywhites was a Dublin team that had beaten Laois by eight points in their encounter at Carlow on 4 May. Reporting on that game, Peadar O'Brien of *The Irish Press* proclaimed that 'Dublin have no chance of regaining the Leinster senior football championship.'

When the sides met at Carlow on 15 June, the Metropolitans did not disappoint as they crashed to an eleven-point defeat. They made no impression against a defence in which Joe McTeague, Pat Nally and John Balfe were outstanding, while Donnelly and Pat Mangan controlled midfield for the Lilywhites. Were it not for the herculean efforts of defenders Patsy Markham, Christy Kane and Mick Kelleher, Dublin's defeat would have been even more embarrassing.

The newspaper previews of the 1969 Leinster Final make for interesting reading. In the *Westmeath-Offaly Independent*, 'Poc Saor' stated matter-of-factly that Offaly would have the measure of Kildare. In the national newspapers, both Mick Dunne and John D. Hickey opted for a Kildare victory, with each acknowledging that much would depend on the psychological approach of the mercurial

Lilywhites. Unsurprisingly, the *Leinster Leader* and *The Nationalist and Leinster Times* plumped for Kildare, with much store being placed on their training regime. Such was the intense nature of their preparation for this game that County Secretary Peter Delaney proudly boasted: 'We have almost 20 players at every training session.'

The early departure through injury of both Pa Connolly and Mick Carolan was a body blow for Kildare but, in truth, Offaly were stronger all round and fully deserved their 3-7 to 1-8 victory. Their 1960–61 full-back line of Paddy McCormack, Greg Hughes and Johnny Egan was rock solid, Willie Bryan controlled midfield and forwards Pat Monaghan, Pat 'Birdy' Keenan and Sean Kilroy tormented the Kildare defence. On a day when luck deserted Kildare, goalkeeper Ollie Crinnigan performed heroically, with Peter Archibald, Kevin Kelly and Jimmy Dalton also catching the eye.

Sean Meade, who had starred for Galway in their three-in-a-row All-Ireland run, played his first, and last, championship game with Donegal against Antrim on 8 June. His hopes of progressing to a quarter-final joust with All-Ireland champions Down were dashed when Gerry McCann pounced for an opportunist goal to give Antrim a two-point win. In rain-drenched conditions at Newry two weeks later, the Antrim men were thoroughly outclassed as Down reinforced their tag as hot favourites to retain their provincial crown. Next in the queue for the champions was a Monaghan side that had failed to impress in their quarter-final win over Armagh. As expected, the Mourne men had little difficulty in progressing as Sean Morgan, Sean O'Neill and Colm McAlarney turned on the style in an emphatic eleven-point win. Only for some great work by Benny Mone, Sean Woods and goalkeeper Paul McCarthy, Monaghan's defeat would have been all the greater.

Down's opponents in the Ulster Final, Cavan, were distinctly unimpressive in their earlier championship games. Notwithstanding their two-point win over Fermanagh at Irvinestown on 15 June, Declan Downs of the *Irish Independent* concluded that they had 'flopped dismally', the only saving grace being the impressive showings of newcomers Ollie Brady and Frankie Dolan. Matters seemed to be getting worse for the men of Breffni when they struggled to score 2-3 against Derry's 0-9 at Clones on 29 June. Beaten in almost every sector, they owed their shot at a replay to centre half-back, Tom Lynch, who defiantly broke up attack after attack. As for their five-point win over Derry in the replay, this was widely attributed to what Mick Dunne of *The Irish Press* described as 'the chronically careless shooting of a remarkably inept Derry team'.

However disappointing Cavan's performance might have been, they could take consolation on at least two fronts. Firstly, they were back in the provincial final and, secondly, Hughie Newman from Ballyhaise produced a stunning tour de force as he completely monopolised midfield proceedings. Maybe, just maybe, they could make a game of it against what the *Sunday Independent*'s Andy Croke decreed the 'team of all the talents'.

From the moment Tommy Johnstone of Fermanagh threw in the ball at Casement Park on 27 July, it was obvious that a shock result was in store. Down goalkeeper Danny Kelly made three great saves in the opening two minutes of the game as Cavan piled on the pressure. Ray Carolan and

Hughie Newman took control at midfield and provided a launching pad for an eager attack in which Steve Duggan, Charlie Gallagher and Gene Cusack were outstanding. While Cavan's victory, on a score of 2-13 to 2-6, was emphatic, it was universally agreed that this was a magnificent game, with Down going down in style, and in a spirit of true sportsmanship.

The first of the All-Ireland semi-finals saw the beaten finalists of 1968, Kerry, face Mayo on 10 August. Based on the dominance of midfielders Mick O'Connell and Din Joe Crowley, Kerry monopolised possession and should have been out of sight long before the end. Their inability to convert possession onto the scoreboard meant that when Des Griffith slammed home a late goal for Mayo, the cat was well and truly among the proverbial pigeons. Kerry held out, but only after Seamus O'Dowd was off target with a late free that would have meant a replay.

A replay was required in the second semi-final when, after fluffing a succession of scoring opportunities, Cavan eventually drew level thanks to the boot of Crosserlough's Gene Cusack. With Tony McTague in irresistible form, Offaly looked likely winners for most of the game, but a Cavan goal from Hugh McInerney set the scene for a pulsating finish to a great game. In the replay on 14 September, the Offaly men again took the early initiative when, as Mick Dunne of *The Irish Press* described it, 'their exuberantly enterprising forward severed the Cavan defence like a surgeon's knife'.

With Sean Evans, Ambrose Hickey and Johnny Cooney lending great support, McTague was again Offaly's chief scoring menace and Cavan's prospects looked bleak when they trailed by two goals at the break. The second half saw a complete turnaround in the possession stakes as Ray Carolan and Hughie Newman took control at midfield. If Offaly's forwards had blossomed in the first half, it was a rock-solid defence that saved them in the second as they held on for a deserved 3-8 to 1-10 victory. Rhode teammates Paddy McCormack and Eugene Mulligan were unbeatable on the right flank, while centre half-back Nicholas Clavin was in imperious form. Cavan contributed handsomely to this brilliant contest, with Tom Lynch, Steve Duggan, Gene Cusack and goalkeeper Paddy Lyons all given high ratings.

THE FINAL – 28 SEPTEMBER

The clash of Kerry, who were seeking their twenty-first title, and Offaly, who had yet to win their first, generated enormous interest in the 1969 decider. That they had never previously met in the championship added further to the novelty of the occasion.

Referencing their twelve-point win over the same opposition in the League Final (Home), most pundits were predicting a Kerry victory. There was a major caveat, however. A leg injury meant that their most influential player, Mick O'Connell, was a doubtful starter and his absence would shift the betting odds considerably. The suspense was heightened when a decision as to whether he would line out was delayed until just before the game. In the event, all Croke Park decibel records were smashed by the thunderous roar that greeted the maestro when he emerged from the tunnel.

As a spectacle, this final fell way below expectations. The near gale-force conditions militated against free-flowing football, but it couldn't account for the amount of fumbling and mishandling in evidence. The record shows that Kerry, at the fourth time of asking, finally captured their twenty-first title on a score of 0-10 to 0-7.

With wind advantage in the first half, Kerry entered the break only three points ahead, and Offaly supporters had grounds for optimism. The second half started ominously for the Offaly men when Johnny Culloty saved brilliantly from Sean Evans. Thereafter, they fought tooth and nail to bridge the gap but Kerry's defence was in a grudging mood. In particular, Tony McTague was well marshalled by Tom Prendergast and this seemed to curb the usual spirit of adventure in Offaly's forward division. Elsewhere, Kerry won the midfield battle decisively but, for once, not on account of O'Connell's efforts. His partner, Din Joe Crowley, produced the performance of his life, fielding majestically and carrying the ball through Offaly's defence at will. His groundwork created the space that allowed Pat Griffin, Liam Higgins and veteran Mick O'Dwyer to outmanoeuvre the Offaly defence.

For Offaly, too many of their players failed to produce the form they had shown throughout the campaign, but time would show that they learned many lessons on that windy September day. As ever, Martin Furlong was outstanding in goal, while Eugene Mulligan, Nicholas Clavin and Mick Ryan formed a brilliant half-back line that conceded just one point to Kerry's highly rated half-forward trio. Willie Bryan showed flashes of the skill and panache with which he would later dismantle Kerry on another All-Ireland day. Their day in the sun would have to wait, however, as the Kingdom celebrated a return to the summit after seven barren years.

FINAL STATISTICS

	Kerry	Offaly
Full-time:	0-10	0-7
Half-time:	0-5	0-2
Scorers:	D.J. Crowley 0-2	T. McTague 0-3 (0-3 frees)
	M. Gleeson 0-2	S. Evans 0-2
	M. O'Connell 0-2 (0-2 frees)	W. Bryan 0-1
	M. O'Dwyer 0-2 (0-1 free)	P. Keenan 0-1
	L. Higgins 0-1	
	B. Lynch 0-1	
Attendance:	67,828	
Referee:	John Moloney (Tipperary)	

FINAL MISCELLANY

- From *The Irish Press* of 27 September: 'The participation of Mick O'Shea and Nicholas Clavin in the football final, as well as the earlier appearance of Kilkenny curate Tommy Murphy in the hurling final and the permission granted to Down's Father Jackie Fitzsimmons to play in the Ulster championship, underlines the growing desire of the Church authorities to involve the clergy more and more in the everyday activities of the laity.'

A footnote advised that all students in Maynooth and All-Hallows had been granted permission to attend the game.

- In the run-up to the final, the GAA took space in the national newspapers to advise would-be patrons about match-day arrangements, confirming that the stands were fully booked, and that Hill 16 and Canal End admission was priced at 7/6 (47 cents). 'Boys' could gain admission for the princely sum of 2/- (13 cents), but there was no reference to 'Girls'. Without the benefit of the smartphone or, apparently, the postal service, the Association also took the opportunity to announce: 'Stilesmen are expected to report for duty at 11a.m.'

- Speaking with Peadar O'Brien of *The Irish Press* moments after the final whistle, veteran Offaly defender Paddy McCormack declared: 'That's the end for me. I'm giving up the game and you can quote me on that.' This seemed a sad way to finish a brilliant inter-county career that had started in 1956 and was now destined to end without the game's ultimate reward. Three years later, the 'Iron Man from Rhode' would be the holder of two All-Ireland medals and would occupy the full-back berth on the All-Star team.

- A second member of Offaly's much vaunted full-back line was very busy after the 1969 Final. The Times showband, managed by Greg Hughes, provided the music at the team's homecoming reception at the Tullamore Harriers Athletic Club.

- The Dublin County Board brought a motion to the GAA's Annual Congress in 1969 proposing the banning of all live television coverage of games.

1969 — THE YEAR THAT WAS

- On 20 July, astronauts Neil Armstrong and Edwin 'Buzz' Aldrin became the first men to walk on the moon. A worldwide television audience of 650 million established a new record, one that wasn't 'eclipsed' until the wedding of Lady Diana and Prince Charles in 1981.

- August 1969 saw unrest in Northern Ireland reach a new high. The British army was deployed on what would become its longest operation. Few foresaw that the 'Troubles' would continue for three decades. In a live television address to the nation, Taoiseach Jack Lynch said that the situation had been caused by the forces of sectarianism and prejudice. Announcing that 'the Irish government can no longer stand by and see innocent people injured and perhaps worse', he disclosed that he had been in contact with the British government to propose the installation of a United Nations peacekeeping force in Northern Ireland.

- 'It is a terrible pity more young girls do not avail of this course which provides excellent training for the future.' This was the view expressed by G. Foley (C.A.O.), at the Meath County Committee of Agriculture meeting of July 1969. Naming the seven girls who declined to take up their scholarship offers, Mr Foley pointed out that 'most of these women expect to get married and a term in a domestic science college … would be a tremendous advantage to them.'

KERRY (WINNERS)

1. Johnny Culloty
(Killarney Legion) Capt.

2. Seamus Murphy
(Camp, also Lispole)

3. Paud O'Donoghue
(Ballylongford)

4. Seamus Mac Gearailt
(An Ghaeltacht, also Gaoth Dobhair, Donegal)

5. Tom Prendergast
(Keel, also Forestry College, Wicklow, Sean Mac Cumhaills, Donegal and Ballingeary, Cork)

6. Mick Morris
(John Mitchels)

7. Mícheál Ó Sé
(An Ghaeltacht)

8. Mick O'Connell
(Valentia, also Waterville)

9. Din Joe Crowley
(Rathmore)

10. Brendan Lynch
(Beaufort and UCC)

11. Pat Griffin
(Glenbeigh/Glencar, also Clonakilty, Cork)

12. Eamonn O'Donoghue
(Ballylongford)

13. Mick Gleeson
(Spa and UCD)

14. Liam Higgins
(Lispole)

15. Mick O'Dwyer
(Waterville)

Subs: Donie O'Sullivan (Spa, also Dr Crokes and Clanna Gael, Dublin); Mick Fleming (Currow and UCC, also St Finbarr's, Cork and Bishopstown, Cork); John O'Keeffe (Austin Stacks); Derry Crowley (Glenflesk); Dom O'Donnell (John Mitchels); Weeshie Fogarty (Killarney Legion); Pat Moynihan (Gneeveguilla); Mick Aherne (Currow); Christy O'Sullivan (Finuge).

OFFALY (RUNNERS-UP)

1. Martin Furlong
(Tullamore)

2. Paddy McCormack
(Rhode)

3. Greg Hughes
(Gaeil Colmcille, Meath, also Kinnegad, Westmeath and Cloghan)

4. Johnny Egan
(Kickhams, Dublin, also Doon)

5. Eugene Mulligan
(Rhode)

6. Nicholas Clavin
(St Carthage's)

7. Mick Ryan
(Sean McDermotts, Dublin, also Doon, Tullamore and Erin's Isle, Dublin)

8. Larry Coughlan
(Eadestown, Kildare, also Killeigh and St Mary's)

9. Willie Bryan
(Éire Óg, also Walsh Island)

10. Pat 'Birdy' Keenan
(Gracefield)

11. Ambrose Hickey
(Daingean)

12. Tony McTague
(Ferbane)

13. Sean Kilroy
(St Carthage's, also Rathcline, Longford)

14. Sean Evans
(Ballyfore, also Edenderry)

15. Johnny Cooney
(Erin Rovers)

Subs: Pat Monaghan (Ballycumber) Played; Frank Costello (St Brigid's) Played; Kevin Kilmurray (Daingean, also Civil Service) Played; Mick O'Rourke (St Mary's, also Killeigh); Joe Flynn (Ballycumber); Brian Guinan (St Mary's); Leo Grogan (Ferbane); Har McEvoy (Éire Óg)

1970

THE CHAMPIONSHIP

There was a certain familiarity about the championship pecking order as the 1970s dawned on the football world. As so often in the past, Kerry entered a new decade as All-Ireland champions, and favourites to retain the Sam Maguire Cup. Other than the perennial banana skin that Cork represented, there were few pretenders to the throne. True, Mayo had shown well when overcoming Down in the League Final, but they had a habit of falling short in the heat of championship battle. Offaly had serious talent but they still needed to step up a gear on their 1969 showing if they were to reach the summit. Of the rest, the likes of Down, Galway, Meath and Kildare were mentioned in dispatches, but few believed that any of these was capable of launching a realistic bid for ultimate honours.

Kerry's Munster semi-final opponents were Limerick, who had earlier scrambled to a one-point win over luckless Waterford at Dungarvan on 10 May. Fresh from their recent Australian trip, the Kerry men showed no mercy at Askeaton on 5 July as they cruised to a fourteen-point win over the hapless Limerick fifteen. If Mick Gleeson grabbed the headlines for his two-goal haul, it was the immaculate form of thirty-three-year-old Mick O'Connell that pleased Kerry supporters most of all.

Also on 5 July, Cork and Tipperary clashed in the second Munster semi-final at Clonmel. Tipperary got off to a flying start, with Michael 'Babs' Keating scoring two goals as Cork struggled to convert their superiority. Two points ahead at the break, the home side still had the advantage when Keating, this time with a blistering shot, again found the Cork net late in the game. Despite playing brilliantly and scoring an impressive 3-1, the unfortunate Keating ended up on the losing side. He didn't even finish as the day's top scorer. This honour went to Cork's Denis Coughlan who, like Keating, was also an outstanding hurler. Notching up a personal tally of 1-10, Coughlan terrorised the Tipperary defence every time he got the ball. Other than the St Nicholas stalwart, Cork had few stars in this 2-15 to 3-9 victory. An injury to Pat Moroney was an unfortunate blow for Tipperary, but their failure to include veteran Patsy Dawson in their original line-out was a bad mistake, and this became abundantly clear when Dawson entered the fray just before half-time.

Consistent with his early season prediction that the 1970 All-Ireland Championship would be a cakewalk for Kerry, Mick Dunne of *The Irish Press* wrote that he would be 'startled' if Cork were to beat Kerry in the Munster Final. We can safely assume that the Clonaslee native retained his usual calm demeanour as the Kingdom strolled to an emphatic 2-22 to 2-9 win over their neighbours. Outstanding contributions from veterans Johnny Culloty, Seamus Murphy, Mick O'Dwyer and Mick O'Connell were lauded after this victory, but the performance of newcomer John O'Keeffe was even more gratifying from a Kerry perspective. Manning the centre half-back position, O'Keeffe was embarking on what would become one of the most accomplished careers ever in the famed green and gold jersey.

Frustration was once again Cork's lot. They could take some consolation from the performances of Billy Morgan, Kevin Jer O'Sullivan and Denis Coughlan, while Barney O'Neill had fielded brilliantly against the mighty O'Connell. It seemed likely, however, that the Kingdom would remain on their provincial perch for some time to come.

Ulster champions Cavan opened their campaign with an easy 3-13 to 1-3 win over Fermanagh at Breffni Park on 7 June. Other than the impressive display of seventeen-year-old Ollie Leddy at midfield, the one-sided nature of this game told little of Cavan's true merit. On the same day at Ballinascreen, Derry overwhelmed a surprisingly weak Tyrone on a score of 3-13 to 0-7. In a game that saw Anthony McGurk make an impressive debut for Derry, Seamus Lagan and Adrian McGuckin provided the midfield launching pad for this facile victory.

Cavan and Derry were now pitted against each other in the Ulster semi-final and they served up a particularly explosive encounter when they met at Irvinestown on 28 June. That Derry won, 1-8 to 1-5, seemed incidental as far as the various newspaper reports were concerned. Describing the scenes as a 'disgrace', John D. Hickey in the *Irish Independent* pulled no punches in condemning the 'tripping, hacking, elbowing, charges of malicious intent and even pulling down by the neck', all of which escaped the ultimate sanction. For Derry, qualifying for their first Ulster Final since 1958, Tom Quinn, Mickey Niblock and Eamonn Coleman were the top performers. Andy McCabe, Brendan Donohoe and Hugh McInerney performed heroically for a Cavan side that never really got into its stride.

On the opposite side of the Ulster draw, opinion was divided as to whether Down or Antrim would progress to the final. The Mourne men hadn't missed a provincial decider since 1957, and they could still call on most of their All-Ireland winning side of 1968. Antrim had laboured in the shadows for many years, but All-Ireland success at Under-21 level in 1969 had many predicting imminent glory for the Glensmen.

Fielding eight of their successful Under-21 team, Antrim opened their account at Ballybofey on 7 June when they had an easy win over Donegal. The national newspapers were unanimous on one point: Antrim's performance was singularly unimpressive and their prospects of capturing the Ulster title were remote in the extreme. While Billy Miller, Tony McAtamney, Frank Fitzsimons and Andy McCallin performed solidly, the overall quality of their play was deemed well short of what would be necessary against Down on 21 June. Of course, one of the great attractions of championship football is its ability to throw up a shock result. Against all predictions, Antrim overcame both Down and the near gale-force conditions as they deservedly won, 2-9 to 1-6. A late goal by McCallin ultimately settled the issue, but the foundation for this win was forged at midfield where Fitzsimons and McAtamney dominated.

Antrim followed their victory over Down with a 2-10 to 1-8 win over Monaghan in the provincial semi-final at Newry on 5 July. Star of the show here was the diminutive Aidan Hamill, scorer of two great goals. Hamill and Owen Roddy tormented the Monaghan defence while, at the other end of the field, Jimmy Ward was the rock upon which most of Monaghan's attacking efforts perished. Another worthy of special mention was centre half-back Billy Miller, whose preparations were not helped by the fact that he lived inside Belfast's curfew zone. (The Falls Curfew was a military siege which saw thousands of nationalists held in the Lower Falls area of west Belfast for two days in early July.) As for Monaghan, the departure through injury of Sean Woods deprived them of their outstanding performer, and any prospect of victory.

Derry were installed as favourites for the Ulster Final clash with Antrim at Clones on 26 July. They fully justified this tag when chalking up an impressive nine-point lead before the break. Thereafter, they struggled inexplicably before finally emerging winners, 2-13 to 1-12, to take their second ever Ulster title. Antrim did have their chances in this scrappy encounter but they couldn't apply the finishing touches when the Derry men completely lost their way in the second half. The performances of Sean O'Connell, Mickey Niblock, Harry Diamond and Malachy McFee were out of the top drawer, but Derry would need a big improvement if they were to trouble Kerry in the All-Ireland semi-final. Though disappointed, Antrim had made great progress and, with such an array of young talent, the breakthrough was surely imminent. Surprisingly, it would be another thirty-nine years before the Glensmen would again line out on Ulster Final day.

When Roscommon beat Leitrim, 4-14 to 1-8, at Carrick-on-Shannon on 7 June, they booked their Connacht semi-final place against league champions Mayo. A midfield masterclass from Dermot Earley, who created opening after opening for forwards Mel Flanagan, M.J. Keane and Mick Fallon, was the main reason for this annihilation of the unfortunate Leitrim. Not even the gallant efforts of Frank Reynolds, Harry Carroll and Joe Gormley could stem the Roscommon tide.

The general view was that Roscommon's prospects against Mayo would depend on two things: dry conditions and a repeat performance from Dermot Earley. While Tuam Stadium was lashed by heavy wind and rain on 21 June, Earley delivered in spades as he inspired the Rossies to a thrilling 2-10 to 1-9 victory. Peadar O'Brien of The Irish Press attributed Roscommon's win to a combination of 'courage, determination and willpower', with Eamonn Beades, Adrian O'Sullivan and Mick Fallon lending most support to the imperious Earley. Apart from defenders Ray Prendergast, John Morley and Ray Niland, Mayo were a major disappointment. Showing his usual penchant for capturing the mood of Mayo's grief-stricken supporters, Sean Rice of The Connaught Telegraph was at his blistering best: 'It was no proof against championship destruction. For the dizzying glory of that National League win two months ago dissolved into black misery on Sunday. Roscommon, young and eager, tore asunder the flimsy fabric of Mayo's recent success, and laid bare the pimples and boils of overconfidence.'

An unfortunate misjudgement by Sligo goalkeeper Peter Brennan resulted in a Galway goal that edged the Tribesmen into the Connacht Final after a particularly dull affair at Charlestown on

The 1970 decider between Kerry and Meath featured Mick O'Dwyer (centre), playing in his eighth All-Ireland Final. Later moving into team management, he would be directly involved in no fewer than twenty senior finals in a lifetime of dedication to the game. *Image courtesy of the GAA Museum at Croke Park.*

28 June. The irony was that Brennan was one of Sligo's best performers in what Peadar O'Brien described as 'the most pathetic game of football I have seen'.

Feeling that the wide-open spaces of Pearse Stadium would suit their young team, Roscommon opted to travel to Galway for their Connacht Final clash on 12 July. Already warm favourites, their prospects brightened further with the news that injury had forced Galway's Jimmy Duggan to cry off. Unfortunately for Roscommon, veteran Pat Donnellan was drafted into the Galway team and he proceeded to turn back the clock with a magnificent exhibition of midfield play. Ably supported by Billy Joyce, Donnellan provided the platform from which Galway, aided by the elements, forged a twelve-point interval lead. There was no coming back for Roscommon and they ended up on the wrong side of a 2-15 to 1-8 scoreline. With Donnellan to the forefront, this was very much a victory for experience over youth, with Cyril Dunne, John and Tommy Keenan all outstanding as Galway marched on to the All-Ireland semi-final.

Reigning champions Offaly and neighbours Kildare were marked out early on as the leading lights in Leinster. Dublin and Meath had long been top dogs in the province, but few among their supporters would have wagered on their 1970 prospects.

However limited Dublin's expectations might have been, they probably stretched beyond their first-round encounter with Longford at Mullingar on 17 May. Their championship journey

Legendary Kerry corner-back Donie O'Sullivan holds the Sam Maguire Cup aloft after his side's victory over Meath in 1970. *Image courtesy of the GAA Museum at Croke Park.*

came to a shuddering halt, however, as Longford deservedly won, 2-14 to 3-8. According to John D. Hickey, this was no yardstick by which to measure Longford's potential – he described Dublin as 'astonishingly inept, a pathetic side, who would scarcely make much of an imprint in the Junior Championship'.

Following up on their first-round win over Dublin, Longford then accounted for Louth by three points in the quarter-final at Croke Park on 7 June. With Jimmy Flynn and Seamus Mulvihill controlling midfield, Longford forwards Tom Mulvihill, Jimmy Hannify and Mick Hopkins picked off the vital scores against an over-stretched Louth defence. The best efforts of Frank Lynch, Leslie Toal, Frank Clarke, Benny Gaughran and the ever-industrious Mick 'Muckle' McKeown were not enough to save the Wee County.

The true test for Longford would be how they fared against Offaly, earlier victors over West-meath. When they met at Croke Park on 28 June, Offaly started in whirlwind fashion and looked to be the team of all the talents. As the game wore on, however, they began to lose some of their lustre and were ultimately fortunate to hold out for a draw.

An intriguing feature of this draw was the manner in which the referee, Brinsley Lowth from Dublin, dealt with a number of indiscretions. Without taking any names or issuing formal warnings, the big man routinely put a paternalistic arm round the shoulders of the culprits. An entirely different approach was adopted for the replay the following Sunday when Martin Meally of Kilkenny took on the refereeing duties. That Offaly won this robust encounter by five points was not the major talking point after the game. After a melee midway through the second half, marching orders were issued to Longford goalie John Heneghan and Offaly forward Johnny Cooney. One newspaper photograph shows Heneghan clutching a very sore jaw. Another depicts a clearly bewildered Cooney being helped to the line by gardaí and team officials. Part, but only part, of the reason for Cooney's state of confusion was explained the following day when referee Meally read a newspaper report on the game. He discovered, to his utter astonishment, that he had sent off the wrong man, and that Ballyfore's Sean Evans had escaped the clutches of the rulebook. The upshot was that Cooney's suspension was quashed, while Evans would have to sit out the Leinster Final.

With Meath trouncing Carlow, 1-17 to 1-4, and Kildare easily accounting for both Wicklow and Wexford, the stage was set for the second of the Leinster semi-finals. All previews had the Lily-whites marked out as favourites to advance, but if they did, they all included the by now standard caveat where Kildare were involved. A team with the talent to beat all before it, they also had the propensity to fold without warning. At Croke Park on 5 July, they duly folded, 0-13 to 1-8. Captur-ing the essence of this encounter, Padraig Puirséal of *The Irish Press* credited Meath's never-say-die spirit against 'the more stylish but less effective Kildaremen'.

When Meath and Offaly lined out for the Leinster Final on 19 July, there was a general expec-tation that a close and entertaining contest was in the offing. The events which unfolded almost defy description. It is safe to say that not one of the 32,085 in attendance had ever witnessed, or would ever witness, a greater sporting contest. A summary account of the game might relay how, in a brilliant game of dramatic twists and turns, the Meath men fell over the line, 2-22 to 5-12. The wondrous nature of the contest had scribes scrambling for new and better superlatives. It would be difficult to improve on a paragraph from the pen of Denis Smyth of the *Meath Chronicle*: 'To assemble an analytical appraisal of this match in any logical form is completely impossible. The dictionary of superlatives necessary to describe accurately a sporting achievement of this magnitude is, unhappily, not in existence. Suffice it to say at this stage that this was the greatest victory achieved by a team in the most fantastic game of football in living memory. It also embodied the most wonderful performance ever turned in by a team on the wrong end of a result.'

Against such a background, it would be wrong to differentiate between the thirty-five warriors who graced Croke Park on the unforgettable day.

There was much less drama involved in Meath's next Croke Park assignment, against Galway in the All-Ireland semi-final. As normal, the men from the Royal County trailed at the break, but a surge of second-half scores propelled them to a comfortable four-point victory. Apart from progressing to the final, the most pleasing aspect of this victory was that, in sharp contrast to the Offaly game, there was no concession of goals on this occasion. Credit for this went to their rock-solid full-back line of Mick White, Jack Quinn and the evergreen Bertie Cunningham.

If Meath's passage to the final was comfortable, Kerry's was a veritable stroll in the park as they outgunned Derry's challenge on a score of 0-23 to 0-10. Not alone did the Kingdom dominate the play generally, their high conversion rate contrasted starkly with the squandermania of a team which managed to fluff two penalties during the game. Impressive throughout the field, there was a familiar ring to Kerry's top performers, as Tom Prendergast, Mick O'Connell, Pat Griffin and team captain Donie O'Sullivan turned on the style. It was a case of back to the drawing board for Derry, whose best were Matt Trolan, Tom McGuinness and the Niblock brothers, Mickey and Hugh.

THE FINAL – 27 SEPTEMBER

Most commentators predicted a Kerry victory in the 1970 showdown. Given the great tradition of the reigning champions, this is hardly surprising. However, the manner of Meath's progress through the championship, particularly the never-say-die spirit that saw them overtake both Offaly and Kildare, persuaded some that they could topple the Kingdom. Notable among these contrarians was seasoned reporter Donal Carroll, whose *Evening Herald* headline comprised a single word: 'MEATH'.

When the big day arrived, Meath duly delivered an outstanding display against the mighty men of Kerry, but this was still not good enough to capture the sport's biggest prize. In the first ever eighty-minute final, the teams exchanged score for score in a first half that saw the sides level six times. The outcome remained in the balance until the final minutes when Kerry, showing greater guile and football power, pulled away. With Meath hanging on to Kerry's coat-tails, it was a typical piece of magic from O'Connell that saw him strike a spectacular point that turned the tide of the game. Two minutes later, John O'Keeffe set up Din Joe Crowley, who raced through the Meath defence before unleashing a piledriver to the back of the Meath net. On a final score of 2-19 to 0-18, Kerry duly took their twenty-second title, a feat that saw them become the leading title winners in either hurling or football.

Most reports on this game acknowledged that Meath shaded matters in the possession stakes, but that Kerry were much more economical in their use of the ball. Their ability to pick off their scores laid the foundation for this latest victory, and none were more impressive than Brendan Lynch and Eamonn O'Donoghue on this front. If the forward division and midfielder O'Connell impressed, their defensive work was also outstanding. Top honours here went to Keel's Tom Prendergast, who embellished a brilliant year with a man-of-the-match display. Johnny Culloty was soundness personified in the Kerry goals, and he received great cover from full-back Paud O'Donoghue and substitute Seamus Mac Gearailt.

Meath contributed handsomely to a highly entertaining and sporting game. Jack Quinn gave yet another masterclass at full-back and he was ably supported by Mick White and Ollie Shanley. Mickey Fay and Tony Brennan were their chief scorers while the energetic Ken Rennicks brought added bite to their forward division.

At the end of a long season that had witnessed more than its quota of scrappy, and sometimes very unsporting, play, the final of 1970 was lauded as a great spectacle. Much of the credit for this was attributed to the steady hand of Dublin referee Paul Kelly, who was known for his ability to impose discipline while still allowing a game to flow.

The Sam Maguire Cup was presented for the forty-third time in 1970. While the first winners, Kildare, had yet to repeat the feat, the second major footballing force of the 1920s were still dining at the top table. Kerry had accepted the trophy for a record fifteenth time. Their nearest rivals on the honours list were Galway, who had reached the summit six times in the same period. Perhaps understandably, Kerry couldn't equal the achievement over the next forty-three years. The poor unfortunate people of the Kingdom would have to suffer the indignity of a forty-four year wait before amassing another fifteen titles!

FINAL STATISTICS

	Kerry	Meath
Full-time:	2-19	0-18
Half-time:	0-9	0-8
Scorers:	M. O'Dwyer 0-5 (0-3 frees)	M. Fay 0-10 (0-8 frees)
	B. Lynch 0-5 (0-1 free)	T. Brennan 0-5 (0-2 frees)
	M. Gleeson 1-1	K. Rennicks 0-2
	D.J. Crowley 1-0	V. Lynch 0-1
	M. O'Connell 0-2 (0-1 free)	
	E. O'Donoghue 0-2	
	L. Higgins 0-2	
	P. Griffin 0-2	
Attendance:	71,775	
Referee:	Paul Kelly (Dublin)	

FINAL MISCELLANY

- The Galway–Roscommon Connacht Final was the first eighty-minute football game. It was also the first Connacht Final to be televised live. On a day of atrocious weather conditions, would-be patrons 'stayed away in their droves'; the attendance of 11,500 was 15,000 down from the previous year's showdown between Galway and Mayo.

- In a tailpiece to his report on the clash between Antrim and Donegal at Ballybofey on 7 June, John D. Hickey of the *Irish Independent* showed his frustration at the lack of punctuality: 'The game started 16 minutes after the throw in time and the second half had to be extended to fifteen minutes to permit the completion of a bingo game for a £50 prize. At the moment I will say no more than that there is a time and place for everything.'

- For the first time in living memory, a football disappeared after going into the crowd at the Canal End. It was something of a trend as twenty-two sliotars had gone AWOL during the hurling final three weeks previously. It wasn't long before the Croke Park authorities invested in protective netting behind the goals.

- On the evening before the final, Kerry attended the *Gaels of Laughter* show, featuring Maureen Potter, at Dublin's Gaiety Theatre. This was the preferred choice of team selector Jackie Lyne.

- The arrival of legendary defender John O'Keeffe on the Kerry team coincided with the departure of their outstanding centre half-back from the 1969 team, Mick Morris. A student at UCC, Morris was advised, in somewhat undiplomatic terms, that since he was not earning a wage, he couldn't expect to receive any travel allowance or compensation when the team embarked on a six-week-long 'world tour' in early 1970. The John Mitchels stalwart promptly called a halt to his time in the Kerry jersey. He went on to forge a very successful golfing career, representing Ireland over fifty times and winning the Irish Close Championship in 1978.

1970 – THE YEAR THAT WAS

- On 6 May, government ministers Charles Haughey and Neil Blaney were asked to resign by Taoiseach Jack Lynch, who accused them of attempting to import arms illegally.

- At a meeting in Maynooth, Ireland's bishops decided to lift the ban on Catholics attending Trinity College, Dublin.

- Singing 'All Kinds of Everything', Dana gave Ireland its first win in the Eurovision Song Contest.

- The world's first jumbo jet, the Boeing 747, went into commercial service on 22 January. Flying between New York and London, it had 332 passengers and eighteen crew on board.

1970 TEAM LINE-OUTS

KERRY (WINNERS)

1. Johnny Culloty
(Killarney Legion)

2. Seamus Murphy
(Lispole, also Camp)

3. Paud O'Donoghue
(Ballylongford)

4. Donie O'Sullivan
(Spa, also Dr Crokes and Clanna
Gael, Dublin) Capt.

5. Tom Prendergast
(Keel, also Forestry College, Wicklow,
Sean Mac Cumhaills, Donegal and
Ballingeary, Cork)

6. John O'Keeffe
(Austin Stacks and UCD)

7. Mícheál Ó Sé
(An Ghaeltacht)

8. Mick O'Connell
(Valentia, also Waterville)

9. Din Joe Crowley
(Rathmore)

10. Brendan Lynch
(Beaufort and UCC)

11. Pat Griffin
(Glenbeigh/Glencar, also Clonakilty,
Cork)

12. Eamonn O'Donoghue
(Ballylongford)

13. Mick Gleeson
(Spa and UCD)

14. Liam Higgins
(Lispole)

15. Mick O'Dwyer
(Waterville)

Subs: Seamus Mac Gearailt (An Ghaeltacht, also Gaoth Dobhair, Donegal) Played; Derry Crowley (Glenflesk); P.J. Burns (Sneem); Paudie Finnegan (Kenmare Shamrocks); Dom O'Donnell (John Mitchels)

MEATH (RUNNERS-UP)

1. Sean McCormack
(Kingscourt, Cavan, also Nobber and Kilmainhamwood)

2. Mick White
(Rathkenny)

3. Jack Quinn
(Kilbride) Capt.

4. Bertie Cunningham
(Ballivor)

5. Ollie Shanley
(Trim, also Duleek)

6. Terry Kearns
(St Vincent's)

7. Pat Reynolds
(Walterstown)

8. Vincent Foley
(Duleek)

9. Vincent Lynch
(Ballinlough)

10. Tony Brennan
(Castleblayney Faughs, Monaghan,
also Enfield and Dunderry)

11. Mattie Kerrigan
(Summerhill)

12. Mick Mellett
(Martinstown)

13. Ken Rennicks
(Bohermeen)

14. Joe Murphy
(Gaeil Colmcille)

15. Mickey Fay
(Trim)

Subs: Peter Moore (Ballinabrackey) Played; Billy Bligh (Dunderry) Played; Eamonn McMahon (Ballivor); Peter Black (Bellewstown); Francis Ward (Gaeil Colmcille); Christy Bowens (Walterstown); Jimmy Fay (Trim); Michael Costello (Dunsany); Alan Burns (Navan O'Mahonys); Denis Gogarty (Dunderry); Tommy Brannigan (Stars of the Sea)

1971

When David Pugh and Gerry Mitchell lined out for Sligo against Roscommon in a Connacht semi-final in Hyde Park on 20 June, they were creating quite a significant piece of history as the first established League of Ireland players to officially play inter-county football.

The irony that it was Sligo who were the first county to integrate League of Ireland players since the 'Ban' had been removed two months earlier was not lost on anyone. They had been one of just two counties (Antrim was the other) at the GAA Congress in Belfast the previous April to oppose its deletion after some sixty-eight years in place. Until then it was, officially at least, against the rules to play or attend other designated sports such as soccer, rugby or cricket while being a GAA member.

Pugh, who had once marked Pele in a club game while playing for Boston Beacons in 1968, and Mitchell were Sligo Rovers regulars and had both played in the 1970 FAI Cup Final. Their addition to the Sligo football team was a welcome one and undoubtedly a factor as they beat Roscommon, by 0-10 to 1-5, in the championship for the first time since 1926. Mickey Kearins chipped in with seven points while Tom Cummins made a spectacular debut.

Mayo had a fixtures schedule that simply wouldn't cut it in the modern game, playing Leitrim in the Connacht first round on 13 June, a game they won by 5-7 to 2-4 and which was seven days out from a League Final against Kerry, delayed because of their tour to San Francisco in March.

Mayo suffered their first ever League Final defeat (0-11 to 0-8), having triumphed in the previous ten, and had little time to recover as they faced Galway the following weekend in the second Connacht semi-final. They were already without Joe Langan, who had picked up a shoulder injury, and lost out to a Frank Canavan goal as Galway won 1-7 to 0-7.

Pugh and another Sligo player, Hugh Quinn, had based themselves in the US for the summer but Sligo were keen to get them back for the final, especially with Jim Colleary missing because of a leg injury. On a sweltering day in Castlebar, Colleary came on to make an impact, Pugh played his part despite having picked up an injury while in Boston but it still took a Kearins equaliser, one of thirteen points he scored, to force a replay after a 2-15 each draw. Galway had led by six points at one stage and, with the influence of the three-in-a-row team waning, it was Joe McLoughlin who stepped up to score eight points, seven from frees.

Galway had too much for Sligo in the replay, winning 1-17 to 3-10 in Castlebar again, but it really should have been much more comfortable as Pugh scored a last-minute goal from a fourteen-yard free to reduce the gap to the minimum. Kearins was quiet this time, Mitchell was

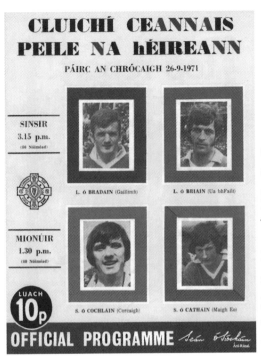

CLUICHÍ CEANNAIS
PEILE NA hÉIREANN

PÁIRC AN CHRÓCAIGH 26-9-1971

SINSIR
3.15 p.m.
(80 Nóiméad)

L. Ó BRADAIN (Gaillimh)   L. Ó BRIAIN (Ua bhFáilí)

MIONÚIR
1.30 p.m.
(60 Nóiméad)

S. Ó COCHLAIN (Corcaigh)   S. Ó CATHAIN (Maigh Eo)

LUACH
10p

OFFICIAL PROGRAMME   Seán Ó Síocháin
Ard-Rúnaí

The cover of the 1971 football final programme. *Image courtesy of the GAA Museum at Croke Park.*

on hand for two goals but Galway wasted a lot on another scorching day, failing to capitalise properly on the midfield dominance of Billy Joyce and Liam Sammon.

The 1971 Championship was a goalfest and it's hard to pinpoint exactly why. The move to eighty-minute games from provincial finals onwards the year before had its impact, but even in regular sixty-minute games, goalkeepers were having their work cut out for them on an increasing basis. There were 106 goals in all from thirty-two championship games played, an average of 3.3 goals per game. Ulster and Leinster had the highest returns with thirty-four each, though Leinster played three more games than Ulster's eight, putting the latter's average at over four goals per game. Only two games, Cork's big Munster Final win over Kerry and Derry's double-scores defeat of Antrim in Ulster, failed to produce a goal.

One of the other striking features of the 1971 Championship was the scheduling, especially in Leinster, which took almost three months to complete after Wicklow and Wexford got it underway on 25 April. Wicklow won by 4-6 to 2-8, a precursor of the flow of goals that was to come.

Meath and Offaly both had to wait eight weeks between their quarter-finals, on 2 May and 9 May respectively, and their semi-finals. Noel Curran's recall for Meath was a factor as he scored 1-4 in a 1-14 to 0-9 win over Westmeath, while Willie Bryan's half-time introduction and Johnny Cooney's goal were decisive as Offaly advanced with a 1-7 to 0-3 win over Longford.

In the preliminary rounds, Enda Condron's marksmanship for Laois stood out, 2-8 from the then clerical student flooring Carlow as he hit half of it before they had even got off the mark. Laois went on to beat Wicklow and then caused one of the shocks of the championship, downing Dublin by 3-8 to 0-13 in a quarter-final in Carlow. Dublin had been league finalists and Laois were coming from Division Two, but once Johnny Lawlor hit the first of his two goals, Dublin's 0-9 to 0-6 interval lead looked increasingly fragile.

In the remaining quarter-final Kildare required a replay to progress past Louth by 0-11 to 1-5 after Kevin Kelly's late equaliser had saved the Lilywhites in the initial 1-7 draw. Prior to their semi-final, chief marksman Jack Donnelly was involved in a car accident, forcing him out for the remainder of the season, but they overcame such a significant loss to beat Meath by 4-8 to 2-12 in a thrilling semi-final. Pat Mangan delivered a tour de force at centre-back as Meath relinquished their provincial crown despite two Tony Brennan goals.

Offaly hadn't looked like future All-Ireland champions earlier in the year but an eight-point semi-final win over Laois in Portlaoise began to change that. And they delivered their biggest statement in the Leinster Final against Kildare with a resounding 2-14 to 0-6 win, the platform of which was the midfield dominance of Bryan and Kieran Claffey. Nicholas Clavin and Kevin Kilmurray were in the US for the summer but were brought home for games and Kilmurray obliged in the final with four points. Offaly were 1-10 to 0-1 ahead at half-time, Kildare's sole score coming from midfielder Hugh Hyland. Murt Connor scored both Offaly goals, Tony McTague was the top scorer with nine points, while Offaly's Jody Gunning and Kildare's Patsy Kelly were sent off.

When Denis Coughlan scored 1-6 for Cork in their Munster semi-final win over Clare in Doonbeg, he, or any colleague or Cork supporter for that matter, could never have imagined that he'd be dropped for the subsequent final against Kerry five weeks later. But on the Tuesday before the final, word filtered out that Coughlan had been omitted by the Cork selection committee, causing a storm that reverberated around Leeside. The omission was baffling as he had scored 4-33 in his previous nine games for his county.

So irate were some of the Cork players at the decision that they convened immediately after training that evening and those present, thirteen, signed a statement subsequently given to the County Board, stating that Coughlan was to be restored. The implications of the 'request' weren't clear but the removal of the selection committee was to be a consideration. There had been suggestions at the time that issues were at play between the board and Coughlan's club St Nicholas, but others from the north city club had been selected on Cork teams. By the following evening, however, the controversy had died down and Coughlan continued to train with the squad.

In the early rounds in Munster, Senan Downes had driven Clare to a 1-9 to 3-2 win over Limerick, a late Eamonn Cregan penalty not enough to rescue the Treaty men. But a Coughlan-inspired Cork were 2-10 to 0-5 winners over Clare in that semi-final.

On the other side, the sending off of Waterford's Achill Lannon had a bearing as Tipperary advanced, while a strong performance by Din Burke at midfield was another factor. But in the subsequent semi-final, Mick O'Dwyer's 1-6 from a penalty and frees gave Kerry safe passage to the inevitable final with Cork.

Cork had beaten Kerry in a league match the previous November, but since their win over Tipperary, Kerry had been crowned league champions with a win over Mayo in a late June final, the conclusion of a competition that had been delayed because of an All-Stars tour to San Francisco that March, a precursor to the official All-Stars tour that commenced in March 1972.

Cork's preparations had intensified for the Munster Final but they were without the promising Declan Barron, Jerry Lucey and the injured Denis Long. The reigning champions then were

Offaly, All-Ireland champions 1971. Back (l–r): Paddy McCormack, Mick O'Rourke, Murt Connor, Kieran Claffey, Nicholas Clavin, Sean Evans, Martin Furlong, Mick Ryan, Kevin Kilmurray; front (l–r): Johnny Cooney, Tony McTague, Willie Bryan, Eugene Mulligan, Martin Heavey, Jody Gunning. *Image courtesy of the GAA Museum at Croke Park.*

favourites and that position appeared to be justified when they led by 0-11 to 0-7 at the break. By then Coughlan was on the field, sprung into action for Connie Kelly after fifteen minutes.

The transformation in Cork after the break was sensational as they put the memory of defeat in the three previous finals to Kerry by a cumulative total of twenty-nine points behind them. Coughlan finished with ten points (eight frees) but the afternoon was one of Ray Cummins' best as he scored six points to rampage through the Kerry full-back line. The Rebel County 'won' the second half 0-18 to 0-3, 0-25 to 0-14 being the final score, with much local commentary firm in the belief that this was shaping to be the best Cork team ever, high praise when previous All-Ireland winners and even back-to-back finalists are considered.

When Cavan played Down in the 1971 Ulster semi-final, rival managers Gabriel Kelly, one of the game's great right corner-backs, and Paddy Doherty, named at left corner-forward for Down, ended up marking each other! The symmetry didn't end there. Both players, icons of the game through the 1960s, had retired after the 1969 Championship but reversed those decisions prior to this game.

Player-managers were becoming a more regular feature in this era but it was Doherty who was happier after a 0-11 to 2-3 win before 20,000 in Castleblayney. It had been a fractious game and the Cavan crowd were furious at an incident that left one of their players with a serious injury.

Earlier in the campaign two Leo McCabe goals helped Armagh to a 4-9 to 2-10 win over Tyrone, while Derry were 4-10 to 1-10 winners over Fermanagh in the preliminary round. There were suggestions prior to their quarter-final with Derry that Antrim would be without Andy McCallin as he concentrated on hurling, but McCallin, who would win a football All-Star on the inaugural team later that year, played. His presence, however, wasn't enough to prevent a 0-8 to 0-4 defeat. In their semi-final against Armagh a late Sean O'Connell goal had steered Derry to a 3-13 to 1-10 win.

Sean O'Neill's influence for Down was all over this provincial championship. Two goals from the maestro helped them to a 3-14 to 3-6 win over Donegal in an opening round, while he was the direct source of three of their four goals in the final against Derry. The game finished 4-15 to 4-11, as Down claimed an eighth Ulster title before 25,000 in Casement Park. Derry had led early but, once O'Neill made the decision to roam, it changed the complexion of the game. His genius helped the Mourne men to dominance in the last twenty-five minutes of the first half as they outscored Derry by 3-6 to 0-3 to lead by 3-11 to 1-7 at half-time. Derry made changes, and Malachy McFee's introduction helped, but the game was out of reach.

Of the four semi-finalists, only Galway retained their provincial title from the previous year, placing them in the path of a more fancied Down who were without Peter Rooney. A colour change saw Galway wear white and Down saffron with black shorts and it was the Connacht champions who adapted best as early chaos reigned in the Down defence. The Mourne men had coughed up four Ulster Final goals and consequently replaced regular goalkeeper Danny Kelly with championship debutant John Harte. That move didn't age well, however, and with two early Galway goals from Emmett Farrell and Pat Burke, Down moved to restore Kelly for Harte after only nine minutes. It had little impact as Galway went on to dominate, their Joyce–Sammon midfield axis thriving. With Tommy Joe Gilmore and Jack Cosgrove locking down the threats from Colm McAlarney and O'Neill, Down's challenge quickly petered out. To compound matters just before half-time, James Morgan was wide from a penalty after Sean O'Neill had been fouled. Jimmy Duggan got Galway's third goal and only two late Down goals prevented a more humiliating defeat than 3-11 to 2-7 before 36,052.

Offaly and Cork met in a championship match for the first time ever in the second semi-final. The counties had contested the 1964 All-Ireland Minor Final with Martin Furlong, Willie Bryan, Eugene Mulligan, Mick Ryan, Tony McTague, Jody Gunning, John Smith and Mick O'Rourke graduating for Offaly, in contrast to Cork who had no link to seven years earlier. Offaly also had Greg Hughes, one of their renowned defenders of the 1960s, back in training since their Leinster title win.

Cork's impressive win over Kerry gave them some hope. However, the experience of being in a final two years earlier and a sense that their team was coming to its peak justifiably made Offaly favourites, a billing they lived up to. The foundations were laid in the first half when they led by 0-9 to 0-4, and despite Jimmy Barrett's goal leaving just two points between them in the closing stages, Offaly's response was swift as Kevin Kilmurray swept in to cancel it out and ensure a 1-16 to 1-11 win. Cork-born McTague led the way for Offaly with nine converted frees.

THE FINAL — 26 SEPTEMBER

For only the third time in the GAA's history, two counties sharing a border were contesting an All-Ireland Football Final. While Offaly and Galway's border had a stronger hurling connection it nonetheless provided a unique feel as Offaly sought to be the fifteenth first-time winners.

The conditions were atrocious as a deluge descended on Croke Park for much of the afternoon where 70,798 were in attendance. At home, it was the first All-Ireland Final broadcast in colour.

Both sides had developed a reputation for attacking and free-flowing football. Offaly, under the guidance of Fr Gilhooley, their minor winning coach seven years earlier, and Alo Kelly had an edge in experience, though Galway could call on four veterans of some or all of the three-in-a-row years – Seamus Leydon, Colie McDonagh, Liam Sammon and Jimmy Duggan. Galway's management team had a stellar feel to it with both Frank Stockwell and Sean Purcell joined by John 'Tull' Dunne and Dunmore's Bertie Coleman.

A swirling wind swept through the ground and Galway had whatever advantage it bestowed in the first half, but they didn't make it count like they might have. Offaly had early goal chances themselves with Johnny Cooney denied by the woodwork and Kevin Kilmurray scoring just after referee Paul Kelly's whistle had blown for a free which Tony McTague converted. But they paid a price when Leydon took advantage of a rare Martin Furlong error when the Offaly keeper lost possession. Galway went on to dominate, leading by 1-6 to 0-4 at half-time. Frank Canavan had a chance to possibly wrap it up just after the break but switching Nicholas Clavin to midfield and bringing in John Smith changed everything for Offaly.

By the sixty-first minute they were level as a relentless Clavin dominated and while Leydon grabbed a second goal to cancel out a subsequent three-point lead, Offaly had the bit between their teeth and finished strongly, sparking celebrations that Croke Park hadn't witnessed for many years.

Fittingly, Paddy McCormack was chaired through the crowd by his fellow players as at last the steely Rhode defender had the All-Ireland medal he had long pursued, having played in the final against Down ten years earlier.

FINAL STATISTICS

	Offaly	Galway
Full-time:	1-14	2-8
Half-time:	0-4	1-6
Scorers:	T. McTague 0-6 (0-5 frees, 0-1 fifty)	S. Leydon 2-3 (0-3 frees)
	M. Connor 1-2	F. Canavan 0-3
	K. Kilmurray 0-2	L. Sammon 0-2 (0-2 frees)
	S. Evans 0-2 (0-1 free)	
	J. Cooney 0-1	
	N. Clavin 0-1	

Attendance:	70,789
Referee:	Paul Kelly (Dublin)

FINAL MISCELLANY

- On Easter Sunday 1971, the GAA took the momentous decision to remove the ban on members participating in 'foreign games'.
- The GAA All-Stars scheme was introduced in 1971. Cork's Ray Cummins achieved the distinction of being chosen at full-forward on both the hurling and football selections. In an era when players were nominated for individual positions, Offaly man Eugene Mulligan's performances were so impressive that he was the only nominee for the right half-back position on the football team.
- When Monaghan hosted Cavan on 13 June, it was the first Ulster Senior Championship game played at Ballybay in forty-five years.
- At Croke Park on All-Ireland day 1971, the GAA sponsored a raffle in aid of 'distress in the Six Counties.' The prizes on offer were:

  First Prize: 24" colour television set

  Second Prize: cassette tape recorder

  Third Prize: lady's electric hair curling set.

1971 — THE YEAR THAT WAS

- Launching its annual campaign for the recruitment of school-leavers, AIB was very precise as regards its requirements. A half-page spread in the Sunday newspapers of 31 May declared, 'We want young men between 17 and 20 with Leaving Certificate or equivalent with passes in English and Maths. Young men with an eye to the future. Young men who know where they're going.'
- On 22 May, members of the Irish Women's Liberation Movement brought contraceptives from Belfast to Dublin on the 'Contraceptive Train'. (At the time contraception was illegal in the Republic.)
- The Eurovision Song Contest, which was broadcast from Dublin on 3 April, was RTÉ's first colour transmission. The cost of producing the programme was £35,000.
- A nine-month-long war between India and Pakistan ended in December 1971, resulting in the establishment of Bangladesh in the territory previously known as East Pakistan.
- In November 1971, an eight-year-old Dublin boy was sentenced to five years' detention in Letterfrack industrial school in Galway for stealing shoes and non-attendance at school. He was not represented in the children's court and neither he nor his parents were aware that any appeal had to be lodged within fourteen days. It's not known how his life progressed, but the *Sunday Independent* reported two years later that he was still in the care of the Christian Brothers at Letterfrack, 190 miles from home.

1971 TEAM LINE-OUTS

OFFALY (WINNERS)

1. Martin Furlong
(Tullamore)

2. Mick Ryan
(Erin's Isle, Dublin, also Doon,
Tullamore and Sean McDermotts,
Dublin)

3. Paddy McCormack
(Rhode)

4. Mick O'Rourke
(Killeigh, also St Mary's)

5. Eugene Mulligan
(Rhode)

6. Nicholas Clavin
(St Carthage's)

7. Martin Heavey
(Rhode)

8. Willie Bryan
(Éire Óg, also Walsh Island) Capt.

9. Kieran Claffey
(Clontibret, Monaghan, also Doon and
Moate, Westmeath)

10. Johnny Cooney
(Erin Rovers)

11. Kevin Kilmurray
(Daingean and UCD, also Civil
Service)

12. Tony McTague
(Ferbane)

13. Jody Gunning
(Rhode)

14. Sean Evans
(Ballyfore, also Edenderry)

15. Murt Connor
(Éire Óg, also Walsh Island)

Subs: John Smith (Gracefield) Played; Paddy Fenning (Tullamore) Played; Noel Kinnarney (St Columba's); Liam Hanlon (Daingean); Larry Coughlan (Eadestown, Kildare, also Killeigh and St Mary's); Daithi Murphy (Gracefield); Seamus Darby (Rhode, also Edenderry); Greg Hughes (Gaeil Colmcille, Meath, also Kinnegad, Westmeath and Cloghan); Sean Lowry (Ferbane, also Crossmolina, Mayo)

GALWAY (RUNNERS-UP)

1. P.J. Smyth
(Tuam Stars)

2. Brendan Colleran
(Mountbellew-Moylough)

3. Jack Cosgrove
(St Nicholas, Cork, also Clifden and
Spiddal)

4. Noel Colleran
(Mountbellew-Moylough)

5. Liam O'Neill
(St Grellan's, also Castlebar Mitchels
and Knockmore, Mayo)

6. Tommy Joe Gilmore
(Cortoon Shamrocks)

7. Colie McDonagh
(Fr Griffin's)

8. Liam Sammon
(Fr Griffin's, also Salthill-Knocknacarra)
Capt.

9. Billy Joyce
(Killererin)

10. Pat Burke
(Corofin)

11. Jimmy Duggan
(Corofin, also Claremorris, Mayo)

12. Michael Rooney
(Cortoon Shamrocks)

13. Emmett Farrell
(St Gabriel's, also Fr Griffin's)

14. Frank Canavan
(Corofin)

15. Seamus Leydon
(Dunmore MacHales, also Nemo
Rangers, Cork)

Subs: Tom Divilly (Caltra) Played; Miko Feerick (Milltown) Played; Gay Mitchell (Dunmore MacHales); Joe McLoughlin (Maigh Cuilinn); Gabriel King (Mountbellew-Moylough); Mickey Byrne (Tuam Stars); Mick Keane (Menlough)

1972

The wonder was that there was an Ulster Championship at all in 1972, such was the spiral of violence and bloodshed that gripped the Six Counties for all of that summer. That year is widely regarded as the worst one of 'The Troubles', the escalation from Bloody Sunday in January leading to the greatest loss of life in any calendar year of the conflict. Hardly a day went by that front-page news was not dominated by the latest atrocity or failed attempts to broker peace or a ceasefire.

By the end of the summer, just as the Ulster Championship was being completed, the British Army were occupying Casement Park in Belfast; it had become a national issue, with Irish government involvement. There was even a protest on the day of the All-Ireland Hurling Final in Croke Park with GAA President Pat Fanning and five vice-presidents in attendance.

Against that backdrop, Down put their title on the line, but it was clear that preparation for teams among 'the Six' was going to be difficult, with many players uprooting to the US for the summer.

Derry were many people's favourites at the outset and they had an emphatic 5-7 to 0-7 win over Fermanagh early on before taking out Antrim by 2-9 to 2-5 in Ballinascreen, with four late points from Sean O'Connell, who hadn't started because of a shoulder injury, making the difference.

On the same side of the draw, Tyrone looked in trouble ahead of their opening game against Armagh as their player drain was so great they had to resort to fourth-choice goalkeeper Martin McCann. Regular goalkeeper Ciaran Harte was exam-tied while second and third choices Anthony Gallagher and Liam Turbett were in the US, along with four other probable starters. But McCann prospered and a youthful Tyrone, with Frank McGuigan (still only seventeen and playing for the minor team) in inspired form on his debut at midfield with partner Brendan Dolan, won by 0-13 to 1-7. It was the catalyst for more and they shocked Derry in the semi-final next time out, 1-8 to 0-9, Frank Quinn getting their decisive goal.

More than half of the Tyrone team was drawn from the Under-21s – Kevin Teague was their only starting forward who wasn't – as players like centre-back Gerry Taggart and Patsy Hetherington, both nineteen, delivered performances to defy their years. The win ensured that Tyrone would contest minor, Under-21 and senior Ulster titles in the same year, a remarkable achievement for a county that hadn't won an Ulster senior title in fifteen years.

A sign of the time was the impact of emigration on Down for the first time, as observed by their then secretary, T.P. Murphy, with Donal and Kevin Gordon both in the US, as they prepared to play Donegal in Ballybofey.

The Donegal team that captured the county's first Ulster title in 1972. Back (l–r): Anthony 'Doonan' Gallagher, Michael Sweeney, Donal Monaghan, Alan Kane, Seamus Bonner, Pauric McShea, Mickey McMenamin, Declan O'Carroll; front (l–r): Martin Carney, John Boyce, Anton Carroll, Frankie McFeely, Brian McEniff, Seamie Granaghan, Joe Winston. *Courtesy Gaelic Art.*

Colm McAlarney was still out with a badly injured arm and Down were a pale shadow of their true selves as Seamie Granaghan pounced on a poor Dan McCartan kick-out for the game's only goal and a 1-8 to 0-8 win for the home side, their first over the Mourne men since 1957. By then Brian McEniff was twenty-nine but had attained status as player-manager and was outstanding at wing-back, as he was throughout the championship.

Cavan comfortably dealt with Monaghan, 3-9 to 0-6, as Monaghan felt the loss of Leaving Cert-tied Felix Mulholland and Kevin Traynor, and that set up a Donegal–Cavan semi-final with two former Cavan All-Ireland winners, Columba McDyer, a Glenties native, and Mick Higgins, helping McEniff with Donegal preparations.

The outcome was the first drawn Ulster semi-final for thirty-nine years, 2-6 to 0-12, with ten points from sharpshooter Joe Winston suggesting Donegal had more of the play. Cavan were much changed, bringing home Frank Dolan and Gene Cusack from the US and introducing St Patrick's All-Ireland Colleges winner Kieran O'Keeffe.

But for the replay Martin Carney was back from the US and he made an impact as Donegal reached their third Ulster Final in ten years, winning 2-11 to 1-9. Again, Winston's accuracy was a key factor, his nine-point haul including seven frees and a converted fifty.

The decision around which team McGuigan would play for on Ulster Final day was left

The Offaly team which retained the title in 1972 by beating Kerry in a replay. Back (l–r): Paddy McCormack, Larry Coughlan, Sean Lowry, Martin Furlong, Sean Evans, John Smith, Mick Ryan, Kevin Kilmurray; front (l–r): Johnny Cooney, Willie Bryan, Paddy Fenning, Tony McTague, Martin Heavey, Eugene Mulligan, Seamus Darby. *Image courtesy of the GAA Museum at Croke Park.*

between senior manager Jody O'Neill and his 1957 Ulster-winning colleague Donal Donnelly. They opted to keep the rising star at his own age group, a big factor in the minor team's 3-6 to 1-6 win over Cavan.

McGuigan then came off the bench in the senior final but Donegal, spurred on by the power of Seamus Bonner at midfield and the defensive strength of Donal Monaghan, Pauric McShea and McEniff, were always good for their 2-13 to 1-11 win, as they became the latest county to win their first Ulster title, leaving just Fermanagh on their own without one. Tyrone led by a point with ten minutes to go but the result hinged on a fortunate goal as a Bonner delivery into the Tyrone goalmouth deceived Harte.

There were ugly scenes in the Connacht semi-final replay. Two weeks earlier, Mickey Kearins, Sligo's player-manager and sole selector at the time, had equalised from a twenty-one yard free in Markievicz Park to force the rematch, but only after Clare-born defender Michael Begley had spared Mayo with a crucial goal-line save from Sligo's Peter Brennan. At Castlebar, Mayo led by 1-5 to 0-7 at half-time but a serious punch-up developed, exacerbated by the crowd, and before play resumed after the break, referee Jimmy Martin called both sides together for a stern talking-to for an estimated three minutes! A former All-Ireland winner with Mayo, Paddy Quinn, full-back on the victorious 1932 and 1936 teams, took to the public address system during the interval to calm the 16,872 attendance, reminding them of the game's 'good name'.

The Mayo management had left record scorer Joe Corcoran off the starting team both days but it was his five extra-time frees, after they had drawn 1-11 to 0-14 in normal time, which got Mayo over the line by 1-18 to 0-17.

It wasn't the only fractious Connacht Championship incident that summer. Mayo referee Michael Connaughton was repeatedly struck after being surrounded by Roscommon supporters in Dr Hyde Park following their side's 3-9 to 2-12 draw with Galway. Roscommon had led by nine points on the three-quarter mark but Galway rallied and some of the home crowd vented their anger at Connaughton over a number of late frees awarded as John Tobin helped himself to 1-9, including the equaliser from a free. Connaughton required a garda escort, supported by Galway players, to get him to the sanctuary of the Galway dressing-room.

Roscommon had beaten Leitrim in the opening round and were spurred on in that first Galway game by a wonderful Mel Flanagan goal following a seventy-yard run. No Roscommon player had been part of a previous championship win over Galway and perhaps inexperience told, but they made no mistake in the replay in Tuam as they won by 1-8 to 0-7, John Kelly's goal proving pivotal. Galway had coaxed John Keenan out of retirement but the general consensus was that justice had been done, giving Roscommon a first championship win over the Tribesmen since 1962.

They carried momentum into the final with Mayo in Castlebar, a first between the counties since 1955, where Dermot Earley gave one of his finest performances at midfield, eventually winning out by 5-8 to 3-10, with John Kelly on the mark for 2-2.

Roscommon, who had lost the Division Two Final earlier in the year to Longford, enjoyed some transformation over the summer months and to have players like Flanagan, Tom Hunt, Kelly and Jimmy Finnegan all based in the county again was a big factor. To beat Galway and Mayo in the same championship year really capped it for them as they claimed a thirteenth Connacht title.

Stung by their 1971 Munster Final loss to Cork, the 1971/72 league took on renewed importance for Kerry and they met that challenge by winning the title the following May with a 2-11 to 1-9 win over Mayo before an attendance of 32,883 in Croke Park. Liam Higgins, with 1-4, and the dominant midfield axis of Mick O'Connell and John O'Keeffe made sure of the title. The distraction of Brendan and Paudie Lynch and Donal Kavanagh having to play an All-Ireland club final in Croke Park against Bellaghy just two days beforehand didn't have the impact Kerry feared (they had lobbied – unsuccessfully – for a different date). That win buoyed the senior team ahead of their challenge to reassert authority in the province.

In the foothills, two Liam Moyles goals secured safe passage for Tipperary to a semi-final at Clare's expense on a 2-10 to 1-6 scoreline. Waterford had a 0-10 to 0-8 win over Limerick in the other quarter-final, Déise goalkeeper John Colbert coming to their rescue on at least five occasions.

Waterford also had to contend without defender Vinny O'Rourke, who was on duty with the Irish amateur boxing team on a US tour and was actually watched by the Kerry football team, on Cardinal Cushing Cup duty in the US at the time, in his middleweight loss to US fighter John Mills in Madison Square Garden.

Waterford got to within a point of Cork when they met in the league but this time lost 2-8 to 0-9 in one semi-final. In the other semi-final Kerry had six points to spare over Tipperary, who spurned four good goal chances including a penalty that goalkeeper Eamonn Fitzgerald saved from Michael 'Babs' Keating, who was otherwise, along with Dinny Burke, impressive for Tipp.

Question marks of age difference surfaced in much analysis of the Munster Final. Kerry were still being driven by thirty-six-year-old Mick O'Dwyer and thirty-five-year-old O'Connell whereas, in contrast, Cork's oldest, at twenty-eight, was Frank Cogan, while they had ten players under twenty-four and an average age of twenty-three.

But Cork had their own concerns: the dual involvement that summer of five players – Denis Coughlan, Seamus Looney, Ray Cummins, Brian Murphy and Teddy O'Brien – and whether that would catch up with them. As it was, O'Dwyer landed ten points for Kerry, nine from frees, as they reclaimed the title by 2-21 to 2-15.

Kerry were now being trained by five-time All-Ireland winner Johnny Culloty since the start of the championship, while Paudie Lynch turned in a man-of-the-match display and substitutes Pat Griffin and Derry Crowley, on for the injured Donie O'Sullivan to police Dinny Allen, made big impacts.

As provincial champions dropped in all three other provinces, first Down, then Galway and finally Cork, just Offaly were left standing when it came to the Leinster Final on 23 July. As champions, Offaly had a bye into the Leinster semi-final that year and so had plenty of time to shake off the apparent lethargy of a league semi-final replay loss to Mayo earlier in the year.

In the meantime two 'new' players had emerged who would go on to play pivotal roles over the next decade and more, Sean Lowry coming in at centre-back and Seamus Darby joining the attack at Murt Connor's expense after an impressive Wembley tournament experience.

Ahead of their semi-final with Meath on 25 June, Paddy Fenning's sending off against Mayo in the league semi-final was overturned, freeing him to play. Meath had beaten Offaly in that epic 1970 Leinster Final and brought some form into the game after beating a Longford team that had gone through the Division Two League unbeaten in nine games.

A 4-9 to 0-5 win over Wicklow in Portlaoise, in which then County Secretary Sean Donnelly, playing at full-forward, scored two goals, and then a 5-5 to 3-7 win over Louth, when Donnelly scored two more goals, earned Longford their quarter-final spot. Kevin Canavan had been outstanding at centre-back in the Louth game, while seventeen-year-old Brendan Smith from Longford Slashers, who had played minor on the day they beat Wicklow, was also introduced. But Meath were a big step up in class and won easily by 0-16 to 1-9, Longford hitting 1-2 in the last five minutes with Donnelly, inevitably, getting the goal, his fifth of their three-match campaign. However, the win only served to give Meath a false sense of security in the meeting of the previous two champions.

Offaly were magnificent, a real statement performance, winning by 2-17 to 3-5 with at least two of the Meath goals of the 'soft' variety. There was real conviction about the champions, who were inspired by Nicholas Clavin, scorer of four points from midfield where he revelled in the freedom after Lowry's introduction to his old centre-back berth.

On the other side of the draw, Sean King's eight points, five from frees, helped Carlow to a 0-16 to 0-9 first-round win over Wexford, a surprise outcome. Three weeks later Laois were 1-7 to 1-5 winners over Carlow, earning a quarter-final against Kildare. That went Kildare's way, 1-11 to 0-7, Pat Dunney's goal on top of a series of Ollie Crinnigan saves making the difference in a bad-tempered affair.

Dublin's build-up had not gone well after a challenge match defeat to Cavan and there were some misgivings about the inclusion of elder statesmen Mickey Whelan, back from the US, and Lar Foley in the team to play Westmeath in their quarter-final. Whelan's travel expenses were covered by the Dublin Supporters club, who marked it with a presentation and photograph that subsequently appeared in the *Irish Independent*. He justified selection, hitting 2-4, including a penalty for a foul on Foley, in a 2-8 to 0-8 win.

In the semi-final against Kildare, however, Whelan never got the same freedom from Joe Doyle and, while they only lost by two points, 0-16 to 3-5, the consensus was that Dublin were miles off and it was never a two-point game with Kildare leading by seven points at one stage. Kildare had Jack Donnelly back almost a year after his car accident while their trainer was Brendan Quinn, 1942 All-Ireland winner with Dublin and team trainer when Dublin won the 1963 All-Ireland title.

At a County Board meeting the following night, Dublin football selector and future chairman Phil Markey hit out at the level of influence that St Vincent's had on football in the city, a reference to a fractious county final the week before as they beat UCD to win their nineteenth title. It had been a spiteful game and most observers saw Vincent's as the aggressors against the students. This included Markey who told the meeting that 'Vincent's are running Dublin football and ruining it.' He said he had left the county final in 'utter disgust with the whole affair and in disgust with the GAA in general'.

Four Vincent's players and one from UCD were called to a disciplinary meeting on foot of referee Paddy Doherty's report. In a stark warning about the future of Dublin football, County Chairman Jimmy Gray warned that 'players at club and county would have to be coached in the fundamentals of the game if Gaelic football was to survive in Dublin'.

There were no such issues in Offaly as they pressed on with back-to-back Leinster titles thanks to a 1-18 to 2-8 win over Kildare in the final. Everything Kildare threw at them they absorbed and the only downside was a serious knee injury to Clavin. But otherwise they were shaping impressively and clearly even better than they had been the year before.

No Leinster county had retained an All-Ireland title since Kildare in 1928 but Offaly put themselves well on course to bridge that gap with a 1-17 to 2-10 All-Ireland semi-final win over Donegal. Compared to their wins over Meath and Kildare in Leinster, this was a much sterner test, above what most expectations of Donegal were. Familiarity with Croke Park had to be a factor for Offaly, having played both Leinster games there in addition to two league semi-finals against Mayo.

Donegal led by a goal early in the second half but between the forty-seventh and sixty-eighth minutes, Offaly scored 1-8 without reply, Kevin Kilmurray's block on Andy Curran and subsequent goal the decisive score in that run.

Paddy McCormack, Offaly's granite-like full-back who was in his sixteenth championship season and a team selector, was outstanding but Donegal gave a great account of themselves with Brian McEniff's performance on Tony McTague a stand-out.

Roscommon were no match for Kerry in the other semi-final before 31,455, Donal Kavanagh's goal giving the Munster champions a 1-22 to 1-12 win at their ease. The laborious nature of the game raised question marks, growing all summer, over the merit of the eighty-minute games in place from provincial finals onwards since 1970. O'Dwyer and O'Connell scored eight and four points respectively but their shooting was off otherwise as even they were impacted by the poor standard.

For Roscommon, Mickey Freyne stood out in a roving role, hitting six points, three from frees, but they were outclassed, setting up a repeat of the 1969 All-Ireland Final.

THE FINAL – 24 SEPTEMBER

Four days after Offaly's semi-final win over Donegal, a picture of Kerry's midfield icon Mick O'Connell and his future wife and Cavan native, Rosaleen O'Reilly, appeared on the front page of the *Irish Independent*, with an interview inside the paper in which O'Connell outlined their relationship and marriage plans. Reserved by nature, he had felt compelled to write in the hope that it would lead to 'no further unnecessary trips down here (Valentia Island) by journalists' and thus his preparation for the All-Ireland Final could proceed 'unhindered'.

But when Kerry drew with Offaly, 1-13 each, in the final the following month, it put the wedding in Killygarry in Cavan firmly in the spotlight as it would take place the day before the replay on Saturday 14 October, with many of the Kerry team present as guests.

As it was, Kerry were somewhat fortunate to get a draw the first day out with Mick O'Dwyer punching a point to level a game they never led. By any consensus it was a poor game, underpinned by the stray shooting of O'Connell and Tony McTague, Offaly's chief marksman, who was off target with up to eight scoreable frees.

Offaly played without injured duo Mick O'Rourke (Achilles) and Clavin (knee) but went five points clear at one stage in the second half when Johnny Cooney punched a goal. Kerry's response was instant, however, with Brendan Lynch, their best player on the day, getting a goal back to keep them in touch. Lynch scored 1-7, 1-4 from play, and it was one of those points on top of that effort from O'Dwyer that brought Kerry to dry land after a sometimes turbulent afternoon for them.

Kevin Kilmurray and Paddy Fenning had given their markers Mícheál Ó Sé and Seamus Mac Gearailt plenty of trouble, while McCormack, Offaly's only survivor from the 1961 team that contested the county's first All-Ireland Final, and Larry Coughlan kept a good handle on Liam Higgins and Mick Gleeson at the other end.

So it was a first All-Ireland Final replay since 1952, a tenth in all and a fifth involving Kerry. In the aftermath there was criticism of Cavan referee Fintan Tierney, with Offaly goalscorer Cooney contending that, with any other referee in charge, 'we would have won fairly and well.'

There was disquiet too over the confined seating arrangements for substitutes who were within earshot of team selectors in conversation about them. Communication to the sideline too was an issue. Even expenses during the All-Star tour to San Francisco the previous March was raised by some players, the $60 given so inadequate that players couldn't buy presents for the families they were staying with.

The seating issue was addressed with changes before the replay. In the meantime Kerry's UCC contingent had more club clashes to deal with, as Paudie and Brendan Lynch and Donal Kavanagh were engaged with the university team in a Cork SFC semi-final against Muskerry on the Sunday before the replay. Kerry chairman Gerald McKenna travelled to Cork on the Saturday night before the game to seek a postponement but it was a journey in vain.

THE REPLAY — 15 OCTOBER

There was no disputing the outcome when they met again, Offaly's 1-19 to 0-13 a crowning glory for this team as they put back-to-back All-Ireland titles together.

They did it the hard way too. On top of being without O'Rourke and Clavin, who did come on but made no impact as the gravity of his knee injury became clear, Offaly lost Cooney and Eugene Mulligan to injury before half-time.

Offaly got the benefit of a kind bounce when a Fenning delivery into the Kingdom goalmouth deceived everyone to put the champions a point clear early in the second half. From there they were imperious, inflicting what is, to the time of writing, Kerry's heaviest All-Ireland Final defeat.

Offaly midfielder Willie Bryan emerged as the game's dominant figure as they hit eight points to Kerry's one in a twelve-minute spell between the forty-ninth and sixty-second minutes. McTague's radar was back in focus too as he scored ten points, nine from frees, while John Smith's switch to centre-back was also hugely influential.

FINAL STATISTICS — DRAW

	Offaly	Kerry
Full-time:	1-13	1-13
Half-time:	0-7	0-5
Scorers:	T. McTague 0-6 (0-6 frees)	B. Lynch 1-7 (0-3 frees)
	J. Cooney 1-2	M. O'Dwyer 0-5 (0-4 frees)
	P. Fenning 0-2	M. O'Connell 0-1 (0-1 free)
	J. Smith 0-2	
	K. Kilmurray 0-1	
Attendance:	73,032	
Referee:	Fintan Tierney (Cavan)	

FINAL STATISTICS — REPLAY

	Offaly	Kerry
Full-time:	1-19	0-13
Half-time:	0-8	0-8
Scorers:	T. McTague 0-10 (0-9 frees)	M. O'Connell 0-7 (0-5 frees)
	P. Fenning 1-1	B. Lynch 0-2
	S. Darby 0-2	M. O'Dwyer 0-2
	M. Connor 0-2	L. Higgins 0-2
	W. Bryan 0-3	
	K. Kilmurray 0-1	
Attendance:	66,136 (replay record)	
Referee:	Patsy Devlin (Tyrone)	

FINAL MISCELLANY

- Writing in *The Irish Press* after Offaly's replay win over Kerry, Sean Diffley captured the ferocity of Paddy McCormack's unique footballing style: 'The Colossus of Rhode defended the Offaly goal with all the tenacity of an ancient mariner repelling boarders. He used everything bar the cutlass.'
- Kerry legend Mick O'Connell and Rosaleen O'Reilly from Cavan were married the day before the replay. Best man was Ned Fitzgerald, former Kerry captain and father of Cahirciveen legend, Maurice.
- Two Kerry lads, finding the gates of Croke Park open on the night of the replay, decided to have their very own kick-around under the moonlit sky. Pat Spillane and Páidí Ó Sé would make ten more visits to Croke Park on All-Ireland day as players, each winning eight Celtic Crosses in the process.
- Paddy McCormack (Offaly) and Mick O'Dwyer (Kerry), both of whom lined out in the 1972 decider, were also team selectors.

1972 — THE YEAR THAT WAS

- In Derry's Bogside on 30 January, a day that would become known as Bloody Sunday, soldiers from the British Parachute Regiment opened fire on civilians who were protesting against internment without trial. A total of twenty-six people were shot, of whom fourteen were fatally wounded. Three days later, the British Embassy building on Dublin's Merrion Square was burned to the ground.
- At the 1972 Olympics in Munich, eleven members of the Israeli team were shot dead by terrorists from the Palestinian Black Sabbath movement.
- When a British European Airways flight crashed at Staines, near Heathrow Airport, on 18 June 1972, all 118 people on board were killed. Among the dead was a delegation of twelve Irish business leaders on their way to Brussels for meetings preparatory to accession to the EEC.

1972 TEAM LINE-OUTS — DRAW

OFFALY

1. Martin Furlong
(Tullamore)

2. Mick Ryan
(Erin's Isle, Dublin, also Doon, Tullamore and Sean McDermotts, Dublin)

3. Paddy McCormack
(Rhode)

4. Larry Coughlan
(Eadestown, Kildare, also Killeigh and St Mary's)

5. Eugene Mulligan
(Rhode)

6. Sean Lowry
(Ferbane, also Crossmolina, Mayo)

7. Martin Heavey
(Rhode)

8. Willie Bryan
(Éire Óg, also Walsh Island)

9. Sean Evans
(Ballyfore, also Edenderry)

10. Johnny Cooney
(Erin Rovers)

11. Kevin Kilmurray
(Daingean and UCD, also Civil Service)

12. Tony McTague
(Ferbane) Capt.

13. Seamus Darby
(Rhode, also Edenderry)

14. John Smith
(Gracefield)

15. Paddy Fenning
(Tullamore)

Subs: Jody Gunning (Rhode) Played; Murt Connor (Éire Óg, also Walsh Island); Nicholas Clavin (St Carthage's); Mick Wright (Daingean, also Celbridge, Kildare); Noel Kinnarney (St Columba's); Liam Hanlon (Daingean); Sean Kilroy (St Carthage's, also Rathcline, Longford)

KERRY

1. Eamonn Fitzgerald
(Dr Crokes)

2. Donie O'Sullivan
(Spa, also Dr Crokes and Clanna
Gael, Dublin)

3. Paud O'Donoghue
(Ballylongford)

4. Seamus Mac Gearailt
(An Ghaeltacht, also Gaoth Dobhair,
Donegal)

5. Tom Prendergast
(Keel, also Forestry College, Wicklow,
Sean Mac Cumhaills, Donegal and
Ballingeary, Cork) Capt.

6. Mícheál Ó Sé
(An Ghaeltacht)

7. Paudie Lynch
(Beaufort)

8. Mick O'Connell
(Valentia, also Waterville)

9. John O'Keeffe
(Austin Stacks and UCD)

10. Brendan Lynch
(Beaufort and UCC)

11. Donal Kavanagh
(Dr Crokes and UCC)

12. Eamonn O'Donoghue
(Ballylongford)

13. Mick Gleeson
(Spa and UCD)

14. Liam Higgins
(Lispole)

15. Mick O'Dwyer
(Waterville)

Subs: Derry Crowley (Glenflesk) Played; Pat Griffin (Clonakilty, Cork, also Glenbeigh/Glencar) Played; Jackie Walsh (Ballylongford and UCD); John Saunders (Rathmore); Mickey 'Ned' O'Sullivan (Kenmare)

1972 TEAM LINE-OUTS – REPLAY

OFFALY (WINNERS)

1. Martin Furlong
(Tullamore)

2. Mick Ryan
(Erin's Isle, Dublin, also Doon,
Tullamore and Sean McDermotts,
Dublin)

3. Paddy McCormack
(Rhode)

4. Larry Coughlan
(Eadestown, Kildare, also Killeigh and
St Mary's)

5. Eugene Mulligan
(Rhode)

6. Sean Lowry
(Ferbane, also Crossmolina, Mayo)

7. Martin Heavey
(Rhode)

8. Willie Bryan
(Éire Óg, also Walsh Island)

9. Sean Evans
(Ballyfore, also Edenderry)

10. Johnny Cooney
(Erin Rovers)

11. Kevin Kilmurray
(Daingean and UCD, also Civil
Service)

12. Tony McTague
(Ferbane) Capt.

13. Seamus Darby
(Rhode, also Edenderry)

14. John Smith
(Gracefield)

15. Paddy Fenning
(Tullamore)

Subs: Murt Connor (Éire Óg, also Walsh Island) Played; Nicholas Clavin (St Carthage's) Played; Mick Wright (Daingean, also Celbridge, Kildare) Played; Noel Kinnarney (St Columba's); Jody Gunning (Rhode); Liam Hanlon (Daingean); Sean Kilroy (St Carthage's, also Rathcline, Longford)

KERRY (RUNNERS-UP)

1. Eamonn Fitzgerald
(Dr Crokes)

2. Donie O'Sullivan
(Spa, also Dr Crokes and Clanna
Gael, Dublin)

3. Paud O'Donoghue
(Ballylongford)

4. Seamus Mac Gearailt
(An Ghaeltacht, also Gaoth Dobhair,
Donegal)

5. Tom Prendergast
(Keel, also Forestry College, Wicklow,
Sean Mac Cumhaills, Donegal and
Ballingeary, Cork) Capt.

6. Mícheál Ó Sé
(An Ghaeltacht)

7. Paudie Lynch
(Beaufort)

8. Mick O'Connell
(Valentia, also Waterville)

9. John O'Keeffe
(Austin Stacks and UCD)

10. Brendan Lynch
(Beaufort and UCC)

11. Donal Kavanagh
(Dr Crokes and UCC)

12. Eamonn O'Donoghue
(Ballylongford)

13. Mick Gleeson
(Spa and UCD)

14. Liam Higgins
(Lispole)

15. Mick O'Dwyer
(Waterville)

Subs: Derry Crowley (Glenflesk) Played; Pat Griffin (Clonakilty, Cork, also Glenbeigh/Glencar) Played; Jackie Walsh (Ballylongford and UCD) Played; John Saunders (Rathmore); Mickey 'Ned' O'Sullivan (Kenmare); Ger Power (Austin Stacks); John Coffey (Beaufort).

1973

Such was the depth of anger among some Donegal County Board officials in the days that followed their 0-12 to 1-7 Ulster quarter-final defeat to Tyrone in Ballybofey that consideration was given to applying to Connacht to contest future provincial championships.

The game had left a sour taste, not the loss itself but the toxic undercurrent on the terraces and on the field where Donegal veteran Neilly Gallagher was left hospitalised with a horrific cut around the eye. Donegal alleged that the twelfth-minute incident was deliberate and had happened off the ball with referee Hugh McPolin's eyes on the play at the other end of the field. Bottles of water, cans and even rocks were hurled onto the field at various stages as tensions escalated. Things got so bad that substitutes declined to warm up.

Privately, Donegal had been expressing concern about the dangers that cross-border games were placing on their supporters and to some extent their players, and this felt like a tipping point. But despite conveying these concerns to the Ulster Council the following day and demanding an investigation into all the incidents that took place, the threat to relocate to Connacht never materialised.

'We have to protect our players from this sort of abuse and it is a terrible thing that we have to admit that we had to fight our way off the pitch on Sunday,' Donegal secretary Frank Muldoon told the *Donegal Democrat*, which led its front page with the potential Connacht move in the week after the game. Tyrone manager Jody O'Neill refuted any contention that his team had been underhand in their approach, stating that 'I never send out a team to do anything except play football.'

On the field, Tyrone had Seamus Donaghy sent off but were fortified by magnificent performances against the reigning champions from midfielders Aidan McMahon and Frank McGuigan, minor captain the previous year. McGuigan was now captain of the senior team, courtesy of his club Ardboe's reign as Tyrone champions, but he took to leadership with ease. It was clear that beyond events in Ballybofey, there was a progressive team developing.

Ballybofey wasn't the only controversy to engulf an Ulster county that summer. Derry had played a league semi-final against Kerry in April that ended acrimoniously as up to 200 of their supporters angrily invaded Croke Park, ostensibly to vent frustration at referee Paul Kelly for his perceived influence as it finished level, Derry's 2-5 to 0-11.

Two Derry players, Chris Brown and Tom Quinn, had been sent off by Kelly, inflaming tensions that got out of hand as seats were ripped up and bottles flung by supporters in the direction of stewards, gardaí and even Director-General Seán Ó Síocháin. Kelly admitted afterwards that he had

A jubilant Billy Morgan raises the Sam Maguire Cup after Cork's victory over Galway in the 1973 decider. *Image courtesy of the GAA Museum at Croke Park.*

been in danger, stating that 'they came like wild animals, not like human beings. Only for the Gardaí, I would have been in serious trouble.'

A long-drawn-out investigation followed, the upshot of which was that Derry refused to play the replay as the then Activities Committee of the GAA broadened disciplinary measures to fine the county £500 and suspend Sean O'Connell for three months, solely on the written evidence of a rival Kerry player. O'Connell subsequently withdrew his services from inter-county football while his club, Ballerin, stood down from activity for the period. The final straw for Derry was Kelly's reappointment for the replay after apparent assurances at a high level that such an appointment would not be made.

Kerry, who had Tom Prendergast suspended for two months, went on to claim the league title and Derry articulated their frustration through several channels afterwards. The team and management, after a challenge against Kildare in May, gave their side of the story, focusing on how O'Connell's suspension was arrived at as they expressed 'grave dissatisfaction' with the treatment meted out to him. 'It was extremely vindictive to suspend a player indefinitely on the allegations of (a Kerry player). We believe that the GAA has been greatly degraded when one informs on another,' read a statement, signed by captain Gerry O'Loughlin, manager Harry Cassidy and selector Harry Gribbin.

A month later the Derry County Board presented their findings. 'We reject utterly the contention

Left: Acknowledged as one of the best dual-code referees, John Moloney from Bansha in Tipperary tosses the coin before the 1973 decider between Cork and Galway. Rival captains (l–r) Billy Morgan (Cork) and Liam Sammon (Galway) look on. *Image courtesy of the GAA Museum at Croke Park.*

Below: Cork, All-Ireland champions 1973. Back (l–r): Donie O'Donovan (team coach), Denis Long, Ray Cummins, Jimmy Barry-Murphy, John Coleman, Dave McCarthy, Declan Barron, Ned Kirby, Denis Coughlan; front (l–r): Jimmy Barrett, Connie Hartnett, Kevin Jer O'Sullivan, Billy Morgan, Frank Cogan, Brian Murphy, Humphrey Kelleher. *Image courtesy of the GAA Museum at Croke Park.*

of the Activities Committee that the alleged rough tactics of the Derry team communicated itself to the Derry supporters,' part of their lengthy statement read. 'In an effort to blacken further the good name of Derry in GAA circles, some sociological claptrap was trotted out and an attempt was made by some journalists to relate what happened in Croke Park to the political situation in the Six Counties.'

Consequently, a fine Derry team showed signs of fragmentation in the Ulster Championship. They beat Monaghan 1-7 to 0-4 in Castleblayney but subsequently lost to Down, 1-12 to 0-9, as suspensions, Mickey Niblock's soccer exploits in the US and injuries weakened them.

In the previous rounds Down had beaten Armagh and then Cavan, inflicting only a fourth first-round loss on the Breffni men in a century and a first since 1966.

Tyrone's progress continued unimpeded on the other side with a 1-15 to 0-11 win over Fermanagh, thanks to another Donaghy goal and another tour de force from McGuigan at midfield. Fermanagh had reached an Ulster semi-final for the first time in seven years thanks to a 3-9 to 4-4 win over Antrim, with Eamonn McPartland scoring all three goals in the opening seventeen minutes.

Only on the eve of the Ulster Final was Tyrone defender Mickey Joe Forbes suspended by the Ulster Activities Committee, arising out of their Ballybofey inquiry, and with Colm McAlarney back, Down had some grounds to be optimistic.

But Tyrone's form lines, which had seen them beat Down in the Division Two League, the League Final and the McKenna Cup, held up with a 3-13 to 1-11 win before 30,000 in Clones, as Sean McElhatton's brace of goals proved crucial, giving them a first provincial title in sixteen years.

In the previous four years that Roscommon were Connacht champions, they had successfully defended the title (1944, 1947, 1953 and 1962). But at no stage in their semi-final, not even when they trailed by 0-7 to 1-3 at the break in Hyde Park before 15,000 spectators, did that sequence look like continuing as a resurgent Galway emerged 1-13 to 1-8 winners.

Galway had ridden their luck a little in their opening game against Sligo, their 3-6 to 1-9 win in Tuam framed by fortuitous goals for Johnny Coughlan, Michael Rooney and Liam Sammon. At one stage, Sligo had led by 0-6 to 0-2.

On the other side of the draw, Leitrim's ebbing competitiveness was reflected in a twenty-four-point beating by Mayo who ran in seven goals (7-6 to 0-3). It doubled the gap from two years earlier when Mayo had won by 5-7 to 2-4. But for many fine saves from their goalkeeper Noel Crossan, Leitrim would have suffered an even heavier defeat.

The game is never recognised as the great Packie McGarty's inter-county sign-off – that came two years earlier – but the forty-year-old was on the bench as an unused substitute that day, a twenty-fourth and last campaign of involvement. Three of Mayo's goals came from Willie McGee, a survivor, along with John Morley, Tom Fitzgerald, Johnny Carey and Joe Corcoran, from Mayo's last provincial title win four years earlier. But McGee's prolific streak deserted him in the final when he was denied by Galway goalkeeper Gay Mitchell on at least two occasions, as the Tribesmen landed a 1-17 to 2-12 win in Castlebar to take their thirty-first title. Galway led by

Cork and Galway players appear to focus on everything except the ball in this action shot from the 1973 Final.
Image courtesy of the GAA Museum at Croke Park.

eleven points at one stage in the second half but were clinging on at the end as Mayo, stirred by Sean O'Grady's new midfield partnership with John Morley, made a charge to outscore their neighbours by 2-5 to 0-2 in the last twenty-five minutes.

Offaly began the defence of their Leinster title with the weight of recent history stacked against them. Not since 1938 had a county in the province completed a three-in-a-row. Dublin, Meath and Offaly had all achieved two titles in a row on more than once occasion, but none had managed to add a third since Laois in 1938. And they made quite the inauspicious start when defeating a Danny Nugent-inspired Louth in the quarter-final by 1-8 to 0-8, Willie Bryan's move to midfield and goal making the difference.

Louth had provided the big talking point in the four-team preliminary round which they emerged from by knocking Dublin out of the championship after a replay. It was a reflection of how far Dublin were falling that they had found themselves in the preliminary round in the first place and then lost to the Wee County by 1-8 to 0-9 before 10,000 in Navan.

In truth, it should never have even gone to a replay. Bartle Faulkner had rescued Louth, on a seven-match unbeaten run, with a late equaliser but they had been the dominant team, spurred on by Tony Hoey's early goal.

Paddy O'Brien and Frank Murray from a penalty hit back to give Dublin some momentum, but despite fielding nine players that would start and win an All-Ireland Final more than twelve months later, it would have been rough justice had Dublin prevailed.

Meath had lost some of their lustre since the 1970 All-Ireland Final and there was little sign of any progression when they scraped past Westmeath by 1-6 to 0-8 thanks to a goal from Matt Kerrigan. Among the debutants for Meath on the day was the former Roscommon player Pat McManus.

Nine points from Wicklow's Peter Clarke wasn't enough to prevent a 3-15 to 0-14 defeat to Laois and with Sean Donnelly retiring after fourteen years, Longford were no match for a wasteful Kildare side that triumphed in Athy by 0-13 to 0-8. And yet Kildare, in keeping with the growing trend of having a player, Pat Mangan, as manager, were off the pace when they met Offaly in their semi-final, losing 1-15 to 2-6. They looked well placed at the break, just 0-9 to 1-3 behind with the wind to come, but a Johnny Cooney goal, his lob deceiving the Kildare defence, stretched an Offaly lead that couldn't be reeled in.

Kerrigan's introduction for Meath made the difference again as they beat Laois by 2-17 to 1-11, a result few could have seen at the break when Laois led by 2-8 to 1-8 after playing with the wind. For Offaly it was a fifth successive Leinster Final appearance against a Meath side that had lost five of their seven Division Two League games.

Both counties made transatlantic travel arrangements in the build-up, with Kevin Kilmurray and Kevin McConnell flown home. And it was McConnell who was happier at the break as Meath led by 1-7 to 1-5.

Galway, All-Ireland Finalists 1973. The Galway footballers of the early 1970s suffered the agony and frustration of losing the finals of 1971, 1973 and 1974. Back (l–r): Tom Naughton, Joe Waldron, Morgan Hughes, Jimmy Duggan, Gay Mitchell, Liam O'Neill, Tommy Joe Gilmore, Jack Cosgrove; front (l–r): Michael Rooney, Johnny Coughlan, Maurice Burke, Brendan Colleran, Liam Sammon, Billy Joyce, Johnny Hughes. *Sportsfile.*

Offaly changed jerseys during the interval, switching from all white to white with a green front-ing, but the change in the champions was more than cosmetic as they overwhelmed Meath, hitting 2-16 over the next forty minutes. Tony McTague landed eleven points but was also the subject of an off-the-ball blow just before the interval that enraged the Offaly support and roused their players.

It was a statement performance from Offaly, now without Paddy McCormack, who was forced to retire – he made a brief comeback in 1974 – with an eye injury picked up in a Grounds Tournament game at the end of the previous year. The game saw Nicholas Clavin return from a knee injury in the 1972 Leinster Final that had kept him out for a year, apart from an appearance as a substitute in the All-Ireland Final replay against Kerry ten months earlier.

Clare's 0-18 to 1-5 Munster quarter-final win over Waterford in early June placed Cork playing and coaching great Eamonn Young in something of a dilemma. He had been helping out with Clare but progression now put him in the pathway of his native county, not a position he was prepared to countenance. By agreement, he stepped aside for the semi-final two weeks later, a day when the Rebels hinted at things to come with a 2-14 to 0-3 win, both goals from Billy Field and Jimmy Bar-rett coming in a three-minute period before half-time. Field was making his debut and posted 1-8 (0-6 from frees) to illustrate his talent.

Tipperary had Michael 'Babs' Keating back for their quarter-final with Limerick and his 1-1 helped to secure a 4-13 to 1-7 win on a day when Paudie Blythe hit three goals and Johnny Cum-mins landed seven points. 'Babs' had been suspended for four months for an incident in a league hurling match the previous December against Cork but here his distribution was a class apart. In their semi-final with Kerry, however, they were overwhelmed by 3-11 to 0-5 in Tralee as Mickey 'Ned' O'Sullivan struck for two goals.

Kerry themselves were on the receiving end of a goal blitz like no other in the Munster Final before 28,859 as Cork hit five in the opening twenty-four minutes in the Athletic Grounds to lead by 5-3 to 0-2. The promise of the previous decade of dominance of underage competitions – up to twelve of the squad had All-Ireland minor medals while another ten had All-Ireland Under-21 medals – looked like it was ready to translate into something much more tangible.

But by the sixty-first minute Kerry, remarkably, were back to within five points and threatening, with Cork captain Billy Morgan forced to make a save from John Egan on his knees to prevent further erosion. It had the desired effect. Kerry scored just one point in the closing nineteen min-utes as Cork served notice of real intent with a 5-12 to 1-15 win over the previous year's beaten All-Ireland finalists.

Central to their success was the impact of Jimmy Barry-Murphy, the talented nineteen-year-old who was making his championship debut and lit up the ground with his movement and dash to score one goal and create another, as his switch with full-forward Ray Cummins paid dividends, troubling the Kerry full-back line who had clearly been expecting something different.

It is considered one of Morgan's best displays in an illustrious career as he thwarted both Mick

O'Dwyer and Mickey 'Ned' O'Sullivan in the opening eight minutes, prior to that save from Egan. In fact, Donal Kavanagh's fifty-third minute goal was Morgan's first concession in four Munster finals that he had played in at the Athletic Grounds. Field, Barrett (two) and Denis Long got the other four goals while Cummins enjoyed another fine Munster Final against Kerry, finishing with four points.

Cork's All-Ireland semi-final was a first championship meeting with Tyrone. Conditions were difficult and the new Munster champions had to deal with the perception that away from their home ground, the Athletic Grounds, they weren't near the force they were at home.

Tyrone were on a seventeen-match unbeaten streak, and with midfielder Aidan McMahon cleared to play after picking up an injury against Down, their optimism grew. And for a long time they hung in, three Cork goals in the last ten minutes giving a different impression on the scoreboard than how the match had evolved. It had been emphatic but nothing like the 5-10 to 2-4 scoreline suggested.

Cork lost Field to a suspected leg fracture, and with his having already scored 2-14 in the championship that was a blow. Barry-Murphy brought his goal tally to three in two championship games with a brace, both coming in those closing stages. And Cummins, who had his best game in either hurling or football that year, got the first goal as they established control. Cork's win, watched by 28,997, headed off a controversy as Tyrone had sixteen players on the field for a three-minute spell in the first half.

A week earlier, Galway had dethroned Offaly, 0-16 to 2-8, in the first semi-final, before 36,705. Offaly had won their three previous All-Ireland semi-finals and brought much experience – captain Pat Keenan was their only player without an All-Ireland medal. And when they drew level going into the fourth quarter after a McTague goal and Sean Evans point made it 0-11 to 1-8, the prospects of a three-in-a-row remained on course. But Galway asserted themselves impressively, with Liam Sammon and Jimmy Duggan rampant through midfield. It was Sammon who got the insurance point after an Evans goal had again brought Offaly back into it and, for the first time since 1956, Galway and Cork would contest an All-Ireland Final.

THE FINAL – 23 SEPTEMBER

The challenge to the Galway players was simple – beat Cork by twelve points and the keys of a new house were theirs. Even by modern standards such a carrot would be grossly out of place in a game largely semi-professional in approach but still rooted in amateur ethos. 'Rewards', even on a small scale, are rare, not to mention what was on offer when Galway auctioneer Tom Colleran threw down the gauntlet to the county's footballers in the week leading up to the final.

The rationale was simple. Galway had registered eighteen wides in their semi-final win over Offaly and Colleran felt an incentive could focus their minds that bit more. What had started out initially as an apparent joke developed to the point where Colleran made enquiries about insurance for the cost of houses for all, which would have amounted to around £200,000 in total, with an insurance premium of £7,000 to £10,000. The GAA was aghast at such a proposal but there was nothing in its rules to prevent it. Director-General Seán Ó Síocháin was particularly scathing, suggesting it was a 'publicity gimmick' that was 'in very bad taste at a time when so many families can't get homes'.

The proposal never went ahead. And Galway never came close to beating Cork by twelve points. Quite the opposite in fact, as they felt the full force of a Cork team that the former Taoiseach and All-Ireland winner in 1945, Jack Lynch, described beforehand as the county's best ever team. He was just as adamant in the aftermath of a resounding seven-point win.

As a portent for what was to come, the respective cumulative goals were accurate pointers as to where the difference would lie. In their three games Cork had scored 12-36, one goal to every three points scored. Galway had scored just five goals in their four games, 5-52 in all, while conceding 6-37.

Cork's capacity to score goals was clear and they didn't disappoint on that front, with Barry-Murphy continuing his scintillating form with a goal inside ninety seconds after Galway had opened the scoring. Watched by 73,308, the largest All-Ireland Final crowd at the time since the capacity at Croke Park was reduced in 1965, Cork were supreme in building up a 1-9 to 0-3 lead after twenty-eight minutes. All the doubts around their ability to deliver when the pressure was really on began to abate. For years they had been stockpiling All-Ireland success at minor and Under-21 level and it appeared only a matter of time before they'd make that breakthrough. However, the issue of dual players weighed heavier on Cork than any other county and it seemed to restrict their footballers when they should have been at their best.

But 1973 felt different. Billy Morgan had captained Nemo Rangers to an All-Ireland club title earlier in the year and was captain of the county, providing experience, assurance and leadership when big moments were upon them. Morgan was one of three survivors, along with Frank Cogan and Denis Coughlan, from their previous All-Ireland Final appearance against Meath six years earlier. In Donie O'Donovan they had a trainer held in high esteem and in Barry-Murphy they had a young man with an X factor rarely seen at this level before. His impact was seismic. He exuded class and style and it was easy to see why, even then, he would become a Rebel legend in the years that followed.

Galway had lost John Tobin to injury and frankly never really threatened, despite closing to three points at one stage in the second half, having been behind by 1-10 to 0-6 at the break. Tom Naughton got their first goal and even then there was a question mark over it, with Morgan querying whether it had crossed the line after the initial effort had struck an upright.

Naughton and Liam Sammon had been troubling Kelleher and John Coleman in the central attacking positions, but switching Declan Barron back to the defence for the last quarter was an inspired move from the Cork sideline.

Ultimately Barry-Murphy's second goal on seventy-two minutes, a score for the ages, decided it. Jimmy Barrett got a third and with Morgan saving from Maurice Burke, Jimmy Duggan and Colie McDonagh throughout, Galway were largely kept at arm's length. No wonder Sammon visited the winning dressing-room afterwards to present his rival captain with the match ball.

It was Cork's first All-Ireland success in twenty-eight years and finally delivered on the promise of the previous decade.

FINAL STATISTICS

	Cork	Galway
Full-time:	3-17	2-13
Half-time:	1-10	0-6
Scorers:	R. Cummins 0-8 (0-6 frees)	M. Hughes 0-7 (0-6 frees)
	J. Barry-Murphy 2-1	T. Naughton 1-0
	J. Barrett 1-2	J. Hughes 1-0
	D. Long 0-3 (0-2 frees)	M. Burke 0-2
	D. Coughlan 0-1	J. Duggan 0-2
	D. Barron 0-1	T.J. Gilmore 0-1
	N. Kirby 0-1	L. Sammon 0-1
Attendance:	73,308	
Referee:	John Moloney (Tipperary)	

FINAL MISCELLANY

- Running onto the pitch at Croke Park on 23 September, Cork captain Billy Morgan was wearing scapulars given to him by P.A. 'Weesh' Murphy, who had become unwell and died at the hurling final three weeks earlier. The same scapulars were worn by 'Weesh' when he led Cork to All-Ireland victory in 1945.
- There was no popping of champagne corks in the victorious dressing-room after the 1973 Final. Instead, the exhausted Cork men launched into tubs of ice cream in an effort to quench their burning thirst.
- Manchester United manager Tommy Docherty and his assistant Pat Crerand attended the All-Ireland Final. Guests of Mick O'Connell and Ned Fitzgerald, they were on their way to Lisbon to attend Eusébio's testimonial. The visitors were hugely impressed by Cork's Ned Kirby and Billy Morgan, while O'Connell declared that he had witnessed 'the finest performance I have seen from a Leeside team'.
- The case of the missing number 13 jersey caused consternation in the Cork team hotel prior to the All-Ireland Final. It transpired that the jersey had been loaned for a display in Clery's window on O'Connell St for the weekend but inadvertently left there when other items were being returned on Saturday evening. An SOS, involving leading GAA officials and local gardaí, was sent out but even then the difficulty of locating security and keys to access the window display consumed time. With no replacement number 13 jersey, anxiety built but the window display was eventually opened and the jersey delivered back to the Skylon Hotel just as Cork were making the short trip to Croke Park.

1973 — THE YEAR THAT WAS

- In a referendum on 10 May 1972, over 83% of the electorate had voted in favour of entry into the Common Market. Ireland formally joined the EEC on 1 January 1973.
- In July 1973, Ireland abolished the provision under which women employed in the public services were obliged to resign when they married.
- In April, the Minister for Education, Richard Burke, removed the requirement to obtain a minimum D grade in Irish in order to pass the Intermediate and Leaving Certificate examinations.
- An oil embargo imposed by the Organisation of Arab Petroleum Exporting Countries in October resulted in unprecedented queues at petrol stations throughout the country.
- There was no shortage of fuel for the helicopter which landed in the exercise yard of Mountjoy Prison on 31 October. To the acute embarrassment of the Irish government, three IRA prisoners made a daring aerial escape from confinement.

1973 TEAM LINE-OUTS

CORK (WINNERS)

1. Billy Morgan
(Nemo Rangers) Capt.

2. Frank Cogan
(Nemo Rangers)

3. Humphrey Kelleher
(Millstreet)

4. Brian Murphy
(Nemo Rangers)

5. Kevin Jer O'Sullivan
(Adrigole)

6. John Coleman
(Millstreet)

7. Connie Hartnett
(Millstreet)

8. Denis Long
(Millstreet, also Austin Stacks, Kerry)

9. Denis Coughlan
(St Nicholas)

10. Ned Kirby
(Grange, also Glanworth)

11. Declan Barron
(Bantry Blues)

12. Dave McCarthy
(Clonakilty and UCD)

13. Jimmy Barry-Murphy
(St Finbarr's)

14. Ray Cummins
(St Michael's)

15. Jimmy Barrett
(Nemo Rangers)

Subs: Seamus Coughlan (Nemo Rangers) Played; Donal Hunt (Bantry Blues) Played; Mick Scannell (Naomh Abán) Played; Noel Murphy (Bishopstown and UCC); Robert Wilmott (Bandon); Teddy O'Brien (St Nicholas)

GALWAY (RUNNERS-UP)

1. Gay Mitchell
(Dunmore MacHales)

2. Joe Waldron
(Milltown and UCD)

3. Jack Cosgrove
(St Nicholas, Cork, also Clifden and Spiddal)

4. Brendan Colleran
(Mountbellew-Moylough)

5. Liam O'Neill
(St Grellan's, also Castlebar Mitchels, Mayo and Knockmore, Mayo)

6. Tommy Joe Gilmore
(Cortoon Shamrocks)

7. Johnny Hughes
(Mountbellew-Moylough)

8. Billy Joyce
(Killererin)

9. Jimmy Duggan
(Corofin, also Claremorris, Mayo)

10. Maurice Burke
(Corofin)

11. Liam Sammon
(Fr Griffin's, also Salthill-Knocknacarra) Capt.

12. Michael Rooney
(Cortoon Shamrocks)

13. Johnny Coughlan
(St Grellan's)

14. Tom Naughton
(Annaghdown)

15. Morgan Hughes
(Killererin)

Subs: Frank Canavan (Corofin) Played; Colie McDonagh (Fr Griffin's) Played; Martin Noonan (St Michael's); John Dillon (St Gabriel's); John Tobin (Tuam Stars); Michael Geraghty (Glenamaddy, also Dunmore MacHales); Gabriel King (Mountbellew-Moylough); Emmett Farrell (St Gabriel's, also Fr Griffin's)

1974

By 1974 it had become apparent to legislators that the game needed 'cleaning up'. A Rules Revision Committee was convened and by Congress that April they had proposed a series of sweeping measures that were designed to transform and eliminate some of the 'darker arts'.

Among them was a ban on the 'third man' tackle (a fair charge would in future be defined as side to side with one foot on the ground), the exclusion of any opponent from the small parallelogram (fifteen yards by five yards) before the arrival of the ball, a ban on charging the goalkeeper, the moving forward of the ball by ten yards for dissent, dismissal for persistent fouling and an expansion of the second parallelogram or penalty area to fourteen yards by twenty-one yards. Restoration of the hand pass, in addition to the existing fisted pass, was also cleared for a twelve-month trial period.

Naturally, it led to concerns that such 'sanitisation' would weaken one of the game's pillars, its physical engagement. And initially it was the monitoring of the flight of the ball relative to the positioning of the player making his way into the small 'square' that troubled referees, with leading exponent John Moloney suggesting at one stage that a third umpire, in addition to the existing two, would be required for added vigilance.

But as the championship took hold it was the return of the hand pass and the expansion of the second parallelogram that would have the most significant impact, with penalties a recurring theme right from the off until Dublin's Paddy Cullen knocked out Galway's Liam Sammon's effort for a fifty in the All-Ireland Final, arguably the game and the season's defining moment.

Who could have envisaged how the season would turn out when Dublin set off in the foothills of the Leinster Championship? The Dubs had again been pitched into a preliminary group with Carlow, Louth and Wexford, an indication of how far they had fallen in the preceding years. Kevin Heffernan had taken charge and on the same day that Kerry beat Roscommon in the League Final, Dublin got their campaign underway with a 3-9 to 0-6 win over Wexford, Bobby Doyle scoring two goals including a 'new' penalty.

Prior to that Louth had beaten a Cyril Hughes-inspired Carlow (3-14 to 3-7), who had themselves scored from two penalties, Willie Doyle converting one and connecting with the rebound from another as it became obvious how great the adjustment was going to be.

Inevitably a penalty, this time scored by Brian Mullins, featured in Dublin's 'surprise' win over Louth in the second round, reversing the previous year's result, but the chief catalyst was the return after a two-year absence of Jimmy Keaveney and with nine points, a combination of frees and play, the logic of Heffernan's persuasion was clear.

Dublin were quietly building momentum and it carried into the quarter-final against reigning provincial champions Offaly, seeking four-in-a-row, which Dublin edged by 1-11 to 0-13 after the sides had been level seven times. Bernard Brogan had a big impact off the bench in the second half and the pivotal moment came at the end when Sean Lowry was stripped of possession by Stephen Rooney and Mullins set up Leslie Deegan for the winning score.

Kildare had beaten Longford in their opening game, 2-10 to 0-11, and having overcome Dublin in the Division Two League Final earlier in the year they were justifiably confident of a repeat. But in truth they were no match as a Mullins penalty was decisive in a 1-13 to 0-10 win, booking a first provincial final for the Dubs in nine years. Heffernan's influence and exploitation of the hand-pass rule were evident with the volume of games helping to develop a stronger unit.

Meath opened their campaign with a 3-8 to 0-7 win over Westmeath and followed up with a ten-point win over Laois. Gerry Farrelly's goal was decisive but Laois themselves had six clear-cut goal opportunities.

The midfield dominance of Mullins and Rooney was a key factor in Dublin's thirtieth Leinster success against Meath before 37,067, a provincial final crowd that signalled another sign of a city's

The Jacks are Back! Back (l–r): Stephen Rooney, Anton O'Toole, Robbie Kelleher, Jimmy Keaveney, Tony Hanahoe, Paddy Cullen, John McCarthy, Alan Larkin, Bobby Doyle; front (l–r): Brian Mullins, Georgie Wilson, Paddy Reilly, Sean Doherty, David Hickey, Gay O'Driscoll. *Image courtesy of the GAA Museum at Croke Park.*

football uprising. Dublin won by 1-14 to 1-9 and the five-point margin didn't flatter them, despite being behind at half-time and only hitting the front in the fifty-sixth minute.

The year saw the departure of two of Kerry's greats, Mick O'Dwyer bowing out after scoring two points from full-forward in a league defeat to Cork, and Mick O'Connell signing off after coming on as a late substitute in the Munster Final against the same opponents.

By then Cork had become the dominant force, All-Ireland champions the previous year, and despite a less than convincing effort in the Wembley Tournament Final against Galway two weeks earlier they still scored a resounding 3-14 to 2-2 win over Tipperary in their opening provincial game. Tipp, hampered by injuries to 'Babs' Keating and Jim Kehoe, didn't score until a John Cummins point early in the second half.

Michael Hackett's goal had helped Waterford overcome a Limerick team featuring hurling giant Pat Hartigan at full-back, but they were hit for seven goals by Kerry in their semi-final (7-16 to 0-8).

Mikey Sheehy and Páidí Ó Sé both made championship debuts that day and Sheehy celebrated with two goals, booking his team's place in the final against Cork, only the second time in their history that the Rebels, as All-Ireland champions, had faced Kerry in a provincial final.

Some 49,822 set a new attendance record in a rain-soaked Killarney but the home crowd were left disappointed as Cork ran out seven-point winners (1-11 to 0-7). Kerry had led by 0-6 to 0-4 at the break but essentially it was over at that point with Billy Morgan saves from John Egan and Mickey 'Ned' O'Sullivan serving to deflate before Cork used the significant wind advantage to drive home dominance. Dave McCarthy's goal sealed it and Kerry were left with much to ponder for the future as they reflected on only a second successive championship defeat to their neighbours.

Out west, Galway were seeking a fourth Connacht title in five years and got off on the right note with a 3-11 to 0-13 semi-final win over Mayo before 20,000 in Tuam on a day that Tommy Joe Gilmore and Jimmy Duggan were dominant.

Mickey Kearins was Sligo's player-manager and sole selector as they beat Leitrim thanks to Michael Laffey's 2-4. Leaving Cert student Mickey Martin impressed on his championship debut for Leitrim, the beginning of a career that would last almost two decades.

It took a replay for Roscommon to thwart Sligo, a dour and physical affair with fifty-five frees as they met for a fourth time in a matter of months, this time going head to head with the West Germany–Netherlands World Cup Final. The Dermot Earley–Gerry Beirne midfield axis gave Roscommon an edge en route to a 0-13 to 0-8 win after they had drawn, 1-11 to 2-8, in the first game.

A week later, before 25,000 in Pearse Stadium in Salthill, another dominant Gilmore display saw Galway retain the title, 2-14 to 0-8, with penalties again being influential, Liam Sammon converting two, in contrast to Mickey Freyne's point from his, a telling difference. For many, it was a strong statement from Galway in light of their previous year's All-Ireland Final defeat to Cork.

The Ulster Championship had been placed in some doubt over the freezing of petrol supplies as action by the Ulster Workers Council in opposition to the Sunningdale Agreement intensified. But

If Kevin Heffernan was the brains behind Dublin's resurgence in the 1970s, his St Vincent's clubmate Brian Mullins was its beating heart. Here, Mullins is in typically determined mode against Galway in the 1974 Final. Johnny Hughes (number 7) and Tommy Joe Gilmore are the Galway players. *Image courtesy the GAA Museum at Croke Park.*

when it got underway in June, Down eased past Armagh by 1-10 to 0-6 in the preliminary round thanks to Mickey Cunningham's goal, courtesy of an astute Sean O'Neill flick. Meanwhile, late Anthony McGurk and Gerry O'Loughlin goals within sixty seconds gave Derry a 3-6 to 0-8 win over Monaghan.

Down pressed on to beat Cavan, 2-8 to 0-12, in their quarter-final. Colm McAlarney had been out of action for almost two years with a broken arm that required three surgeries, but his introduction sparked Down, and with his first touch midway through the second half he goaled, putting the Mourne men in front for the first time since the eighth minute. It earned them a semi-final spot against Derry which they negotiated comfortably, 1-12 to 0-7, with O'Neill's goal a game breaker to put them into a fifteenth Ulster Final in seventeen years.

On the other side, Donegal were drawn to play Tyrone in the quarter-final, somewhat inevitable after the violence on and off the field that had marred their meeting a year earlier. But this time in Omagh there was relative peace, with a goal from Donegal's Kieran Keeney paving the way for a 1-9 to 0-8 win. Donegal's progress continued with a thumping semi-final win over Antrim, Fermanagh's quarter-final conquerors, with Seamus Bonner hitting four goals as they won by 5-9 to 1-7 in Clones. Despite their relative lack of recent success by comparison to Down, Donegal were Ulster Final favourites, but their reputation as a second-half team was tested extensively when they had to dig out a 1-14 to 2-11 draw, with an equaliser from Neilly Gallagher almost on the final whistle.

A week later Down's lead was nine points at one stage but two Bonner penalties helped to bring them level before Keeney, hero against Tyrone, popped up again for another decisive goal and the county's second Anglo Celt Cup.

Cork had lost their seven previous championship meetings with Dublin, but as reigning champions and on the back of an impressive Munster Final win over Kerry they were favourites to progress in the first of the All-Ireland semi-finals. But Dublin were only ever behind early, as they improved once again with Mullins and Rooney again dominant at midfield.

It took the brilliance of Billy Morgan and Declan Barron to keep Cork in touch after they had trailed by three points at the break. It ebbed and flowed with goals – first Anton O'Toole, then Jimmy Barry-Murphy from a penalty – and controversy, as Cork appeared to have had sixteen players on the field with Ned Kirby not yet off by the time his replacement at full-forward, Martin Doherty, was fouled in the large parallelogram.

Inevitably it was another penalty that eased Dublin concerns, Mullins converting his third of the campaign in the sixty-seventh minute to propel Dublin to a first All-Ireland Final in eleven years.

The toll of injuries to Bonner and player-manager Brian McEniff, taking both out for the second half, was too much for Donegal in the second semi-final against Galway. Bonner had scored an eighth goal of the championship in the sixteenth minute – his third from a penalty – to help halt early Galway momentum generated by a John Tobin goal as they led by seven points. But a collision with Galway goalkeeper Gay Mitchell saw Bonner removed with a rib injury while McEniff followed eight minutes later with a hand injury.

Galway led by 2-7 to 1-6 at half-time and made certain of their passage to a third final in four years when Tobin added a second goal – he scored 2-6. They had some anxious closing moments as Martin Carney rallied Donegal from midfield, but Sammon's influence was profound as he finished with 0-3.

THE FINAL – 22 SEPTEMBER

The story goes that when the Dublin bus pulled in to Nowlan Park for one of those pre-Christmas Division Two League games in late 1973, they couldn't find a parking spot, such was the crowd that had gathered in their thousands for a local championship match. By throw-in time for their game, however, the place had emptied, leaving just a few knots of observers behind. It felt like the right illustration for where Dublin football was at that time, with interest at an all-time low.

Heffernan had been appointed that September, having turned the job down initially because of a commitment to St Vincent's. But the pressure to turn their ailing football predicament around was strong and there was common consensus that only he could even attempt a revival from where they were.

With him were Lorcan Redmond and Donal Colfer as selectors, the choice of chairman Jimmy Gray as the old top-heavy selection committees were dispensed with. The process was more stream-lined, with Heffernan as the most powerful voice and chief arbiter, and a new way of doing business was created that has largely shaped the sideline dynamic for much of the last half century.

Fast forward a year and Dublin were transformed, a team embracing new athleticism and powers of communication that had taken out the winners of the last three All-Ireland titles, Offaly (1971 and '72) and Cork (1973).

In their way was Galway, back in a third final in four years and a team with considerably more experience. Jimmy Duggan, Colie McDonagh and Liam Sammon were all involved in the 1966 squad, the last time Galway had won an All-Ireland, while only Pat Sands and John Tobin, injured for the '73 final, did not have All-Ireland Final experience. In contrast no Dublin player had contested an All-Ireland Final and only Georgie Wilson had a Railway Cup medal.

The match had drawn huge interest abroad with the availability of live coverage for the first time via satellite on telecast in cinemas and theatres in the major US cities, New York, Boston, Philadelphia and Chicago. At home much of the pre-match talk focused on an injury that Brian Mullins had carried, but on the day he was fit and hugely influential as Dublin's capacity to flip reputations all that summer continued.

Penalties had dominated the championship and inevitably it was one awarded to Galway in the twelfth minute of the second half that pivoted this game spectacularly, with Sammon's shot tipped around by Paddy Cullen for a fifty. The Dublin goalkeeper read his opponent's mind astutely, having closely studied his technique in the build-up.

The interchanging between Dublin's forwards had been troubling for Galway, yet they led by 1-4 to 0-5 at half-time, thanks to Michael Rooney's goal from Sammon's cross. Galway had Tommy Joe Gilmore to thank for thwarting a promising position that John McCarthy had found for himself in the first half and there was just a point between them when Sammon was hauled down for the penalty, Gay Mitchell having earlier saved smartly from Bobby Doyle.

Cullen's save from the penalty spurred Dublin to the next three points, Galway got the next two to level, 1-6 to 0-9, but Dublin, as they had done all season, finished with a flourish to herald the beginning of one of the great eras in football.

FINAL STATISTICS

	Dublin	Galway
Full-time:	0-14	1-6
Half-time:	0-5	1-4
Scorers:	J. Keaveney 0-8 (0-5 frees)	M. Rooney 1-1
	B. Mullins 0-2	T. Naughton 0-2
	D. Hickey 0-2	J. Duggan 0-1
	A. O'Toole 0-1	J. Tobin 0-1 (0-1 free)
	J. McCarthy 0-1	J. Hughes 0-1 (0-1 fifty)
Attendance:	71,898	
Referee:	Patsy Devlin (Tyrone)	

FINAL MISCELLANY

- Kevin Heffernan's sporting achievements were not confined to managing Dublin to an All-Ireland title that year. He also won the captain's prize at Clontarf Golf Club on the morning of their Leinster semi-final.
- Reporting on Dublin's first-round victory over Wexford, Gerry McCarthy of *The Irish Press* wrote, 'on the evidence of this hour they can be written off as serious challengers for Offaly's provincial crown.' More than six years would elapse before the Metropolitans would next lose a Leinster Championship game.
- An ancient English law which stipulated that no money could change hands at any Sunday sporting fixture created a problem for the London County Board when it hosted an inter-county double-header at Wembley Stadium on 26 May. Not to be outdone, the board's chairman and Drom & Inch native, Paddy Ryan, devised an ingenious solution. Announcing that the practice of selling match tickets would be dispensed with, the wily chairman made arrangements for the production of 45,000 programmes which were 'sold' to would-be patrons in advance.
- Brian Mullins and John Tobin may have been rivals on All-Ireland day, but they were housemates in Limerick where they were both students at the National College of Physical Education. Dublin panellist Fran Ryder also lived under the same roof.

1974 — THE YEAR THAT WAS

- On the evening of Friday 17 May, three bombs exploded in Dublin and one in Monaghan, killing thirty-four people and leaving 300 injured. Almost twenty years later, the Ulster Volunteer Force (UVF) claimed responsibility for this atrocity.
- On 9 July, the longest bus strike in Dublin's history ended after a sixty-five-day stoppage.

- Having been under pressure for several months in the wake of the Watergate break-in revelations, and under threat of impeachment, US president Richard Nixon resigned from office on 8 August. Defiant to the end, he made a TV and radio address to the American people, proclaiming that this decision was 'abhorrent to every instinct in my body'.

- A government-sponsored bill to legalise the sale of contraceptives was defeated by fourteen votes in the Dáil on 16 July. It wasn't the result of the vote that hit the news headlines, rather the fact that Taoiseach Liam Cosgrave broke ranks and voted against the motion. The Dáil debate on this bill makes for interesting reading. Many TDs argued that it was simply not possible to avoid the sale of aids to unmarried people. Deputies Oliver J. Flanagan and Michael Kitt were strongly of the view that to permit contraceptives to be available, even in a restricted way, was something that 'would damage the quality of life in the country.'

1974 TEAM LINE-OUTS

DUBLIN (WINNERS)

1. Paddy Cullen
(O'Connell Boys)

2. Gay O'Driscoll (St Vincent's) | 3. Sean Doherty (Ballyboden St Enda's) Capt. | 4. Robbie Kelleher (Scoil Uí Chonaill)

5. Paddy Reilly (St Margaret's) | 6. Alan Larkin (Raheny) | 7. Georgie Wilson (O'Dwyers)

8. Stephen Rooney (O'Dwyers) | 9. Brian Mullins (St Vincent's and Thomond College)

10. Bobby Doyle (St Vincent's) | 11. Tony Hanahoe (St Vincent's) | 12. David Hickey (Raheny)

13. John McCarthy (Garda, also Na Fianna) | 14. Jimmy Keaveney (St Vincent's) | 15. Anton O'Toole (Synge Street)

Subs: Dave Billings (St Vincent's); Kevin Synnott (Lucan Sarsfields); Brendan Pocock (St Vincent's); Paddy Gogarty (Raheny); Leslie Deegan (St Vincent's); Brendan Donovan (Crumlin); Pat O'Neill (UCD, also Civil Service); Jim Brogan (Oliver Plunketts); Fran Ryder (St Vincent's and Thomond College, also Ballymun Kickhams)

GALWAY (RUNNERS-UP)

1. Gay Mitchell
(Dunmore MacHales) Capt.

2. Joe Waldron
(Milltown)

3. Jack Cosgrove
(Spiddal, also Clifden and St Nicholas, Cork)

4. Brendan Colleran
(Mountbellew-Moylough)

5. Liam O'Neill
(Knockmore, Mayo, also St Grellan's and Castlebar Mitchels, Mayo)

6. Tommy Joe Gilmore
(Cortoon Shamrocks)

7. Johnny Hughes
(Mountbellew-Moylough)

8. Billy Joyce
(Killererin)

9. Michael Rooney
(Cortoon Shamrocks)

10. Tom Naughton
(Annaghdown)

11. Jimmy Duggan
(Corofin, also Claremorris, Mayo)

12. Pat Sands
(Ballygar, also Fr Griffin's)

13. Colie McDonagh
(Fr Griffin's)

14. Liam Sammon
(Fr Griffin's)

15. John Tobin
(Tuam Stars)

Subs: Jarlath Burke (Killererin) Played; Martin Noonan (St Michael's); John Dillon (St Gabriel's); Michael Geraghty (Dunmore MacHales, also Glenamaddy); Declan Smyth (Tuam Stars); Emmett Farrell (St Gabriel's, also Fr Griffin's)

1975

It was, *The Kerryman*'s John Barry concluded, an ominous sign when Kerry lost a National League quarter-final to Division Two side Meath on 23 March, with one of their poorest performances for many years. The 0-11 to 0-6 defeat told only some of the story of just how inept Kerry had been.

'I don't think anybody in their right senses could come out now and say the Kerry team, as presently constituted, is going to win an All-Ireland this year or in the immediate future. No way,' declared Barry beneath the blunt headline, 'Utter Disaster'.

Mick O'Dwyer barely had his feet beneath the manager's desk at that stage and by his own admission came away from Croke Park with misgivings about what lay ahead. O'Dwyer had packed up playing for Kerry the year before and, with Johnny Culloty stepping aside as trainer, he had accepted chairman Gerald McKenna's invitation to take the reins that spring.

He was Under-21 manager in 1974 and many of the All-Ireland winning Under-21 team from 1973 had graduated in the two years since as the pace of change in personnel accelerated. But like Barry, few could have envisaged what lay ahead and not even Meath's subsequent league win, beating Dublin in the final, could change that.

In the meantime, O'Dwyer attended a coaching conference in Gormanston, hosted by his old adversary, Down's Joe Lennon, who was a PE teacher at the famed boarding school. A reluctant attendee, he accompanied Mickey 'Ned' O'Sullivan, himself a PE student at the time, where they were treated to a coaching session with the Dublin players delivered by Kevin Heffernan as part of the conference.

It's hard to square that in a modern context and perhaps too much is made of O'Dwyer's presence in Meath that weekend, but Kerry's approach was transformed as the manager, sensing a requirement to surpass Dublin's physical fitness condition, introduced a training regime that was groundbreaking in the game for its intensity and repetition.

The approach was one that O'Dwyer had previously adopted in Waterville when, as player-manager, to compensate for a numbers and consequently talent deficit, they made their gains on staying power. Thus, he'd 'train the life out of him', as he'd put it himself.

At one stage in the build-up to the Munster Championship they trained for twenty-seven nights consecutively. All the time O'Dwyer knew that by pushing boundaries he was doing so with a group of enthusiastic young men who could absorb it. Some veterans of previous campaigns were omitted

Dublin centre-back Alan Larkin has a bird's-eye view of how Kerry captain Mickey 'Ned' O'Sullivan was floored by Sean Doherty in the early minutes of the 1975 Final. After this rather inauspicious introduction, O'Sullivan and Doherty went on to become lifelong friends. *Image courtesy of the GAA Museum at Croke Park.*

from O'Dwyer's panel and there were only four survivors from Kerry's previous All-Ireland Final starting team in 1972 – John O'Keeffe, Brendan and Paudie Lynch and Donie O'Sullivan (Mickey 'Ned' O'Sullivan and Ger Power were substitutes that year) – when the provincial championship campaign got underway in June.

Kerry's opening game was against Tipperary and there was no shortage of suggestions locally that it could be their only one, such was the pall of doom that had descended after the Meath defeat three months earlier. But John Egan's 2-3, on a day when O'Keeffe and Paudie Lynch were missing, helped Kerry to pull away and win by 3-13 to 0-9 in Clonmel, with Pat McCarthy's switch to midfield from centre-forward also pivotal.

Cork, bidding for a first ever provincial three-in-a-row, eased past Clare by 1-16 to 0-7 in the other half of the draw, setting up a 13 July final, and in the meantime Kerry prepared for that with a challenge against Dublin in Tralee, a 1-23 to 1-10 win over the All-Ireland champions that convinced O'Dwyer he had them on the right path.

The Munster Final against Cork provided further validation as 43,295 in Killarney watched a home team, featuring nine of the 1973 All-Ireland Under-21 winning side, build a commanding 1-7 to 0-3 lead, despite Mikey Sheehy missing a penalty – Cork's Jimmy Barry-Murphy had one saved by Paudie O'Mahony too. Pat Spillane got the decisive goal and Kerry's half-back line – Páidí Ó Sé, Tim Kennelly and Ger Power – really left their mark.

The Connacht Championship saw London enter a team at provincial level for the first time since 1908. London had won an All-Ireland junior three-in-a-row from 1969 to 1971 and that fuelled interest in bigger challenges.

After a number of failed Congress attempts to gain entry in the years beforehand, Connacht Council had cleared the way the previous October and, managed by Derry man Brian Devlin, they played Mayo in MacHale Park on 25 May, achieving respectability in front of a 5,000 crowd as they lost by 4-12 to 1-12.

London had encountered the usual logistical problems of trying to convene training sessions in a city of its size but for four weeks beforehand they met twice a week in Wormwood Scrubs. In their panel was Vincent Ryan from Kilmeena, who had captained the Mayo minors to an All-Ireland Final defeat just a year earlier. Sligo's Jim Colleary was also on board.

Gerry Farrelly, a regular with Meath at the time, top scored with 1-8 but Mayo pressed on and made the final with a 1-12 to 1-9 win over a Roscommon side hampered by an injury to Dermot Earley, who played but could not make the impact expected of him. It was a poor match and the twenty-six wides overall, nineteen in the second half, were a concern for Mayo.

In the other semi-final, Sligo prevailed over Galway for the first time in twenty-eight years, with

Sligo, Connacht champions 1975. Back row (l–r): John Brennan, Aidan Caffrey, Tom Cummins, Mattie Hoey, Des Kerins, Frank Henry, Tom Colleary; front (l–r): Mattie Brennan, Paddy Henry, James Kearins, Michael Laffey, Mickey Kearins, Barnes Murphy, Robert Lipsett, Johnny Stenson. *Picture courtesy of the* Western People.

a 1-13 to 0-6 win before 8,000 in Markievicz Park. Mickey Kearins was unplayable, especially in the second half when he struck nine of his ten points, six from play, as they exploited the absence of Galway's John Tobin and Jimmy Duggan.

It set up a first Sligo–Mayo Connacht Final since 1932 and there were 15,500 present as Sligo took an early initiative and led by six points at one stage in the second half, thanks to a Frank Henry goal.

But Mayo, without the injured Eamonn Brett, hit back and with Seamus Reilly policing Kearins well and J.P. Kean giving Sligo's player-coach and centre-back Barnes Murphy trouble, they hit seven unanswered points before Henry's leveller.

The general consensus was that Sligo had blown a glorious opportunity, especially with the replay two weeks later in MacHale Park. But if anything Mayo had less experience, with nine of the 1974 All-Ireland Under-21 winning side on board and only Willie McGee with a Connacht senior medal. By contrast, Kearins was in his fourteenth season and used all his guile to win and then convert a penalty just after half-time in the replay as he helped himself to 1-4.

But their momentum was short-lived and Mayo were ahead by two when Kearins teed up Des Kerins for a game-changing goal, his third in three championship games. This time Sligo saw it out, sparking great celebrations as Kearins was shouldered high off the field to salute what was the county's second ever provincial title, the last having been won in 1928. A civic reception in Sligo the following Sunday recognised the importance of such a landmark triumph.

Dublin's defeat in that Tralee challenge didn't take too much out of them for their Leinster title defence as they recorded back-to-back wins for the first time in twelve years. There had been signs of wear and tear in their opening game as Wexford hit them for 3-10 in Dr Cullen Park, but with Jimmy Keaveney posting ten points and goals from David Hickey, Martin Noctor, John McCarthy and Tony Hanahoe, allied to Bernard Brogan's midfield dominance, the result was never in doubt.

The untidiness continued in the semi-final, when a ten-point lead early in the second half against Louth in Navan, before 31,200, was whittled down to one as Louth took advantage of John McCarthy's sending off in the fifty-third minute. Dublin lived dangerously and might well have surrendered their crown but Hanahoe's creation of a goal for Keaveney at the end gave them a 3-14 to 4-7 win.

Meath bounced into the provincial campaign on the back of a first league title since 1951 but they paid a price for overconfidence when Louth took them out in the quarter-final, 0-15 to 1-9. Ironically, Louth had done the same to Longford in the 1966 Leinster Championship when they too were league champions.

Louth opened their campaign with a 2-22 to 2-6 win over a Wicklow team featuring Paul McNaughton who, in between an FAI Cup Final appearance with Shelbourne and a Leinster senior cup semi-final with Greystones, managed to make his inter-county senior debut with his native county at full-forward. That game took place in Croke Park, giving the future Irish rugby international the distinction of playing at what were then the three citadels of Irish sport (Dalymount Park and Lansdowne Road being the other two) in a matter of just a few weeks.

Kilkenny were back in a Leinster senior football championship for the first time in twelve years and, not unexpectedly, their interest didn't last beyond their opening game against Westmeath, which they lost by 2-14 to 2-2 after struggling to put a team together from the twenty-eight players originally named. Longford recalled 1968 provincial winner Jimmy Hannify, but to little avail as they lost heavily to Laois, while Wexford nudged past Carlow in their first round, courtesy of Diarmuid Clancy's late winner.

In the other quarter-finals, Offaly needed a replay to advance past Laois (3-14 to 3-7), thanks to Murt Connor's hat-trick, while Kildare, led by Arthur French with six points, eased past Westmeath, 1-15 to 1-8. Goals from Ray O'Sullivan and a Pat Dunney penalty kept up Kildare momentum in a 2-11 to 0-11 semi-final win over Offaly, giving them a first Leinster Final with Dublin since 1928, a year they looked back on with such fond memories.

But there was to be no repeat as Dublin, stung by the concession of seven goals in their two previous games, found their form before 44,182 in Croke Park. Kildare weren't helped by Bryan O'Doherty's dismissal by referee Brendan Hayden and by half-time they were 2-6 to 0-2 adrift.

Brian Mullins was immense, scoring two goals, as his midfield partnership with Brogan blossomed. They were 3-13 to 0-8 winners, dispelling any notion that their appetite had been sated the previous year.

Not since 1966 had a team successfully defended an Ulster title and that was the fate endured by Donegal when they lost to Cavan by 0-15 to 0-13 in a quarter-final in Ballybofey, where the Breffni men were maintaining an unbeaten record. Ollie Leddy's midfield dominance, until he sustained a head injury, was a key factor for Cavan who trailed by five points at the break.

In the preliminary round, Armagh had beaten Fermanagh but Derry showed clear signs of what was to come in their subsequent quarter-final when, guided by thirty-eight-year-old Sean O'Connell, playing in a nineteenth championship, they won by 2-15 to 1-7.

Down had it all too easy, 3-12 to 0-7, against Antrim, while Monaghan's 0-13 to 1-5 win over Tyrone brought Jody O'Neill's five-year spell as the Red Hand coach and sole selector to an end.

A late Peter Stevenson penalty saved Derry blushes against Monaghan in their semi-final as they drew 1-11 each in Dungannon. Monaghan had been bringing well-known showband singer, Ballybay's Gerry Finlay, back from Catskill in New York for games, and he was again involved for the replay as they took a six-point lead at one stage thanks to a Gerry McCague goal. But Derry powered ahead to record a 0-14 to 1-6 win, strongly influenced by Gerry McElhinney's move to midfield.

Down's 1-13 to 1-10 win over Cavan in the other semi-final put them in a third successive provincial final where once again they came up short. Missed penalties were a feature of the summer and Dan McCartan's set Down off on the wrong note when they trailed by 1-8 to 1-5. Derry dominated midfield through Tom McGuinness and Eugene Laverty, with O'Connell setting up McElhinney for their goal and a 1-16 to 2-6 win in Clones, giving them a third Ulster title.

A spectre of violence, emanating from Hill 16 where Dublin supporters were camped, hung over

Derry's All-Ireland semi-final with the All-Ireland champions on Sunday 24 August. The trouble began even before the main event when the minor semi-final between Tyrone and Kildare had to come to a halt for up to four minutes just after half-time when bottles and missiles rained down from the terrace, forcing the players to take cover.

Order was restored but only briefly, and throughout the senior semi-final there was an undercurrent with the hooligan element on 'the Hill' causing chaos at every opportunity. Eventually, it spilled out on to the field when, with a few minutes remaining, some began throwing stones and bottles at Derry supporters in the Hogan Stand. Three gardaí and a Cavan-based priest were among those who sustained nasty injuries from the missiles hurled. With just thirty-five gardaí on duty inside the ground, it took time to bring the situation under control, and inevitably led to a review of security and crowd control measures on Hill 16.

The game itself reinforced Dublin's position as the dominant team as an Anton O'Toole goal helped them to a four-point interval lead. O'Toole added a second goal and Tony Hanahoe was also on the mark to seal it in the forty-sixth minute.

Derry did provide resistance and the talent of McElhinney, an Ulster youth boxing champion who would later play professional soccer for Bolton Wanderers among other clubs, as well as Northern Ireland, was in full view when he scored the point of the afternoon.

Despite the 3-13 to 3-8 scoreline it was a poor match, with sixty-six frees awarded, raising fresh questions about the direction in which the game was headed.

It set up the first Dublin–Kerry All-Ireland Final for twenty years, Kerry, as expected, having comfortably dealt with Sligo in the other semi-final two weeks earlier. In truth, it was an impossible game for Sligo to prepare for given the carnival atmosphere in the county after their Connacht triumph. And yet Kerry, for all their dominance, were largely unimpressive, scoring all three goals in the last ten minutes with Egan getting two and Spillane also on target.

It didn't help that Kearins had a penalty saved by O'Mahony early on while player-manager Murphy would reflect years later on sideline changes made, in his absence, that he felt didn't have the desired effect. He had brought the legendary Galway trainer John 'Tull' Dunne and Brian McEniff, Donegal's player-manager for their Ulster title a year earlier, for added assistance that afternoon but their advice had gone largely unheeded. Still, Kerry's powerful Pat McCarthy–Paudie Lynch midfield axis was instrumental as they eased to a 3-13 to 0-5 win.

THE FINAL – 28 SEPTEMBER

The perception around the glory of Kerry–Dublin All-Ireland finals at the time was a little misleading. This was just the sixth final meeting between them and only the second in fifty-one years, the 1955 Final being the other.

The demand for tickets beforehand was as intense, it seemed, as it had ever been, yet curiously the official attendance was recorded as 66,346, well below the 73,000 capacity. There had been a hike in ticket prices to £1.50 and £3, with some reportedly changing hands with touts for up to £20, but on the day there were empty spaces.

The adverse weather may have been a factor; so too, perhaps, security fears after the events of the Dublin–Derry semi-final, with up to 200 gardaí on duty on the day of the match.

Whatever the reason, it didn't impact on the quality of the match as Kerry's improvement through the season continued. It's rare that a Kerry team would be considered such outsiders and have such a deficit in experience, with only Brendan and Paudie Lynch and John O'Keeffe having previous final exposure. For the fourth consecutive match they didn't concede a goal, completing a championship shut-out, Dublin's eleven points bringing Kerry's overall concession to 0-36, nine points per game on average.

In contrast, Dublin had conceded 10-33 in their four games, so suspicions around their defence beforehand were well held as Kerry hit them for two goals. The first, from John Egan, came early when he exploited indecision between Paddy Cullen and Gay O'Driscoll as they moved to deal with a Mikey Sheehy free, to pounce for a goal after only three minutes.

Dublin had taken a somewhat surprise decision to recall John McCarthy, suspended for much of the summer after being sent off against Louth in an earlier round, at Bobby Doyle's expense, and their attack just never functioned against an impressive Kingdom rearguard, with only Paddy Gogarty of the six starting forwards scoring from play.

By half-time Kerry were 1-6 to 0-4 clear and were winning all the major individual duels, John O'Keeffe on Jimmy Keaveney, Páidí Ó Sé on David Hickey and Paudie Lynch and Pat McCarthy on any number of different Dublin midfield permutations.

Kerry captain Mickey 'Ned' O'Sullivan, who had spent four of the six weeks between the semi-final and final touring Europe, was in flying form early on but was knocked unconscious in a seventeenth-minute collision with Dublin full-back Sean Doherty as he embarked on another electrifying run, resulting in an overnight stay in the Richmond Hospital. He didn't come around until some forty-five minutes after referee Johnny Moloney had called time, by which time Pat Spillane, as the other representative from the Kenmare district, had deputised as captain to receive the cup.

Spillane also came out to half-forward, where O'Sullivan had been operating to great effect, and everywhere Kerry just seemed to have athletic superiority as they made their young and energetic legs count.

Dublin kept in touch for much of the second half, but Kerry's Ger O'Driscoll, O'Sullivan's replacement, got a second goal to make safe a twenty-third All-Ireland title.

FINAL STATISTICS

	Kerry	Dublin
Full-time:	2-12	0-11
Half-time:	1-6	0-4

Scorers:		
	M. Sheehy 0-4 (0-3 frees)	J. Keaveney 0-6 (0-6 frees)
	B. Lynch 0-3 (0-2 frees, 0-1 fifty)	P. Gogarty 0-2
	J. Egan 1-0	B. Mullins 0-1
	G. O'Driscoll 1-0	B. Pocock 0-1
	P. Spillane 0-3	B. Doyle 0-1
	D. 'Ogie' Moran 0-2	
Attendance:	66,346	
Referee:	John Moloney (Tipperary)	

FINAL MISCELLANY

- In the wake of the county's heavy defeat against Kerry in the All-Ireland semi-final, there was an air of despondency in Sligo GAA circles. *Sligo Champion* journalist Jim Gray certainly didn't pull any punches in his report on the game, commenting, 'It would be an unwarranted compliment to say that most of the Sligo players played badly.' The achievement of bridging a forty-seven-year gap seemed to merit less attention than the theory that Kerry were far from world-beaters. The men from the south-west could only manage to collect eight All-Ireland titles over the next twelve years!

- The 1975 Championship has given the GAA world what are probably two of its most viewed YouTube clips ever. One shows referee Brendan Cross skating to the scene of the exchange of some friendly gunfire between Dinny Allen and Páidí Ó Sé during the Munster Final. Not to be outdone, Sean Doherty's All-Ireland Final 'tackle' on Mickey 'Ned' O'Sullivan has given these great friends celluloid immortality.

- At twenty-six, Brendan Lynch was the oldest member of the winning Kerry team. He also became the only man to win All-Ireland medals in sixty-, seventy- and eighty-minute finals on the field of play.

1975 – THE YEAR THAT WAS

- The Dutch businessman Dr Tiede Herrema was abducted by members of the Provisional IRA at Castletroy on the morning of 3 October. The kidnappers demanded the release of three named Republican prisoners and threatened to execute their hostage. They were eventually tracked down to a house in Monasterevin, County Kildare, where, after an eighteen-day siege, Dr Herrema emerged unhurt.

- As General Franco lay critically ill, heir-designate Prince Juan Carlos took over as provisional head of state in Spain. Franco had ruled the country with an iron fist for well over thirty years.

- After nineteen years, five months, four weeks and one day, the Vietnam War came to an end on 30 April when the Democratic Republic of Vietnam captured the city of Saigon. There were almost 3.5 million casualties, of which 58,000 were American soldiers.

- Near Newry in the early hours of 31 July, the minibus carrying the members of The Miami Showband, one of the country's most popular musical acts at the time, was stopped by gunmen wearing British Army uniforms. Two were killed when a bomb they were planting went off prematurely. In the ensuing chaos, the remaining gunmen opened fire, killing three members of the band and wounding two others.

1975 TEAM LINE-OUTS

KERRY (WINNERS)

1. Paudie O'Mahony
(Spa)

2. Ger O'Keeffe
(Austin Stacks)

3. John O'Keeffe
(Austin Stacks and UCD)

4. Jimmy Deenihan
(Finuge)

5. Páidí Ó Sé
(An Ghaeltacht)

6. Tim Kennelly
(Listowel Emmets)

7. Ger Power
(Austin Stacks)

8. Paudie Lynch
(Beaufort and UCC)

9. Pat McCarthy
(Sallins, Kildare, also Churchill)

10. Brendan Lynch
(Beaufort)

11. Denis 'Ogie' Moran
(Beale and UCD)

12. Mickey 'Ned' O'Sullivan
(Kenmare) Capt.

13. John Egan
(Sneem)

14. Mikey Sheehy
(Austin Stacks)

15. Pat Spillane
(Templenoe and Thomond College)

Subs: Ger O'Driscoll (Valentia) Played; John Bunyan (Ballydonoghue); John Long (An Ghaeltacht); Batt O'Shea (Churchill); Jackie Walsh (Ballylongford and UCD); Donie O'Sullivan (Spa)

DUBLIN (RUNNERS-UP)

1. Paddy Cullen
(O'Connell Boys)

2. Gay O'Driscoll
(St Vincent's)

3. Sean Doherty
(Ballyboden St Enda's) Capt.

4. Robbie Kelleher
(Scoil Uí Chonaill)

5. Paddy Reilly
(St Margaret's)

6. Alan Larkin
(Raheny)

7. Georgie Wilson
(O'Dwyers)

8. Brian Mullins
(St Vincent's and Thomond College)

9. Bernard Brogan
(St Oliver Plunketts)

10. Anton O'Toole
(Synge Street)

11. Tony Hanahoe
(St Vincent's)

12. David Hickey
(Raheny)

13. John McCarthy
(Garda, also Na Fianna)

14. Jimmy Keaveney
(St Vincent's)

15. Paddy Gogarty
(Raheny)

Subs: Bobby Doyle (St Vincent's) Played; Pat O'Neill (UCD, also Civil Service) Played; Brendan Pocock (St Vincent's) Played; Leslie Deegan (St Vincent's); Kevin Synnott (Lucan Sarsfields); Stephen Rooney (O'Dwyers)

1976

Those who have suffered the agony of losing an All-Ireland Final speak, if they speak at all, about the bitter disappointment in the immediate aftermath of the game. This is followed by a craving to avoid any company that might seek to relive the action or fret about the might-have-beens that could have changed the result. In short, refuge is sought in hibernation. The time for analysis and planning for 'next year' can wait until the long winter evenings.

As in so much else, Kevin Heffernan was different. The official record shows that the 1976 Championship got underway on 9 May. In reality, it began within three hours of John Moloney blowing the final whistle on 28 September 1975. The Dublin manager piled his charges onto the team bus and proceeded to bring them on a 'mystery tour'. As they drove slowly around the Kerry team's hotel, the players had to endure the raucous sounds of wild celebration. Heffo's 1976 campaign had begun.

THE CHAMPIONSHIP

The renewal of the Kerry–Dublin rivalry was a real shot in the arm for Gaelic football. What turned out to be two of the finest teams ever to grace Croke Park, managed by two icons of the game, had emerged from nowhere to play at a pace and intensity never previously seen. Most punters expected, and hoped, that the fourth Sunday in September would deliver another mouth-watering clash between these great rivals.

Dublin's journey through Leinster saw them face Longford at Mullingar on 27 June. Whatever confidence an earlier twenty-five point hammering of Kilkenny had instilled in the Longford men, it quickly dissipated in this lopsided encounter. According to Con Kenealy of the *Irish Independent*, it was clear after ten minutes that 'the only possible surprise would be if the Dublin team missed the coach home'. If Jimmy Keaveney's haul of 3-4 hit the headlines, it was the performance of heretofore unknown newcomer Kevin Moran that probably pleased the Dublin mentors most. As for Longford, veteran Jimmy Hannify and corner-forward Liam Tierney performed best on this day of carnage.

Laois emerged four-point victors after a scrappy encounter with Kildare at Carlow on 20 June, the decisive goal being a brilliant effort by Graiguecullen's Willie Brennan. The performances of teenagers Tommy Shaw and Johnny Crofton were, apart from the usual brilliance of goalkeeper Ollie Crinnigan, the only positives in yet another tame championship exit for the Lilywhites.

As they prepared for their semi-final clash with Dublin, the Laois men would be pinning much of their hope on the telepathic combination play of forwards Tom Prendergast, Mick Fennell and

414

Baptism of Fire. When teenager Charlie Nelligan was introduced as a replacement goalkeeper for the injured Paudie O'Mahony during the 1976 decider, he could hardly have imagined that he would have to face Dublin sharpshooter Jimmy Keaveney for a penalty. Unsurprisingly, Keaveney's effort was a veritable bullet to the roof of the net. *Sportsfile.*

Brennan. The trio managed to notch a total of ten points, but this was not enough to negate the efforts of Dublin's slick forward machine where, once again, Keaveney was the outstanding figure in this 3-12 to 0-11 victory. Aside from progressing to their third successive provincial decider, Dublin could be happy that they had inserted another vital cog in their rebuilt defence, with Whitehall's Tommy Drumm joining fellow novice Kevin Moran in the half-back line. Of some consolation for Laois was the midfield mastery of Kieran Brennan and Bobby Millar over no less a pairing than Bernard Brogan and Brian Mullins.

When Meath faced underdogs Wicklow at Croke Park on 9 May, they could not have expected to be trailing 1-5 to 0-1 after just twenty minutes, with Mick O'Toole their chief tormentor. Wicklow continued to pile on the pressure for the remainder of the first half, but incredibly wasteful shooting, and a deftly taken Cormac Rowe goal, meant that their lead was reduced to a single point at the interval. There was a major turnaround in the second half, however, with Robbie McMahon and Ken Rennicks the key men as Meath eventually pulled through, 2-13 to 1-10.

At Croke Park four weeks later, Meath scrambled past Offaly on the flattering scoreline of 3-8 to 0-8, thus advancing to the provincial semi-final. In an otherwise unremarkable encounter, this game saw seventeen-year-old Rhode man Johnny Mooney make his championship debut.

Wexford were deemed no-hopers when they opened their account against Westmeath at Athy on

9 May. Not alone did they breeze through this game, they then proceeded to give Louth a 0-15 to 1-8 footballing lesson at Croke Park on 20 June. Their most impressive performer on this journey to the Leinster semi-final against Meath was dual star Martin Quigley, with Mick Carty, Eddie Waters and long-kicking Brian Furlong also to the fore. While a scoreline of 2-14 to 1-9 suggests otherwise, Meath's semi-final win over Wexford was far from comfortable. The early dominance of Watty French and Mick Carty at midfield faded in the second half as newcomer Dermot Rennicks swung the possession stakes in favour of the Meath men. The full-forward line of Colm O'Rourke, Cormac Rowe and the evergreen Matt Kerrigan capitalised fully, notching 0-11 between them.

'Lucky Dublin. Unlucky Meath.' This was the verdict of Padraig Puirséal of *The Irish Press* when reigning Leinster champions Dublin edged Meath, 2-9 to 1-9, in their Croke Park showdown on 25 July. A missed penalty by Colm O'Rourke was the focus of much post-match analysis, but the irony was that O'Rourke was Meath's leading light on the day. As for Dublin, many 'experts' now asserted that they were on the wane, and that the Sam Maguire Cup was beyond their reach.

Predicting an emphatic victory for the local favourites in their Connacht semi-final clash with Roscommon, Jim Gray of *The Sligo Champion* felt it was 'unlikely that any Sligo team in the past has approached a championship with as much optimism'. A week later, the unfortunate man was acknowledging that 'the execution axes are swinging … for a particular sports scribe who put his head on the chopping block'.

Following up on his impressive form against London earlier in the championship, it was John 'Jigger' O'Connor who inflicted most of the damage on the Sligo men.

Elsewhere in Connacht, a Mickey Martin-inspired Leitrim showed impressive form when ousting Mayo, 2-8 to 0-10, in their rain-soaked Carrick-on-Shannon replay on 30 May. The suggestion that Mayo might have been a tad overconfident gained currency when the *Western People* published its calendar of sporting events in the days prior to the game. This proclaimed that the Mayo–Galway semi-final would take place at Castlebar on 6 June.

It was to Carrick-on-Shannon that the Tribesmen headed on 6 June, where they were expected to face stiff resistance against a cock-a-hoop Leitrim fifteen. The *Leitrim Observer* predicted a crowd of 10,000 if weather conditions were favourable. This turned out to be well wide of the mark – over 15,000 patrons turned up to witness what was expected to be a ding-dong affair. Bigger, stronger and faster, Galway powered their way to a twenty-two point victory, the result being a foregone conclusion from the opening minutes. Late in the game the chief focus of interest centred on the roof of the stand which buckled under the weight of rival supporters. It took the old reliable loudspeaker to persuade enough climbers to abandon their perch, and so avoid possible disaster.

In appalling conditions at Tuam on 18 July, Galway maintained their form and had little difficulty in overcoming neighbours Roscommon in the provincial decider. The experienced Jimmy Duggan was the fulcrum around which much of Galway's play revolved and there was a growing optimism that the Tribesmen could prove a stern test for Dublin next time out.

The Dublin team that beat Kerry in the 1976 decider, thus reversing the result of the previous year. Back (l–r): Kevin Moran, Anton O'Toole, Sean Doherty, Jimmy Keaveney, Paddy Cullen, John McCarthy, Tommy Drumm, Bernard Brogan, Bobby Doyle; front (l–r): Brian Mullins, Robbie Kelleher, Pat O'Neill, Tony Hanahoe, David Hickey, Gay O'Driscoll. *Courtesy Gaelic Art.*

Based on their extraordinary run in 1975, Kerry were expected to saunter through the Munster Championship with some ease. Their opening game was in the semi-final against Waterford, who had four clear goals to spare over Tipperary when they met earlier. Unfortunately for the men from the Déise, Kerry took up where they had left off the previous September. With their forwards in top gear, and Pat Spillane in overdrive, the Kingdom romped to a 3-17 to 0-6 victory.

As per usual, Cork were expected to progress to a Munster Final showdown with their great rivals. A goal in the dying seconds by Michael Greene gave Clare the slimmest of victories over Limerick, and their ticket for the right to face Cork in the provincial semi-final. Here, Cork had little difficulty overcoming the Clare challenge as they eased to a 2-15 to 1-10 victory. Apart from outstanding displays by Tom Creedon and Denis Long, there was no great sense of urgency in Cork's performance. The consensus was that Kerry's already rosy prospects of retaining their Munster title were more secure than ever.

The Munster Final took place at the new state-of-the-art Páirc Uí Chaoimh on 11 July. Despite the overwhelming view that Kerry would prevail, the novelty of the stadium was expected to attract a huge crowd. This it did, but while the official capacity was adequate to accommodate the over 50,000 who turned up, unforgiveable stewarding failures created chaos. Over 3,000 supporters ended up huddled along the sidelines for the entire duration of the game. The match itself was somewhat fractious but lacked in quality football. That it ended in a draw, 0-11 each, was generally considered not just a fair result, but an opportunity for the protagonists to redeem themselves.

For the replay on 25 July, Cork retained home advantage. In contrast to the drawn encounter, this turned out to be a classic, complete with a strong element of controversy. The men in red took the initiative and remained firmly in control until midway through the second half. Despite the outstanding work of Pat McCarthy and Pat Spillane, it was not until the introduction of 'super sub' Sean Walsh that the pendulum began to swing in Kerry's favour. Walsh scored 1-3, his goal being awarded controversially when the umpires deemed that Brian Murphy had held the ball over the line as he attempted to block a piledriver from the Kerins O'Rahillys man. Further Kerry pressure in the dying minutes resulted in Spillane grabbing the equaliser, thereby bringing the game to extra time.

Many reports on the game suggested that Kerry had the psychological advantage as extra time loomed. That they struck five points to Cork's one within minutes of the restart seems to support this theory. Cork, however, continued to create chances, with Declan Barron and Jimmy Barry-Murphy each coming close to finding the Kerry net.

As an illustration of the quality of the 1976 Munster Final, it is worth quoting the verdict of Gerry McCarthy of *The Irish Press*: 'Words fail to describe the tension, excitement, thrills, misses, joy, despair and confusion of a game that will never be forgotten.'

After this unexpected scare, Kerry could finally look forward to facing the champions of Ulster in the All-Ireland semi-final.

Since the days of Cavan's near-monopoly, winning back-to-back Ulster championships had become a notoriously difficult challenge. While Derry had proven very worthy winners in 1975, and could boast of having a very strong panel, the strength of the competition within the province left no room for complacency.

The preliminary round clash between Armagh and Fermanagh was widely expected to be a routine task for the men from the Orchard County. When the half-time whistle sounded the Fermanagh men, with midfielders Fionn Sherry and Gerry Gallagher dominating and Aidan Lunny in scintillating scoring form, held an eleven-point advantage. Armagh gradually began to close the gap in the second half and eventually stumbled over the line for victory, thanks to a late point from Noel Marley.

If Armagh supporters were unhappy with their team's less than impressive form against Fermanagh, their quarter-final performance against Derry at Omagh on 13 June would bring them to the depths of despondency. The scoreline of 1-19 to 2-1 was an accurate reflection of the yawning gap in class between the teams. While this game was little more than a training run for Derry, they could take special encouragement from the performances of Adrian McGuckian and newcomer Colm McGuigan.

The winners of the Tyrone–Monaghan quarter-final would provide the next opposition for Derry. At Dungannon on 6 June, a tour de force from half-forward Brendan Donnelly was the key to Tyrone's unexpected three-point victory. An early goal by Phelim Hugh Forbes, capitalising on a great centre from Donnelly, gave the Tyrone men an advantage they would hold throughout the game.

Other than qualifying for their second successive Ulster Final, there was little about their 0-12 to 0-8 win over Tyrone at Clones on 27 June that would have pleased Derry. In a lethargic performance on a scorching day, the performances of Anthony McGurk, Mickey Moran and especially Tom McGuinness were the only redeeming features.

The opposite side of the Ulster draw saw Cavan and Down, victors over Donegal and Antrim respectively, emerge to contest the second semi-final. Commenting on Cavan's emphatic 1-18 to 0-10 victory over the Mourne men, *The Irish Press* opined this was very much a triumph of strength over subtlety. It went on to note that Cavan's strategy was to leave 'no doubt that the cudgel rather than the rapier was to be their means of subduing the opposition'. Whatever about Cavan's strong-arm tactics, there was little doubt about the refinement of Steve Duggan's play, the wily corner-forward notching a total of ten points, six of which came from open play.

Clones was the venue for the Derry–Cavan Ulster Final on 18 July. Following the example set in Munster and Connacht, this provincial showdown also ended in a draw, 1-8 each. In a dour, uncompromising affair, red-hot favourites Derry could thank their brilliant centre half-back Anthony McGurk for a second bite of the cherry at the same venue the following Sunday.

As was the case in Munster, an utterly forgettable draw was followed by a replay of the highest quality. Derry eventually prevailed, after extra time, on a score of 0-22 to 1-16. In contrast to the drawn game, there were heroic performances all round, with Anthony McGurk again being singled out for special mention.

The stage was now set for the All-Ireland semi-finals, with Kerry expected to account for Derry while most pundits favoured Dublin to progress at the expense of Galway.

When referee Paddy Collins blew the half-time whistle at Croke Park on 8 August, Derry led 0-9 to 0-8 against the reigning All-Ireland champions. The introduction of Sean Walsh coincided with a dramatic improvement in Kerry's performance and, with an avalanche of goals, they ran out convincing 5-14 to 1-10 winners. Mikey Sheehy was top scorer with 3-3 but Kerry had outstanding performers in every sector and were now installed as warm favourites to retain their title. Soccer star Gerry McElhinney was Derry's best on a most disappointing day but his uncertain future as a Gaelic footballer didn't augur well for the county.

The second football semi-final, between Dublin and Galway, took place on 29 August. As a football game, this encounter defied description. A flavour of the proceedings can be gleaned from Donal Carroll's report in the *Irish Independent* which referenced how 'punching, hacking, elbow jabs, tripping, pushing, holding and almost every provocation open to man was tried in an effort to sustain the notion that the end justifies the means'.

Few denied that Dublin's three-point victory was fully deserved. Fewer still thought that Dublin could mount any meaningful challenge in their September showdown with the men from the Kingdom.

THE FINAL — 26 SEPTEMBER

A common theme in the lead-up to the 1976 Final was that, to have any prospects of success, Dublin's newly minted half-back line of Tommy Drumm, Kevin Moran and Pat O'Neill would have to come up trumps. They did not disappoint. The ball was hardly in play when Moran gave notice of intent when he powered out of defence in a slick passing movement, firing a proverbial rocket which missed the target by mere inches.

In an all-action performance, the Dubs took the honours, 3-8 to 1-10. Their goals came from Keaveney, Mullins and the ever-industrious John McCarthy. Every man chased every ball, and every Kerry man, as if his life depended on it. Mullins and Brogan were imperious at midfield. Sean Doherty was a commanding figure in a solid full-back line. The forward line, in which Jimmy Keaveney and Anton O'Toole shone brightest, created panic in the Kerry defence. While all of their experienced hands contributed handsomely, it was the outstanding display of newcomer Moran that captured most of the headlines.

As always, Kerry were gracious in defeat and offered no excuses. Their captain, John O'Keeffe, put in a tremendous performance at full-back. 'Ogie' Moran did well, especially when moved to midfield. Elsewhere, Pat Spillane and John Egan performed heroically on a day when the Kingdom were simply not good enough to withstand the Dublin onslaught.

This was Dublin's first championship win over Kerry since 1934 and their first in a final since 1923. Team manager Kevin Heffernan savoured this victory more than most. Referring to the disappointment of losing to the Kingdom in 1955, he proclaimed that he had waited twenty-one years for this result.

Perhaps the most colourful description of the importance of beating Kerry in a final came from ace marksman Jimmy Keaveney. When RTÉ's Mick Dunne asked how he felt about finally turning the tables on the old enemy, the response was: 'I don't care if I never win another bloody match!'

FINAL STATISTICS

	Dublin	Kerry
Full-time:	3-8	0-10
Half-time:	1-5	0-5
Scorers:	J. Keaveney 1-2 (1-0 penalty, 0-1 free)	M. Sheehy 0-3 (0-2 frees)
	B. Mullins 1-1	D. Moran 0-2
	J. McCarthy 1-1	P. Spillane 0-2
	T. Hanahoe 0-1	J. Egan 0-1
	B. Brogan 0-1	B. Lynch 0-1
	D. Hickey 0-1	M. O'Sullivan 0-1
	A. O'Toole 0-1	
Attendance:	73,588	
Referee:	Paddy Collins (Westmeath)	

FINAL MISCELLANY

- Kerry goalkeeper Paudie O'Mahony suffered the misfortune of tearing his Achilles tendon after just nineteen minutes of play. Describing the excruciating pain, the Spa clubman recalled: 'The minute I fell I thought I had been hit by a bullet.'

- Kerry native and international athlete Tom O'Riordan was one of the leading sportswriters of his generation. In his *Irish Independent* preview of the match, he resorted to the Olympic Games when describing Pat Spillane's extraordinary stamina. Drawing a comparison with the Finn who had annexed two gold medals at each of the 1972 and 1976 Games, O'Riordan referred to the Templenoe dynamo as 'an outsized Lasse Virén'.

- When Cavan and Donegal met in the Ulster quarter-final at Breffni Park on 30 May, referee Tommy Johnstone inadvertently blew the half-time whistle after thirty minutes' play instead of the stipulated thirty-five. The embarrassed Fermanagh man realised his error only after the rain-drenched players had taken refuge in the dressing-rooms. After three minutes, the teams were recalled to play out the remainder of the first half, which period didn't produce any scores.

- A year-end review of the 1976 campaign would most likely have led to very different predictions as regards the future prospects of Armagh and Cork. The men from the Orchard County had a largely forgettable run, culminating in managing just three scores as they exited the championship at the hands of Derry. From this low base, they succeeded in powering through to the All-Ireland Final of 1977. Cork were decidedly unlucky not to relieve Kerry of their Munster crown in 1976. Surely success was just around the corner, with no less an authority than Mick O'Dwyer repeatedly labelling them 'the second-best team in Ireland'. But Cork would wait another seven years before they would again claim a Munster title.

- The 1976 Final was a milestone in terms of television coverage as it was beamed to millions of viewers around the globe. BBC 2 showed the game live, while it was also carried on closed-circuit TV in the US and the UK. Among the venues where the match could be seen were Irish clubs and centres in Slough, Manchester, Birmingham, Coventry and Northampton. In the US, colleges in New York, Pittsburgh, Chicago and Boston also carried the game live.

1976 – THE YEAR THAT WAS

- Two weeks after his arrival in Ireland, British ambassador Christopher Ewart-Biggs was killed when an IRA landmine exploded under his car at Sandyford, Dublin on 21 July. Twenty-six-year-old civil servant Judith Cooke also died at the scene.

- President Cearbhall Ó Dálaigh resigned from office following remarks made by Minister for Justice Paddy Donegan about the President's decision to refer the Emergency Powers legislation to the Supreme Court.

- Commerce was severely disrupted throughout the summer of 1976 when bank staff went on strike from 28 June to 6 September.

- Following on from an eye-watering 20.88% in 1975, the rate of price inflation in Ireland in 1976 fell to 17.99%.
- Named after the outbreak at an American Legion convention in Philadelphia, Legionnaires' disease was first identified in 1976.

1976 TEAM LINE-OUTS

DUBLIN (WINNERS)

1. Paddy Cullen
(O'Connell Boys)

2. Gay O'Driscoll
(St Vincent's)

3. Sean Doherty
(Ballyboden St Enda's)

4. Robbie Kelleher
(Scoil Uí Chonaill)

5. Tommy Drumm
(Whitehall Colmcilles and TCD)

6. Kevin Moran
(Good Counsel)

7. Pat O'Neill
(UCD, also Civil Service)

8. Brian Mullins
(St Vincent's and Thomond College)

9. Bernard Brogan
(St Oliver Plunketts)

10. Anton O'Toole
(Synge Street)

11. Tony Hanahoe
(St Vincent's) Capt.

12. David Hickey
(Raheny)

13. Bobby Doyle
(St Vincent's)

14. Jimmy Keaveney
(St Vincent's)

15. John McCarthy
(Garda, also Na Fianna)

Subs: Fran Ryder (St Vincent's and Thomond College, also Ballymun Kickhams) Played; Paddy Gogarty (Raheny) Played; Jim Brogan (St Oliver Plunketts); Paddy Reilly (St Margaret's); Brendan Pocock (St Vincent's); Leslie Deegan (St Vincent's)

KERRY (RUNNERS-UP)

1. Paudie O'Mahony
(Spa)

2. Ger O'Keeffe
(Austin Stacks)

3. John O'Keeffe
(Austin Stacks)

4. Jimmy Deenihan
(Finuge)

5. Páidí Ó Sé
(An Ghaeltacht)

6. Tim Kennelly
(Listowel Emmets)

7. Ger Power
(Austin Stacks)

8. Paudie Lynch
(Beaufort)

9. Pat McCarthy
(Sallins, Kildare, also Churchill)

10. Denis 'Ogie' Moran
(Beale and UCD)

11. Mikey Sheehy
(Austin Stacks)

12. Mickey 'Ned' O'Sullivan
(Kenmare) Capt.

13. Brendan Lynch
(Beaufort)

14. John Egan
(Sneem)

15. Pat Spillane
(Templenoe and Thomond College)

Subs: Charlie Nelligan (Castleisland Desmonds) Played; Sean Walsh (Kerins O'Rahillys) Played; Ger O'Driscoll (Valentia) Played; John Long (An Ghaeltacht); Tony O'Keeffe (Austin Stacks); Jackie Walsh (Ballylongford and UCD); Vincent O'Connor (Dingle); Barry Walsh (Ballylongford and UCD)

1977

In October 1976, a meeting of the Dublin senior football team was convened on a Tuesday evening in the Gresham Hotel on O'Connell Street. There Kevin Heffernan dropped the bombshell that, just weeks after their second All-Ireland title in three years, he was stepping down as manager.

There was shock, naturally, and emotion, but above all else, mystery. Why now, when all the momentum was theirs and there was more, surely, to give?

Heffernan had been at the coalface of Dublin football for decades and when he came back in 1974 he had set himself a three-year target. With his goals reached his race, then, was run, he clearly felt.

Quite quickly Tony Hanahoe was appointed as player-manager, not an uncommon phenomenon at the time, with Lorcan Redmond and Donal Colfer remaining on as selectors.

Would the departure of Heffernan have an immediate impact? Dublin still reached a League Final the following spring, losing to Kerry, but quickly put that behind them, and despite the presence of some of the team on the All-Star tour to the US that May, they enjoyed a 1-14 to 2-8 win over Kildare before 12,000 in Navan in their quarter-final, the opening game of their latest defence. The lead had been nine points at one stage but Kildare, without Pat Dunney who had broken an ankle while on hurling duty with the All-Stars, rallied.

Kildare had beaten Kilkenny by 4-13 to 2-4 in their opening game, though Kilkenny had shown some flickers of light with a tournament win over Carlow prior to the championship. Still, Carlow recovered to beat Longford after a replay in their opening game, Willie Cullen scoring 2-7 between both games, to set up a quarter-final with Meath.

For that game Carlow brought back thirty-four-year-old Pat McNally after a six-year absence, but with Cormac Rowe, Mattie Kerrigan and Ollie O'Brien in inspired form they hit 1-13 between them of Meath's total in a 1-18 to 0-7 win and shaped like Dublin's biggest challengers.

Offaly had been losing altitude after those heady days at the start of the decade but they eased past Wicklow, 0-19 to 0-7, in the first round. They ran out of road in their quarter-final with Wexford, however, a shock 4-6 to 2-10 defeat, with the winners getting two goals each from dual player Martin Quigley and Ger Howlin in Croke Park.

That set up a semi-final with Dublin in Carlow. Wexford were being managed by Seamus Keevans, whose brother was a Christian Brother in a Dublin school at the time and happened to be in Parnell Park on schools-related business in the lead-up to the semi-final at the same time as a Dublin practice match against St Vincent's was taking place. Consequently, the match was halted

Dublin and Armagh march behind the Artane Boys' Band prior to the 1977 Final. *Sportsfile*.

over 'concern', the *Irish Independent* reported! No chances were being taken.

Dublin need not have worried as goals from Tony Hanahoe, John McCarthy and Bobby Doyle, on top of an outstanding defensive display from Robbie Kelleher, gave the champions a 3-11 to 0-6 win. They had David Hickey sent off, along with Wexford's Brian Furlong, as things got fractious but Hickey received just a two-week ban and was eligible for the final.

There was controversy prior to Louth's opening round win over Westmeath when J.P. O'Kane transferred to the Wee County from Antrim. The GAA's Activities Committee approved the transfer in time despite objections from Antrim over residency and other issues. O'Kane made a positive impact in a 2-9 to 0-12 win, with Leslie Toal delivering an imperious defensive performance for the winners. But 2-4 from Willie Brennan was the spur for Laois in a 4-15 to 1-16 quarter-final win over Louth, setting up a semi-final with Meath.

Meath didn't have an emerging Colm O'Rourke with them that season because of a bad knee injury but they did have Ken Rennicks back after a near twelve-month absence with a leg injury and he contributed 1-9 in a 3-20 to 1-13 win, with Mayo-born John Gibbons scoring the other two goals. That set up a second successive final with Dublin, and Meath went in with some hope, having beaten them in the 1975 League Final and again in the 1976 O'Byrne Cup and league.

But Anton O'Toole sent Dublin on their way to a fourth successive provincial title with a punched goal that Meath protested at the time was thrown. Meath dominated possession in the second half and came within a point and Dublin required a magnificent block from Fran Ryder on Rennicks to preserve their lead before two late Jimmy Keaveney points from difficult angles ensured a 1-9 to 0-8 win before 46,044 spectators.

By any stretch, you couldn't have given Armagh a prayer ahead of the 1977 Ulster Championship, especially when they drew Cavan in their opening round. Twelve months earlier they had been humiliated, 1-19 to 2-1, by Derry, the reigning Ulster champions who then went on to put back-to-back provincial titles together by winning that 1976 title. It was Armagh's second successive defeat to that Derry team and it appeared to leave them with remote hope of a recovery in the years ahead.

Cavan had forced a replay out of Derry in the '76 Ulster Final and that strong form line should have given them a decisive edge when they met Armagh in the Athletic Grounds in June. With Cavan establishing a swift nine-point lead, that view was thoroughly reinforced. Just before half-time, though, Armagh won a penalty which Paddy Moriarty took but Cavan goalkeeper Aidan Elliott saved, only for Moriarty to follow up and score from the rebound.

From a seemingly hopeless predicament then, Armagh sensed renewal and produced a stunning second half, 'winning' it by 1-12 to 1-1, 2-14 to 1-12 overall, an outcome that served to electrify the county's support. For the first time in many years Armagh genuinely felt they were on to something.

Gerry O'Neill, a teacher in St Colman's, Newry and older brother of then Nottingham Forest

The Armagh team which lost out to Dublin in the 1977 Final. Back (l–r): Peter Trainor, Sean Devlin, Larry Kearns, Brian McAlinden, Tom McCreesh, Colm McKinstry, Kevin Rafferty; front (l–r): Noel Marley, Denis Stevenson, Joe Kernan, Jimmy Smyth, Paddy Moriarty, Jim McKerr, John 'Joey' Donnelly, Peter Loughran. *Sportsfile.*

soccer player and Northern Ireland international Martin, was back as manager to bring a new level of organisation and tactical awareness.

It was a statement performance, one they followed through on with a four-point win over Monaghan in Dungannon in the semi-final, an afternoon marred only by a dislocated shoulder sustained by Tom McCreesh, the team's elder statesman, who had battled through many lean years and had just a couple of Railway Cup medals (1966 and 1970) with Ulster to show for it.

A formidable defender, thirty-six-year-old McCreesh had been living in Virginia where he was a bank manager and playing with the local club, Ramor United. He was coveted regularly by Cavan at the time but his loyalty to Armagh, in pursuit of an Ulster title, was unyielding. Fresh doubt about his participation in the final, because of the injury, cast a cloud over the team's preparations. Still, Armagh were into a first Ulster Final since 1961, chasing a first Ulster crown since 1953, a place they hadn't thought they could be just a few weeks earlier.

On the other side of the draw, Down had reshaped under the management of the legendary James McCartan, who had taken over months earlier from Jackie Fitzsimons, installing his brother Dan and cousins Dominic McCartan and Val Kane as his selectors. They were 3-9 to 0-7 quarter-final winners over Fermanagh, setting up a semi-final against Derry, who had to draw on all their craft to see off Donegal in a preliminary round and Tyrone in a quarter-final.

It took Seamus Lagan's goal – he scored 1-5 on the day – to make the difference against a Donegal side that had Martin Carney as its catalyst, but Derry had been somewhat lethargic, perhaps still reeling from the two-month suspension handed out by their County Board to Peter Stevenson for an alleged incident in a club game.

Frank McGuigan's absence, as he remained in the US, made Derry strong favourites to see off a Tyrone side underpinned by two sets of three brothers, Trillick's Donnellys – Sean, Tom and Brendan – and Augher's McKennas – Dessie, Willie and Eugene. It wasn't so straightforward for Derry, though, and it required 2-5 from Brendan Kelly for them to book a safe passage on a 3-10 to 1-11 scoreline.

It was nowhere near as free flowing in the semi-final. Down were without the injured Liam Austin so Donal Gordon and Willie Walsh were paired together in a new-look midfield. But a game marked by some sixty-seven frees and countless wides fell Derry's way, 0-10 to 0-8.

Subsequently, the GAA issued a new directive to crack down on the personal foul, something prevalent across the board, by giving a warning first, then a booking and finally dismissal, removing dependency on a referee's mental recall.

Having lost in both previous years by double figures to Derry, there were still misgivings about Armagh against a team bidding for only the second three-in-a-row in Ulster, post Cavan dominance.

Derry didn't bring home Kelly and Mickey Moran, star of the win over Down in the semi-final, from the US. They had conceded only one goal in their three previous championship games but by half-time that had doubled as Moriarty and Noel Marley struck for an Armagh team with serious momentum.

McCreesh had defied all medical analysis to take his place and the more Derry 'tested' his shoulder, the more, it seemed, he thrived and was by general consensus the game's outstanding player.

Derry were at arm's length and Armagh consolidated their dominance to see out the game comfortably, winning 3-10 to 1-5 to spark further euphoria. From nowhere, they had taken the province by storm.

They've been part of the Connacht Championship for almost half a century and have only had three wins in that time, but London's first came just three seasons in when they shocked Leitrim by 0-9 to 0-6 in Carrick-on-Shannon in mid May. That it took them another thirty-six years to win another championship game – this time over Sligo – puts this victory in context.

Twelve months earlier they had been well beaten by Roscommon, but with Mickey Martin, Leitrim's rising attacking star, touring the US with the All-Stars at the time, opportunity knocked for the Exiles. The home side figured that if they could not beat London without Martin they had no business playing Galway in the next round, but they had not played a competitive game since the end of January, a National Football League Division Two play-off defeat to Donegal, while their team featured quite a sprinkling of players who would go on to win a Connacht Under-21 title that year.

London's preparations lacked sufficient game time too but they prepared hard and had some of their team that had won a trio of All-Ireland junior titles between 1969 and 1971, among them Jerry Mahoney from Renard in Kerry, considered one of their best ever players.

There were other Kerry men pivotal to their success – Billy O'Connell, Tim Shanahan and John Mahoney – while Eamonn Brett, who had played on the Mayo team that beat London in their first ever Connacht Championship match two years earlier, had also moved over. There were even two Leitrim players involved, Gerry Keegan and Sean Harte, while Mick McGovern was the only London-born player, a former professional soccer player with Queens Park Rangers and Swindon Town in the 1960s and early 1970s.

London's win was built on the platform of Jerry Mahoney and Tony Flavin, another Kerry man, at midfield. It set up a semi-final against Galway in Ballinasloe a month later and briefly London were dreaming big when they led by 1-3 to 1-2 after twenty minutes. But Galway were 2-3 to 1-5 ahead at the break and the introduction of Tom Naughton for the second half stirred things further as they hit six points in a row to win by 5-13 to 1-9.

Roscommon had to play Mayo in their Connacht quarter-final without John O'Gara and Gerry Beirne, but inevitably Dermot Earley, starting at right half-forward, stepped up to deliver a big performance, contributing eight points (seven frees) in a 0-16 to 0-13 win in Castlebar. Goals either side of half-time against Sligo before 7,000 in Dr Hyde Park saw the home side through to the Connacht Final on a 2-9 to 1-6 scoreline.

Galway were looking for a fourth win over Roscommon in eight years and this was a repeat of the 1976 Final. They were buoyed by two opportunist Brian Talty goals and they led by five points, but Roscommon were resilient and when Mickey Freyne hit the winning point for a 1-12 to 2-8 win before 15,000 in Dr Hyde Park, it gave them their thirteenth provincial title.

It was a train journey like no other on the Saturday before the Munster Football Final in mid July as the Cork squad headed west to Killarney. All week, and indeed for weeks before that, tension had been building because of the players' liaison with Three Stripe International, the company that had the sportswear franchise for Adidas in Ireland. Earlier that year Dinny Allen had been approached by representatives of the company for the supply of gear in exchange for some promotional work. Cork players had to supply much of their own gear at the time but Billy Morgan saw it as an opportunity to raise their standards and adopt a more professional approach. Thus, agreement was reached for the supply of boots, shorts and socks. But that put them on a collision course with the Cork County Board, as Adidas were a German manufacturing company and GAA rules only permitted the use of Irish-produced gear where it was possible.

The selection committee were also divided on it and some Adidas gear was worn in Cork's semi-final against Clare, but matters reached a tipping point as they prepared to play Kerry. The players were told that any further breach after Clare would merit a suspension. Billy Morgan and Jimmy Barry-Murphy were among those reluctant to push through with it for the game in Killarney but others were more hawkish and a decision was reached to wear Adidas shorts on the day.

On the journey to Killarney, Cork officials made pleas to desist, even going as far as purchasing plain white shorts before they left the city. But there was no relenting, the Adidas shorts were worn, Kerry dished out a 3-15 to 0-9 defeat and team members were suspended for six months at a subsequent board meeting. The suspensions did not extend to club duty, nor did they apply to dual players Barry-Murphy and Brian Murphy, who had an upcoming All-Ireland hurling semi-final against Galway. If they wanted to return they had to give an undertaking not to wear or promote Adidas gear again and that was given, but only after further brinksmanship right up to and beyond the hurling semi-final. In fact, it wasn't entirely settled until late September, when that undertaking was formally accepted.

For Kerry, the second half in Killarney was a procession as they scored 3-11, having been 0-8 to 0-4 behind. Cork, with their supporters outnumbering the home crowd considerably, were impressive in the first half but once a Sean Walsh goal put Kerry ahead in the fortieth minute, the floodgates opened. Pat Spillane terrorised the Cork defence with his running, Walsh drifted to midfield from full-forward to cause them further trouble and John Egan and Spillane added their second and third goals. 'Something of the fire and determination of 1975 was back today,' defender Ger O'Keeffe declared afterwards.

In the early rounds Clare ultimately took care of Waterford by 1-18 to 3-6, a game that referee George Ryan concluded five minutes too early with Clare ten points clear. After Waterford protests, the remaining five minutes were played out with the Déise getting two Vinny Kirwan goals thirty seconds apart.

In the other quarter-final Tipperary had too much for Limerick, 4-10 to 1-5, with Laois-born garda Harry Mulhaire helping himself to two goals.

Clare's semi-final with Cork was switched to Limerick from Fermoy to facilitate a double header with the Tipperary–Clare hurling replay. Cork were too strong, with Barry-Murphy scoring a goal and setting up Dinny Allen for another before Michael Downes, who would later play for Meath, grabbed a late goal after a rare Morgan error.

Kerry had fourteen points to spare over Tipperary, for whom Gene McGrath was outstanding at midfield, as he had been against Limerick. Kerry's Barry Walsh hit 2-3 from corner-forward as a Jack O'Shea–Páidí Ó Sé midfield partnership was tried out for the first time in championship.

Armagh looked to be heading out of the championship when they found themselves seven points down in the first All-Ireland semi-final before 32,601 with just sixteen minutes remaining. But a restructuring after McCreesh departed saw Paddy Moriarty switch to centre-back which paid dividends, and when Moriarty scored a penalty in the fifty-seventh minute after Kevin Rafferty was fouled, the mood changed. Roscommon, playing in their first All-Ireland semi-final for five years and with Harry Keegan, Pat Lindsay, Tom Heneghan, Earley and Freyne as survivors, had led 2-7 to 1-4 thanks to goals from Earley and Eamonn McManus. But now they were under pressure and parity came when Jimmy Smyth, who had one of his greatest Armagh games that day, landed an equaliser for a 3-9 to 2-12 finish and a first All-Ireland semi-final replay since 1969.

The replay two weeks later wasn't televised live because of a clash with the final round of the Irish Open golf tournament, with Roscommon making two changes, John McDermott coming in for Gerry O'Dowd and Mick Keegan for Richard O'Beirne. Jim Finnegan was ruled out for Armagh so Sean Devlin replaced him, with McCreesh moving to full-back and Moriarty staying at centre-back.

The crowds came in their droves, over 43,000 this time, but saw no goals as Armagh edged out the Connacht champions by 0-15 to 0-14 to reach a first All-Ireland Final since 1953.

There waiting for them were Dublin who, in between the drawn and replayed semi-final, had won their own epic battle with Kerry. A game for the ages that still resonates to this day, it had everything as two sides that had beaten each other in championship games in the previous two seasons went at it with a 'winner takes all' feel to it.

Sean Walsh and Jimmy Deenihan were both declared fit for Kerry beforehand after being injury doubts, while Bernard Brogan came back from Cherbourg in France where he had been working on the construction of an oil rig destined for the south coast. Robbie Kelleher came from San Francisco where he had got married the previous week.

Kerry had won their two previous league meetings since the '76 All-Ireland Final and were buoyed by the emphatic nature of their win over Cork. Before 54,974 enthralled supporters, a record for a semi-final in the era of live television, Dublin trailed by three points at half-time before a McCarthy goal, Dublin's first, brought parity. Brogan had come on for Ryder in the twenty-fifth minute to partner Brian Mullins and it was ebb and flow in a thrilling second half before finally Dublin surged with Hickey and Hanahoe goals. To top it all Hanahoe then sealed it with a point for a 3-12 to 1-13 win. Mullins had been majestic while O'Toole kicked four points.

'We will talk by winter firesides of an afternoon touched by magic when two teams got locked in a confrontation frightening in the intensity of its climax, something beyond a normal match,' Raymond Smyth wrote eloquently in the *Irish Independent*. To this day it remains a reference point for the era.

THE FINAL – 25 SEPTEMBER

Try as Armagh did to guard against the conviction of most that the final had already been played when Dublin beat Kerry in that memorable semi-final, it was impossible to prevent reality taking hold as they were crushed by twelve points.

The enthusiasm generated by Armagh in reaching their first final in twenty-four years was one of the reasons that prompted the GAA to make a final all-ticket for the first time. Prior to that only the Hogan and Cusack Stands required ticket entry, with the Hill and Canal Ends on a first come, first served basis until they were at capacity. But often crowds exceeded capacity, and conscious of the support expected for Armagh, the GAA made a snap decision in the weeks leading up to it.

The impact was that far too many tickets got into the hands of touts who subsequently couldn't sell them as supporters without them took the advice not to travel to Dublin that day. Others with tickets stayed away too and the upshot was that a game that was in such demand had an attendance of 66,542, the second lowest in twenty-five years. Maybe it was a good thing because it was so one-sided as Dublin, from the start, imposed their will impressively. They were ruthless.

Playing with the wind, it was Jimmy Keaveney, on the way to recording the highest individual score in an All-Ireland football final (2-6), who got an early goal, cutting in from the sideline from a tight angle to deceive Armagh goalkeeper Brian McAlinden with a looping shot. Was it an effort for a point? According to Joe Kernan, Armagh midfielder on the day, the St Vincent's man would admit to that many years later! But the impact was huge and by the break Dublin were 3-6 to 1-3 ahead, Armagh's goal coming from Moriarty's converted penalty.

Keaveney's second goal came early in the second half after a magnificent Dublin move, helping them into a 4-8 to 1-3 lead. Kernan played his heart out even when it was clear that they could never rescue a hopeless situation and he struck for two second-half goals to help reduce the gap to eight points before Dublin took off again. Bobby Doyle finished the rout in the sixtieth minute with a fifth goal that helped to establish the highest ever All-Ireland final score then and even to the time of writing, a distinction shared with Kerry's 4-15 in the 2006 Final. Paddy Cullen denied a second Moriarty penalty with a late save.

The ease of Dublin's win renewed calls for an open draw while Armagh manager O'Neill suggested the following day at the official GAA reception for the teams in the Garda Club on Harrington Street in the capital that Dublin were the 'team of the century'. However, the years that followed would soon change that thinking.

FINAL STATISTICS

	Dublin	Armagh
Full-time:	5-12	3-6
Half-time:	3-6	1-3
Scorers:	J. Keaveney 2-6 (0-4 frees)	J. Kernan 2-1
	B. Doyle 2-2	P. Moriarty 1-0 (1-0 penalty)
	J. McCarthy 1-2	P. Loughran 0-2 (0-2 frees)
	D. Hickey 0-1	P. Trainor 0-1
	A. O'Toole 0-1	S. Devlin 0-1
		J. Smyth 0-1 (free)
Attendance:	66,542	
Referee:	John Moloney (Tipperary)	

FINAL MISCELLANY

- With a tally of 2-6, Dublin's Jimmy Keaveney set a new individual scoring record for a final. The previous record-holder was Galway's Frank Stockwell, who scored 2-5 in the 1956 decider against Cork.
- Within months of the 1977 All-Ireland Final Kevin Moran had signed for Manchester United and would go on to have a very successful professional career, winning seventy-one caps for the Republic of Ireland.
- For only the second time ever, a total of eight goals were scored in the final. In 1948, Cavan beat Mayo on the extraordinary scoreline of 4-5 to 4-4.
- Winners Dublin lined out with the same fifteen players as had started the 1976 Final, emulating the feat of Kildare when they won in 1927 and 1928.
- The Church of Ireland was officially represented at an All-Ireland Final for the first time. The Dean of St Patrick's Cathedral, Dr Victor Griffin, was among the GAA's VIP guests.

1977 – THE YEAR THAT WAS

- In the lead-up to the general election in June 1977, Fianna Fáil leader Jack Lynch expressed confidence that his party could win up to seventy-seven Dáil seats and so return to power. Despite the protestations of Minister for Finance Richie Ryan, Lynch argued that the country could well afford to borrow the funds necessary to finance an election package which included the abolition of motor tax and domestic rates. The electorate's response was emphatic: Fianna Fáil won eighty-four seats and entered government with an overall majority of twenty.
- The 'King of Rock and Roll', Elvis Presley, passed away on 16 August. The official cause of death was a heart attack, but doctors said this was probably brought about by an addiction to prescription barbiturates.

- In Marseilles on 10 September, Tunisian-born Hamida Djandoubi became the last man to be executed by guillotine.
- On 2 April, Red Rum won the Aintree Grand National for an unprecedented third time.

1977 TEAM LINE-OUTS

DUBLIN (WINNERS)

1. Paddy Cullen
(O'Connell Boys)

2. Gay O'Driscoll
(St Vincent's)

3. Sean Doherty
(Ballyboden St Enda's)

4. Robbie Kelleher
(Scoil Uí Chonaill and TCD)

5. Tommy Drumm
(Whitehall Colmcilles and TCD)

6. Kevin Moran
(Good Counsel)

7. Pat O'Neill
(UCD, also Civil Service)

8. Brian Mullins
(St Vincent's)

9. Bernard Brogan
(St Oliver Plunketts)

10. Anton O'Toole
(Synge Street)

11. Tony Hanahoe
(St Vincent's)

12. David Hickey
(Raheny)

13. Bobby Doyle
(St Vincent's)

14. Jimmy Keaveney
(St Vincent's)

5. John McCarthy
(Na Fianna, also Garda)

Subs: Alan Larkin (Raheny) Played; Paddy Reilly (St Margaret's) Played; Jim Brogan (St Oliver Plunketts and TCD) Played; Paddy Gogarty (Raheny); Brendan Pocock (St Vincent's); Fran Ryder (St Vincent's, also Ballymun Kickhams); Norman Bernard (St Vincent's); Michael Hickey (Raheny); Liam Egan (Scoil Uí Chonaill); Dermot Maher (Kilmacud Crokes)

ARMAGH (RUNNERS-UP)

1. Brian McAlinden
(Sarsfields)

2. Denis Stevenson
(Sarsfields)

3. Tom McCreesh
(Ramor United, Cavan, also Crossmaglen Rangers)

4. Jim McKerr
(Clan na Gael)

5. Kevin Rafferty
(Maghery)

6. Paddy Moriarty
(Wolfe Tones)

7. John 'Joey' Donnelly
(O'Neills, Blackwatertown)

8. Joe Kernan
(Crossmaglen Rangers)

9. Colm McKinstry
(Clan na Gael)

10. Larry Kearns
(Crossmaglen Rangers)

11. Jimmy Smyth
(Clan na Gael)

12. Noel Marley
(Ballyhegan Davitts)

13. Sean Devlin
(Armagh Harps)

14. Peter Trainor
(Carrickcruppen)

15. Peter Loughran
(Carrickcruppen)

Subs: Jim Loughran (Carrickcruppen) Played; Sean Daly (Armagh Harps) Played; Frank Toman (Clann Eireann) Played; Malachy Heaney (Maghery); Eamonn O'Neill (Sarsfields); Noel O'Hagan (Clan na Gael); Thomas Cassidy (Crossmaglen Rangers); Jim Finnegan (St Killian's, Whitecross); Redmond Scullion (Pearse Óg); Raymond Kelly (Mullaghbawn); Fran McMahon (Culloville Blues)

CONCLUSION

So that's the first fifty years of those who 'chased Sam' documented.

In 2027, the GAA President of the day will present the Sam Maguire Cup to the winning captain for a 100th time. At the time of writing, a further four counties – Donegal, Derry, Armagh and Tyrone – had claimed 'Sam' for the first time, bringing to sixteen the number overall. Wexford, Limerick and Tipperary won All-Ireland titles in the years before 1928.

The years since 1978 have seen great changes in Gaelic football, with the athleticism and power of Dublin giving way to an even more athletic Kerry team which also prioritised possession to progress the game during that much revered first period.

Those breakthrough years for that Ulster quartet, 1992–1993 and 2002–2003, marked a new development in the sport. The dominance that Dublin have had over football for the last decade again transformed the game and brought it to the next level.

The shape of Gaelic football has changed dramatically from decade to decade and this last decade has perhaps witnessed the greatest acceleration of all. It will continue to evolve. Modern players make a lifestyle choice when they step into an inter-county dressing-room, their devotion to the cause of a county team requiring much more time than those years that we have just documented. But that cause still remains the same. That prize, out of reach for so many, still remains a distant dream for most and an aspiration for all.

Charting the journey of the first fifty years has been a privilege, and recalling the high and lows of its pursuit, with some social context added, opened eyes. 'Sam' has the capacity to change lives and break hearts in equal measure. It has a hold on the Irish sporting psyche like no other silverware.

ACKNOWLEDGEMENTS

Records for Gaelic games are notoriously hit and miss. There is no central database and it's not possible, for example, to press the click and control buttons to establish what player has the most championship appearances or provincial medals. Historical results and team lists can be trial and error, varying from county to county.

Nonetheless, within every county there is invariably a figure or two of 'authority', who can be relied upon to give a definitive judgement on the games, teams and players of earlier generations.

Their diligent work to capture and record their county's tradition and build its archive may be a labour of love. More importantly, however, it helps fill a gap that isn't always recognised and recorded in the detail it should be. This is of inestimable value in bringing the GAA's glorious past to life. Their work has been invaluable, their authority unimpeachable, as *Chasing Sam Maguire* came to fruition.

From George Cartwright in Cavan, himself the author of two invaluable books on his county's glorious past, to James Rocke in Mayo and Tony Conboy and Colm Hennelly in Roscommon, their knowledge and capture of the past was truly amazing. John Phelan's record of Laois GAA is a model. Pat Donegan is the definitive voice on Offaly GAA's archive, while Padraig Foy and Ciarán Reilly's excellent *Faithful Pioneers* filled in many gaps. Eoghan Corry followed his detailed history of Kildare GAA with a broader sweep on the games at national level. Brian Willoughby and Noel Hynes, authors of *Guardians of the GAA*, were a rich source of invaluable detail.

Is there anyone that knows the landscape of the GAA in the west, or indeed anywhere, better than Jim Carney, the former *Tuam Herald* sports editor and well known *Sunday Game* presenter and commentator? Tim Slattery carries the same authority in Kerry and, with the county's stature in the game during the period, his validation carried much weight.

Joe Ó Muircheartaigh, co-author of *Princes of Pigskin*, that superbly detailed account of a century of Kerry footballers, also gave invaluable input, as did Seamus Mac Gearailt and Micheál Ó Sé.

Hugh Gribbin, Derry's 1958 full-back, and his son, also Hugh, kindly provided critical detail for that year. Brendan Cummins and Mick O'Brien of Meath, Jim O'Sullivan in Cork, J.P. Graham in Monaghan and the late Paddy Clarke in Louth all provided key pieces of information. When Paddy died in 2018, his family presented his wonderful collection of Louth GAA records to local journalist Joe Carroll, another great source for this project.

It was our very good fortune to benefit from all their hard work and perseverance.

The gathering of old photographs and programmes is never straightforward but George Cartwright, James Laffey (*Western People* editor and author of *The Road to 51*), Joe Carroll, Jimmy Wren, Peter Shields (Gaelic Art), Larry Hyland and Ray McManus (Sportsfile) could not have been more helpful. Thanks also to Elizabeth Kirwan, Curator at the National Photographic Archive, and to Barbara Bonini who gave us outstanding support and advice.

Martin Breheny, Gerry Buckley, Hugh Cawley, Brían Clarke, Jim Crowley, Tom Duffy, Gus Fitz-patrick, Roddy Guiney, Noel Fox, John Hackett, Orla Heffernan, Jerome Higgins, Mattie Kilroy, Gearóid Mac Gabhann (RIP), Peter McConnon, Linda McCoy, Liam McDonagh, Ger McDon-ough, Pete McGrath, Dominic McPhillips, Brian Neilan, George Ormsby, Liz Reilly and Terry Reilly were also helpful in providing and piecing information together.

Niamh McCoy and Adam Staunton at the GAA Museum in Croke Park were always accessible and hugely supportive, likewise Joanne Clarke before them.

We are indebted to Larry McCarthy (President, GAA), Tom Ryan (Director General, GAA) and Peter McKenna (Stadium & Commercial Director, Croke Park) and to Paraic Duffy (former Director General, GAA) for their encouragement and very practical support.

A special word of thanks to Brenda Burke at PwC who, with unfailing good humour, worked tirelessly in developing the early templates and drafts.

The support of Tommy Drumm (Collen Construction), John Tuffy (Padraic Tuffy Limited), Ray-mond Conlan (N. Conlan & Sons), Rory O'Dwyer and Neville Cavanagh (NKC) and the partners at PwC is gratefully acknowledged and appreciated.

Our editing team at The O'Brien Press have steered us on a steady path, even when we were tempted to stray from time to time. Natasha Mac a'Bháird's attention to detail, recall and ability to knit the years together, between text and team lists, has been phenomenal. It was never an easy task but, armed with a deep passion for the GAA, she committed to it with great patience and profes-sionalism to pull it all together. Paula Elmore provided expertise, advice and strong leadership on all aspects of the project, and particularly so on the sourcing and selection of photographs.

The O'Brien Press is a name that is synonymous with book publishing in Ireland and our first conversations were with the late Michael O'Brien, the company's founder and a true giant in the industry. Michael took a keen interest in the project from the outset, not just from a commercial perspective, but based on what he regarded as its cultural significance. His son Ivan now steers the ship and we thank him for his invaluable guidance and advice.

Lastly, for their patience and perseverance since the idea of putting clubs to names was first conceived a decade ago, we thank our families from the bottom of our hearts. That the project grew exponentially was something they, and we, could not have envisaged.

When 'Sam' was in its infancy, Olive Reilly was assured by Dermot that this would be nothing more than a hobby to while away a few hours during his retirement. This was far from the reality. For her unwavering love and support throughout, he is truly grateful. Thanks also to their children, Deirdre, Diarmuid and Finian, and their families, for their great enthusiasm for the project and their ongoing support and encouragement.

Likewise, Colm would like to thank Frances Keys and their daughters, Danielle and Lauren, who were unrelenting in their encouragement, lending support and assistance with great humour, love and enthusiasm. Their technical assistance is always greatly appreciated.

INDEX

Photographs are indicated by page numbers in **bold**. To distinguish teams from towns where both appear in the index, teams appear with the county in brackets and towns appear with the county after a comma, for example 'Ferbane (Offaly)' [team] and 'Ferbane, Co. Offaly' [town].

Abbeydorney (Kerry), 267
Aberfan disaster, 325
Academy Awards, 27
Acton, Tom, **167**, 169, 172, 188
Adams, Billy, 142
Adidas, 428
Adrigole (Cork), 250, 335, 394
Aer Lingus, 78, 154, 179
Aghaderg (Down), 275, 283, 344
Aghagallon Shamrocks (Antrim), 215
Aghamore (Mayo), 188
Ahascragh (Galway), 95–6, 240
Aherne, Jim, 126, 149, 157
Aherne, Mick, 353
Aherne, Pat, 292
Aintree Grand National, 334, 432
Air Corps, 124, 149, 188, 196, 213, 232, 259, 284, 292, 335
air travel, 78, 148, 154, 161, 179, 362, 381
Aldridge, Seamus, 308
Aldrin, Buzz, 346, 352
Ali, Muhammad, 308
All-Star teams, 352, 366, 370, 379, 423, 427
Allen, Dick, 48
Allen, Dinny, 376, 412, 428, 429
Allen, Norman, 226, **226**, 232
Anglo Celt, 17, 25, 26, 32–3, 38, 52, 59, 66, 77, 81, 101, 106, 114, 126, 130, 131, 135, 137, 147, 162–3, 170, 192, 201, 219, 227, 270, 311, 316, 331
Annaclone (Down), 73, 275, 283
Annacurra (Wicklow), 259, 300
Annaghdown (Galway), 111, 118, 124, 395, 404
Annascaul (Kerry), 86–7, 96–7, 105, 111, 117, 141, 155–6, 164
Antrim
  1920s, 17, 24

1930s, 31, 37–8, 42, 48, 56, 92
1940s, 106, 116, 126, 130, 134, 144, 150, 151–2, 159–60, 165, 173
1950s, 184–5, 192–3, 199, 208, 218, 221, 227, 236, 239, 246, 255
1960s, 269, 285, 306, 311, 321, 331, 340, 349
1970s, 355–6, 362, 364, 365, 368, 372, 387, 399–400, 409, 419, 424
Antrim County Board, 151, 322
Aodh Ruadh (Donegal), 215, 268, 301, 309, 317, 325
Archbold, Jim, **135**
Archibald, Peter, 319, 349
Ardagh (Limerick), 95–6
Ardboe (Tyrone), 384
Ardcath (Meath), 180, 197, 205–6
Ardfert (Kerry), 117, 214, 224, 267, 345
Ardglass (Down), 344
Ardgroom (Cork), 241, 250
Ardnacrusha power plant, 27
Ardnaree Sarsfields (Mayo), 172, 188, 196
Armagh
  1920s, 11, 17, 24
  1930s, 31, 38, 42, 49, 55–6, 66, 73, 80–1, 92, 101, 103
  1940s, 106, 113, 121, 126, 134, 144, 150, 159, 173
  1950s, 13, 185, 192, 199, 200, 207–8, 208, 209–15, 218–19, 227, 236, 254, 262
  1960s, 277–8, 282, 285, 296, 311–12, 322, 349
  1970s, 367, 372, 387, 399, 409, 418, 421, **424**, **425**, 425–7, 429–32
Armagh County Board, 38
Armagh Harps (Armagh), 215, 432
Armagh Observer, 275
Armstrong, Kevin, 106, 130, 150, 160, 227

Armstrong, Neil, 346, 352
Army, 17, 28, 35, 41, 47, 79, 132–3, 141, 149, 163, 171, 181, 204–6
Army Metro, 70, 79
Arrigan, Paddy, 29, 36
Artane Boys Band, 32
Arthurs, Gerry, 17
Arva (Cavan), 87–8, 132–3, 149, 163, 171, 181, 204–6
Asdee (Kerry), 27, 34, 40, 46
Ashe, Mick, 269
Ashe, Tom, 214, 224
athletics, 20, 45, 77, 110, 222, 240, 316, 344
Athlone (Westmeath), 284
Athlone Town FC, 179
Athy (Kildare), 28, 41, 63, 67, 70
atomic bomb, 147
Atticall (Down), 344
Auschwitz, 123
Austin, Liam, 426
Austin Stacks (Kerry), 27, 34, 40–1, 46, 86–7, 96–7, 105, 111, 117, 141, 224, 232, 292, 309, 317, 353, 363, 382–3, 394, 413, 422
Australia, 333, 336, 354
Austria, 95

Bailieboro (Cavan), 21, 54, 69, 87–8, 132–3, 149, 163, 171, 181, 204–6, 292, 306
Baily, Jimmy, **23**, 27, 34
Balfe, John, 348
Balla (Mayo), 78, 95–6, 111, 118
Ballaghaderreen (Mayo), 172, 185, 188, 196, 249, 268, 301, 309, 317, 325
Ballerin Sarsfields (Derry), 259, 385
Ballina, Co. Mayo, 162, 222
Ballina Herald, 72
Ballina Stephenites (Mayo), 47, 78, 172, 188, 196

Ballinabrackey (Meath), 197, 326, 334, 363

Ballinacor (Wicklow), 240

Ballinagh (Cavan), 181, 204–6, 249

Ballinaheglish (Roscommon), 132–3, 141, 155–6

Ballinameen (Roscommon), 132–3

Ballinamore (Leitrim), 273

Ballinasloe Mental Hospital (Galway), 62, 95–6

Ballinderry (Derry), 259

Ballingeary (Cork), 345, 353, 363, 382–3

Ballinlough (Meath), 105, 180, 197, 205–6, 223, 363

Ballinrobe (Mayo), 47, 78

Ballintober (Roscommon), 132–3, 141, 155–6

Ballintubber (Mayo), 172, 188, 196

Ballivor (Meath), 180, 197, 205–6, 223, 326, 334, 363

Ballybay (Monaghan), 35

Ballyboden St Enda's (Dublin), 403, 413, 422, 432

Ballyboughal (Dublin), 288, 300

Ballybrittas (Laois), 79

Ballybunion (Kerry), 27, 34, 40, 46

Ballycastle (Mayo), 47, 78, 172, 188, 196

Ballyconnell (Cavan), 132–3, 149, 163, 171, 181

Ballycumber (Offaly), 353

Ballydonoghue (Kerry), 155–6, 160, 164, 224, 240, 268, 276, 309, 317, 413

Ballyfermot Gaels (Dublin), 300

Ballyferriter (Kerry), 62, 86–7

Ballyforan (Roscommon), 141

Ballyfore (Offaly), 353, 359, 371, 381–2

Ballygar (Galway), 240, 268, 301, 309, 317, 325, 404

Ballyhaise (Cavan), 21

Ballyhaunis (Mayo), 47

Ballyhegan Davitts (Armagh), 432

Ballyjamesduff (Cavan), 78

Ballyjamesduff, Co. Cavan, 76

Ballykinlar (Down), 275, 283, 344

Ballylongford (Kerry), 46, 83, 86–7, 96–7, 105, 111, 117, 141, 212, 214, 224, 232, 309, 317, 345, 353, 363, 382–3, 413, 422

Ballymacelligott (Kerry), 27, 34, 268, 292

Ballymacnab (Armagh), 215

Ballymaguigan (Derry), 259

Ballymartin (Down), 275, 283

Ballymun Kickhams (Dublin), 403, 422, 432

Ballymurray (Roscommon), 132–3, 141

Banba (Dublin), 149, 163, 171, 181, 204–6

Banbridge (Down), 275

Bandon (Cork), 250, 335, 394

Bangladesh, 370

Banks, Tommy, 119, 122, 123, 124

Bannister, Roger, 222

Bantry Blues (Cork), 335, 394

Barden, Brendan, 313, 329, **337**

Barnard, Christiaan, 334

Barrett, Bill, 29

Barrett, Jimmy, 368, **386**, 390, 391, 392, 394

Barrett, Jo Jo (Kerry: 1950s–1960s), 243, 292, **303**, 309, 313, 317

Barrett, Joe (Kerry: 1920s), **23**, 27, 34, 40, 46

Barrett, John, 289, 296

Barrett, Tommy, 41

Barrett, Tony, 307, 320

Barrett, Vincie, 278

Barron, Declan, 366, **386**, 392, 394, 400, 418

Barrow, Clyde Chestnut, 62

Barry, John, 405

Barry, Mick, 29

Barry-Murphy, Jimmy, **386**, 390, 391, 392, 394, 400, 407, 418, 428, 429

Bashford, Johnny, **176**, 180

basketball, 258

Baston, Vin, 213

Beades, Eamonn, 356

Beahan, Kevin, **243**, 244–5, 247, 249, 280, 304

Beale (Kerry), 413, 422

Beann Eadair (Dublin), 63, 95–6, 111, 118, 124, 232, 259

Beatles, The, 308

Beaufort (Kerry), 63, 86–7, 96–7, 105, 111, 117, 141, 267, 276, 292, 309, 345, 353, 363, 382–3, 413, 422

Beckett, Derry, 145, 146, 147, 149

Beggan, Paddy, 105

Beggs, Bobby, **56**, 60, 63, 65, 72, 93, 95–6, 107, 111, 115, 116, 118, 121–2, 123, 124

Begley, Michael, 374

Begley, Paddy, 71, 106

Behan, Mick, 28

Behan, Paddy, 199, 258

Behan, Simon, 258, 280, 300

Beirne, Gerry, 398, 427

Beirne, Ray, 193

Beirne, Richard 'Dickie', 292

Beirne, Vinny, 155–6

Beisty, Paddy, 141

Bell, Jack, 189

Bellaghy Wolfe Tones (Derry), 259

Bellewstown (Meath), 334, 363

Belmullet (Mayo), 47

Belturbet (Cavan), 132–3, 149, 163, 171, 181

Belturbet Rory O'Moores (Cavan), 215

Benson, Des, 132–3, **166**, 171

Bere Island (Cork), 149

Bergman, Ingrid, 123

Bermingham, Paddy, 124

Bermingham, Tom (Cork: 1960s), 335

Bermingham, Tom (Waterford: 1950s), 254

Bernard, Dennis, 235, 241, **244**, 250

Bernard, Norman, 432

Berry, Jack, 348

bicycles, 61, 76, 103, 115, 116, 121, 125, 130

Billings, Dave, 403

Biro, Laszlo Jozsef, 95

Birrell, Bill, 54

Bishopstown (Cork), 309, 317, 335, 345, 353, 394

Black, Peter, 334, 363

Black Sabbath movement, 381

Blackrock College (Dublin), 195

Blaney, Neil, 362

Blessing, Louis, **50**, 54, 56, **65**, 69, 73, **81**, 83, 84, 87–8

Blessing, Noel, 242

Bligh, Billy, 363

Bloody Sunday, 372, 381

Blueshirts, 61

Blythe, Paudie, 390

Bogart, Humphrey, 123

Bohane, Mick, 305

Bohermeen (Meath), 363

Boland, Colm, 123, 124

Boland, Eamon, 128, 132–3, 134, 137, 141, 155–6, 198, 200

Boland, Eugene, 174

Bolton Wanderers FC, 410

Bonner, Seamus, **373**, 374, 400

Bornacoola (Leitrim), 155–6

Boston, 401, 421

Boston Beacons FC, 364

Bourke, Dermot, 39, 41, 43

Bourke, Seamus, 108, 112

Bowens, Christy, 363

Bowler, Teddy, 317, 345

boxing, 77, 308, 376, 410

Boyce, John, **373**

Boyd, Des, 155–6

Boylan, Paddy, **65**, 67, 69, **81**, 83, 84, 87–8, 114, 121, 128, 132–3, 149

Boyle (Roscommon), 63, 141, 155–6

Boyle, Eddie, 68, 99

Boyle, Jimmy 'Cookie', 227

Boyle, Johnny, **226**, 230, 232, 245, 251, 255, 256, 258, 259

Boyle, Sean, 187, 189

Bracken, Mickey, 271

Bracken, Paddy (Laois: 1960s), 337

Bracken, Paddy (Westmeath: 1930s), 43

Bracken, Paddy (Westmeath: 1950s), 261

Bracken, Pat, 288

Bracken, Seamus, 37

Bradley, Dick, 173

Bradley, Tommy, 32, 33, 35

Bradley, Vincent, 173

Brady, Aidan, 242, 287, 292

Brady, Bernard, 296, 322

Brady, Jim, 262

Brady, Mickey (Cavan: 1960s), 285

Brady, Mickey (Offaly: 1960s), 272, **278**, 280, 282, 284

Brady, Ollie, 349

Brady, Paddy (Cavan: 1930s), **50**, 54

Brady, Paddy (Meath: 1950s), 223

Brady, Phil 'Gunner', 149, **158**, 163, **166**, 168, 170, 171, 178, 181, **199**, 199, 202, 204–6, 207, 227, 229

Brady, Tom (Cavan: 1930s), 54

Brady, Tom (Waterford: 1960s), 346

Brannigan, Harry, 35

Brannigan, Tommy, 363

Bratton, Jack, 212, 215, 219

Bray Emmets (Wicklow), 87–8

Breen, Dinny, 43, 65

Breen, Patsy, 259

Brennan, Declan, 202, 205–6

Brennan, Des, **56**, 63

Brennan, Frank, 227

Brennan, Jim, 132–3

Brennan, Joe (Carlow: 1940s), **135**

Brennan, Joe (Dublin: 1950s), **226**, 232, 259

Brennan, Joe (Laois: 1930s), 79

Brennan, John, **407**

Brennan, Kieran, 336, 337, 415

Brennan, Mattie, **407**

Brennan, Michael 'Cussaun', 51, 53, 54, 62

Brennan, Peter, 356–7, 374

Brennan, Sean, 301

Brennan, Tom 'Click', 16, 17, 22, 43

Brennan, Tony, 320, 326, **328**, 332, 334, 361, 363, 366

Brennan, Willie, 414, 424

Brereton, Sean, **278**, 280, 281, 282, 284, 287

Breslin, Cormac, 250

Breslin, Eamonn, 300, 308

Breslin, John Joe, 292

Brett, Eamonn, 408, 427

Brett, Paddy, **72**, 78

Brewster, Mick, 269, 277, 321–2

Brick, Willie, 59

Briens, Johnny, 141, 155–6

Briody, Eugene 'Sammy', 54

British Army, 33, 372, 381

British Commonwealth, 40, 179

Brogan, Bernard, 397, 408, 409, 413, 415, **417**, 420, 422, 429, 432

Brogan, Seamus, 273

Brogan, Jim, 403, 422, 432

Brosnan, Con, **23**, 27, 29, 34, 40, 46

Brosnan, Jim, 211, 214, 224, 231, 232, 235, 262, 267, 276, 315

Brosnan, Mick, 214

Brosnan, Paddy 'Bawn', 96–7, 109, 111, 115, 117, 121, 138, 141, 155–6, 164, 186, 190, 193, 200

Brosnan, Sean, 84, 86–7, 93, 96–7, 102, 105, 106, 109, 111, 115, 117, 121, 136, 141

Brosnan, Tim 'Timineen Deas', 141, 164

Brown, Chris, 384

Brown, Tom, **56**

Browne, Har, 30, 37, 49, 79

Browne, Jack, 30

Browne, Noel, 196

Browne, Tom, 288, 297, 304, 326

Browne, 'Weasel', 66

Bruer, Ned 'Dinger', 272

Bruton, Pat, 334

Bryan, Willie, 260, 349, 351, 353, 365, 366, **367**, 368, 371, **374**, 379, 381–2, 388

Bryansford (Down), 275, 283

Buckley, Bobby, 214, 216, 224, 232

Buckley, Mick, 20, 28

Buckley, Pat, 320

Bunyan, John, 413

Burgess, Eamonn, 288

Burke, Derry, 141

Burke, Dinny, 366, 376

Burke, Frank, 54, 62

Burke, Harry, 30, 39, 41, 82, 119

Burke, Jarlath, 404

Burke, John (Clare/Galway: 1930s–1940s), 71, 91, 92, 93, 95–6, 108, 111, 115, 116, 118

Burke, John (Kerry: 1960s), 309, 317

Burke, Maurice, **389**, 392, 395

Burke, Mick, 322, 329, 330, **330**, 331, 332, 335

Burke, Paddy, 150, 152, 155–6

Burke, Pat, 368, 371

Burke, Richard, 394

Burke, Tom, 45, 47, **58**, 72, **72**, 78

Burns, Alan, 363

Burns, Bobby, 313, **337**

Burns, Eddie, **270**, 275

Burns, Leo, 126

Burns, Mickey, **337**

Burns, P.J., 363

Burrows, Seanie, 317, 330, 345

Butterly, Paddy, 191, 250

Byrne, Frankie, 176, **176**, 177, 178, 180, 192, 197, 223

Byrne, Gay, 291

Byrne, Jim (Monaghan: 1960s), 269

Byrne, Jim (Wexford: referee), 15, 33

Byrne, Jimmy (Kildare: 1930s), 70

Byrne, Mick 'Huckle' (Louth: 1950s), 189

Byrne, Mickey (Galway: 1970s), 371

Byrne, Mickey (Longford: 1960s), 313

Byrne, Micky (Carlow: 1940s), 112, **135**

Byrne, Paddy, 41, 70, 74

Byrne, Pat 'Babby', 90

Byrne, Patsy 'Bunny', 189

Byrne, Tommy, 134, **167**, 172, 188

Caffrey, Aidan, **407**

Caffrey, Tom 'Skinner', 57, 65, 82

Cahirciveen (Kerry), 41

Caherdaniel (Kerry), 34, 40, 46

Caherlistrane (Galway), 240

Cahill, Mick, 136, 190

Cahill, Tom, 132–3

Callan, Eugene, 57, 99

Callanan, Eugene 'Nudge', 16
Caltra (Galway), 371
Caltra-Ahascragh (Galway), 54, 62
camogie, 179, 239
Camp (Kerry), 27, 34, 41, 86–7, 96–7, 105, 111, 117, 214, 224, 232, 267, 276, 292, 309, 317, 345, 353, 363
Campbell, Joe Henry, 55
Campbell, Pat, 215
Campbell, Seamus, 55
Campbell, Tom (Cavan: 1920s), 21
Campbell, Tommy (Cavan: 1950s), 184
Campbell, Tommy (Tyrone: 1950s), **233**
Canavan, Frank, 364, 369, 371, 395
Canavan, Jarlath, 111, 118, 123, 124, 168
Canavan, Kevin, 376
Canning, Patrick, 31
Canovee (Cork), 250
capital punishment, 308, 432
Caragh (Kildare), 20, 28, 41
Carbery, Jack, 177
Carbury (Kildare), 20, 28, 41, 43, 280
Cardinal Cushing Cup, 376
Carew, Tommy, 321
Carey, Hugo, 52, 54, 57, 62
Carey, Jarlath, **270**, 275, 277, 282, 283
Carey, Johnny, 318, 347, 387
Carey, Peter, 271
Carley, Mick, 272, 288, 303, 320
Carlos, Bill, 114, 120, 128, 132–3, **136**, 138, 141, 151, 155–6, 160
Carlos, John, 344
Carlow
    1920s, 26
    1930s, 65, 68, 82, 90, 99
    1940s, 112–13, 114, 119, 120, 125, **135**, 136–8, 139, 151, 158, 167, 176
    1950s, 182, 190–1, 199, 218, 225, 244, 251, 260
    1960s, 271, 280, 287, 297, 299, 303, 313, 320, 336, 348
    1970s, 359, 365, 377, 396, 409, 423
Carlow County Board, 26
Carmody, Jer, 86
Carna (Galway), 54
Carney, Jackie, **58**, **72**, 75, 78, **167**, **191**
Carney, Martin, **373**, 373, 400, 426
Carney, Pádraig, 165, **167**, 168, 169, 170, 172, 174, 185, 188, 190, **191**, 194, 195, 196, 198

Carolan, Edwin, 83, **158**, 163, **166**, 171, 181, **199**, 200, 202, 204–6
Carolan, Hugh B., 21
Carolan, Jim, 326
Carolan, John, 21
Carolan, Mick, 251, 280, 287, 297, 321, 349
Carolan, Paddy (Cavan: 1950s), **199**, 204–6
Carolan, Pat (Meath: 1940s–1950s), **176**, 180, 197, 205–6
Carolan, Ray, 285, 286, 306, 311, 331, 341, 349, 350
Carrantryla (Galway), 301, 309, 317, 325
Carrickcruppen (Armagh), 432
Carrickmacross (Monaghan), 35
Carrickmore (Tyrone), 236
Carrickshock, Co. Kilkenny, 103
Carrigan Commission Report, 69
Carrigtwohill (Cork), 240
Carroll, Anton, **373**
Carroll, Bill, 87–8
Carroll, Christy, 217, 218, 284
Carroll, Donal, 286–7, 306, 324, 360, 419
Carroll, Harry, 356
Carroll, Joe, 192
Carroll, Johnny, 305, 320, 329, **330**, 332, 335
Carroll, Tom, 250
cars, 20, 77, 85, 204
Carty, Dave, 304, 326, 334
Carty, Mick, 416
Casablanca (1942), 123
Casey, Bill (Dublin: 1960s), 300
Casey, Bill (Kerry: 1930s–1940s), 86–7, 96–7, 99, 102, 105, 111, 117, 121, 141, 152, 153, 155–6, 164
Casey, Johnny, 95–6, 111, 118, 124
Casey, Mick (Dublin: 1930s), **56**, 59, 63, 71
Casey, Mick (Offaly: 1950s–1960s), 218, 225, 272, **278**, 281, 284, 288
Casey, Ned 'Togher', 149
Casey, Paddy, 177, 217, 218, 225
Casey, Willie, **191**, 195, 196, 208, 229, 264, 303
Casserly, Jack, 141, 149
Cassidy, Dick, 105
Cassidy, Harry, 259, 385
Cassidy, Jim, 269, 285
Cassidy, John Joe, 163, **166**, 171, 181, **199**, 200, 204–6

Cassidy, Mick, 124
Cassidy, Thomas, 432
Castlebar Mitchels (Mayo), 47, 75, 78, 172, 188, 196, 241, 249, 300, 371, 395, 404
Castleblakeney (Galway), 118
Castleblayney (Monaghan), 35
Castleblayney Faughs (Monaghan), 326, 334, 363
Castledermot (Kildare), 41, 70
Castlegar (Galway), 103
Castlegregory, Co. Kerry, 220
Castlegregory (Kerry), 124, 223, 267, 276
Castleisland, Co. Kerry, 249
Castleisland Desmonds (Kerry), 86–7, 97, 105, 141, 155–6, 214, 224, 232, 267, 276, 292, 309, 317, 422
Castlerahan (Cavan), 54, 69, 149, 163, 171, 181, 204–6, 268
Castletown (Laois), 79
Castletown (Meath), 105, 180, 197, 223
Castletownbere (Cork), 250
Castlewellan (Down), 275, 283, 344
Catholic Church, 55, 69, 148, 196, 258, 351–2, 362
Catholic Truth Society, 95
Caulfield, Mick, 188
Cavan
    1920s, 11–12, **14**, 17–21, 24, 26
    1930s, 31–2, 36, 38, 42, 44, 49, **50**, 51–4, 55–6, 59, 60, **65**, 66, 67–9, 71, 73, 75, 80, 81, **81**, 83–8, 92, 94, 101, 103
    1940s, 12, 106, 107, 108, 113–14, 121, 123, 126–33, **126**, **127**, 134–5, 137, 139, 144–5, 146–9, 150, **158**, **159**, 159–63, 165–6, **166**, 168–71, 173, 177–81, 431
    1950s, 11, 182, 184–5, 192–3, **199**, 199–206, 207–8, 218–19, 227–9, 236, 246, 254–5, 262, 263
    1960s, 269–70, 277, 282, 285–6, 289, 296, 306, 311–12, 316, 322, 330–1, 339–40, 341, 349–50
    1970s, 355, 367, 370, 373–4, 377, 387, 399, 409, 418, 419, 421, 425, 426
Cavan County Board, 31–2, 55, 77, 85, 114
Cavan Harps (Cavan), 163, 171, 181
Cavan Slashers (Cavan), 21, 54, 69, 87–8, 124, 132–3, 163, 171, 181

Cavanagh, Frank 'Dizzer', **56**, 60, 63
Cavanagh, Paddy, **56**, 60, 63
Cavanagh, Sean, 149
Celbridge (Kildare), 381–2
Chambers, Michael, 338
Chanders, Pat 'Cuddy', 67, 70
Charlestown Sarsfields (Mayo), 47, 78, 124, 172, 188, 196, 240
An Chéad Cath (Galway), 54, 62, 95–6, 111, 118, 124, 141, 240, 268
Cheshire, Paddy, 250
Chicago, 401, 421
China, 180, 258, 267
Christie, Mick, 217, 242, 252
Christie, Paddy, 217, 242, 286
Church of Ireland, 431
Churchill (Kerry), 224, 413, 422
Churchill, Winston, 110, 148
cigarettes, 53, 117, 204, 240
Citizen Kane (1941), 117
Civil Service, 124, 132–3, 149, 155–6, 163, 171, 172, 181, 187, 188, 189, 196, 204–6, 214, 224, 353, 371, 381–2, 403, 413, 422, 432
Civil War, 40
Claffey, Kieran, 366, **367**, 371
Clan na Gael (Armagh), 215, 432
Clancy, Dermot, 143
Clancy, Diarmuid, 409
Clane (Kildare), 70
Clann Éireann (Armagh), 432
Clann na Gael (Kilkenny), 214, 224
Clann na nGael (Roscommon), 292
Clanna Gael (Dublin), 63, 69, 70, 87–8, 124, 149, 163, 171, 180, 181, 197, 204–6, 223, 232, 250, 259, 267, 276, 292, 300, 309, 317, 345, 353, 363, 382–3
Clara (Offaly), 284
Clare
    1920s, 15, 22, 26
    1930s, 43, 48, 64, 71, 82, 89, 98
    1940s, 106, 113, 120, 150, 157, 167, 173
    1950s, 183, 190, 209, 213, 216, 228, 233–4, 243, 254, 262
    1960s, 289, 293, 304, 312, 319, 329, 338, 346
    1970s, 366, 375, 390, 406, 417, 428–9
Claremorris, Co. Mayo, 76
Claremorris (Mayo), 47, 78, 172, 188, 196, 325, 371, 404
Clarenbridge (Galway), 103

Clarke, Frank, 336, 359
Clarke, Jack, 21, **50**
Clarke, Jim (Kildare: 1950s), 236
Clarke, Jim (Meath: 1930s–1940s), 102, 105, 125
Clarke, John, 223
Clarke, Patsy, 132
Clarke, Peter, 389
Clarke, Vincent, **199**, 204–6
Claudy (Derry), 259
Clavin, Nicholas, 350, 351, 353, 366, **367**, 369, 371, 377, 378, 379, 381–2, 390
Cleary, Sean, 301, 303, 306, 309, 317, 325
Clegg, Herbie, 21
Clements, Eamonn, **270**, 275
Clery's department store, Dublin, 20, 187, 393
Clifden (Galway), 371, 395, 404
Clifford, Gerry, 304
Clifford, Johnny, 123, 124, **136**, 141
Clifford, Richard, 27
Clinton, Mark, 105
Cloghan (Offaly), 284, 353, 371
Clogherinkoe (Kildare), 280
Clonakilty, Co. Cork, 85
Clonakilty (Cork), 126, 147, 149, 224, 232, 309, 317, 335, 345, 363, 382–3, 394
Clonbur (Galway), 54, 240, 292
Clonduff (Down), 275, 283, 344
Clones (Monaghan), 35, 149, 163, 171, 181, 204–6
Clonoe (Tyrone), 49
Clontarf Golf Club, 402
Clontarf Gun Club, 180
Clontibret (Monaghan), 371
clothing, 20, 61–2, 104, 130–1, 154
Clounmacon (Kerry), 214, 224, 232
Cluskey, Paddy, 99
Cluxton, Stephen, 83
Clynch, Willie, 105
Cody, Kathleen, 179
Coen, Michael, 309
Coen, Sean 'Blackie', 300
Coffey, John, 383
Coffey, Kevin, 264, 265, 267, 273, 276, 278, 292, 293, 309
Cogan, Frank, **330**, 331, 333, 335, 376, **386**, 392, 394
Cogley, Mitchel, 225, 226, 273, 304, 314
Colbert, John, 375

Cole, Mickey, 344
Coleman, Bertie, 369
Coleman, Christy, 105
Coleman, Eamonn, 355
Coleman, John, **386**, 392, 394
Coleman, Matt, 65
Coleman, Patsy, **243**, 245, 249, 272
Colfer, Donal, 401, 423
Colleary, Jim, 364, 407
Colleary, Tom, **407**
Colleran, Brendan, 371, **389**, 395, 404
Colleran, Enda, 301, 306, 309, 314, 316, 317, **319**, 323, 325, 347
Colleran, Joe, 59, 63
Colleran, Luke, 22, 38, 43
Colleran, Noel, 347, 371
Colleran, Paddy, 16, 17, 24, 29, 30, 38, 43
Colleran, Seamus, 240, 268
Colleran, Tom, 391
Collier, Pat 'Red', 304, 321, 323, 326, **328**, 328, **329**, 329, 332, 334
Collins, Jim, 277
Collins, Paddy (Mayo: 1930s), **58**, 78
Collins, Paddy (Westmeath: referee), 419
Collins, Tom (Kerry: 1950s), 267
Collins, Tom (Roscommon: 1940s), 155–6, 160
Collins Barracks (Cork), 149, 214, 224, 232, 241, 250
Colreavy, Tom, 242, 279
Comerford, George, 22, 43, **56**, 58, 59, 63, 64, 71, 82, 89
Comiskey, Alphonsus 'Fonsie', 126, 149
Commercials (Cork), 149
computers, 196, 334
Conaty, Seamus, 269–70
Concannon, Sean 'Scan', 301
Condon, Eddie, 141
Condron, Enda, 365
Cong, Co. Mayo, 196
Congo, 275
Conlon, Andy, 17, 21
Conlon, Tom, **183**, 183, 189, 209, **243**, 245, 247, 249
Connacht Council, 98, 151, 302, 407
Connacht Tribune, 57, 60–1, 190, 266, 272, 302, 315, 323
Connaire, Mick, 51, 52, 54, 62, 65, 93, 95–6, 109, 111, 121–2, 123, 124
Connaught Telegraph, 29, 37, 51, 57, 65, 75, 80, 165, 198, 310, 316, 327, 339, 356

Connaughton, Mick, 302, 318, 375
Connell, Jack, 20
Connell, Paddy, **176**, 178, 179, 180, 183, 197, 205–6, 223
Connellan, Peter, 133, 141
Connolly, Charlie, 62, 95–6, 111, 114, 118, 124, 126
Connolly, Des, 191
Connolly, Kevin, 167, 211
Connolly, Liam, 293
Connolly, Pa, 280, 297, 321, 349
Connolly, Paaks, 260
Connolly, Tom, 278
Connolly, Willie, **50**, 54, **65**, 67, 69
Connor, Mick, 20, 28
Connor, Murt, 366, **367**, 371, 376, 381–2, 409
Connors, Wally, 346
Conroy, Dick 'Boiler' (Offaly: 1930s), 82
Conroy, Dickie (Offaly: 1950s), 225
Conroy, Jack, 196
Conry, Tommy, 132–3
Constitution of Ireland, 85
contraception, 69, 370, 403
Convery, Jack, 144
Conway, Dan Joe, 27, 34
Conway, Pat (Mayo: 1950s), **191**
Conway, Patsy (Tipperary: 1960s), 305
Cooke, Judith, 421
Cooley Kickhams (Louth), 189, 249
Cooney, Johnny, 350, 353, 359, 365, **367**, 369, 371, **374**, 379, 381–2, 389
Cooney, Paddy, 288
Cootehill (Cavan), 21, 54, 69, 204–6
Corballa (Sligo), 172
Corcoran, Joe, 264, 318, 327, 347, 375, 387
Corcoran, Seamus, **135**
Cordal (Kerry), 267, 276, 292
Corey, Paddy, **233**
Corish, Brendan, 324
Cork (city), 61–2
Cork (team)
    1920s, 16, 17–18, 22, 29
    1930s, 36, 43, 48, 59, 64, 71, 81–2, 89, 98, 103
    1940s, 106, 113, 116, 120, 123, 126, 127, 130, 134, 135–6, **143**, **144**, 145–9, 150, 157, 165, 168, 173–4, 177
    1950s, 183–4, 190, 200–1, 209, 216, 228, 234–5, 237–41, 243–4, **244**, 246–50, 254, 262

1960s, 272, 278–9, 289, 293–4, 304, 305, 308, 312–13, 319, 320, 322, 329–30, **330**, 331, 332–5, 338, 346
1970s, 354–5, 365, 366–7, 368, 375, 376, **386**, **388**, 390–4, 398, 400, 406–7, 417–18, 421, 428–9
Cork County Board, 366, 428
Cork Examiner, 25, 48, 81, 110, 145, 200–1, 246, 265, 266, 272, 279, 289, 293, 299, 307, 313, 320
Cornafean (Cavan), 11, 21, 54, 67, 69, 77, 87–8, 132–3, 149, 163, 171, 181, 204–6
Cornafean, Co. Cavan, 11, 201
Corofin (Galway), 54, 62, 91, 95–6, 111, 118, 240, 268, 317, 325, 371, 395, 404
Corr, Peter, 125
Corrigan, Aidan, **199**, 204–6
Corroon, Christy, 320
Cortoon Shamrocks (Galway), 371, 395, 404
Cosgrave, Liam, 324, 403
Cosgrove, Jack, 347, 368, 371, **389**, 395, 404
Costello, Frank, 353
Costello, John A., 179
Costello, Michael, 363
Costello, Tom, 232
Cotter, Eddie, 228
Cotter, Tim, 64
Coughlan, Ben, 288
Coughlan, Denis, 329, **330**, 335, 354, 355, 366, 367, 376, **386**, 392, 394
Coughlan, Johnny, 387, **389**, 395
Coughlan, Larry, 287, 329, 353, 371, **374**, 379, 381–2
Coughlan, Seamus, 394
Courell, Gerald, 17, 22, 43, 44–5, 47, **58**, 65, 67, 78, **167**, 190, **191**
Cousteau, Jacques, 131
Cox, Frank, 155–6
Coyle, Jackie, 240, 268
Coyle, Jimmy, 74, 82, 90, 99, 125
Coyle, Terry, 42, **50**, 52, 54
Crawley, Jack, 73, 107
Creagh, Dick, 17
Creaven, Ronnie, 290, 292, 339, 347
Creedon, Johnny, 228, 238, 239, 241
Creedon, Tom, 417
Cregan, Eamonn, 312, 313, 366
Creggs (Roscommon), 292
Creighton, Jim, 37

Cremin, Gus, 152, 153, 155–6
Crerand, Pat, 393
Cribbin, Larry 'Hussey', 266
cricket, 36, 364
Crinnigan, Ollie, 321, 349, 377, 414
Croagh Patrick, Co. Mayo, 213
Crofton, John (Kildare: 1930s), 70, 100
Crofton, Johnny (Kildare: 1970s), 414
Croghan (Cavan), 54, 69, 87–8, 132–3, 171
Croghan (Roscommon), 155–6, 292
Crohan, Pat, 173
Croke, Andy, 265, 297, 322, 331, 341, 346, 349
Cromwell, Paddy, 326, 334
Crone, Caleb, 123, 124, 149, 150
Cronin, Jim, 127, 149, 150, 200, 213
Cronin, John, 209, **210**, 211, 212, 213, 214, 220, 224, 228, 232, 235
Cronin, Paddy, 149, 200
Cross (Cavan), 21, 54, 69, 87–8, 132–3
Cross, Brendan, 412
Crossan, Noel, 387
Crosserlough (Cavan), 21, 54, 69, 87–8, 350
Crosshaven (Cork), 335
Crossmaglen Rangers (Armagh), 215, 432
Crossmolina (Mayo), 47, 78, 155–6, 172, 188, 196, 268, 371, 381–2
Crowe, M.F., 324
Crowe, Tom, 21, **50**, 54
Crowley, Con, 297
Crowley, Derry, 353, 363, 376, 382–3
Crowley, Din Joe, 345, 346, 350, 351, 353, 360, 363
Crowley, Jim, 27, 217, 225, 226, **226**, 229, 230, 232, 235, 245, 251, 252, 256, 257, 259
Crowley, John, 335
Crowley, Noel, 173
Crowley, Tadhg, **143**, 147, 149, 168
Crubany (Cavan), 132–3, 135
Crumlin (Dublin), 403
Crumlin Independents (Dublin), 20, 79
Cryan, Columba, 242, 252, 264
Cryan, Tom, 236
Cuban Missile Crisis, 291
Culhane, Tom, 59, 71, 82
Culkin, Johnny, 37, 47
Cullen, Paddy, 396, **397**, 401, 403, 411, 413, **417**, 422, 430, 432

Cullen, Sean, 57
Cullen, Terry, 77
Cullen, Tommy, 271, **278**, 282, 284, 288
Cullen, Willie, 423
Culleton, Jackie, 143
Culligan, Jim, 66
Cullinane, Des, 149
Culloty, Johnny, 228, 230, 232, 266, 267, 273, 274, 276, 281, 289, 290, 292, **303**, 309, 315, 317, 342, 345, 351, 353, 354, 361, 363, 376, 405
Culloville Blues (Armagh), 432
Cully, Barney, 129, 132–3, 137, 149, 171
Cully, Michael, 87
Cullyhanna (Armagh), 215
Cummins, Jack, 100, 105
Cummins, Jimmy, 287, 321
Cummins, Johnny, 390, 398
Cummins, Larry 'Pop', 132–3, 134
Cummins, Pat, 280, 287
Cummins, Ray, 367, 370, 376, **386**, 390, 391, 394
Cummins, Tom, 364, **407**
Cunniffe, Frank, 95–6, 111, 118, 123, 124
Cunningham, Bertie, 297, 304, 326, **328**, 328, 333, 334, 360, 363
Cunningham, Joe, 208, 215
Cunningham, Mickey, 399
Cunningham, Sean, **243**, 247, 249
Cunningham, Tom, 234, 243
Curley, Eamonn, 280, 290, 292, 310
Curragh (Kildare), 87–8, 132–3, 149, 163, 171, 181
Curran, Andy, 378
Curran, J., 66
Curran, Jimmy, **191**, 196, 229
Curran, Noel, 321, 322, 323, 326, **328**, 328, 332, 333, 334, 365
Currow (Kerry), 309, 317, 345, 353
Curry (Sligo), 63
Curtis, Joe, 18, 19, 20, 28
Cusack, Gene, 350, 373
Cusack, John (son of Michael Cusack), 108
Cusack, Johnny (Cavan: 1940s–1950s), 181, **199**, 204–6
Cusack, Michael, 108
Cusack, Pat, **58**
Cushenan, Mick, 236, 246
Czechoslovakia, 104, 343–4

D-Day, 140
Daingean (Offaly), 284, 353, 371, 381–2
Daingean Reformatory, 343
Dalai Lama, 267
Dalton, Davy, 218, 236
Dalton, Jim (Kildare: 1930s), 70
Dalton, Jimmy (Kildare: 1960s), 349
Daly, Gerry, 236, 240
Daly, James, 57, 62
Daly, Jim 'Dealers', 182
Daly, Mickey, 344
Daly, Peter, **278**, 281, 284
Daly, Seamus, 172
Daly, Sean, 432
Dana, 362
Danagher, Gus, 288, 293, 304, 305
dancing, 69
Darby, Peter, 326, **328**, 334
Darby, Seamus, 83, 371, **374**, 376, 381–2
Darcy, Gerry, 132
Darcy, Johnny, **135**
Darver Volunteers (Louth), 189, 245, 249
Davey, Gerry, 298, 300
Dawson, Patsy, 305, 319, 354
de Barra, Eamon, 52
de Gaulle, Charles, **305**
de Valera, Éamon, 130, 131, 148, 162, 222, 267, **271**, 275, 325
Dead Sea Scrolls, 163
Deane, Rory, 182, 209
Deegan, Leslie, 397, 403, 413, 422
Deenihan, Jimmy, 413, 422, 429
Deignan, Jim, 163
Deignan, Simon, 126, 132–3, 135, 146, 147, 149, 157, **158**, 161, 163, **166**, 171, 177, 181, 186, 187, 193, **199**, 204–6, 213, 220, 221
Delaney, Bill, 75, 79, 82, 90, 108, 143, 152, 158, 168
Delaney, Chris, 49, 79, 82
Delaney, Jack, 37, 75, 79, 82, 90
Delaney, Mick, 79, 82
Delaney, Noel, 260, 261, 297, 304, 313
Delaney, Paddy, 225
Delaney, Peter, 349
Delaney, Teddy, 261
Delaney, Tom (Laois: 1930s, defender), 79, 82, 92
Delaney, Tom (Laois: 1930s, goal-keeper), 79
Delany, Ronnie, 240

Deneher, Dan, 163
Denmark, 140
Denvir, Kieran, **270**, 275
Derry (city), 372, 381
Derry (team)
1920s, 17
1940s, 144, 150, 173
1950s, 13, 184, 192, 199, 208, 218, 227–8, 236, 246, **252**, 255–9, 262, 336
1960s, 269–70, 277, 296, 330, 340–1, 349
1970s, 355, 356, 360, 365, 367–8, 372, 384–7, 399, 409–10, 418–19, 421, 425, 426–7
Derry County Board, 385–7, 426
Derry People, 139
Desertmartin (Derry), 259
Devin, Kevin, 105, 108
Devine, Jackie, 313, 329, **337**, 337, 341
Devine, John 'Lefty', 195
Devlin, Brian, 407
Devlin, Eddie, **233**, 246
Devlin, Jim, **233**, 237
Devlin, Packy, 17, 18, 21, **50**, 52, 54, **65**, 69, **81**, 84, 87–8
Devlin, Patsy, **233**, 236
Devlin, Seamus, 277
Devlin, Sean, **425**, 429, 432
Diamond, Harry, 356
Diffley, Sean, 380, 429
Dillinger, John, 62
Dillon, Bill, 81, 84, 86–7, 96–7, 99, 102, 105, 111, 117, 121, 141
Dillon, Dermot, 224, 232
Dillon, John, 395, 404
Dillon, Kevin, **330**, 335
Dillon, Tom 'Pook', 217, 238, 240
Dingle (Kerry), 27, 34, 40, 46, 86–7, 95–7, 99, 102, 105, 111, 115, 117, 118, 121, 124, 141, 155–6, 164, 214, 224, 232, 267, 422
Dingley, Marcus, 272
Dinneny, Mick, **50**, 54, 56, **65**, 69, **81**, 87–8
Divilly, Tom, 371
Dixon, Henry, 172, 188, **191**, 194, 196
Dixon, Paddy, **176**, 178, 180, 194, 197, 205–6, 221
Djandoubi, Hamida, 432
Docherty, Tommy, 393
Dockery, Des, 242

Dr Crokes (Kerry), 27, 34, 40–1, 46, 86–7, 96–7, 105, 111, 117, 118, 124, 141, 155–6, 164, 214, 224, 232, 267, 276, 292, 309, 317, 345, 353, 363, 382–3

Dodd, Noel, 271

Doheny's (Cork), 149, 224, 232, 241, 250, 335

Doherty, Eugene, 228

Doherty, Martin, 400

Doherty, Paddy, 255, **270**, 270, 273, 274, 275, 281, 282, 283, 296, 306, 311, 312, 344, 367, 377

Doherty, Padraig, 196

Doherty, Sean, **397**, 403, **406**, 411, 412, 413, **417**, 420, 422, 432

Doherty, Tommy 'Long', 259

Doherty, Tommy 'Wee', 255, 256, 259

Dolan, Brendan, 372

Dolan, Dessie, 320

Dolan, Frankie, 349, 373

Dolan, Gerry, 141, 152, 155–6

Dolan, Joe, 264

Dolan, Pete, 174

Dolan, Terry, **65**, 69

Dolan, Tommy, 328

Dolphins (Dublin), 41, 63

Donaghy, Pat, **233**

Donaghy, Seamus, 384, 387

Donaghmore (Meath), 105, 180, 197, 205–6, 223

Donegal
1920s, 24
1930s, 37–8, 42, 55, 66, 73, 80, 92, 94, 101
1940s, 106, 114, 121, 135, 139, 144, 150, 165, 173
1950s, 192, 227, 246, 262
1960s, 269, 296, 306, 311, 316, 322, 331, 341, 349
1970s, 355, 362, 368, 372–4, **373**, 378, 384, 399–400, 409, 419, 421, 426, 427

Donegal County Board, 384

Donegal Democrat, 311, 384

Donegan, Paddy, 421

Donlon, John, 313, **337**

Donnellan, John, 268, 280, 301, 307, 309, 310, 315, 317, 323, 325

Donnellan, Mick, 22, 51, 52, 54

Donnellan, Pat, 279, 297, 299, 301, 309, 315, 317, 318, 323, 325, 347, 357

Donnelly, Aidan, 300

Donnelly, Brendan, 418–19, 426

Donnelly, Dinny, 251, 304, 326

Donnelly, Donal, **233**, 374

Donnelly, Frankie, 218, **233**, 236, 246, 254

Donnelly, Har, **278**, 280, 282, 284

Donnelly, Harry, 320

Donnelly, Hugh, **233**

Donnelly, Jack, 321, 328–9, 348, 365–6, 377

Donnelly, John 'Joey', **425**, 432

Donnelly, Pat 'Red', 102, 105

Donnelly, Sean (Longford: 1960s–1970s), **337**, 337, 376, 389

Donnelly, Sean (Tyrone: 1950s), **233**, 237

Donnelly, Sean (Tyrone: 1970s), 426

Donnelly, Tom, 426

Donnelly, Tony, 90, 100, 101, 102, 105, 107, 108

Donoghue, Eamonn, 227

Donoghue, P. *see* McManus, Fr Michael

Donohoe, Bertie, 315

Donohoe, Brendan, 355

Donohoe, Paschal, 240

Donohoe, Peter, 133, 149, **158**, 160, 161, 163, 165, **166**, 169, 171, 173, 181, **199**, 204–6, 227

Donovan, Brendan, 403

Donovan, Jim, 228

Doogue, Ned, 251

Dooley, Leo, 272

Doon (Offaly), 284, 353, 371, 381–2

Doonan, Willie, **158**, 163, **166**, 171, 181

Doran, Liam, 260, 261, 288

Doris, Davy, 302

Dougan, Danny, 306

Douglas, Danny, 23, 79, 83

Dowd, Tom, 44, 63

Dowdallshill (Louth), 189

Dowling, Eddie, 153, 155, 160, 161, 164, 224

Dowling, Frank 'Sambo', 67, 70

Dowling, Jack, 267, 276

Dowling, Jim Joe, 67, 70

Dowling, Jimmy, 335

Dowling, John (Kerry: 1950s–1960s), 224, 228, 230, 232, 265, 267, 274, 276, 279

Dowling, John (Offaly: referee), 274, 321, 324

Dowling, Fr William, 239

Dowling, Willie, **56**, 60, 63

Down
1920s, 24
1930s, 31, 38, 42, 56, 73, 80
1940s, 106–7, 113, 121, 134–5, 144, 165
1950s, 185, 192, 199, 218, 254, 255, 262–3, 265, 336
1960s, 13, 269–70, **270**, **271**, 273–5, 277–8, **279**, 280, 281–3, 285–6, 296, 297–8, 299, 306, 311, 312, 314, 318, 321, 322, 324, 330–1, 339, 340–4, 346, 349–50
1970s, 354, 355, 367, 368, 372–3, 387, 399, 409, 419, 426

Downes, Michael, 429

Downes, Paddy, 262

Downes, Senan, 338, 366

Downey, Paddy, 245, 259, 298, 300

Downpatrick (Down), 107, 259, 344

Downs, Declan, 349

Doyle, Bernie, 264

Doyle, Bobby, 396, **397**, 401, 403, 411, 413, **417**, 422, 424, 430, 432

Doyle, Joe, 321, 377

Doyle, John, 112, **135**, 137

Doyle, Mattie, **135**

Doyle, Miko (Kerry: 1920s–1930s), **23**, 27, 34, 40, 45, 46, 61, 71, 76, 86–7, 94, 96–7

Doyle, Miko (Kildare: 1950s), 235

Doyle, Paddy, 43

Doyle, Paul, 15, 18, 19, 20, 25, 28, 30, 37, 38, 41

Doyle, Willie (Carlow: 1970s), 396

Doyle, Willie (Down: 1960s), 344

Drogheda Independent, 58, 66, 68, 74, 75, 125, 127, 166, 182, 186, 187, 209, 272

Dromara (Down), 275, 283

Dromtarriffe (Cork), 149, 241

Drumbo (Cavan), 21

Drumconrath (Meath), 189, 249

Drumkilly (Cavan), 84, 87–8, 132–3

Drumlane (Cavan), 54, 87–8

Drumlish (Longford), 111, 118

Drumm, Tommy, 415, **417**, 420, 422, 432

Drumree (Meath), 180, 326, 334

Duagh (Kerry), 232, 267, 276, 292

Dublin (city), 12, 19, 27, 46, 53, 86, 116, 117, 139, 179, 213, 299, 300, 316, 324–5, 362, 381, 393, 402

Dublin (team)
  1920s, 15, 19, 23
  1930s, 30, 36–7, 43–4, 49, 51, 55,
    56, 57–8, 59–63, 65, 71, 74, 82,
    89, 99
  1940s, 107, 113, 114, 116, 119–24,
    120, 125, 136–7, 139, 142, 151,
    176, 179, 213
  1950s, 182, 198, 209, 213, 217, 222,
    225, 226, **226**, 229–32, 233,
    235, 239, 245, 251–2, **252**, 255,
    256–9, 260, 261, 264
  1960s, 269, 270–1, 280–1, 285, 288,
    289, **294**, **295**, 296–300, 303,
    304, 308, 313–14, 318, 320–1,
    328, 336, 348
  1970s, 13, 325, 357–8, 365, 377,
    388–9, 396–8, **397**, 400–3, 405,
    406, 408, 409–13, 414–15,
    416, **417**, 419–22, 423–4, **424**,
    429–32
Dublin bombing, 402
Dublin County Board, 139, 352, 377
Duff, Jim, 205–6
Duff, Tom, 218, 223
Duffy, Eddie, 264
Duffy, Jimmy, 33, 35
Duffy, P.J., 35
Duffy, Peter, 35
Duffy, Vincent, 107, 134
Duggan, Jimmy, 123, 318, 323, 325,
    339, 341, 347, 357, 368, 369, 371,
    389, 391, 392, 395, 398, 401, 404,
    408, 416
Duggan, Joe, 108, 109, 111, 115, 118,
    123, 124
Duggan, Nealie, 228, 241, **244**, 248,
    250
Duggan, Steve, 331, 350, 419
Duke, P.J., 149, **158**, 161, 163, **166**,
    169, 171, 177, 178, 181
Duleek (Meath), 105, 205–6, 223,
    326, 334, 363
Dullaghan, Bertie, 250
Dunboyne (Meath), 197, 202, 205–6,
    223
Dundalk Democrat, 81, 121, 126, 336
Dundalk Gaels (Louth), 189, 250
Dundalk Young Irelands (Louth), 189,
    240, 247, 249–50, 267, 268, 276,
    292, 309
Dundas, Ray, 311
Dunderry (Meath), 326, 334, 363
Dundon, Jack, 137

Dundrum (Down), 275, 283
Dungannon Clarkes (Tyrone), 49
Dungarvan (Waterford), 27, 34, 40,
    46
Dungloe (Donegal), 172, 188, 196
Dunhill (Waterford), 214, 224, 232
Dunican, Jack, 37, 43, 65
Dunleavy, 'Big' Tom, 159, 190, 198
Dunlop, Frank, 184
Dunmanway, Co. Cork, 11
Dunmore MacHales (Galway), 54, 62,
    72, 95–6, 111, 124, 240, 268, 297,
    301, 309, 315, 317, 325, 339, 369,
    371, 395, 395, 404
Dunne, Andy, 65
Dunne, Bernard, 70
Dunne, Cyril, 299, 301, 302, 307, 309,
    317, 318, 322, 325, 341, 357
Dunne, Eddie (Kerry: 1940s), 141
Dunne, Eddie (Laois: 1960s), 288
Dunne, John 'Tull', 54, 57, 60, 62, 91,
    94–6, 108, 111, 115, 118, 146,
    242, 369, 410
Dunne, Maurice, 142
Dunne, Mick, 219, 225, 226, 227, 229,
    257, 302, 314, 322, 324, 336, 337,
    348, 349, 350, 354, 420
Dunne, Paddy (Galway: 1950s), 264,
    268
Dunne, Paddy (Westmeath: 1950s),
    226
Dunne, Peter 'Peenie', **278**, 284
Dunne, Tom, 336
Dunney, Pat, 321, 377, 409, 423
Dunphy, Patsy, 324
Dunsany (Meath), 363
Dunsford (Down), 344
Dunshaughlin (Meath), 223, 326, 332,
    333, 334
Durcan, Ned, 190, 205–6
Durkin, Billy, 188
Durnien, Tommy, 144
Durnin, Morgan, 15
Durnin, Ned, 209, 220, 223

Eadestown (Kildare), 353, 371, 381–2
Eagleson, George, 321
Earhart, Amelia, 86
Earley, Dermot, 327, 356, 375, 398,
    407, 427, 429
Easter Rising, 27, 324
Eastern Command (Galway), 240
Edenderry (Offaly), 284, 353, 371,
    381–2

Egan, John (Kerry: 1970s), 390–1,
    398, 406, 410, 411, 413, 420, 422,
    428
Egan, John (Mayo: 1930s), 47
Egan, Johnny (Offaly: 1960s), **278**,
    280, 284, 288, 349, 353
Egan, Liam, 432
Egypt, 334
Éire Óg (Offaly), 353, 371, 381–2
El Guerrouj, Hicham, 222
electricity, 26, 27, 53, 123, 196
Elizabeth II, 204
Elliott, Aidan, 425
Ellistown (Kildare), 20, 28, 90
Elphin (Roscommon), 132–3, 141,
    155–6, 292
emigration, 249, 372
Emo (Laois), 326
Enfield (Meath), 326, 334, 363
Ennis, Co. Clare, 131
Erin Rovers (Offaly), 353, 371, 381–2
Erin's Hope (Dublin), 36, 47, 54, 70,
    78, 95–6, 224, 232, 240, 292, 309
Erin's Isle (Dublin), 259, 353, 371,
    381–2
Erin's Own (Kells, Meath), 21, 54,
    69, 87–8
Eucharistic Conference, 46
European Economic Community
    (EEC), 249, 381, 394
Eurovision Song Contest, 362, 370
Eusébio, 393
Evans, Sean, 350, 351, 353, 359, **367**,
    371, **374**, 381–2, 391
Evening Herald, 46, 139, 360
Everest, 213
Evers, Frank, 237, 240, 265, 268, 272
Ewart-Biggs, Christopher, 421
exhibition matches, 36, 161, 233

Fagan, Frank, 167
Fagan, Jack, 326
Fagan, James, 326
Fahy, M. *see* McManus, Fr Michael
FAI Cup, 364, 408
Fallon, John Joe, 155–6
Fallon, Mick (Galway: 1940s), 124
Fallon, Mick (Roscommon: 1970s),
    356
Falvey, Jackie, 117, 155–6
Falvey, Mick, 122, 123, 124, 136
Fane, Jack, 44, 57
Fanning, Pat, 372
Farmers' Party, 131

Farnan, Paddy, 256, 257, 259, 288
Farragher, Johnny, 332
Farrell, Emmet, 368, 371, 395, 404
Farrell, James, 223
Farrell, Jimmy, 268
Farrell, Joe, 35
Farrell, Paddy, **135**
Farrell, Tom, 301
Farrelly, Gerry, 397, 407
Farrelly, Seán, 21
Farrelly, Thomas, **176**, 180
Fr Griffin's (Galway), 204–6, 240, 268, 301, 309, 317, 325, 371, 395, 404
Faughnan, Jack, 279, 294
Faulkner, Bartle, 388
Fay, Benny, 21
Fay, Harry, 245
Fay, Jimmy, 363
Fay, Mickey, 361, 363
Feely, Des, 280, 287, 292
Feely, Don, 280, 287, 290, 292
Feeney, Ger, 79
Feerick, Miko, 371
Fenlon, Paddy, 217
Fennell, Mick, 336, 414
Fenneral, Mick, 28
Fenning, Paddy, 371, **374**, 376, 379, 381–2
Ferbane, Co. Offaly, 148
Ferbane (Offaly), 353, 371, 381–2
Ferguson, Des 'Snitchie', 225, **226**, 229, 232, 235, 245, 257, 259, 297, 300
Fermanagh
1930s, 31, 42, 48–9, 55, 66, 80, 92
1940s, 144–5, 159
1960s, 269, 277, 285, 296, 311, 321–2, 324, 331, 340, 349
1970s, 355, 367, 372, 374, 387, 399–400, 409, 418, 426
Fermi, Enrico, 123
Fermoy (Cork), 149, 335
Ferriter, Mick, 59, 60, 62, 81–2, 86–7
Ferriter, Sean, 296, 322, 341
Fethard-on-Sea boycott, 249
Fianna Fáil, 46, 130, 203, 222, 431
Field, Billy, 390, 391
film, 27, 104, 117, 123, 162
Fine Gael, 61, 131, 148, 179, 222, 324
Finlay, Gerry, 409
Finn, Mick, 149
Finnegan, Eugene, **65**, 69, **81**, 85, 87–8, 132–3
Finnegan, Jim (Armagh: 1970s), 429, 432

Finnegan, Jimmy (Roscommon: 1970s), 375
Finnegan, Joe, 35
Finnegan, Paudie, 363
Finneran, Tom, 320
Finucane, Mick, 156, 164
Finuge (Kerry), 34, 41, 46, 353, 413, 422
Firies (Kerry), 214, 224, 232
First World War, 33
Fisher, Christy, 24, 35, 42
Fitzgerald, Dick, 32
Fitzgerald, Eamonn (Kerry: 1930s), 34, 40, 45, 46
Fitzgerald, Eamonn (Kerry: 1970s), 376, 382–3
Fitzgerald, Gearoid (Dublin/Kerry: 1930s), 59, 63, 81–2, 86–7
Fitzgerald, Gerald (Dublin: 1930s), 51
Fitzgerald, Gerry (Dublin: 1940s), 124
Fitzgerald, Jim 'Bawn', 105, 111, 232
Fitzgerald, Joe, 122, 123, 124
Fitzgerald, Maurice, 380
Fitzgerald, Ned, 232, 380, 393
Fitzgerald, Niall, 235, 239, 241, **244**, 248, 250, 322
Fitzgerald, Noel, 184
Fitzgerald, Paddy, 124
Fitzgerald, Tom, 387
Fitzgerald, Tony, 313
Fitzpatrick, Frank, 21, 24
Fitzpatrick, Gus, 18, 20, 28
Fitzpatrick, James, **270**, 275
Fitzpatrick, Morgan, 191
Fitzpatrick, Paddy, 106
Fitzpatrick, Willie, 132–3
Fitzsimons, Frank, 355
Fitzsimons, Jack, 296, 321, 351, 426
Fitzsimons, Pat, **270**, 275
Fitzsimons, Paul, 171, 181, **199**, 204–6
Flaherty, Jimmy, 169, 324
Flanagan, Bernard, 223
Flanagan, Hugh, 277
Flanagan, Mel, 356, 375
Flanagan, Mick, 172, 186, 188, **191**, 193, 194, 196, 227
Flanagan, Oliver J., 403
Flanagan, Paddy, 225–6
Flanagan, Sean, 134, 165, **167**, 170, 172, **184**, 185, 186–7, 188, **191**, 196, 227, 229
Flannelly, Patsy, 37, 47, 57, **58**, 65, **72**, 73, 75, 78, 110

Flavin, Jackie, 46, 87, 91, 94, 95–6, 111, 118, 123, 124
Flavin, Tony, 427
Fleming, Alexander, 20
Fleming, Mick, **303**, 305, 309, 317, 345, 353
Fleming, Seamus, 337
Fletcher, Matt, 113, 122, 124
Flood, Danny, 287, 297
Flood, Mickey, 249
Flood, P.J., 296
Flood, Sean Óg, **243**, 249, 251
Flynn, Cathal, 242, 252, 254, 264, 294, 295
Flynn, J.J., 177
Flynn, Jim 'Red' (Sligo: 1920s), 17
Flynn, Jimmy (Longford: 1960s–1970s), 313, **337**, 341, 359
Flynn, Joe, 353
Flynn, Johnny, 289
Flynn, Paschal, 288, 298, 300
Flynn, Seamus, **337**
Fogarty, Weeshie, 353
Foley, Des, 257–8, 260, **287**, 291, **294**, 296, 298, 299, 300, 314
Foley, Joe, 348
Foley, Johnny, 212, 214
Foley, Lar, 257, 259, 296, 300, 377
Foley, Vincent, 326, 363
food, 34, 46, 104, 116, 140, 162, 187, 203–4, 231
foot-and-mouth disease, 112–13, 116
Football Association of Ireland (FAI), 231
Foran, Aidan, 197
Foran, Sean, 271, 272, **278**, 284
Forbes, Mickey Joe, 387
Forbes, Phelim Hugh, 418
Forde, Jim, 47
Forde, John (Mayo: 1920s), 17
Forde, John 'Denny' (Mayo: 1940s–1950s), **167**, 172, 187, 188, **191**, 196
Forde, Tom, 17
Fordstown (Meath), 180, 249
foreign dances, 69, 77
foreign games ban, 94, 95, 117, 120, 213–14, 308, 325, 364, 370
Forestry College (Wicklow), 345, 353, 363, 382–3
Four Roads (Roscommon), 141, 155–6
Fox, Frank, 52, 54, 57, 60, 62, 72, 110
Fox, Jim, 70
Fox, Joe, 120

Fox, Larry, 260, **278**, 284
Fox, Noel, 258, 288, 289, 298, 300, 303
Fox, Pat, 21
Foxford (Mayo), 78
Foynes, Co. Limerick, 148
Fraher, Dan, 324
France, 104, 110, 429, 432
Franco, Francisco, 77, 412
Frazer, Bertie, 47
Freaney, Cyril, **226**, 232
Freaney, Ollie, 217, **226**, 229, 232, 255, 257, 259, 260, 264
French, Arthur, 409
French, Watty, 416
Frenchpark (Roscommon), 155–6
Freyne, Mickey, 378, 398, 427, 429
Freyne, Sean, 213
Friel, Liam, 254–5
Fuerty (Roscommon), 132
Furbo (Galway), 118, 124
Furlong, Brian, 416, 424
Furlong, Jim 'Sacker', 99, 112, 119
Furlong, Martin, 351, 353, **367**, 368, 369, 371, **374**, 381–2
Furlong, Mick, 217
Furlong, Tommy (Cork: 1950s), 241, **244**, 247–8, 250, 262
Furlong, Tommy (Offaly: 1960s), 288

GAA Central Council, 31, 38, 66, 77, 85, 92, 94, 103, 110, 112, 114, 128, 129, 152, 211, 333
Gaeil Colmcille (Meath), 232, 259, 284, 300, 353, 363, 371
Gaelic League, 69, 163
Gaelic Weekly, 239, 343
Gaels of Laughter, 362
An Gaeltacht (Kerry), 124, 309
Gaffney, Gertrude, 115
Gaffney, Hubert, 227, 229
Gaffney, Mick, 216
Gagarin, Yuri, 283
Gagnan, Emil, 131
Gaiety Theatre, Dublin, 362
Gallagher, Anthony, 372
Gallagher, Anthony 'Doonan', **373**
Gallagher, Brian, **199**, 204–6, 236, 262
Gallagher, Charlie, 236, 262, 263, 285, 311, 312, 331, 350
Gallagher, Gerry, 418
Gallagher, Hudie Beag, 106
Gallagher, Jackie, 264
Gallagher, Jim, 246
Gallagher, Neilly, 384, 400

Gallagher, Sean, 150, 321
Gallagher, Tommy, 322
Galligan, Peter Paul, 132–3, 149
Galway
  1920s, 14, 16–17, 22
  1930s, 29, 33, 37, 42–3, 50–4, 55, 57, 59–62, 64–5, 68, 71, 72–3, 80, 91, 92–6, 98
  1940s, 107, 108–11, 114–18, **120**, 120–4, 126, 130, 134, 145, 151, 159, 168, 174
  1950s, 185, 190, 198, 208, 216–17, 219, 226–7, 236–40, 242–3, 246, 252–4, 255, 263–4, 265–8, 269
  1960s, 269, 272–3, 279–80, 285, 286–7, **295**, 295, 297, 298–301, 302–3, 306–9, 310–11, 314–17, 318–19, **319**, 322–5, 327, 338–9, 341–2, 346–7
  1970s, 123, 354, 356–7, 360, 361, 362, 364–5, 368, 369–71, 375, 387–8, **388**, **389**, 391–5, 396, 398, 400–4, 407–8, 416, 419, 427–8
Galway Gaels (Galway), 54, 62
Gandhi, Mahatma, 170
Gannon, Bill 'Squires', 13, 15, 18, 20, 28, 41
Gannon, Jack, 47, **58**
Gannon, Val, **158**, 163, 171
Gaoth Dobhair (Donegal), 317, 345, 353, 363, 382–3
Garda, 17, 21, 27, 28, 34, 35, 40, 46, 54, 62, 63, 69, 70, 78, 79, 86–8, 118, 124, 132–3, 141, 155–6, 163, 171, 172, 181, 188, 196, 204–6, 214, 240, 241, 250, 268, 403, 413, 422, 432
Garnish (Cork), 241
Garrett, Mick, 251, 268, 295, 298, 301, 309, 314, 317
Garry, Michael, 209
Garryowen (London), 292
Gartland, Mick, 288, 304
Gartland, John, 57
Garvey, Batt, 151, 155–6, 161, 164, 167
Gaughran, Benny, 320, 359
Geaney, Con, 41, 46, 86–7, 97
Geaney, Dave, 262, 267, 288, 289, 292, 317
George VI, 204
Geraghty, Andy, 37
Geraghty, Brian, 301, 309, 317
Geraghty, George, 289, 292, 302, 338

Geraghty, Johnny, 303, 306, 307, 308, 309, **312**, 315, 317, 322, 323, 325
Geraghty, Michael, 395, 404
Geraghty, Mickey, 67, 70, 157–8
Geraghty, Ollie, 334
Geraghty, 'Spog', 66
Geraldines (Dublin), 27, 41, 54, 62, 63, 86–7, 95–7, 105, 110, 111, 117, 118, 123, 124, 124, 141, 155–6, 164, 189, 214, 224, 232, 249, 267, 276
Germany, 53, 77, 95, 104, 110, 117, 123, 131, 325
An Ghaeltacht (Kerry), 267, 276, 292, 317, 345, 353, 363, 382–3, 413, 422
Ghana, 249
Gibbons, Hugh, 132–3, 134, 137, 141, 155–6
Gibbons, John, 424
Gibbons, Paddy, 235
Gibney, Jack, 89
Gibson, Sean, 150, 185
Gilheany, Seamus, 31, **50**, 55
Gill, Jimmy, 174
Gillen, Larry, 271, 313, **337**
Gillen, Mickey, 57
Gillen, Tony, 259
Gilmartin, Liam, 128, 132–3, 134, 137, 141
Gilmore, Brendan, 313, **337**, 395
Gilmore, Tommy Joe, 368, 371, **389**, 398, **399**, 401, 404
Gilroy, Jackie, 258
Gilsenan, Mattie, 101, 102, 105, 107
Gilvarry, Joe 'Joko', 151, **167**, 172, 188, **191**, **192**, 193, 194, 195, 196
Gilvarry, Johnny, **167**, 172
Gilvarry, Paddy, 172
Glanmire (Cork), 241
Glanworth (Cork), 394
Glasgow Celtic FC, 147
Glasgow Herald, 282–3
Gleeson, Liam, 316
Gleeson, Mick, 353, 354, 363, 379, 382–3
Glenamaddy (Galway), 395, 404
Glenbeigh/Glencar (Kerry), 292, 309, 317, 345, 363, 382–3
Glenfesk (Kerry), 363, 382–3
Glenn (Down), 275, 283, 344
Glenties (Donegal), 163
Glenview (Cork), 241, 250
Glenville (Cork), 335

Glin (Limerick), 71

Glynn, Brendan, 268

Glynn, Frank, 132–3, 141

Glynn, George, 344

Glynn, Jimmy, 317

Gneeveguilla (Kerry), 345, 353

Goff, Matt, 18, 20, 28, 38, 41, 66, 67, 68, 70

Gogarty, Denis, 363

Gogarty, Paddy, 403, 411, 413, 422, 432

golf, 36, 228, 362, 402, 429

Gone with the Wind (1939), 104

Good Counsel (Dublin), 422, 432

Goode, Declan, 106

Goodison, Willie, 143, 166

Goodwin, Joe, 277

Gordon, Donal, 372, 426

Gordon, Kevin, 372

Gorman, Dick, 125

Gormanston College, Co. Meath, 11, 405

Gormley, Joe, 356

Gormley, Patsy, 255, 259, 262

Gould, Mick, 241, **244**, 250

Goulding, Eamonn, 241, **244**, 250

Gowna (Cavan), 69, 87–8

Grace, Micheál, 218, 220, 223, 251

Gracefield (Offaly), 284, 353, 371, 381–2

Graham, Christy, 28

Graiguecullen (Laois), 79, 83, 90, 414

Granaghan, Seamie, **373**, 373

Grange (Cork), 335, 394

Gray, Jim (journalist), 412, 416

Gray, Jimmy (Dublin: 1950s), **226**, 232, 377, 401

Greally, Jimmy, 177

Greally, Mick, 240, 242, 268

Greaney, Jack, 95–6

Great Depression, 27

Great Famine, 157

Great Leap Forward, 258

Greenan, Josie, 133

Greene, Michael, 417

Greene, Seamus, 198

Greene, Tommy, 271, **278**, 281, 282, 284, 297

Greene, Vincent, 285, 322, 340

Grey, Tom, 295

Greystones (Wicklow), 408

Gribbin, Hugh Francis, **253**, 255, 256, 259, 385

Gribbin, Owen, 256, 259

Gribbin, Paddy, 259

Gribbin, Roddy, 144, 227, 228, 246

Grier, Tom, 47, **72**, 75, 78, 80

Griffin, Pat, 293, **303**, 307, 309, 317, 329–30, 345, 351, 353, 360, 363, 376, 382–3

Griffin, Ralph, 62, 93, 95–6

Griffin, Victor, 431

Griffith, Des, 347, 350

Griffith, Eddie, 47

Griffith Barracks (Dublin), 20

Grogan, Christy, 292

Grogan, Leo, 353

Grogan, Patsy, 285

Guinan, Brian, 353

Guinane, Sean, 98

Guiry, Monty, 293

Gunning, Jody, 366, **367**, 368, 371, 381–2

Gusserane (Wexford), 99, 167

Gypsum Rovers (Meath), 171, 181, 204–6

Hackett, Michael, 398

Hadden, Tony, **270**, 273, 275, 281, 283, 285

Halpenny, Bill, 105, **176**, 180

Halpenny, Michael, 116

Halpin, Paddy, 77

Hamill, Aidan, 356

Hamill, Liam, 285

Hamilton, Michael, 157

Hanahoe, Tony, **397**, 403, 408, 410, 413, **417**, 422, 423, 424, 429, 432

Hand, Christo, **176**, 180, 193, 194, 197, 205–6

Hanley, Cormac, 310

Hanley, Mick, 217

Hanley, Paddy 'Dickie', 141

Hanley, Pete, **303**, **305**, 309

Hanley, T.J., 47

Hanlon, Donie, 271, **278**, 284

Hanlon, Liam, 371, 381–2

Hannafin, Dermot, 190, 214

Hanniffy, Liam, 190

Hannify, Jimmy (Longford: 1930s–1940s), 90, 116, 118, 136

Hannify, Jimmy (Longford: 1960s–1970s), 90, 313, 329, **337**, 337, 341, 359, 409, 414

Hardy, Mick, 168

Hardy, Tom, **199**, 204–6

Harkins, Syd, 82

Harney, Des, 278

Harold, Jim, 261, 270

Harrington, Gus, 305

Harrington, Pádraig, 228

Harrington, Paddy, 228, 237, 239, 241, **244**, 248, 250, 262, 289

Harrison, Seamie, 236, 237

Harte, Ciaran, 372, 374

Harte, John, 368

Harte, Peter, 285, 331

Harte, Sean, 427

Hartigan, Bernie, 312

Hartigan, Pat, 398

Hartnett, Connie, **386**, 394

Hartnett, Josie, 216

Harty, Fred, 116

Hastings, Liam, 165, 172, 188, **191**, 196

Hatton, Jimmy, 324

Haughey, Charles, 362

Haughey, Pádraig 'Jock', **226**, 232, 256, 257, 259, 264

Haughian, John, **270**, 275, 283

Haughney, Mick 'Cutchie', 79, 158

Hawaii, 267

Hayden, Brendan, 260, 287, 299, 409

Hayden, Tom, 264

Hayden, Tony, 254

Hayes, Flor, 305, **330**, 335

Hayes, Jack, 20, 28, 41

Hayes, Maurice, 269

Hayes, Peter, 119

Hayes, Sean, 202

Healy, Con, 85

Healy, Mick, 27, 46

Healy, Paddy, 149

Healy, Sean, 124

Healy, Tadhg, 85, 86–7, 105, 109, 111, 117, 136, 137, 141

Heaney, Malachy, 432

Hearns, Dick, 77

Hearty, Joe, 57

Heavey, Bill, 132–3, 155–6

Heavey, Martin, **367**, 371, **374**, 381–2

Heavey, Mattie, 141

Heeran, Paddy, 35

Heery, Seamie, **176**, 177, 180, 183, **192**, 197

Heffernan, Kevin, 225, 226, **226**, 230, 231, 232, 235, 245, **252**, 256–7, 259, 288, 297, 325, 396–7, 400–1, 402, 405, 414, 420, 423

Hegarty, Christy, 196

Henderson, Isaac, 215

Heneghan, John, **337**, 359

Heneghan, Tom, 429

Henry, Frank, **407**, 408
Henry, Paddy (Dublin: 1940s), 122,
    123, 124
Henry, Paddy (Sligo: 1970s), **407**
Herlihy, Donal, 241
Herrema, Tiede, 412
Heslin, John, 174
Heslin, Leo, 242, 254
Hetherington, Patsy, 372
Hetherton, Seamus, **199**, 204–6, 227
Hickey, Ambrose, 350, 353
Hickey, David, **397**, 403, 408, 411,
    413, **417**, 422, 424, 429, 432
Hickey, John D., 193, 194, 211–12,
    219, 221, 228, 230, 237, 238, 244,
    264, 273, 274, 296–7, 329–30,
    338, 341, 347, 348, 355, 358, 362
Hickey, Leo, 288, 299, 300
Hickey, Michael, 432
Hickey, Paddy, 43, 49, **56**, 63
Higgins, Charlie 'Chuck', 228, 255,
    259
Higgins, Christy, 66, 70, 90
Higgins, Frank (Offaly: 1960s), **278**,
    284
Higgins, Frank (Tyrone: 1950s), **233**,
    236
Higgins, George, 17, 22, 29
Higgins, Greg, 317
Higgins, Jack, 15, 18, 20, 24, 28, 30,
    39, 41, 66, 67, 70
Higgins, Liam, 351, 353, 363, 375,
    379, 382–3
Higgins, Mick, 52, 54, 60, 62, 95–6,
    111, 132–3, 135, 145, 146, 149,
    160, 161, 163, **166**, 168, 169, 170,
    171, 178, 181, **199**, 199, 201, 202,
    204–6, 207, 307, 313, 373
Higgins, William A., 21
Hillary, Edmund, 213
Hinchion, John Joe, **244**, 250
Hiroshima, 147
Hitler, Adolf, 53, 77, 103, 148
Hoare, Owensie, 132–3, 141, 155–6,
    266
Hoare, Seamus, 296, 322
Hoban, Phil, 47
Hoban, Tommy, 134
hockey, 214
Hoey, Mattie, **407**
Hoey, Paddy, 32
Hoey, Tony, 388
Hogan, David, 44
Hogan, Eddie 'Cran', 280

Hogan, Tommy, 71
Holden, Paddy, 280, 288, 289, 297,
    298, 300, 303, 304
Holland, Kieran, 64, 66
Holly, Pat, 126
Hollywood, 27, 104, 117, 123, 200
Holocaust, 123
Hopkins, Mick, 336, **337**, 337, 359
horse racing, 334, 432
Hosey, Willie, **135**
Houlihan, Joe, 42, 56, 92
house prices, 53, 171, 240, 300
Howard, Tom, 288
Howley, Alfie, 319
Howlin, Billy, 112
Howlin, Ger, 423
Hoy, Harry, 278
Hughes, Cyril, 396
Hughes, Danny, 311
Hughes, George, 126
Hughes, Greg, **278**, 280, 282, 284,
    288, 349, 352, 353, 368, 371
Hughes, Jim, **135**
Hughes, Johnny, **389**, 395, **399**, 404
Hughes, Morgan, **389**, 395
Hughes, Pat, 348
Hughes, Stephen 'Faun', 158
Hughes, Tommy, 54, 62
Hunt, Donal, 394
Hunt, Tom, 375
Hunterstown Rovers (Louth), 249
hurling, 14, 53, 67, 68, 77, 94, 103,
    116, 123, 130, 145, 146, 147, 213,
    221, 238, 239, 266–7, 291, 324,
    333, 351, 354, 362, 368, 370, 372,
    428, 429
Hussey, Paddy, 267
Hyde, Douglas, 95
Hyland, Hugh, 366
Hynan, Bill, 24, 28, 30, 39, 41

Iceland, 140
Inchicore Hibernians (Dublin), 300
India, 163, 170, 267, 370
inflation, 422
Irish Independent, 15–16, 24, 25, 26,
    52, 56, 71, 74, 91, 92, 93, 98, 100,
    107–8, 109, 110, 113, 115, 116,
    138, 140, 145, 151, 153–4, 157,
    160, 161–2, 174, 177, 178, 182–3,
    184, 190, 193, 194, 204, 207, 209,
    214, 216, 219, 221, 225, 230, 234,
    236–7, 240, 244, 264, 266, 272,
    273, 274, 290, 296–7, 304, 306,

310, 314, 324, 331, 333, 338, 347,
    348, 349, 355, 362, 377, 378, 414,
    419, 421, 424, 430
Irish Press, 40, 42, 44, 51, 66–7, 68, 71,
    74, 75, 80, 82, 84, 85, 86, 92, 93,
    98, 101, 107, 108, 113, 114, 125,
    128, 130, 136, 138, 145, 146, 150,
    154, 160, 162, 168, 169, 170, 178,
    187, 191, 194, 199, 201, 202, 218,
    219, 220, 221, 225, 227, 229, 236,
    237, 238, 244–5, 252, 257, 260,
    266, 277, 286–7, 289, 296, 299,
    300, 302, 308, 310, 312, 314, 322,
    324, 336, 337, 338, 340, 348, 349,
    350, 351–2, 354, 356, 359, 380,
    402, 416, 418, 419
Irish Republican Army (IRA), 324–5,
    394, 412, 421
Irish Times, 18, 103, 142
Irish Women's Liberation Movement,
    370
Irwin, Bill, 15
Irwin, Paddy, 188, **191**, 194, 196
Islandeady (Mayo), 172, 188, 196
Israel, 170, 334, 381
Italy, 69, 104, 131

Jackson, Bill, 132–3, 141, 155–6
Japan, 147
jazz, 69
Jennings, Terry, **226**, 232
John XXIII, 203, 300
John Mitchels (Kerry), 27, 34, 40–1,
    46, 86–7, 96–7, 105, 111, 117, 141,
    155–6, 164, 214, 224, 232, 267, 276,
    292, 309, 317, 345, 353, 362, 363
Johnson, Ed, 286
Johnson, Kevin, 105
Johnstone, Tommy, 349, 421
Jones, Iggy, 165, **233**, 236, 237, 254
Jordan, 334
Jordan, Paddy, 172, **191**, 195, 196
Joy, Jimmy, 120, 122, 123, 124
Joyce, Billy, 357, 365, 368, 371, **389**,
    395, 404
Joyce, Johnny, **253**, 255, 256, 257, 259,
    271, 288
Joyce, Liam, 78
Joyce, Ted, **135**
Juan Carlos I, 412
Judge, Jim 'Blackie', **243**, 249

Kane, Alan, **373**
Kane, Christy, 288, 300, 348

Kane, George, 272, 288

Kane, Val, 296, 344, 426

Kanturk (Cork), 335

Kavanagh, Brian, 225

Kavanagh, Dan, 116, 118, 123, 124, 141, 155–6, 164, 184

Kavanagh, Dermot, 245

Kavanagh, Donal, 375, 378, 379, 382–3, 391

Kavanagh, Ger, 143

Kavanagh, Jackser, **56**

Kavanagh, Patrick, 103, 334

Keadue (Roscommon), 155–6

Keady Michael Dwyers (Armagh), 215

Kean, J.P., 408

Keane, Connie, 36, 48

Keane, M.J., 356

Keane, Mick, 371

Keane, Seamus, 292

Keane, Sean, 164

Kearins, James, **407**

Kearins, Mickey, 286, 294, 302, 310–11, 318, 338, 364, 374, 398, **407**, 408, 410

Kearney, J.D., 116

Kearney, Jim, 105, **176**, 178, 180

Kearney, Joe, 16

Kearney, Sean, 319

Kearns, Larry (Armagh: 1970s), **425**, 432

Kearns, Larry (Meath: 1960s), 326

Kearns, Peadar, 198

Kearns, Terry, **328**, 332, 333, 334, 363

Keating, Jim 'Tipper', 79

Keating, John, 293, 305

Keating, Michael 'Babs', 293, 304, 319, 346, 354, 376, 390, 398

Keating, Mick (Dublin: 1930s), 44, **56**, 59, 60, 63

Keating, Mick 'Tipper' (Laois: 1930s), 49

Keatings (Dublin), 63

Keaveney, Jimmy, 397, **397**, 403, 408, 411, 413, 414, 415, **417**, 420, 422, 424, 430, 431, 432

Keeffe, Danno, 201

Keegan, Gerry, 427

Keegan, Harry, 429

Keegan, Mick, 429

Keel (Kerry), 155–6, 345, 353, 361, 363, 382–3

Keeley, Sean, 240, 268, 301

Keenan, Donal, 121, 126, 128, 132–3, 138, 141, 155–6

Keenan, John, 279, 301, 309, 310, 315, 317, 323, 325, 327, 339, 341, 347, 357, 375

Keenan, Pat 'Birdy', 349, 353, 391

Keenan, Tommy, 309, 317, 325, 357

Keeney, Kieran, 399, 400

Keevans, Seamus, 423

Kehoe, Eamonn, 225

Kehoe, Jim, 398

Kehoe, Paddy, 167, 235, 236

Kelleher, Denis 'Toots', 238, 239, 241, **244**, 248, 250

Kelleher, Humphrey, **386**, 392, 394

Kelleher, Joe, 52, 54, 62

Kelleher, Mick, 348

Kelleher, Robbie, **397**, 403, 413, **417**, 422, 424, 429, 432

Kelliher, Brendan, 155–6

Kells (Meath), 21, 54, 69, 87–8, 105

Kells Harps (Meath), 180, 197, 205–6, 223

Kelly, Alo, 369

Kelly, Anna, 162

Kelly, Billy, 167

Kelly, Brendan (Cavan: 1940s), 132–3, 149, 163

Kelly, Brendan (Derry: 1970s), 426

Kelly, Charlie, 124

Kelly, Connie (Cavan/Meath: 1940s–1950s), 149, 197, 200, 202, 205–6

Kelly, Connie (Cork: 1970s), 367

Kelly, Cyril, 240

Kelly, Danny (Armagh: 1960s), 278

Kelly, Danny (Down: 1960s–1970s), 341, 344, 349, 368

Kelly, Frank, 198

Kelly, Gabriel, 262, 263, 285, 296, 331, 367

Kelly, Gene, 200

Kelly, Hugh, **233**

Kelly, Jimmy (Kilkenny: 1930s), 103

Kelly, Jimmy (Offaly: 1940s), 142, 143

Kelly, John, 290, 292, 375

Kelly, Kevin, 321, 349, 365

Kelly, Luke, 112, **135**, 136, 137, 167

Kelly, Martin, 54, 57, 60, 62, 95–6

Kelly, Michael 'Murt', **56**, 59, 63, 81–2, 86–7, 92, 93, 96–7, 102, 105, 111, 113, 114, 117, 138, 141

Kelly, P.J. 'Purty', 47, **58**, **72**, 78, 80

Kelly, Paddy, 54

Kelly, Patsy, 366

Kelly, Paul (Donegal: 1960s), 296

Kelly, Paul (Dublin: referee), 361, 369, 384–5

Kelly, Raymond, 432

Kelly, Sean, 209, 214, 224

Kenealy, Con, 414

Kenmare (Kerry), 214, 224, 232, 382–3, 413, 422

Kenmare Shamrocks (Kerry), 309, 345, 363

Kenna, Jack, 260, 261, 288, 304

Kennedy, Frank, 262

Kennedy, John, 266, 268

Kennedy, John F., 275, 291, 298, 299–300

Kennedy, Paddy (Galway: 1930s), 95–6

Kennedy, Paddy (Kerry: 1930s–1940s), 85, 86–7, 96–7, 102, 105, 111, 115, 117, 141, 152, 153, 155–6, 160, 164

Kennedy, Paddy (Sligo: 1950s), 190

Kennedy, Paddy 'Beefy' (Dublin: 1940s), **120**, 121, 123, 124

Kennedy, Robert, 343

Kennedy, Seamus, **270**, 275

Kennedy Committee, 343

Kennelly, Brendan, 221–2

Kennelly, Colm, 212, 214, 216, 221–2, 224, 232

Kennelly, Tim, 407, 413, 422

Kenny, Billy, **167**, 172, 185, 186, 188, 195

Kenny, Henry, 47, **58**, 67, **72**, 73, 75, 78, 107, 145

Kenny, J.J., 324

Kenny, Jack, 47

Kenny, Kieran, 17

Kenny, Mickey, 292

Kenny, Tony, 280, 292

Keogan, John, 132–3

Keogan, Terry, **199**, 204–6

Keogh, Harry, 198

Keogh, Ned, 198

Keogh, Paddy, 143

Keogh, Tom, 15, 20, 67, 70, 74, 75, 76, 79, 82

Keohane, Joe, 71, 86–7, 93, 96–7, 102, 105, 109, 111, 115, 117, 136, 137, 138, 141, 155–6, 157, 164

Kerins, Des, **407**, 408

Kerins O'Rahillys (Kerry), 27, 34, 40–1, 46, 86–7, 96–7, 105, 111, 117, 141, 155–6, 164, 214, 224, 232, 267, 276, 309, 317, 345, 418, 422

Kernan, Frank, 215
Kernan, James, 24
Kernan, Joe, **425**, 430, 432
Kerr, Mickey, **233**
Kerrigan, Dan, **81**, 85, 87–8
Kerrigan, Mattie, **328**, 332, 334, 363, 389, 416, 423
Kerry
  1920s, 12, 13, 14–15, 19, 22, **23**, 24–7
  1930s, 12, 13, 29, 32–4, 36, 38–41, 43, 44–6, 48, 51, 55, 58–9, 60, 64, 71, 75, 76, 81–2, 83–7, 89, 92–7, 98–9, **99**, 101–5
  1940s, 12, 106, 108–11, 113, 114–17, 120, 121, 123, 126, 130, 134, 136, 137–41, 145, 150, 151, 152–6, 157, 160–4, 165, 167–8, 173
  1950s, 183–4, 185, 186, 190, 193, 200, **207–8**, 209, **210**, 211–14, 216, **217**, 219–24, 228–32, 233–5, 243, 254, 255–6, **261**, 261–2, 264, 265–7
  1960s, 12, 269, 272, 273–6, 278–9, 280, 288–92, 293–4, 297, **303**, 304–9, 312, 313, 314–17, 318, 319–20, 329–30, 338, 341, 342–5, 346, 350–3
  1970s, 13, 249, 325, 354–5, 360–3, 364, 365, 366–7, 375–6, 378–83, 384–5, 390–1, 398, 400, 405–7, 410–13, 414, 417–18, 419–22, 423, 428, 429–30
Kerry Champion, 33, 77–8, 173
Kerry County Board, 32, 64, 85, 316
Kerryman, 22, 24, 25, 61, 89, 108, 110, 121, 145, 222, 229, 266, 405
Keys, Gerry, 219, 228
Khrushchev, Nikita, 291
Kickhams (Dublin), 34, 54, 62, 95–6, 240, 284, 353
Kiely, Benedict, 221
Kilbeg (Meath), 105
Kilbride (Meath), 205–6, 326, 334, 344, 363
Kilclief (Down), 275, 344
Kilcloon (Meath), 223
Kilconly (Galway), 95–6, 111, 118, 124, 344
Kilconnell (Galway), 124
Kilcoyne, Mick, 43
Kilcummin (Kerry), 27, 34, 40, 46, 214, 224, 317, 345

Kildare
  1920s, 11, 13, 14–16, **16**, 17–20, 22–8, 431
  1930s, 30, 32, 36, 37, 38–41, 43, 49, 55, 57, 60, 66–70, 71, 74, 89–90, 91, 100
  1940s, 107, 110, 113, 119, 125, 130, 136, 142–3, 151, 157–8, 166, 176
  1950s, 182, 191, 198, 218, 225, 235–6, 237, 244–5, 251, 254, 258, 260
  1960s, 271–2, 280, 287–8, 297, 313, 318, 320, 321, 328–9, 336, 348–9
  1970s, 354, 357, 359, 365–6, 377–8, 385, 389, 397, 409, 410, 414, 423
Kildare Round Towers (Kildare), 20, 28, 41, 70, 79
Kilduff, Paddy, 98
Kilgannon, Padraig, 286
Kilkeel (Down), 275, 283
Kilkenny
  1920s, 23, 26
  1930s, 30, 37, 67, 68, 103
  1940s, 113, 130, 142, 213
  1960s, 287, 299, 333
  1970s, 409, 414, 423
Kilkerrin-Clonberne (Galway), 54, 62, 95–6, 111, 309, 317, 325
Kill (Cavan), 132–3, 181
Kill (Waterford), 335
Killala (Mayo), 172, 188, 196
Killalon (Meath), 326
Killanny (Monaghan), 35, 63
Killarney, Co. Kerry, 32, 116, 213
Killarney Legion (Kerry), 86–7, 96–7, 105, 117, 141, 155–6, 164, 214, 224, 231, 232, 267, 276, 292, 309, 317, 345, 353, 363
Killeavy (Armagh), 215
Killeevan Sarsfields (Monaghan), 35
Killeigh (Offaly), 353, 371, 381–2
Killererin (Galway), 309, 371, 395, 404
Killeshandra (Cavan), 21, 54, 69, 87–8
Killinkere (Cavan), 132–3, 149, 163, 171, 181, 206
Killoran, Jimmy, 294
Kilmacud Crokes (Dublin), 432
Kilmainhamwood (Meath), 180, 197, 205–6, 326, 334, 363
Kilmessan (Meath), 105
Kilmore (Roscommon), 95–6, 111, 118, 124

Kilmurray, Kevin, 353, 366, **367**, 368, 369, 371, **374**, 378, 379, 381–2, 389
Kilnaleck (Cavan), 132–3, 149, 163, 171, 181, 204–6
Kilrea Pearses (Derry), 259
Kilroy, Paddy, 17, 33, 35
Kilroy, Sean, 349, 353, 381–2
Kilrush Shamrocks (Clare), 149
Kiltimagh (Mayo), 47, 78
Kilwarlin (Down), 275, 283
Kinahan, John, 177
Kinahan, Sean, 217, 218
King, Gabriel, 371, 395
King, Martin Luther, 343
King, Mick, 134
King, Sean, 377
Kingscourt (Cavan), 87–8, 171, 181, 204–6, 326, 334, 363
Kinlough, Bill, 132–3
Kinlough, Frankie, 126, 127, 128, 132–3, 137, 141, 155–6
Kinnarney, Noel, 371, 381–2
Kinnegad (Westmeath), 95–6, 111, 118, 124, 284, 353, 371
Kinnerk, Bill, 46, 84, 86–7, 96–7
Kirby, Ned, **386**, 393, 394, 400
Kirwan, Billy, 243, 244
Kirwan, Gerry, 240
Kirwan, Sean, 242
Kirwan, Tom, 293
Kirwan, Vinny, 428
Kissane, Jack, 240, 242, 264, 265, 268
Kissane, Mick, 258, 298, 300
Kitt, Liam, 118
Kitt, Michael, 403
Knock, Co. Mayo, 110, 222
Knockbride (Cavan), 132, 204–6
Knockmore (Mayo), 371, 395, 404
Knocknagoshel (Kerry), 86–7, 96–7, 105, 111, 117, 141, 155–6, 164, 214, 224, 232
Korean War, 187
Kyne, Bernie, 289, 290, 292

Labasheeda (Clare), 95–6, 111, 118
Labour Party, 131, 324
Lacken (Mayo), 78, 188, 196
Laddy, Pat, 21
Laffey, Jimmy, **191**
Laffey, Michael, 398, **407**
Laffey, Peter, 57, **58**, **72**, 75, 78, 80
Lagan, Seamus, 355, 426
Laide, Mick, 268

Lambe, Peter, 35, 63
Lambe, William 'Bunny', 136, 139
Landers, Bill 'Lang', 46, 51
Landers, John Joe 'Purty', **23**, 25, 27, 33, 34, 40, 44–5, 46, 59, 83, 84, 86–7, 93, 96–7
Landers, Tim 'Roundy', 39, 40, 44–5, 46, 81, 84, 86–7, 105, 117
Langan, Joe, 303, 318, 364
Langan, Tom, 165, **167**, 172, **183**, 185, 188, 190, **191**, **192**, 193, 194, 196, 216, 227, 229
Lannon, Achill, 366
Laois
    1920s, 14, 19, 23–4
    1930s, 13, 30, 37, 43, 49, 57, 66, **73**, **74**, 74–9, 82–3, 89, 90–1, 92, 99–100, 388
    1940s, 107–8, 112, 119, 125, 130, 136, 143, 151, 152, 157–9, 167, 176
    1950s, 191, 192, 209, 251, 260–1
    1960s, 288, 297, 303–4, 308, 313, 320, 336–7, 348
    1970s, 365, 366, 377, 389, 397, 409, 414–15, 424
Laois County Board, 196
Larkin, Alan, **397**, 403, **406**, 413, 432
Larkin, Gene, 278
Larkin, John, 139
Lascaux cave paintings, 110
Latton O'Rahillys (Monaghan), 35
Laune Rangers (Kerry), 96–7, 117, 124, 155–6, 164, 309, 317
Laverty, Eugene, 409
Laverty, Harry, 296
Lavery, George, 255, **270**, 274, 275, 277, 281, 283
Lavey (Cavan), 181, 204–6
Lavey (Derry), 259
Lavin, Jim, 225, **226**, 232
Lawler, Johnny, **135**
Lawlor, Gabriel, 336
Lawlor, John, 336, 365
Lawlor, Tom, 117
League of Ireland, 364
Leaney, Christy, 257, 259
Leaving Certificate, 78, 370, 373, 394
Leddy, Ollie, 355, 409
Lee, Sean, 300
Lee, Tom, 29
Leech, Liam, 304, 320, 336
Leech, Tommy 'Trixie', 37, 54
Leeds United FC, 231

Lees (Cork), 132–3, 141, 155–6, 241, 250
Leicester Young Irelands, 259
Leinster Council, 65, 113, 119, 120, 130, 313
Leinster Express, 20
Leinster Leader, 15, 18, 349
Leixlip (Kildare), 20, 28, 41, 70
Leitrim
    1920s, 16–17, 22
    1930s, 29, 37, 43, 50, 57, 64, 94
    1940s, 120, 126, 159, 168, 174
    1950s, 216, 227, 237, 242, 252–4, 264
    1960s, 273, 279, 286, 294–5, 302, 310, 318, 327, 338, 346
    1970s, 356, 364, 375, 387, 398, 416, 427
Leitrim (Down), 275, 344
Leitrim Observer, 56–7, 254, 416
Lemass, Seán, 69, 316
Lenehan, Kevin 'Gus', 209, 218, 220, 223
Leningrad, siege of, 117
Lennon, Joe, **270**, 275, 281, 283, 313, 343, 344, 405
Letterfrack industrial school, 370
Levey, Ignatius, 110
Leydon, Seamus, 297, 299, 301, 309, 317, 318, 323, 325, 338, 369, 371
Liddy, Sean, 228
Limerick
    1930s, 36, 43, 59, 64, 67, 71, 82, 89, 98
    1940s, 106, 145, 167, 174
    1950s, 216, 243
    1960s, 312–13, 319, 329–30
    1970s, 354, 366, 375, 390, 398, 417, 428
Limerick County Board, 214
Lincoln City FC, 275
Lindsay, Pat, 429
Linehan, Sean, 149
Lipsett, Robert, **407**
Lisnabuntry (Cavan), 54, 69, 87–8
Lisnaskea (Fermanagh), 144
Lispole (Kerry), 86–7, 96–7, 105, 111, 117, 141, 155–6, 164, 267, 276, 292, 309, 317, 345, 353, 363, 382–3
Liston, Sonny, 308
Listowel, Co. Kerry, 130–1
Listowel Emmets (Kerry), 96–7, 105, 111, 117, 224, 267, 276, 292, 413, 422

Locke, Sammy, **23**, 27, 34
Loftus, Mick, **191**, 195, 196, 295, 308, 315, 327
Loftus, P.J., 310, 327
Loftus, Willie, 327
London (city), 110, 204, 250, 362
London (team), 402, 407, 416, 427
London County Board, 402
Lonergan, Matty, 254
Lonergan, Pat, 59
Long, Denis, 366, **386**, 391, 394, 417
Long, John, 413, 422
Long, Ned, 260
Long, Tom, 155–6, 164, 264, 265, 267, 276, 288, 289, 290, 292, 293, **303**, 309
Long Kick Championship, 61
Longford
    1920s, 15, 23, 26
    1930s, 30, 89–90, 99
    1940s, 107, 119, 125, 136, 142, 176
    1950s, 190–1, 198, 218, 225, 235, 251, 261
    1960s, 270–1, 280, 288, 297, 313–14, 318, 320, 328–9, 336, **337**, 337, 341, 348
    1970s, 357–9, 375, 376–7, 389, 397, 408, 409, 414, 423
Longford County Board, 198
Longford Leader, 15, 271, 313
Longford Slashers (Longford), 376
Longstone (Down), 275, 283
Longwood (Meath), 197
Looney, Seamus, 376
Los Angeles, 45
Loughglynn (Roscommon), 292
Loughinisland (Down), 275, 283, 344
Loughman, John, 101
Loughran, Jim, 432
Loughran, Joe, 90, 101, 105, 108
Loughran, Noel, 250
Loughran, Peter, **425**, 432
Louisburgh (Mayo), 78, 172, 188, 196
Lourdes, 231
Louth
    1920s, 14, 15, 23, 26
    1930s, 30, 36, 43, 49, 55, 57–8, 65–6, 68, 74, 76, 82–3, 90, 99
    1940s, 107, 113, 125, 127, 136, 139, 142, 151, 158, 165, 166, 167, 168, 176
    1950s, 13, 182–3, 185, 186–9, 191, 198–9, 209, 211, 213, 217, 225, **243**, 244–5, 246–50, 251–2, 260

1960s, 271–2, 280, 288, 297, 304, 320–1, 327–8, **328**, 336–7
1970s, 359, 365, 376, 388–9, 396–7, 408, 416, 424
Louth County Board, 336–7
Lovett, Declan, 345
Lowney, Joe, 240
Lowry, Sean, 371, **374**, 376, 377, 381–2, 397
Lowth, Brinsley, 359
Lucan Sarsfields (Dublin), 403, 413
Lucey, Jerry, **330**, 333, 335, 366
Lucey, Jimmy, 292, 317
Lucey, Noel, 292
Lucey, Vincent, 309, 313, 317
Lundy, Eamonn, **270**, 275, 283
Lunny, Aidan, 418
Lynch, Batt, 198, 242
Lynch, Brendan (Kerry: 1960s–1970s), 338, 341, 342, 345, 353, 361, 363, 375, 379, 382–3, 406, 411, 412, 413, 422
Lynch, Brendan (Roscommon: 1940s), 132–3, 141, 155–6
Lynch, Frank, **243**, 248, 249, 251, 272, 280, 320, 359
Lynch, Hughie, 105
Lynch, Jack, 145, 146–7, 149, 258, 334, 352, 362, 392, 431
Lynch, Jim, 294
Lynch, John, 292
Lynch, Michael (Down: 1940s), 107
Lynch, Michael (Meath: 1960s), 326
Lynch, Mick (Cavan: 1950s), 246
Lynch, Mick (Cork: 1950s), 241
Lynch, Patsy, 19, 21, **50**, 54, 69, **158**, **166**
Lynch, Paudie, 375, 376, 379, 382–3, 406, 410, 411, 413, 422
Lynch, Roger, 189
Lynch, Timmy J., 155–6
Lynch, Tom, 285, 286, 349, 350
Lynch, Vincent, 363
Lynch, William, 64
Lyne, Dinny, 138, 141, 155–6, 161, 164
Lyne, Jackie, 141, 150, 155–6, 161, 164, 186, 190, 193, 214, 224, 244, 248, 362
Lyne, Mikey, 83, 86, 105, 117
Lyne, Tadhgie, 211, 212, 214, 224, 228, 230, 232, 255, 265, 267, 276
Lyng, Johnny, 177
Lyons, Austin, 334
Lyons, Paddy, 350

Lyons, Tim 'Tiger', 267, 273, 276, 281, 289, 290, 292
Lyster, Jack, 226

McAlarney, Colm, 321, 330, 331, 341, 344, 349, 368, 373, 387, 399
McAleer, Jim, **233**
McAleer, Mickey, 33, 35
McAlinden, Brian, **425**, 430, 432
McAlinden, Leo, 174
McAlinden, Pat, 344
McAllister, Seamus, 269
McAndrew, John, 188, 190, **191**, 195, 196
McAndrew, Pat, **167**, 168, 169, 172
McArdle, Jim, **243**, 245, 250
McArdle, John, 311
McArdle, Mick, 185, 255
McArdle, Paddy, 187, 189, 199
McAree, Harry, 311
McAtamney, Tony, 306, 331, 355
McAteer, Brian, 173
McAuley, John, **270**, 275
McAuliffe, Dan, 232, 262, 265, 267, 276, 288, 289, 292
McAuliffe, Finbarr, **244**, 250
McAuliffe, Tony, 96–7, 105, 111, 117
McBreen, Johnny, 215
McCabe, Andy, 355
McCabe, James, 181, **199**, 204–6
McCabe, Leo, 367
McCaffrey, Ivan, 264
McCaffrey, P.J., 285
McCague, Gerry, 409
McCallin, Andy, 355, 368
McCallin, Jim, 331
McCallin, Joe, 150, 165, 192
McCann, Dermot, 259
McCann, Gerry, 349
McCann, Martin, 372
McCann, Ned, 44, 49, **56**, 63
McCann, Tom (Down: 1940s), 107
McCann, Tommy (Dublin: 1940s), 124
McCarney, Peter, 126
McCartan, Dan, **270**, 275, 281, 282, 283, 322, 344, 373, 409, 426
McCartan, Dominic, 426
McCartan, James, 255, 263, **270**, 270, 273, 274, 275, 278, 281, 282, 283, 296, 306, 330, 426
MacCárthaigh, Ceallacháin, 163
McCarthy, Charlie, 35
McCarthy, Dave, **386**, 394, 398
McCarthy, Gene, 289, 335

McCarthy, Gerry, 243, 338, 402, 418
McCarthy, John (Dublin: 1970s), **397**, 401, 403, 408, 411, 413, **417**, 420, 422, 424, 429, 432
McCarthy, John (Kerry: 1960s), 309
McCarthy, John (Kilkenny: referee), 324
McCarthy, Martin, 105, 138, 141
McCarthy, Mick, **244**, 250
McCarthy, Pat, 406, 410, 411, 413, 418, 422
McCarthy, Paul, 349
McCarthy, Sean, 86–7, 111, 117
McCarthy, Tadhg, 51, 54, 59, 62
McCarthy, Toss, 287
McCashin, Gerry, 283
McCloone, Mickey, 322
McClorey, John, 107
McCloskey, Dermot, **233**
McClurg, Noel, 322
McConnell, Kevin (Meath: 1940s–1950s), **174**, **176**, 180, 194, 197, 205–6, 223
McConnell, Kevin (Meath: 1970s), 389
McConnon, Peter, 32, 35
McConville, Dan, 106
McConville, Ray, 344
McCormack, Jim, 319
McCormack, Larry, 235, 236
McCormack, Paddy (Offaly: 1950s–1970s), 251, **278**, 280, 282, 284, 287, 288, **347**, 349, 350, 352, 353, **367**, 369, 371, **374**, 378, 379, 380, 381–2, 390
McCormack, Paddy 'Butcher' (West-meath: 1950s), 226
McCormack, Sean, 326, **328**, 334, 363
McCormack, Stephen, 319
McCormack, Terry, 107
McCorry, Bill, 173, 185, 212, 215
McCorry, Frank, 150
McCorry, Jim, 306
McCorry, John, 285
McCowell, John, 313
McCoy, Barney, **243**, 249
McCreesh, Pat, 215
McCreesh, Tom, 296, **425**, 426, 427, 429, 432
McCudden, Tommy, 340
McCullough, Jim, 42, 56, 66, 74, 81, 101
McDarby, John 'Mallet', 79, 82
McDermott, Derry, 132–3, 141, 155–6

McDermott, Jackie, 227

McDermott, John (Roscommon: 1970s), 429

McDermott, John Bosco (Galway: 1960s), 301, 309, 317, 325

McDermott, Peter, 158, 159, 176, **176**, 178, 180, 194, 197, 200, 205–6, **207**, 213, 218, 220, 223, 228, 238, 275

McDonagh, Colie, 323, 325, 347, 369, 371, 392, 395, 401, 404

McDonagh, Mattie, 236, 238, 240, 268, 298, 301, 307, 309, 310, 317, 323, 325, 338–9

McDonagh, Michael 'Hauleen', 264, 268

McDonagh, Pat, 'Big', 118, 124

McDonagh, Pat, 'Small', 95–6, 111, 115, 118, 122, 124

McDonald, Brian, 298, 300, 304

McDonald, Frank, 302

McDonald, Joe 'Rexie', **73**, 76, 79

McDonald, Mick, 260

McDonald, Fr T., 24, 26

McDonnell, Eamon, 66

McDonnell, Jim (Cavan: 1950s–1960s), 263, 270, 285, 286, 289

McDonnell, Jim (Louth: 1940s–1950s), 176, 189, 209, 228–9, **243**, 245, 247, 249

McDonnell, Johnny, 15, **56**, 60, 63

McDonnell, Matty, **176**, 180, 197, 205–6, 223, 225, 226

McDonnell, Mickey, 189, 199

McDonnell, P.J., 62

McDonnell, Paddy, 15, 23, 37, 44

McDonnell, Tommy, 66

McDyer, Columba, **158**, 162, 163, 373

McElhatton, Sean, 387

McElhinney, Gerry, 409, 410, 419

McElroy, P.J., **270**, 275, 283

McElroy, Seamus, 311

McEniff, Brian, **373**, 373, 374, 378, 400, 410

McEnroe, Bartle 'Batty', 181, **199**, 203, 204–6

McEnroe, Hughie, 102, 105

McEnroe, James, 181

McEntee, Sean, 203

Mac Eoin, Sean, 148

McEvoy, Har, 353

McEvoy, John, 28

McEvoy, Mal, 211, 212, 215, 218, 262

McFadden, Joe, 316

McFee, Malachy, 356, 368

McFeely, Brendan, 316

McFeely, Frank, 296, 316, **373**

MacGabhann, Liam, 201

McGarty, Packie, 216, 227, 242, 252, 253–4, 264, 272, 279, 294, 327, 387

McGauran, Jimmy, 95–6, 109, 111, 116, 118, 123, 124

Mac Gearailt, Seamus, 12, 317, 320, 345, 353, 361, 363, 379, 382–3

McGearty, Patsy, 205–6, 218, 220, 221, 223

McGeary, Johnny, 277–8

McGee, Eugene, 343

McGee, Willie, 387, 408

McGeough, John, **158**

McGonagle, William, 343

McGovern, Con, 111

McGovern, Mick, 427

McGovern, Owen Roe, 149, **158**, 163, 169, 171, 181

McGovern, Terry, 313, **337**

McGovern, Vincent, **50**, 51, 52, 54, **65**, 69

McGowan, Jim 'Tot', **58**, **72**, 78

McGowan, Kevin, 295

McGrane, Pat 'the Red Fella', 35

McGrath, Con, 177, 184

McGrath, Gene, 429

McGrath, Hilary, 344

McGrath, Sean, 340

McGuckin, Adrian, 355, 418

McGuigan, Colm, 418

McGuigan, Frank, 372, 373–4, 384, 387, 426

McGuinness, Jim, **226**, 229, 232

McGuinness, Johnny, 35

McGuinness, Larry, **176**, 180, 197

McGuinness, Tom (Derry: 1970s), 360, 409, 419

McGuinness, Tommy 'Boiler' (Meath: 1930s), 66, 101, 102, 105

McGuirk, Willie, 251

McGurk, Anthony, 355, 399, 419

McHugh, Danny, 310, 311

McHugh, Tom, 240

McIlduff, Ciaran, 331

McIlkenny, Mick, 236

McInerney, Hugh, 350, 355

McInerney, Martin, 338

McIntyre, P.J., 313, 345

McIntyre, Paddy, 110, 119

McKane, Des, 288, 298, 300, 303

McKay, Eamonn, **270**, 275, 283

McKay, John, 291

McKearney, Hughie, 200

McKee Barracks (Dublin), 20, 28, 41

McKeever, Dinny, 256, 258, 259, 277

McKeever, Jim, 227, 228, 246, **252**, 255, 256, 259, 277, 283

McKeever, Peter, 205–6

McKenna, Dessie, 426

McKenna, Eugene, 426

McKenna, Gerald, 379, 405

McKenna, John, 269

McKenna, Peter, 128

McKenna, Willie (Tyrone: 1940s), 134

McKenna, Willie (Tyrone: 1970s), 426

McKenna Cup, 24, 66, 81, 387

McKeon, Mickey, 57

McKeown, Mick 'Muckle', 304, 320, 359

McKerr, Jim, **425**, 432

McKevitt, Jim, 74

Mackey, Mick, 145

McKinstry, Colm, **425**, 432

McKnight, Felix, 262

McKnight, John, 212, 215, 218, 262

McLarnon, Patsy, 255, 259

McLean, Fr Lucius, 283

McLoughlin, Brendan, 227

McLoughlin, Eddie, 92

McLoughlin, Frank, 308, 309, 325

McLoughlin, Gerry, 43, 49, 63, 107

McLoughlin, Jimmy, 107

McLoughlin, Joe, 364, 371

McMahon, Aidan, 384, 391

McMahon, D.J., 183

McMahon, Eamonn (Armagh: 1950s), 212, 215

McMahon, Eamonn (Meath: 1970s), 363

McMahon, Eddie, 42, 92

McMahon, Fran, 432

McMahon, Garry, 254, 265, 267, 276, 290, 291, 292

McMahon, Pat, 338

McMahon, Robbie, 415

McMahon, Seamus, 311

McMahon, Willie 'Terry', 71

McManus, Eamonn, 429

McManus, Fr Michael, 22, 30–1

McMenamin, Mickey, **373**

McNally, Pat, 423

McNamara, Brian, 181

McNamara, Danny, 197

McNamara, Michael 'Pop', 172
McNamee, Paddy (Cavan: 1930s), **50**, 54, **65**, 69, 87–8
McNamee, Paddy (GAA President), 115
McNaughton, Paul, 408
McNeill, Des, 306
McNicholas, Tom, 76, 78
McNutt, Mickey, 144
McPartland, Eamonn, 387
McPhillips, Frank, 300
McPolin, Hugh, 384
McQuaid, John Charles, 231, 258
McQuillan, Jack, 132–3, 134, 137, 141, 155–6, 160
Macroom (Cork), 241, 250
McRory, Art, 343
McShane, Mick, 35
McShea, Pauric, 311, **373**, 374
McSorley, Brian, **233**
McStay, Gerry, 215
McTague, Tony, 329, 348, 350, 351, 353, 366, **367**, 368, 369, 371, **374**, 378, 379, 381–2, 390, 391
McTeague, Joe, 321, 348
McTiernan, Mick, 327
McVeigh, Liam, 185
McWey, Brendan, 191
Maddenstown (Kildare), 20, 28, 41
Magee, M.J. 'Sonny', **50**, 51, 52, 54, **65**, 67, 69, **81**, 83, 84, 87–8
Magee, Noel, 225
Magennis, Aidan, **243**, 249
Maghera (Cavan), 21, 171, 181, 204–6
Maghery (Armagh), 432
Magnier, Dave, 149
Maguire, Brendan, 11, 199, 201, 202, 205–6
Maguire, Des, 11, 181, **199**, 201, 204–6
Maguire, Jimmy, 41, 67, 68, 70
Maguire, Liam, 11, **199**, 201, 204–6, 278
Maguire, Seamus, 132–3
Maguire, Sean, 277
Maguire, Tom, 219, 228, 286, 289
Maher, Chris, **135**
Maher, Dermot, 432
Maher, Nicky, **226**, 229, 232
Mahon, Cyril, 286, 292, 302
Mahon, Jack, 237, 238, 240, 242, 265, 268
Mahoney, Jerry, 427
Mahoney, John, 427

Mahony, Denis 'Danno', **226**, 229, 230, 232
Maigh Cuilinn (Galway), 371
Malcolmson, George, 21
Malone, Frank, 18, 20, 25, 28, 41
Malone, John Joe, 112
Malone, Tommy, 142–3
Manchester United FC, 393, 431
Mandela, Nelson, 308
Mangan, Bill, 18, 20, 68, 70
Mangan, Jack, 190, 216, **234**, 237, 238, 240
Mangan, Pat, 321, 348, 366, 389
Mangan, Tom, 262, 289, 304
Manning, Sean, **226**
Mannion, Liam, 240, 268
Mannion, Mickey, 91, 95–6
Mantua (Roscommon), 141, 155–6
Mao Zedong, 180, 258
Markey, Paddy, 187, 189, 199
Markey, Pat, 167, 209
Markey, Phil, 377
Markham, Patsy, 348
Marley, Noel, 418, **425**, 426, 432
marriage bar, 258, 394
Marron, Dessie, 237, 245
Martin, Bob, 90, 110, 151
Martin, Jimmy, 311, 374
Martin, John Willie, 132–3, 149
Martin, Mick (Dublin: 1940s), 116–17
Martin, Mickey (Leitrim: 1970s), 398, 416, 427
Martin, Ned, 176
Martin, Paddy, 20, 25, 28, 41, 66, 70, 74
Martin, Rogie, 270
Martinstown (Meath), 326, 334
Mason, Billy, 33, 35
Masterson, Joe, 216
Masterson, Paudge, 21
Masterson, Peter, 16
Matthews, Paul, 41, 66, 68, 70
Mattock Rangers (Louth), 334
Maynooth College, Co. Kildare, 213, 290, 307, 352, 362
Mayo
    1920s, 17, 22, 24
    1930s, 29, 30, 32, 36, 37, 38, 42–3, 44–7, 50–1, 55, 57, **58**, 61, 64–5, 67, 68, 71, **72–3**, 72–3, 75–8, 80, 83, 91, 94, 98, 101
    1940s, 107, 114, 120, 126, 134, 145, 151, 159, 165, **167**, 168–72, 174, 177, 431

    1950s, 185, 186–8, 190, **191**, 193–6, 198, 208–9, 213, 216, 227, 229, 230, 236, 242, 252, 264
    1960s, 12, 272, 279, 286, 295, 302–3, 310, 318, 327, 331–2, 338, 339, 346–7, 350
    1970s, 354, 356, 364, 366, 374–5, 376, 387–8, 398, 407, 408, 416, 427
Mayo Abbey (Mayo), 172, 188, 196
Mayo County Board, 101, 165, 185
Mayobridge (Down), 344
Meade, Sean, 268, 279, 301, 309, 317, 325, 349
Meade, Ted, 90, 105
Meally, Martin, 359
Meaney, James, 70
Meaney, Johnny, 41
Meath
    1920s, 15, 22–3
    1930s, 30–1, 37, 40, 43, 49, 55, 57, 65–6, 68, 74, 90, 99–105
    1940s, 107–8, 119, 125, 136, 142, 158–9, 160, 165, 166, 170, 176, **176**, 177–80
    1950s, 11, 182–3, 191–2, 193–7, 198–9, 200, 201–6, 209, 213, **217**, 218, 219–23, 225–6, 245, 251, 261
    1960s, 270, 280, 287, 296–7, 304, 306, 308, 313, 318, 320, 321, 322–6, 327–9, 331–4, 336, 348
    1970s, 354, 359–63, 365, 366, 376–7, 389–90, 397–8, 405, 408, 415–16, 423, 424
Meath Chronicle, 22–3, 26, 57, 103, 119, 179, 194, 195, 199, 200, 219, 220, 221, 270, 359–60
Meath County Board, 22
Mee, Dick, 223
Meegan, Paddy, **176**, 180, 197, 205–6, 218, 220, 223
Meehan, Jim 'Red', **176**, 180, **243**, 247, 249
Meehan, John, **176**, 180
Mehigan, P.D., 18
Mellett, Mick, 326, **328**, 332, 334, 363
Melly, Mick, 73, 106
Menlough (Galway), 301, 371
Merrigan, Andy, 348
Metcalf, Paddy, 225
Miami Showband, 413
Michael Glavey's (Roscommon), 292
Mickey Mouse, 20

Middletown Eoghan Rua (Armagh), 215

Miles, Patrick, 41

Millar, Bobby, 415

Miller, Billy, 355, 356

Miller, Bob, 261

Milligan, Jim, 341, 344

Mills, John, 376

Millstreet (Cork), 149, 241, 250, 293, 394

Milltown (Kildare), 20, 28, 41

Milltown (Galway), 204–6, 301, 309, 317, 325, 371, 395, 404

Milltown-Castlemaine (Kerry), 149, 155–6, 214, 224, 232, 309, 317

Miltown Malbay (Clare), 63

Mitchell, Brian, 292

Mitchell, Dermot, 52, 54, 62

Mitchell, Gay, 371, 387, **389**, 395, 400, 401, 404

Mitchell, Gerry, 364–5

Mitchell, Joe, **65**, 69, 87–8

Mitchell, Paddy, 95–6, 111, 118

Mitchelstown (Cork), 241, 250, 335

Moate (Westmeath), 371

Mockler, Dick, 29

Moclair, Paddy, 44–5, 47, 57, **58**, **72**, 75, 78, 98, 107

Molloy, John, **65**, 69

Molloy, Peter, 177

Moloney, John, 332, **386**, 396, 411, 414

Monaghan
  1920s, 17, 24–5, 26
  1930s, 13, 31–5, 36, 38, 42, 49, 55–6, 66, 71, 73, 80, 92, 94, 101
  1940s, 106–7, 113–14, 126, 134–5, 144, 150, 159, 165, 173
  1950s, 185, 192, 199–200, 207, 218, 227, 236, 246, 254–5, 263
  1960s, 269, 277–8, 296, 306, 311, 321, 331, 340, 349
  1970s, 356, 370, 373, 387, 399, 409, 418–19, 426

Monaghan, Donal, **373**, 374

Monaghan, Pat, 349, 353

Monaghan Argus, 254

Monaghan bombing, 402

Monaghan County Board, 31–2

Monaghan Harps (Monaghan), 35

Monasterevin, Co. Kildare, 412

Mone, Benny, 349

Mongey, Billy, 78

Mongey, Eamonn, 165, **167**, 168, 172, 185, 187, 188, **191**, 196

Monk, Alfie, **243**, 245, 249, 251

Monks, Billy, **226**, 232

Mooney, Johnny, 415

Mooney, Peter, 236

Mooney, Ray 'Gu', 176, 189

Moore (Roscommon), 132–3, 141, 155–6, 292

Moore, John 'Buller', **135**, 137

Moore, Michael, 301, 308

Moore, Mossie, 155–6

Moore, Pat 'Archie', 280, 287

Moore, Paud, 236

Moore, Peter, 304, 321, 322, 323, 326, **328**, 334, 363

Moore, Sean, 237, 239, 241, **244**, 250

Moran, Denis 'Ogie', 290, 413, 420, 422

Moran, John Oliver, 287, 292

Moran, Kevin, 414, 415, **417**, 420, 422, 431, 432

Moran, Lee, 79

Moran, Mick (Westmeath: 1960s), 272

Moran, Mickey (Derry: 1970s), 419, 426

Moran, Mickey (Mayo: 1930s), 30, 37, 47

Moran, Sean, 47

Morgan, Billy (Cork: 1960s–1970s), 320, 330, **330**, 333, 335, 346, 355, **385**, **386**, 390–1, 392, 393, 394, 398, 400, 428

Morgan, Billy (Longford: 1960s) 271

Morgan, Breen, **270**, 275, 283

Morgan, Charlie, 17

Morgan, Dan, 73

Morgan, Dónal, **50**, 54, **65**, 69, **81**, 87–8, 132–3

Morgan, Gene, 212, 215

Morgan, James, 368

Morgan, John (Cavan: 1920s), 17, 21

Morgan, John 'Boiler' (Louth: 1950s), 189

Morgan, Sean, 349

Morgan, Tom, 322

Moriarty, Eddie, 216, 227, 229

Moriarty, Johnny, 105

Moriarty, Paddy, 425, **425**, 426, 429, 430, 432

Moriarty, Sean, 124

Moriarty, Tom (Cork/Kerry: 1950s), 201, 209, 211, 220, 224, 228, 232

Moriarty, Tom (Meath: 1950s), 218, 220, 223

Morley, John, 318, 327, 331–2, 347, 356, 387–8

Moroney, Pat, 354

Morris, Brendan, 259

Morris, Davy, 43, 49

Morris, Frank, 54

Morris, Jim, 112, **135**, 136, 167

Morris, John 'Suck', 143

Morris, Mick, **303**, 309, 317, 345, 353, 362

Morris, P.J., 54

Morris, Seamus, 171, 181, **199**, 204–6, 208, 228

Morris, Tony, 286, 289

Mother and Child scheme, 196

Moules, Eamon, 322

Mountbellew-Moylough (Galway), 189, 249, 301, 309, 317, 325, 371, 395, 404

Mountjoy Prison, 53, 394

Mountnugent (Cavan), 54, 69, 78, 87–8, 132–3, 149, 163, 171, 181, 197, 204–6

Moylan, Mick, 225, **226**, 232

Moyles, Liam, 375

Moyna, Mackie, 200

Moyna, Tommy, 200

Moynalty (Meath), 105, 180, 197, 205–6, 223

Moynihan, Pat, 345, 353

Moyvane (Kerry), 27, 34, 40, 46, 86–7, 95–7, 111, 118, 124, 214, 224, 232, 276, 309, 317

Mulderrig, Mick (Mayo: 1930s), 47

Mulderrig, Mick (Mayo: 1950s), 185, 188, **191**, 195, 196

Mulderrig, Sean, **167**, 172, 188, **191**, 194, 196

Muldoon, Frank, 384

Mulhaire, Harry, 428

Mulhall, Bill, 107

Mulhall, Eddie, 337

Mulhall, Seamie, 191

Mulhall, Tommy, 67, 70

Mulholland, Colm, 256, 259

Mulholland, Felix, 373

Mulholland, Liam, 259

Mulholland, Ned, 93, 95–6, 111, 118, 124

Mullagh (Cavan), 132–3, 149, 163, 171, 181, 204–6

Mullaghbawn (Armagh), 432

Mullahoran (Cavan), 54, 67, 69, 87–8, 132–3, 149, 163, 171, 181, 204–6

Mullan, Brian, 259
Mullaney, Noel, 272
Mullen, Mick, 264
Mulligan, Eugene, 350, 351, 353, **367**, 368, 370, 371, **374**, 379, 381–2
Mulligan, Seamus, 278, 311
Mulligan, Tom, 176
Mullins, Brian, 396, **397**, 397–8, **399**, 400, 401, 402, 403, 409, 413, 415, **417**, 420, 422, 429, 432
Mullins, Mick 'Butcher', 348
Multyfarnham College (Westmeath), 309
Mulvany, Harry, 17, 21
Mulvany, Paddy, 304, 326, **328**, 334
Mulvany, Tom, 21
Mulvey, Johnny, 310
Mulvihill, Seamus, 359
Mulvihill, Tom, 341, 359
Munnelly, Dick, 47
Munnelly, Josie, **58**, 65, **72**, 75, 78, 80, 172
Munnelly, Paddy 'Captain', 43, 44–5, 47, **58**, **72**, 75, 78
Munster Council, 211
Munterconnaught (Cavan), 54, 204–6
Murphy, Andy, **135**
Murphy, Barnes, **407**, 408, 410
Murphy, Bennie, 322
Murphy, Bob, 96–7
Murphy, Brendan, 149
Murphy, Brian, **330**, 335, 376, **386**, 394, 418, 428
Murphy, Daithi, 371
Murphy, Denis, 241
Murphy, Dickie, 344
Murphy, Donie, 186, 190, 212, 214, 224, 228, 231, 232
Murphy, Gerry, 215
Murphy, J.J., 304
Murphy, J.P., 21, 37, 41, **50**
Murphy, Jack, 112, 123, 124
Murphy, James 'Jas', 157, **210**, 211, 214
Murphy, Jimmy, 17, 21
Murphy, Joe, 363
Murphy, John, 330, 341, 342, 344
Murphy, Larry, 135
Murphy, Leo, 255, 263, 269, **270**, 274, 275, 277, 283, 286, 322
Murphy, Miah, 126
Murphy, Mick (Kerry: 1950s), 214, 224, 232
Murphy, Mick (Westmeath: 1960s), 320

Murphy, Noel, 394
Murphy, P.A. 'Weesh', 145, 147, 149, 190, 393
Murphy, Paddy, 241
Murphy, Pat (Armagh: 1950s), 215
Murphy, Pat (Limerick: 1960s), 312
Murphy, Seamus, 254, 262, 267, 274, 276, 292, **303**, 309, 317, 338, 345, 353, 354, 363
Murphy, Sean, 212, 214, 216, 224, 230, 232, 254, 264, 265, 266, 267, 276
Murphy, T.P., 372
Murphy, Tommy 'Boy Wonder', **74**, 82, 83, 86, 90, 92, 107, 112, 125, 151, 152, 191
Murphy, Val, 304
Murray, Alf, 81
Murray, Brendan, 255, 259
Murray, Dan, 237, 241, **244**, 250
Murray, Dom, 157
Murray, Frank, 389
Murray, Jimmy, 12, 128, 132–3, **137**, 141, 151, 152, 155–6, 160, 290
Murray, Josie, 242, 254, 294, 295
Murray, Paddy 'Cocker', 185
Murray, Phelim, 132–3, **136**, 141, 151, 155–6
Murray, Sean (Longford: 1960s), 313, 328, **337**, 341
Murray, Sean 'Yank' (Dublin: 1950s), 251, 255, 259
Murtagh, Dom, 320
Mussen, Kevin, **270**, 274, 275, 283
Mussolini, Benito, 69
Myers, Bill, 83–4, 85, 86–7, 96–7, 105, 111, 115, 117
Myers, Jack, 85
Myles, Tony, 202
Mythen, Paddy, 129

Na Fianna (Dublin) 232, 259, 292, 300, 403, 413, 422, 432
Naas (Kildare), 20, 28, 41, 67, 70, 180, 197, 205–6
Nagasaki, 147
Nallen, John, 227, 268
Nally, Pat, 321, 348
Nally, Vincent, 318
Naomh Abán (Cork), 335, 394
Naomh Mhuire, Drogheda (Louth), 180, 249
National College of Physical Education, 402

National Film Institute, 162
National Football League, 80, 91, 94, 165, 182, 193, 195, 200, 213, 226, 244, 248, 254, 269, 293, 318, 350, 354, 356, 364, 366, 375, 376, 384–7, 396, 397, 400, 405, 408, 423, 424, 427
Nationalist (Tipperary), 29
Nationalist and Leinster Times, 26, 75, 82, 112, 119, 136, 260, 280, 349
Naughton, Tom, **389**, 392, 395, 404, 427
Navan, Co. Meath, 103
Navan Gaels (Meath), 105
Navan O'Mahonys (Meath), 180, 197, 205–6, 223, 249, 363
Navan Parnells (Meath), 105, 180, 197, 223
Nealon, John, 346
Nealon, Ted, 208
Nelligan, Charlie, 249, **415**, 422
Nelson's Pillar, Dublin, 324–5
Nemo Rangers (Cork), 301, 309, 317, 325, 335, 371, 392, 394
Nerney, John Joe, 137, 141, 155–6
Nestor, Brendan, 51, 54, 60, 62, 72, 93, 95–6, 109, 111
Nestor Cup, 253
neutrality, 148
New York, 12, 27, 40, 69, 90, 110, 148, 157, 160–4, 194, 195, 233, 248, 271, 293, 308, 362, 401, 409, 421
Newbridge (Derry), 259
Newell, Martin, 301, 302, 309, 315, 317, 325
Newman, Hughie, 349–50
Newport, Tony, 234, 272
Newry Mitchels (Down), 275, 283, 344
Newry Shamrocks (Down), 275, 283, 344
Newtown Blues (Louth), 249, 292, 336
Niblock, Frankie, 227
Niblock, Hugh, 360
Niblock, Mickey, 355, 356, 360, 387
Niland, Ray, 356
Nixon, Richard, 275, 403
Nobber (Meath), 180, 197, 326, 334, 363
Noctor, Martin, 408
Nolan, Joe, 280
Nolan, Mick, 303
Nolan, Peter, 225, 251, 271

Nolan, Willie, **278**, 284
Noonan, Martin, 395, 404
Noone, Mickey, 29
Norgay, Tenzing, 213
Norman, Peter, 344
North Atlantic Treaty Organisation (NATO), 180
North Korea, 187
nuclear power, 123
Nugent, Danny, 388
Nulty, Frank, 105
Nunan, Matt, 59
Nuremburg War Crimes Tribunal, 154

Oates, Barney, 198
O'Beirne, P.J., 77
O'Beirne, Richard, 429
O'Boyle, Br William, 107
O'Brien, Danny, 269
O'Brien, Dermot, **243**, 245, 247, 248, 249
O'Brien, Dom, 251
O'Brien, Hugh, 47
O'Brien, Jimmy, 198
O'Brien, Josie, 345
O'Brien, Larry, 223
O'Brien, Micheál (Meath: 1940s–1950s), **175, 176**, 180, 194, 197, 205–6, 223
O'Brien, Mick (Meath: 1960s), 326, 334
O'Brien, Mick 'Ginger' (Dublin: 1920s–1930s), 23, **56**, 63
O'Brien, Ollie, 423
O'Brien, Paddy (Dublin: 1970s), 389
O'Brien, Paddy (Kerry: 1930s), 87
O'Brien, Paddy 'Hands' (Meath: 1940s–50s), **175, 176**, 177, 180, 183, **192**, 197, 199, 202, 205–6, 218, 219, 221, 223
O'Brien, Peadar, 260, 277, 348, 352, 356–7
O'Brien, Sean, 205–6
O'Brien, Teddy, 376, 394
O'Brien, Tim 'Sambo', 79
O'Brien, Tom, 205–6, 219, 223
O'Brien, Willie, 100, 105
O'Byrne Cup, 424
O'Callaghan, Bernie, 276, 305, 307, 309, 317
O'Callaghan, J.P. 'Doc', 132–3, **136**, 138, 141, 155–6
O'Callaghan, Pat, 20
O'Callaghan, Tim, **244**, 250

Ó Caoimh, Pádraig, 26, 40, 160, 162
O'Carroll, Declan, 341, **373**
O'Carroll, Sean, 33, 35
O'Connell, Billy, 427
O'Connell, Denis 'Rory', 27, 34
O'Connell, Michael, 310
O'Connell, Mick, 234, 235, **261**, 262, **263**, 264, 265, 266, 267, 272, 273–4, 276, 279, 289, 290, 292, 293, **303**, 307, 309, 315, 317, 319, 338, **339, 340**, 341, 345, 346, **347**, 350, 353, 354, 360, 363, 375, 376, 378, 380, 382–3, 393, 398
O'Connell, Moss, 267
O'Connell, Paddy, 319
O'Connell, Sean, 246, 255, 256, 259, 262, 356, 368, 372, 385, 409
O'Connell Boys (Dublin), 403, 413, 422, 432
O'Connor, Andy, 268
O'Connor, Brendan, 302
O'Connor, Charlie, 155–6
O'Connor, Dee, **23**, 27, 34, 40, 46, 118
O'Connor, Din, 149
O'Connor, Gerry, 286
O'Connor, Harry, 132–3
O'Connor, J., **23**
O'Connor, Jack, 46
O'Connor, Jerdie, 276, **303**, 305, 309, 317
O'Connor, Joe, 74, 82, 107, 110, 119
O'Connor, John 'Connie', 95–6, 111, 124
O'Connor, John 'Jigger', 416
O'Connor, Kieran, 309
O'Connor, Mick, 244
O'Connor, Paddy, 124
O'Connor, Rory, 181
O'Connor, Teddy, 155–6, 164
O'Connor, Tom (Offaly: 1930s), 90
O'Connor, Tom 'Gega' (Kerry: 1930s), 87, 96–7, 99, **100**, 102, 105, 109, 111, 115, 117, 152, 155–6, 161, 164, 168
O'Connor, Vincent, 422
Ó Dálaigh, Cearbhall, 421
O'Dea, Niall, 228
O'Dempseys (Laois), 326
O'Doherty, Bryan, 409
O'Donnell, Dom, 309, 345, 353, 363
O'Donnell, Jimmy, 254, 306
O'Donnell, Seamie, **243**, 247, 248, 249
O'Donnell, Sean, 296

O'Donnell, Tim, **23**, 27, 34, 39, 41, 46, 59, 86–7
O'Donnell, William 'Bruddy', 141, 155–6, 160, 164, 168
O'Donoghue, Eamonn, 338, 345, 353, 361, 363, 382–3
O'Donoghue, John, 304
O'Donoghue, Nick, 155–6
O'Donoghue, Paud, **303**, 305, 309, 317, 320, 345, 353, 361, 363, 382–3
O'Donoghue, Vincent, 214
O'Donovan, Dermot, 250
O'Donovan, Donie, 173, 174, **386**, 392
O'Donovan, Fachtna, 145, 149
O'Donovan Rossa, Antrim (Antrim), 275, 283
O'Donovan Rossa, Magherafelt (Derry), 259
O'Dowd, Gerry, 429
O'Dowd, Harry, 242
O'Dowd, Mick, 57
O'Dowd, Nace, 198, 217, 242
O'Dowd, Seamus, 327, 350
O'Dowda, Brendan, 139
O'Dowda, Callum, 139
O'Driscoll, Gay, **397**, 403, 411, 413, **417**, 422, 432
O'Driscoll, Ger, 411, 413, 422
O'Driscoll, Michael 'Moll', 145, 149
O'Driscoll, Paddy, 209, 239, 241, **244**, 248, 250, 254, 262
O'Driscoll, Tadhg, 145
O'Dwyer, Mick, 243, 254, 264, 265, 267, 274, 276, 278, 290, 292, 293, **303**, 309, 314, 317, 325, 338, 341, 345, 351, 353, 354, **357**, 363, 366, 376, 378–9, 380, 382–3, 391, 398, 405–6, 421
O'Dwyers (Dublin), 403, 413
Offaly
1930s, 30, 37, 43, 49, 65, 74, 82, 89–90, 100
1940s, 107–8, 110, 119, 125, 136, 142, 143, 151, 158, 166, 177
1950s, 182, 198, 209, 217–18, 225, 235–6, 244, 251, 260
1960s, 271, 273, **278, 279**, 280–4, 285, 287–8, 297, 308, 313, 321, 328–9, 336–7, 348–9, 350–3
1970s, 13, 354, 357, 359–60, 365, 366, **367**, 368–71, **374**, 376–82, 388, 389–90, 391, 397, 409, 415, 423

Offaly Independent, 148
O'Flaherty, Paddy, **226**, 232, 256, 259, 264
O'Gara, John, 427
O'Gorman, Jimmy 'Gawksie', 85, 86, 105, 108, 111, 115, 117, 141
O'Gorman, Michael, 86
O'Gorman, Thady, 85
O'Grady, Donal, 311
O'Grady, Paddy, 149
O'Grady, Sean, 387
O'Grady, Tony, 213
O'Hagan, Art, 173, 185, 208, 209–11, 215, 218
O'Hagan, John Joe, **233**
O'Hagan, Noel, 432
O'Hagan, Patsy, **270**, 275, 283, 296
O'Hanlon, Jim, 269
O'Hanlon, Mick, 215
O'Hara, Fr Eddie, **58**
O'Hara, Gerald, 203
O'Hara, Pat, 193
O'Hare, Dan, 73
O'Hare, Joe, 215
O'Hare, John, 73, 134
O'Hare, Tom (Down: 1930s), 73
O'Hare, Tom (Down: 1960s), 296, 341, 344
O'Hehir, Michael, 92, 138, 146, 161, 195, 334
O'Higgins, Tom, 324
oil embargo, 394
O'Kane, Hugh, 262
O'Kane, J.P., 424
O'Kane, Willie, 277
O'Keeffe, Dan, 39, 40, 46, 86–7, 96–7, 102, 105, 111, 117, 141, 155–6, 157, 164
O'Keeffe, Frank, 155–6, 157, 164
O'Keeffe, Ger, 413, 422, 428
O'Keeffe, John, 353, 354–5, 360, 362, 363, 375, 382–3, 406, 411, 413, 420, 422
O'Keeffe, Kieran, 373
O'Keeffe, Tony, 422
O'Kelly, Sean T., 179
Oldcastle, Co. Meath, 11, 201
Oldcastle (Meath), 11, 27, 34, 40, 46, 105, 149, 180, 181, 197, 204–6
O'Leary, Cathal, **226**, 232, 245, 256, 257, 259, 261, 264, 280, 288, 289
O'Leary, Frank, 293–4, **303**, 309
O'Leary, Gerry, 82
O'Leary, Tim, 86–7, 93, 96–7

O'Leary, Willie, 293, 304, 305
Oliver Plunketts (Dublin), 403, 413, 422, 432
Oliver Plunketts (Louth), 132–3, 163, 171, 181, 189, 204–6, 249
O'Loughlin, Gerry, 385, 399
O'Loughlin, Joe, 20, 25, 28
O'Loughlin, Mick, **330**, 333, 335
O'Loughlin, Paddy, 18, 20, 28, 30, 32, 39, 41
Olympic Games, 20, 45, 77, 240, 344, 381, 421
O'Mahony, Garry, 220, 224, 232
O'Mahony, John, **330**, 332, 335
O'Mahony, Paudie, 407, 410, 413, 421, 422
O'Malley, Donogh, 334
O'Malley, Gerry, 198, 227, 242, 281, 286–7, 289, 290, 292, 295, 302
O'Malley, Kieran, 260, 287
O'Malley, Mick, 78, 107
O'Malley, Seamus, 47, **72**, **73**, 76, 78
Ó Muircheartaigh, Mícheál, 179
O'Neill, Albert, 23, 28
O'Neill, Barney, 355
O'Neill, Bernie, **329**, **330**, 335
O'Neill, Billy, 219, 240
O'Neill, Dan, 216, **243**, 245, 247, 248, 249
O'Neill, Des, 143
O'Neill, Donal 'Marcus', 232, 234–5
O'Neill, Eamonn, 432
O'Neill, Leo, 257, 259
O'Neill, Liam, 371, **389**, 404
O'Neill, Gerry (Armagh: 1950s), 185, 211, 215, 425–6, 430
O'Neill, Gerry (Derry: 1950s), 257, 259
O'Neill, Harry 'Red Dog', 150
O'Neill, Humphrey, 149
O'Neill, Jody, **233**, 236, 246, 247, 263, 373, 384, 409
O'Neill, Joe, 240
O'Neill, Kevin, **270**, 275, 283, 285
O'Neill, Liam, 347, 395
O'Neill, Martin (soccer player/manager), 257, 426
O'Neill, Martin (Wexford: 1930s), 43, 49
O'Neill, Martin Óg (Wexford: 1960s), 280
O'Neill, Mick, 49
O'Neill, Owen Roe, 229
O'Neill, Pat (Armagh: 1940s–1950s), 173, 208, 215

O'Neill, Pat (Dublin: 1970s), 403, 413, **417**, 420, 422, 432
O'Neill, Pat (Tipperary: 1940s), 139
O'Neill, Sean, 262, 265, **270**, 270, 275, 281, 282, 283, 285, 286, 296, 312, 331, **340**, 341, 342, 343, 344, 349, 368, 399
O'Neill, Terence, 316
Operation Overlord, 140
O'Raghallaighs (Louth), 189
Oran (Roscommon), 132–3, 141, 155–6, 292
O'Regan, Martin 'Bracker', 36, 40, 46, 96–7, 105
O'Reilly, Benny, 21
O'Reilly, Brian, 163, **166**, 171, **199**, 202, 204–6
O'Reilly, Christy, 102, 105
O'Reilly, Gerry, 245, 260
O'Reilly, Hugh Barney, 285
O'Reilly, Hugh Paddy, 69, 87–8
O'Reilly, Hughie, 21, **50**, 52, 54, **65**, 66, 67, 69, 81, **158**
O'Reilly, John (Cavan: 1920s), 21
O'Reilly, John (Laois: 1930s), 79
O'Reilly, John Joe (Cavan: 1930s–1940s), **81**, 83, 87–8, 107, 114, 121, 128, 132–3, 135, 147, 149, **158**, 161, 163, **166**, 166, 169, 171, 177, 181, 203
O'Reilly, John Joe (Cavan: 1960s), 331
O'Reilly, Michael, **50**
O'Reilly, Ned, **65**, 69
O'Reilly, P.A., 149
O'Reilly, Packy Joe, 21
O'Reilly, Peter, 107, **120**, 122, 124, **226**
O'Reilly, Phil, **278**, 284
O'Reilly, Rosaleen, 378, 380
O'Reilly, T.P., 121, 126, 129, 132–3, 149, **158**, 160, 163, **166**, 171, 181
O'Reilly, Tom, 'Big', **50**, 53, 54, **65**, 66, 67, 69, 73, **81**, 83–4, 87–8, 107, 114, **127**, 127, 128, 129, 132–3, 137, 149, **158**, 163
O'Reilly, Tom, 'Small', **50**, 54, **65**, 67, 69, 87–8, 163
Organisation of Arab Petroleum Exporting Countries, 394
O'Riordan, Jerry, 292
O'Riordan, Tom, 338, 421
Ormonde, Sean, 254, 289
Ormsby, George, 45, 47, 57, **58**, 65, **72**, 78, 94

Ormsby, Mickey, 47
O'Rourke, Brian (Carlow: 1940s), **135**
O'Rourke, Brian (Roscommon: 1930s), 132–3
O'Rourke, Colm, 299, 416, 424
O'Rourke, Fergus, 294
O'Rourke, Hughie, 209
O'Rourke, James, 280
O'Rourke, Mick, 353, **367**, 368, 371, 379
O'Rourke, Ollie, 200
O'Rourke, Paddy, 200
O'Rourke, Vinny, 376
Ó Ruairc, Mícheál, 23, 27, 34
Ó Sé, Páidí, 380, 398, 407, 411, 412, 413, 422, 429
Ó Sé, Mícheál, 345, 351, 353, 363, 379, 382–3
O'Shea, Batt, 413
O'Shea, Brendan, 214, 224
O'Shea, Colm, **244**, 250
O'Shea, Derry, 309, 315, 317
O'Shea, Dinny, 232
O'Shea, Jack, 429
O'Shea, Jerome, 214, 224, 228, 230, 232, 256, 267, 274, 276, 281
O'Shea, Jim, **56**, 59, 63
O'Shea, Joe, 23
O'Shea, John 'Thorny', 315, 317
O'Shea, Mick *see* Ó Sé, Mícheál
Ó Síocháin, Seán, 333, 384, 392
O'Sullivan, Adrian, 356
O'Sullivan, Bernie, 241
O'Sullivan, Charlie, 83, 86–7, 92, 96–7, 101, 105, 109, 111, 113, 117
O'Sullivan, Christy, 353
O'Sullivan, Con, 278, 305, **330**, 332, 335, 338
O'Sullivan, Daniel, 224
O'Sullivan, Denis, **303**, 307, 309, 313, 317, 345
O'Sullivan, Dermot, 241
O'Sullivan, Donal (Cork: 1930s), 48
O'Sullivan, Donal (Cork: 1950s), 241, **244**, 250
O'Sullivan, Donie (Kerry: 1960s), 290, **303**, 307, 309, 317, 345, 353, **358**, 360, 363, 376, 382–3, 406, 413
O'Sullivan, Eamon, 231, 290, 293
O'Sullivan, Eugene, 95–6
O'Sullivan, Gerald, 164, 214, 224, 232
O'Sullivan, Joe (Cork: 1950s), **244**, 250

O'Sullivan, Joe (Kerry: 1920s–1930s), **23**, 27, 34, 40, 46, 51
O'Sullivan, Kevin Jer, 355, **386**, 394
O'Sullivan, Mickey 'Ned', 382–3, 390, 391, 398, 405, **406**, 406, 411, 412, 413, 422
O'Sullivan, Mike, 345
O'Sullivan, Murty, 326, 334
O'Sullivan, Owenie, 205–6
O'Sullivan, Paddy (Carlow: 1940s), **135**
O'Sullivan, Paddy (Cork: 1960s), 278
O'Sullivan, Paud, **23**, 27, 34
O'Sullivan, Ray, 409
O'Sullivan, Stevie, 278
O'Sullivan, Teddy, 155–6, 164, 183
O'Sullivan, Timmy, 276, 292, 309
O'Sullivan, William, 32
O'Toole, Anton, **397**, 400, 403, 410, 413, **417**, 420, 422, 424, 429, 432
O'Toole, Eddie, 54
O'Toole, Frank, 20
O'Toole, Matt, 105
O'Toole, Mick, 415
O'Tooles (Dublin), 36, 63
Oughterard (Galway), 47, 54, 62, 78, 95–6, 111, 118, 124, 240, 301, 309, 317
Owens, Jesse, 77

Padraig Pearse's (Roscommon), 292
Pakistan, 163, 370
Palestine, 381
Palmer, James 'Mixie', 214, 220, 224, 228, 230, 232, 248
Parker, Bonnie Elizabeth, 62
Parks, Rosa, 231
Parnells (Dublin), 124
Peacock, Paddy, 191
Peadar Mackens (Dublin), 124
Pearse Óg (Armagh), 432
Pele, 364
Perry, Paddy, 63
Phair, Packy, **50**, 54, **65**, 69, 87–8
Phelan, Mick, 261
Philadelphia, 401
Philippines, 195
Phillips, Andy, 245
Philpott, Eric, **330**, 333, 335, 346
Pierce, Jimmy, 117
Pioneer Total Abstinence Association, 140, 180, 222
Pioneers (Dublin), 124
Pittsburgh, 421
Pocock, Brendan, 403, 413, 422, 432

Poland, 104
Portarlington (Laois), 79
Portlaoise (Laois), 20, 70
Potter, Maureen, 362
Powell, Larry, 344
Power, Dick, 36, 48, 64
Power, Ger, 383, 406, 407, 413, 422
Power, Jackie, 145
Power, Jimineen, 244, 272
Power, Liam, 241, **244**, 247, 250, 262
Power, Noel, 243
Power, Seamus, 244
Power, Tom (Tipperary: 1930s), 29
Power, Tom (Waterford: 1960s), 272, 288
Prendergast, Mick, 272
Prendergast, Paddy, **167**, 172, 188, 190, **191**, 195, 196, 227
Prendergast, Ray, 310, 318, 327, 347, 356
Prendergast, Tom (Kerry: 1960s–1970s), 345, 351, 353, 360, 361, 363, 382–3, 385
Prendergast, Tom (Laois: 1970s), 414
Prenderville, John, 45
Presley, Elvis, 431
Price, Sean, 304
Prichard, Peter, 306
Pringle, Peter, 19, 20, 28, 41
Prohibition, 53
Pugh, David, 364
Puirséal, Padraig, 220, 229, 237, 238, 245, 348, 359, 416
Purcell, Sean, 190, 198, 216, 217, **235**, 237, 238, 240, 242, 252, 264, 265, 268, 272, 273, 279, 286, 287, 299, 369
Purdy, John, 344

Queens Park Rangers FC, 427
Quigley, Felix, 321
Quigley, Fintan, 190
Quigley, Jim 'Sogger', 176, **243**, 248
Quigley, John, 348
Quigley, Martin, 416, 423
Quill, James 'Bruddy', 34, 41, 46
Quinlan, Arthur P., 162
Quinlan, John 'Pim', **135**, 136
Quinn, Alec, 185, 246
Quinn, Austin, **184**
Quinn, Brendan, **120**, 122, 124, 298, 328, 377
Quinn, Frank (Leitrim: 1950s), 242
Quinn, Frank (Tyrone: 1970s), 372
Quinn, Gerry, 322, 326, 334

Quinn, Hugh, 364
Quinn, Jack, 304, 306, 321, 322, 323, 326, **328**, 329, 334, 360, 361, 363
Quinn, Jim, 155–6
Quinn, 'Locky', 99
Quinn, Martin, 270, 297, 326, 334
Quinn, Mickey, **233**
Quinn, Paddy (Mayo: 1930s), 45, 47, **58**, **72**, 78, 80, 375
Quinn, Paddy (Tyrone: 1950s), **233**
Quinn, Peter, **167**, 172, 188, **191**, 195, 196
Quinn, Sean, 185, 212, 215
Quinn, Tom, 355, 384

Rackard, Nicky, 143, 221
radio coverage, 46, 53, 83, 125, 138, 146, 154, 161–2, 195
Rae, 'Jimma', 112, **135**, 137
Rafferty, Joe, 213
Rafferty, Kevin, **425**, 429, 432
Raftery, Mick, **58**, 95–6, 109, 111, 115, 116, 118
Raheens (Kildare), 41, 67, 70
Raheny (Dublin), 403, 413, 422, 432
Rahill, Jack, **50**, 54
Railway Cup, 71, 179, 267, 291, 401, 426
Ramor United (Cavan), 426, 432
Ramsey, Alf, 325
Rankins, Dick, 79
Rathangan (Kildare), 20, 28, 41, 70
Rathcline (Longford), 353, 381–2
Rathkenny (Meath), 180, 197, 205–6, 326, 334, 363
Rathmore (Kerry), 345, 353, 363, 382–3
Rathnew (Wicklow), 124
Rattigan, Billy, 223
Ratty, Patsy, 223
Raymond, Mick, 86–7, 96–7, 105, 111
Red Rum, 432
Redmond, Lorcan, 401, 423
Regan, Jack, 186, 189, 199
Regan, Tommy 'Danno', **58**, 72, **72**, 78
Reid, Frank, 186, 189
Reidy, Brendan, 86–7
Reilly, Dessie, 149
Reilly, Gerry, 292
Reilly, Jim, 192, 197, 202, 205–6, 209, 223
Reilly, Joe, 20, 24, 25, 28
Reilly, Ollie, **243**, 249, 272
Reilly, Paddy, **397**, 403, 413, 422, 432

Reilly, Seamus, 408
Rennicks, Dermot, 416
Rennicks, Ken, 363, 415, 424
Revie, Don, 231
Reynolds, Frank, 356
Reynolds, Hubert, 183, 189
Reynolds, Jackie, **243**, 249, 271
Reynolds, Mick (Galway: 1950s–1960s), 268, 295, 298, 301, 303, 306, 309, 314, 317, 325
Reynolds, Mickey (Louth: 1950s), 189
Reynolds, Pat, 306, 321, 322, 324, 326, **328**, 328, 334, 363
Rhode (Offaly), 177, 239, 272, 284, 350, 353, 369, 371, 381–2, 415
Rice, John, 200, 236, 255, 269
Rice, Pat, 255, **270**, 274, 275, 277, 282, 283, 286
Rice, Sean, 327, 339, 356
Richardson, Mick, 124
Ring, Christy, 267
Riordan, Johnny, **23**, 27, 33, 34, 39, 41
Robertstown (Kildare), 67, 70
Roche, Dave, 149
Roche, Ned, 209, **210**, 214, 219, 224, 230, 232
Roche, Pat, 245
Roche, Seamus, 292
Roche Emmets (Louth), 250
Rock, Dean, 291
Roddy, Owen, 356
Rodgers, Antoin, 192
Rodgers, Harry, 132–3
Roe, Jim, **243**, 247, 249
Roe, Nicky, 183, 186, 187, 189
Rogers, 'Buller', 66
Rogers, Jim (Wicklow: 1950s), 245
Rogers, Jimmy (Wexford: 1940s), 166
Rooney, Michael, 371, 387, **389**, 395, 401, 404
Rooney, Pat, 262, 334
Rooney, Peter, 330, 341, 342, 344, 368
Rooney, Stephen, **397**, 397–8, 400, 403, 413
Roosevelt, Franklin Delano, 46
Rooskey/St Barry's (Roscommon), 292
Roscommon
  1920s, 17, 22
  1930s, 29–30, 37, 43, 50, 57, 64, 72, 94
  1940s, 12, 114, 120–1, 125–33, **127**, 134, **137**, 137–41, 145, 151, 152–6, 159, 160, 162, 165, 168, 174

  1950s, 185, 190, 198, 200, 208–11, 216, 226–7, 230, 236–7, 242, 252, 264
  1960s, 12, 273, 279–80, 281, 286–7, 289–92, 294–5, 302, 310, 318, 327, 338–9, 347
  1970s, 356, 357, 362, 364, 375, 378, 387, 396, 398, 407, 416, 427–8, 429
Roscommon County Board, 98
Roscommon Gaels (Roscommon), 292
Rosemount (Westmeath), 176
Rossaveal (Galway), 118, 124
Rosscarbery (Cork), 289
Round Towers, Clondalkin (Dublin), 63
Rowe, Cormac, 415, 416, 423
Rowley, Eddie, 242
Royal Irish Fusiliers, 33
Ruane, Mick, 310, 318
Ruddy, M.J., 318
rugby, 36, 120, 214, 364, 408
Ruske, Bob, 197
Russell, Paul, 12, 22, **23**, 27, 34, 39, 40, 44, 46
Russell Rovers (Cork), 241, 250
Russia see Soviet Union
Rutledge, Sean, 174
Ruttledge, P.J., 76
Ryan, Dan (Kerry: 1920s–1930s), 27, 46, 178
Ryan, Dan (Kildare: 1920s), 20
Ryan, Eamonn, 330, **330**, 335
Ryan, Eric, 235, 237, 241, **244**, 246, 247, 250, 254
Ryan, Frank, 124
Ryan, George, 428
Ryan, Jackie, **23**, 27, 29, 33, 34, 39, 40, 45, 46, 59
Ryan, Jim, 251
Ryan, John (Wexford: 1950s), 236
Ryan, Johnny (Tipperary: 1950s), 261–2
Ryan, Mick, 351, 353, **367**, 368, 371, **374**, 381–2
Ryan, Paddy (Kildare: 1920s), 20
Ryan, Pat 'Darkie', 20, 41
Ryan, Richie, 431
Ryan, Sean (GAA President), 38
Ryan, Sean (Offaly: 1960s), 271, **278**, 280, 281, 284
Ryan, Tom, 139
Ryan, Vincent, 407
Ryan, Willie, 110

Ryder, Fran, 402, 403, 422, 424, 429, 432
Ryder, Mick, 95–6

St Aidan's (Roscommon), 292
St Anne's (Dublin), 300
St Brendan's (Kerry), 267
St Brendan's (Roscommon), 292
St Bride's (Louth), 189
St Brigid's (Dublin), 259, 300
St Brigid's (Offaly), 353
St Brigid's (Roscommon), 141, 292
St Bronagh's, Rostrevor (Down), 275, 283, 344
St Carthage's (Offaly), 353, 371, 381–2
St Columba's (Offaly), 371, 381–2
St Coman's (Roscommon), 132–3, 141, 155–6, 300
St Croan's (Roscommon), 292
St Dominic's (Louth), 249–50
St Dympna's (Dublin), 180, 197, 205–6
St Faithleach's (Roscommon), 292
St Finbarr's (Cork), 149, 241, 250, 309, 317, 335, 345, 353, 394
St Gabriel's (Galway), 371, 395, 404
St Grellan's (Galway), 47, 54, 62, 95–6, 111, 118, 124, 240, 268, 301, 309, 317, 325, 371, 395, 404
St Jarlath's College, Tuam (Galway) 309
St Joseph's (Dublin), 36, 63, 95–6, 111, 118, 249
St Killian's (Armagh), 432
St Margaret's (Dublin), 232, 403, 413, 422, 432
St Mary's (Offaly), 284, 353, 371, 381–2
St Mary's, Ardee (Louth), 149, 163, 171, 181, 189, 249
St Mary's, Bettystown (Meath), 180, 197, 205–6
St Mary's, Caherciveen (Kerry), 124, 141, 214, 224, 232, 267, 276, 309
St Mary's, Granard (Longford), 149, 163, 171, 181
St Mary's, Saggart (Dublin), 124, 259, 300
St Maur's (Dublin), 232
St Michael's (Cork), 241, 250, 394
St Michael's (Galway), 395, 404
St Monica's (London) 284
St Nicholas (Cork), 149, 214, 241, 250, 335, 366, 371, 394, 404
St Oliver Plunketts *see* Oliver Plunketts (Dublin)

St Patrick's (Cork), 241
St Patrick's (Meath), 249, 275, 283, 326, 334, 344
St Patrick's (Roscommon), 132–3, 141, 155–6, 292
St Patrick's College, Cavan, 147
St Peter's, Warrenpoint (Down), 344
St Rynagh's (Offaly), 345
St Vincent's (Dublin), 213, 229, 232, 240, 257–8, 259, 268, 300, 377, 400, 403, 413, 422, 423, 432
St Vincent's (Meath), 196, 268, 301, 309, 317, 334, 363
St Wilfred's (Manchester), 268, 301, 309, 317, 325
Sallins (Kildare), 413, 422
Salthill-Knocknacarra (Galway), 325, 371, 395
Sammon, Liam, 318, 325, 365, 368, 369, 371, **386**, 387, **389**, 391, 392, 395, 396, 398, 400, 401, 404
San Francisco, 364, 366, 379, 429
Sands, Pat, 401, 404
Sands, Tommy, 309, 317, 325
Sarsfields (Armagh), 215, 432
Sarsfields (Kildare), 70, 157, 172, 188, 196
Saul (Down), 344
Saunders, John, 382–3
Sayers, Jim, 158
Scally, Kevin, 225
Scanlon, Brendan, 87–8
Scanlon, Seamus, 227
Scannel, Mick, 394
Scoil Uí Chonaill (Dublin), 403, 413, 422, 432
Scotstown (Monaghan), 171, 181, 204–6
Scott, Walter, 64
Scullion, Alastair, 340
Scullion, Redmond, 432
Scully, Dick, 92
Sean Mac Cumhaills (Donegal), 345, 353, 363, 382–3
Sean McDermotts (Dublin), 63, 78, 95–6, 99, 110, 111, 118, 123, 124, 132–3, 141, 163, 171, 180, 197, 205–6, 215, 223, 249, 259, 292, 300, 353, 371, 381–2
Second World War, 102, 104, 108, 110, 112, 115, 117, 125, 131, 140, 147, 154
Seeley, Brian, 208, 215
Seery, Tom, 37

Seneschalstown (Meath), 326
Sexton, John, 35
Sexton, Sean, 286
Shanahan, Martin, 48
Shanahan, Tim, 427
Shanley, John 'Nipper', 16, 50
Shanley, Ollie, 304, 321, 323, 326, **328**, 333, 334, 361, 363
Shannon, Bill, 310
Shannon Airport, Co. Clare, 334
Shannon Gaels (Roscommon), 292
Shaw, Billy, 74
Shaw, Tommy, 414
Sheehan, John Joe, 212, 214, 220, 224, 232
Sheehan, 'Packo', 191, 235
Sheehan, Tim, 317, 345
Sheehy, Brian, **303**, 309
Sheehy, Joe, 97
Sheehy, John Joe, **23**, 25, 27, 29, 32, 33, 34, 211, 290
Sheehy, Mikey, 83, 398, 407, 411, 413, 419, 422
Sheehy, Niall, 265, 267, 274, 276, 288, 292, **303**, 305, 307, 309, 317
Sheehy, Paudie, 209, 211, 214, 220, 224, 228, 230, 232, 264, 265, 267, 274, 276, 288, 292
Sheehy, Sean Óg, 288, 290, 292
Sheelagh Emmets (Louth), 189
Shelbourne FC, 408
Sheridan, John (Cavan: 1950s), **199**, 206
Sheridan, John T. (Cavan: 1930s), 69
Sheridan, Terry, **158**, 163, 171
Sherlock, Victor, **166**, 168, 169, 170, 171, 178, 181, **199**, 202, 204–6, 219, 228
Sherry, Fionn, 418
Shevlin, Tom, 16–17, 35, 50, 57
Shine, P.J., 292
Shivnan, Michael, 208
shooting, 180
Six-Day War, 334
Skerries Harps (Dublin), 63, 95–6, 111, 118, 124, 259
Skryne (Meath), 105, 180, 197, 205–6, 223, 326, 334
Slator, Jim 'Sal', 79
Slattery, Joe, 82
Sleator, Dick, 139
Sligo
 1920s, 16, 17, 22
 1930s, 29–30, 37, 43, 50, 57, 64, 72, 80, 91, 94, 98

1940s, 107, 120, 134, 151, 159, 168, 174

1950s, 185, 190, 198, 208, 216–17, 227, 237, 242, 252, 264

1960s, 272, 279, 286, 294, 302, 310–11, 318, 327, 338, 347

1970s, 356–7, 364–5, 374–5, 387, 398, **407**, 407–8, 410, 412, 416, 427

Sligo Champion, 29–30, 190, 217, 412, 416

Sligo Rovers FC, 364

Sloan, Brendan, 344

Smallhorne, Jack, **50**, 54, **65**, 69, **81**, 87–8

Smith, Brendan, 376

Smith, Con, 262, 270

Smith, Gerald (Meath: 1950s), 223

Smith, Gerry (Cavan: 1940s), 132–3

Smith, Hugh, **81**

Smith, Jim, 17, 18, 21, 24, 38, 42, **50**, 51, 52, 54, **65**, 66, 68, 69, 80, **81**, 87–8

Smith, John (Down: 1960s), 283

Smith, John (Offaly: 1970s), 368, 369, 371, **374**, 379, 381–2

Smith, Paddy, **81**, 84, 87–8, 108, 126, 128, 132–3, 147, 149, **158**, 163, **166**, 171, 181

Smith, Peadar, 189, **243**, 249

Smith, Peter, 256, 259

Smith, Robert, 69

Smith, Sean *see* Hetherton, Seamus

Smith, Tommie, 344

Smyth, Brian, 176, **176**, 178, 180, 197, 198, 199, 205–6, 218, 219, 223, 272

Smyth, Charlie, **176**, 180

Smyth, Declan, 404

Smyth, Denis, 359–60

Smyth, Hughie, **158**

Smyth, Jimmy, **425**, 429, 432

Smyth, Kevin, 160, **176**, 180, 194, 197, 205–6

Smyth, P.J., 371

Smyth, Raymond, 430

Snee, Michael, 57

Sneem (Kerry), 63, 86–7, 214, 224, 232, 363, 413, 422

soccer, 34, 94, 95, 116–17, 139, 147, 214, 231, 257, 275, 325, 364, 387, 398, 408, 410, 427, 431

Solan, Peter, **167**, 172, 174, 186, 188, 195, 196

Somers, Tom, 99, 112

Somme, Battle of, 131

South Africa, 308, 334

South Korea, 187

Soviet Union, 104, 131, 180, 187, 249, 283, 291, 343–4

Spa (Kerry), 309, 317, 345, 353, 363, 382–3, 413, 421, 422

space exploration, 249, 283, 346, 352

Spain, 40, 77, 412

Spanish Civil War, 77

Spiddal (Galway), 371, 395, 404

Spillane, Pat, 299, 380, 407, 410, 411, 413, 417, 418, 420, 421, 422, 428

Spillane, Tom, 307

Spring, Dan, 41, 86–7, 101, 102, 105, 109, 111

Stabannon Parnells (Louth), 189, 249–50

Stack, Austin, 26

Stack, Bob, **23**, 27, 34, 36, 40, 45, 46

Stack, Gerry, 224

Stack, Sean, 27

Stafford, Jimmy, 286, 296

Stafford, Joe, 121, 126, 127, 128, 129, 132–3, 137, 146, 147, 149, **158**, 161, 163, **166**, 170, 171, 181

Staines air crash, 381

Stalingrad, Battle of, 131

Stanley, Larry, 32

Starlights (Wexford), 223

Stars of the Sea (Meath), 363

Staunton, Joe, 188, **191**, 196

Stenson, Johnny, **407**

Stevens, Paddy 'Staff', 62

Stevenson, Denis, **425**, 432

Stevenson, Peter, 409, 426

Stewart, Mick, 54

Stockwell, Frank, 176, 238, 240, 242, 253, 264, 268, 369, 431

Stokes, Dick, 145

Strabane Chronicle, 49

Stradbally (Laois), 79

Stradone (Cavan), 149, 163, 171, 178, 181

Strokestown (Roscommon), 132–3, 141, 155–6, 292

Stuart, Phil, 256, 259, 262

Sullivan, Charlie, 95–6

Sullivan, Chris, 139

Sullivan, Dinny, 54, 60, 62, 95–6, 109, 111, 115, 118, 145

Sullivan, P.J. 'Peachy', 40, 41

Sullivan, Paul, 304

Sullivan, Tom, 124, 168

Summerhill (Meath), 334, 363

Suncroft (Kildare), 20, 28, 41, 232, 258, 259

Sunday Game, 60

Sunday Independent, 61, 110, 140, 186, 203, 231, 265, 283, 297, 315, 316, 322, 331, 336, 341, 346, 349, 370

Sunningdale Agreement, 398–9

Swanlinbar (Cavan), 149, 163, 171, 181

Swayne, Paddy, 76, 79

Sweeney, Michael, **373**

Sweeney, Ned 'Pedlar', **23**, 25, 27, 33, 34, 41

Sweetman, Gerard, 240

Swindon Town FC, 427

Swinford (Mayo), 172, 188, 196

Swords, Aidan, 240, 272

Syddan (Meath), 105, 180, 197, 205–6, 223

Synge Street (Dublin), 300, 403, 413, 422, 432

Synnott, Jack, 105

Synnott, Joe, 15

Synnott, John, 15

Synnott, Kevin, 403, 413

Synnott, Pat, 300

Synnott, Peter, 44, 63

Syria, 334

Taaffe, Des, **176**, 180, 183, 197, 205–6

Taggart, Gerry, 372

Taggart, Jackie, 218, **233**, 236

Talty, Brian, 427

Tarmon (Roscommon), 62, 95–6, 111, 118, 124, 132–3, 155–6

Taylor, Glenn, 171

Teague, Kevin, 372

Teahan, Ger, 96–7, 117, 150, 155–6, 164

television coverage, 283, 291, 322, 332, 333, 352, 401, 421, 429

Templenoe (Kerry), 413, 422

Templeport (Cavan), 21, 77, 132–3, 149, 163, 171, 181

Thomas Davis (Dublin), 326, 334

Thomond College (Limerick), 403, 413, 422

Thornbury, Art, 17

Thornton, Jim, 125

Thornton, Pierce, 118, 122, 123, 124

Thornton, Sean (Galway: 1940s), 122, 123, 124

Thornton, Sean (Louth: 1950s), 183, 186, 187, 189
Three Stripe International, 428
Tibet, 267
Tibohine (Roscommon), 155–6
Tiernan, Eunan, **158**, 163
Tierney, Fintan, 379
Tierney, Liam, 414
Tierney, Noel, 299, 301, 302, 306, 309, 317, 323, 325
Tierney, Vincent, 198
Tighe, Tony, 135, 147, 149, **158**, 160, 161, 163, **166**, 169, 170, 171, **175**, 181, **199**, 202, 204–6
Timlin, Niall, 331
Timmons, Joe, 218, 256, 259
Timmons, John, 245, 251, 255, 259, 280, 288, 300, 313, 320
Tipperary
1920s, 15–16, 19, 22
1930s, 29, 36, 43, 48, 59, 61, 64, 66, 71, 82, 89, 98–9
1940s, 106, 113, 116, 120, 126, 130, 135–6, 139, 145, 157, 168, 173–4, 179, 213
1950s, 184, 200, 216, 228, 233–4, 254, 261–2
1960s, 272, 288, 293, 304–5, 319, 338, 346
1970s, 354, 366, 375, 376, 390, 398, 406, 417, 428, 429
Tito, 154
Toal, Bennie, 269
Toal, Leslie, 320, 359, 424
Tobin, John, 375, 392, 395, 400, 401, 402, 404, 408
Toman, Frank, 432
Trainor, Peter, **425**, 432
Tralee, Co. Kerry, 110, 293
Traynor, Felix, 69
Traynor, Kevin, 373
Treacy, Ned, 235, 260
Treacy, P.T., 269, 285, 321–2, 324
Treanor, Eugene, 344
Treanor, Jack 'Rock', 35
Treaty of Rome, 249
Treaty of Versailles, 95
Treaty Sarsfields (Limerick), 172, 188
Trim (Meath), 223, 268, 292, 326, 334, 363
Trinity College Dublin, 34, 213, 258, 362, 422, 432
Trolan, Matt, 360
Troubles, 352, 372, 381, 412–13

Tuam Herald, 91
Tuam Stars (Galway), 47, 54, 62, 95–6, 111, 118, 124, 240, 268, 292, 295, 301, 309, 317, 325, 371, 395, 404
Tubridy, Mick, 145, 146, 147, 149
Tuft, Jim, 189
Tullamore (Offaly), 41, 79, 284, 353, 371, 381–2
Tully, Ray, 208, 242
Tullyallen (Louth), 26
Tullylish (Down), 275, 283, 344
Tullyvin (Cavan), 21, 54, 69
Tunney, Tom, 47
Turbett, Liam, 372
Turbett, Thady, **233**, 236, 237, 285
Turley, Tom, 292
Turner, Sean, 235
Tyers, Paddy, 238, 241
Tynan, Mick, 312, 313
Tyrone
1920s, 17, 24
1930s, 42, 48–9, 55, 61, 66, 73, 80, 101
1940s, 113–14, 121, 126, 130, 134, 144, 150, 159, 165, 173
1950s, 184, 192, 207, 218, 227, **233**, 236, 237, 245–7, 254, 262–3, 336
1960s, 269, 277, 285, 311, 321, 324, 331, 343
1970s, 355, 367, 372, 374, 384, 387, 391, 399, 409, 410, 418–19, 426
Tyrone County Board, 49
Tyrrell, Christy, 303, 309, 310, 317, 325
Tyrrell, Pat, 280

Ulster Council, 31–2, 38, 48, 103, 114, 121, 311, 384
Ulster Volunteer Force (UVF), 402
Ulster Workers Council, 398–9
Underwood, Bennie, 112
United Nations, 154, 275, 352
United Stars (Roscommon), 292
United States, 12, 14, 27, 36, 40, 43, 45, 46, 53, 55, 62, 69, 73, 90, 110, 147–8, 157, 160–4, 171, 194, 195, 196, 231, 233, 248, 267, 271, 275, 291, 293, 298, 299–300, 308, 330, 343, 344, 364, 366, 372, 373, 376, 379, 387, 401, 403, 409, 412, 421, 423, 426, 427, 429

Universal Automatic Computer (UNIVAC), 196
University College Cork (UCC), 16, 214, 224, 241, 250, 309, 317, 335, 345, 353, 362, 363, 379, 382–3, 394, 413
University College Dublin (UCD), 34, 35, 40, 46, 63, 69, 132–3, 141, 149, 155–6, 163, 171, 172, 181, 188, 196, 204–6, 214, 215, 224, 232, 267, 276, 353, 363, 371, 377, 381–3, 394, 395, 403, 413, 422, 432
University College Galway (UCG), 54, 62, 95–6, 111, 118, 124, 132–3, 141, 172, 188, 268, 292, 301
Urhan (Cork), 241, 250, 335

Valentia (Kerry), 141, 267, 276, 292, 309, 317, 345, 353, 363, 382–3, 413, 422
Valentia Island, Co. Kerry, 266, 378
Vallely, John, 42, 56, 81, 165, 173
Vichy regime, 110
Vietnam War, 412
Virginia (Cavan), 21, 54, 69, 87–8, 132–3

Waldron, Joe, **389**, 395, 404
Walker, Eddie, 280, 303
Walker, Tom 'Drakes', 65, 90, 112
Wall, Paddy, 181
Wall Street crash, 27
Wallace, George, 300
Walsh, Barry, 422, 429
Walsh, Bobby, 330
Walsh, Dan, 79
Walsh, Eddie, 87, 96–7, 102, 105, 109, 111, 117, 137, 141, 155–6, 161, 164
Walsh, Fintan, 260, 288, 297
Walsh, Jack (Kerry: 1920s–1930s), **23**, 27, 34, 40, 46
Walsh, Jackie (Kerry: 1970s), 382–3, 413, 422
Walsh, Jimmy, 304, 326, 334
Walsh, John Joe, 280
Walsh, Johnny, 44–5, 46, 83, 84, 86–7, 93, 96–7, 105, 111, 117, 141
Walsh, Nick, 44
Walsh, Pa, 346
Walsh, Paddy, 293
Walsh, Sean (Galway: 1940s), 124
Walsh, Sean (Kerry: 1970s), 418, 419, 422, 428, 429

Walsh, Tom (Laois: 1960s), 336, 337

Walsh, Tommy (Kildare: 1960s), 321

Walsh, Willie (Down: 1970s), 426

Walsh, Willie (Waterford: 1920s), 324

Walsh Island (Offaly), 79, 125, 284, 353, 371, 381–2

Walshe, Martin, 18, 20, 39, 41

Walterstown (Meath), 326, 334, 363

Ward, Francis, 363

Ward, Jimmy, 306, 356

Ward, Johnny, 176, 177

Washkansky, Louis, 334

Waterford
1930s, 36, 43, 48, 59, 64, 82
1940s, 106, 150
1950s, 190, 200, 209, 213, 216, 228, 234, 243–4, 248, 254, 262
1960s, 272, 288–9, 293, 304, 312, 319, 338, 346
1970s, 354, 366, 375–6, 390, 398, 417, 428

Watergate scandal, 403

Waters, Eddie, 416

Waters, Peter, 39, 41, 67, 70, 93

Waterville (Kerry), 250, 267, 276, 292, 309, 317, 345, 353, 363, 382–3, 405

Watson, Bertie, 262

Watson, P.J., 302

Watson, Peter, 292

Watterson, George, 106

Weir, Frank, **278**, 284

Welles, Orson, 117

Wellington, Mickey, **56**, 57, 60, 63

Wembley Tournament, 376, 398, 402

Western People, 59, 165, 310, 416

Westerns (Dublin), 180, 196, 240, 249

Westmeath
1930s, 30, 37, 43–4, 49, 65, 74, 99
1940s, 134, 142, 158, 166, 176–7
1950s, 191, 225–6, 261
1960s, 271–2, 288, 303–4, 320, 328, 336, 348
1970s, 359, 365, 377, 389, 397, 409, 415–16, 424

Westmeath County Board, 179

Westmeath-Offaly Independent, 348

Weston, John, 29, 43

Westport (Mayo), 47, 78, 172, 188, 196

Wexford
1920s, 15, 19
1930s, 30, 33, 36–7, 43, 44, 49, 57, 65, 68, 82, 89, 99, 100–1
1940s, 107, 112, 119, 136, 142–3, 146, 151, 166–7, 176
1950s, 182, 191, 199, 209, 221, 225, 235–6, 238, 244–5, 248, 260
1960s, 280, 287, 304, 313, 320, 336, 348
1970s, 359, 365, 377, 396, 402, 408, 409, 415–16, 423–4

Whan, Jimmy, 262, 296, 311

Wheeler, Tom 'Towe', 20, 28

Whelan, Ciaran, 299

Whelan, Marcus, 232

Whelan, Mickey, 261, 280, 298, 299, 300, 377

Whelan, Mossy, **226**, 229, 232, 257, 259

Whelan, Paddy, 15

Whelan, Peter 'Peenie', **135**, 137

White, Frank, 208, 217

White, Georgie, 243, 262

White, James, **65**, 69, 87–8

White, Mick, 326, **328**, 333, 334, 360, 361, 363

White, Paddy 'Boiler', 157–8

White, Stephen, 166, 183, 189, 209, **243**, 245, 247, 249

White, Vincent, 69, **81**, 84, 87–8

Whitecross (Armagh), 432

Whitehall Colmcilles (Dublin), 422, 432

Whitney, Brian, 340

Whitty, Paddy, 34, 39, 40, 46

Whyte, Tony, 290, 292, 295, 310, 339

Wickham, Brendan, 159

Wicklow
1930s, 68, 85, 90
1940s, 142, 143, 158
1950s, 182, 218, 225, 245, 260
1960s, 271, 313, 320, 328, 348
1970s, 359, 365, 376, 389, 408, 415, 423

Williams, Jim, 64, 98, 139

Williamstown (Galway), 301, 309, 317, 325

Wilmott, Robert, 394

Wilson, Georgie, **397**, 401, 403, 413

Wilson, Gerry, 215

Wilson, John, 134, 147, 149, **158**, 163, 171, 246

Wilson, Marcus, 235, 251, 257, 259

Wilson, Tim, 287

Wilson, William G., 69

Winston, Joe, **373**, 373

Winters, Dick (Mayo: 1930s), 78

Winters, Dick (Tipperary: 1940s), 136

Wizard of Oz, The (1939), 104

Wolfe Tones (Armagh), 215, 432

Wolfe Tones (Galway), 46, 62, 63, 87, 95–6, 111, 118, 124

Woods, Johnny, 288

Woods, Pat, 250

Woods, Peter, 177

Woods, Sean, 340, 349, 356

World Cup (soccer), 34, 325, 398

Wrenn, Charlie, 260, 271, **278**, 284, 288

Wright, Mick, 381–2

Wright, William, 247

Wynne, Sean, 188, 190, **191**, 196

Young, Eamonn, 126, 146, 149, **244**, 390

Young, Joe, 240, 242, 253, 265, 268

Young, John, 21

Young, Seamus, 259

Young, Willie, 18, 21, **50**, 54, **65**, 69, **81**, 87–8, 266

Young Irelands, Cushinstown (Meath), 180, 197, 205–6, 223

Yugoslavia, 154, 231